THE FABULOUS FLOATING HORSES

Comprehensive guide to 30 SOFT-GAITED breeds

"A *Living* Epic"

Barbara Weatherwax

Forward by
Elizabeth Graves

MARKWIN PRESS

Reno, Nevada

Acknowledgments

First of all, thank you to my dear sister, Loraine Costa and to friends who have encouraged me over the last nine years to complete this project. The list of thank you's continues: Skeeter Savage, who took over all the telephoning and supported me in so many ways; Liz Graves, whose expertise continues to amaze me and whose generosity is constant; all the horse lovers who shared their photographs; the professional photographers who were generous enough to let us use their wonderful photos; the Breed Associations who provided information, photographs, and enthusiasm; Colin Dangaard, who never lost faith; and finally to my own horses, who thrill me every morning when I walk into the barn to serve up breakfast.

About the Author

Barbara Weatherwax has never been far from a horse. In the months before she was born her parents rode horseback and took sleigh rides in the Illinois forest preserves. Her father propped her up on a horse before she could walk. By the age of three she was riding. Her childhood memories revolve around her love of horses. While other girls played with dolls, she made up games to play with bridles and saddles. It surprised no one that as an adult she became a devoted horsewoman.

She attended Loyola University and earned a bachelor's degree in Theater Arts. While teaching in Los Angeles inner-city schools she maintained a separate career as an actress and singer in musical theater. Upon retirement from teaching she manufactured custom horse tack and established a popular tack store, *The Saddle Tree*, in the San Fernando Valley.

When Los Angeles freeway construction blocked many of her favorite horse trails, she moved to the great blue-sky country of Washoe Valley, nestled below the Sierra Mountains. With a stable of soft-gaited riding horses and a horse trailer, riding opportunities became virtually unlimited. She introduced the extraordinary qualities of the soft-gaited horse to new acquaintances and riding groups throughout the region. Since she used Australian-made saddles exclusively, she called her ranch Ophir Hill Station—the word "station" being a homestead or farm down under. She considers a soft-gaited horse and an Australian saddle the best possible combination for trail riding.

With her advocacy for pleasure-riding horses, her place became a magnet for horse lovers searching for information. Over and over again she explained the difference between a running walk and a rack, and a fox trot versus a saddle gait. Her reputation as a wise and insightful teacher spread quickly. Her enthusiasm for sharing her expertise spurred the nine-year project of deep and careful research study resulting in this book. She is encouraged that this publication will carry her accumulated knowledge to a large audience so that equestrians can better understand and enjoy *The Fabulous Floating Horses*.

Barbara has examined horses throughout the United States and holds multiple credentials to inspect for the Kentucky Mountain Saddle Horse Association, the American Spotted Horse Association, the Spotted Saddle Horse Breeder and Exhibitor Association, the Tiger Horse Association, the Missouri Fox Trotting Horse Breed Association, and the Kentucky Natural Gaited Horse Association. She has also judged Paso Finos, Peruvian Pasos, Spotted Saddle Horses, Kentucky Mountain Horses, Tennessee Walkers and Icelandics in non-pointed, all-breed gaited shows and is the state representative for the Mountain Pleasure Horse Association.

Credits

Editor: Robin Swados
Designer: Barbara Weatherwax
Illustrations: Barbara Weatherwax
Cover photographer: Melinda Williams
Cover Photo: Largo stallion, Eclipse's Cassino Pisadas
Printer: Don Junowich – Print Management Services
Publicist: Colin Dangaard
ISBN 0-9740793-0-8
LIBRARY OF CONGRESS 2003109080
Published by **MARKWIN PRESS**, Reno, Nevada
Printed by Daehan Printing Company in Korea

© 2003 All rights reserved. No part of this book may be reproduced or utilized in any form or by any means, electronic or mechanical, including photocopying, recording or by any information storage and retrieval system, without permission in writing from the publisher.

Forward

    In watching this project grow from its initial rough draft, I knew it was a book that would fill a need within the gaited horse community. I always wondered why no one else had ever done a book like this before, and with that thought I began to understand that it needed just the right person to bring it to life, in just the right way. I came to understand it was a person such as Barbara Weatherwax to get this special task done. There was no one else who could do a book like this, the way Barbara could.

    In her lifelong journey through the horse, Barbara is just the kind of person we all should be lucky enough to experience as we find and build lifelong friendships, owning and sharing the love and joys of the gaited horses that come into our lives.

    This book tells just what it's all about. No matter what breed of gaited horse a person may choose as their own, there is a common ground that brings us together through the desire to understand them better. This is a book that will benefit everyone regardless of their level of experience. It's not just a vehicle of entertainment but one of gaining more knowledge. The information it contains is vast and excellent. The large amount of photography it contains is what brings it all together, making it complete and unique.

    This book re-enforces everything that is so special and dear to me about the gaited horse experience.

    Thank you, Barbara, for sharing and bringing it together for all of us, as well as our horses.

    You will always be a hero and a champion - for the horse, for me, and for everyone else whose lives you have touched.

Elizabeth Graves
April 2003

To the reader........

This book grew out of my lifelong passion for the soft-gaited horse. My intention is to share the joy, and at the same time, pass on information gathered over the course of many years.

The soft-gaited horse is a natural wonder. There are so many choices for the horse fancier. Within the ranks of soft-gaited horses, one can find any size, any color and a multitude of gaits. Remember, it doesn't have to be a bad horse to be the wrong horse; conversely, it doesn't have to be a great horse to be the right horse. The important issue is that the horse and horse rider/owner be well-matched . Soft-gaiteds, as a category, are kind by nature. It's important to know there are many more attributes that constitute a terrific partner.

I've divided this book into three sections. In Part I, I examine issues that relate to gaited horses as a category. In Part II, I present the many different breeds that share one important characteristic: soft-gaiting. In Part III, I look at several activities and associations focused on the soft-gaited horse.

Much of the material I cover is in response to the overwhelming amount of misinformation out there regarding the soft-gaited horse. If "all about horse" books mention gaited horses, they refer to the soft gaits as being artificially trained rather than natural. It is true that some trainers use dreadful methods to "set" gaits; but I view that as an aberration, a display of human ignorance, and not a legitimate part of the horses in any breed.

For many reasons, a registration that labels a horse " soft-gaited" may be no guarantee that the animal has a solid, true 4-beat gait. Sometimes horses can be pushed at a young age into developing bad habits. Often they are purchased and ridden by untrained riders who don't understand how to ride correctly. Sometimes these horses are advertised as "anybody can ride," which is usually not true. Last, but not least, some horses have a stronger, more dominant gaiting gene than others.

English riding lessons are a great way to start. Learn about the tools of riding - hands, legs and seat. Learning to post can only improve your riding skills to develop balance and security. There are accommodations for riding the gaiteds, but it's easier and quicker to make the transition from an English walk-trot horse. *There are no short-cuts.* The pleasure and comfort derived from a soft-gaited horse can be awesome. Believe me, it's worth the preparation.

It's also important to ride some really good horses. Learn what the ideal is. I've seen lots of disappointment and frustration from folks who went out and bought a "bargain" horse before they really knew what they were doing. It's very difficult to learn correctness from a horse that for one reason or another, doesn't have a strong 4-beat gait. There is an abundance of well-gaited desirable horses out there. Don't settle!

You can read *The Fabulous Floating Horses* from cover to cover – or in bits and pieces – or just pore over the pictures. Whichever you choose, please enjoy and appreciate these marvels of horse flesh!!

Barbara

ZANE'S BLUE MAX D
May 15, 1973 – August 20, 2001

DEDICATION

In 1986 my life was forever changed and enriched when I met the powerful and charismatic Fox Trotter, Zane's Blue Max D.

I had been interested in soft-gaited horses all my life. My mom and dad both rode saddle horses before I was born. But it was the Blue who opened my eyes to the amazing buffet of choices in the soft-gaited world.

Every time I sat on the Blue's back - from the very first time those many years ago, to the last time, in the summer of 2001 - I experienced his magic. As I stepped into the stirrup, I felt his motor engage. His strength and brio provided extraordinary exhilaration and his exciting animation was matched by his sweetness and kind nature.

What adventures we had! Blue had a passion for any new trail. His spectacular gait gobbled up the miles, and his curiosity gave a zest to every new bend in the road. That big motor of his kept him up front of any group, and the pace he set was a challenge to all the other horses.

Blue never met a horse he didn't like. Horses who didn't get along with any other horse would respond to Blue's overtures with friendliness. During his last few years, we utilized his social skills by putting him in charge of our equine day-care program. Our youngsters went directly to Blue when they were weaned. He obviously enjoyed the babies but was serious about "manering" them. Oh, those fortunate colts and fillies who learned the tricks of the trade from the master himself!

Blue had a remarkable 28 years on this earth. He touched many hearts. He was the love of my life from the moment we met. We were friends, we were partners, he was my spirit. When he and I moved to Washoe Valley, Nevada in 1989, he became king of the hill and the unquestioned head of the herd as it grew. He was always there for me as I ventured into new horse-related activities. He watched as horses came and went. As horses arrived from the Midwest and found new families in Northern Nevada, it was the Blue who showed potential buyers just what a soft-gaited horse could do.

There's a certain consolation in knowing I never took our partnership for granted. Blue was my claim to fame in the soft-gaited horse world. His life was a testament to his parentage. His sire was the celebrated Zane Grey. Blue was born as a part of Zane Grey's last foal crop. There aren't many Fox Trotters of note living today that don't boast of Zane Grey blood – and he was the Blue's dad.

Blue's dam was also exceptional. She was the first mare to be honored by The Horseman's Association of Middle Missouri for her get. Mares are too frequently underappreciated when laurels are being handed out because the numbers of their offspring are limited. Admittedly, they can't have the impact on a breed that a stallion can. But Blue's mom, Sugar Cookie, produced such outstanding horses, she could not be overlooked. The Blue was her first.

Blue's last summer was spent enjoying the warm breezes at his Washoe Valley home, where he meandered through the trees and napped outside my office window. He had numerous trips to Washoe Lake and ran free and unencumbered while I rode another horse along with him. The vision of his joyful energies rolling in the sand and grabbing a bite of grass before he launched off in a cloud of dust are forever in my heart. His precious presence will always be with me and with all the lucky folks who were touched by him. He is present on each page of this volume.

ABOUT … "A *Living* Epic"

The Fabulous Floating Horses is a book designed to grow. The world of the soft-gaited horse is entering into a renaissance. Every day, horse fanciers are turning their attention to the soft-gaited breeds. Riders who never dreamed they would be considering a soft-gaited horse and first-time horse owners who are new to horses in general, are discovering these smooth-going beauties.

With this amazing growth pattern, new breeds are being developed, and existing breeds are facing demands for more individual horses. As a category, the soft-gaited breeds are under tremendous pressure to expand.

During the nine years I spent creating *The Fabulous Floating Horses*, the face of the soft-gaited horse community has changed a great deal. Who can know exactly where we're headed? Because of these exciting developments, this volume has been designed to "grow" with the industry.

As new breeds are introduced, and as current information changes, new chapters will be offered to the book owners. **There will also be an ongoing request, by the author, for personal stories of adventures and relationships with soft-gaited horses. Pictures and stories that are selected will be edited and available in future installments of *The Fabulous Floating Horses*.**

When this initial volume is purchased, it is recommended that the enrollment form, found in the back of the book, be filled out and mailed to the printed address, to insure the owner is contacted about any new offerings. We will make every effort to keep information updated on the web page: www.thefabulousfloatinghorses.com

The Fabulous Floating Horses is the premier volume for the soft-gaited owner and fancier. We look forward to your participation! Enjoy!

PART ONE
THE SOFT-GAITED HORSE

1. Soft-Gaited Horses: The Well-Kept Secret 10
2. Are They Really Different? 16
3. Choreography: How The Horse Moves 32
4. Choosing A Horse: The Adoption Process 56
5. Care and Maintenance Of The Soft-Gaited Horse 64
6. Tack: Clothes That Make The Horse 80

PART TWO
THE BREEDS

7. Mountain Pleasure Horse 96
8. Kentucky Mountain Saddle Horse 114
9. Rocky Mountain Horse 134
10. Kentucky Natural Gaited Horse 152
11. Tennessee Walking Horse 166
12. Missouri Fox Trotting Horse 188
13. Spotted Saddle Horse 208
14. Paso Fino Horse 228
15. Peruvian Paso Horse 252
16. American Paso Largo Horse 272
17. McCurdy Plantation Horse 294
18. Mangalarga Marchador Horse 308
19. American Curly Horse 320
20. Icelandic Horse 336
21. Tiger Horse 352
22. Walkaloosa Horse 364
23. Tiger Horse Registry 374
24. Gaited Morgan Horse 388
25. Spanish Mustang Horse 400
26. Racking Horse 416
27. Part Walking Horse 426
28. Florida Cracker Horse 434
29. Spanish Gaited Pony 442
30. American Saddlebred Horse 448
31. Registries In The Making: Sorraia, Tennuvian, Montana Travler Gaited Morab, Spotted Mountain Horse 460

PART THREE
ASSOCIATIONS AND ACTIVITIES

32. The Pleasure Trail: A Place To Shine 470
33. Let's Show Our Horses 490
34. NASHA: North American Single-Footing Horse Association 504
35. NATRC: North American Trail Ride Conference 516
36. AGHA: American Gaited Horse Association 518
37. Gaited Horses on the NET 520
38. United Mountain Horse 522
39. Hollywood Horses 524
40. Moms and Babies 526

REFERENCE / DIRECTORIES

Breed Characteristics 535
Associations and Registries 536
Breeder & Trainer Directory 538
Professional Photographers 546
Bibliography 548
Index 549

Gaited Horse Breeds Tree

- Paso Largo
- Tennuvian
- Racking Horse
- Tiger Horse
- Kentucky Mountain Saddle Horse
- Brazilian Marchador
- Sorraia
- Rocky Mountain
- Paso Fino
- Standardbred
- Columbiano Paso
- American Saddle Horse
- Florida Cracker
- Fox Trotter
- American Saddlebred
- Peruvian Paso
- Mountain Pleasure Horse
- Morgan
- Narragansett Pacer
- Tennessee Walker
- French Canadian Horse
- American Indian Horse
- Canadian Pacer
- Bidet D'Allure
- Spanish Mustang
- Icelandic
- British Cob
- Spanish Jennet
- Scottish Galloway
- Barb
- Irish Hobbie
- English Palfrey

PART ONE

THE SOFT-GAITED HORSE

1. Soft-Gaited Horses: The Well-Kept Secret

2. Are They Really Different?

3. Choreography: How The Horse Moves

4. Choosing A Horse: The Adoption Process

5. Care And Maintenance of the Soft-Gaited Horse

6. Tack: Clothes That Make The Horse

SOFT-GAITED HORSES: THE WELL-KEPT SECRET

CHAPTER 1

Ophir Hill Station Herd
Owner: Barbara Weatherwax

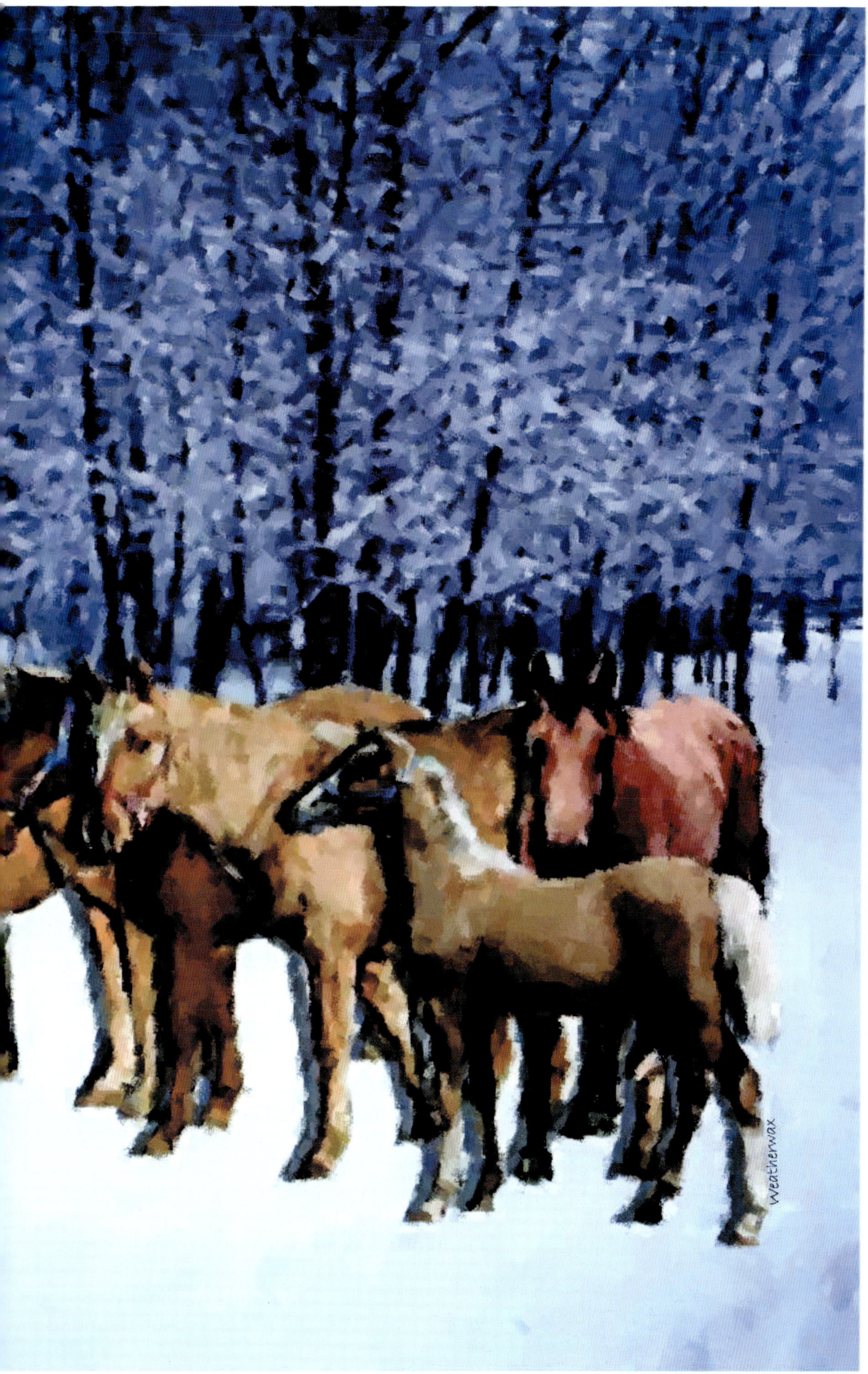
Weatherwax

Chapter 1 SOFT-GAITED HORSES: The Well-Kept Secret

Horses enrich our lives in so many ways. Because of careful selection in breeding programs throughout the centuries, there is a horse for every conceivable purpose. From battle to plow, from sport to show, horses have been our willing partners throughout the development of our civilization.

How do the *Fabulous Floating Horses* fit into the picture? For as long as there has been recorded information on horses - both traditional[1] and written - there have been gaited horses. If the horse was your only mode of transportation, wouldn't you want it to be as comfortable as possible? The ability to transport us in comfort is the foundation for the soft-gaited horses being a true cohort to humankind since the beginning of time.

The Akhal-Teke is a breed that has been around for 3,000 years. This horse, originally bred in the Turkmenistan Desert, has a gaited strain, which has been identified by E. Gus Cothran, Ph.D., director of the equine blood typing lab at the University of Kentucky.

Moving forward in time to 850 B.C., the Greek poet Homer, author of the Iliad and Odyssey, used the word *podarge* to describe certain horses. The translation of *podarge* is

The Akhal-Teke, an ancient breed, has a gaited strain that has contributed to other gaited breeds. Pictured is the stallion DORKUSH, 3rd place winner at the World Championship in Moscow 2000. Photo: Ganna Zernova, Ph.D.

swift-foot or rack.

From 500 A.D., the English Pacer was known throughout the British Isles as the principal means of transportation. In 847 A.D., the Vikings colonized Iceland. They brought with them Galloway horses from Scotland and Hobbies from Ireland, soft-gaited breeds that were to become the ancestors of the Icelandic horses we know today.

From 1096, on the British Isles, there were three categories of horse. The *courser* type was the predecessor of the race horse, since it was used to carry messages for the military and the politicians. The *destrier* was a large horse similar to our draft horses. This horse was important to the knights, in full armor, going into battle. It was important because of its size and strength, but it was not a comfortable horse to ride. For this reason, the knights also owned a *palfrey*, or soft-gaited horse, for transportation. Stories have been handed down describing knights riding their palfrey while their squire rode the destrier. When they got to the city gates, they swapped horses so the knight could make a grand entrance on his fine big horse. In 1340, Geoffrey Chaucer mentioned the palfreys in his *Canterbury Tales*.

In 1492, Columbus came to America where there was not a horse to be found. But

The Sorraia appears to be the predecessor of many light horse breeds. Prehistoric cave paintings in south Iberia, like Escoural in Portugal and La Pileta in Spain, give us evidence of the early existence of these important equines. As it is not unusual for a Sorraia to be gaited, there is a possibility that it is a source of the soft gait in horses. Photo: Courtesy of Hardy Oelke

---

[1] Usually means information handed down orally from generation to generation

A modern Canadian Horse has changed little from the French Canadian Horses of the 18th century. Many pure-bred French Canadian horses were entered into the early stud books of the Morgan, Standardbred, and American Saddlebred. Photo: Dennis Dyck, of the Lazy D Ranch in Rosemary, AB Canada. (See Chapter 24.)

in subsequent trips he brought many of the finest horses obtainable from the Iberian Peninsula, the Spanish Jennets. This was an important event, because the soft-gaited Spanish Jennet was to make an invaluable contribution to the future of the soft-gaited horses in the Americas.

In early 17th century Europe, the ratio of soft-gaited to walk-trot horses was 80/20. By the early 18th century, the soft-gaited horse had all but disappeared in Europe. As cities developed, the need for wagons and carts expanded. It was no longer necessary for a horse to be smooth and comfortable if it was pulling a carriage with no one on its back. The more animated, showy prancing walk-trot horse became coveted and prized. At the same time, the passion for racing horses continued.

In the early 1600s, the French horses, the Breton and Norman, began their journey to the new world. The Norman horses, in particular, had evidence of oriental blood, which came from a strain out of Andalusia, Spain. These horses, along with the Dutch Friesian, constituted the foundation for the Canadian Horse.

The Canadian horses contributed many of the important characteristics we enjoy in our modern soft-gaited horses. They had pluck, vigor and constitutions of iron. Many pure-bred French Canadian horses were entered into the early stud books of the Morgan, Standardbred, and American Saddlebred, all foundation breeds of the soft-gaited horses of today.

The early 18th century brought the Scottish Galloways and Irish Hobbies to North America. William H. Robinson, governor of Rhode Island, utilized the soft-gaited Galloways, Hobbies, Andalusian Spanish Jennets, and Canadian Horses for his breeding program in Narragansett County. Governor Robinson was an affluent planter who owned a very large plantation. He needed an easy-going horse that would be close to the ground and smooth to ride. Local tradition ascribes to him the creation of the pride and joy of Narragansett, the Narragansett Pacer.

A well-known horseman of the period described the horse thus: They have handsome foreheads, the hindquarters are narrow

The Canadian Horses passed on many important characteristics to our present-day soft-gaited horses - namely, pluck, vigor and iron constitutions. The Morgan horse, which figures prominently in early soft-gaited breed stud books, was a direct descendant of these tough and talented French Canadians.

and the hocks a little crooked which is here called sickle hocked, which turns the hind feet out a little; their color is generally, though not always, bright sorrel; they are very spirited and carry both head and tail high. But what is most remarkable is that they amble with more speed than most horses trot, so that it is difficult to put some of them upon a gallop. Notwithstanding this facility of ambling, where the ground requires it, as when the roads are rough and stony, they have a fine, easy single-footed trot.[2] These circumstances together with their being very sure-footed, render them the finest saddle horses in the world; they neither fatigue themselves nor their rider.

The Narragansett Pacer was important to the future of the soft-gaited horses in the Americas. From that little spot in Rhode Island, they found their way in all directions. A customs report from the early 1700 s shows a sale of 7,130 Narragansetts to the British West Indies in one year alone.

The American Colonial Military appreciated the comfortable ride of the Narragansett Pacer so much that they provided them to their remount stations located throughout North and South America. As roads improved throughout the colonies and the east coast, the horses were dispersed to Canada, the Midwest and the West.

For pure pleasure, this remarkable category of breeds, developed in the Americas, has been maintained here in the Americas. The soft-gaited plantation horses were designed to provide comfortable and efficient transportation over roadless terrain. They could also be hitched to the plow to plant the fields or pull the buggy to town for supplies.

The same horses were spruced up and decked out to take the family to church. With their kind and pleasant nature, they provided companionship and a willingness to participate.

A number of these special soft-gaited breeds carry the name of the area that has fostered their survival. The Missouri Fox Trotter, the Tennessee Walker, the Peruvian Paso, the Kentucky Mountain Saddle Horse, the Florida Cracker and the Puerto Rican or Colombian Paso Finos all carry regional identity in their names.

It is important to know that the ability to perform the soft gaits is in the genes. In other words, these gaits are totally natural and inborn. It is almost impossible to teach these

Soft-gaited horses come in all colors. Several colors are shown above: 1) BAY; 2) PALOMINO ROAN; 3) BLACK; 4) BLACK & WHITE SPOTTED; 5) LIGHT PALOMINO 6) CHOCOLATE WITH FLAXEN MANE AND TAIL; 7) PALOMINO; 8) DARK SORRELL; 9) GREY; 10) BUCKSKIN; 11) STRAWBERRY ROAN; 12) CHESTNUT.

---

[2] It might be noted that the single-footed trot Livingston refers to describes the soft-gaited 4-beat diagonal fox-trot we know today.

gaits to a horse that does not possess the soft-gaited gene.

The soft-gaited horse can demonstrate the walk, canter and gallop of a "regular" horse. Rather than trot, however, these soft-gaited horses perform various soft gaits for their "second gear." These gaits are accomplished by having at least one foot on the ground at all times. This produces a way of going that is animated and dramatic to the eye, but extremely smooth and comfortable to the rider.

Many people discover soft-gaited horses after they have suffered an injury that keeps them from riding a walk-trot horse.

There is a good deal of variation among the soft-gaited or plantation[3] breeds. Every equine color is available, plus colors seldom found in walk-trot horses, such as the chocolate body with white mane and tail found in the Rocky Mountain horses, or the burgundy-colored Marchadors from Brazil or the iridescent champagne-colored Tennessee Walking horse.

These horses come in all sizes too. Kentucky Mountain Saddle Horses can be registered in class B as small as 11 hands (44 inches), and it would not be uncommon to find a 17+ hand Tennessee Walker.

There are also variations in the ability to travel different topographies. The Paso Finos and Mountain Horses excel in rough mountainous regions. The Peruvian Pasos fly over flat terrain and the Tennessee Walkers (also known as Turn-Rows) can travel at a fast clip over narrow flat paths.

Part II of this book takes a close look at each of 30 soft-gaited breeds. The family tree of this equine sub-species is full of exciting and talented horses. Many variations have been developed from the magic soft-gaited gene. As more people become aware of the joys of ownership and associating with these special horses, their popularity is spreading. Once this well-kept secret is out of the hat, folks will find out what was almost lost back in the seventeenth century. Thanks to the Americas, the soft-gaited breeds are alive and well, so enjoy!

Breed-specific body types are available in assorted packaging: 1) BLACK & WHITE SPOTTED SADDLE HORSE; 2) BUCKSKIN MOUNTAIN HORSE; 3) LIGHT PALOMINO MOUNTAIN HORSE; 4) GOLDEN PALOMINO ICELANDIC HORSE; 5) Lp TIGER HORSE; 6) BAY SPOTTED SADDLE HORSE; 7) CREMELLO PERUVIAN PASO; 8) GREY RACKING HORSE; 9) CHESTNUT WALKING HORSE; 10) BAY PERUVIAN PASO.

[3] Most of the soft-gaited horses were cultivated for work on plantations in the New World (Western Hemisphere), after the arrival of the Europeans.

ARE THEY REALLY DIFFERENT?

CHAPTER 2

Fox Trotter, FRF GOLD DUST
Photo: Dawn Lindsay

McCurdy - ROSE, with friends.
Photo: Gale Johnson

Chapter 2
Are They Really Different?

It's important to remember that all the rules of horse safety apply to soft-gaited horses. Beginners are cautioned to take it easy, learn the rules of safety, and remember a horse is a horse.

TEMPERAMENT

The soft-gaited horse is warm-blooded.[1] Unlike some other breeds in that category, the soft-gaited horse is bred to be a docile and devoted companion to man. Each of the soft-gaited registries boasts that their horse is the most kind-tempered and cooperative. If you look at the jobs each horse is asked to accomplish, you can see the important role temperament plays.

The development of the Americas was closely linked with the equine. The horse of that era was able to plow the land, or be hitched to a wagon or buggy to carry the family to town, church, or a new homestead. With few roads open to carriages and the like, the horse was also expected to provide personal transportation in a comfortable and efficient fashion over hill and dale, making the trail as they went.

History tells us of the demise of the soft-gaited horse for general use in Europe by the end of the 17TH century. If it weren't for the plantations in the New World, those precious soft-gaited genes might well have been lost.

A Tennessee Walker is handsome and talented in harness as well as under saddle.

---

[1] Warm-blooded is a blend of hot-blooded and cold-blooded. They have the animation of the hot bloods, and the easier disposition of the cold.

A good disposition and smooth way of going are Apparent in this photo of Henry Elam aboard a Mountain Horse. The inset photo shows Mr. Elam in 1967.

The personal relationship between man and horse necessitated a willing and pleasant temperament in the horse. With such a solid foundation, it's easy to see why a kind disposition is honored in the soft-gaited horse. Within each registry's guidelines, you will find the desire to maintain and encourage an even-tempered and cooperative horse.

The pleasure riders of today have the same requirements for a calm and patient horse. Many folks discover the choices offered within the soft-gaited category when they are older and finally find the time and resources to own and enjoy a horse. Often the passion for horses has been dormant while families were raised and careers were pursued. What better choice is there to reignite the joy in a relationship with horses?

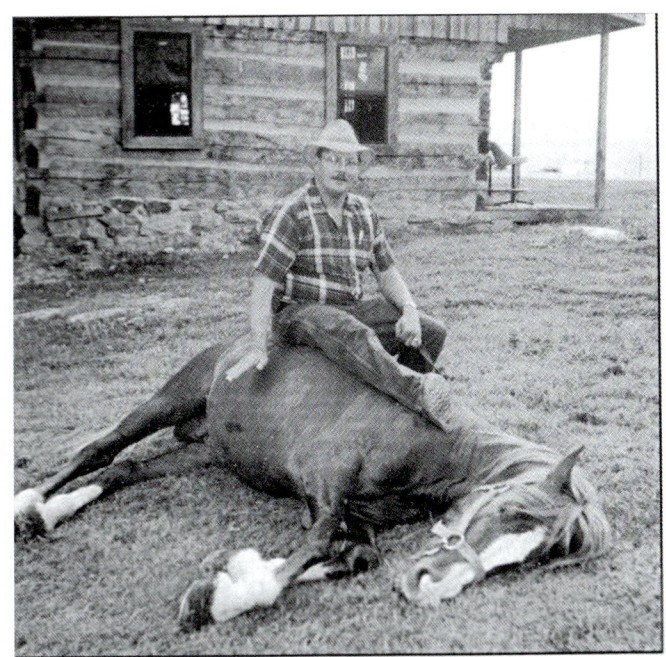

Paul Stamper is standing a stallion of the same bloodlines as found in horses owned and bred by his great-grandfather.

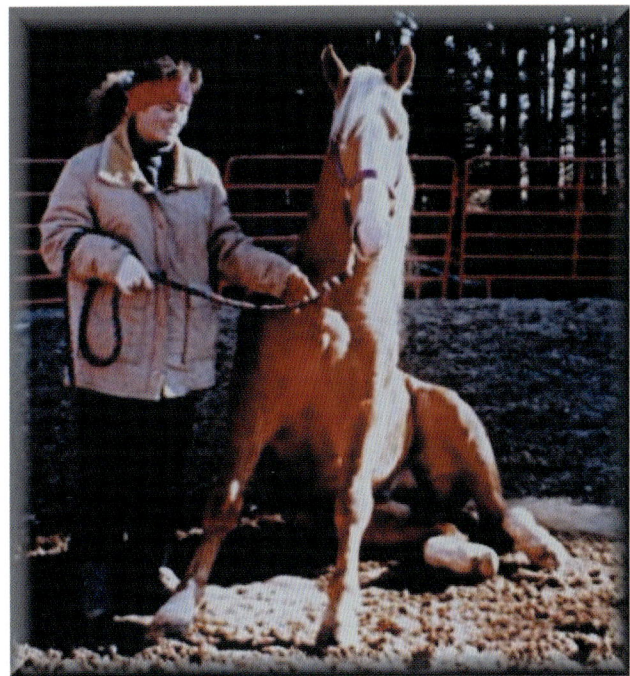

The Neidert Family is proud of the dispositions of their stallions (Julie with Goble), and their breeding facility, Gaitway Farm, in Wausau, Wisconsin.

The soft-gaited horse is also the perfect companion to the young. There are numerous choices within the breeds for a horse of smaller stature that can be suitable as a teacher but also usable as the child grows. Hours of pleasure are in store for all the human generations to experience together. The soft-gaited horse is a package of fun, safety and comfort, just waiting to be opened!

The horse is an extremely emotional and sensitive creature. People who have experienced the pleasure of owning and enjoying the soft-gaited horse all seem to have their own stories describing some area of the horse's amazing disposition. It is not unusual to see a toddler perched on the back of a stallion. These horses often make great "baby sitters." The Breed Chapters in this book will present numerous special horses and the people who love them as told through personal stories.

Truly the era of sound, comfortable, easygoing horses is getting underway. It is valid to say much of the growth is due primarily to the disposition and cooperation of the soft-gaited horse itself. The United States Forestry Service of the Interior makes frequent use of

Soft-gaited horse enthusiasts are eager to share the experience with the youngest of their loved ones. Pictured is surely "the littlest cowgirl," on WOODWIND'S SHOWTIME, a three-year-old Mountain Pleasure gelding.

Yearlings WOODWIND ELAINA and WOODWIND JULIAN, owned by Dr. Joyce Doonan and Will Ferguson.

The Ectomorph body type shows up often in the Tennessee Walkers, the Saddlebreds and the McCurdy Plantation horses. These can be tall and narrow with a long neck and long legs.

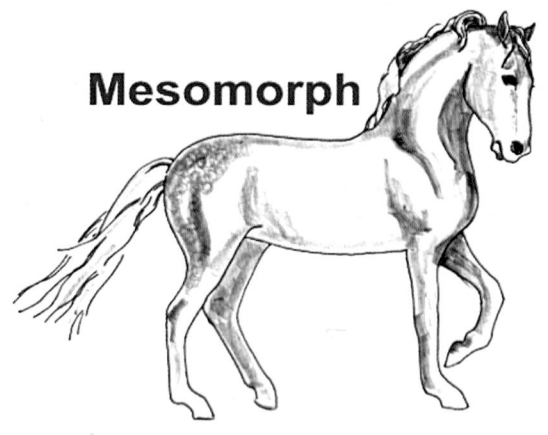

The Mesomorph body type can be found in many soft-gaited breeds. But it is particularly apparent in the Paso Finos, the Brazilian Marchadors and the Gaited Morgans. Their body type is definitely muscular.

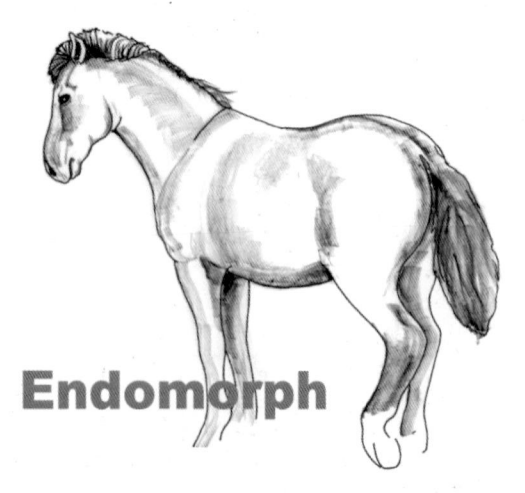

The Endomorph is chunky, round and substantial. The body type is often seen in the Mountain Horses, the Bashkir Curly and the Icelandics.

the Fox Trotter. The foresters do this as much for the animal's calm nature as for their comfortable way of going. Registries such as the one for the Kentucky Mountain Saddle Horse won't consider a horse for registration unless it demonstrates a "gentle and willing disposition." For the last four hundred years, the Peruvian Paso breeders have rejected any horse for their breeding programs that was in any way difficult in disposition. They strive for "brio," which is a noble spirit never to be out of hand.

CONFORMATION

There are certain basic conformation characteristics that can be found in any breed of horse. The *mesomorph* is a muscular horse. The *ectomorph* is a narrow angular horse. The *endomorph* is a round, plump, stocky horse. The world of soft-gaited horses encompasses all three different body types. The primary concern is balance. This is a quality desirable in any horse.

It might be helpful to think of a horse as an athlete. Whether used for a competitive sport or as a companion on the trail, the important element in equine conformation is its athletic ability. This ability does not develop in a vacuum. The bottom line is conformation. To move well, a horse must be balanced according to its individual build.

It is true that the show ring is a perfect place for breeders to show the result of their careful selection. The pleasure trail is, however, the ultimate goal for the soft-gaited horse. It is on the trail that the soft-gaited horse shows its mettle. Just think about what the trail can hold for you and your horse - uneven footing, ups and downs, waterfalls, waterflows and still water that needs crossing. This is where excellent conformation is critical. To be successful on the trail, a horse must have a good mind, a willing attitude and well-balanced conformation.

"Symmetry," as described by Webster, is an arrangement characterized by balance and harmonious proportions. To have symmetry, a horse must have balance between the hind quarters and the front end. If it has a round stout rear end, it would fall out of balance if its neck and shoulders were slender and lean. Likewise, if it has a broad chest and thick neck, a narrow back end would not complete a picture of balance.

Another important aspect of balance is found in bone structure. The legs are the most apparently visible facet of the bone structure. A horse should display enough "bone" to support its body style. The legs of a horse are the foundation of its physical structure. It is important for a horse to have a strong foundation.

The skeletal structure or bone of a horse is inherited. It does not, however, determine the ability to perform the soft gaits. Gaiting is in the genes. What bone does allow is the facility for different gaits once the gene is present.

Gaiting requires participation of the whole body. There are four main categories describing the horse's way of going: 1) the convex, or dorsal flex which is roundly collected; 2) the concave, or ventral flex which is strung out; 3) the combination of the first two, 4) a level back.

The convex, or dorsal flex type travels in a very collected fashion. The neck is arched, the body is rounded and the head is carried in a vertical position. This type is found most often in the "trotty" type horse, or the Fox Trotter, Mountain Horse or the Paso Fino.

The concave, or ventral flex type is more commonly found in other soft-gaited horses. This horse travels with a hollow back and a neck that is not overly flexed at the poll. Its head is held rather high and can be either pointed out or vertical. The hind end on this animal tends to be behind the horse. This way of going facilitates the performance of the pace and the stepping pace.

The middle, or square gaits such as the paso llano and the running walk require a level back.

The combination of concave and convex allows the horse to travel with characteristics of both types. It is also important to note that an individual horse can move in all four ways. To trot or foxtrot, it simply rounds its back and tucks its neck. To perform the lateral gaits, it hollows out its back and picks up its head. Some of the soft-gaited breeds are so set in their body type that it is more difficult for them to perform more than their predisposed gait.

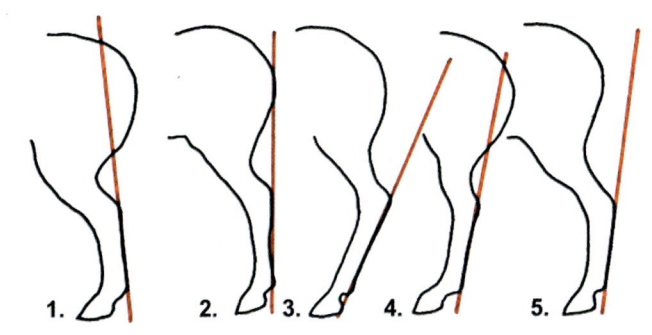

Rear Legs: 1. Too straight. 2. Well balanced. 3. Sickle-hocked. 4. Underslung hind legs. 5. Stance too open.

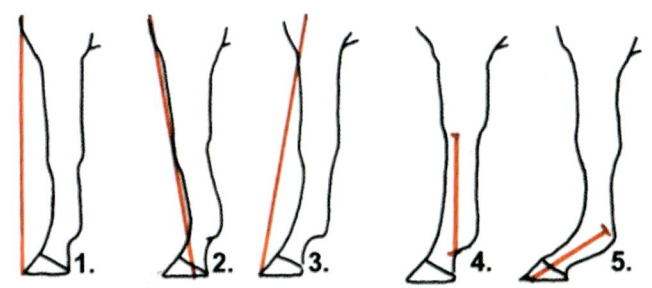

Front Legs: 1. Straight front legs. 2. Buck-kneed. 3. Calf-kneed. 4. Cannon bone too long. 5. Coon-footed.

Hoof: 1. Regular pastern. 2. Stumpy pastern. 3. Sloping pastern. 4. Foot broken forward. 5. Foot broken back.

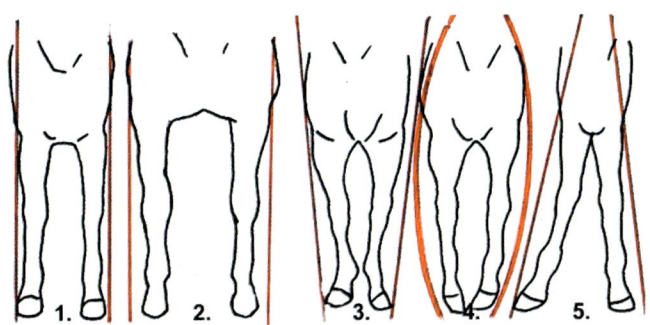

Front View: 1. Balanced chest and base. 2. Too wide in front (slows down movement). 3. Wide chest and narrow base (horse may paddle). 4. Narrow base with pigeon toes. 5. Narrow chest and wide base (often seen in immature horses).

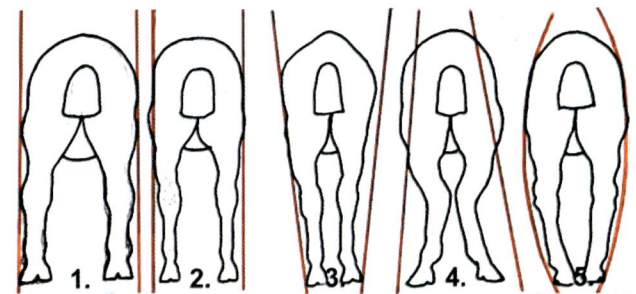

Rear View: 1. Too wide behind (horse will travel spraddled out). 2. Well balanced. 3. Narrow base, narrow in stifle and rafter-hipped. 4. Cow-hocked and splay-footed. 5. Out at the hocks, with pigeon toes.

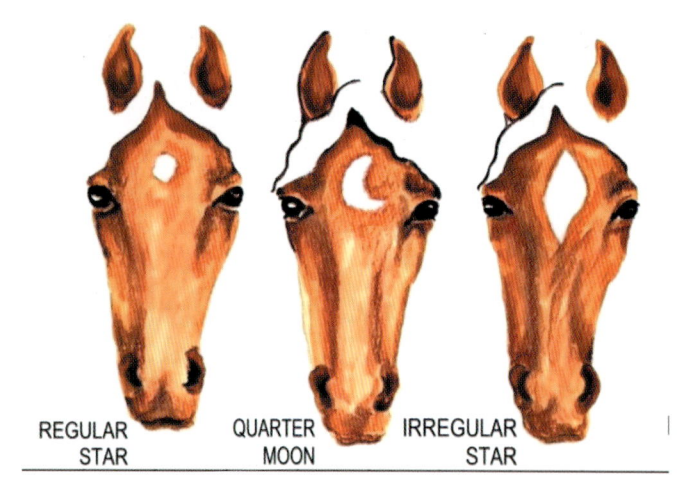

REGULAR STAR QUARTER MOON IRREGULAR STAR

FLEUR-DE-LIS STRIP SNIP

People who have not experienced the "soft-gaited horse" are somewhat amazed at the bonding that goes on between horse and owner. These gaited beauties revel in the joy of companionship with their "people."

A horse with a long back, a flat or horizontal pelvis, and a long tibia producing proportionally long back legs, will find it difficult to round its back and get under itself. Similarly, a horse with a short neck will have difficulties flexing that neck.

STRIPPED HOOF CORONET 1/2 PASTERN HEEL

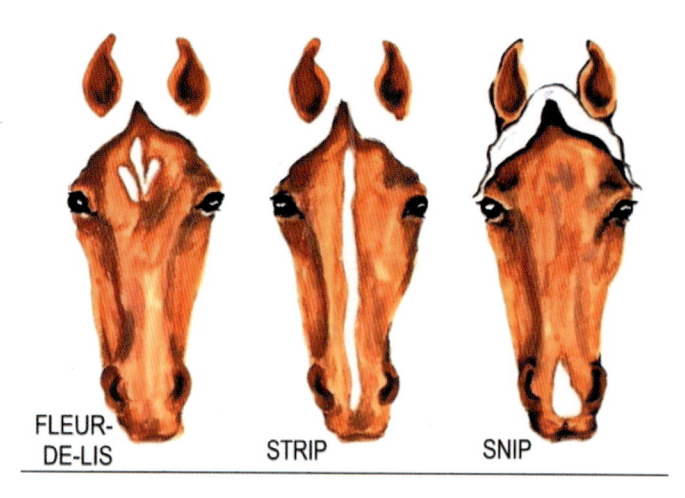

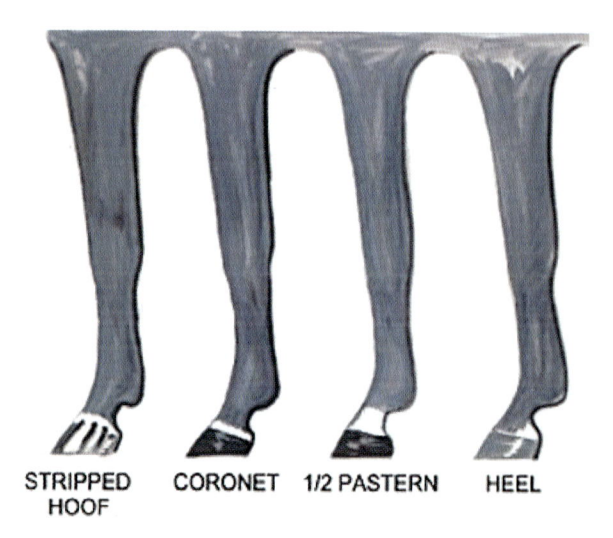

Body type, however, impels rather than compels. The degree and type of training will effect these natural abilities in any given horse. If the bone is the foundation for the horse, it will indeed influence its way of going.

There are other characteristics that are equally important. The brain, nervous system and muscles will definitely impact movement. Think about all that goes on when a horse takes a step. Its movement is caused by losing

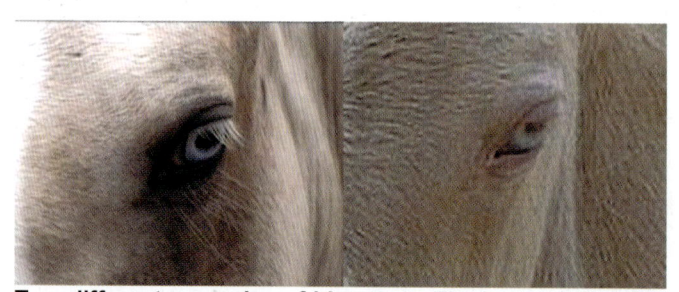

The middle, or square gaits such as the paso llano and the running walk, require a level back. Photo: Forrest Bliss

Two different examples of blue eyes. The horse on the left is a palomino and the skin exhibits normal pigmentation. The eye on the right belongs to a cremello that has the characteristic lack of pigment in its skin.

22

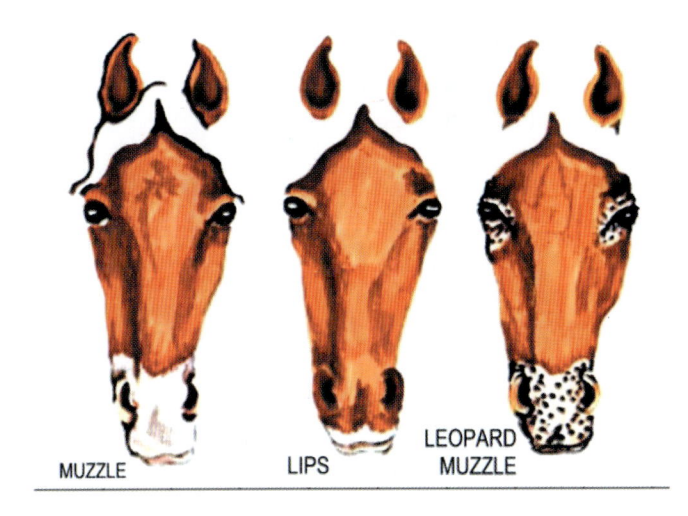

MUZZLE — LIPS — LEOPARD MUZZLE

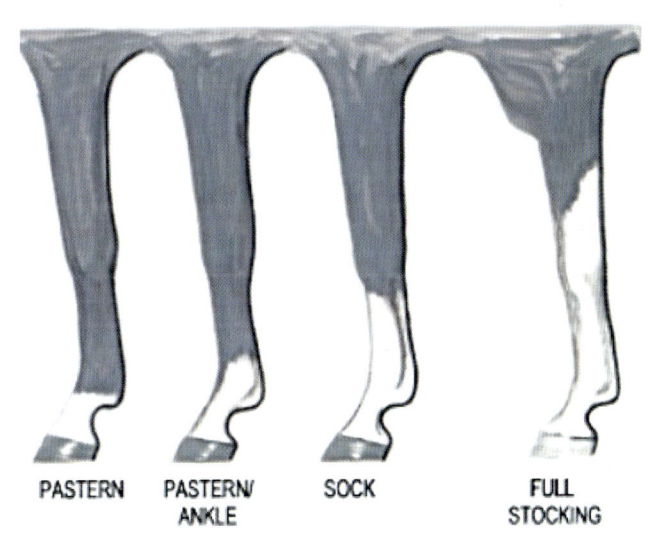

STAR, STRIP, SNIP — BLAZE — BALD FACE

PASTERN — PASTERN/ANKLE — SOCK — FULL STOCKING

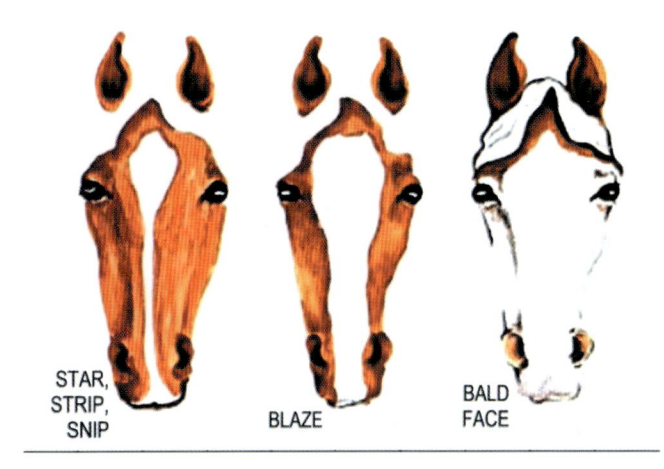

Three distinct colors seen on these three horses from Tetonia Ranch in Idaho.

its equilibrium and then by regaining it. It has to move its weight from the foot that will be leading out. Then it must raise its head and neck, round its back and lower its hind quarters. Only then will it be able to take that step and move out. In this one simple undertaking, we see the important role played by the nervous system and muscles as directed by the brain. Where the bone is a given, the muscles can be conditioned and developed within the limitations of their design.

No optical illusion here, just brothers out for a run. (MPHA) WOODWIND BEN and (KMSHA) ANDRE.

ROWDY and his offspring are known for their dazzling speed. See chapter 26.

23

COLORS

The soft-gaited horse comes in all horse colors. The Mountain Horses of Kentucky are known for their unusual chocolate body with a flaxen or white mane or tail. They do, however, come in other colors - chestnut, palomino, black, grey, roan, cremello, buckskin and bay.

The Tennessee Walkers have the overo gene in their foundation stock and that pinto characteristic is still present. During the 1940's, a very popular stallion, Midnight Sun, infused a strong black gene into the breed. Looking at the world grand champion Tennessee Walkers, from 1939 to 1990, forty-six horses were honored. Of these winners, twenty-nine were black, twelve were dark chestnut, four were bay and one was white.

The Tennessee Walker registry does honor other colors such as grey, palomino, roan, and sabino. Since the popularity of the spotted horses hit the state of Tennessee, there are now tobiano horses in their registry. One color that is exclusive to the Tennessee Walker is the exotic iridescent champagne.

The Fox Trotter boasts a true rainbow of colors available in the breed. Their list of champions includes bays, blacks, palominos, cremellos, chestnuts of all hues, dun buckskin, grey, white and pintos; both tobiano and overo.

Spotted Saddle Horses come in all the color variations associated with the pinto. Tobiano, overo and sabino are found in both piebald (black and white), and skewbald (any color combined with white, other than black).

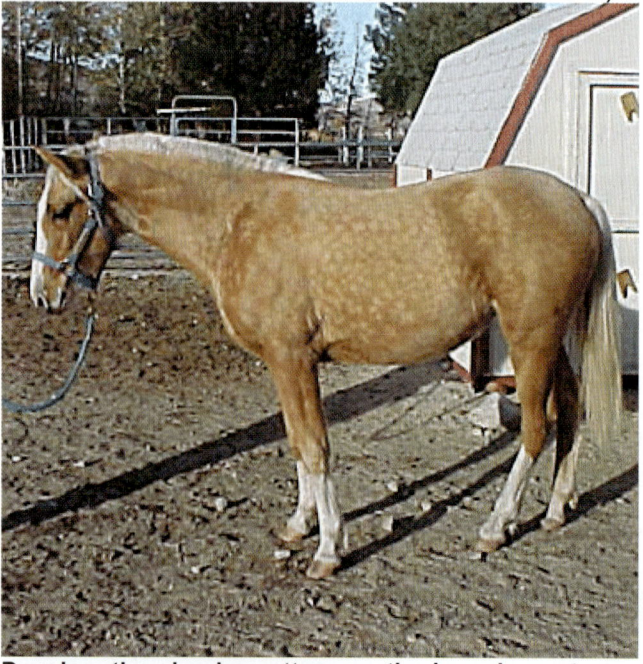

This beautiful Paso Fino stallion from the Remolino Ranch in Northern Nevada displays an eye-catching grey color. Photo: Forrest Bliss

The Cremello is a unique color. When a cremello is bred to a chestnut, there is 100% palomino offspring. With the popularity of palomino, cremello breeding stock is certainly in demand. STAR'S APRIL ROSE, a two-year-old Mountain Horse, is pictured above.

Dapples, the circular pattern on the horse's coat, are a sign of excellent condition.

Black is definitely a popular color found in the Tennessee Walking Horse. However, all horse colors are accepted, including spotted and champagne.

The Racking Horse may be black, bay, sorrel, chestnut, brown, grey, yellow and sometimes even spotted. The Paso Fino recognizes all equine colors with or without white markings.

In the Peruvian Paso, you can find jet black to creamy white, as well as various shades of grey, roan, buckskin, or dun and palomino. White on the face and legs below the knees and hocks is acceptable, but white on the body or above the knees and hocks will be a penalty to breeding stock in horse show classes.

The new Spotted Mountain Horse Registry honors any spotted markings on the Mountain Horse.

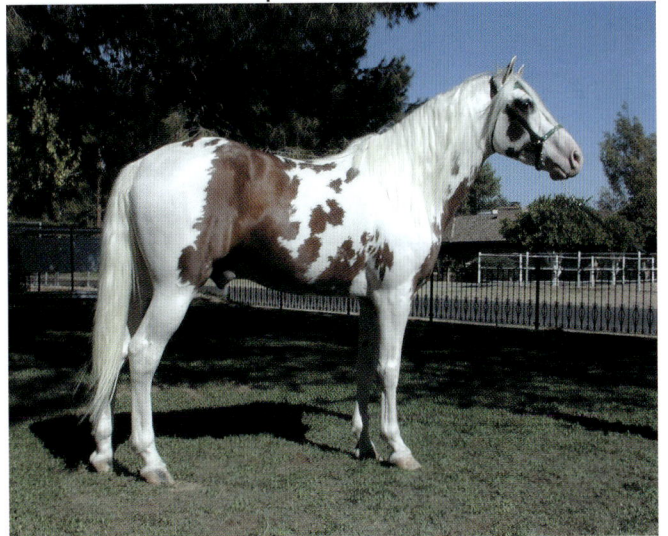

The Florida Cracker's colors are any color common to the horse. However, solid colors, roans and greys are predominant.

The Icelandic horse also comes in all imaginable colors. You can find pinto, chestnut, bay, black, buckskin, blue and red dun and palomino. The Icelandics can even be found with Appaloosa type spotting, although it is rare.

The Mangalarga Marchador's coloring is extensive and varied. They come in every known equine color including spotted and solid. Due to their isolation within Brazil for two hundred years, they also have developed colors not known in North American horses such as a stunning burgundy.

The Tiger horse is distinguished by its Leopard Complex gene (Lp). This gene is responsible for the manifestations of the Appaloosa characteristic. The horses can be of any base color except pintado, grey or genetic

The Spotted Saddle Horse is truly the "sports model" of the soft-gaited family. Pictured is REVELRY'S LITTLE BANDIT, from Mane Gait Farms in Glendale, Arizona. Owned by Lisa Brown.

Tennessee Walking Horses have an exclusive on the exotic champagne coloring.

Chestnut, of all hues, is desired coloring for the Peruvian Paso. All other colors are accepted, except pinto or excessive white markings.

white. Maximum contrast within the coat is considered desirable.

The Tennuvian's coloring follows that of their foundation stock. A blend of the Tennessee Walker and the Peruvian Paso, the Tennuvian exhibits colors of those found in either parent breed.

The Walkaloosa is also a combination of established breeds. The Tennessee Walker and the Appaloosa lend their color characteristics to the Walkaloosa.

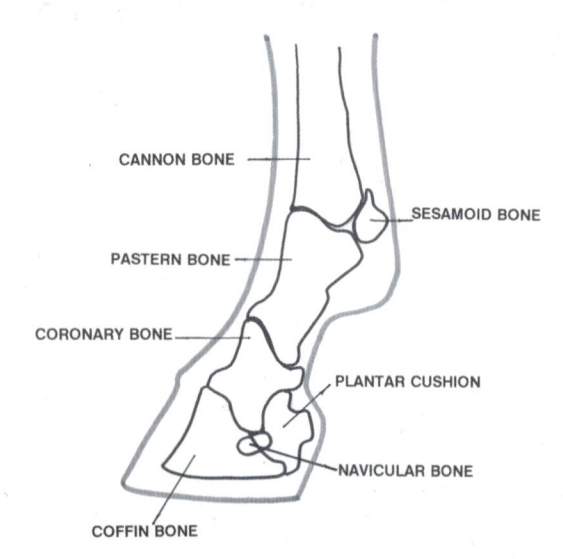

Correct angle of foot is an important safeguard to soundness. The fragile bones of the horse's foot are of primary importance to its long-lived serviceability.

HOOVES AND HOOF CARE

One of the most controversial areas for the soft-gaited horse owner is how to maintain proper foot health for their horse. Numerous sources incorrectly assume it is the shoeing that creates the magic soft gaits. The truth is, the unique soft-gaits are natural to these horses. The gait is in the gene and not nailed to the foot.

That being said, it is important for a gaited horse to be correctly shod. Traditionally, the Peruvian Paso is shown without shoes. Many horses that have healthy hard feet can be ridden without shoes. (The abrasive quality of the riding surface should be considered.) But it is critical that all horses have their feet trimmed or shod on a regular basis. If a horse is used as a pleasure horse over all terrains, shoes are a must, or sore-footedness or lameness may occur. But keep in mind, that the shoes are to protect the hoof and allow the farrier to control the growth and angle of the hoof, not to artificially create gait.

The most important element of hoof care is to maintain a proper angle. The individual degree of angle is based on the conformation of the individual horse. Both

It can be somewhat surprising to see such contrasting color between a mare and her foal.

shoulder angle and pastern/fetlock angle should be taken into consideration when determining the hoof angle. Soft-gaited horses usually do better with a little more foot than a Quarter horse or Arabian, but allowing the foot to grow extra long in the toe that isn't matched with adequate heel can cause unwanted stress on the ligaments. Feet should be checked regularly for unwanted debris such as manure, gravel or nails.

SPECIAL TALENTS

The soft-gaited horse as a category, certainly has special characteristics that are definitely exclusive to the individual breeds. Their orientation to their "people" will continue to set them apart from other horses.

One extra special talent that is only recently becoming addressed is the gaited horse's ability to attain great speed in their "second gear." Racking Horses and Tennessee Walking Horses have had speed racking classes at most of their shows for years. The North American Single-Footing Horse Association has a speed gait class that is catching fire! Imagine, a gaiting horse achieving speeds matching cantering horses.

This tremendous speed is attracting a whole new audience to the soft-gaited horses. Serious breeders welcome the challenge of breeding for speed, because it's one talent that definitely has to be bred into the horse. There isn't much you can do to increase a horse's ability to travel at a high speed if it isn't in the genes.

So the renaissance of the soft-gaited horse is at hand. The myths are beginning to be dispelled. The soft-gaited horse is not a hot-house creature, only suited to the show arena. Where these horses shine is on the trail, in competition, as family mounts, and because of their ability to amaze a crowd with their speed. As life becomes more complicated, and city life more hectic, experiencing nature in the company of a companion horse is certainly a special opportunity of enjoyment. These are "using horses" and they're certainly up to the challenge!

The dark chocolate body and flaxen or white mane and tail are commonly found in the Rocky Mountain Horse.

Kentucky Natural Gaited stallion, TREVER, carries on the tradition of working side by side with his owners Greg and Sara Jenkins at Jenkins Pleasure Gait Farm in Salyersville, Kentucky.

An Icelandic on his way to be filmed performing the tolt for the gaiting chapter (Chapter 3) in this book. Owner: Elisabeth Haug

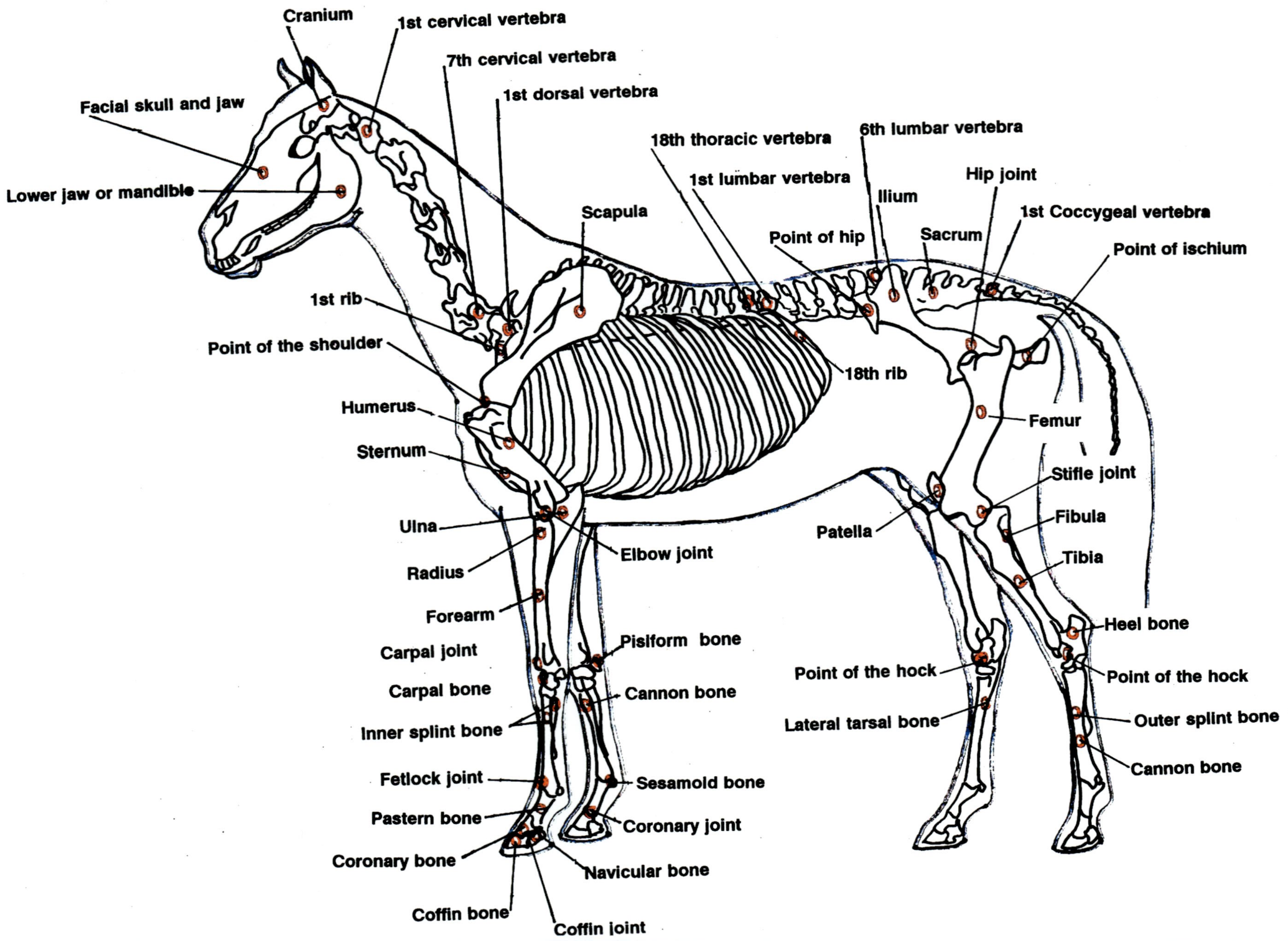
Cranium
1st cervical vertebra
7th cervical vertebra
1st dorsal vertebra
Facial skull and jaw
Lower jaw or mandible
18th thoracic vertebra
6th lumbar vertebra
1st lumbar vertebra
Ilium
Hip joint
Scapula
1st Coccygeal vertebra
Point of hip
Sacrum
Point of ischium
1st rib
Point of the shoulder
18th rib
Humerus
Femur
Sternum
Stifle joint
Fibula
Ulna
Patella
Elbow joint
Radius
Tibia
Forearm
Heel bone
Carpal joint
Pisiform bone
Point of the hock
Carpal bone
Cannon bone
Point of the hock
Lateral tarsal bone
Inner splint bone
Outer splint bone
Cannon bone
Fetlock joint
Sesamoid bone
Pastern bone
Coronary joint
Coronary bone
Navicular bone
Coffin bone
Coffin joint

29

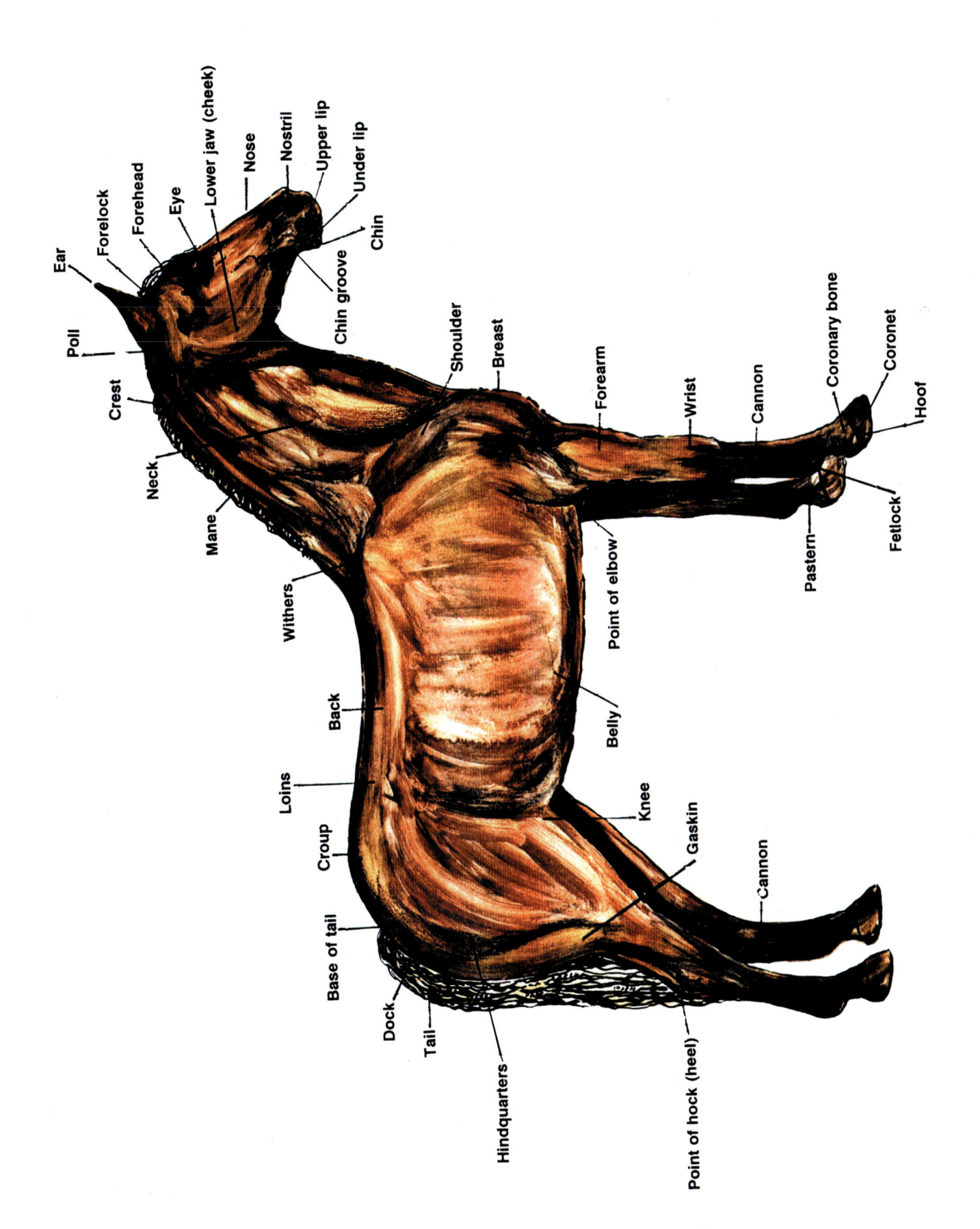

The **YEARLING'S** mouth shows wear in the central and intermediate temporary incisors. The corner incisors are nearly touching and there are signs of the first permanent premolars pushing their way through.

When the horse reaches **TWO YEARS OLD**, there is evidence of full wear in the mouth. It will resemble the mouth of a five-year-old, but the teeth are only temporary. By the time the horse reaches 2 _ years, the permanent teeth will begin erupting over the temporary ones.

A **THREE YEAR OLD** will show full wear in the central incisors, and by 3 _ years the permanent intermediate incisors will be coming in. By **FOUR YEARS**, both the central and intermediate incisors have been replaced. The canine teeth (also known as trushes) make their appearances in MALE horses at the age of FIVE.

By **SIX YEARS**, the top corner incisors are developing hooks because of their contact with the lower corner incisors. The cups on the underside of the incisors begin to disappear at this point, starting with the lower centrals.

After six years of age, accuracy of determining age through the teeth becomes more difficult. Generally, the teeth begin to slant outward and usually by the **TWELVTH YEAR** the horse has a "smooth" mouth because the cups on the incisors have all but disappeared.

After **TWENTY YEARS**, teeth may become shorter and more triangular in shape on the wearing surface. These mouths may appear to be much younger if the horse has had excellent care and allowed to graze and provided with grains accompanied by a good healthy life.

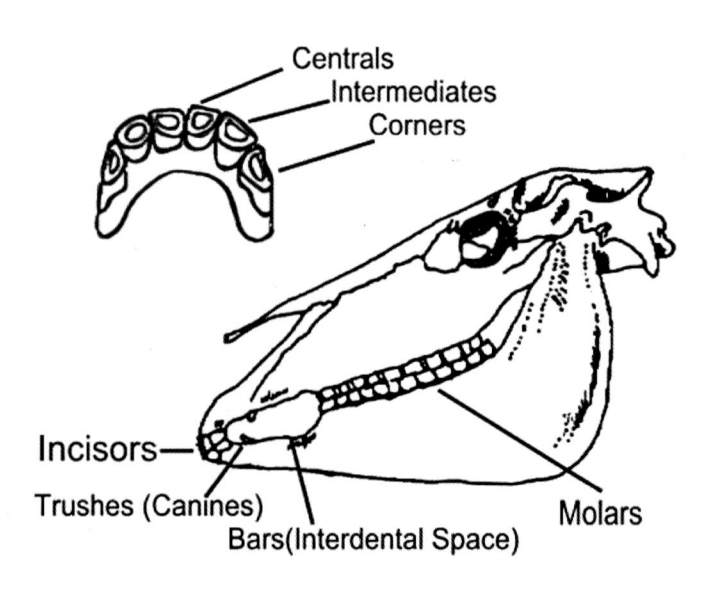

**Teeth courtesy of SKEETER'S COUNTRY GIRL,
A Kentucky Mountain Saddle Horse owned by
Skeeter Savage of Smith, Nevada.**

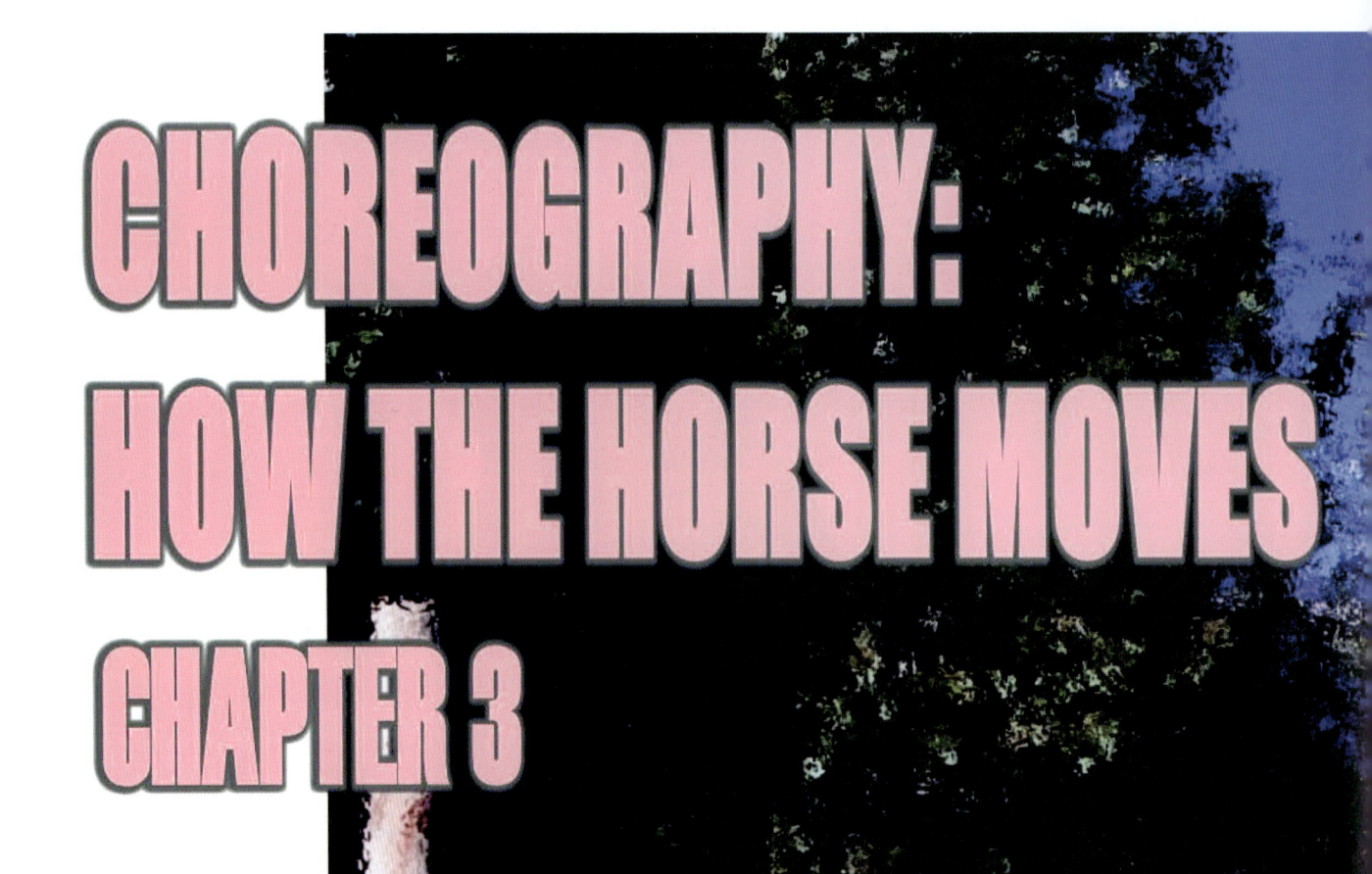

CHOREOGRAPHY: HOW THE HORSE MOVES
CHAPTER 3

Kentucky Mountain - STERLING SILVER
Photo: Loraine Costa

LATERAL 2-BEAT	LATERAL 4-BEAT	SQUARE 4-BEAT	DIAGONAL 4-BEAT	DIAGONAL 2-BEAT
PACE	ANDADURA IMPERFECTA	WALK	TROCHE	TROT
HUACHANO		RUNNING WALK		HARD TROT
		FINO	BATIDA	
ANDADURA	STEPPING PACE	CORTO		
		LARGO	BROKEN TROT	TROTE
CAMEL	SLICK PACE	RACK		
		TOLT		
HARD PACE		PASO LLANO	FOX TROT	
DEAD PACE	BROKEN PACE	SINGLE FOOT		
		EVEN GAIT		
FLYING PACE		SQUARE GAIT		
		SADDLE		
	SOBREANDANDO	PICADA		
		AMBLE*		

*Archaic.- Belonging to an earlier time - characteristic of language that was once common.

Chapter 3 CHOREOGRAPHY:
How The Horse Moves

The soft-gaited horse moves in a unique fashion that produces a definite four-beat rhythm when it performs the pleasure gaits. This is natural to these soft-gaited breeds. The ability to move in this special fashion is in their genes. These gaits can't be taught, but they can be refined.

Since most soft-gaited horses have the ability to perform more than one of these specialized gaits, it is vital for them to be trained to stick to one at a time. For riders new to soft-gaited horses, it is easy to become bewildered by the horse's "shifting gears."

As an observer, when you first start studying the gaits, don't get discouraged if you can't tell what gait a horse is performing. At first, all you will see is flurry of legs. Your work is to better understand the basic classifications of a horse's way of going. The five categories of "second gear" movement are: 1) Lateral 2-beat. 2) Lateral 4-beat. 3) Square 4-beat. 4) Diagonal 4-beat. 5) Diagonal 2-beat.

What do lateral, square and diagonal mean? In a *lateral* gait, the horse's movement is initiated when the front leg on one side corresponds with the movement of the rear leg on the same side. In a *diagonal* gait, the horse's movement is initiated when the front leg on one side corresponds with the movement of the rear leg on the opposite side. In a *square* gait, each foot acts independently in a defined sequence while maintaining an even distribution of movement.

The common gaits of the soft-gaited breeds can be placed in one of these five categories: **1) Lateral 2-beat.** Here there is an obvious two-beat sound because the lateral hooves leave the ground and return to the ground simultaneously. With these gaits, at one moment, all four hooves are off the ground between "landings." Gaits included in this category are the pace, dead pace, and flying pace. In these gaits, the rider is moved from side to side as the horse "lands," with a wide

In the Flying Pace, the Icelandic horse displays all four feet off the ground between strides. The lateral movement is very easy to see.

range of comfort; from the jarring of the hard pace to the extreme speed that produces the Icelandic's smooth-flying pace known as the "Gait of the Gods."

2) Lateral 4-beat. With these gaits, there is an offbeat four-beat sound. The lateral hooves leave the ground together but land separately. The degree of smoothness varies in the horse's individual ability to maintain a constant rhythm. Gaits in this category are the Sobreandando, andadura imperfecta, stepping pace, slick pace, and broken pace. The sound of these gaits is sometimes described as rectangular.

3) Square 4-beat. These gaits are square as in four-cornered evenly spaced footfalls. Some registries describe these gaits as lateral because an argument can be made that the lateral hooves leave the ground "almost" simultaneously. But actually, as in the walk, these gaits are performed with each hoof acting independently. In these gaits, the horse maintains ground support with one or more feet on the ground at all times. This explains the outstanding comfort and smoothness of a square 4-beat gait like the walk, running walk, fino, corto, largo, rack, tolt, paso llano, single

Here we see evidence of a square gait. The lateral legs on the horse's left side appear to be moving together. However where the front foot is off the ground, the rear is grounded. In a square gait, all four feet act independently.

foot, even gait, square gait, saddle gait, picada and amble.

4) Diagonal 4-beat. This unique way of going produces an offbeat rhythm as the diagonal legs pick up almost at the same moment but land separately.(The Fox Trotting breed describes this trademark gait by echoing the sound of the gait: "hunk o' meat and two potatoes.") Gaits that conform to this footfall pattern are the foxtrot, troche, batida, and broken trot.

This is an example of a trot, or 2-beat diagonal gait. It has a two-beat cadence. The right front and the left rear feet leave the ground together and hit the ground together (as seen in the illustration). The left front and right rear feet leave the ground together and hit the ground together.

5) Diagonal 2-beat. The gaits in this category are the trot, hard trot, and trote. Although the soft-gaited horses can certainly perform the two-beat diagonal gait at liberty, it is almost always discouraged under saddle. Exceptions to this are the Colombian Paso Finos that have a category known as the "trote y gallope" horses which are shown and ridden in a trot and contribute to the gene pool that can "square up" pacey horses. Another exception is an advanced horse used for cross-purposes such as dressage.

Armed with this information, how do we therefore identify the gait being performed? First, standing far enough away to see several strides, you focus on only one hoof. Watch it leave the ground and watch it land. Feel the rhythm of the movement. Gradually, expand your vision to include another hoof. Begin with the lateral hooves. Concentrate only on the two hooves on the same side of the horse nearest you. Now watch to see when they leave the ground. Don't bother with when they strike the ground - *yet*. Are they leaving at the same or very nearly the same time? If they are, then you are looking at a lateral or square gait. If the rear hoof on one side and the front hoof on the other side are leaving at the same time, then it is a diagonal gait. Once you know this much, then follow the information given in this chapter to identify the specific gait.

Distinguishing the different gaits from the perspective of being in the saddle is perhaps a more difficult challenge. Many riders are simply satisfied if the ride is smooth.

The best way to expand your expertise is to have someone who knows and recognizes correct gait coaching you from the ground. Then it's up to you to memorize the feel and sound of the footfall.

This chapter will isolate the various steps these Fabulous Floaters are able to accomplish. The photographs of each gait represent one stride. Focus on the front leg nearest you and follow it through the series of pictures. You will see that the horse keeps at least one hoof on the ground at all times. At no time do all four hooves leave the ground in a four-beat gait. Each gait has its own attitude. The body posture and carriage all contribute to the performance of the individual gait.

Are there any similarities between walk-trot horses and soft-gaited horses? Yes - all horses have one 4-beat gait in common. It is the walk.

The **WALK** is a gait that all horses perform in the same manner. A walk is four-cornered, with each hoof leaving the ground and then hitting the ground independently. The horse always has two or three hooves on the ground at once. There is alternation between two front and one rear and two rear and one front. Each hoof is off the ground for the same interval of time. This is what produces a smooth, even and comfortable gait.

The difference in smoothness and comfort between the walk and the trot is the same difference in smoothness and comfort between the trot and the running walk, rack, fox trot, paso llano, paso fino, tolt, saddle gait and the rest of the soft gaits particular to the breeds presented in this book.

In order to learn to distinguish the gait, let's begin by taking a close look at the trot. The trot is a gait that is familiar to most horseback riders.

The **TROT** is the only true diagonal gait. It has a 2-beat cadence. The right front and left rear hooves leave the ground together and hit the ground together. The left front and right rear hooves leave the ground together and hit the ground together. At one moment in the gait, all four hooves are off the ground. This means the horse will "land" on the two diagonal hooves at the same time. This produces a jarring effect upon the rider.

The trot is a comfortable gait for the horse to perform, but one that demands practice and skill to ride properly. The trot necessitates posting by the rider in order to absorb the percussion created by the horse. In posting, the rider sits and rises from the saddle in rhythm to the footfalls of the horse. In advanced dressage training, the rider is taught to "sit the trot" and absorb the percussion with his or her body. Throughout the trot, a definite two-beat rhythm is evident.

In the **FOX TROT**, the hooves leave the ground diagonally as in the trot, but they hit the ground squarely as in a walk. The 4-beat gait is accompanied by a vertical head nod. The right front and left rear hooves leave the ground almost together. The right front hoof hits the ground when the left rear hoof is approximately half-way through its stride. The left rear hoof hits the ground while the left front hoof is still on the ground. It appears to be taking a long step in front and quicker step in back with the hind quarters displaying an apparent up-and-down movement. This action is repeated with the left front and right rear hooves. The rear hoof is off the ground twice as long as the front. It is common for the horse to "cap its tracks" with no evidence of overstride. Capping its tracks means the rear hoof lands on the track left by the front hoof.

This is the classic silhouette of a Missouri Fox Trotter performing the foxtrot. The diagonal legs are forward (right front and left rear). It looks like the horse is walking in front and trotting behind.

The **FOX WALK** has the same footfall as the foxtrot, but the speed is much slower. It might look like a walk, except for the deep head nod that accompanies the fox walk.

The **FLAT WALK** should be true, bold, smooth, and four-cornered. Each hoof leaves and strikes the ground independently at equal intervals. It is accompanied by a vertical head nod that comes from the shoulder and involves the entire head and neck. The horse should pull with its front legs and push with its rear legs. The rear hooves should track straight and move close to the ground with minimal hock action, keeping the croup level smoothly and effortlessly. The action of the back hoof stepping over the front track is known as overstride. A six-to-ten-inch overstride is normal in the flat walk.

The **RACK** is a smooth, bold, 4-beat gait. When a horse is racking, both its right hooves leave the ground together. The right rear hoof hits the ground when the right front hoof is at its highest point. The right front hoof hits the ground while the right rear hoof stays on the ground; this is repeated with the left hooves. The hooves leave the ground laterally and hit the ground bilaterally. The hooves leave the ground like a pace and hit the ground like a 4-beat walk at equal intervals. There is no nodding of the head, but there is a great deal of action in the rear end. The horse appears to be taking short steps, jumping from one hoof to the other as it moves. The timing is equally distributed, 1-2-3-4. The rack is even, and square.

The **RUNNING WALK** is a smooth gliding gait. It is executed freely, with loose and easy manner of movement. It involves pulling with the front legs and pushing and driving with the rear. It is the same gait as the flat walk, but with a noticeable increase in speed and overstride. The head should continue to nod while performing the running walk, even though the nod will be quicker and more shallow. A twelve-to thirty-inch overstride is normal in the running walk.

The powerful forward motion of the Tennessee Walker is seen in this silhouette of the great stallion HAYNES PEACOCK. The signature gaits of the soft-gaited breeds have a distinctive "attitude" specific to the gait.

The **SLOW SADDLE GAIT**, often known as the **AMBLE**, is a smooth, 4-beat gait and almost the same as the rack. The hooves leave the ground and hit the ground the same as in the rack. The difference is that the slow saddle gait is a shorter, faster stride, with little or no overstride and the horse has little or no head shake.

The **PASO LLANO** (PAH-so YAH-no) is the signature gait "pisos" (PEE-sos) of the Peruvian Paso. In the paso llano, or "smooth walk," the horse's knee and hock on the same side appear to be joined together, but the hooves do not strike the ground at the same time. An even 1-2-3-4 cadence can be heard. The hind hoof strikes the ground just before the front hoof. The longer path traveled by the front hoof is a key to the gait. As the rear hoof glides straight forward, the front hoof arcs out, then strikes the earth squarely a split second after the rear one. This gait is most easily recognized when there are three hooves on the ground, one in the air and the staccato rhythm of the "paca, paca" sound.

The **SOBREANDANDO** (so-bree-un-DON-doe) is generally a faster 4-beat gait with enough hesitation between laterals to make it closer to the pace. It is often described as a stepping pace. As the horse gaits, the knee and hock joints on the same side should move as if joined by a rod; the hooves do not strike the ground simultaneously because of the longer path traveled by the front hoof. There is an exaggerated "termino" or winging action in the front legs as they move out to the side from the shoulder.

While the sound of the paso llano is square, the sound of the Sobreandando is rectangular.

The **FINO, CORTO, LARGO** (FEE-no, COR-toe, LAR-go) are three speeds of the same Paso 4-beat square gait displayed by the Paso Fino horses of Puerto Rico. The footfall of this gait is left rear, left front, right rear, right front, etc. The cadence of the 1-2-3-4 beat is rhythmic, with equal time intervals between hoof beats that are perceptibly equal. The horse maintains a fairly stiff neck carriage, and a slight up-and-down motion in the hind quarters. There is usually a slight "winging" motion in the front legs.

The Paso Columbiano's gaits are described as **TROCHE Y GALLOPE** (TRO-chee ee gal-O-pay), which means Fox Trot and

Canter, and **TROTE Y GALLOPE** (TRO-tee ee gal-O-pee), which means Trot and Canter.

The **TOLT** is a gait peculiar to the Icelandic Horse. The footfall is that of the running walk or single-foot. The conformation and "way of going" of the Icelandic give the gait the unique appearance of what is known as the tolt. The desired form of the tolt is a combination of a high-stepping, accentuated show tolt and the smoother and more rider-friendly utility tolt.

The suppleness and stride are highly valued. What is more important is the ability to stretch at high speed. It is the stretch rather than the actual speed that is important.

The **STEPPING PACE** is a gait that is frequently mistaken as a pure pace. The overall appearance of the horse is of one performing the pace. The action is indeed lateral. The legs on each side move "almost" together. In some examples of the stepping pace, it has to be observed on slow motion film to see the hooves striking independently. The sound of 4 beats ranges from sounding clearly 4-beat to almost a 2-beat cadence.

This moose performs a picture-perfect pace. The camel is another non-horse that naturally paces.

The **PACE** is the one true lateral gait. It has two beats. The front right and rear right hooves leave the ground at the same time and strike the ground at the same time. The left side works in the same manner. The horse will swing its head and neck from side to side as it moves. It may also appear to swing its hind quarters from side to side. Together, there is a definite 1-2 beat.

At one moment, mid-stride, the horse is suspended in air as in the trot. This means the horse will land on the two lateral hooves at once, creating a definite rocking sensation for the rider. Depending on the horse, the rider could experience either a bouncing or a float.

The pace is the "parent" of all the specialized soft gaits, but it is not desirable in its pure form in any of the *FABULOUS FLOATING HORSES*, except occasionally in the Peruvian Paso and the Icelandic.

In the Peruvian Paso, the pace, or **HUACHANO** (watch-AH-no), is honored if it follows in line after the Sobreandando when exhibiting the "thread" of the horse's gaits.

In the Icelandic, the pace is displayed in the **FLYING PACE** which is known as the "Gait of the Gods." But the pace must be "flying." Slow pace is only useful for transport purposes and is not very pleasant to sit.

Like the walk, the canter (known in Western terminology as the lope) and gallop are common to all horses.

The **CANTER/LOPE** is a 3-beat, smooth rolling rocking-chair motion. One hind hoof sets down (beat one); the other hind hoof and its diagonal front set down simultaneously (beat two); the other front hoof sets down (beat three); all four hooves clear the ground for a split second, and then the sequence begins again. The front hoof that hits last determines the lead.

The **GALLOP** occurs when the canter is extended from a 3-beat to a broken cadence 4-beat, as in a run.

Some gaits defy being named.

HOW DOES THE 4-BEAT GAIT DEVELOP?

The walk, common to all horse breeds, is the foundation for all the 4-beat gaits. For the young gaited horse, the most productive time is spent performing the walk. The walk is ideally suited to develop the musculature needed to perform the "second gear" 4-beat gait.

How much time should be spent practicing the walk? As much as possible. Start with a relaxed easy walk and gradually push the horse up to speed. Work the horse at a rapid walk. Push the edge of speed without letting the horse actually hit that second gear. This is where you will best develop not only stamina, but a consistent even gait.

Many trainers from different breeds suggest working the horse in sand, high grass, and up and down hills. These areas all help the horse to develop its own rhythm and strength of musculature.

While the canter is a gait that has been fairly controversial for some of the gaited horse breeds, more recently it is becoming accepted as a fine developer for both body and mind.

When a horse is not under saddle, it can display amazing agility and body flexibility. Make use of that physicality when you're on its back.

The canter can actually relax a horse physically and at the same time stimulate its mind and body coordination to identify and perform the correct lead. It is important not to let the horse slip into a canter from its second gear. If you use the canter in training, always ask for it specifically, and only from a stand or a walk. Never allow your horse to break out of its 4-beat gait into the canter. The canter must be taught as an individual gait — never as an extension to the 4-beat gait.

If a trainer pushes for speed at the second gear, or asks or the second gear too quickly, the horse is likely to develop "hitches." Many will get trotty or pacey and some will throw in a few canter steps as it gaits. Any of these problems should alert the trainer that the horse is trying to produce the speed or gait before its musculature is ready. If you find that your horse is making these false steps, go back to the walk.

When a horse is allowed to perform its gait incorrectly, it is the same as *teaching* the horse to gait incorrectly. At the first misstep, pull up and return to the walk. Be sensitive to know the optimum speed that the individual horse can best perform its gait. Once you experience the smooth and synchronized sensation of a properly performed 4-beat gait, it is up to you to insist on that correct gait from your horse. You may have to bump it up or pull it back to stay in "the groove." Careful attention to this at the beginning of your association with the individual horse, will reward you with a lifetime of wonderful rides.

When in doubt, return to the walk. Maintaining a brisk walk on many trail rides can be the best prescription for "setting" gait.

On the following pages, you will see 16 gaits exhibited side by side, 4 gaits at a time. There are sixteen frames for each gait. Each frame represents one full stride of the particular gait. Follow from left to right across four pages to see the leg action involved in performing these "second gear" gaits. The two legs farthest from you have colored wraps.

In studying these pictures, you can see how the soft-gaited horse keeps at least one foot on the ground during each stride. Pay particular attention to the comparison of the trot and the foxtrot. These are both diagonal gaits, but here you will see how they differ from each other. You will also see the similarity between the walk and the flat walk. Body language and speed are also obvious elements in the variation and appearance of gait.

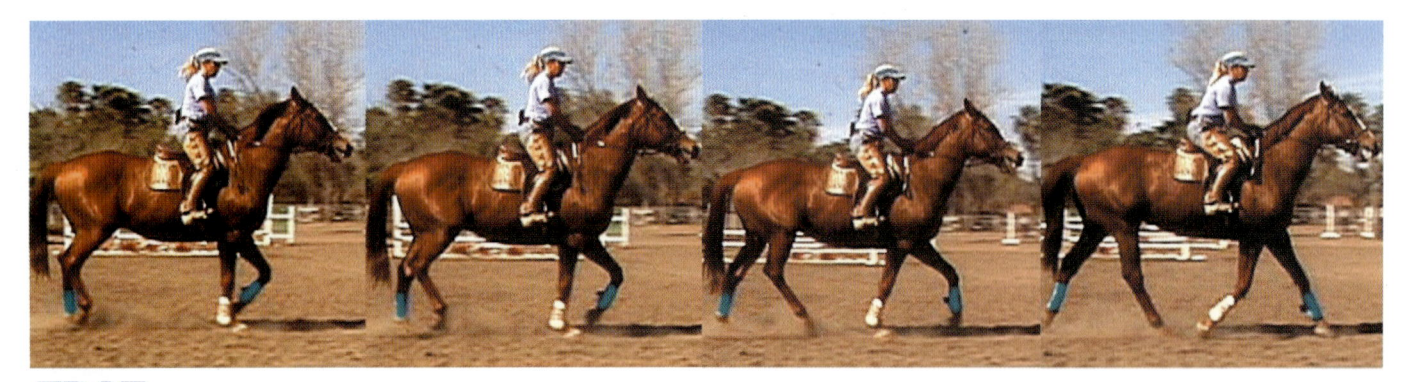

TROT

FOXTROT

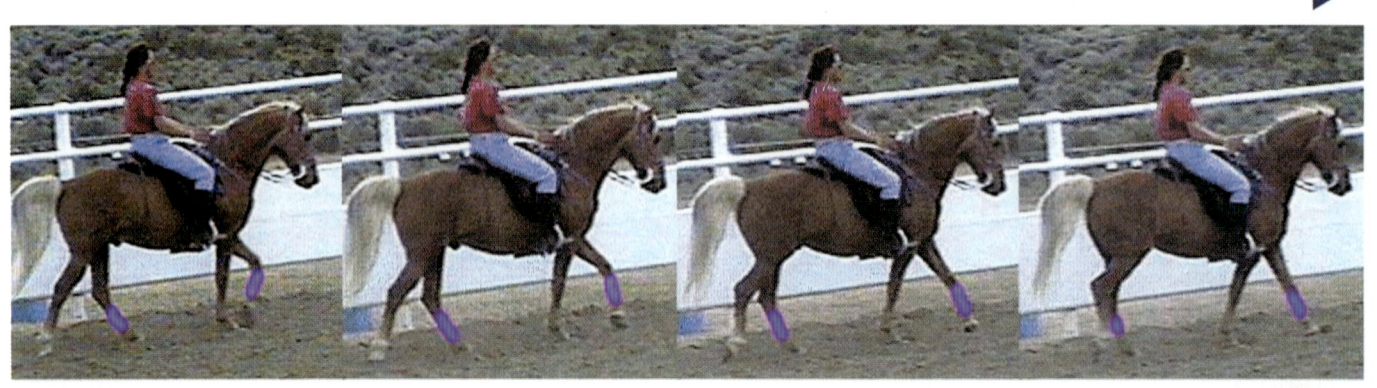

WALK

FLAT WALK

TROT

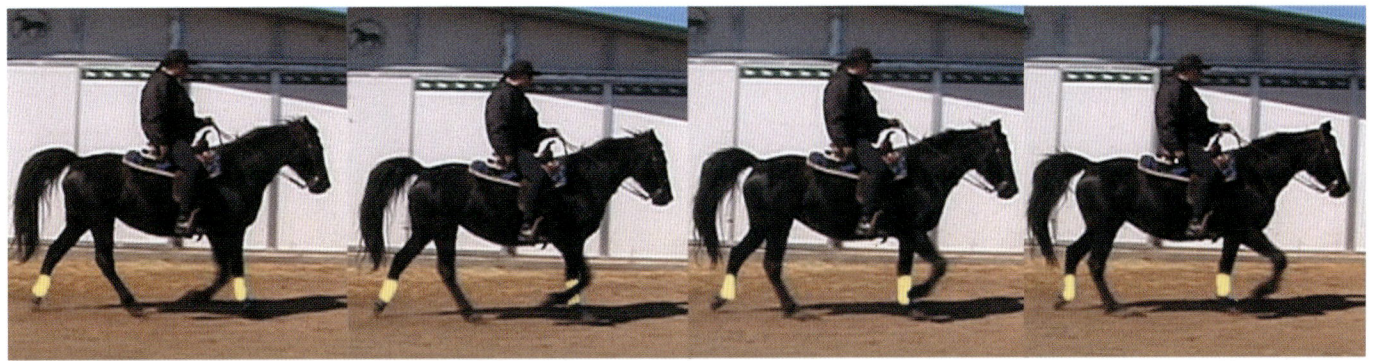

FOXTROT

WALK

FLAT WALK

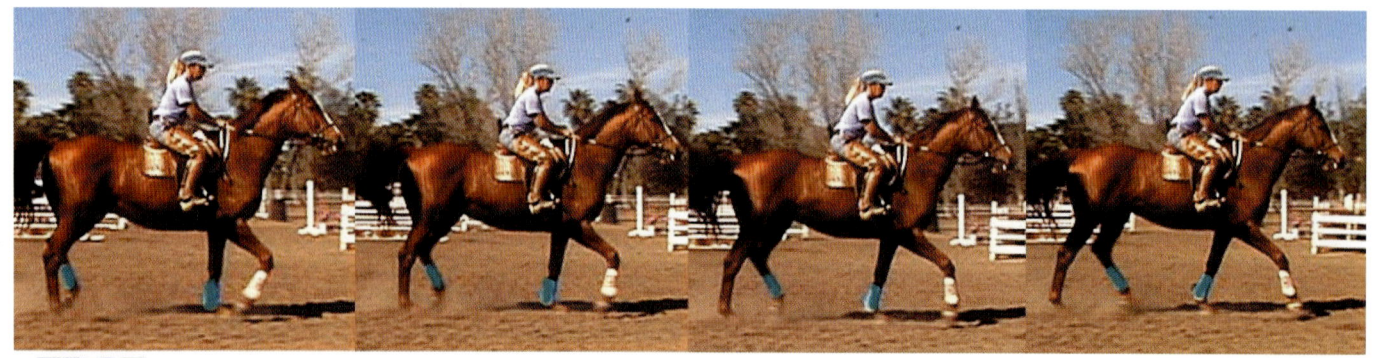

TROT

FOXTROT

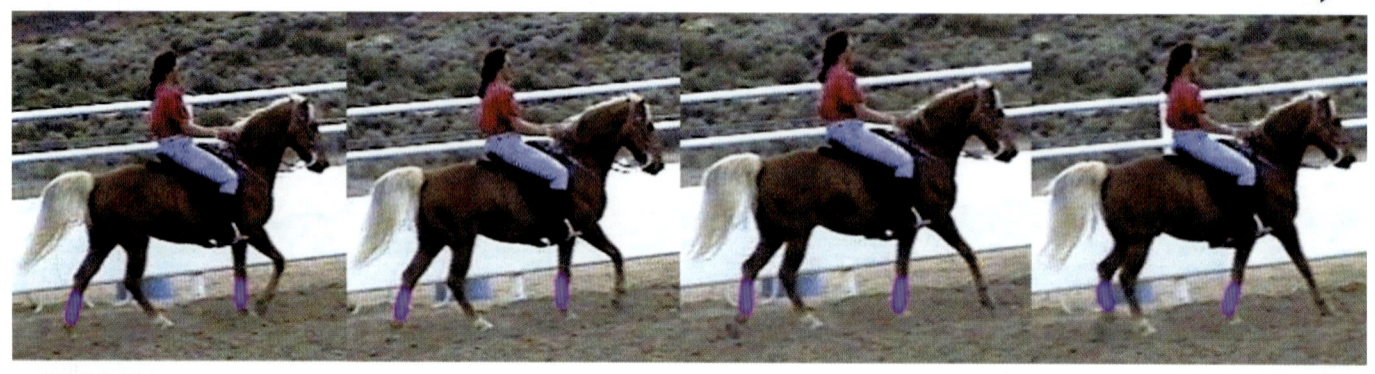

WALK

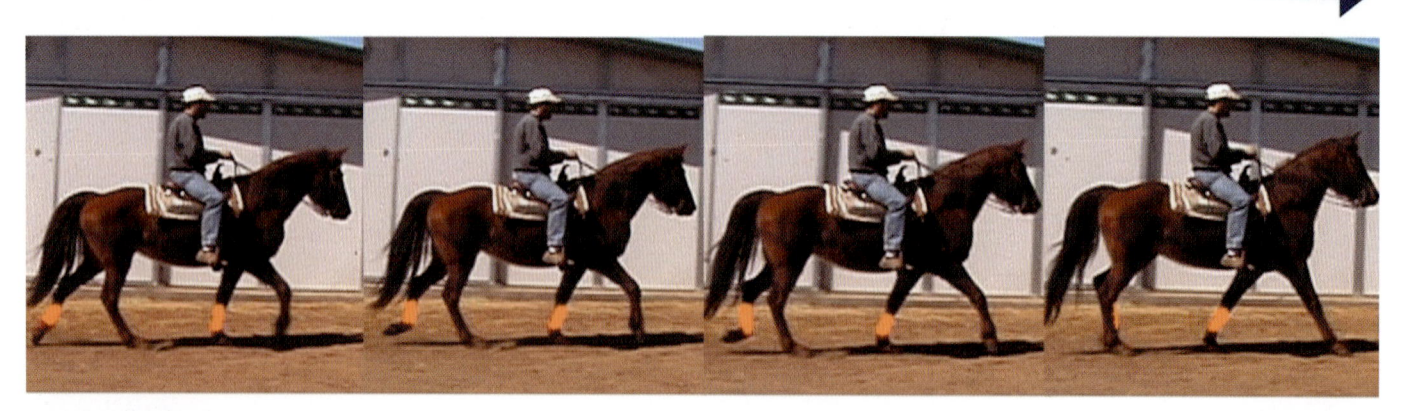

FLAT WALK

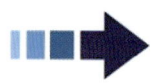

TROT

FOXTROT

WALK

FLAT WALK

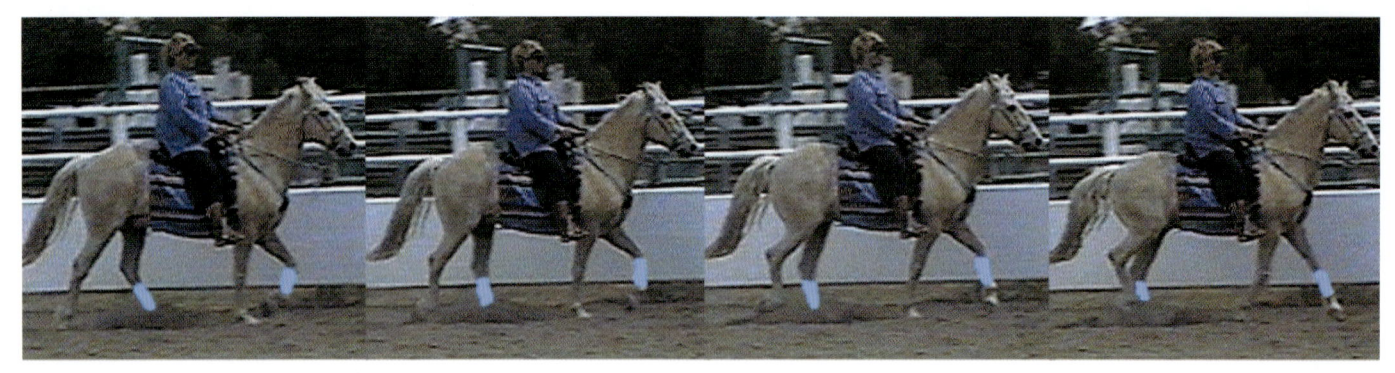

SADDLE GAIT

RACK

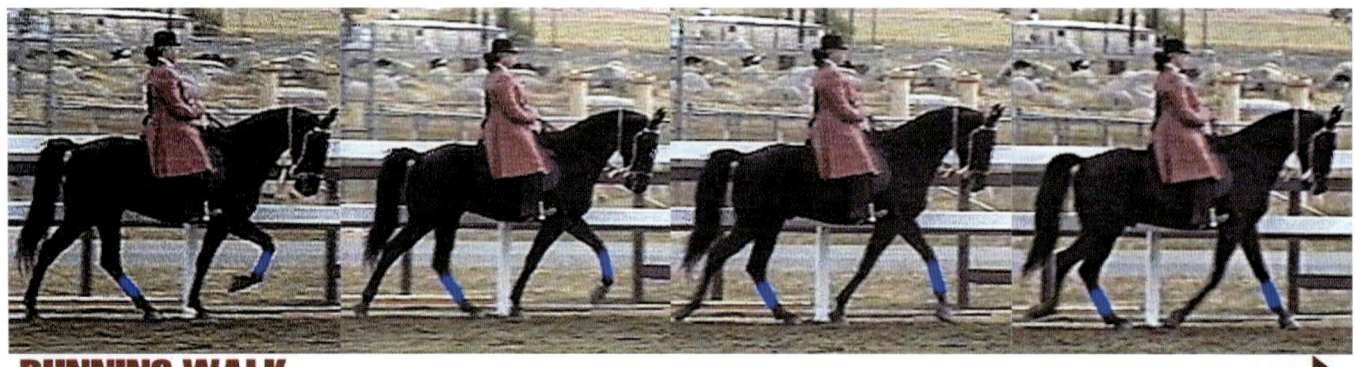

RUNNING WALK

PASO FINO

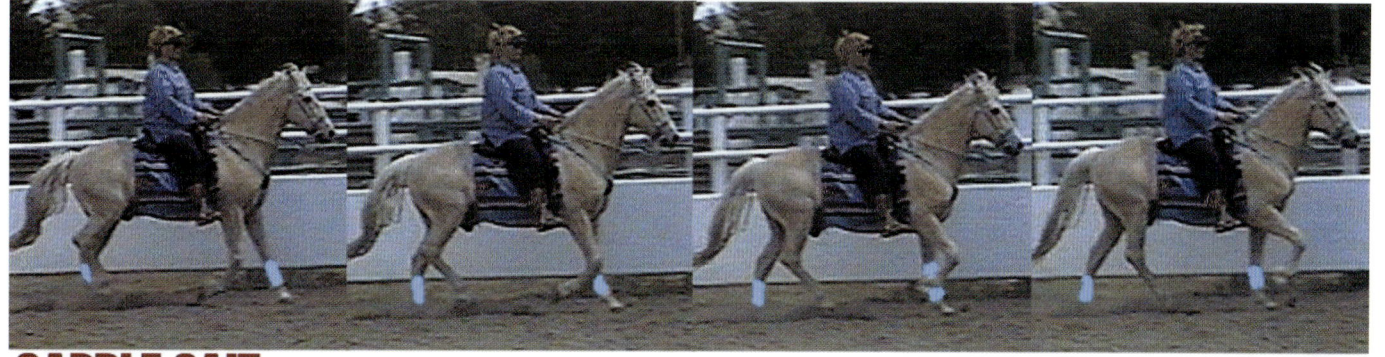

SADDLE GAIT

RACK

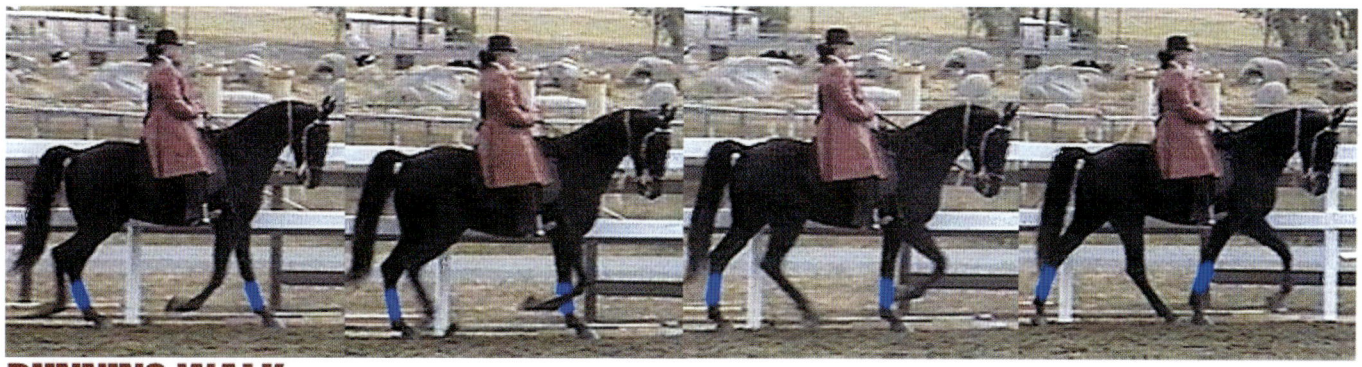

RUNNING WALK

PASO FINO

45

SADDLE GAIT

RACK

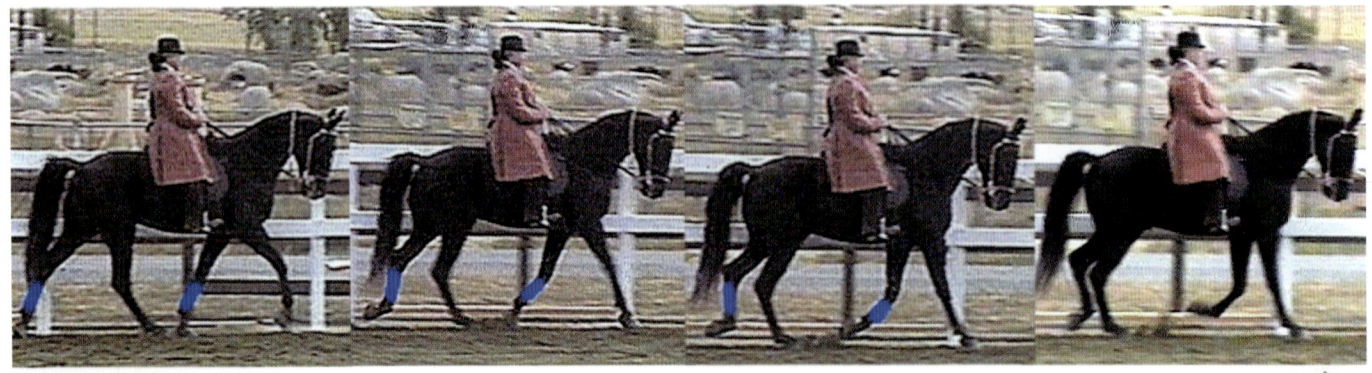

RUNNING WALK

PASO FINO

46

SADDLE GAIT

RACK

RUNNING WALK

PASO FINO

47

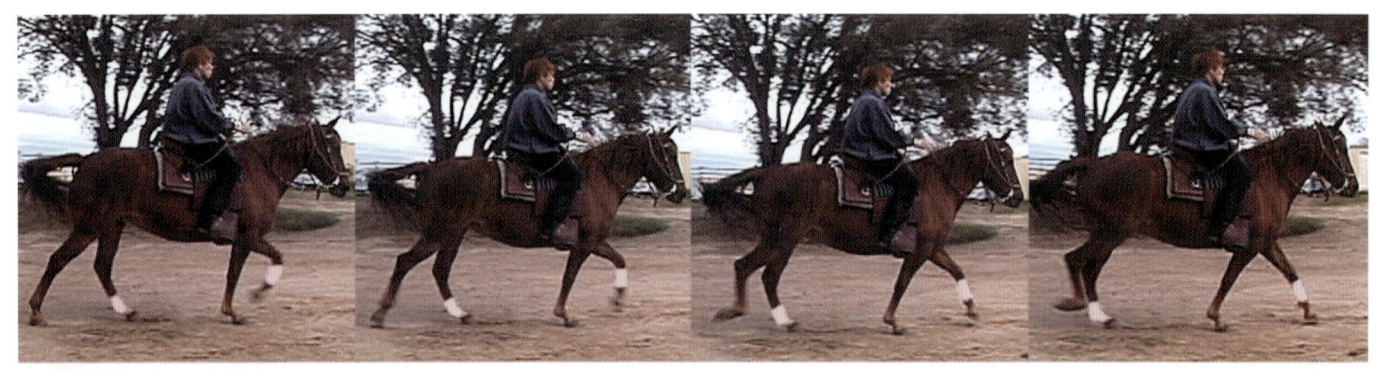

PASO LLANO

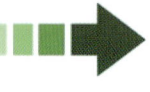

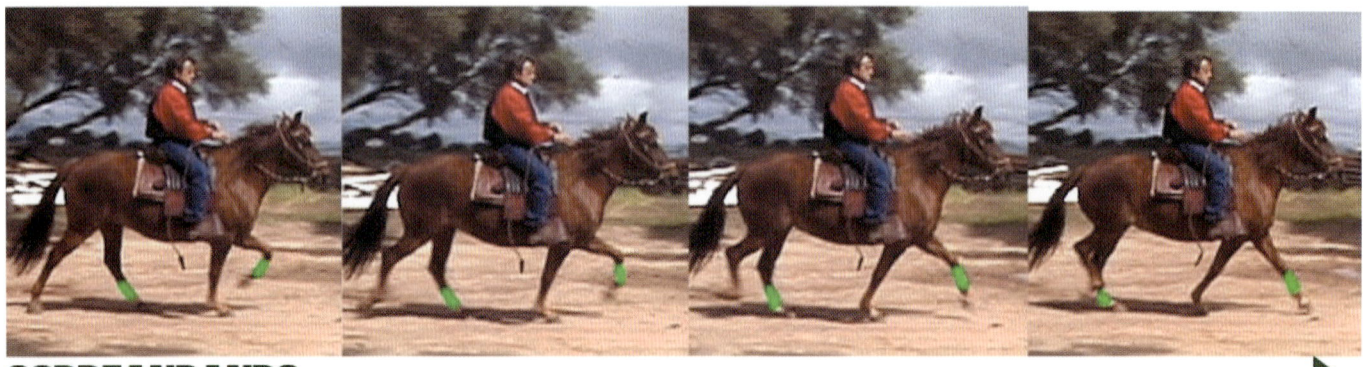

SOBREANDANDO

TOLT

FLYING PACE

48

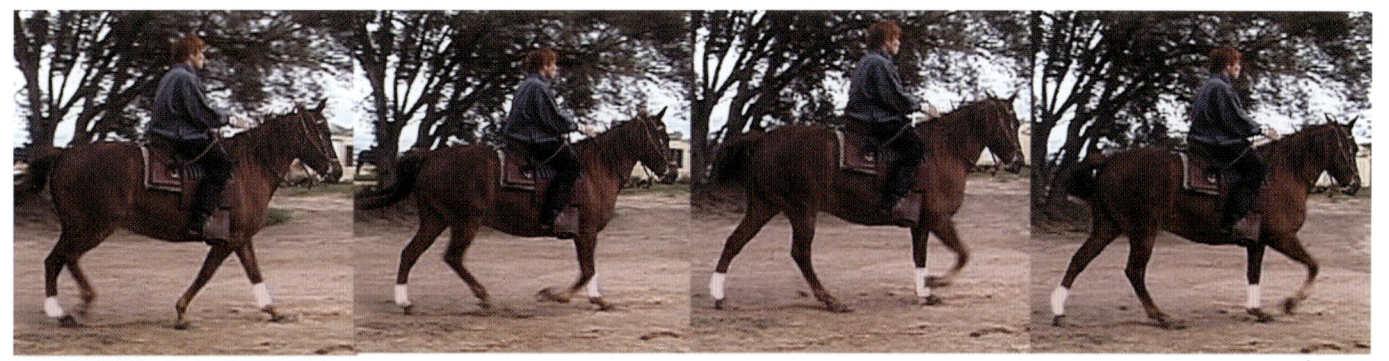

PASO LLANO

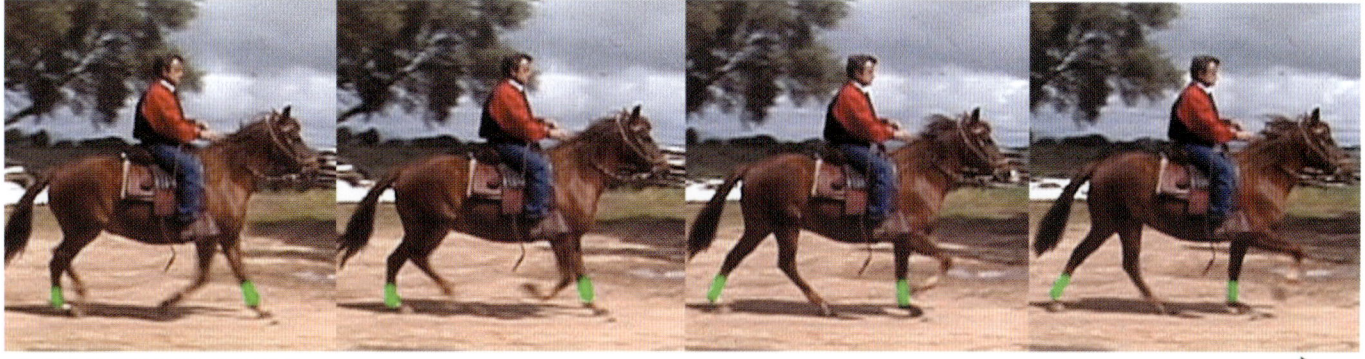

SOBREANDANDO

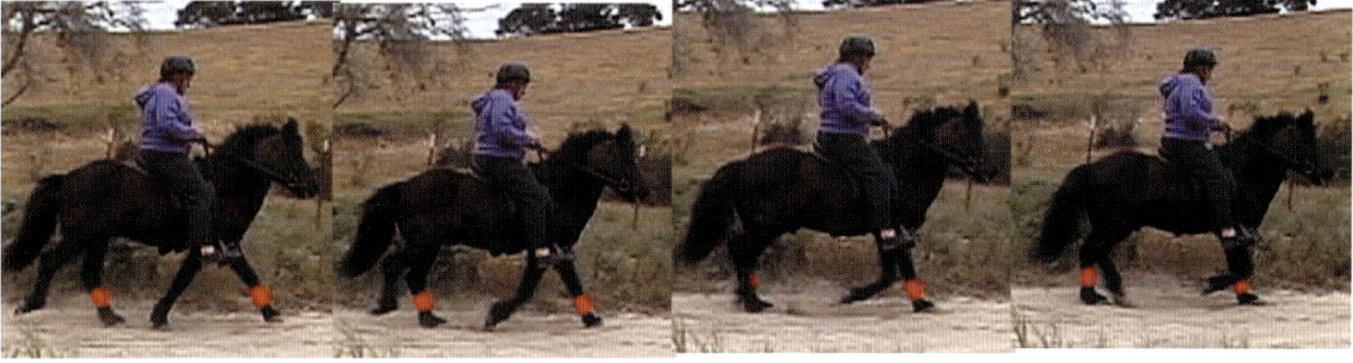

TOLT

FLYING PACE

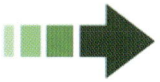

49

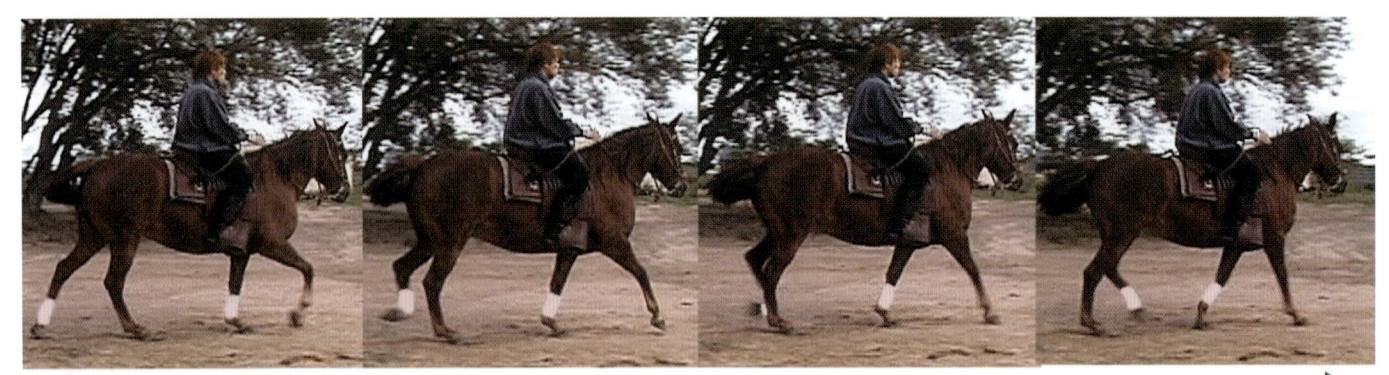

PASO LLANO

SOBREANDANDO

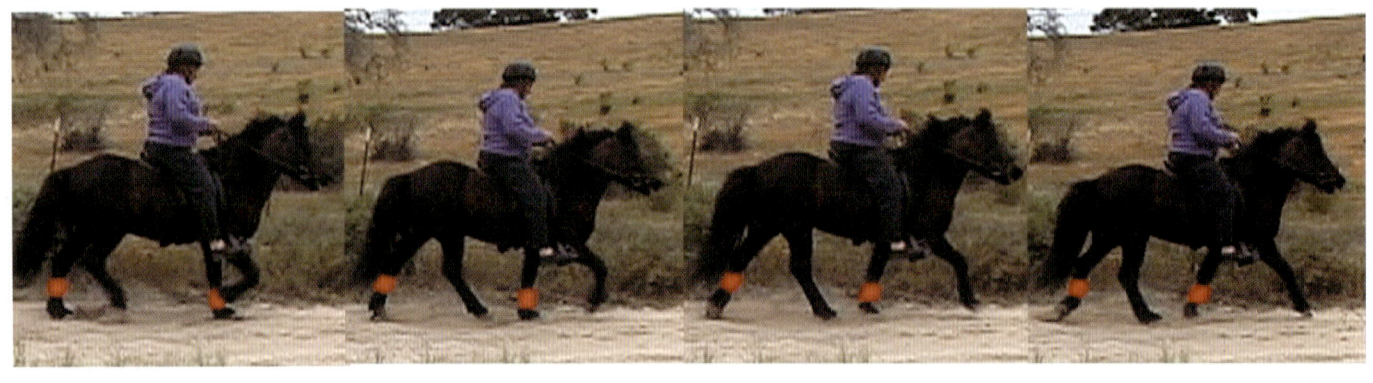

TOLT

FLYING PACE

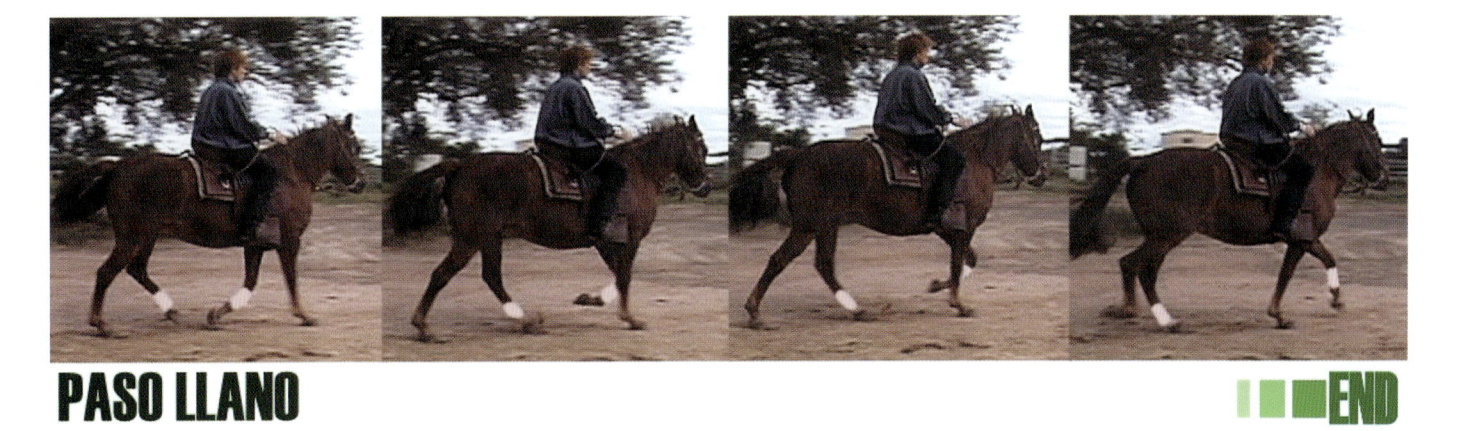

PASO LLANO

SOBREANDANDO

TOLT

FLYING PACE

51

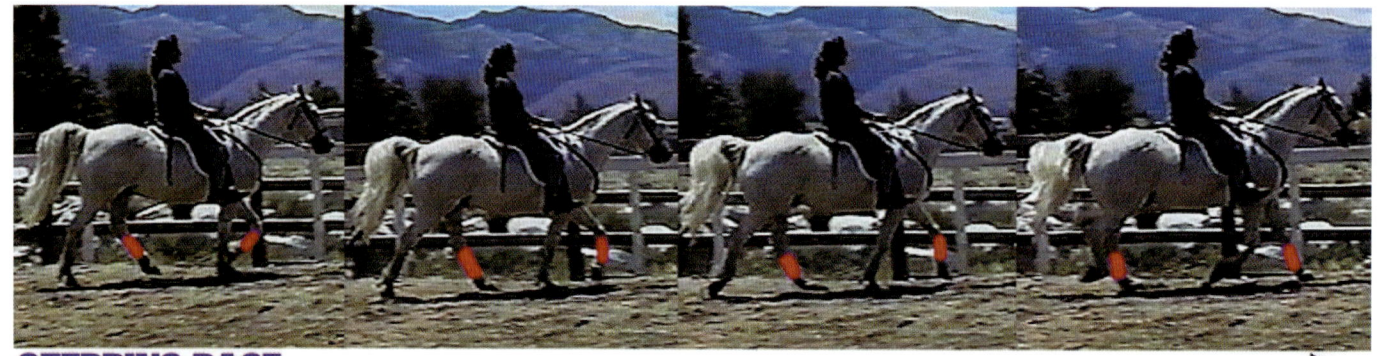

STEPPING PACE

LARGO

CANTER

GALLOP

STEPPING PACE

LARGO

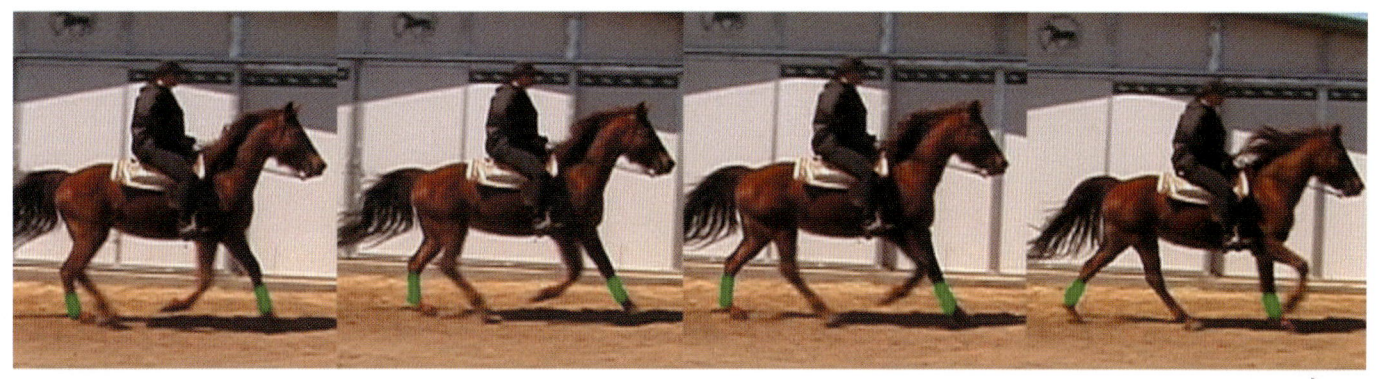

CANTER

GALLOP

STEPPING PACE

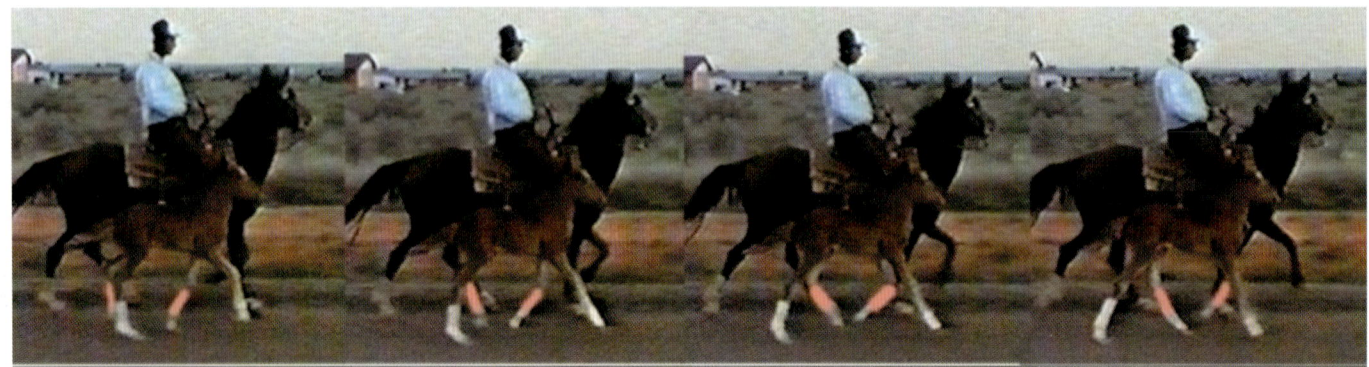

LARGO

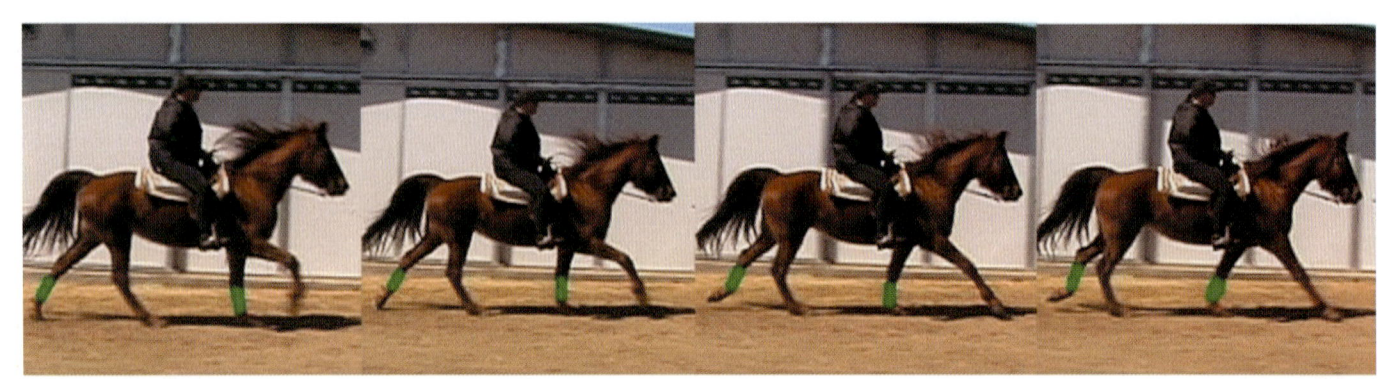

CANTER

GALLOP

STEPPING PACE

LARGO

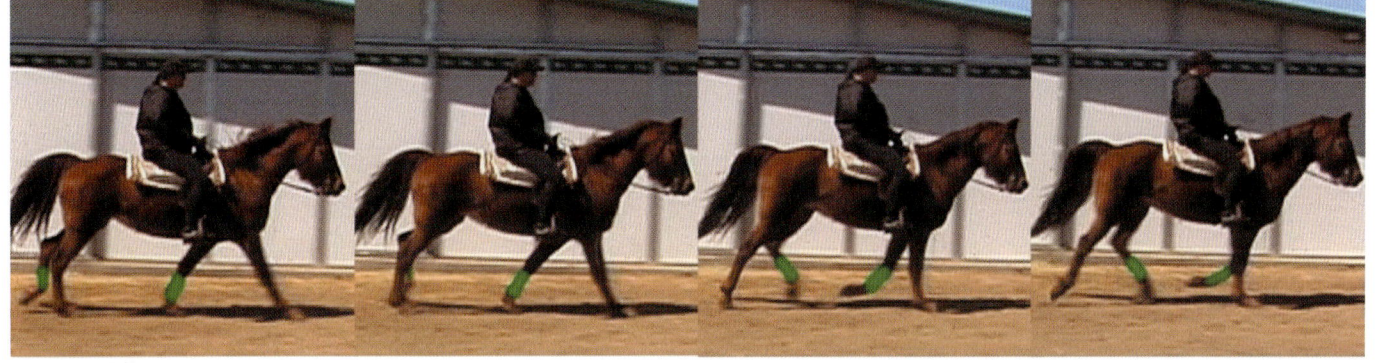

CANTER

GALLOP

CHOOSING A HORSE: THE ADOPTION PROCESS
CHAPTER 4

Logan & Derek Padget, and cousin Jacob

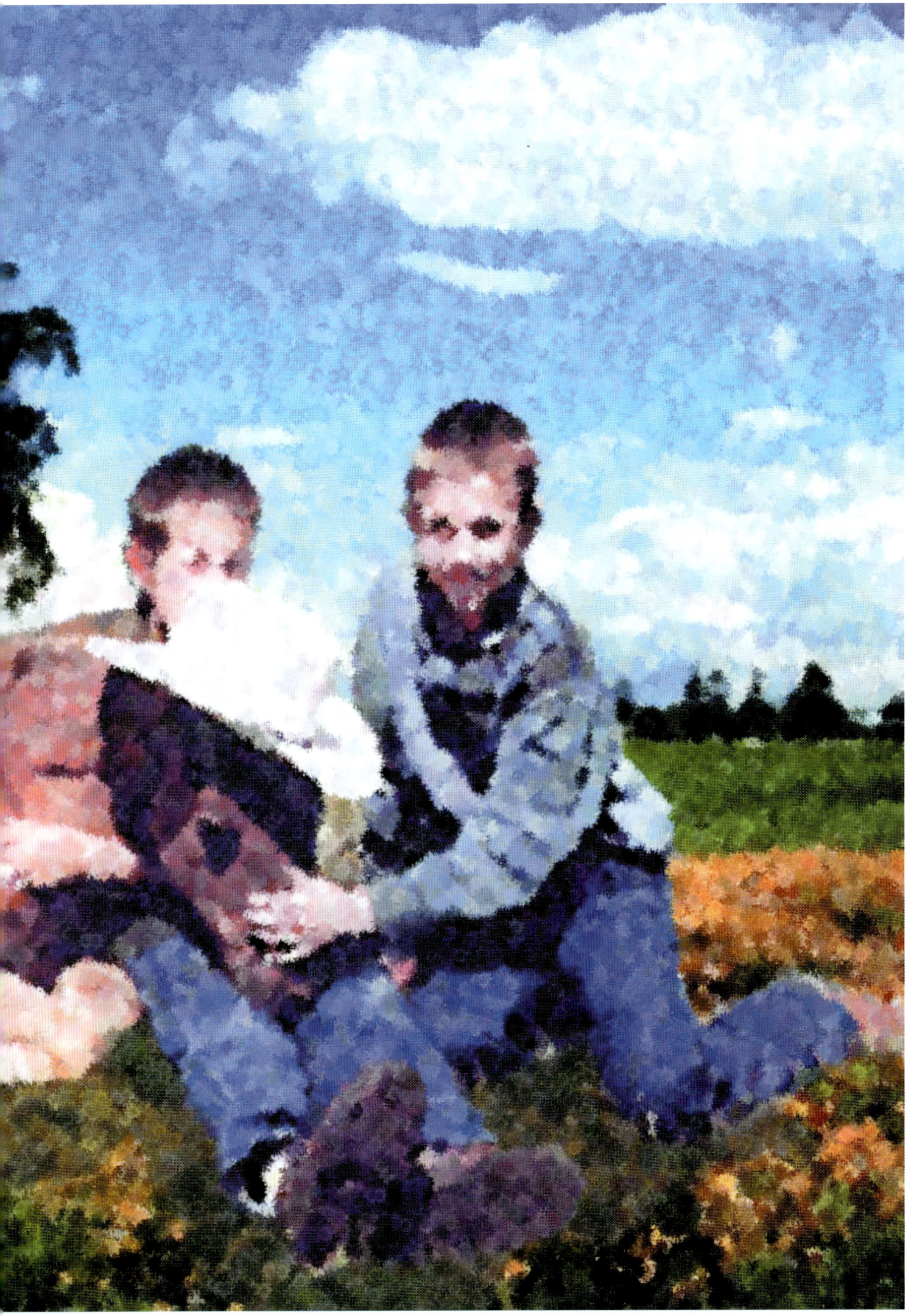

Chapter 4 CHOOSING A HORSE: THE ADOPTION PROCESS

Deciding you want to own a soft-gaited horse is sure to change your life. While the concerns you have are not altogether different from any other horse purchase, there are definite priorities. After the practical considerations are met, your decision will be subjective. Unlike some of the other competitive and sport horses, the soft-gaited horse is primarily a companion horse. *It doesn't have to be a bad horse to be the wrong horse.* It is important that you make an honest and thorough examination of your personal assets and expectations. Clarifying this **before** you begin will simplify your search.

An honest evaluation of your skills and desires will lead you to the right horse. (It doesn't have to be a bad horse to be the wrong horse – and sometimes a great horse can be the wrong horse). If you want to compete in champagne classes, (pictured), then look for a talented smooth horse that likes to show.

Take your time when choosing a horse for your very own. It's an important decision. Act in haste, regret in leisure. You may want a horse that is a "babysitter" or a horse with which you can stretch your skills a bit, but avoid a horse beyond your capabilities or power of control. Never assume that a novice horse and a novice rider can "grow" together.

You would be well-advised to make a fun project out of the process. Look at lots of horses. Even if you "fall in love" with the first horse you see, look at more. You may go back to the first one, but at least you will be making an informed decision.

The first questions to ask are:

1) **Why do you want a horse?**
   Is it a replacement horse? For your child? For social participation? For a hobby? As a companion? To fulfill a dream? For competition? To show?

2) **What is an honest estimate of your horsemanship?**
   Are you a beginner? Are you advanced? Could you train a young horse? Have you had training? Have you ridden soft-gaited horses?

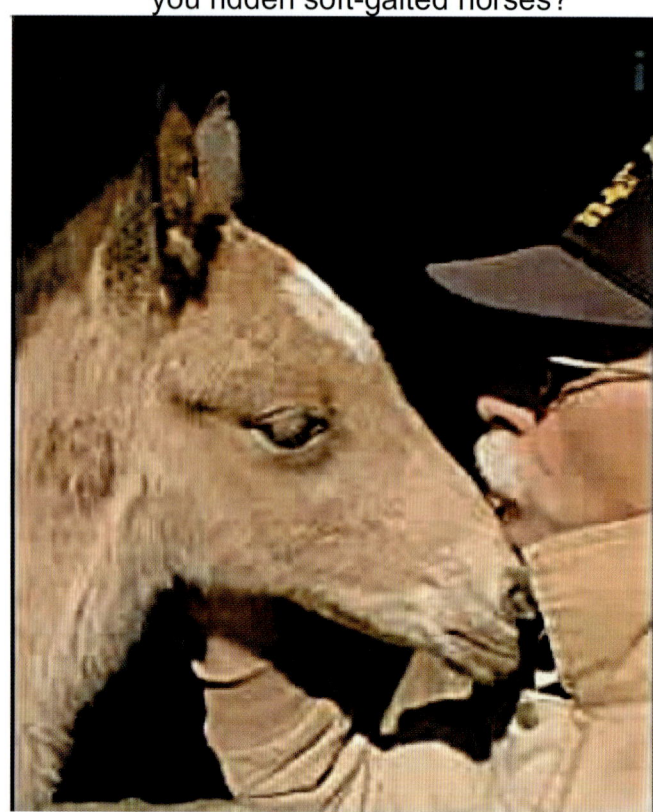

A young horse may seem like a more affordable choice, but carefully evaluate the costs of training and maintenance until the horse is ready to ride. If you are an experienced trainer, a young horse can be an excellent option. Even if the costs are similar, it may be helpful to pay them incrementally, rather than all at once. Here we see a 2-hour-old foal getting a kiss from Will Ferguson

3) **What is your personality?**
   Are you high-strung? Are you a relaxed rider? Are you competitive? Are you quiet natured? Are you boisterous? Are you timid?

4) **What are your physical chacteristics?**

Are you petite? Are you heavy? Are you tall? Are you short? Your weight and height must be in line with the height and weight of your horse. But keep in mind, the height of a horse does not determine how much weight it can carry. If you are heavy, you don't necessarily need a tall horse, but rather a strong one. Conformation and bone are more important than height. A short stout horse is much easier for a short stout person to mount and dismount. A feather-weight person will have little trouble jumping up onto a super tall horse.

A good trail horse has to be the best of any breed. When you're out there on the trail, you have to count on your horse's sound mind and excellent conformation.

5) **What kind of riding will you do?**
Competitive trail riding? Shows? Sport? For pleasure riders: Is the terrain mountainous? Flatland? Hilly? Desert? Rocky? Farmland? All of the above?

6) **Do you want to show?**
Breed specific? All breed? Halter? Versatility?

7) **Do you want to breed?**
Mare? Stallion? Do you know what to look for in a pedigree?

8) **Are you competitive?**
You need a horse with a competitive nature.

9) **How much can you spend?**

Take into consideration upkeep and training as well as purchase price. Take a careful look at Chapter five in this book: Care and Maintenance. If you have no intention of showing or breeding, there are some wonderful animals available without papers that will be a perfect match for you. Don't assume that either the most expensive or the least expensive might be the best horse for you.

Group trail riding can be fun and satisfying. Visiting with friends as you glide along on your "Fabulous Floater" is an exhilarating experience!

Set your budget according to your financial position and don't allow the heat of the moment to get you in over your head. Spending more than you can afford is sure to lessen the pleasure in the long run. Take someone along to help you stick to your planning schedule. (Another person can also be a second set of eyes that may see things you miss.)

Now that you have a true picture of yourself, the horse that will best suit you is becoming more clearly defined. It's time to begin thinking about where you will start to look. Your search will depend on which part of the country you live in. Certain areas will have a concentration of specific breeds and other areas will be pretty sparse. States like Missouri, Tennessee, Arkansas, and Kentucky have public sales for soft-gaited trail horses. Be forewarned that attending an auction or public sale may leave you vulnerable to impulse. You may find yourself the owner of a horse you know nothing about, or one that you haven't even ridden.

Other sources are breeders, dealers, personal recommendations and private parties (via newspaper ads, videotapes, and the Internet). For a full-rounded search, you may wish to utilize all these sources.

Visiting a breeder can be an excellent way to get acquainted with a particular breed.

Breeding facilities will usually have only one breed. Most dealers in soft-gaited horses will specialize in one or two breeds. Newspaper ads will be breed specific and personal recommendations will usually address one breed. Following through on all of these leads will certainly expose you to more than one of the soft-gaited breeds. Even though, as a category, these horses have much in common, there are breed-specific qualities that will have particular interest and appeal for you.

With the scarcity of soft-gaited horses in many parts of the country, you may have to rely on choosing a horse from a video tape. Don't panic, it can work out beautifully. Making use of the mail and telephone, you can learn a lot about, if not the specific horse, the owner of the horse. If finances allow, it would be ideal to be able to travel to see the horse before the purchase is made. But if you can't, make sure you review the tape carefully. If possible, have someone who has an expertise in soft-gaited horses review the tape with you. Make sure there is a provision in the contract that will protect you if the horse arrives and doesn't measure up to what was promised. Evaluate the horse on tape the way you would in person.

With a candidate horse in front of you, what are you looking for? How does this horse correspond to your preliminary want list: What are some specifics you may want to review?

All equine colors are available within the soft-gaited breeds. Be careful not to pass over a perfect horse because you are color-blind. You can't ride a color!

The color of a horse is one characteristic that has very little to do with the quality and nature of the animal. No one has ever ridden a color, and yet many people will pass up the perfect horse because it isn't the color they were looking for. Try to ignore the color until you have examined all the other attributes. As you complete your search, you might use color to tip the scale among your finalists.

Unless you have established a reasonable preference for the sex of your horse, try to keep this characteristic out of the initial decision making. So what is important? Temperament leads the list. The soft-gaited horses are bred for good temperament, but there are still lots of different personalities. Handle the horse. Watch its body language. Watch its eye. Is it responding to you in a positive fashion? Is the horse selling itself?

Once you decide you like the horse, take a good look at its conformation. *Trail horses have to be the best of any breed.* A trail horse must have sound conformation, solid bone, a good mind, and brio. Study Chapter two, "General Characteristics," as a guideline for these qualities.

How old is the horse? A young horse will usually cost less than one that is fully trained, but if you are unable to make the time or don't have the skill to do the training yourself, remember that good training is expensive.

Don't discount the older horse. A mature animal can be very serviceable and provide lots of pleasure.

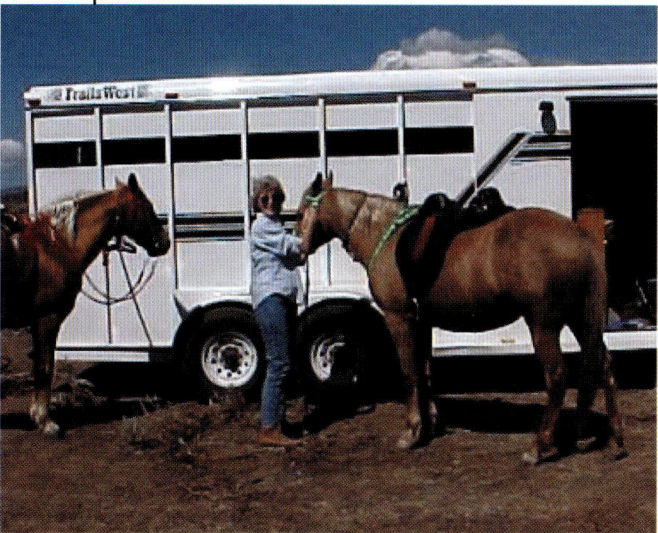

If you have to trailer to ride, finding a horse that is comfortable trailering is important to you. Make sure your candidate horse is at ease in your particular trailer. Pictured is Jacqueline Scott with Kentucky Golden Daisy.

What experience has the horse had? How are its manners? Is it safe on the trail? Is it safe in traffic? Is it easy to shoe, clip or to trailer? Is it at ease with new surroundings? If the answers to these questions are in keeping with your expectations, have the owner ride the horse for you. Watch as the horse is tacked up. See the way it interacts with its owner. Does it stand still to be mounted? Does it listen to the rider? Is it having a good time?

If the answers satisfy, it's time to ride the horse yourself. Now it's all up to you. Up to this point, you listen to others. But the final decision must be yours. How does it feel? Do you feel comfortable and safe? Are you a match?

If you are convinced you have a match, it's time to call your vet for the medical appraisal of the horse. The pre-purchase exam should be specific to your intended use of the horse. You will be paying for this service, and it is a good opportunity to initiate an association with a veterinarian if you haven't had one before. Be careful to explain what you are looking for, and agree on the cost of the exam in advance.

Unfortunately, most veterinarians are not especially familiar with the soft-gaited horse. If your veterinarian hasn't had much experience with them, be careful to point out to him or her exactly what they are looking at. When they ask you to trot the horse down

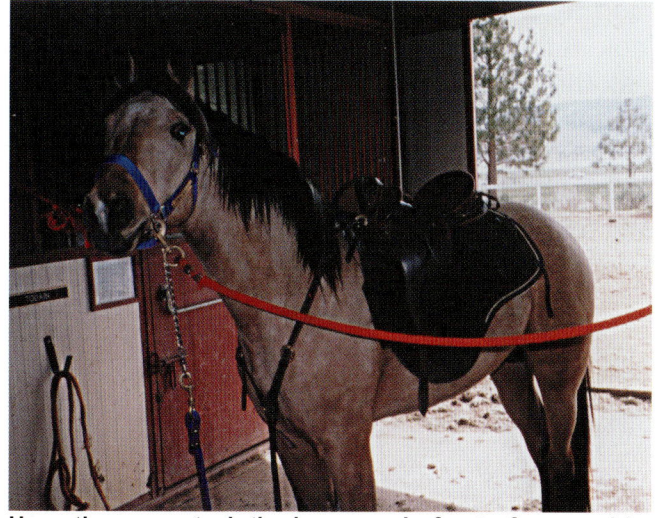

Have the owner tack the horse up in front of you and be careful to watch the way the horse responds to being handled. Is it cinchy? Is it easy to bridle? Does it enjoy the company of humans?

the road, let them know it is natural and normal for the horse to nod its head in rhythm to its gait. A nodding head on a walk-trot horse can indicate lameness. The soft-gaited horse may also nod its head as it walks and flat walks. If the veterinarian doesn't know this, he or she might not pass the horse in its stress test.

Sometimes a full-sized horse, rather than a small horse or pony, is the best choice for a child. The most important factor is the horse's ability to bond.

Know what ailments are likely in a given area and have the horse tested for them. You may wish to administer a blood test to look for equine infectious anemia or other illnesses as well as drug screening. Along with heart and lung testing, you will want the veterinarian to look at the horse's eyes and teeth and hooves. Ask the owner or dealer for a history of shots, worming and shoeing for the horse. If you are purchasing a stallion or mare for breeding purposes, you will certainly want to include a test for equine viral arteritis and fertility exams.

The pre-purchase exam will not give you a simple yes or no. What it does provide is an evaluation of the horse's health at the time of purchase. This should give you valuable information to decide if the horse is suitable for your intended use.

Once the decision is made, it's time to make plans to bring the horse to its new home. Whether you're taking it to your home or to a boarding facility, you will want to make the homecoming a pleasant and reassuring experience for the horse. The premises should be prepared well in advance of the horse's arrival. If you are a first-time horse owner, you would be well advised to review the laws in your area concerning horsekeeping. As a horse owner you are responsible to ensure that gates and fencing are secure. Usually you will be liable for any damage your horse causes if it leaves your property "on its own."

Plan to bring the horse home as early as possible in the day. The more time the horse can spend in its new surroundings in the daylight, the better. If it has had to make an extended trip, give it time to settle in before you ask it to take you on a long trail ride. This is a time to put your common sense and good instincts to use. Let the horse tell you when it's ready to go into full gear.

Well, you've done it! Now enjoy the flush of new horse ownership!

Ken and Gloria Harris with Fox Trotter, PISTOL PETE.

"Soft-gaiteds" are a family's best friend. Pictured is the Lincoln family with Kentucky Mountain Horse CANDY.

Joyce Doonan with blue-eyed WOODWIND'S HOLLY

Running free at Woodwind Farms

KENTUCKY GOLDRUSH with Steve Martin and son, Evan

Shiela Schwadel's curious Fox Trotter

Will Ferguson with his grandaughter aboard a Mountain baby

The Spradlins aboard their gaited gems

Kellie Rahm with ORATANA ROCKET'S JET

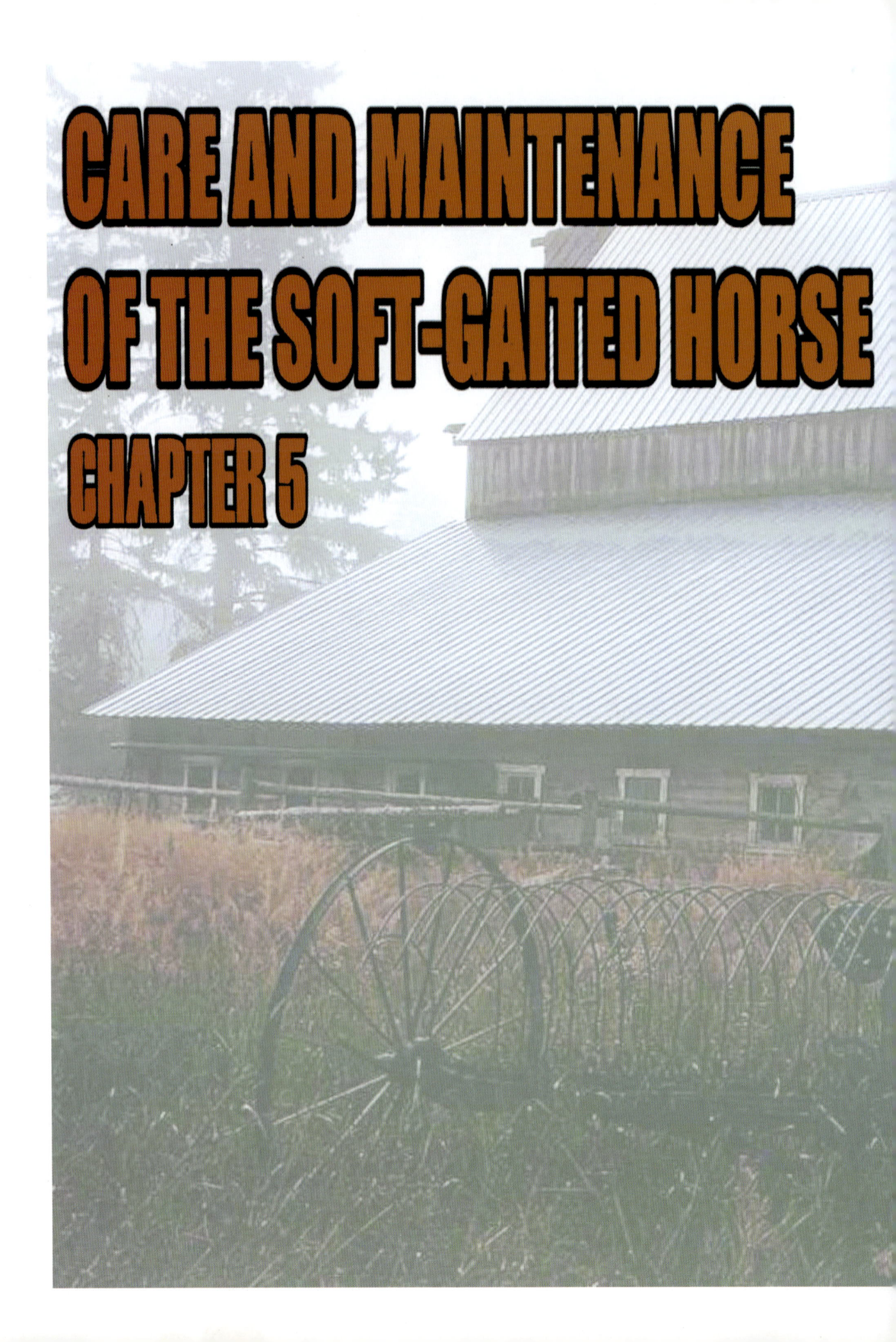

CARE AND MAINTENANCE OF THE SOFT-GAITED HORSE
CHAPTER 5

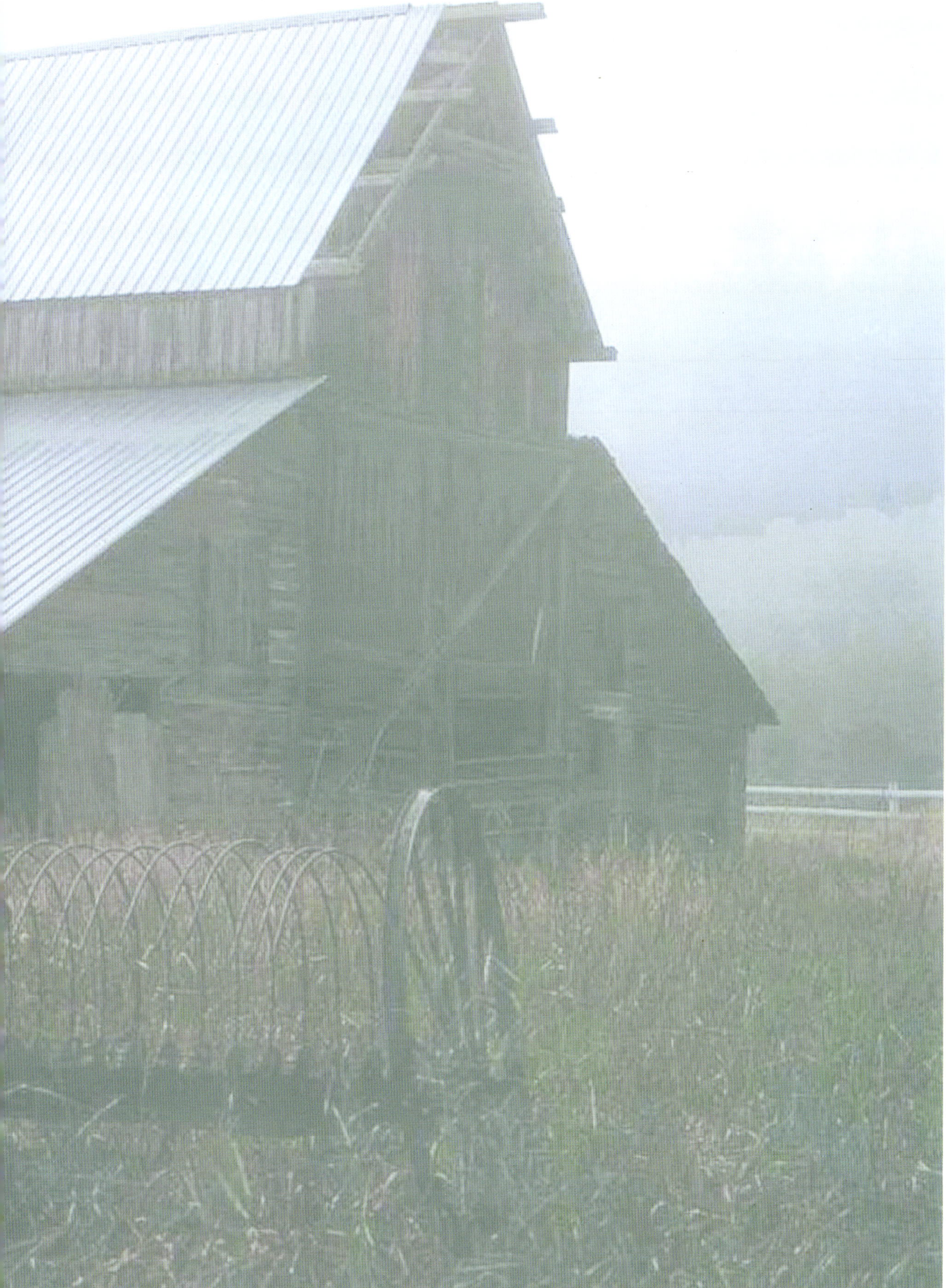

Chapter 5 CARE AND MAINTENANCE OF THE SOFT-GAITED HORSE

There are two basic categories in caring for a horse - housing the horse at a boarding stable, and housing the horse at your home (or someone else's home). If the horse is to be kept in a boarding stable, there are serious questions to ask and things to look for when choosing a facility.

First of all, pick a boarding stable as close to your home as possible. It takes time to bond with your soft-gaited horse, so it's important to spend time together. The bonding

After the initial attraction, you begin the serious process of developing a bond with your horse. As with personal relationships, a connection with your horse takes true dedication.

process occurs on and off the trail, on and off the saddle. Some of the most productive time can be spent brushing, lunging, touching or simply talking to, or feeding treats. Riders tend to spend more time with the horse when it is housed close by.

To begin your search, go to each prospective stable and spend time walking around to get the "feel" of the place. Look at the horses and pay attention to their apparent health and energy. Ask other horse owners how they feel about the general quality of the horse care provided. If you are pleased with the overall appearance of the facility, it's time to ask specific questions of the proprietors.

1) How often and when are the horses fed?
2) What kind of feed is used?
3) What is the water source (automatic or barrel?)
4) Are salt blocks provided?
5) Are grain, vitamins and bran mash available?
6) Will they worm the horses?
7) Will they exercise or turn out?
8) What facilities are available to the boarders?
   - Round pen
   - Arena
   - Hot walker
   - Pasture stalls, barns, corrals
   - Wash rack (hot or cold water)
9) Are tack lockers or tack rooms available?
10) Is there a grooming area? Are there cross ties? Electric outlets?
11) What kind of security is provided?
12) What safety regulations are required?
13) What type of insurance protection is in place?
14) How accessible are the trails?
15) Is there storage parking available for horse trailers?
16) How often are the corrals cleaned out?
17) Is there farrier service available?

A hot walker allows you to hook up your horse and let it exercise itself, freeing you to clean your corrals, or tack or simply sit near-by to chat with your equine friend.

If you use this list as an outline, it should give you a basis for comparison with your stable choices. Remember, if you are a first-time horse owner, people are going to come out of the woodwork to give you "helpful suggestions." Listen to everyone, but trust yourself to make your decisions based on what seems reasonable to you and your horse's individual needs. Be flexible and receptive to new information. Allow yourself to change your mind. Don't believe information must refer to you and your horse simply because you read it in a book. If you keep an open mind, you will eventually arrive at a system of horsekeeping that works for you.

Here's a collection of ideas designed to increase the enjoyment and ease of maintenance. To both the new owners and old-timers, use these suggestions as a guideline. **It's up to you to develop your own style of horsekeeping.**

SUGGESTIONS FOR CORRAL CONSTRUCTION

It might appear that wood posts and boards would be the easiest to construct and the most efficient type of corral design. Wood can be an attractive perimeter fencing. However, using wood to enclose a limited area (12'x 24' or 24'x 48' etc.) may invite trouble if your horses are wood-chewers. Many horses can become chewers if they are bored or under-used.

Pipe corrals can be erected or rearranged in minutes, and at the same time, they are extremely strong and safe "containers."

Metal pipe corrals are the only truly maintenance-free way to house a horse. There is no painting or upkeep; being modular, they're flexible and can "grow" with you. This affords you the opportunity to add and remove sections or to change the configuration altogether. With pipe there is no wood to be eaten, eliminating costly and frequent repairs.

Pipe corrals can be a safety aid in the event a horse casts itself. To cast means the horse rolls over into a position that keeps it from rolling back or getting up. It can roll up against a fence and find that its legs are tangled in the fence itself. If this happens with a pipe corral, just grab your socket wrench and undo the section that will free the struggling horse.

Wooden barns can be a source of constant repair and expense. There's a little "termite" in most horses.

If a horse casts itself in a stall or other fixed structure, be extremely careful not to get in the path of struggling legs. Keep a long rope around for times like this. Carefully slip a loop over a hind leg and from a safe distance, tug at the horse until it can change its direction and get up on its own. Don't tie anything onto the horse. The horse may react to its fear in a dangerous fashion, and you don't want to be attached to the horse, or attach anything to the horse that will accelerate its fear once it is on its feet.

There are now plastic-coated wood fencing and other high tech products on the market. Many are cosmetically attractive and suitable if there is no need for flexibility and cost is not an important factor.

Plastic-coated fencing is ideal for perimeter fencing. It is attractive and permanent.

If you have to keep dogs out of the horse area, you may want to consider wire fencing. There is a heavy field wire on the market that has 2" x 4" openings. It is installed like chain link, but it isn't flexible like chain link, so horses can't lean on it and stretch it or get their feet caught in it. It doesn't have the portability of pipe, but if you need the dog safety, it is a good option.

If you want to keep dogs or other critters out of the corrals, 2" x 4" wire stretched like chain link fencing is an excellent choice.

A portion of the corral should be converted to provide shelter. Feeder units and water should be located in the shelter or barn areas.

Take a good look at anything in your corral area that might be chewed on. This includes trees, fence posts, or wooden barn siding. It's easier to chew-proof it before you bring in the horses. Repair and replacement can be both costly and time-consuming. A light-weight chicken wire can be strapped around the trunks and exposed limbs of trees. Be careful to allow for growth in young trees. If the tree is very young, or freshly planted, it is best to construct a framework around the tree to prevent the horses from reaching it. Remember to take into account the length of their necks.

If you want to protect a tree within a horse area, place the fencing far enough from the tree to allow for the neck reach of your horses. An exposed tree in a corral is unfortunately an eaten tree.

Sheet metal or chicken wire will also protect flat surfaces. Metal corners for sheetrock are well-suited to protect wooden corners. Bitter-tasting preparations can also be painted on, but they tend to wear off. Most horses will not pursue their chewing if the wood is protected from the start. Don't let them develop the bad habit of wood chewing.

Slope for drainage should be carefully considered. Foul weather is sure to find low spots in your corral, creating mud holes and unnecessary slush.

FEED AND FEEDING

A horse should be fed twice daily, at regular times. The feed must be clean and dry. Make sure you store your hay under a roof or keep it well covered with a tarpaulin. Unexpected rain or accumulated moisture can ruin tons of hay. Mold can be white or black and usually has a "sulfur-like" odor. So get in the habit of sniffing and looking at each flake of hay as you feed it. If in doubt, don't take chances. Any wet or moldy hay may cause colic, which could result in the death of your horse.

It is best to put the feed in either a manger or some container, rather than directly on the ground. Horses that are fed on the ground are more vulnerable to types of sand colic. As they nibble at the small leaves and stems of their hay, they are also inhaling dirt

A stanchion has to be installed in cement to be truly efficient, but it is a super safety device for medical exams and bathing.

fragments that may collect in their stomach and eventually threaten their well-being.

Hay is the main portion of a horse's diet. Depending on the size of the horse and the amount of work it is doing, a horse requires twenty to thirty pounds of feed per day. Don't rely on a "flake"[1] as the correct amount; with some bales, a flake can be too light or too heavy.

---

[1] When the hay is baled in the field, it is folded by the machinery into a rectangle bale. The folding creates "flakes" that will vary according to the texture and moistness of the hay in the field.

Different types of hay and different types of baling are available according to your geographical region. Midwest and Eastern horsekeepers are familiar with large rolls of hay, while in the west, the 75# to 150# rectangle bales are common. Your job is to find out what the desirable feed is in your area.

Many people are happy feeding cubes or pellets instead of hay. These are compressed hay products that can be fed in weighted amounts. There is reportedly more efficient control of protein intake. Users claim there is less manure produced, which would indicate the food value of the cubes/pellets is being efficiently processed by the horse's system. Some horses eat the pellets too quickly, and have been known to suffer from

Truck tires make excellent feeders. They keep the feed nearer the ground and have no metal parts to injure the horse.

"choke," which can have serious consequences. Other arguments against pellets include an increase in wood-chewing and other boredom-related habits. If you live in a high-wind area, cubes may be the ideal feed, as regular hay can blow away. It is important that you make careful decisions that are in keeping with the specific needs of both you and your horse.

It's best to call your local feed stores and have them describe and explain your local hay to you. Then, through trial and error, you can develop your own system.

Salt is also essential to the horse's diet. A trace mineral salt block from the feed store will fit in a special holder, which can be mounted on a wall near the manger and out of the weather. Keep fly spray away from the block as well as from all other feed and water. If a horse is kept in pasture, a salt block should be placed in an area that can be monitored.

Carefully ration the amount of grain you feed. Most horses do not require grain unless they are being worked heavily. Too much grain can cause founder and/or azoturia (tying up), either of which may result in losing the animal.

After a long trail ride, you may wish to give your horse a cup or so of grain as a "thank you," but fight the urge to grain too heavily on a regular basis. Find another "treat" that your horse will appreciate. A carrot[2] treat on the trail or after a ride can give a quick sugar hit and a little moisture. Be careful that your horse doesn't become aggressive or "mouthy" about treats. If it does, it's best to discontinue hand feeding until the horse learns to respect you.

A hitching post can also include chains for crossties. It is a good idea to anticipate your horse's chewing instincts by wrapping the cross-bar with sheet metal.

---

[2] Don't give any treat if the horse is breathing heavily. It is too easy for the horse to inhale a piece of food into its windpipe.

Simple and efficient crossties can be accomplished by sinking peeler cores and attaching chains and hooks.

Remember, these suggestions are for soft-gaited pleasure horses. The guidelines for grain feeding are different for high-impact race horses or three-day eventers in training. As with people, nutrition needs differ between Olympic runners and Sunday joggers.

Bran, both wheat and rice, is a valuable source of protein and minerals. Rice bran is very rich and is fed to fatten and condition the coat. Wheat bran has provoked a bit of debate. Many feed wheat bran as roughage to clean out the digestive tract and yet in some areas, the natural nutrients in the feed would make feeding bran undesirable altogether. But if you should decide to feed bran, know that some horses eat two cups of bran per day and never have a colic problem. Other horses do well being fed a larger dose only once a week. There are also two camps of opinion regarding the choice of feeding bran dry or mixed with water. A good solution is to add the bran to equal amounts of warm water. It is comforting to both horse and owner to feed a nice warm treat, especially in cold weather.

Once a month, it is a good idea to feed psyllium husk powder (or pellets). This helps clean out the intestines – especially in sandy

When building a corral, it's a good idea to include small openings that allow a person quick exit, but not large enough for a horse to use.

areas where sand colic is prevalent. There are a number of products on the market that contain psyllium husk. It also comes in pure form and can be added to the bran and grain mixture.

Another product that aids in a horse's intestine health is beet pulp. This is an inexpensive and tasty addition to the horse's regular diet.

If your horse shows signs of sand collection in its stomach, it's a good idea to put some of its fresh manure in a plastic bag and add some water and shake it up a bit. Let it set for a while and see if there is sand settling in the bottom of the bag. If there is sand, your vet may recommend the use of psyllium husk in the horse's feed for a period of twenty-one days to really clean the intestinal track.

Feed stores have shelves full of vitamins. Decide which is right for your horse as you would for yourself. If your regular feed is wholesome and healthful, there probably isn't much need for additives. With the wide variety of products available, you will find something that works well for you and your horse. Yucca and vitamin E are good for older horses, as is a general "one-a-day" type vitamin.

It is best to feed a horse in a covered or protected area. Water should be clean and fresh. Wherever possible an automatic waterer is helpful. Check it often (at each feeding) to make sure it is working correctly. If you keep water in a barrel or other container, check it regularly for freshness. Feed usually finds its way into the water supply and can quickly sour the standing water. If the water becomes cloudy or colored, it is time to empty the container, hose it out, and refill with fresh water.

Never let a horse drink a lot of water directly after it has been exercised and is still hot. A short drink is ok, but wait until it has cooled down before you let it drink its fill.

PREVENTATIVE MAINTENANCE: AVOID POSSIBLE TROUBLE

Be familiar with your horse's habits and appearance. Know how much weight it should be carrying, how much food it usually eats, how much water it drinks, and how much manure it usually passes. Any changes in behavior or appearance could signal the start of illness. Ask your vet to show you how to check your horse's pulse and respiration. Learn what its pulse and respiration are at rest, so you can have something to check against when the horse is stressed.

Your feed store has shelves full of various products for your horse. Don't "fall into the guilt traps" of spending too much on additives. If your local hay is nutritious and water is available and clean, additives may not be necessary. This is something best discussed with your veterinarian.

First of all, a clean corral eliminates many flies. A fly mask is good protection during periods of high fly infestation. A fly net blanket works against flies and protects against sun bleaching of the coat and offers shade for sensitive eyes.

Make a habit of noticing what is going on in the horse area. Always investigate any unusual commotion, whether during the day or during the night. Know that horses are accident prone, so it's important to maintain a tidy horse area. Keep litter picked up; check often for broken fences and projecting nails. Avoid feed containers with sharp corners. If you have a horse that likes to open latches, use sturdy snap fasteners on gates and doors. Check the horse area for poisonous plants, which may include some common weeds and many garden plants. Do not leave any poisons or fly spray near your horses.

MAINTENANCE PROBLEMS

The most common complaints about horses are flies, odor and dust. To keep these problems under control, pick up manure once a day. Hold it in covered containers until it can be removed from the premises, or spread it out in an open area to dry out. Periodically the manure can be turned into the soil. It is an excellent additive to your arena or bridle path and it softens the earth for the foot-fall of the horse. It's also great for a garden or compost pile.

Flytraps can be used to reduce fly count. Fly spray systems are also available. In addition to your routine stable sanitation and spray, you can make your horse more comfortable during fly season[3] with a daily application of body wipe or body spray. Not all sprays are recommended for application on the skin. Keep fly dope away from eyes, nose and mouth. Many horses display an allergy to fly spray, and break out in little bumps. Watch out for these negative reactions. There are many different types of fly spray including "Skin So Soft," an Avon product for humans that also works well on horses. You're sure to find a product that will be successful with your horse.

Standing urine that turns into a mud condition should be dug out and replaced with sand or decomposed granite. In poor drainage areas, it's a good idea to dig down about two feet. Fill the hole with one foot of gravel and one foot of decomposed granite. Materials such as lime or feldspar can be used to reduce odor. During dry weather, dusty areas should be wet down at least once a day. Ring areas should always be wet down prior to being used.

1) Correct: smooth side of bolt toward horse. 2) Incorrect: the bolt sticking out inside corral. 3) Wire ends waiting to snag. 4) More wire tips sticking out at a gate passageway are hazardous to both humans and equines.

---

[3] It is also wise to keep on hand a product for wounds that also repels flies.

TENDING TO YOUR HORSE'S PERSONAL COMFORT

Most horses like the Farnam fly mask. In fact, many times the horse will push its face into the masks just to get it on quicker. The face mask also acts as a sunblock. Net blankets are also available to protect the horse's body from flies. For colored horses such as black and palominos, these blankets also give protection from the sun's ability to fade color.

IMPORTANT SUPPORT PROFESSIONALS

Your horse will need worming, immunizations and a dental exam at regularly scheduled times. Consult your vet for timings. Attention to these routine matters may prevent illness. It's a good idea to have a backup vet for those emergencies when your regular vet is busy or out of town. Ask every horse owner you know for their recommendations. Pay attention to the names you hear more than once, whether the report is positive or negative.

Horses need shoeing every six to eight weeks. **Even if your horse goes barefoot, it needs regular trimming.** The most important thing you can do for your horse's feet is to provide regular maintenance. Make cleaning their feet with a hoof pick a regular habit when brushing or preparing to ride. Keep a covered container of oil or hoof preparation, along with a stiff bristled brush, available at your grooming area. Brush the hoof at the hairline and on the underside. If you make regular foot care a habit, your horse's feet should remain healthy.

Do not let the horse stand constantly in manure. This may result in an unpleasant ailment called "thrush," characterized by a bad smell and possible infection.

A horse's hoof should be trimmed to match the angle of its shoulder. The bottom of the foot should be flat and strike the ground evenly. If you hire a farrier who wants to get "clever" and fool around with the angulation or weight of the shoes, be on the alert. The reason for trimming and shoeing is to keep the horse sound and ready to ride where and when you want. The support area of the heel moves forward as the foot grows longer. Maintaining the proper angle of the foot is fundamental to keeping the horse's weight distributed evenly. A horseshoe is supposed to be comfortable.

Regular farrier visits are of primary importance. Even if you choose to keep your horse barefoot, regular professional trimmings are imperative.

Stress increases as toe length increases.

As the toe gets longer, the stress on the leg muscles increases. Imagine walking with shoes that are several inches longer than you normally wear. *For every half inch of toe length too long there is double the amount of stress on the horse's tendons and ligaments.*

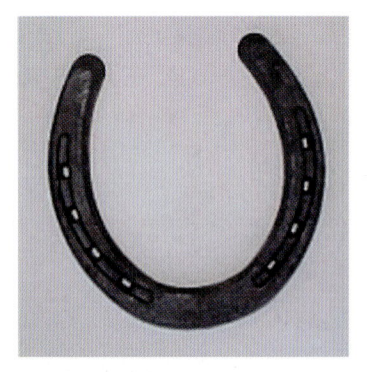

REGULAR FLAT SHOE: Suitable for most gaited horses.

HALF-ROUND SHOE: This shoe allows a horse to break in any direction. It is an excellent choice for a horse that is suffering from navicular damage. It permits a faster break-over to keep a horse more comfortable.

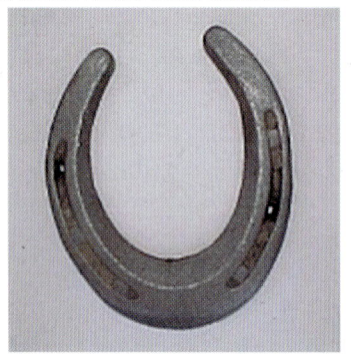

TOE-WEIGHTED SHOE: In some schools of thought this shoe is believed to encourage lift and extension. Used on the front feet, it can make it easier for a pacey horse to gait. Used on the back feet, it can assist a trotty horse.

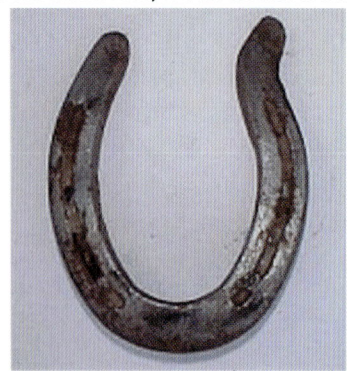

SHOE WITH HEEL TRAILER: It is a pivot for a foot that tends to swivel.

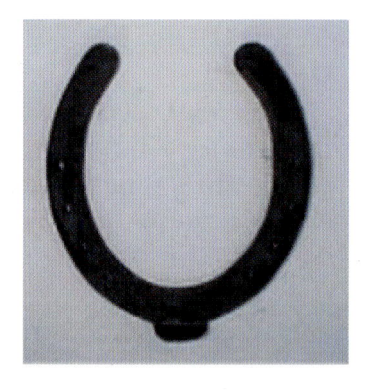

SHOE WITH TOE CLIP: Designed for horses that scoot or slide their feet. The clip keeps the shoe from sliding backwards.

EGG-BAR SHOE: Allows more solid support in the hind end of the foot. Excellent for horses with weak suspensor muscles.

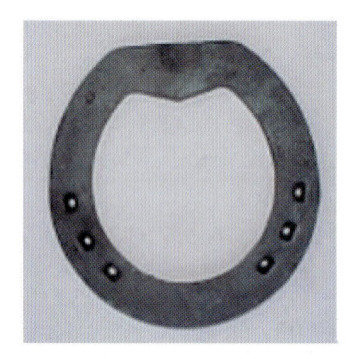

D-BAR SHOE: Serves the same purpose as the egg-bar shoe.

Unfortunately, some horses require more elaborate shoes than are pictured on this page. If this is the case, be prepared for more expenses and the possibility of future unsoundness. **The desirable horse is one that has gait bred into it, not nailed on to it.**

The most important thing is to make sure your horse is on a regular schedule of foot care – including both trimming/shoeing and the consistent use of a hoof pick. When in doubt, ask your farrier how to use the hoof pick properly.

COMMON HORSE AILMENTS

These include wounds, sprains and colic (bellyache), plus various diseases. Check your horse daily for scrapes, cuts, swellings, lameness, unusual heat, and runny discharges from the eyes and nose. When in doubt, call the vet.

Colic can develop suddenly and is life-threatening. Always be alert for these warning signs: refusing to eat, pacing, pawing, frequent getting up and down, continued rolling, anxious attention to the belly, inability to defecate. Some causes are worms, poor feed, sudden change of feed, or intestinal blockage resulting from a foreign object or greedy feeding, or sand.

Take care not to let your horse get into your grain supply. Be careful when allowing your horse to free-feed in a field of green grass. Limit the time, beginning with twenty minutes or so. Rich fresh grass can cause colic If you believe your horse is suffering from colic, call the vet at once. Stay with the horse and keep it on its feet. Walk the horse. Allow it only water until the vet approves feeding. Much of the damage caused by colic is due to the reaction the horse has to the discomfort. This is why it is important to stay with the animal and protect it from self-inflicted damage.

Founder is a condition caused by the same events that initiate colic. *Founder* and *Laminitis* are terms used to describe a condition usually confined to the front feet, but it can affect all four feet. The feet become hot due to the inflammation and increased arterial blood supply. The horse experiences tremendous pain. In severe cases, its hoof or hooves may actually separate and fall off. The inflammation has nowhere to go within the hard covering of the hoof and may split open. Founder can be both acute and chronic, depending on the severity of damage. In any event, the veterinarian should be called at once.

Always keep a kit with up-to-date supplies at the horse area. Access to a hose and cold running water is extremely useful for cleaning wounds. Never apply a disinfectant if the wound may need stitching. If the wound is severe enough to need stitching, wash it off and call the vet immediately. There is a window of time when stitching is possible. Once the wound has been invaded by medication, the veterinarian will not be able to close it by stitching.

Running water from a hose is also useful to reduce swelling of the legs due to strain or injury.

Here is a list of items that will be welcomed in an emergency. It's important to routinely check the contents for freshness and usability.

It's a good idea to have a blanket and perhaps even a hood available to fit your horse for those times when extra cold weather becomes wet. If the horse's coat gets soaked to the skin, there is no natural insulation.

In normal dry conditions, a horse is best left to its own natural thermostat; but if the horse gets soaked to the skin, then you should have a warm-fitting blanket at the ready.

- A horse thermometer. Make sure you attach a cord to it. You never know when you may need a handle. **Know the horse's temperature before you call the vet.**
- Scissors
- A supply of clean rags or paper towels
- Roll of gauze
- Wound powder
- Antiseptic ointment
- Hydrogen peroxide
- Iodine cleaning solution
- Epsom salts for soaking some foot infections
- Fly repellant roll-on (for use around eyes, mouth and wounds)
- Sterile gauze squares
- Q-tips
- Liniment for sore muscles and tired or swollen legs
- Colic remedy (Dipyrone)
- Needles and syringes
- Vet wraps
- Bute
- A timer (can be a kitchen timer)
- Clean bucket
- Stethoscope

COOLING DOWN

Never put the horse away after a ride while it is hot or sweaty, or has a high pulse or respiration. Always finish the ride or the workout by walking your horse for at least ten minutes. In hot weather, the horse will appreciate a sponge or hose bath, followed by a pass with the sweat scraper. In the cold season, use a cotton blanket on the horse after the ride. This makes it easier for the horse to utilize its body heat to dry out. Remove the blanket the next morning or when the horse is dry to the skin.

TO BLANKET OR NOT TO BLANKET

There are valid reasons for keeping a horse blanketed, but there are also legitimate reasons for not blanketing. If the horse is a show or competition horse that is kept in a barn with all the accompanying upkeep, blanketing will keep the horse's coat slick and showtime ready. If the horse is primarily a pleasure horse, it may be best to forget the blanket. Left unblanketed, the horse's natural body thermostat can control hair growth and other physical survival mechanisms. Once the blanketing process interferes with this natural ability, the horse owner assumes the ongoing responsibility of providing artificial thermostat control.

Soft-gaited horses are sensitive to climate and environment. Use common sense when moving horses from one climate to another.

A moderate body clip will make it easier to wick body moisture during a cold weather ride.

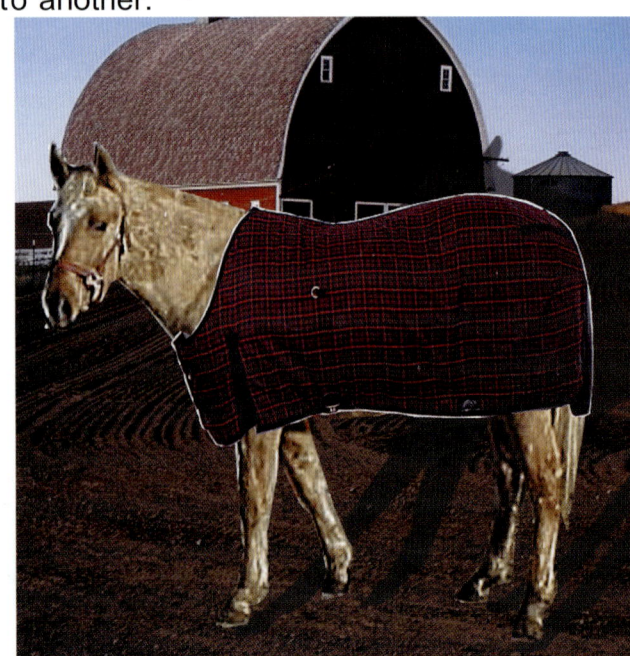

A cotton blanket after a cold-weather ride will assist a horse in utilizing its own body heat. (Helps in a trailer too.)

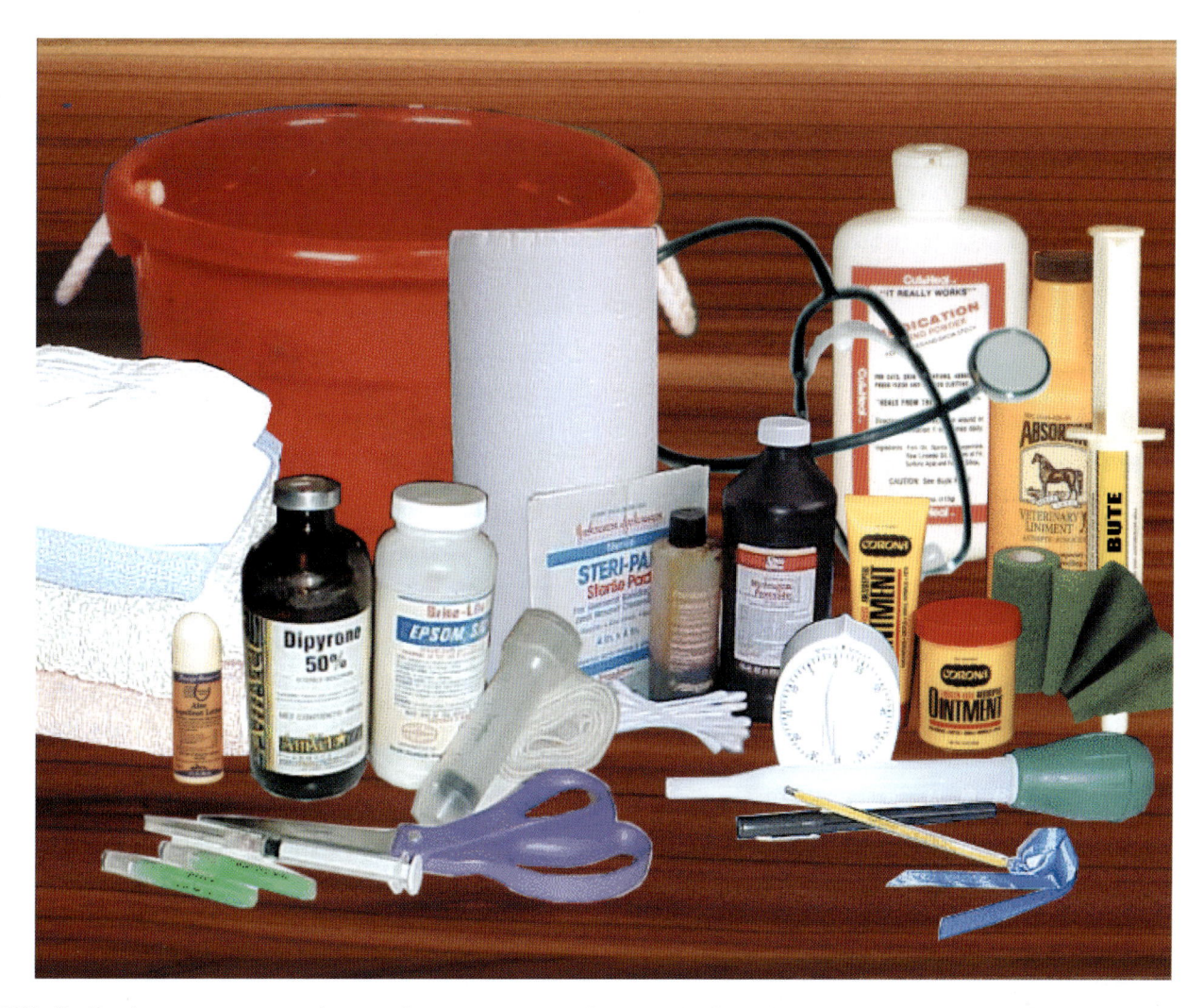

ROW 1) Bucket, paper towels, stethoscope, wound powder, liniment, bute. ROW 2) Towels, roll-on repellant, dipyrone, epsom salts, gauze roll & squares, Q-tips, iodine Iodine cleaning solution, peroxide, antiseptic ointment, vet wraps ROW 3) Needles and syringes, scissors, timer, baster, thermometer (with a tail).

For instance, if you live in a snow-type winter environment, avoid bringing a new horse in from a warm, southern climate after the first frost of the winter season. A horse needs time to upgrade its system for the cold winter months. One season of putting a blanket on, taking it off, mending it, and keeping it clean will usually convince horse owners of the truth in going with "the natural way."

It is important, though, to own two blankets for your horse. One is the cotton blanket to be used after a ride in chilly weather. This light-weight sheet is also just right to protect the horse from drafts when you are trailering home after a cold-weather ride.

The second blanket should be a heavier, water-resistant one. This blanket should be available for use when needed. An especially cold and blustery winter storm, or an icy rain are just two reasons your horse might need some extra protection.

If the horse is ridden frequently in cold weather, there are various clipping patterns that will aid in its cooling down. Long, bushy hair designed for warmth can also create the problem of moisture retention. It becomes more difficult to dry a horse as its coat becomes thicker. If the moisture can drain to a bare portion of the horse's body, it speeds up the cooling-down procedure.

GROOMING

Horses like to be kept as clean as possible. They appreciate frequent brushing. They welcome a warm-water rinse in warm weather. Before brushing the mane and tail with a pin brush, it helps to spray them with a grooming product like Show Sheen. A conditioner eliminates lots of broken ends.

Some soft-gaited breeds such as the Fox Trotter and the Tennessee Walker are trimmed with a long bridle path. Pictured is Missouri Fox Trotter RED WING'S STRIKE THE GOLD.

Some breeds, such as the Mountain Horses and Paso Finos, leave the mane and forelock their natural length. Pictured is Mountain Pleasure Horse CROWN ROYAL.

Braiding mane and tail after cleaning and brushing helps to grow them long and full. The hair should not be left wrapped without frequent (daily) rebraiding and brushing. Use rags or braiding tape to fasten each braid. If the hair is left braided until it gets "woolly," it will break the hairs.

Be careful not to spray Show Sheen or other "glossy" conditioners where you will be placing the saddle. It will make the hair slick and cause the saddle to slip.

Clipping is not necessary, but it really improves the overall appearance of your horse. Tradition with some of the soft-gaited horses calls for a bridle path that is clipped a bit longer than the universal ear-length. Other breeds such as the Mountain and Paso horses don't trim a noticeable bridle path. The muzzle, lips, throat and fetlock are trimmed. Many show horses are trimmed inside the ear but it is not desirable with pleasure horses. Ear hair protects the horse's ears out on the trail, in the elements. The edges of the ears can be trimmed to create a neater appearance without defeating the protective purpose of the hair. It's advisable to leave the fetlock hair on trail horses to protect the fetlocks. Decide what is reasonable for your horse and create a grooming ritual that can be easily maintained.

Here is a list of suggested grooming items to keep at your grooming area:

- Hoof pick
- Curry comb
- Mud brush
- Finishing brush
- Pin brush (for mane and tail)
- Shedding blade
- Fly spray
- Show Sheen
- Terry towel
- Combination brush and curry mitt
- Sweat scraper
- Horse first aid kit
- Shampoo (a citronella based shampoo in summer will discourage flies)
- Cream rinse
- Petroleum Jelly
- Container of oil and a stiff bristled brush for foot care (thrush remedy is good too)
- Turkey baster (for administering hoof care)
- Electric Clippers

79

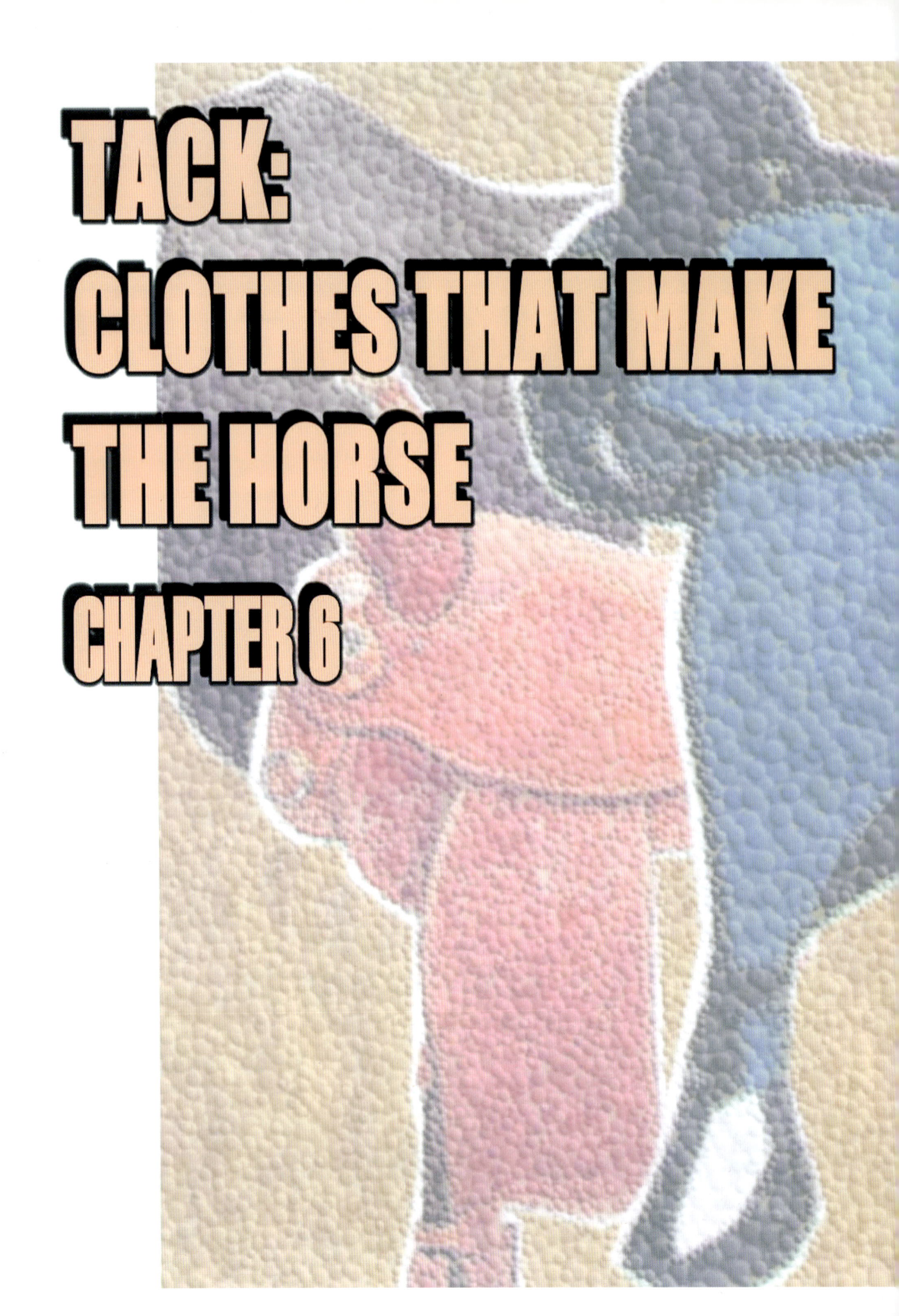

TACK: CLOTHES THAT MAKE THE HORSE

CHAPTER 6

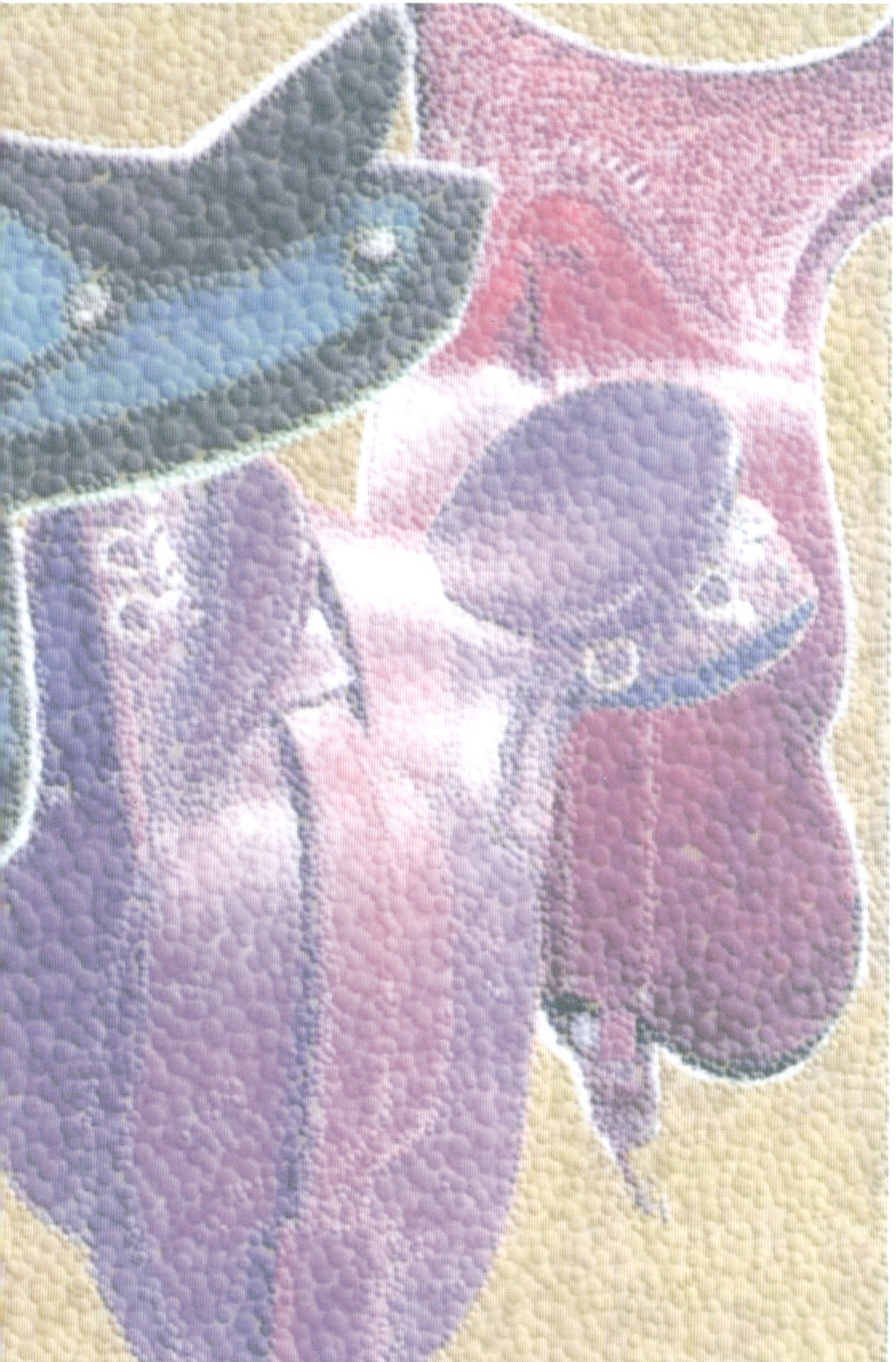

Chapter 6 TACK:
CLOTHES THAT MAKE THE HORSE

It's been said that the clothes make the man. To a great extent, tack does make the horse. Properly fitted saddles and bits are fundamental to the "pleasure" in pleasure riding for both horse and rider.

There is so much to know about tack. Information on the different riding disciplines and their tack requirements could fill many, many volumes. In this chapter, we will take a look at only that tack directly related to the soft-gaited horses. In the show arena, most soft-gaited registries utilize English, Western and Breed-specific saddlery. On the trail, Australian saddles are gaining popularity. Sidesaddles and harness are seen both in and out of the show arena.

Western saddles have a number of designs suitable to gaited horses - the reining and show saddle, the A-fork ranch saddle, the generic show pleasure saddle and the hornless endurance saddle. Western saddles are also available in synthetic and chrome tanned leathers for trail and sport.

Saddle leather has traditionally been vegetable tanned. Chrome tanning is a chemical tanning process that is much quicker and generally used for clothing, shoes, and furniture. With chrome tanning, much thinner cuts of leather can be produced, making it quite cost-effective.

Pictured is Racking Horse ROLEX with Pam Stubbs riding in a Pleasure Racking Class in Georgia. Pam is wearing Western attire that matches the horse's Western tack. Photo: Sandra Hall.

This lovely Tennessee Walker is wearing a Lane Fox flat seat saddle, popular with saddle-seat exhibitors. Photo: Forrest Bliss

English tack and attire hasn't changed much since this example from the early 1930's. Pictured is the author's father, Earl Thompson, on his gaited Standardbred, Kenny.

82

This is the same horse seen on the previous page. Here we see English attire and English tack as worn by Pam Stubbs and her Racking Horse ROLEX. Photo: Sandra Hall.

Most saddle leather takes a month to tan (New Zealand leather, used for Australian-made saddles, takes up to eighteen months to tan, which makes it a high quality and "forgiving" product).

English saddles also come in a variety of styles. The dressage is probably the most popular for gaited horses because the jumping, close-contact and forward-seat English saddles tend to throw the rider forward. Many show riders make use of the Lane Fox flat-seat saddle in "saddle seat" classes. The English saddles made of synthetic fabric are also frequently being used for trail and sport.

The Trail category includes a variety of different saddles - an officer's saddle, built on a swivel tree; the Buena Vista, generally associated with the Tennessee Walkers; the McClellan saddle, with its military design; and the Paragon saddle, popular for use in field trials.

The Australian saddle also comes in different shapes and styles. The Super Drafter is the traditional design; the giltrow has felt-covered bars; the Endurance poley has lower poleys to accommodate a standing rider; the J.S. Champion has a wood-and-steel tree and deep-slung seat; and synthetic Aussie saddles like the Wintec are also available.

No matter the saddle type, the important concern is fit. What are the points to be considered? First of all, the skeleton of a horse is designed to protect and support its internal organs. The vertebrae is connected to its skeleton in only two places. At the wither, it is called the thoracic vertebrae and at the pelvis, the lumbar vertebrae. The vertebrae is not designed to support weight from above, but the thoracic vertebrae, which is over the rib cage,

The author rigged out in English tack and attire circa the 1940's. Barbara is riding QUEENIE, a Tennessee Walker.

Peruvian tack on NASHA registered, CM NAVAJO, son of EASY FALCON, owned by Mimi Busk-Downey.

is best equipped to carry a saddle and rider. So it's important that the saddle rests just behind the wither and not too far along the spine.

It is also important to examine the saddle for any defects. Even though tremendous strides have been made in sports equipment in general, saddle making has not benefited, for the most part. In fact, mass production might be blamed for a lessening of quality.

It is important to make sure there is enough saddle for the rider. A super-light saddle might seem like a good choice, but it is more important for there to be enough contact area to distribute the rider's weight. Some of the synthetic saddles are much too light for adult riders.

Pads can be critical to a correct fit. The saddle should fit the horse, and the pad should never be used to improve the fit. All too often, the use of a pad will complicate the fitting of a saddle. If you were to run a foot race, and your shoes didn't fit, could you make it all right by wearing big fat socks? Adding a pad to an ill-fitting saddle may temporarily improve things. When the addition of a pad alters the fit of the saddle things may appear to be improved. Actually it's only the position of pressure points that has changed, and the improvement will last only until the new areas have become sore.

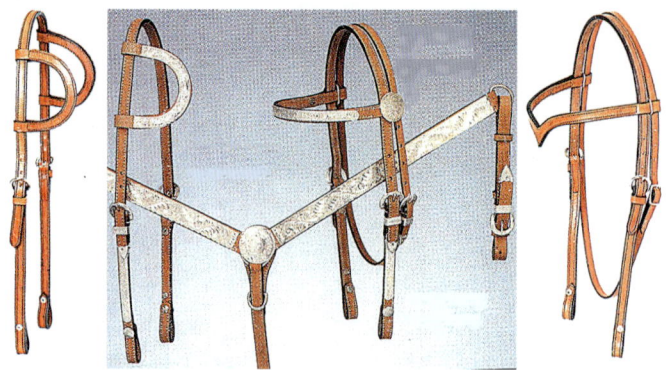

From left to right Western headstalls. Double ear; single ear; brow band; Vbrow band; and a Western breast collar.

Some of the soft-gaited breeds allow the use of a Western saddle and an English headstall. Two-handed reining is also allowed. Classes that are labeled "Western" must have tack that matches and if the horse is wearing a shank bit, only one hand may be used.

Early training often utilizes many different pieces of tack. Here we see an officer's saddle, side pull headstall with long reins. The trainer, Billy Odom, is driving the young horse from the ground.

Spotted Saddle Horses use Western tack and attire exclusively. (English caveson accepted.)

Three English bridles commonly used with the gaited horse; and a halter bridle popular with trail riders.

The Paso Fino horses and riders have a distinctive appearance. The tack and attire makes a crisp and elegant presentation that compliments the showy carriage and appearance of the Paso Fino horse. Pictured are Joe Leisek, from Nevada, and Janice Russ from California.

The Paso Fino horses are ridden with a dressage saddle. Many models are manufactured in Columbia, but traditional dressage saddle made in Germany and England are also popular.

Pads can create even more problems with saddles that are too narrow than with those that are too large. Adding a thick pad to a saddle that is too narrow causes even more pressure on the withers. Muscles can actually atrophy along the side of the withers due to continued use of this ill-fitting tack. Adding pads under a saddle that is too large may cause the saddle to slip and roll out of place.

If you take care with the fitting of your saddle, the rewards are many. A comfortable horse is less apt to have behavior problems. Rather than showing open sores, muscle damage and pain, it will often affect performance and behavior. If your horse can't seem to relax, or displays lameness, stumbling, tripping or excessive shying, if it can't travel in a straight line or grinds its teeth, swishes its tail or generally displays a bad attitude, take a careful look at the fit of your saddle.

ENGLISH SADDLERY IN THE SHOW RING

Where English saddles are called for in the soft-gaited horse show arena, the saddle of choice is the dressage saddle or the flat seat Lane fox.

In truth, the flat-seat saddle is rarely a comfort to horse or rider. As the name implies,

Husband and wife team Barbara and Jim Alexander of Carson City, Nevada, make a great picture of the typical arena wear when competing with the Peruvian Pasos. The Alexanders have a Peruvian Paso breeding facility, Clear Creek Ranch, in Northern Nevada.

Honored Judge and enthusiastic breeder of Peruvian Paso horses for more than three decades, Hugh Richardson shows us how not to sit a saddle. The Peruvian tack and attire is traditional, somewhat complicated and extremely attractive.

Peruvian Paso breed-specific tack and attire (clockwise): Hat, saddle, bridle, wooden stirrups, guarnicion, and poncho. Courtesy Hacienda La Encantada and Albert Lummis from Austin, Texas.

the design of this saddle is flat. The seat is flat and the bars under the saddle have little padding giving a flat appearance. Traditionally, no cloth pad is used under the saddle in the show ring. This gives a slick appearance and hopefully doesn't do much damage during the brief time it is worn.

WESTERN SADDLES IN THE SHOW RING

The Spotted Saddle Horse and the Missouri Fox Trotter are shown with a Western saddle. The actual type is not specified - only that it be a Western type with a horn.

The saddles most frequently seen are the show and pleasure saddles. The short back of the Fox Trotter makes the barrel or contest saddle a good choice.

If showing your horse is a viable option, it is advisable to check with the individual breed registry for their requirements. Most registries have strict policies for both tack and attire.

BREED-SPECIFIC SADDLERY IN THE SHOW RING

The Peruvian Paso horses are best recognized in the show ring with their elaborate saddles and Peruvian costume. They do show in both English and Western tack as well.[1]

The Paso Fino horses are shown in a breed-specific saddle. Frequent use is made of the dressage saddle with the rider dressed in the official Paso Fino show costume. The cutback park saddle, and the English pleasure saddle are also acceptable. A forward seat saddle is allowed where jumping is required.

---

[1] See Chapter 15 for further information on Peruvian Tack.

SADDLERY ILLUSTRATIONS

WESTERN:

Reining & Show Saddle
Bull-hide covered hardwood tree. Smooth suede covered seat. In-skirt dee riggings and leather covered stirrups. About 33 pounds.

Ranch Saddle
A-Fork tree. Slick seat with leather covered pelican riggings. Metal deep roper stirrups. About 40 pounds.

Show & Pleasure Saddle
Quarter horse tree. Smooth suede covered seat. In-skirt dee riggings. Leather covered stirrups. About 22 pounds.

Endurance Saddle
Figerglass covered hard wood tree. Quilted leather seat _ conventional rigging. Ralide pleasure stirrups. About 23 pounds.

Pleasure Saddle
Cordura nylon and chrome tanned leather. Quarter horse bars and 7/8 rigging. Ralide pleasure stirrups. About 15 pounds.

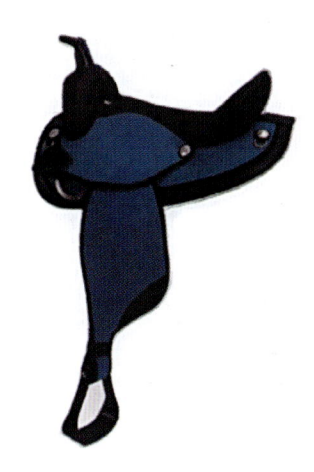

ENGLISH:

Dressage Saddle
Padded knee roll.

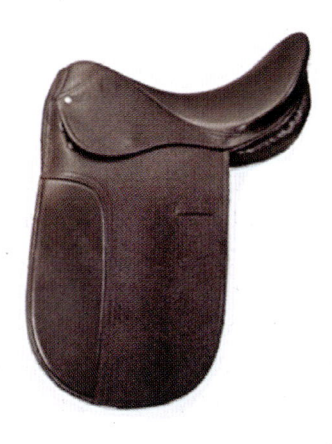

Lane Fox or Saddle Seat Saddle
Full-cut back pommel.

Orthoflex
Standard Patriot smooth black upholstery cowhide stitch-down with in-flap English rigging

Paragon Saddle
Field trial usage. Padded seat and flaps with moderate knee rolls.

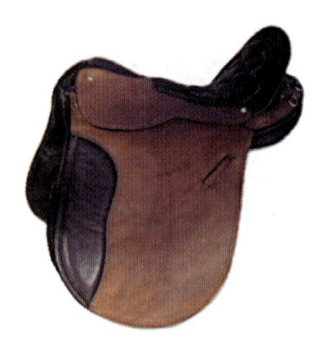

Dragoon
Ladies' side saddle. Two horns on near side with a balance strap.

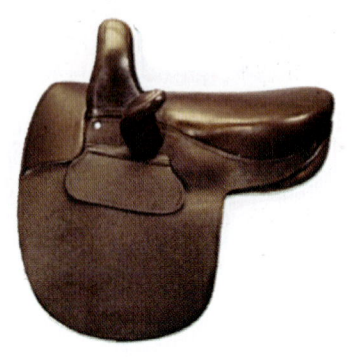

TRAIL:
Officer Saddle
Built on a swivel tree with light swing fenders. The panels are replaceable; the seat is a hammock suspension-style.

Buena Vista Saddle
Built on a Ralide tree with English-type stirrup leathers with fenders and hooded stirrups.

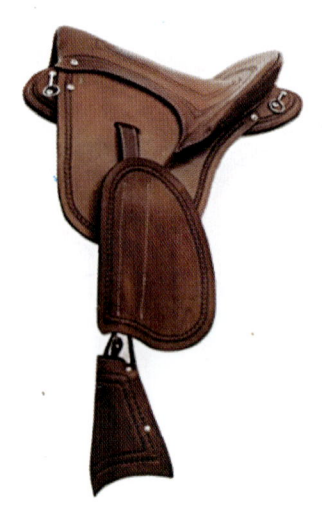

McClellan Saddle
Made on traditional designs with a large open area and no skirt. Adjustable rigging. About 18 pounds.

JS Champion
Australian saddle built on a steel-reinforced wood tree. Has either conventional hair stuffed under panels or fleece lined for "round" horses.

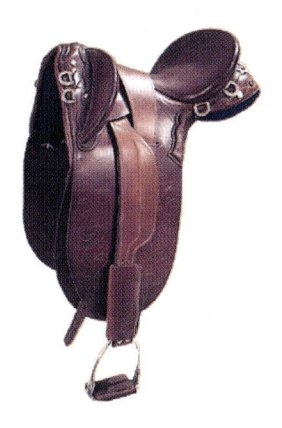

The Colt Giltrow
Felt covered bars, deep seat. Rigged with a western-style cinch. About 19 pounds.

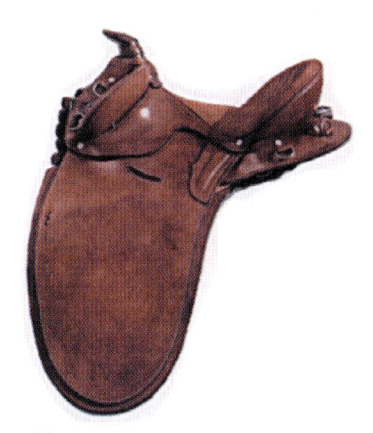

Endurance Poley
Low knee pads. Can go with or without surcingle. English-style girth. About 14 pounds.

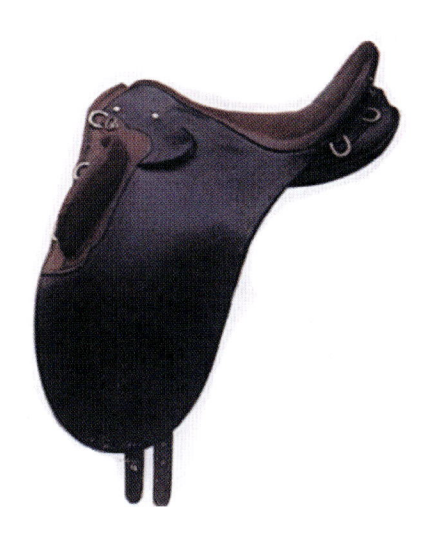

Classic Camp Drafter
The "ringer" has a wood and steel tree. Seat formed by webbing strung across a steel hoop. Four gullet sizes, six seat sizes. 20 pounds.

Enduro
Adjustable (or removable) poley. Web-strained wood and steel tree. About 20 pounds.

Plantation Saddles
Two examples of antique saddles from Kentucky. The workmanship is stunning. These have been the saddle of choice for the gaited horse for over a century. Courtesy of Nelson Francis, Slayersville, Kentucky.

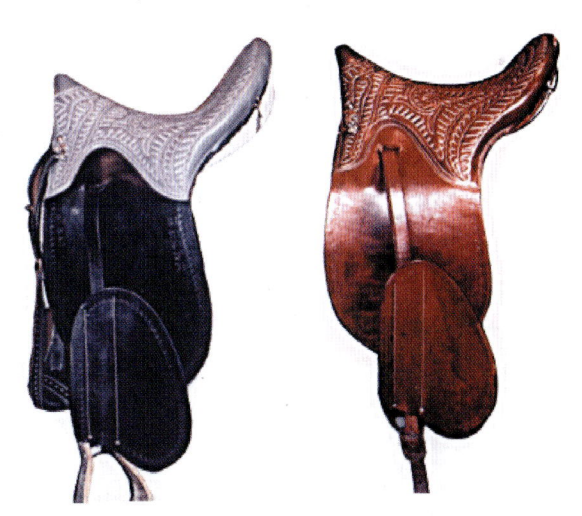

The off-side of the Australian saddle's rigging is similar to an English saddle. The on-side shows the girth being attached to the surcingle.

Australian Saddles and Soft-Gaited Horses: A Combination That Works.
The Author expresses a personal opinion from years of experience.

"My joyful experience with soft-gaited horses has endured for many decades. I have used many different saddles. Once I discovered the Australian stock saddle in the 80's, I knew I would never use anything else.

Many of the breeds require specific saddlery in the show ring. Unfortunately, in the show ring, tradition has taken the place of common sense. On the trail we can put the horse's well-being first, and it's here that the Australian stock saddle is brilliant.

The relationship between the Australian stock saddle and the soft-gaited horse is no accident. The stock saddle is designed for the way Australians ride. Although there are no soft-gaited horses in the Outback, their way of working cattle requires two major gaits from the stock horse - the walk, and the gallop. Stockmen walk tracking cattle, and when they catch up with them, they gallop to turn the mob, and thus contain them. As they say in the bush: "Somebody trotting someplace hasn't made up his mind whether he wants to get there sooner or later."

This high priority on a good walk is not only reflected in the design of the Australian stock saddle, but a fast walk on a horse will fetch a higher price than a fast gallop. So those of us who enjoy our soft-gaited horses can benefit from a saddle designed by countless "down under" stockmen over 200 years ago!

The Australian stock saddle is, in fact, the only saddle ever designed for the primary purpose of keeping a rider seated, safe and comfortable. Western saddles were designed for roping, English saddles for jumping, dressage saddles for dressage, race saddles for racing, and so on. Thus the Australian saddle is unique to the trail, evolving to fit perfectly.

To enjoy trail riding, it is important to have true athletic equipment. There are great demands made on the musculature of a soft-gaited horse. Imagine, for every two footfalls of a trotting horse, the soft-gaited breeds step four times. There is a lot going on under that saddle, and it is critical that the saddle doesn't interfere with the action of the horse.

First of all, the skeleton of a horse is designed to protect and support its internal organs. The vertebrae is connected to the skeleton on only two places. The vertebrae is not designed to support weight from above but the thoracic vertebrae, which is over the rib cage, is best equipped to carry a saddle and rider.

Since the back of a gaited horse is characteristically short, the Australian stock saddle is a beautiful accommodation. It tucks into the natural pocket just behind the wither and the configuration of tree and padding displaces the rider's weight evenly. It creates an air channel over the spine.

The seat design places the rider closer to the horse's center of gravity and off the kidneys. It supports the rider at the back, and cuts in at such a way that the riders' legs can go slightly forward.

In terms of comfort, this puts the rider not just on his or her backside, but on some of the thigh, greatly increasing the bearing surface of the rider on the saddle. And for the horse, this means a load more evenly distributed.

With endless tree and seat sizes, the needs of all of our diverse body types (both horse and rider) are met by the Australian stock saddle.

The Australian hunt breast collar supports the position of the saddle without interfering with the horse's shoulder movement."

Fitting the withers of a horse is the most critical stage in fitting an Australian stock saddle. Shown above are the examples of three widths: wide, standard, and narrow.

BITS AND BITTING

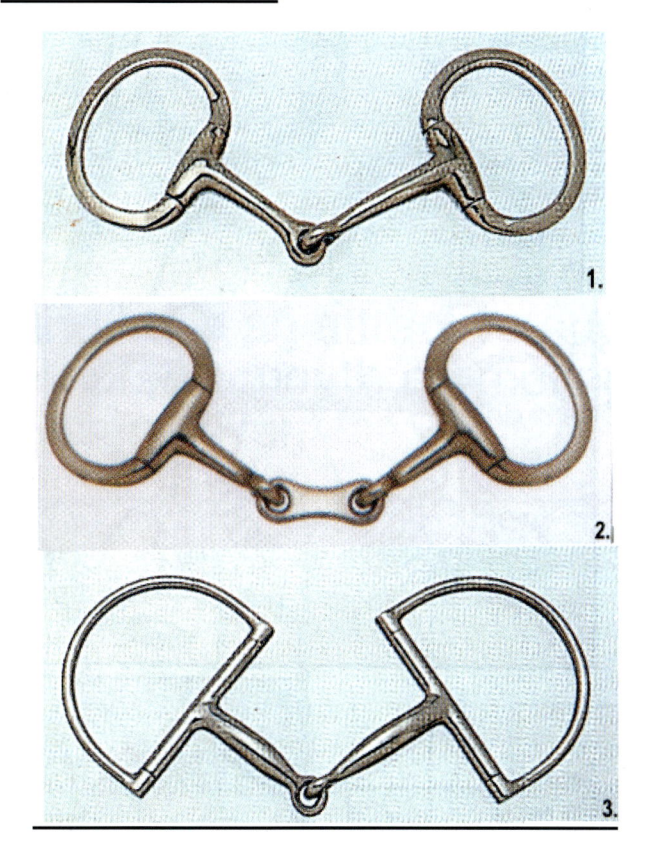

1. Stainless steel Egg Butt bit. 2. Egg Butt Dr. Bristol bit.
3. D snaffle bit.

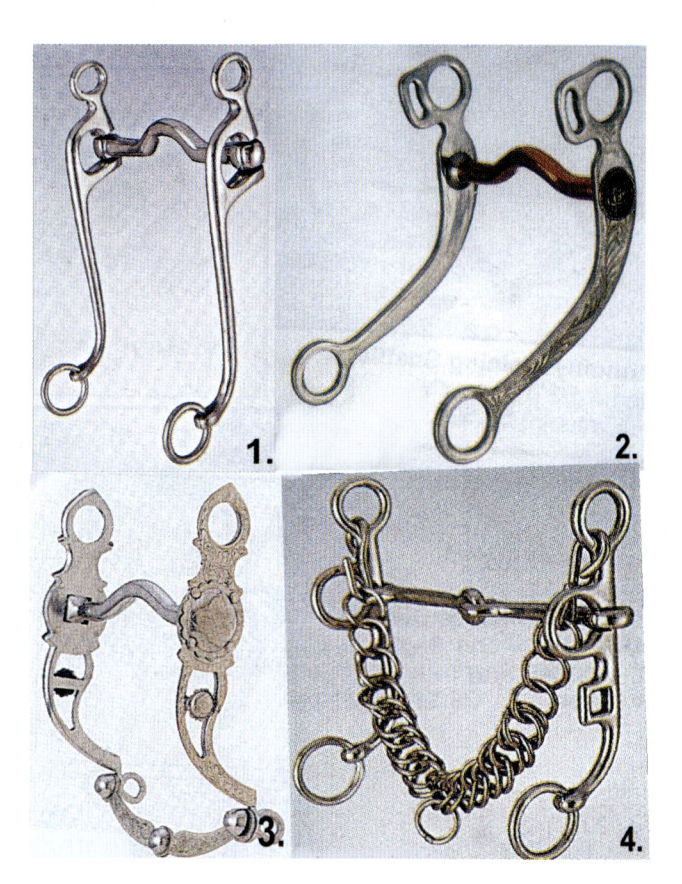

1. "Tennessee Walker" bit with swivel cheeks. 2. A copper mouth aluminum working bit. This is considered a Western bit, and it has slots for a Western-type curb strap. 3. A German silver show bit with engraved sides. 4. An Argentine bit. This bit can be used as a snaffle by attaching the reins to the loops at the mouth piece; or it can be used as a shank bit by attaching the reins to the lower loops.

Choosing the correct bit is extremely important. It's almost like choosing the right shoes for a long-distance runner. Comfort and communication are critical. There is no "universal bit." The structure of the horse's mouth, and the job the horse is supposed to perform, determines the best selection.

The snaffle bits are frequently a good choice for a young horse.[2] A snaffle bit is one that allows direct contact by the reins to the mouth. It can have either a solid mouthpiece or a broken mouthpiece. The determining factor is direct contact. For horses with a low roof to their mouth, the Dr. Bristol snaffle maintains the benefits of the snaffle while eliminating the risk of the joint of the mouthpiece poking into the roof of the mouth.

As with the rest of your tack choices, there are many books and resources to study the use of bits. It's often said that the important element of bit science is the use of your hands. This being said, good trainers will not automatically move on to a "stronger" bit without taking a careful look at the behavior, and determining a solution that addresses more than simply the bit used.

Strap-goods selection, like bridles and halters, all come in several types of materials. Leather, of course, is traditional, and used almost exclusively for the show ring. Nylon and Biothane are popular for trail, endurance and "everyday" use.

---

[2] Many horses will be kept in a snaffle bit for their entire career.

Halters and bridles and other "strap-goods" come in different materials. Leather and nylon are both serviceable. It is important to keep these clean.

Whatever your choice, leather or synthetic, it is important to keep it clean. Soap and water are your friends. The synthetic can go into the washing machine, and the leather should be washed by hand. *Never oil leather goods without first washing them.*

CLEANING YOUR TACK

Many myths exist with regard to cleaning leather saddles. Some cowpokes insist that cleaning a saddle ruins the hide. The truth is, leather does best when you keep it clean and well-oiled.

Never clean leather with harsh detergents or hot water. Natural soaps such as Murphy's Oil soap, liquid glycerin soaps or glycerin bars with lukewarm water are best. Don't soak the leather, but don't be afraid to get it wet. Remember, saddle leather is skin; it is very durable, but do not subject it to harsh scraping or brushing with wire brushes.

Never oil dirty leather. As the oil is drawn into the leather, it sucks the dirt with it. If you can imagine dirt particles as the rough-sided sharp-edged specks that they are, then you can see how much damage they can do to the structure of the leather. Any use of the leather will cause dirt particles to simply cut away at the fibers of the leather from the inside out. When you oil clean leather, the oil is drawn into the leather and is able to lubricate and extend its life.

It is also important to keep your fabric tack clean. It will maintain its usefulness and extend its life. Dirt particles have the same cutting properties in fabric as they do in leather. Nylon halters and leads, saddle pads, fabric girths and any other nylon items should be machine washed frequently in cool water using a gentle soap. Never use detergent. Detergent has a heat-producing agent that is difficult to rinse out. In saddle pads, it could produce heat on the horse's back.

Here are suggested supplies to be gathered:
- Two-gallon pail of lukewarm water
- One cup of Murphy's Oil Soap, or liquid glycerin soap or bar of glycerin soap
- A sponge
- A soft fingernail brush
- Terry rags or towel
- Saddle oil: i.e. Liddy Oil or Hydrophane (avoid neetsfoot oil and the rest of the "dirty" oils)
- Soft cloth such as flannel, for applying oil
- Metal polish
- Disposable gloves

STEP ONE: Find an area where you can set up a stand to hold your saddle. If you are inside, you might want to put a plastic drop-cloth under your stand. If your saddle is very dirty, remove the top layer of dust and dirt with a clean rag. Then gather the cleaning tools listed above and you are ready to begin.

STEP TWO: Soak the sponge in warm water and rinse the entire saddle. Take extra care to wet the backside of the flaps, or any area that directly touches the horse and collects deposits of salt, oils and dirt. Avoid soaking the serge covering or fleece under the padding/panels.
a) If you are using Murphy's Oil Soap, pour a cup of the soap into warm water.
b) If you are using liquid glycerin, wet your sponge thoroughly with warm water and pour the soap directly onto the sponge as needed throughout the cleaning process.
c) If you are using bar soap, wet your sponge thoroughly with warm water and work up a lather, rubbing the bar into the sponge. Continue adding water and suds throughout the cleaning process.

STEP THREE: Work the suds into the leather. If the saddle is very dirty, a grey film may appear on the leather. Using plenty of soap, gently scrub the surface with the brush. The leather is clean when the film is gone and the pores of the leather can be seen. Sometimes it is easier to clean the saddle in sections. **Never "soak" leather.** As each section is cleaned, wipe the leather dry with the terrycloth towel or rag.

STEP FOUR: When the entire saddle is clean, rinse the leather by wiping with a damp sponge and towel-dry the surface. It is important not to let the leather dry before covering the surface with saddle oil. If it does dry, the pores close down and the leather will be dry from the inside out. If part of the leather does dry out during the cleaning process, dampen it again before applying the oil.

STEP FIVE: Oil the leather by wiping a moderate amount of oil over all leather surfaces. Do not wipe off.

STEP SIX: Set the saddle stand where the saddle can dry naturally - in an open room, outside on a porch, etc. Overnight is usually enough time to accomplish this. When the saddle dries it may have spots that appear drier than others. More oil will remedy this. If too much oil is applied simply buff it away after it has had ample time to thoroughly penetrate the leather. Your saddle may require three oilings before you see that all the oil has been absorbed and there is nothing but a slight residue to wipe away.

After the first cleaning/oiling of your saddle, you may substitute beeswax compound for an even softer, more lasting finish.

STEP SEVEN: Between cleanings, it is important to keep your saddle covered and free of dust and dirt. Dust acts like a sponge on the surface of leather, actually drawing the oils and life out of it. A soft bristled paintbrush is helpful in regular quick cleaning. Brush the entire surface of the saddle after each use. Pay special attention to all the folds and crevices.

In your tack room, you can keep a sponge in a covered bucket of Murphy's Oil Soap mixed with water. That makes it easy to run the dampened sponge over the entire sad-

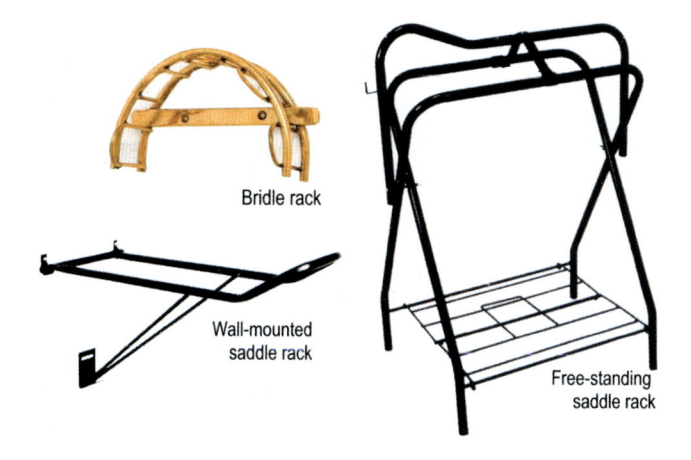

Bridle rack

Wall-mounted saddle rack

Free-standing saddle rack

It is recommended that you store your saddle on a stand, making sure it is covered with some kind of cloth. Stands come in all varieties – both standing and hanging. Your bridle will always be ready to use if you keep it hanging in a clean, dry area. Proper maintenance of your tack will prolong its usefulness.

dle and then cover it with a cloth between rides. Take the time to quickly run the sponge over your bridle, breast collar and any other leather items. It will extend the life of all your tack by keeping it dust free.

Whatever tack you decide is best for you and your horse should be fitted properly. It will last longer and give you better service if you keep it as clean as possible.

It is recommended that you store your saddle on a stand, making sure it is covered with some kind of cloth. There are saddle covers available, but the important thing is keeping something between your saddle and dust. If space is an issue, take a look at the various hanging saddle racks that, in effect, utilize air space.

Bridles and halters and various kinds of training equipment will serve you better if they are hung in a clean, dry area. Unfortunately, most tack rooms inside the barns, which are natural sources of dust and dirt. So keeping tack dust-free is truly a challenge. Keeping your bridles and saddles organized, will certainly help.

You can always hang bridles and halters on a nail in the wall, but a rounded headstall holder will avoid the possibility of the leather breaking down when hung to bend sharply over a nail. Something as simple as a coffee can, nailed in place, will serve the same purpose as more costly tack room accessories.

CARTS AND CARTING

Our wonderful soft-gaited horses make terrific cart horses. The Tennessee Walker is one breed that includes carting in its versatility competition. Photo: Rick Osteen

Lowell May out for a spin with his Mountain Pleasure stallion, EMERALD FIRE. Mr. Lowell and EMERALD FIRE have driven the Governor down the streets of Lexington on parade.

Carting can be great fun. It's a lovely way to share our horses with non-rider friends. Sitting in a buggy, watching the animation of a soft-gaited horses is an awesome experience for both "old-timer" and novice.

Carriage Clubs can be a source of pleasure and challenge, and several breeds have carting classes in their shows as part of their versatility programs.

The maintenance of both harness and cart are the same as the rest of your tack. Keep them clean, well oiled and covered. The weather can really wear away not only at the finish of your cart, but its safety capacity as well.

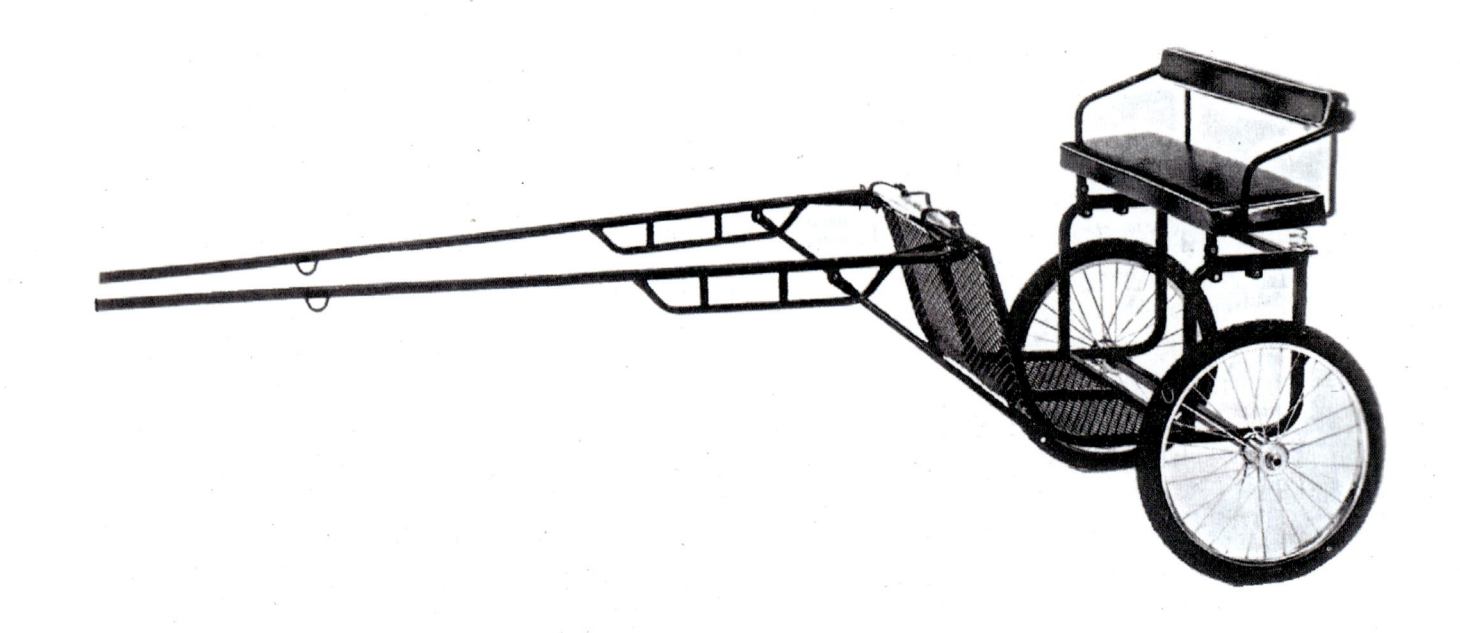

PART TWO
THE BREEDS

7. Mountain Pleasure Horse
8. Kentucky Mountain Saddle Horse
9. Rocky Mountain Horse
10. Kentucky Natural Gaited Horse
11. Tennessee Walking Horse
12. Missouri Fox Trotting Horse
13. Spotted Saddle Horse
14. Paso Fino Horse
15. Peruvian Paso Horse
16. Largo Horse
17. McCurdy Plantation Horse
18. Mangalarga Marchador Horse
19. American Curly Horse
20. Icelandic Horse
21. Tiger Horse
22. Walkaloosa Horse
23. Tiger Horse Registry
24. Gaited Morgan Horse
25. Spanish Mustang Horse
26. Racking Horse
27. Part Walking Horse
28. Florida Cracker Horse
29. Spanish Gaited Pony
30. American Saddlebred Horse
31. Registries In The Making: Sorraia, Tennuvian, Montana Travler, Gaited Morab, Spotted Mountain Horse

MOUNTAIN PLEASURE HORSE

CHAPTER 7

Mountain stallion, GOLDFINGER
Owner: Ronnie Little

HEIGHT: 14.2 Hands & up

GAIT: Mountain Walk, Mountain Gait

COLOR: Any color (White markings limited)

TRAIT: "Boy Scout" Breed

Chapter 7 The Mountain Pleasure Horse

Long before the Civil War, the amazing Mountain Horse of Kentucky was being developed. In the early 1700's the governor of Rhode Island brought Scottish Galloways, Irish Hobies, and Spanish Jennets to Narragansett County. He needed an easy-going horse that would be close to the ground and smooth to ride. He more than accomplished this by producing the pride and joy of Narragansett, the Narragansett Pacer.[1]

The Narragansetts became the most sought-after commodity shipped to the West Indies and other South American destinations. Different areas created special laws directed at the import of Narragansett Pacers. Surinam only allowed a ship to dock if it had equine cargo aboard. If a vessel contained at least 60 horses, many areas did not charge trade permits.

There were ships specially designed for equine transport. They were known as "horse jockeys." Each horse to be shipped required 110 gallons of water, 500 pounds of hay and 10 bushels of oats. Successful delivery of each horse depended on careful attention. Such care demonstrates how prized these Narragansetts were.

The horses that didn't survive the trip were used as food. Indirectly, the trip itself contributed to the "weeding out" of the lesser animals. Only the strongest survived. The hardiness of today's Mountain Horses pays tribute to that hardiness.

Many of the Narragansetts were sold to Canadian locations where they were developing the Canadian Pacers. Many of these Can-

---

[1] The term "pacer" was used to denote gaited horses of all types, not simply the hard pace that the word describes today.

Stallion, NERO, owned by Hiram and Shirley Combs.

Champion stallion, GOBLE, at the Minnesota Horse Expo

Stallion, EMERALD FIRE, parading with Governor and Mrs. Paul Patton and owners Mr. & Mrs. Lowell May in the 2001 Lexington Christmas Parade.

98

Stallion, SUNDANCER, owned by William Ferguson.

The Mountain Pleasure comes in all colors including this eye-catching dappled buckskin.

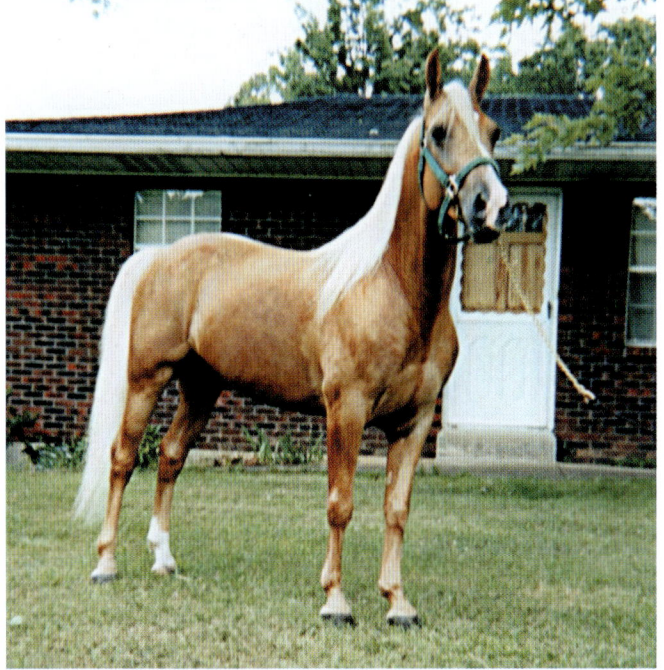

GOBLE son, STAR DUST, winner of the MPHA 2001 Highpoint award. Photo: owner Glen Peck

adian horses were brought back to the Colonies and bred back to the original Narragansetts. These horses in turn found their way to other locations across the North American continent.

For many years, it was believed the Narragansett Pacer had become extinct, diluted into all the other soft-gaited breeds developed in the Americas. But there is evidence to support the theory that the settlers moving into the rugged mountains and desolate hollows of the Eastern Kentucky Appalachians brought the Narragansetts with them. These horses were eventually to become the foundation stock for the Mountain Horses of Kentucky.

Other contributors to the development of the Mountain Horses must have stemmed from a more ancient bloodline perhaps brought to the Appalachians by the early Scottish settlers. The gene that produces the unique chocolate body with flaxen or white mane and tail is limited to very few sources. It passed on the special color gene through the Narragansett, but the high incidence of the color present in the Kentucky Mountain Horses suggests a more direct line was indeed found.

Spanish Jennet blood was also handed down through the Narragansetts. Their medium size, heavy manes and tails, bone structure, heavy muscling in chest and hindquarters, the angle of the shoulder, all leave evidence that the Narragansetts found their way to the protective anonymity of the Appalachian Mountains.

The farmers of Eastern Kentucky came to depend on these horses for their very survival. It was imperative that the horse consistently display a number of qualities.

An even, cooperative disposition was the primary concern. Animals that didn't have heart and a true willingness were not used for breeding. The horse had to be an "easy keeper." They could only be fed what they could forage during the cold winter. Those that weren't strong enough to flourish on this basis didn't survive.

The smooth, 4-beat gait was also considered a necessity. Rougher horses were put to the plow, but the super-smooth horses

Important foundation stallion GOLDFINGER, 1972-2002. Sire of over 120 offspring registered with MPHA. Proudly owned by Ronnie Little of Pomeroyton, Kentucky. GOLDFINGER was buried on the farm where he had stood at stud for 26 years.

Promise of the life with horses seen in this early photo of Ronnie Little, respected breeder and promoter of the Mountain Horse, and owner of the great stallion GOLDFINGER.

with great heart, disposition and stamina were the ones chosen to reproduce. Eventually a consistently high quality became the norm.

Those horses were not being bred in great numbers. The community was not a wealthy one. A farmer could afford to produce only the horses that would be put to use. Extra mouths to feed were luxuries not affordable to these hard-working individuals. A good riding mare would not be bred and taken out of commission if she was needed for work.

Only in the mid-20TH century did financial incentives encourage the production of an extra horse here and there. During the 1940's, they could expect to get $1,100 for a good saddlehorse. With that money, they could purchase a whole farm.

Families might keep such an "extra" horse around to sell to the "drummers," or salesmen, that acted as agents for the wealthy folk of Virginia and Tennessee.

Unlike the rich tobacco planters of Tennessee, the mountainmen of Kentucky needed a horse that could do it all. This horse could work, babysit and still be the ideal horse for their personal riding enjoyment. It's been

GOLDFINGER sired twins, born to a 20-year-old mare when GOLDFINGER was 28 years old. (Owned by Charlie Short and pictured with Mike Wattenberger.)

A dappled palomino son of GOLDFINGER. GOLDFINGER'S DELIGHT

Stallion, GOLDFINGERS STAR, official flag horse to the state of Kentucky. Owned by Nora Deaton.

Foundation stallion, GOBLE, standing at Gaitway Farm in Wausau, Wisconsin.

said that "this horse is a curious mixture of family pet and farm implement."

There are still folks around who are descendants of families long involved with the Mountain Horses. There are many stories surrounding the mystique of special horses, their progeny, and the people who treasured them.

Marion Stamper, born in 1913, tells of his father, grandfather, and great grandfather whose lives were all involved with the breeding and trading of the Mountain Horses.

Mr. Stamper said, "We didn't have much time for pleasure, except maybe on Sundays. Horses up here had to work for a living —they still do, for that matter. No one could afford a horse that only rode good – but wouldn't work. People up here had families to feed. There weren't grocery stores in those days. You ate what you grew. We all had big families that had to eat come winter."

Quoting from Alfred Prewitt, resident of Mt. Sterling, Kentucky: "My family has been raising these horses since way before the

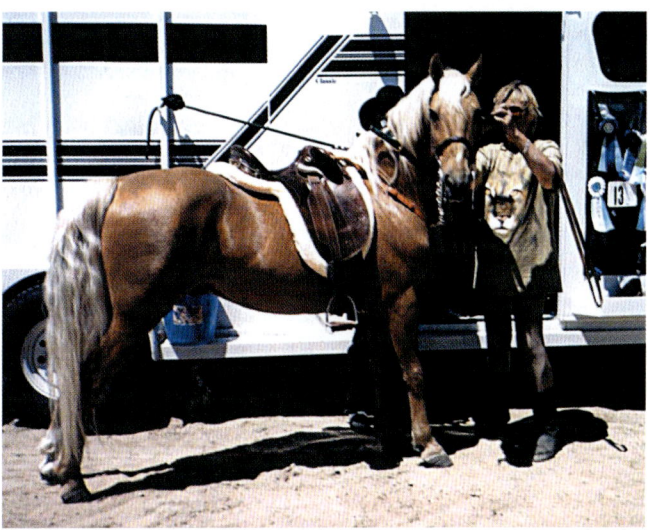

GOBLE daughter, WIND BENT LEXUS.

Stallion, CLEMONS THUNDER, show ready with owner, Barbara Weatherwax.

101

War. There's a family story about a great, great grandmother of ours, Anne Kenney. They say she saw a horseman trotting real fast up the road towards her. "Where are you going in such a hurry?" she asked the rider. "Mr. Lincoln's dead. Mr. Lincoln's dead!" he answered.

"They say she said, 'Well, you will be too, riding on a horse like that. Go down to the barn and get yourself a good one. Just leave yours there.' A month later he brought the horse back and asked to buy it, but Anne refused to sell."

The measure of a good Mountain Horse was whether you could ride 95 miles in a day. It was bred for easy riding, but could step out and cover some ground. It was a horse you could ride all day and had the temperament to do anything you want. Kentucky horse owners immediately culled the horses that did not suit their purposes. A single-use horse was a luxury they could not afford. A single-use horse would be sold to an unsuspecting "flatlander."

Quoting from Marion Stamper: "The big Mt. Sterling court days were held once a month. We all used to drive our stock over there to sell, you know. It was funny when we had to drive turkeys in a flock. We were all on horseback, trying to keep the turkeys – or whatever we were wanting to sell – herded

Stallion, CROWN ROYAL, standing at Willow Creek Farm, Cynthiana, Kentucky. Owner Lonnie Potter.

Stallion, YANKEE CLIPPER, with Yvonne Henson up during a 31 Mile endurance race in 2001. Owner: Raymond Setters. Photo: Becky Siler

Mike Wattenberger aboard SHORT'S GOLD MINE, owned by Charles Short, breeder of the well-known stallion GOLDFINGER. Photo: Pam Ervin

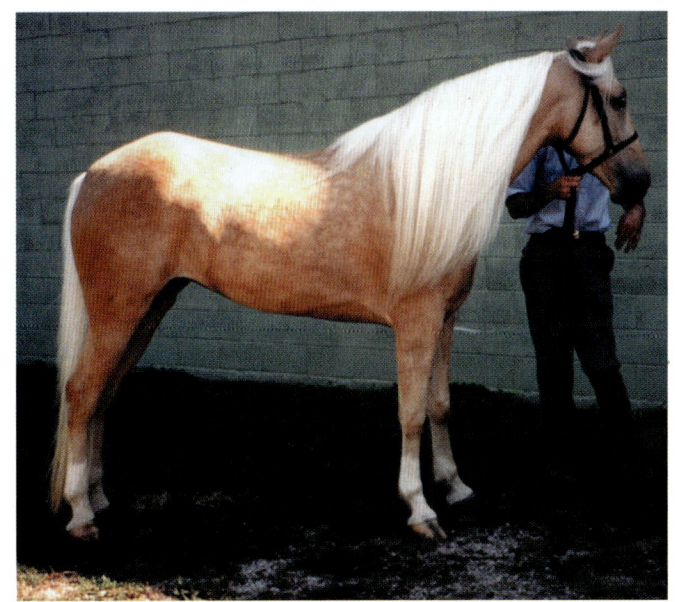

A young palomino Mountain Pleasure gelding.
Photo: Ann Thompson

Charlie Short, a WWII Vet, at 79, on his stallion SHORT'S GOLD MINE, carrying the WWII flag.

together. But, come nightfall, or even a real dark rain cloud, the turkeys would all fly up in the trees to roost, and you stopped right where you were, because they weren't coming back down again until daylight. So we had lots of places along the route to put up our horses and us."

Quoting Dr. Gordon Layton, equine veterinarian from Paris, Kentucky: "The original settlers of these hills came here from other colonies. This was frontier country in those days. They were independent kinds of folks. They had their own ideas and kept to themselves. They didn't like to fool much with people. They could do just about anything. They made what they needed. If they couldn't make it, they did without it. Some people might call them backward in some ways, but they still didn't need civilization to be productive. They made these harsh mountains and climate provide for them and their families, and they wouldn't have it any other way."

Quoting Paul Stamper, Marion's son: "Only a few people ever bothered keeping track of the bloodlines, since it was really a community thing. Someone along the creek had a good stallion, the kind whose colts worked good and rode the best. Mare owners

Cliff Clemons with his stallion, MOSES. Photo: Liz Graves

Mare, GOLDIE, mother to Mountain Pleasure foundation stallion, MOON.

Stallion, MOON, at 23 months of age.

Stallion, MOON, at 17 months of age.

Stallion, MOON, at six years of age.

along the creek bred to him. Everyone mostly stayed around their own branch. The Eastern Kentucky horsemen lived pretty well within their hollows and creeks."

Quoting Roy Coffey, born in 1918, and breeder of the old "country horse" for most of his life: "The first Mountain Horse I ever had was known in those days as a black squirrel. She was a very good gaited horse. We wanted them to rack and the old fashioned running walk. We trained them to that. A pace was something that we absolutely didn't want. And if one would pace, we did something to stop it from pacing. I got a young horse from that black squirrel mare. He was one of the best saddle horses I ever sat on. Or as good.

And that horse racked, and I mean he racked smooth, he'd rack slow, he'd rack fast, and he had that old fashioned nod like our Grandfathers used to ride. You'd get on one of them and he'd nod for you from here to Salyersville. He'd never get out of breath if you used him and kept him in good shape."

Quoting James H. Finch, nephew to Jasper Jones and life-long breeder and owner of Mountain Horses, describing the Jasper Jones' "Buckey" horse: "My uncle kept him until he was 31 or 32. He worked him all the time. He worked him with a big mule to mow down the hills. He was a good work-horse. He had no pace whatever. He had the old-time running walk. He nodded his head some, and

The great stallion MOON, at 27 years of age.

Will Ferguson, aboard his stallion SUNDANCER.

when he dropped into that gait you could just ride him from there on. He wouldn't break going down the hill. He'd cross ditches and just keep that gait. If he ever trotted, I never did see it.

"Glenn Lacy will tell you about the time he rode Buckey across a bridge in the dark. He said the bridge had holes all in it and it was the darkest night he ever saw. He said he didn't know whether to try and lead him across, so he just stayed on and turned his reins loose. Said Buckey put his nose right down to the bridge and felt with his foot...as he put his foot down, he'd feel for that hole. All this with just a halter around him. A child could handle him. A very intelligent horse."

Marion Stamper tells another story that illustrates the intelligence of the Mountain Horse. "There were lots of salesmen who'd travel around here back several years ago. There was a train in Campton. Well, this old sorrel horse belonged to the livery stable in Hazel Green. They'd lease the sorrel horse to a salesman to ride to the trail in Campton. When he got there, what he was told to do was to tie the reins to the saddle horn and turn the horse loose, and he'd come right on back to the stable. You could see that old horse a-coming home regular. Probably 15 to 18 miles. Lots of folks would try to catch that old horse. Some because they wanted him, and some just for meanness, or to see if they could - but no one ever did."

Well, if no one ever caught the old sorrel horse, the Mountain Horse certainly caught the fancy of the "outsiders." Hubbard B. Spencer, born in 1892, was perhaps a major contributor to the expansion of awareness about the Mountain Horse. He shared with his father John, and his son, Hub Jr., the art of riding those rugged Kentucky mountains, buying those splendid horses, and selling them to a waiting out-of-state public.

Quoting Hub Jr.: "I delivered two or three perfectly matched palomino horses up in Pennsylvania to a horse broker named Fisher. They were sold to Roy Rogers. I know what another breed says, but I am the one who personally delivered the horses. They were definitely Mountain Horses. I know, because I was there."

The Spencers were personally responsible for railcars full of horses being sent to Tennessee in loads of 75 to 100. These horses, nurtured in Kentucky, became foundation stock for other breeds in neighboring states.

On September 29, 1994, a proclamation was made by the Governor of Kentucky, Brereton Jones:

To all whom these present shall come:

"The horsemen of Eastern Kentucky developed a type of horse, known as the Mountain Pleasure Horse, to be smooth of gait, gentle of disposition, willing to work and surefooted as necessary for mountain terrain; and this Mountain Pleasure Horse has been carefully and closely bred for over 160 traceable years along the original Kentucky Mountain bloodlines; and blood-typing research by the University of Kentucky has shown the Mountain Pleasure Horse to be the parent stock of all the American gaited horse breeds and now therefore, I Brereton C. Jones, Governor of the Commonwealth of Kentucky, do hereby recognize the Mountain Pleasure Horse."

The Mountain Pleasure Horse Registry was founded in 1989 to foster and protect the stability of the Mountain Horse for generations to come.

The logo of the Mountain Pleasure Horse Registry.

In June of that year, the founding members were Gordon Layton, Harvey Prewitt, Larry Combs, Aleitha Davis, Brenda Blakemore, Paul Stamper, and Harvey's brother Alfred Prewitt. Gordon Layton was elected president, and with his board of directors, began registering horses and attracting members. By the following February, 140 horses had been approved.

The Mountain Pleasure Horse Registry is a nonprofit registry dedicated to the development and promotion of the horse in which the natural gait and amiable disposition breeds true. To ensure that these two key attributes are not diluted by ill-advised breeding, all horses submitted for registration with the Mountain Pleasure Horse Association (MPHA) must be inspected, videotaped and approved for registration by the Board of Directors.

Stallion, EMERALD FIRE, owned by Lowell May, representing the breed at the Equine Affaire in Columbus, Ohio, 2001.

Mike Wattenberger parading with his stallion, GOLDRUSH, son of SHORT'S GOLD MINE. Photo: Pam Ervin

CROWN ROYAL, standing at Willow Creek Farm, owned by Lonnie and Milyne Potter, proudly wearing "the colors."

To further ensure the integrity of this breed, all horses accepted for registration must be blood-typed before registration papers will be issued, in order to prove parentage. This blood typing project, directed by Dr. Gus Cothran from the University of Kentucky, progressed to the point that he was able to identify genetic markers that classified the Mountain Pleasure Horse as a distinct breed.

As the registry developed, important decisions were made about the desired horses. They would not allow "field inspections." They wanted no preferential handling of inquiries to the Association. The rules would be simple, straightforward, and applied equally to everyone. There would be no "preferred color!"

Although the owners of Mountain Pleasure Horses do like to "show off" their horses, they will be quick to tell you these are not really "show horses." Their beauty, smoothness of gait and responsiveness under saddle can be observed in the show ring, but the real proof of this breed's value is on the 100-mile trailride or at the backyard birthday party when the youngster becomes acquainted with his or her first mount.

This could be called the "baby-sitter breed," because they are so much in demand for children's first mounts. One Mountain Pleasure Horse owner dubbed them "the Boy Scout Breed" because they are honest, loyal, trustworthy and reliable. The nickname seems to have stuck. With its natural gait and willing disposition, the Mountain Pleasure Horse is waiting, whether you ride once a week or once a month. Its general conformation is described in the bylaws of the MPHA:

1. Horses must exhibit good disposition.
2. Horses must demonstrate the recognized gait under saddle. The recognized gait is defined as follows:
   An evenly spaced, four-beat lateral gait with moderate forward speed and extension, without exaggerated knee or hock action. The gait should be smooth, supple, cadenced and animated, with the horse collected and balanced and

WOODWIND KEEPER at 18 months with owner, Will Ferguson.

The Mountain Pleasure Horse has a beautiful appearance in or out of the show ring. Pictured is Sarah Nickell on the stallion, GOLDFINGERS STAR.

The author with two GOLDFINGER fillies: HONEY DEW, owned by Lynne Peleshuck of Washoe Valley, Nevada; and HONEY JO, owned by Desirai Schild of Chubbuck, Idaho.

Stallion, SARGE, son of GOLDFINGER, owned by Sue Stewart, at the '95 Hoosier Horse Fair.

BABY DOLL, three time MPHA Halter Grand Champion. Owned by Lowell May of Salyersville, Kentucky.

exhibiting symmetry in flexion and extension. The key trait of the Mountain Pleasure Horse is the way in which the natural gait breeds true. Proper breeding will enhance this and other desirable characteristics in successive generations. To this end no action devices, aids or harsh training methods are permitted.

3. Horses must be of solid body color. Horses with excessive white above the knees or hocks are registerable as Mountain Pleasure Horses, but not desired in breeding stock, or in shows. White on the face (defined by a line from one corner of the mouth) and white on the lower lip (defined by a line from one corner of the mouth to the other, and including the area forward of that line), will not figure in the 20 square inches of allowable white. However, all other white on the head will figure in the 20 square inches allowed, and bald-face horses are not desirable as Mountain Pleasure Horses. Standard recognized colors of the Mountain Pleasure Horse include, but are not limited to, bay, black, chestnut, sorrel, roan, grey, buckskin, palomino and chocolate.

Brenda Wattenberger on her golden mare. Mt. Sterling, Kentucky. Photo: Pam Ervin

4. The average size of the Mountain Pleasure Horse is 15 hands, although there is no registry limit on how tall or short the horse may be.
5. Horses must exhibit a reasonable amount of "eye appeal."

To encourage the breeding of the Mountain Horses, the Mountain Pleasure Horse Association currently publishes a newsletter for members, maintains a web page, an annual Stallion Directory, organizes MPHA classes at horse shows and sponsors an annual MPHA Classic Horse Show in September each year, and is affiliated with UMH (see Chapter 38). Through breeding, they strive to produce an animal that meets the highest standards of this breed, a horse for all occasions and people.

Organizing a registry is no small task. Gathering information about the genealogy of a breed that has been developing for so many years is extremely complex.

Many of the foundation horses had the same or similar names. Horses were frequently named for their color, i.e. Silver, Ginger, Bucky (buckskin), Copper, Star, or Snip. Horses were also given "important" names like Rex and Major. Fortunately, outside the hollow, horses were referred to by the name of the owner - Little's Silver, Cabell's Rex, Chaney's Palomino Mare or simply a Stamper stallion or Cabell's Good Yellow Mare.

The rich golden palomino coloring is frequently exhibited on the Mountain Pleasure Horse, WOODWIND'S WINTER STAR, a three-year-old filly.

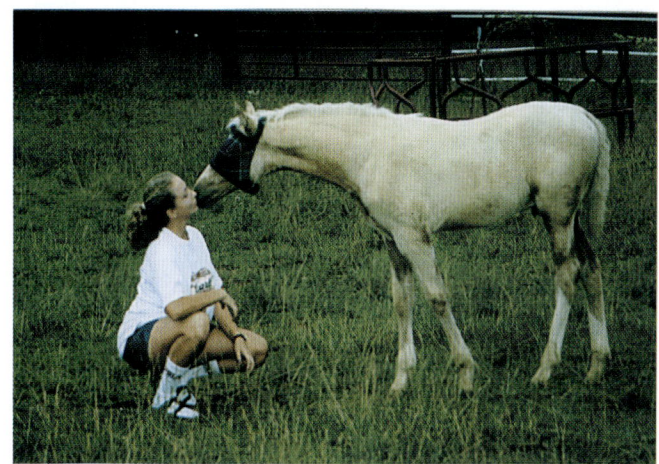

This photo truly demonstrates the family orientation of this lovely breed. Pictured is Jenna Ratliff, the fifteen-year-old granddaughter of the prominent Mountain Pleasure horse breeder, Ronnie Little, and her weanling colt, a great-grandson of the important stallion, GOLDFINGER.

F & R'S RED FLAME, owned and pictured with Shelly Spradlin at their Idaho home.

Stallion, SPIDER, standing at The Wright Place, owned by Renee Wright of Wellington, Kentucky.

The Mountain Pleasure Horse has a disposition so willing to participate and please its human. Photo: MPHA

MOUNTAIN BOURBON, owned by Jamie Lee Derickson.

Stallion, YANKEE CLIPPER as a three-year-old. Owner: Raymond Setters. Photo: Tom Cannon

These clarifications in names have been helpful in outlining the family trees. Tracing the bloodlines would have been difficult for anyone unfamiliar with the actual horses or their owners. For outsiders it would have been impossible. For the mountain horsemen themselves, these horses were completely distinct.

Owners and fanciers of these horses are quick to describe the accomplishments and unbelievable feats that were commonplace. Tradition keeps many stories. A favorite question is, "Who is your favorite Mountain Pleasure Horse?"

Quoting Stanley Franklin, a banker, farmer and MPH owner residing in Kentucky: "My friend and I went to see 'Old Bucky,' one of the sires of the foundation stock of this breed. He had not been ridden for about two years. My friend was using an old wooden milk crate to aid in getting on the horse. The crate broke and he fell directly under the horse in a very dangerous position. 'Old Bucky' very calmly stepped aside not to harm my friend and looked at him, as if to say, 'Are you hurt?'"

Quoting Dr. Gordon Layton, equine veterinarian and founding member of the MPHA: "One time we had a reporter from a Louisville television station come do a feature on Mountain Pleasure Horses. He decided he wanted to do the 'close' on horseback. We hooked a shank to either side of the stallion Rusty Go Boy's halter, and put the reporter up bareback on Rusty's back. We knew we might be in trouble when the reporter almost rolled off the other side. But Rusty suffered through four takes before the reporter finally 'got it right!'

Quoting Tracy Petrie about her remarkable stallion, Moon: "He's got more heart and soul than I've ever known. He consistently reproduces his strength and temperament and I enjoy owning his offspring because they're so easy to work with. We use him to breed, he's my personal riding horse, and he's my 8-year-old daughter's best friend in which I would truly trust her life with him. He will lay down, play dead, sit up like a dog, shake…it doesn't get much more versatile than that."

Quoting Al Prewitt, founding member of the MPHA who has owned Mountain Horses since 1928: "Having a good disposition was a must with the Prewitt children growing up; and if a horse didn't have it, it was soon sent elsewhere. One horse tangled himself in barbed wire and stood still for 16 hours until someone came to help. Another time, two children, under the age of four, wandered into the stall of a 7-year-old stallion. The horse entertained the children for about 30 minutes, never hurting them."

Al goes on to describe a horse he had in 1950: "I had a horse named Blue that won the Walking and Plantation Walking Horse Stake all in one night at the Montgomery County show. After the show, I drove cattle daily, with the same horse, until I joined the military."

Mountain Horse enthusiast Paul Stamper has also owned and enjoyed these horses all of his life. He is actually standing at stud, some of the same bloodline stallions that his great grandfather owned.

Of course, ownership of this lovely breed is not limited to the oldtimers. Like the rest of the soft-gaited horses, the Mountain Pleasure Horse is being enthusiastically received by folks who are not only new to the Mountain Horse, but new to horses as well. The following is a typical story as told by Margaret Layton:

"It all started with Peaches, a young palomino mare that was purchased for the grandson's 4th birthday. The grandfather had looked high and low for a horse for his grandson's birthday. He found that one breed's temperament wasn't right, another breed was too nervous, still another was priced too expensively. The horse he finally chose, the one that sounded just right, was Mountain.

"When the birthday arrived, the young Mountain mare was brought up to the back yard and she proceeded to endure a procession of eight riders. Five of those riders were under the age of seven. Two of the others were greenhorn adults who had not ridden in years. One rider knew what he was doing. The mare patiently carried the little ones and endured the bravado of the adults who thought they knew what they were doing, and then put on quite a show for all when the experienced rider got on her.

"And the grandfather? He hadn't ridden

Stallion, EMERALD FIRE, the "pride and joy" of owner Lowell May, has won MPHA Conformation Grand Champion three times – and under saddle Champion, once.

Charles Short with SHORT'S GOLD MINE a 4-year-old stallion – son of GOLDFINGER out of MANDY CLAY.

The Mountain Pleasure Horse is known as the "boy scout" breed, because they are honest, loyal, trustworthy and reliable. Photo: Courtesy MPHA

A kind nature is evident in the face of this youngster with partially blue eyes, frequently found in horses with MOON in their background.

A pair of palominos courtesy of the Ratliff Family.

a horse in at least 25 years, maybe longer, and didn't plan to start then. But he tried out the mare, and a couple of weeks later ended up buying a gelding for himself to ride, and then several brood-mares, and then stallions, and then…Let that be fair warning to you parents and grandparents out there!"

The Mountain Pleasure Horse has become associated with the Governors of Kentucky as well as the State itself. In 1994, Governor Brereton Jones made the proclamation recognizing the breed, and the Mountain Pleasure Horse has become the official horse to carry Kentucky Governors in parade venues.

The Mountain Pleasure Horse Association will continue to hold the standard of the Mountain Horse well into the future.

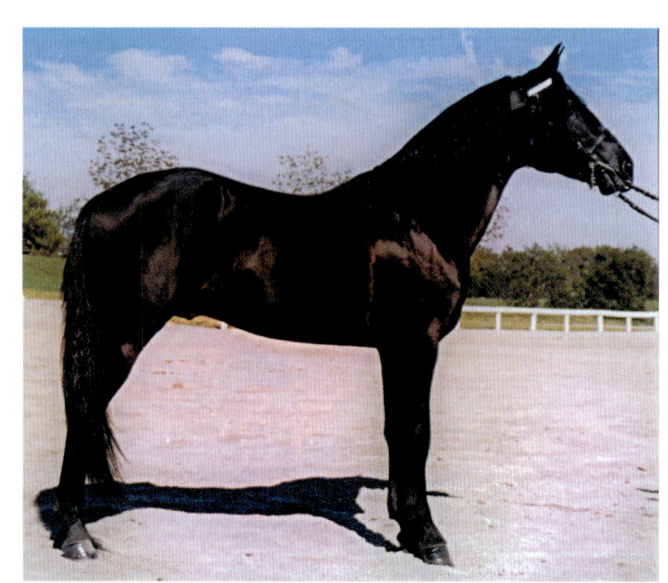

GOLDFINGERS STAR with Sarah Nickell, up.

Stallion, JAKE'S BLACK SHADOW, son of YANKEE CLIPPER, out of MY LADY CHARMIN (MPHA Champion Mare at the first annual MPHA Fall Classic Show in 1991.) Owned by Jake Rose of Olympia, Kentucky.

MOUNTAIN MUSIC
Elen & Charlie Kentnor

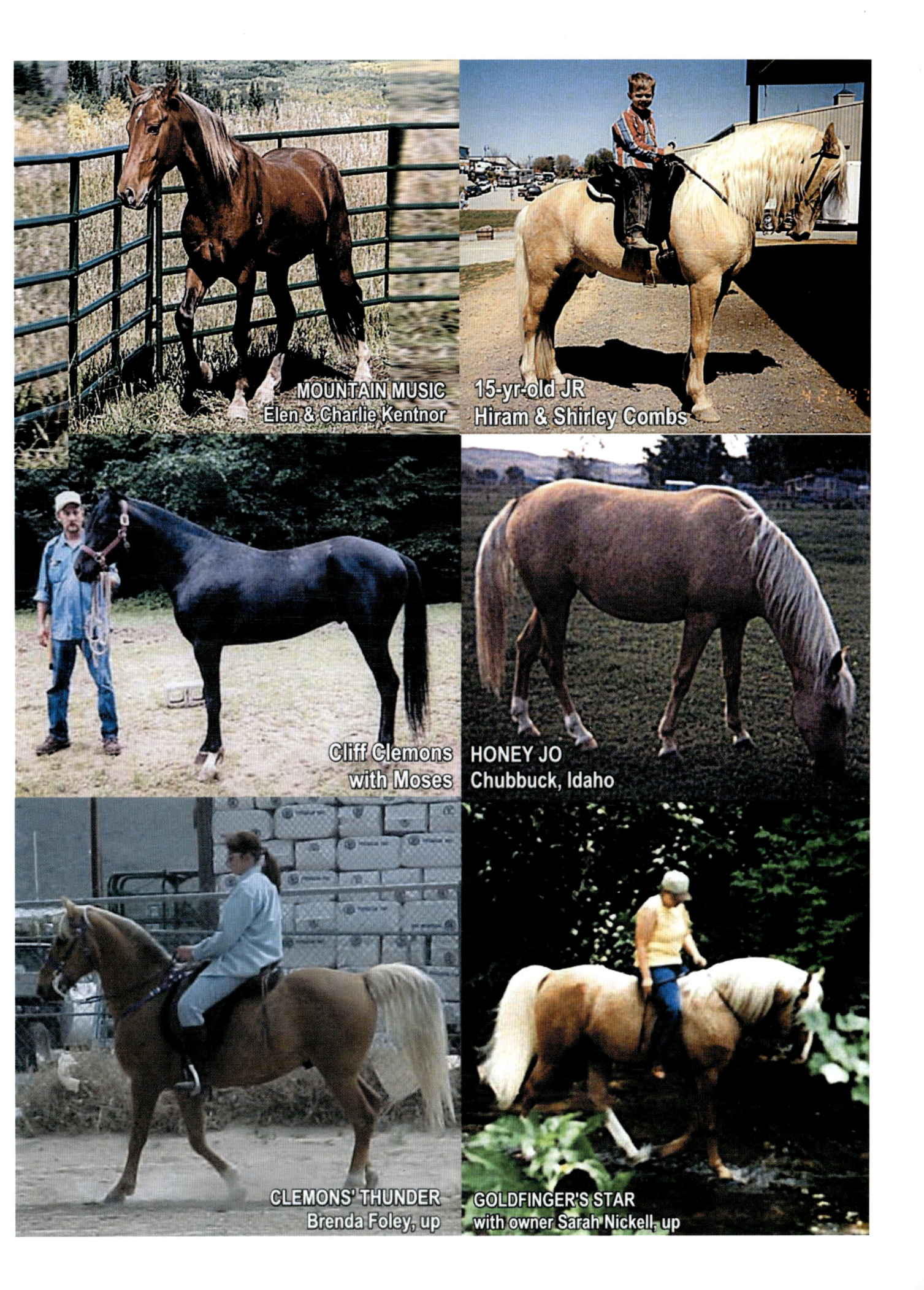

15-yr-old JR
Hiram & Shirley Combs

Cliff Clemons with Moses

HONEY JO
Chubbuck, Idaho

CLEMONS' THUNDER
Brenda Foley, up

GOLDFINGER'S STAR
with owner Sarah Nickell, up

KENTUCKY MOUNTAIN SADDLE HORSE

CHAPTER 8

Mountain stallion, GENERAL JACKSON
Owners: Desirai & Ron Schild and Barbara Weatherwax
Photo: Bob Langrish

HEIGHT: Class A - 13.3 & up
Class B - 11 H -13.3

GAIT: Trail Walk, Show Walk, Show Gait

COLOR: Any color, white markings limited

TRAIT: People Oriented

**Chapter 8
The Kentucky Mountain Saddle Horse**

There were no horses in the Americas when Columbus arrived with his soft-gaited Spanish horses. The very development of this country is reflected in the evolution of the gaited horse.

Early on, the New England colonists were exporting Pacers to the other colonies, the West Indies, the French West Indies, the Dutch Islands, Martinique, Guadeloupe, Dominica, Santa Domingo, Curacao, Bonaire, Aruba and Surinam.

At the same time, horsemen in the Colonies, particularly those from Rhode Island, were importing Scottish Galloways, Irish Hobbies and Spanish Jennets into Narragansett County. With such a brisk trade exchange for molasses being brought back to the colonies, the Governor of Rhode Island spearheaded the development of what was to become known as the Narragansett Pacer. While the southern states were amassing great wealth through the production of crops such as tobacco and cotton, a New England aristocratic society was being developed with wealth acquired from breeding fine horseflesh.

The Narragansett Pacers must have been extraordinary saddle horses. According to a Custom ledger of the period, the New England Colonies shipped 7,133 horses in one year to the British Islands alone. The Narragansetts were known for their remarkable ambling gait, tremendous stamina and sure-footedness.

These horses were described by a well-known horseman of the period as the finest

↓ Nine-year-old Brenda Wattenberger aboard the stallion, STERLING SILVER, a full brother to GOLDFINGER. Brenda's dad, Charlie Short, raised both horses. STERLING SILVER was his first stallion out of McGUIRE'S ROCK and SHORT'S BESS. SHORT'S BESS was a sorrel Mountain mare that Charlie Short had purchased for $225 she produced 17 foals for Short. GOLDFINGER was SHORT'S BESS'S last foal.

At the time, Charlie Short's father thought him "plum silly" for buying a mare at that cost. He thought it was outrageous! For that $225 he could have purchased a team of mules to work, instead of a riding mare. But for Charlie Short, it was a great beginning for an important and wonderful line of Mountain Horses. GOLDFINGER offspring are currently found and registered in most Mountain Horse Registries.

Stallion, WOODWIND KEEPER, from Woodwind Farm in Wytheville, Virginia. Owned by Dr. Joyce Doonan and Will Fergeson

little saddle horse that has ever been known. They were able to cover rough ground at a steady and rapid pace.

Many people believe the Narragansett Pacers became extinct. Some believe the Narragansett blood was diluted into all the other soft-gaited breeds developed in the Americas. But now we have convincing evidence to support the theory that the Narragansetts were brought into the rugged mountains and desolate hollows of Eastern Kentucky Appalachians by settlers moving west from the New England Colonies. Early descriptions of the Kentucky Mountain horses are a match for the Narragansetts.

The Kentucky Mountain horses became partners in survival with the farmers of Eastern Kentucky. Only the most suitable and fit horses could survive under the difficult conditions inherent to the mountainous regions of Kentucky. They would be fed what they could forage during the cold winter. Those that did have the strength to survive went on to flourish in the Kentucky hills. Rich tobacco planters of

The logo of the Kentucky Mountain Saddle Horse Association Registry.

Tennessee could afford to have horses for various purposes. The men of Kentucky, on the other hand needed a horse that could do it all.

The Mountain Horse more than met the challenge. It could work, babysit, and still be the ideal horse for personal riding and enjoyment. These easy-natured, warm-blooded mountain horses were held in high esteem. The finest among them were cherished and bred. If any records were kept, they were usually verbal. Many of the old timers whose fathers and grandfathers owned such horses have stories and pictures that tell of their horse's ancestry, breeding patterns, and characteristics.

In modern times, the gene pool that created these wonderful animals nearly became depleted, seriously threatening their existence. A number of Kentucky residents who had grown up with the Mountain Horses

Three major influences on the Mountain Horses: Carl Vivian, Sam Clemons and Jr. Robinson.

Stallion, MARTIN LUTHER, from KB Stables owned by Kim and Bruce Harrison of Oconomowac, Wisconsin.

realized they could no longer take them for granted without making an effort to protect them.

The Kentucky Mountain Saddle Horse Association (KMSHA), was born out of the keen horsemanship and determination of one man, Robert "Jr." Robinson. His vision and concern for "the horse" has brought the registry to the place of strength and health it enjoys today.

Quoting Robinson: "Well, I've been with these horses all my life. I was brought up with these horses. They were primarily a workhorse. My father and I worked these horses and used them for all purposes. We pleasure rode them, we worked them; back then, we rode a lot. I rode horses to the store myself and just got out on Sunday and rode around."

"We wanted to preserve this horse, so we started the Kentucky Mountain Registry. We hope these horses satisfy their owners.

Robert "Jr." Robinson, founder and continuing "Guiding Light" of KMSHA.

CLEMON'S THUNDER with Steve Foley, up.

FANCY MAY with Herbert Staggs, up.

OPHIR HILL'S GINGER with Skeeter Savage, up.
Photo: Forrest Bliss

TRIPLE S LADY KATE with Joe Morgan, up.
Photo: Forrest Bliss

SUMMER SPIRIT with Beverly Frost, up.
Photo: Forrest Bliss

KENTUCKY GOLDEN DAISY with Kelsey Olsen, up.
Photo: Forrest Bliss

We try to breed for gentle horses, for good temperament and a good smooth 4-beat gait. If you don't register a good product, you're defeating your purpose. We want the horse to be the winner."

Robinson had participated in the formation of other Mountain Horse registries. There was, however an area of disagreement that he wished to address with KMSHA. "In the other registries, the smallest horse they would register was 14:2 H tall. But we had so many good 4-beat gaited horses that came in under that size."

Robinson's decision to embark on the enormous responsibility of forming a registry was sealed when he bred the horse General Jackson. This gorgeous, well-gaited, flashy stallion stood a sturdy and strong 13:3 H tall. Robinson is quick to point out that Jackson is a short horse, not a small horse. This is a solid horse in the tradition of the Narragansett. Many of the shorter horses seem to be the most talented in gaiting.

KENTUCKY GOLDRUSH with Barbara Weatherwax, up.
Photo: Forrest Bliss

J. LEE'S ROCK-IT, two-time Kentucky State Champion. Classic Farms, Mechanicsburg, Pennsylvania. Photo: Bob Langrish

After Robinson and his volunteers registered the local native Mountain Horses as a foundation, the Registry was then open to receive other horses possessing the same traits. By grouping horses with like-characteristics, a gene pool has been formed from which owners of mares and stallions may review and select compatible breedings for their horses.

Through selective breeding of foundation horses with similar approved stock, the smooth gait and gentle disposition can be insured among the horses of the Association for generations to come.

This approach to breed-development has been followed by other important registries. The Missouri Fox Trotter breeders kept their books "open" for more than 30 years. Welcoming "outside" blood that is consistent with the standard of the registry should limit the chance of abnormalities due to lack of variety in breeding options.

Originally, the height of the Kentucky Mountain Saddle Horse was defined as 13:3 H and up. However, it was discovered that many of these gaited native Mountain Horses were somewhat less than the required 13:3 H. These horses clearly demonstrated the 4-beat gait and other desired characteristics of the Kentucky Mountain Saddle Horse. In fact the original stock, the Narragansetts, were short and stout in structure.

Due to numerous requests from KMSHA members and non members, Class B was

SANTA ANNA, Classic Farms. Photo: Bob Langrish

ZSA ZSA, Classic Farms. Photo: Bob Langrish

G V MAN'S MASTERPIECE, Skeeter Savage, up.

Stallion, COMANCHE CHIEF, owned by Woody and Sheila Isaac of Wellington, Kentucky.

Stallion, JOE BANJO, 2001 Sam Tuttle Award Winner, standing at Classic Farms, owned by Dave and Sue Stefanic, owners of the KMSHA Registry.
Photo: Bob Langrish

SKEETER'S COUNTRY GIRL, with Kelsey Olsen, up.

Stallion, JERICHO, from Turning Point Training owned by Shawneen Magrum.

opened in January 1992. While Class A consists of horses from 13:3 H with no upper limit in height, Class B consists of horses from 11H to 13:3H. Other than height, both classes A and B require the same standards for registration.

To qualify for registration, the horse must display the following characteristics: 1) Show a gentle and willing disposition; 2) Demonstrate, under saddle, evidence of a natural, smooth, even 4-beat saddle gait; 3) Be of any color (may have white on the face and legs, but is limited to 36 square inches of white on the body only in the area behind the breast bone and under the ends of the rib cage); 4) Height be not less than 11H (44 inches) for Class B, or 13:3H and up for class A; 5) Be of good conformation.

Foals born of KMSHA-registered sires and dams may be temporarily registered from birth. For permanent registration, however, they will be required to demonstrate the above characteristics when put under saddle at two years of age or older and approved by a KMSHA examiner.

The response to the formation and registration of the Kentucky Mountain Saddle Horse has been one of enthusiasm and great interest. By June 1989, a few months after KMSHA's inception, eleven horses had been registered. These included three stallions, one gelding, and seven mares.

By 1996, a mere seven years after the beginning of the Registry, KMSHA had registered more than 4,000 horses not only within

Stud colt, BUD LIGHT, owned and bred by Vernon Brewer, of Jackson, Kentucky. Vernon is an examiner and supporter of the Kentucky Mountain Saddle Horse.

Kentucky, but also in numerous states throughout the United States and parts of Canada, Germany and Austria.

First-time owners of Kentucky Mountain Saddle Horses and new members are frequently in their upper 30's and older. Many of them are thrilled at having "found" these horses and are purchasing one or more for their children and or grandchildren. This exemplifies the temperament and ease of gait of the Kentucky Mountain Saddle Horse.

The Kentucky Mountain Saddle Horse should exhibit a medium bone structure on a sturdy and graceful body. They must have the proper proportions to make a strong agile

Shawn Magrum of Turning Point Training and Gaited Horses in Lodi, Ohio riding her stallion JERICHO.

Tami Lynn Arndt aboard her double-registered (KMSHA & TWH) stallion in Wheatland, Wyoming.

Jason Stefanic riding JOE BANJO at Classic Farm in Mechanicsburg, Pennsylvania. Photo: Bob Langrish

Owners of the Kentucky Mountain Saddle Horse Registry and Association from left to right: Greg & Danette Williams, Linn & Bill Compton, Dave Stefanic, Peggy & Dale Dransfield.

Four-month-old stud colt, OPHIR HILL'S HIGHLANDER, owned by Barbara Weatherwax, a KMSHA examiner.

horse, and a powerful hindquarter with a long underline and short back. They have well-developed long muscle groups that create a build so strong that even the smallest animal can carry the largest adult easily. They have a straight head profile, a broad chest and short canon bones. They have a longer tail bone than many other breeds, and carry them like a flag. Characteristic of the warm-blooded horse, the Kentucky Mountain Saddle Horse has an abundant long flowing mane and tail that frequently have natural ringlets. The coat, as well as the mane and tail of many Kentucky Mountain Saddle Horses is uncommonly silky soft and luxuriant.

Gelding, SYLVESTER, with owner/rider Gloria Harris from Reno, Nevada, up.

4-year-old Stallion, SOUTHERN FIZZ G. with rider 6-year-old Kelsey Olsen.

ROBINSON'S SUNDOWN ROCKY

ANNA'S EL CHICO

A lovely buckskin

ADAMS' SASSY

OPHIR HILL'S GINGER

OPHIR HILL'S GINGER

GENERAL JACKSON

ROBINSON'S REX

All body colors are available in the Kentucky Mountain Saddle Horse -Palomino, bay, buckskin, black, chestnut, sorrel and chocolate. The mane and tail colors range from red to flaxen to black.

The disposition must be the highest concern. All horses registered should be sensitive and calm in all phases of handling and riding. They tend to be very sensitive to humans. This amazing natural bonding toward people will cause them to follow a stranger around in a pasture as if the person were a long-time buddy. With such a sensitive and curious nature, they have an abundance of personality and style.

These horses are capable of doing just about anything any other horse can do but they excel as a companion and a sensible responsive trail horse. Their way of going makes the breed well-suited to distance riding at a comfortable rate of speed with a constant, rhythmic cadence to the gait. The Kentucky Mountain Saddle Horse is genetically gaited, performing the saddle gait (or single-foot) from birth. The Kentucky Mountain Saddle Horse

GV MAN'S MASTERPIECE, "SAM", with Skeeter Savage and Kelsey Olsen, up. (South Lake Tahoe, California) Here SAM is four years old.

GV MAN'S MASTERPIECE. From the top: Two weeks old, two months old, six months old, two years old.

Sonia Scott aboard DAISY.

has an incredibly silky smooth glide-like action with four distinct hoof beats. The more evenly spaced the rhythm, the better.

Each horse has a slightly different way of going, which depends on the conformation of the horse and the strength of the gait gene it inherited. Basically, the gait is a smooth, bold, 4-beat gait. The right front and hind feet leave the ground almost together.

Then the right rear foot hits the ground first, when the right front foot is at its highest point, midway through the arc of the stride. The right front foot hits the ground while the right hind foot is still on the ground. This is repeated

Jason Royer riding an all spruced up DAISY, competing at the Northern Nevada All-Gaited Horse Show.
Photo: Forrest Bliss

with the left feet. The feet leave the ground like a pace and hit the ground like a 4-beat walk at equal intervals. There is no nodding of the head, but there is a great deal of bobbing of the rear end accompanied with minimal hock action. The horse appears to be walking in "fast forward motion."

There should be a minimal waste of energy in the Kentucky Mountain Saddle Horse's performance, the ideal being that the horse appears to skim over the ground grace-

Stallion, SOUTHERN FIZZ G. from Carson City, Nevada.

Bonnie Robinson, founding "heart" of KMSHA.

CHEEKS ROCKY, sire to ONE CLASSY FELLOW, pictured below.

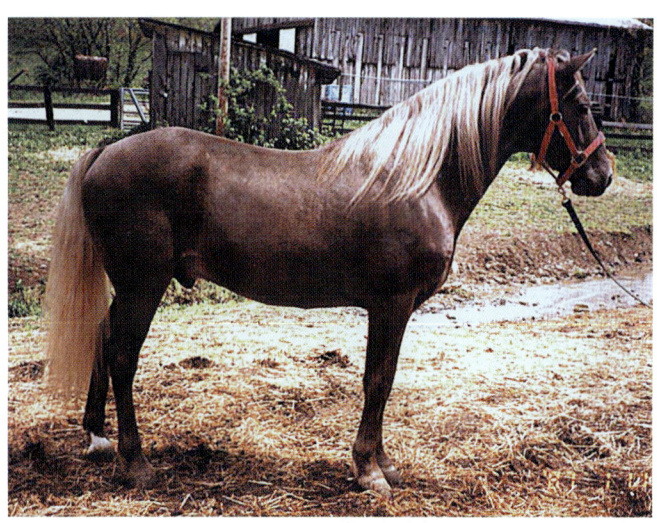

Stallion, AMIGO BLUE, outstanding sire standing at Hawk Hill Farm – owners Bonnie & Jr. Robinson.

gracefully. In the speed form of the gait, these horses usually move faster than other horses can canter or lope.

Quoting Kentucky Mountain Saddle Horse breeder Kathee Jennings of Kenosha, Wisconsin, "In their preferred gait, the Mountain Saddle Horses have incredibly smooth, glide-like action that almost causes you to have to look down to make sure you are moving!"

There is evidence that Kentucky Mountain Saddle Horses tend to be long-lived, often leading useful lives into their 30's. As a result, they mature over a longer period of time than other horses generally do. They frequently do not reach full growth until their fifth or sixth year, but are suitable emotionally and physically for light riding as early as two years of age.

They are tough horses and easy keepers who thrive on a modest diet. They may even get too fat on a diet recommended for horses their size. It seems they have a built-in energy mechanism. They needed it to survive in the early settlements of the Appalachian mountains. Since they are of a cold-blooded nature, they have a very low-key response to stimuli, and their reaction to surprises, as a

Stallion, ONE CLASSY FELLOW, KMSHA World Champion 1998, and Rocky Mountain MASTER STALLION, with KMSHA Association founder Robert "Jr." Robinson, up.

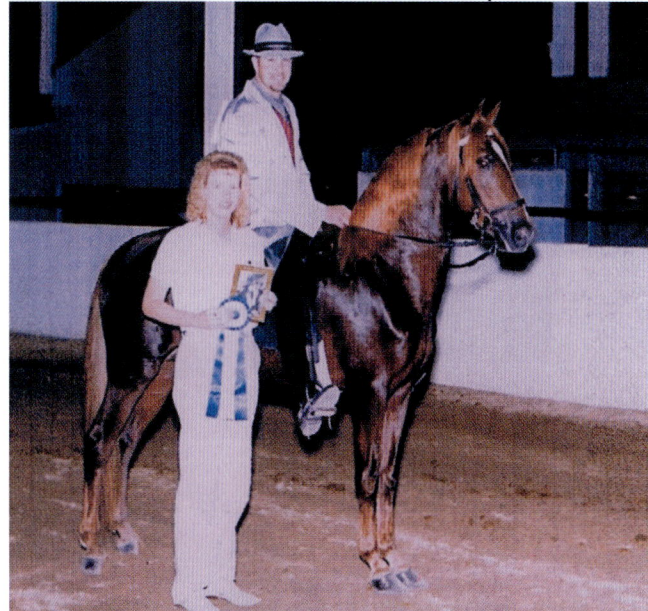

HAWK HILL'S TRACKER, 2-year-old UMH World Champion and son of ONE CLASSY FELLOW, (pictured to the left). Photo V. W. Perry

CHAMP
Photo: Ann Thompson

DAISY
Photo: Ann Thompson

SONNY
Photo: Bob Langrish

ROCKIT
Photo: Bob Langrish

GENERAL JACKSON
Photo: Bob Langrish

TESS
Photo: Ann Thompson

PRINCE CHOCO
Photo: Desirat Schild

group, is generally of a more sensible than fearful nature. In other words, they don't tend to blow up in stressful situations the way many other horses will. They stand their ground and work out their fear so that the rider doesn't lose control.

Due to the overwhelming appreciation for these beautiful native Mountain Horses and the comparative scarcity of available horses, the demand for the Kentucky Mountain Saddle Horse has actually begun to overtake the stock available. It is not unusual for breeders to have reservations on file for foals that are yet to be born.

The KMSHA has drawn to it true horsemen who have risen to the challenge and opportunity of not only "rescuing" the mountain-bred horses, but expanding their treasured talents as well.

A tremendous responsibility lies with the KMSHA Examiners' conscientious selection of quality horses with excellent gait and disposition as well as good conformation. The quality of horses today will no doubt mold the quality of the Kentucky Mountain Saddle Horse in the future.

The three gaits of the KMSH are the Kentucky Mountain Show Walk (collected gait with moderate speed), the Kentucky Mountain Saddle gait (collected gait with more speed), and the Walk (relaxed walk where there is minimal contact with the reins). The horse must demonstrate a distinct difference in speed between the three gaits when called for.

1. Form should not be sacrificed for speed.
2. The horse must be consistent in its four-beat gaits; breaks in the gait will be penalized.
3. Factory-weight standard keg shoes - on all four feet – are to be worn in the show ring, or the horse may be shown completely barefoot.
4. A horse that "wings" or "paddles" in the forelegs will not be penalized in the show ring.
5. Scoring of the horse's gait in the show ring is 60% ; conformation is 30% ; and temperament is 10% (i.e. behavior).

A KMSHA Evening Show in 1994.

CRF BOUNTY HUNTER with trainer, Sandy McCart.

Kristen Lucasey, at 18 months of age, loving her favorite Mountain Horse.

6. There is no limit on how high the horse breaks (i.e. forelegs), but it must be fluid, natural, consistent, and without exaggeration.

The excellent qualities of the Kentucky Mountain Saddle Horse are beautifully described in this personal essay written by Desirai Schild, a breeder and KMSH enthusiast from Chubbuck, Idaho:

"Until we met Chico, my husband Ron and I thought stories about quiet gentle stallions, even Kentucky Mountain horses, were nice fairytales designed to sell stock.

"At best, we're farming novices. Our interest in sweet stallions came about a year after we bought some bred Mountain mares. That's when it finally occurred to us that we would need a stallion around to insure our herd's continued growth.

"Our obvious problem was that we were just learning how to cinch a saddle, so hand-breeding a horse was a little beyond our expertise. We needed a stud who would not take advantage of our inexperience. In most breeds, that would be laughable, but Kentucky Mountain horses are special.

"Sandy McCart, my long-suffering trainer, logged hundreds of miles across Kentucky, seeking a sweetheart stallion. Enter Anna's El Chico, age 8. It was love at first sight, at least on my part. I was awed by the blue-black coat, muscular frame and quiet, inquisitive eyes peeping through a thick forest of forelock. Here was every horse lover's dream - The Black Stallion. I thought Chico was way too good for me. I'm sure he agreed, but was too much a gentleman to say so. He gave me a bemused look as I dragged up a chair to help hoist my substantial, 40-something frame onto the saddle. His eyes widened, but he never moved as I used his mane to pull myself astride that slippery English saddle seat.

Three of Desira Schild's lovely Mountain Horses, SONJA, CHICO; and STRAWBERRY (Photo: Miller Photo, Pocatello, Idaho)

"He walked gently on command. When asked, he gaited flawlessly. I got so excited, I lost a stirrup. As I reached for that, I dropped a rein. I yelled, 'Whoa,' pulling the remaining rein. Chico spun faster. Only centrifugal force kept me in the saddle. My trainer barked, 'stop pulling, sit still.' I did, and Chico stopped. He stood motionless as I crawled, trembling, up his neck to retrieve the rein. He knew he had a fool for a passenger, but instead of taking advantage, he took extra care to keep me safe for the rest of the ride. That made my decision and sealed his fate. He soon made the journey from Kentucky to Idaho.

"Chico has become a bit of an attraction in the west. His sweet disposition and obvious kindness to me charms people at shows, expos, and on trail rides. I often catch folks sneaking a look under his tail to make sure this gentle giant really is a stallion. Once that's confirmed, they usually want to book a breeding to him.

"That turned out not to be a problem either. Chico is as polite to mares as to people. He is so gentle and mannerly, I am able to hand breed him by myself. Chico is an excellent representation of the Kentucky Mountain breed and one of the best friends I've ever had.

"Every horse-crazy little girl dreams of having a beautiful, black stallion who loves her best. I can tell you the realization of that dream is even sweeter when the horse-crazy girl has become a grandma. And, I know, it could only be realized with the most gracious gentleman from the gentlest of all breeds."

**ANNA'S EL CHICO – KMSHA stallion
with Desirai Schild, Chubbuck, Idaho.**

Sandy McCart with SONNY

Sandy McCart supplies one of the most important ingredients for developing a sound and respected Registry: professionalism.

A lifelong horse lover, Sandy first began training gaited horses when she was working at the Kentucky Horse Park in Lexington. The Rocky Mountain Horse was her first, but eventually she found her way to the Kentucky Mountain Saddle Horse.

At Sandy's lovely Harrodsburg, Kentucky farm, she follows her daily routine of consistent, gentle and thoughtful training. Her equine students are brought along to be natural and dependable examples of the best in Mountain horses.

Sandy McCart aboard COPPER'S PRIDE.

Sandy McCart competing in a side-saddle class on HOPE SPRINGS CAPER in 1992.

CLASSIC SQUIRREL with Sandy McCart up. Photo: V.W. Perry

A morning workout at Sandy's Harrodsburg farm.

132

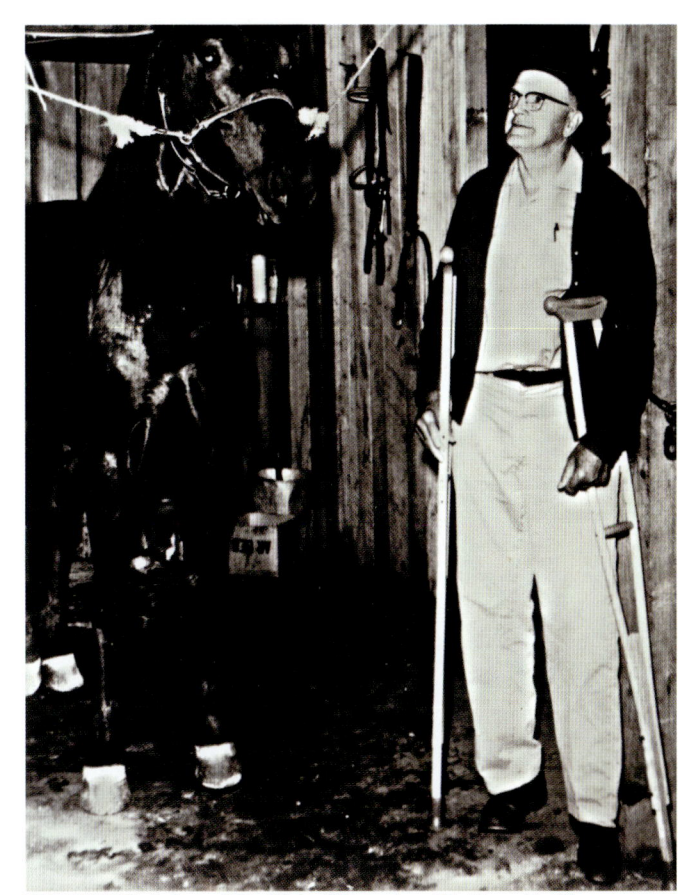

THUNDER (sire of Smith's Ginger) with Sam Tuttle.

SMITH'S GINGER (sire of SONNY) with Mr. J.B. Smith.

SONNY (sire of SONNY'S THUNDER).

SONNY'S THUNDER Sandy McCart in the saddle.

Today, the Kentucky Mountain Saddle Horse Association Registry represents selected bloodlines from all corners of the Mountain Horse family.

Pictured on this page are four generations of Mountain stallions - Thunder, the sire of Smith's Ginger, the sire of Sonny, the sire of Sonny's Thunder.

Through the KMSHA, these bloodlines are not only surviving, but thriving. The information provided by E. Gus Cothren, Ph.D., from his studies of genetics at the University of Kentucky, is being used as a guideline for future breeding programs. The recommended number of eight to ten thousand breeding mares will be observed before the books are officially closed. At that time, the Kentucky Mountain Saddle Horse will achieve breed status. But both management and members agree that there is no hurry. The focus is on the long-term vitality and protection of this very special "Jewel of Kentucky."

ROCKY MOUNTAIN HORSE

CHAPTER 8

Rocky stallion, GRANDVIEW'S CANDY MAN
Owner: Sandee Roberts

HEIGHT: 14:2 Hands - 16:0

GAIT: Trail Walk, Show Walk, Pleasure Gait

COLOR: Any color, except pinto

TRAIT: Gentle Disposition

Chapter 9 The Rocky Mountain Horse

Serendipity is the happy result of almost accidental circumstances. It's luck plus good timing - being at the right place at the right moment. The word perfectly describes the origins of the Rocky Mountain Horse. There were so many times along the road toward the development of a registry, that all could have been lost. But the Rocky Mountain Horse was to be.

It all began with the Mountain Horses of Kentucky.[1] These horses secured the survival of the farmers and miners of Eastern Kentucky. They were integral members of the family, and a high priority was set on their preservation.

The second stage in the development of the Rocky Mountain Horse began in Estill County, Kentucky. The year was sometime during the 1890's. A family from Virginia had traveled to the Rocky Mountain area and were on their way back home by way of Log Lick, Kentucky. They spent the night with a family called Tuttle. In the morning, before they traveled on, they sold the colt that had been at their mare's side to the Tuttles. This colt grew up to sire two important stallions. One stayed with the Tuttle family in Estill County; the other one stood in Clark County.

The offspring of these two studs were so distinctive that they were called Rocky Mountain horses, because of the Rocky Mountain origin of their sire.

The question remains: Where did the original colt come from? What blood flowed

A Pryor Mountain stallion. Note the eel stripe down his back, and zebra stripes on his front legs.

Natural Bridge State Park, Kentucky.

An American Bashkir Curly youngster owned by Johnny R. Brooks from Mountain View, Missouri. See Chapter 19 for more information on the Curlies.

---
[1] See Chapter 7 in *The Fabulous Floating Horses*.

ROCKIN' DOBBIN, 2002 International Grand Champion, from Williamsburg, Indiana. Owners: Mike & Diana Medler. Photo: Jim Hargrove

TOM'S PRIDE from Cypress Lakes Stables and Al Prewitt.

LITTLE DOC from Gaitway Farm in Wausau, Wisconsin.

through this prepotent stallion?

Tradition tells us that this animal came from the west. Most stories describe him as Spanish in type. A Spanish type from the west could have been from numerous sources.

One such source was the Pryor Mountain herd. They were found along a major Crow and Shoshone migration route in the Rocky Mountains. The population itself was founded by Spanish-type horses owned by these tribes. This included sloping croup, low-set tail, deep body, narrow chest, broad forehead but narrow face and muzzle (from front view), eyes placed well on the side of the head with small ears that hook inward at the tips. Their exact gait was not described, but it was said to be comfortable to ride, being extremely smooth.

Although these horses are found in most colors, chocolate body with flaxen mane and tail is not one of them. The classic color of the Rocky Mountain Horse (chocolate body with flaxen or white mane and tail), must have come from the Mountain stock or the Denmark-bred Saddlebred. Only these horses carry that color gene. The Pryor horses are feral horses with a primitive predilection to the dun and grulla and black colorings.

Another western horse that could have fathered the mysterious stud colt of Log Lick Kentucky is the American Bashkir-Curly.[2]

There are several characteristics common to the Bashkirs and Rockys. Although they are more commonly found as chestnut, bay or light brown, Bashkirs have been known to be chocolate of body with flaxen manes and tails.

The hooded eyes, divided mane and spiral curls in the tail are found in many Rockys. Bashkirs are also known to have an abiding love of people, and uncanny intelligence, stamina, sure-footedness, exceptionally strong hooves, a compact physique, a thick mane and tail, and are easy keepers - all traits that are synonymous with Rocky Mountain Horses.

---

[2] See Chapter 19 in *The Fabulous Floating Horses*.

SMITH HIGH CALIBER "MAGIC" from Manteca, California, is owned by Phyllis Rocha and ridden by Mikal Spooner.
Photo: Forrest Bliss

SUMMER SPIRIT with Beverly Frost. From Triple S Mountain Horses; Bert and Paula Morgan.
Photo: Forrest Bliss

Although these horses did not range within the Rocky Mountains, they were native to Nevada. It is very probable that individual horses could have found their way into the Rocky Mountain area.

Taking another look at the possibilities, the Virginia family that brought this mysterious horse from the Rocky Mountain territory may have simply been returning to Virginia with the same horses they brought with them in the first place. Could it be that this Rocky Mountain horse was simply an offspring of Mountain horses that made the trip from Virginia to the Rockies and back home again by way of Log Lick, Kentucky? After all, the blood of the Mountain Horses carries the same Spanish and Saddlebred markers found in the Rocky Mountain horses. Prepotent stallions rarely appear from nowhere to reproduce themselves faithfully. They are more often the product of either intentional or accidental line-breeding. Could this father of a breed have developed from within the breed?

We never will know the exact origins. But we do know that in 1918, Sam Tuttle bought a two-year-old mare that was a descendent of the original stallion purchased by the Tuttle family from the Virginia family. She was dark in color, and her name was Lucy.

Sam brought this young mare to the Calloway Creek farm of Henry Hinz, where she was bred to the "Hinz Stud." The background of this animal is not documented, but it is said to have been of paso type. This mating was to produce the wonderful stallion Tobe. We have to assume that Tobe was to become the sire to Old Tobe who was born in 1927 and lived to become the major influence into the Rocky Mountain gene pool until his death in 1964 at age 37. Old Tobe is considered the foundation sire of the breed.

Old Tobe was a chocolate horse with flaxen mane and tail. He was surrounded by stories that celebrated his good nature. During the days that Sam owned Old Tobe, Sam also owned as many as 52 Rocky Mountain Horses. At that time he had the riding concession at the Natural Bridge State Park in Kentucky. A main feature of the park was the opportunity to ride one of the Rocky Mountain Horses.

One difficulty in making an exacting step-by-step outline connecting the foundation stock with the horses of today, is the frequent use of some of the same names. Sam Tuttle called his favorite stallions Tobe, although he did have other stallions, namely Thunder, King Tut and his uncle's horse Bob. (Bob was actually an American Saddlebred registered as "Chester Dare Peavine.") Sam and his daughter Laura Louise enjoyed showing the five-gaited Saddlebreds.

Most of Tuttle's stock was kept in the pasture and Tuttle, knowing his stock so well,

Jake Rose aboard BLUE RAIN before the stallion was sold to Kellie Bretthauer in Newport, Washington.

Sandy McCart aboard stallion, SONNY, son of SMITH'S GINGER.

would list the sire of each foal according to the characteristics of the foal itself. One such son of Old Tobe was bred to a mare named Honey and produced a stud colt that would be named Tobe. This horse was the sire of the sons of Tobe that actually can be traced as foundation sires of the modern breed.

Although Sam Tuttle was clearly the father of the breed, we have other individuals to thank for developing the horse we know today. Several gentleman horsemen bought young stallions from Tuttle and can be credited with actually maintaining the breed characteristics in the animals they produced.

Some of the individuals who owned Tobe sons were: Sam Clemons, who owned Clemons' Tim; Charles Kilburn, who owned Kilburn's Chocolate Sundown; E.R. Davis, who had both Maples Squirrel and Yankee; and Jim Sewell, who owned Sewell's Sam.

One stallion that was not a Tobe son but still a product of Tuttle's breeding program was Ginger, who was sired by Thunder and his dam was Black Beauty. Ginger was purchased from Tuttle by one of Tuttle's oldest friends, J.B. Smith, who bought Ginger a 1 _-month-old stud colt in 1963.

Smith said Tuttle had about forty mares for sale. He asked $100 a head. If you bought something, Tuttle would buy you a milkshake to seal the deal.

Tuttle would send his dog out into the herd to pick out the individual he was looking to sell or trade. Smith said Tuttle didn't do anything but trade. He didn't believe in work. Smith quotes Tuttle as saying, "Work don't suit me."

Smith said after his purchase of Ginger, he bought two or three horses from Tuttle each year. He would pay $100 each, have a $40 feed bill, and then sell it in the spring for $250.

It wasn't until the early 70's that Smith bought his first mare from Tuttle, but he continued to be a major contributor to the breed via his wonderful stallion, Ginger. There were many years when Ginger would be bred to 40 local mares.

Although both J.B. Smith and Ginger are gone, their offspring are still important to the Rocky Mountain Breed. J.B.'s sons Ray and Jesse follow in their dad's footsteps as Rocky Mountain breeders. And Ginger's sons Sonny and Thunder are still producing wonderful Mountain Horse progeny.

Another important collaboration was the one between Sam Tuttle, Sam Clemons and the great stallion "Clemon's Tim," born in 1970. Tim was sired by Tobe, and his mother is listed simply as "Tuttle Stock."

Tim was one of two Tobe sons born that year that Sam Tuttle had picked out for himself. He promised his good friend Sam Clemons that he could have his pick of the two stud colts. When Tuttle gave his word, he stuck by it.

Tim and Sam Clemons made a grand picture together. Clemons was a big man, both in stature (6'4") and in reputation. When asked why he didn't show his stock he replied, "Yes, I show horses. Come to my barn, and I'll show them to you."

Tim was a lovely chocolate horse with a flaxen mane and tail. He has sired countless quality Rocky Mountain Horses. Owners of Tim offspring sing his praises for passing on his super kind disposition.

One of Sam Tuttle's closest friends and fellow horseman was Charles Kilburn. Kilburn's association with Tuttle began in 1958 when he bought a Tobe daughter, Nance. Further purchases of mares Tillie, Nellie, Bird and the stallion, Major, expanded the Kilburn herd. In 1970, Kilburn's Chocolate Sundown was born. He was a direct descendant of Nance 1 and Tobe.

Tuttle was so pleased with Kilburn's Chocolate Sundown that he arranged for Kilburn to bring "Chocolate" to Tuttle's farm and Sam would stand him. Sam Tuttle called Chocolate Sundown the Ohio Horse. He bred him to hundreds of Mountain mares over the years.

The great stallion TIM. Son of Tobe and sire to a great many lovely and successful offspring. TIM is well-known for passing on his extremely kind disposition.

Stallion, JOHNNY WALKER BLACK. Sire: Grand Champion, **JOHNNY WALKER.** Dam: Grand Champion, **HILLS MISS KIT.**

Sam Clemons, owner of the stallion TIM and strong promoter of the Rocky Mountain Horses. When asked why he didn't show his stock he replied, "Yes, I show horses. Come to my barn, and I'll show them to you."

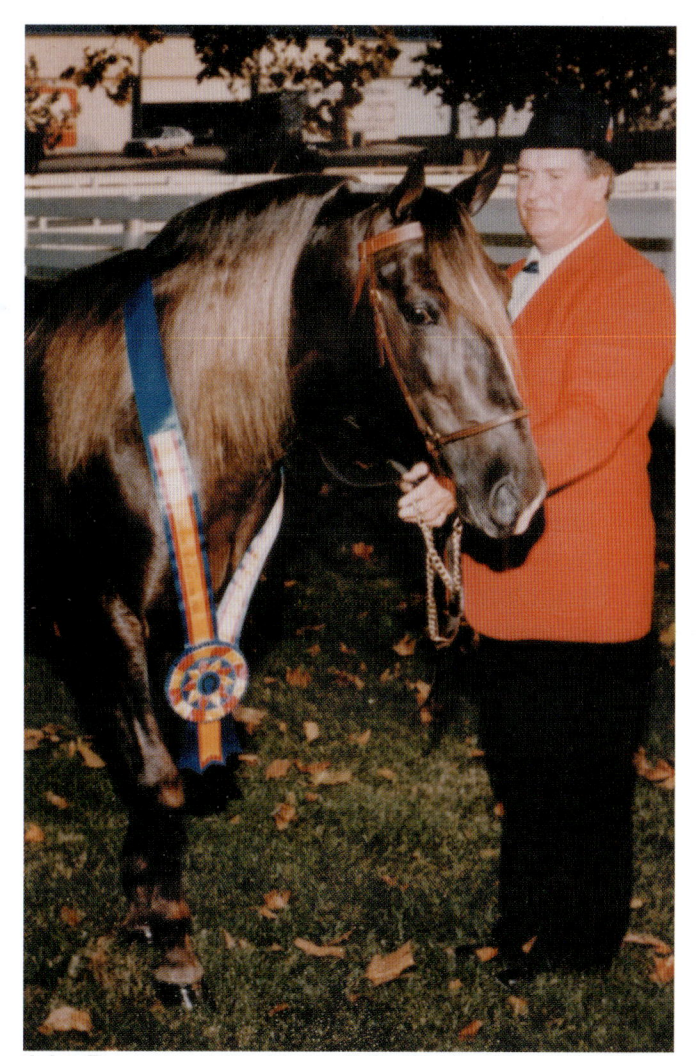

Jake Rose, past president of the Rocky Mountain Horse Association, with one of the sons of CLEMON'S TIM, BLUE RAIN.

Breeder and Rocky Mountain Horse enthusiast, Dan Fehringer, who with his brother Ed, has introduced the Rockies to American Falls, Idaho.

CLEMMONS TIM
- **Blue Rain**
- **Grandview Candyman**
- **Kojak**
- **Clemon's Nick**

KILBURN'S CHOCOLATE SUNDOWN
- Johnson's Toby
  - Woosley's Rocky
  - Rocky Top
  - Johnson's Moonbow
  - Robinson's Sundown Rocky
- Choco
  - Coco
  - Doc
    - Choco Doc
  - Vergeland Jake
    - Tom's Pride
- Sundown Rocky
  - Kizme Kate At Sundoown
- Nuncio
  - Hope Springs Orbit
  - Nuncio's Silver Fable
  - Barlow Chief
  - Green Meadows Cappuccino
- Dan's Dusty Action
  - La Fayettes General

YANKEE
(The Broodmare Stallion)

SEWELL'S SAM
- Buddy Roe
  - Billy Graham
  - Magic Rhythm
  - French's Buddy
  - French's Stormy
  - Sebastians Mountain King
  - Perdue's Rocky Dancer
  - Maximotion
- Broken Bone's Sam'son
- French's Coco
- Kellys Champ
  - Lucky Strike

MAPLES SQUIRREL

- Maple's Fancy
- Tobe's Chocolate Chip
- Castille

SONS OF TOBE: THE SONS ARE IN BOLD RED, THE GRANDSONS ARE IN BLACK, THE GREAT GRANDSONS ARE BLUE, THE GREAT, GREAT GRANDSONS ARE GREEN.

Jim Sewell with a CHOCO daughter. Jim owned the youngest of TOBE's sons, SEWELL'S SAM, who was sire to the "sire of champions," BUDDY ROE.

Barry Neidert aboard the stallion JOHNNY WALKER BLACK at Kentucky Horse Park in Lexington. Barry is owner of Gaitway Farm, home of stallions GOBLE and MAXIMOTION.

Quoting Charles Kilburn, "Sam was interested in the gait more than the color. He wanted a shorter stride. Didn't like a long stride. He used a lot of these horses up there at Natural Bridge for a lot of new riders. Chocolate always produced the gait Sam liked best. Chocolate would throw a lot of color, but he'd also throw some sorrels and blacks. He usually put a snip on them, too. Tobe didn't put a snip on them, and would always throw the chocolate color with flax manes and tails. The gait is the reason Sam liked to breed to Chocolate."

As of 1995, there were 900 descendents that trace back to Chocolate Sundown and his son Sundown Rocky (owned by Jr. Robinson of Irvine, Kentucky).

1971 was the year of "Yankee's" birth. His sire was Tobe, and his dam was "Bay Beauty," who was sired by "Old Bob," an old-time Saddlebred. Yankee holds the distinction of being the last stallion that Sam Tuttle stood at stud. Unlike the other important stallions that were sons of Tobe, Yankee moved through several owners. As a three-year-old, he was sold to Cecil McCall as a horse for daughter Diane. Both Diane and her father, Cecil, were responsible for training the young Rocky Mountain stallion in less than a week. Diane rode Yankee frequently with simply a halter and bailing twine reins. They were a fine pleasure pair.

The Neiderts on a pair of Rocky Mountain Horses.

But when Sam Tuttle's stud Tobe died, the McCalls sold Yankee back to Tuttle. Yankee went on to become important in the development of the breed. He was known as "the Broodmare Stallion," because of the numerous fillies he threw. When Tuttle could no longer care for Yankee, he sent him off to the Kentucky Horse Park, where he became known as the "Fairgrounds Horse," but before Sam died, he sold Yankee back to Diane McCall.

McCall leased and later sold Yankee to E.R. Davis of Paris, Kentucky. In 1991, Davis sold Yankee to Jennifer Bush, who lives near St. Louis, Missouri. Yankee now calls Missouri home and continues to contribute to the Rocky Mountain gene pool.

In 1973, Tobe was bred to Goodpastures Maude and produced Maples Squirrel. Maude's papers indicate she was sired by "The" Black Squirrel. But a search of Black Squirrel's papers in his registry (American Saddlebred), shows his birth year as 1876. There is, however, little doubt that Maude's family tree is part of the Black Squirrel line. Maples Squirrel lived with Mr. and Mrs.

Julie Neidhert with one of her favorite geldings, WILLY WONKA, atop Hat Mountain in South Dakota. "They say you only need one horse; but it's not possible when you have Rockies! They are very addicting!"

E.R. Davis at Horseplay Farm in Paris, Kentucky until his death in 2001.

The Rocky Mountain Horse makes a handsome cart horse as seen in this photo from Gaitway Farm.

SMOKEY & WILLY WONKA, two 6-year-old geldings on a day trip where they encountered free roaming cattle, deep river crossings, steep mountain trails, and challenging terrain that they took in stride!

143

Stallion, SONNY, owned by Dave and Sue Stefanic at their Classic Farms of Mechanicsburg, Pennsylvania.

Stallion, JERICHO. From Turning Point Training Center. Owned and photographed by Shawneen Magrum.

Stallion, BLUE RAIN, four-time International Grand Champion, owned and photographed by Kellie Bretthauer.

Clifford Clemons aboard stallion, NICK.

The youngest of Tobe's remaining sons is Sewell's Sam. He was foaled in 1975 and is owned by Jim Sewell. Sewell is a well-known horseman of great integrity and horse sense. Like other owners of Tobe sons, Jim Sewell was also a good friend of Sam Tuttle and has remained active in the development of the Rocky Mountain breed.

One of Sewell's Sam's sons was the "sire of champions," Buddy Roe owned by Carl Vivian. Buddy Roe's story is that of the other "second generation" horses.

Without getting lost in this parade of wonderful horses, let's look at how the actual Rocky Mountain Horse Association came to be.

During the early and middle eighties, many Mountain Horses were being produced by the sons and offspring of Tobe. But without a registry, these animals were simply considered grade. In particular, out-of-state buyers wanted to invest in horses that were backed by an official registry.

In 1983, Rea Swan began her search for the scattered Rocky Mountain Horses. By

144

Fran Odom aboard MAGIC RHYTHM. Fran and her husband Billy own Odom's Mountain Horses in California. Photo: Forrest Bliss

Stallion DOC, Rocky Mountain Horse Association Sire of the year, 2001. Owned by Classic Farm in Mechanicsburg, Pennsylvania.

Stallion, TOUCH OF CLASS. Sanderosa Farms, Weimar, Texas, James and Suzanne Sanders. 2000 International Reserve Conformation Champion.

Stallion, SUDDEN IMPACT, from Rocky Knoll Farms and standing at Van Bert Farms in Stanton, Kentucky. High Point stallion 2000. Photo: V.W. Perry

1985, she had logged close to 100,000 miles in Kentucky and Ohio alone.

In 1986, at the Clark Rural Electric Building in Winchester, Kentucky, a meeting of several interested and concerned horsemen took place to examine the options for protecting the Rocky Mountain horses. Rea Swan and her husband David were prime movers in gathering these special individuals together, and laying the groundwork for this assembly.

At this first meeting, three men were asked to accept the daunting task of seeking out eligible candidates for this new registry throughout the area. These men were Larry Combs, Junior Robinson and Carl Vivian.

Quoting Carl Vivian: "We ran ads in all the little local papers trying to locate people that had these horses. Then we'd go and look at the horse to see if it would qualify. We had set up some standards at the meeting, and later on the phone. The horse would have to be at least 14:2 hands, couldn't have too much white on it, couldn't show any genetic defects, had to gait – things like that."

Vivian continues: "Was it ever a lot of work! You'd either get a call from someone, or you'd hear So and So had a horse like that, and you'd go look at it. Then you had to ask

Stallion, CHOCO, owned by Jim Sewell.

the man if he wanted to get that horse registered. It was a seven day a week job for two years – maybe more – looking for horses that would qualify. I'd say we got maybe two or three hundred registered. We had to turn down about as many that didn't meet the requirements too."

So, with thanks to this hardy handful of folks: Rea and David Swan, Larry Combs, Junior Robinson, Carl Vivian, Wendell Johnson and other local enthusiasts, the future of the Rocky Mountain Horse had been secured.

Even at this point, it remained to be seen just what a treasure had been rescued. Enter Gus Cothran, Ph.D., head of the University of Kentucky Veterinary School's Equine Blood Typing Research Center. His Genetic studies have shown the Rocky Moun-

The lovely face of stallion, MAXIMOTION, son of BUDDY ROE and two-time RMHA International Conformation Stallion Champion. Owned by Gaitway Farms in Wisconsin.

tain Horse to be genetically different and a true breed.

The Rocky Mountain Horse is extremely adaptable to different uses and environments. It flourishes in most climates and under the most varied of conditions. This makes it desirable to horse enthusiasts from all over the

Fran Odom at her Mountain Horse Farm in Oakdale, California, playing with a herd of youngsters.

Nathan and Courtney with seven-month-old BONFIRE, at Wildfire Farm in Viola, Arkansas. Owner: Bonnie Hodge

MY MARIA, RMHA International Reserve Champion mare under saddle and over all at the age of three.

Stallion, BLUE RAIN, son of CLEMON'S TIM, bred by Jake Rose and owned by Kellie Bretthauer. Quoting Kellie: "Our goal is to raise horses that have a great disposition, gait and conformation. These horses are born naturally gaited, moving from speeds of 7 to 20 miles per hour. They are excellent pleasure mounts. They are also used in parades, showing, driving, endurance, and even farmwork. Their size ranges from 14:r to 16 hands, and they are easy keepers. Willingness to learn and a friendly disposition are breed characteristics.

After his years of living in Kentucky and being the star of the Jake Rose Stables, BLUE RAIN moved to Newport, Washington and KB Mountain Horses in the care and expertise of Kellie Bretthauer and her family, who are all involved in the showing and enjoyment of the Rocky Mountain Horses.

United States, Canada and Europe as well. Breeders maintain lists for available foals. The supply has simply not kept up with the demand.

So what is it about this breed that has caught the fancy of so many horse-lovers? First of all, it is known for its gentleness. They are easy keepers and wonderful riding horses with strong hearts and endurance abilities.

Sam Tuttle would decide which horses stayed and which were sold by the way they responded to his training style. He broke most of his Rockys with a hay bailing string that he doubled and put underneath their neck.

Not only are the Rockys superior in disposition, their overall appearance is most

Jake Rose all decked out for the costume class on his Rocky Mountain Horse.

A group of lovelies from Cypress Lakes Stables owned by Al Prewitt from North Carolina.

MY FAIR LADY   FINAL ANSWER   TOP OF THE LINE   MY FAIR LADY
These foals are from Gaitway Farm, owned by the Neidert Family in Wausau, Wisconsin.

Stallion, MAXIMOTION

2-year-old Kristen and her mom Rebecca Lucasey riding ROCKIN' ROCKETTE

Three generations: Grandmom Fran, Daughter Rebecca, and Granddaughter Kristen, enjoying the horses at Odom Rocky Mountain Horse Farm, in California.

Stallion, ROCKIN' DOBIN. Photo: Jim Hargrove

STROKING COMMOTION, Vernon Stamper, up.

Stallion, BLUE RAIN, with owner Kellie Bretthauer, up.

pleasing. They have ears that have a little bit of foxtail curve at the top and a bold, almond eye that is frequently hooded. Their face is neither convex nor concave, but rather wide at the nose with elliptical nostrils. Their forelip is somewhat extended, giving a pouty look. The chin is "teacup," which could give the appearance of a parrot mouth. (However, a look at the teeth will dispel that idea.) Their shoulder forms a 45-degree angle, the withers are broad and their back is short. Their chest should be broad and their bones are of medium density and size.

The Rocky Mountain Horse is sturdy enough to pull a plow, stylish enough to drive to town, and gentle enough for the kids to ride bareback down to the fishing hole.

Quoting author Jeri Smith, "There probably should be a warning label attached to each Rocky Mountain Horse. Caution: Do not ride this horse unless you want to buy it. And do not buy this horse unless you have room for an entire herd."

The Rocky Mountain Horse Association bylaws are specific in describing their purpose. "The Association is dedicated to the preservation, breeding, development and promotion of the Rocky Mountain Horse in which the natural gait breeds true."

Proper breeding will enhance this and other desirable characteristics in successive generations. To this end, no action devices, aids, or harsh training methods are permitted. "Through breeding, we, the members of the Association, strive to produce an animal that meets the highest standards of this breed - a horse for most occasions and all persons."

The Rocky Mountain Horse naturally demonstrates a smooth, ambling gait which glides forward and in which one can count four distinct hoof-beats that produce a cadence of near equal rhythm.

The Rocky Mountain Horse moves his feet with minimal knee and hock action. Because this gait does not waste motion, it enables the horse to travel long distances with minimal fatigue.

The conformation of the Rocky Mountain Horse will be as follows: The height of the horse will be no less than 58" (14:2 hands), and no more than 64" (16 hands).

This "backstage" masterpiece was taken of the Colors being carried by a Rocky Mountain Horse from Al Prewitt's Cypress Lakes Stables in North Carolina.

They should have medium sized bones with medium-sized feet in proportion to the body; a wide and deep chest with a span between the forelegs. The fore and hind legs should be free of noticeable deformity. The horse should have sloping shoulders (ideally with an angle of 45 degrees), bold eyes and well-shaped ears, and a face which is neither dished nor protruding. The head should be medium-sized in proportion to the body with medium jaws.

The neck should be gracefully arched, medium in length and set on an angle to allow a natural carriage with a break at the poll. The horse must have a solid body color. There shall be no white above the knee or hock except on the face where modest amounts of white markings are acceptable. Excessive facial markings such as a bald face are not acceptable.

Stallion, NUNCIO'S OZARK WILDFIRE, son of NUNCIO, and great grandson of YANKEE, owned by Bonnie Hodge, author of *Rocky Mountain Horses*, a comprehensive book about all facets of the breed. Rhodge.88@juno.com

COPPER'S PRIDE
by REB'S BIG SHOT
by SEBASTION'S COPPER

KENTUCKY NATURAL GAITED HORSE

CHAPTER 10

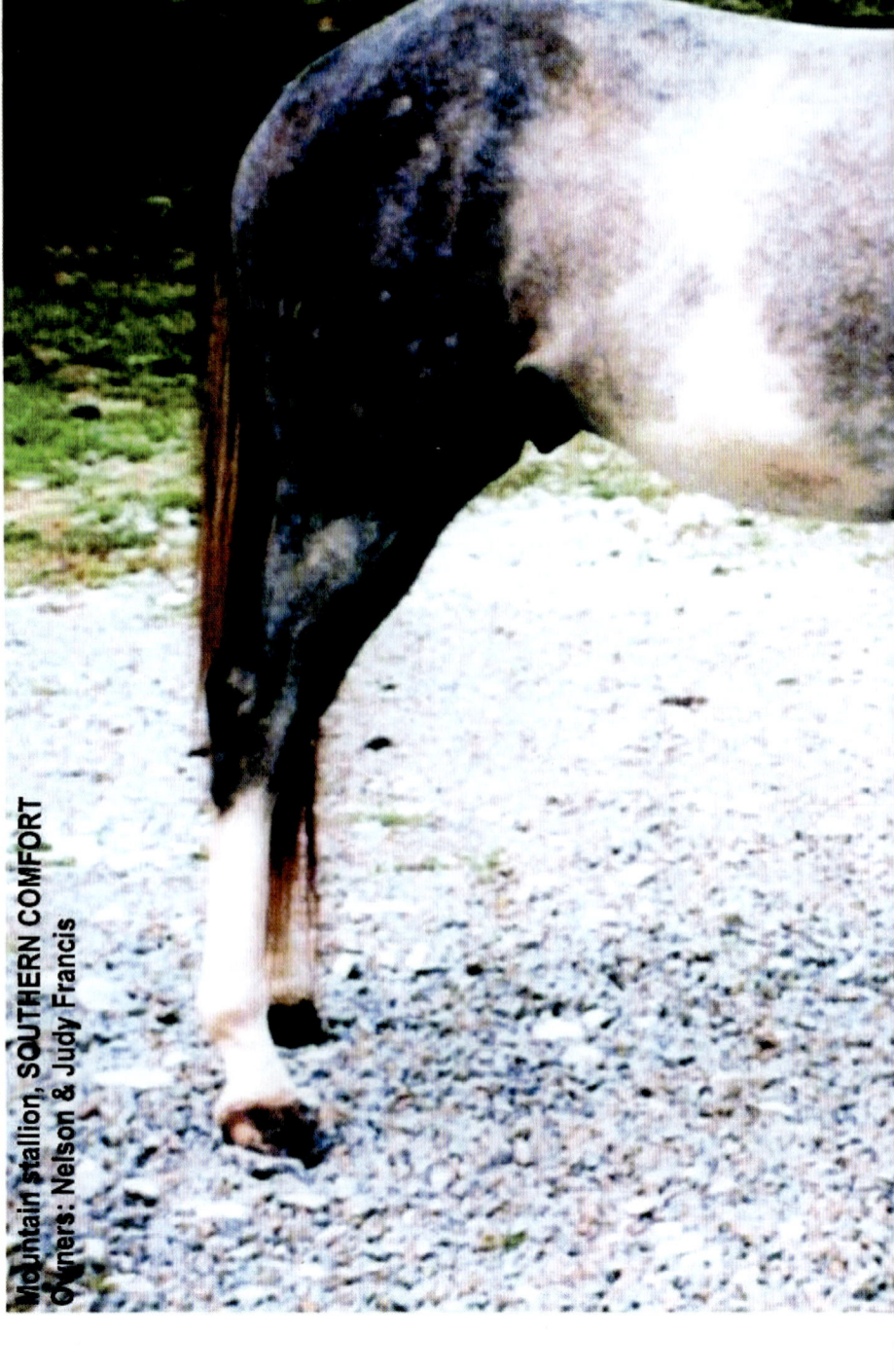

Mountain stallion, SOUTHERN COMFORT
Owners: Nelson & Judy Francis

HEIGHT: 14:2 and up

GAIT: Saddle gaits

COLOR: All equine colors

TRAIT: Comfortable

Chapter 10 The Kentucky Natural Gaited Horse Association

The history of the Mountain Horses of Kentucky has been related in chapters seven, eight and nine in this book. In this chapter, the Kentucky Natural Gaited Horse Association will be presented as an important vehicle to protect and promote all of the horses of Mountain heritage.

All of the Mountain Registries have the same basic stock as their source. They have, however, each addressed specific characteristics of the horse. It is this specific focus of each Registry that is actually developing unique breeds.

Jr. Robinson was prompted to establish the Kentucky Mountain Saddle Horse Association because he felt strongly about including the shorter horse. The Rocky Mountain Horse Association thought it important to preserve the bloodlines of the stallion "Tobe," owned by Sam Tuttle. The Mountain Pleasure Horse Association extols their horse as the foundation for all other gaited breeds currently popular in the United States.

The Kentucky Natural Gaited Horse Association came into existence through the insight and resolve of longtime Mountain Pleasure Horse owner and breeder, Nelson Francis. Francis was determined to acknowledge Mountain Horses of all colors.

FANCY by MOON II, with Greg Jenkins. (FANCY can rack at a clip of 20 mph)

DUSTY ROSE and FANCY. (DUSTY ROSE is a granddaughter of GOLDFINGER, and FANCY is a granddaughter of MOON.)

DUSTY ROSE by GOLDFINGER STAR at 4 years old with Willie Ramey.

CONNELLY'S TRIGGER by LITTLE TRIGGER with Marcus Connelly up (mid 1950's)

Center: **COFFEE 'S DYNAMITE** with Woody Hopkins up. Circa 1962.

CONNELLY'S RANGER with Marcus Connelly up in the late 1970s. The Mountain Horse has been an important part of the families in Kentucky for decades.

When Nelson's registered Mountain Horses[1] occasionally produced spotted horses, he was unable to register them with the existing associations due to their ban on white markings.

Nelson's determination to provide legitimization for his horses drew him to the study of genetics at the University of Kentucky under the direction of Gus Cothran, renowned expert.

In establishing the Kentucky Natural Gaited Horse Association (KNGHA), Nelson headed the first registry to see the need for mapping and tracking the Mountain Horse through the use of DNA testing which would provide a factual foundation. He was determined to more accurately identify what exactly needed to be preserved when one says, "We need to preserve the Mountain Horse."

Quoting Nelson: "Through DNA testing, the picture will start to develop with the markers of certain horses that produce the better qualities of good gait, good disposition and good conformation. It's the genes that are the making, so the horses that throw a good percentage of these qualities will be a focus of our breeding programs. You have to look toward the future; and we're doing that now. Testing for DNA is the way of the future."

Through the DNA process, the University of Kentucky will work toward identifying the Mountain Horse markers and will

---

[1] Nelson Francis has been involved with the breeding of Mountain Horses for the greater part of his life. He follows in the footsteps of his father and grandfather, who were also breeders of Mountain Horses.

SHAWNEE by SOUTHERN COMFORT out of PRECIOUS.

The Logo of the KNGHA.

Nelson Francis with PONY GIRL by F& R FLAME.

have the ability to accurately define the foundation stock or contributors of the Mountain bloodline. Identifying such genes as gait, color, and disease are also a top priority for the University and the KNGHA. The movement from general blood typing to DNA has been recognized as an essential element of this breed's survival.

    The KNGHA has tackled this task with determination and perseverance. The Association's ability to move the Mountain into the 21ST century began in July 2000. The Association has worked diligently to rally membership support and knowledge to best serve this breed. The KNGHA membership reaches outside the boundaries of Kentucky and as the membership grows, so will the development of state chapters. State chapters will assist in continually monitoring the progress of the Mountain Horse in their area as well as others and develop ideas and tasks to better preserve this bloodline. These state chapters will have the ability to show the Mountain Horse in Association shows within their state. Members will not need to travel hundreds of miles to Kentucky to participate and enjoy, the spirit of the Mountain Horse with others.

    The KNGHA recognizes and honors the Mountain Horse bloodline without discriminate-

Jenkins Family members with their Mountain Horses, both palomino and spotted.

156

ing against excessive white or patterns of color. A true Mountain Horse will demonstrate the breed's characteristics despite the color or the pattern of its coat.

Quoting Nelson Francis: "As the 20TH century came to a close, it was obvious there was no more need for the Mountain Horse to carry out the tasks of his ancestors such as plowing the fields or maneuvering the family over the rough terrain of Appalachia. As a result, the Mountain Horse's often hidden talents and versatility have begun to surface and become recognized. Their ability to be used in field trials due to their surefootedness, their ability to be versatile in the arena of dressage, their intelligence and genetic makeup lets them become acclimated to all types of terrain and climates."

The "old-time" Saddlebred is a horse that shares much of the same history and bloodline as the Mountain Horse. Through the KNGHA, some of those bloodlines will be reintroduced to the modern Mountain Horse's pedigree.

One such "crossover" is a young double-registered (KNGHA and Saddlebred) horse named Charles Denmark Dare. This is a registered American Saddlebred (5-gaited). His lineage dates back to the foundation horse Kentucky Ghost. Dare was bred and raised by Paul Hamilton out of Marshfield, Missouri, who has been line breeding for three generations.

Hamilton was not looking for current Saddlebred conformation but rather for the

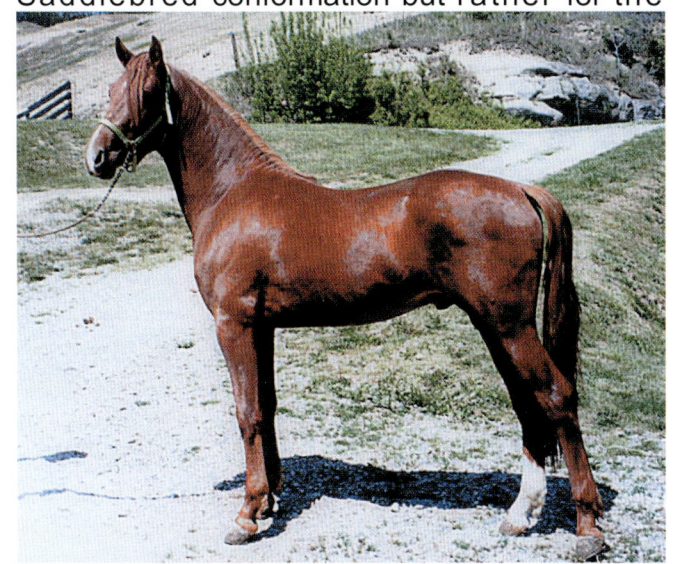

CHARLES DENMARK DARE (double registered as both KNGHA and Saddlebred.

MOON II's SHINING SUN, as a baby, displaying his immature coloring. (See photo below to find out how the color matured).

Mountain Horses have the same types of color changes found in other breeds. It is not unusual to have a brown colt grow into a grey horse; or a light colt mature into a dark horse. Frequently the palomino horse will darken with age, and many horses will display a much lighter coat during the winter.

MOON II's SHINING SUN showing off his lovely mature dark palomino coloring.

SUGAR COOKIE, KNGHA filly with her mother owned by Desirai and Ron Schild, Chubbuck, Idaho

quality he enjoyed as a younger man.

His search brought him to the farm of Nelson Francis and the stallion F&R Red Flame. Hamilton leased the young stallion to breed to his mares for a season. In turn, Nelson bought the colt Charles Denmark Dare to enhance his own Mountain Horse breeding program.

Quoting Francis: "Dare carries important genes that will improve the breeding over the years. Perhaps he carries the bloodlines that generations ago contributed to the development of the Mountain horse. With the use of this stallion, we are going full circle and bringing his genes along with his full pedigree back into the KNGHA Registry."

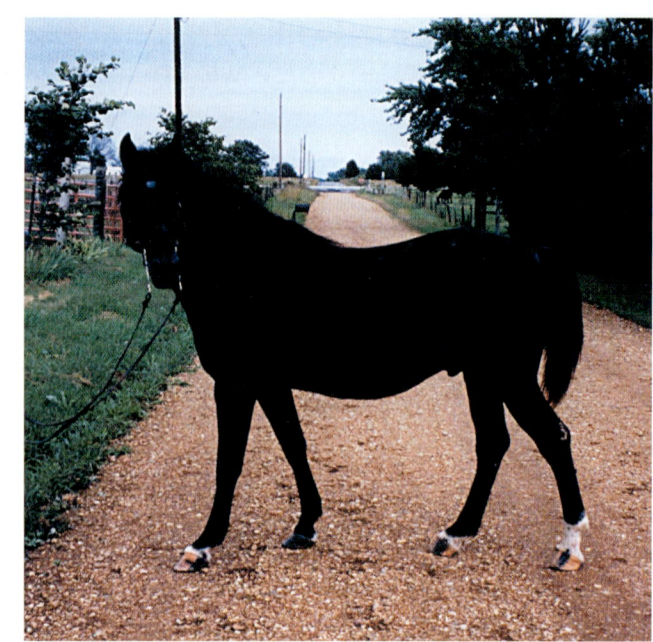

SPARKY DENMARK DARE, a Saddlebred foundation Horse to the Mountain Horses (5 gaited), owned by Paul Hamilton from Marshfield, Missouri.

The foundation horses of the contemporary Mountain Horses were indeed varied. One such horse was Little Trigger, foaled in 1945. His mother was a spotted pony and his father was Jasper Jones' Bucky.

Little Trigger was a consistent producer of quality gaited horses. He was a leading sire in the late 40's, throughout the 50's and even into the 60's. He died at 29. He was ridden hard as a young horse by a doctor who used

Charlie Francis with a work stock mare that produced gaited offspring, circa 1969.

158

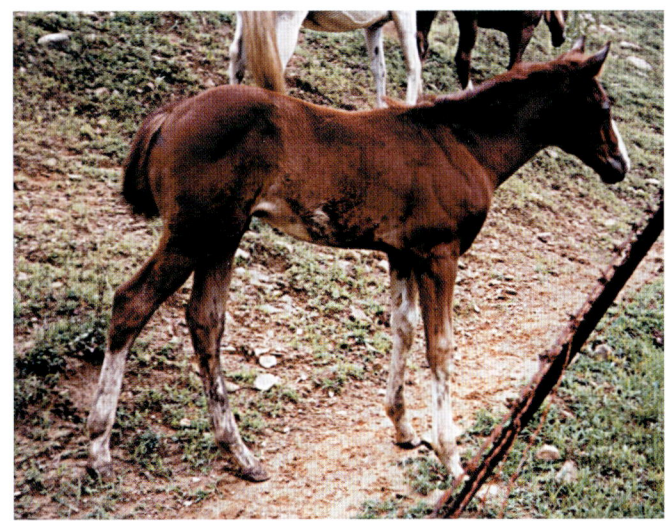

SOUTHERN COMFORT as a foal. It's amazing that this colt grew into the grey stallion seen to the right.

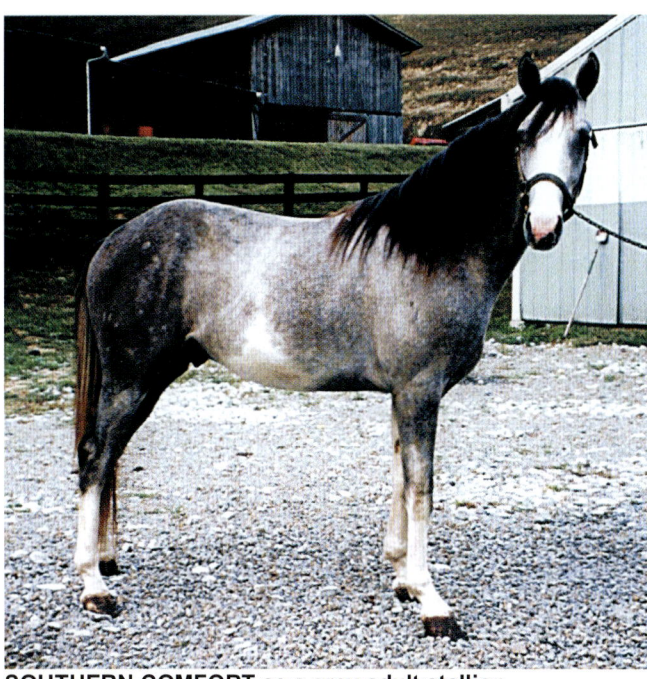

SOUTHERN COMFORT as a grey adult stallion.

him for house calls. In fact, he was ridden hard by all seven sons in the Connelly family.

The Connellys ran a stallion barn during the 50's and 60's. Everybody in the county bred to Little Trigger.

Quoting Francis: "He was like the ultimate stallion because he produced a consistent gait. He only stood 14 to 14:2, but you could breed him to the bigger mares and get a refined colt. He was a small horse, but he was consistent in producing those gaits. He was also a contributor to refining the horse from the big heavy workstock to the more medium- boned. Little Trigger was just a terrific horse."

Little Trigger was also a speed racker. It's said he could travel at some 20 mph. There's a story about a man coming to one of the Mountain Horse competitions and boasting about his speed horse, claiming that no horse would dare compete against him. Marcus Connelly had Little Trigger, now 18 years old and 'not prepared.' He was brought down from the barn to take up the challenge. Well, Little Trigger won.

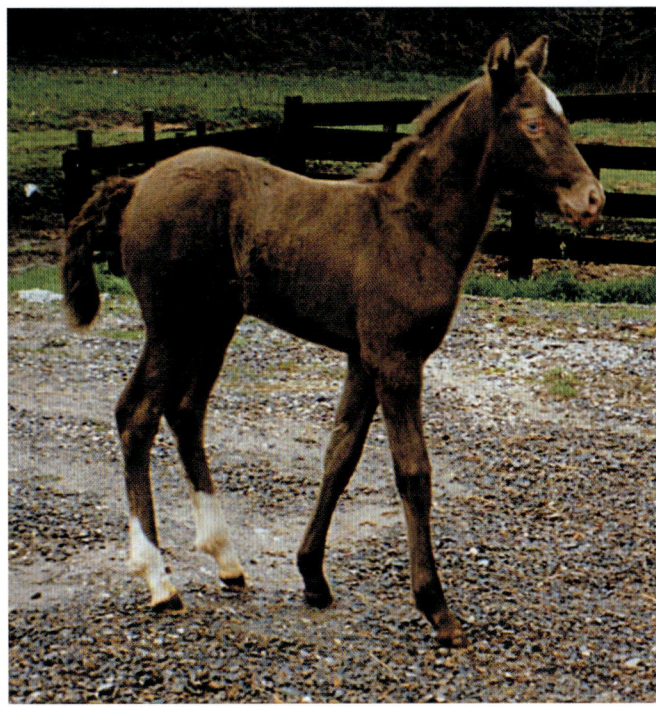

Another example of unique color changes. This colt, JADE is seen to the right with his adult coloring.

JADE sporting his adult coloring.

Nelson Francis began his breeding program with a Little Trigger daughter, Trigger's Betsy, in 1961. Betsy's dam was a grey dappled mare, said to be half draft and half Arabian. Betsy was the mother of Fritz Delight and grandmother to Fritz Banner, who won the 3-year-old Reserve Championship at the Mountain Pleasure Classic show of 1993.

The KNGHA honors the "true Mountain heritage at its best" and is dedicated to preserving, promoting, and enhancing the blood-

This filly, RAVEN, is double registered with KNGHA and KMSHA. By MAPPLE SQUIRREL out of GOLDFINGER'S HONEY JO.

Mother, baby, and a gathering of Mountain Horses

FAITH OF MIDNIGHT, GERTRUDE'S DANCE, SUMMER RAIN, LADY JANE and LANDY PEDDLER enjoying a nap in the sun.

Dale Hall riding MOON II, son of MOON, a foundation sire in the Mountain Pleasure Registry.

Marion Cantrell riding BUCK'S MAJOR.

line of the Old Mountain Horse. It is a not-for-profit organization, incorporated and registered in the Commonwealth of Kentucky. Its focus is on acknowledging the Mountain Horse as a legendary part of the history in the hills and mountains of Eastern Kentucky. It is anxious to to share its goals with all who are interested in preserving the mountain breed's original qualities and by promoting the breed to be a national show horse status.

Brent Francis riding AL CAPONE.

Nelson Francis riding THIRA.

Stallion AL CAPONE

Al Capone is a premier KNGHA breeding stallion. To quote Nelson Francis: "Al Capone is 15:3 and is proven to be a better producer in the Mountain Horses – with class. He was raised by Kelly Stevens of Slayersville. Capone's grandmother was out of Coffee's Dynamite, a palomino mare. He was sired by Wilson's Buck out of the old line of Mountain Horses. He ties in between the Coffee line, Connelly Trigger horses, and the Saddlebreds. This gives him a little more neck, and a little more front end. He presents himself well."

. The KNGHA will accept all horses of Mountain breeding into the Association, providing foundation registration requirements are met. Most important on its agenda is the

HONEY with MAGIC MAN by AL CAPONE.

The Kentucky Natural Gaited Horse Association has spread throughout the country as seen here with **KENTUCKY GOLDRUSH, who lives in Nevada.** Photo: Loraine Costa.

preservation of the breed's beautiful conformation, calm temperament, good disposition and natural gaits.

Registration requirements consist of:

1. The horse must demonstrate a natural four-beat gait. This gait is of equal or near-equal cadence, whereas one can count four distinct hoof beats in a rhythmic manner, with a flowing extension.

2. Meeting the minimum height requirement of 14:2 hands, for stallions and 14:0 hands, for mares and geldings.

3. Verification of belonging to the Mountain bloodline will be made through DNA testing, at the owner's expense. DNA testing is not required on geldings.

4. Color is not a criterion for registration. All colors and patterns of color will be accepted.

BROWN SUGAR with Wayne Jenkins up.

The KNGHA plans to work to make the Mountain Horse a trusted household name. An essential element in accomplishing this goal is to work with the American Livestock Breed Conservatory (ALBC) to establish the Mountain Horse as a recognized breed of a steadily growing population. The KNGHA has already made great strides toward building a strong factual foundation for the Mountain Horse of today. The establishment of the third generation is well underway in this Association with aspirations of many more generations to come.

RED BARON & MOUNTAIN MAN with Sara Jenkins enjoying the awesome trails of Kentucky.

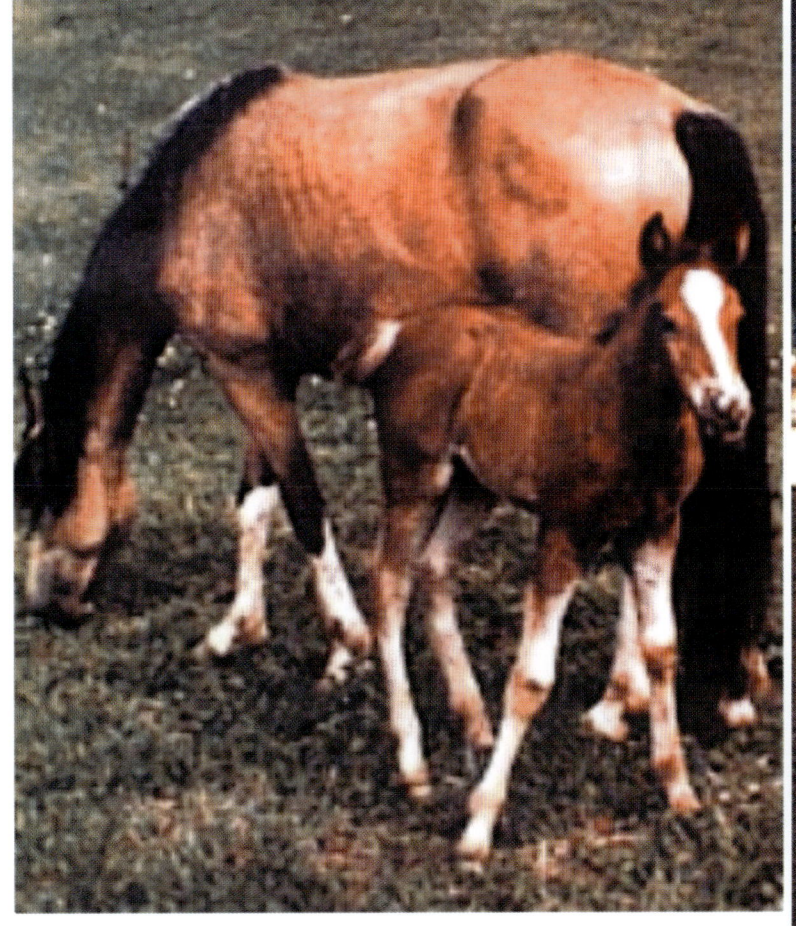

Above: "Moon" daughter, "Precious" with colt "Fritz Banner." (foaled 1990)

Right: "Fritz Banner" with Nelson Francis up, winning reserve 3-year old Championship at the MPHA Classic of 1993.

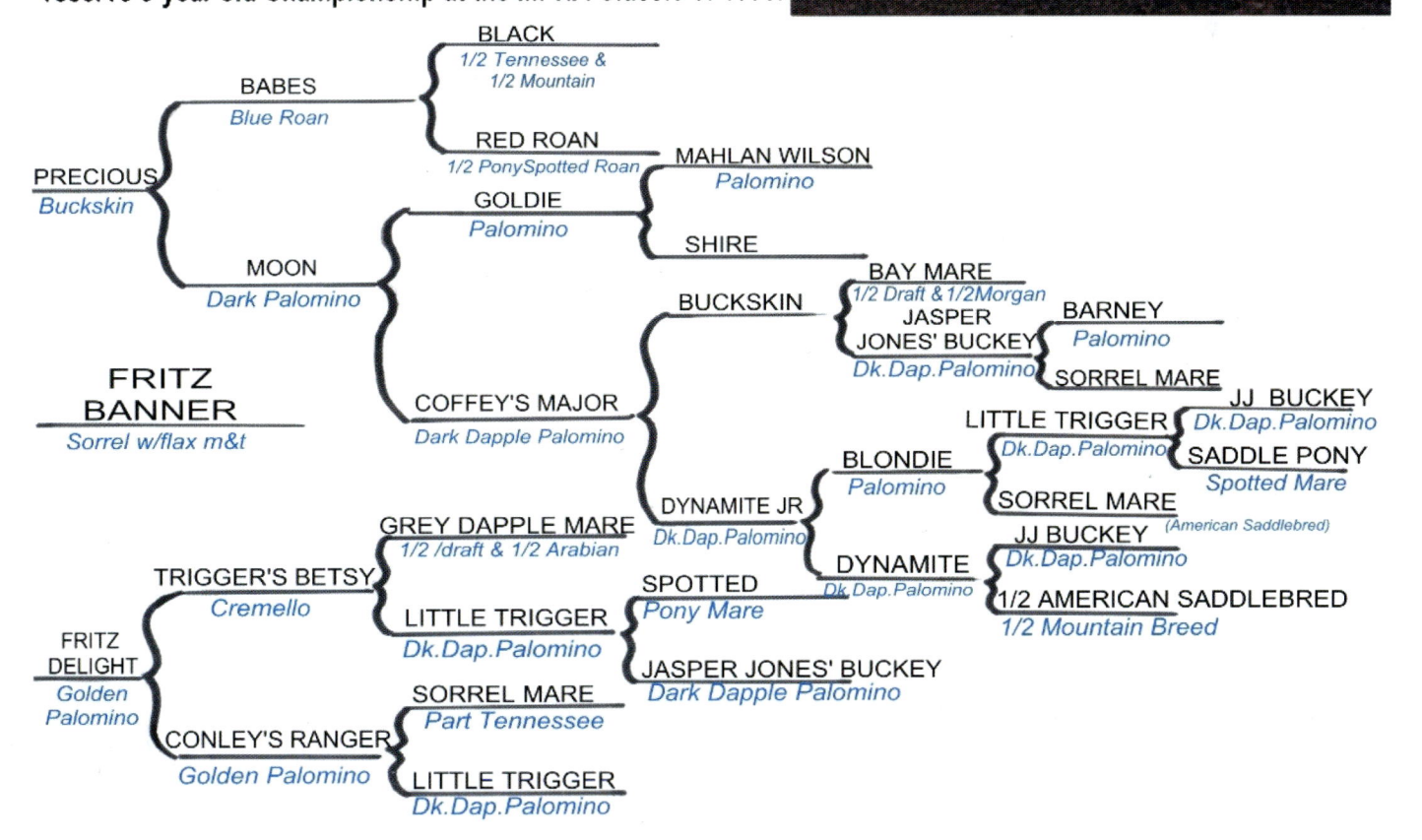

FRITZ BANNER
Sorrel w/flax m&t

- **PRECIOUS** *Buckskin*
  - **BABES** *Blue Roan*
    - **BLACK** *1/2 Tennessee & 1/2 Mountain*
    - **RED ROAN** *1/2 Pony Spotted Roan*
  - **MOON** *Dark Palomino*
    - **GOLDIE** *Palomino*
      - **MAHLAN WILSON** *Palomino*
      - **SHIRE**
    - **COFFEY'S MAJOR** *Dark Dapple Palomino*
      - **BUCKSKIN**
        - **BAY MARE** *1/2 Draft & 1/2 Morgan*
        - **JASPER JONES' BUCKEY** *Dk. Dap. Palomino*
          - **BARNEY** *Palomino*
          - **SORREL MARE**
      - **DYNAMITE JR** *Dk. Dap. Palomino*
        - **BLONDIE** *Palomino*
          - **LITTLE TRIGGER** *Dk. Dap. Palomino*
            - **JJ BUCKEY** *Dk. Dap. Palomino*
            - **SADDLE PONY** *Spotted Mare*
          - **SORREL MARE** *(American Saddlebred)*
        - **DYNAMITE** *Dk. Dap. Palomino*
          - **JJ BUCKEY** *Dk. Dap. Palomino*
          - **1/2 AMERICAN SADDLEBRED** *1/2 Mountain Breed*

- **FRITZ DELIGHT** *Golden Palomino*
  - **TRIGGER'S BETSY** *Cremello*
    - **GREY DAPPLE MARE** *1/2 draft & 1/2 Arabian*
    - **LITTLE TRIGGER** *Dk. Dap. Palomino*
      - **SPOTTED** *Pony Mare*
      - **JASPER JONES' BUCKEY** *Dark Dapple Palomino*
  - **CONLEY'S RANGER** *Golden Palomino*
    - **SORREL MARE** *Part Tennessee*
    - **LITTLE TRIGGER** *Dk. Dap. Palomino*

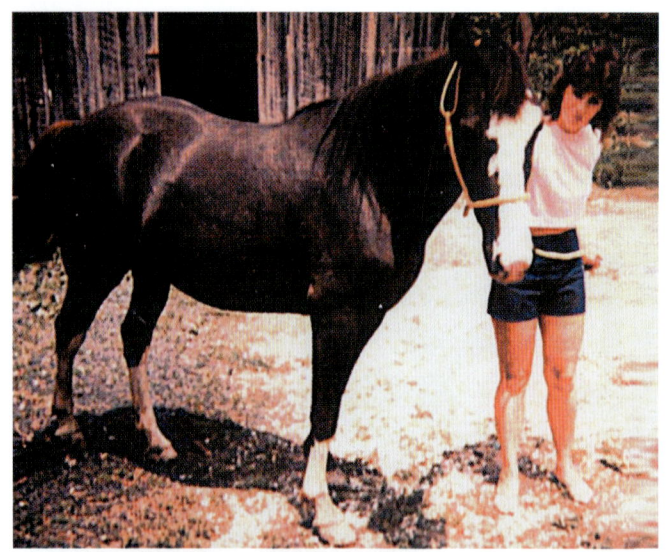

BABES in 1978. (Dam of PRECIOUS)

COFFEY'S MAJOR (foaled 1967)
Sire : DYNAMITE JR. – Dam: A Buckskin Mare

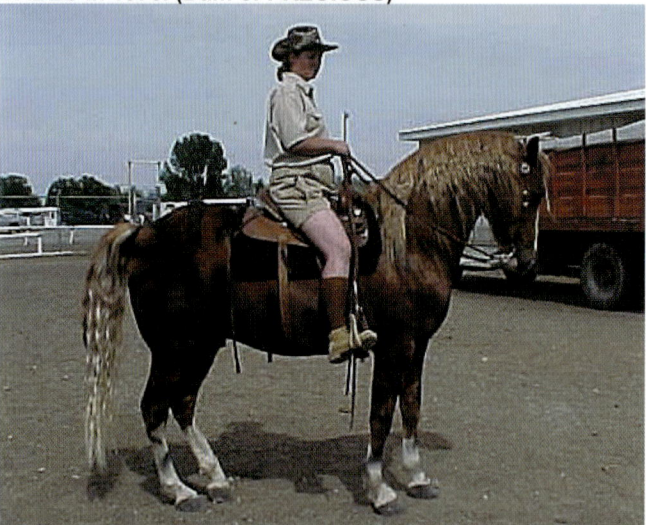

F & R'S RED FLAME impersonating a Tiger Horse with owner Shelly Spradlin competing in a costume class.

DYNAMITE JR. in 1966 (foaled in 1960) Sire: DYNAMITE – Dam: BLONDIE

Judy and Nelson Francis on their Kentucky Natural Gaited Horses

FRITZ DELIGHT with John Russel Connelly up (1977)

164

Sara Jenkins on TRIGGER
Washington, D.C.

Greg Jenkins on BUCK's MAJOR as a 3-yr-old - a brother to AL CAPONE, son of WILSON'S BUCK and grandson of MOON.

BANNER'S BLONDIE and FAITH OF MIDNIGHT, by AL CAPONE

FRANCIS PATCHES at 3 yrs. out of BLACK BABY by FRITZ BANNER.

MOON II'S GINGER by MOON II (BANNER'S uncle) is a hand taller than her half sister, PATCHES

Bobby Joe Bradley with Jared on DUSTY ROSE

THIRA with Nelson Francis

Sue Stuart on MAJOR, Wayne Jenkins on DUSTY ROSE, Greg Jenkins on Fancy, and Dale Hall on SHADOW.

TENNESSEE WALKING HORSE

CHAPTER 11

Tennessee Walker, Delight's Super Star
Owner: Tom & Judy Henry
Photo: Rick Osteen

HEIGHT: 14:3 - 16 Hands

GAIT: Flat walk, Running walk, Canter, Gallop

COLOR: Any equine color

TRAIT: Elegance/Kindness

Chapter 11 The Tennessee Walker

The Tennessee Walking Horse is the first horse to be officially named for a state. It's understandable why many folks associate soft gaits with the Tennessee Walker. In 1935, the original registry was established through a state charter in Lewisburg, Tennessee, by the governor, Jim Nance McCord and well-known horseman, Burt Hunter.

However, the breed didn't begin with the registry. In the mid-1800's, the horse was known as the American Saddle Horse. Developed as a utilitarian plantation horse, this Tennessee gem carries the blood of Standardbreds, Morgans, Copperbottoms, Pilots, Mountain Slashers, Thoroughbreds, Canadian Pacers and Narragansett Pacers, Hals, Brooks, Whips and Bullets.

In 1899, a major change was made in the rules for showing Saddle Horses. As the need for truly serviceable horses diminished, and the desire for flash and showiness increased, a split in the breed occurred. Many breeders went in the direction of the big showy trotting horse that became known as the American Saddlebred. Others retained the soft-gaited gene, maintaining the horse that was to become the Tennessee Walking Horse.

The history and development of this wonderful breed is best told through the stories of several of the foundation stallions and mares.

Allan F-1, the first important sire of the Tennessee Walker breed, was known throughout his life as Black Allan. His story epitomizes the strength and courage of the breed. Black Allan was foaled in Lexington, Kentucky in 1886. During his first seventeen years, Allan changed hands eleven times. Once he was traded for a heifer, a filly and twenty dollars; once for a black jack; once for a work mule and another time for a small mare. Allan was a Standardbred who wouldn't trot. It's no wonder no one knew what to do with him.

Black Allan was sired by Allandorf and born to Maggie Marshall, a mare with strong Narragansett Pacer blood via her grand sire,

ALLAN F-1 founding father of the Tennessee Breed.
Painting: Courtesy of TWHBEA and Kim Abney

SUN'S FIERY TRIBUTE, owned by Tom and Donna Doran of Hemet, California, with Beth Jennings up. Notice the easy comparison of this horse and the great ROAN ALLEN, as seen on the facing page.

Black Hawk.

As Black Allan's name suggests, he was a black horse. He had a white sock on his near hind foot and a white blaze on his face. His disposition was excellent. He was described as possessing a good even temper and an admirable undemanding character. Living an undistinguished life for seventeen years without being gelded certainly substantiates any claims to a pleasant disposition. This terrific attitude permeates the breed today. In fact, Tennessee Walkers are one of the most naturally good-natured of all the breeds.

By 1903, Black Allan had reached rock bottom for a stallion. He had become known as the "old teaser." He was used to tease mares being bred to jacks producing mules. Then, as fate would have it, Black Allan was sold to James R. Brantley for $110. Brantley had a keen eye for horses and quickly realized his luck in making such a fine bargain.

Black Allan was soon a part of Brantley's breeding program. He was bred to Tennessee mares of great lines: Denmarks, Stonewalls, Bullets, Trimmers, Hals, Mountain Slashers, Donalds, Brooks, Hals, Boone's Grey Johns, Copperbottoms, Morgans and animals with similar blood.

Allan was a gentle, dependable horse. Brantley's son French, rode the stallion to School at Beech Grove where the horse was left tied to a tree during school hours.

Allan's chief gait under saddle was a running walk which he performed comfortably and smoothly. It was said that Allan could pace faster than most horses could gallop.

Seven months before he died, Black Aallen was purchased by Albert Dement, a close friend and fellow horseman to James Brantley. During this final period of his twenty-four-year life, Black Allan was bred to 111 mares.

"He was the gamest horse I ever saw," was the eulogy given by his trainer, Jack Grider. He went on to say, "We challenge anyone to fault Allan, he was 15 hands and a

Caylin Hester with PRIDE'S PUSHY MASTERPIECE, and the family dog, Stroika. This 2-year-old stallion is from Woodview Stables in Morrow, Ohio.

Foundation stallion, ROAN ALLEN, had the roan coloration, with flaxen mane and tail and wide blaze on his face that is found again, almost 100 years later on the horse seen on the facing page. Painting: Courtesy TWHBEA and Kim Abney.

ALLERNON, with three-year-old Becky Benson, up. The willing and kind disposition found in the Tennessee Walker make it an ideal choice for children. Photo: Rick Osteen

little over. He had smart ears, a perfect head, wonderful eyes, full and well-set body, a long rangy neck, beautiful mane and a foretop, a divided sloping shoulder, and a breast that belongs to an outstanding Tennessee Walking Horse. He had fine body lines: a short back, a long belly, well-coupled, smooth hips and rump, a natural set long heavy tail. The abundant style he shows in head and neck, smooth limbs, cordy muscles, good foot and bone, his superb gaits, his easy, graceful way of going into the fast running walk justify our statement that he was as fine as they make them."

Quoting a letter from J.E. Willis who owned Allan when the horse was fifteen years old: "Speaking further of Allan, he was a grand little horse, something more than fifteen hands high. In conformation, he was about perfect and at the time I owned him, in 1901, had a heavy, long flowing mane and a superb tail that almost touched the ground and he carried it naturally in royal style. His walking gait was fast, smooth and natural, with a rising sensation that gave the rider a continuing thrill. The one and only time I had him in harness was to an ordinary buggy, and when jogging,

CRYSTAL GAYLE, owned by Beth Jennings. Photo by Bob Hess.

VENTURE'S REWARD, owned by Pauline Rounds of California, with Beth Jennings up. Photo: Rick Osteen.

VENTURE'S REWARD, Supreme Versatility Award Horse owned by Pauline Rounds being ridden by Beth Jennings.

CLASSY'S GLORY, Winner of the Challenge of the Breeds at Del Mar, California. Owner Teresa Scheirer and ridden by Cindy Scheirer. Photo: Rick Osteen.

Tennessee Walkers are shown in both English and Western Tack. Photo: Forrest Bliss

Saddle Seat English presentation emphasizes the stylishness of the Tennessee Walker. Photo: Forrest Bliss

Photo: Forrest Bliss

he had an open trot and showed more speed pacing than was safe over the rough streets of Manchester. He was kind and gentle and very responsive to the rein both under the saddle and in harness."

Of 11,800 pedigrees listed for the horses registered and recorded in the first five stud books issued by the original registry, more than 10,000 showed Allan blood, and 2,785 actually bore his name in some way.

Quoting Ben A. Green from the *Biography of the Tennessee Walking Horse*: "What a phenomenon. How great he would have been with a 24-year life spent in the Brantley-Dement domain, instead of passing those seventeen lost years of wandering as an unwanted horse. He helped bequeath to future generations the running walk gait that must be maintained as the Tennessee Walking Horse heritage."

Let's take a look at Allan's get. These outstanding horses had positive impact on the development of the Tennessee Walking Horse. Son, Roan Allen was a prolific stallion who was solid and talented in his ability to gait. He could perform seven distinct gaits and knew the cue for each.

ORATANA ROCKET'S JET, owned by Kellie Rahm of Oregon.

EBONY'S ROCKY BOY owned by Midge McGoldrick of Anza, California. Photo by Rick Osteen.

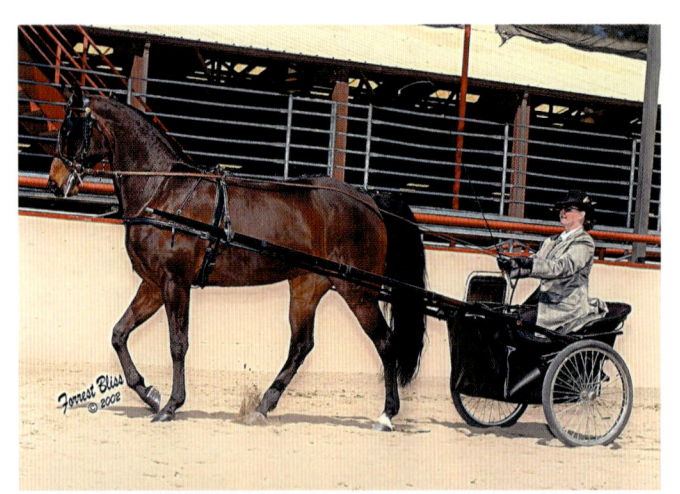

Photo: Forrest Bliss

VENTURE'S REWARD, with Beth Jennings driving. This horse is one of the few who have been awarded the title of Supreme Versatility Champion Tennessee Walking Horse. Owner: Pauline Rounds. Photo: Rick Osteen

The Tennessee Walker is a frequent choice for folks who enjoy driving.

Roan Allen was born on May 23, 1904. His owner, James Brantley, believed the roan colt was very unusual. Quoting Mr. Brantley: "He possessed a rare quality in conformation, a very long and finely pro-portioned neck, sloping shoulders, perfect head, quick sharp ears, short back, very heavy flaxen mane, water-spout flaxen tail, rear stockings, forsocks, broad blaze face, and carried his head high. My first memory of him was when he was only a few hours old, and like all colts, gazing into a world truly new. Frankly, the looks and pride of this little fellow impressed me very much, and I was indeed happy with his general appearance, and tried to visualize him as a horse. My real thrill came as he gamboled around his mother, showing a burst of speed, with a long overreach, nodding his head with coltish legs beating in perfect form, a true running walk."

Henry Davis was selected to show Roan Allen. As he remembered the great horse: "Roan Allen's pictures don't do him justice. He was a good-looking horse with a great deal of natural style, was high-headed and proud in motion. He was six years old the fall I showed him, and we put him in five-gaited classes and harness classes and won with him too. He could rack and trot well enough to beat Roe's Chief. Roe's Chief was an important

Stallion MY COLONEL HEADMAN, owned by TamiLynn Arndt, stopping for a visit with his son, LITTLE JOE.

Dean and Kathy Kaminski at the Oregon State Expo.

Saddlebred stallion owned by Tom Hays of Lynchburg, Tennessee. He won in combination classes and harness classes, and wore harness well."

Albert Dement tried to purchase Roan Allen from James Brantley on several occasions, but Brantley had always regretted the sale of Allan F-1 to Mr. Dement and never parted with Roan Allen.

Henry Davis, rider and trainer of Roan Allen said that Brantley loved the horse as a member of the family and truly believed in his greatness.

Quoting Brantley about Roan Allen: "He could show in more different classes at the best shows in his day, and win more of them than any horse that ever lived. Frankly, I always gave him credit for having abundant brains, and I still consider him the smartest horse, with the best disposition of any horse I had ever seen."

Roan Allen was only 21 years old when he had to be destroyed after having his leg broken by a kicking mare. But what a tremendous legacy he left. There are over 30 stallions registered to Roan Allen in the stud books of the Walking Horse Breeder's Association. Roan Allen proved to be among the greatest of the great, because his daughters were just as outstanding as his sons.

Some of Roan Allen's famous get were: Wilson's Allen – sire of five World Grand Champions, including Midnight Sun.

Katie O'Brien, from Reno, aboard HEAVENLY STAR.

Brenda Foley, aboard 17-hand Walker, JASON.

This lovely jet black Walker exhibits the characteristic long stride. Photo: Forrest Bliss

Merry Boy – sire of two World Grand Champions including Merry Go Boy.
Hall Allen – sire of Red Ice, Champion stallion at the 1940 Celebration.
Brantley's Roan Allen Jr. – sire of many outstanding show and brood animals.
Maud Gray – in her day, never lost a ribbon when she entered the show ring. After a long career as a broodmare, she was described as a 19-year-old: "She is a beautiful roan, both hind stockings, bald, and with a flaxen mane and tail. Her conformation is of the true type for a broodmare. Her state of preservation is remarkable, and she carries her years most lightly. Her manners are those of the "lady" that she is, and she can still "walk" with the best of them."

Another son of Allan F-1 was the very beautiful and strong Hunter's Allen (F-10), who was born in 1906. Hunter's Allen, named for his owner Burt Hunter, had tremendous stamina. His trainer, Fred Walker, preferred to ride Allen to the show grounds rather than send him by train. The distance from his home stable to the State Fair was about sixty miles. Walker would hitch him up with another horse and

Beth Jennings riding the popular stallion, SHADOW'S DOUBLE TROUBLE. Photo: Forrest Bliss

The great stallion, MIDNIGHT SUN, sired by WILSON'S ALLEN and out of RAMSEY'S RENA. His name appears on many, many current papers registered with the Tennessee Walking Horse Breeders and Exhibitors Association. Photo: Courtesy of TWHBEA and Kim Abney

JUBILEE'S SAVANNAH ROSE, owned by Elise Parrish, of Temecula, California being shown by Beth Jennings. Photo: Forrest Bliss

DOUBLE ENTENDRE, owned by Tim Jennings of Hemet, California with Tom Doran, up. Photo: Forrest Bliss.

PRIDE'S DOUBLE DOWN, owned by Corie Narvaez, with Beth Jennings, up. Photo: Locke Photography

drive him, or ride him all the way to the "big show."

Once, when Walker was already at the showgrounds in Nashville, he and a buddy decided to visit young ladies back in Wartrace. This was a distance of fifty miles on today's roads. They hitched Allen with another horse and drove to Wartrace and back to Nashville. They returned to the fairgrounds after daylight. Allen was entered in and won his classes that night.

Hunter's Allen's story exemplifies the durability and brio of the true Tennessee Walker. Listen to the words of Mr. Hunter: "I appreciate the opportunity of telling the story of my sorrel stallion, Hunter's Allen F-10, who we call "Little Allen." I rode him for many years, and he was just as supple, with as quick an ear and the same gait, as a three-four-or five-year-old. From the age of 16 to 20, he was as grand a saddlehorse as ever lived, regardless of his years."

Before reviewing more of these important foundation horses, let's take a look at one of the breeders responsible for establishing the breed.

As early as 1905, Albert Dement felt that a breed of horses could be produced that would perform the running walk, not only naturally, but predictably. Before Dement began his breeding program, producing foals

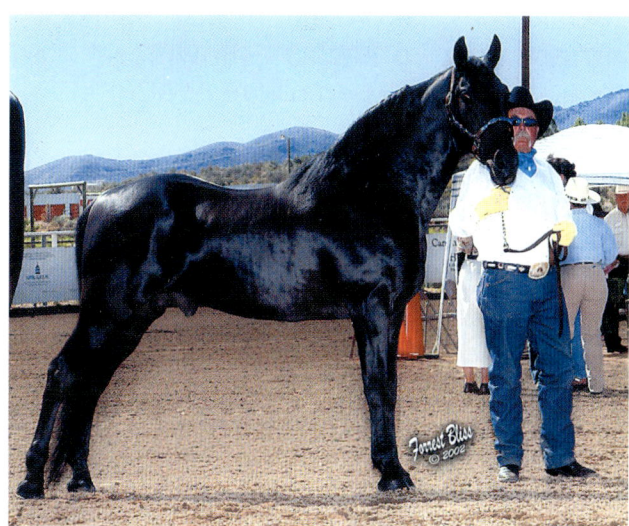

Stallion, **SOUL'S GOLD**, owned by David Palmer of Kentucky, registered TWHBEA, KMSHA, RHBA, and PHBA.

Stallion **EBONY'S OVERDRIVE**, with owner Dan B. Cripps. Photo: Forrest Bliss

Mother, Sharon Henson, and daughter, Kellie Rahm, on their Tennessee Walking Horses.

Elizabeth Graves decked out in English Day Coat and Tack. Photo: Darlene Wohlart

Colin Dangaard and friends, all on Tennessee Walking Horses, enjoying his first "gaited horse" experience.

SHADOW'S E MOTION, owned by Pauline Rounds, from La Cresta, California.

with head nod and overstride was a hit-and- miss proposition.

In 1905, Dement had high hopes for a lovely three-year-old mare who had won every competition he had entered her into. Her name was Nell Dement, by Donald out of Flax.

Dement's intention during his early breeding experiments was to produce a little more finish for his Walking Horses. He thought the five-gaited horses would serve this purpose. However, he discovered after several trials that mating of this type did not produce horses with the desired nodding walk.

After several failures, Dement bred Nell to Allan F-1. The product of this mating was perhaps the greatest showmare ever produced. Merry Legs was foaled in April of 1911.

Merry Legs was a big mare, standing 15:2 hands and weighing 1200 pounds. She was described in the Echo of Hoofbeats as a straightgoing mare with no amble whatsoever. She had lots of head motion, a good long neck, perfect ears, and large eyes truly as great as any ever displayed by Tennessee Walking Horses. Anyone could ride her because she had perfect manners, and was gentle as could be.

While Nell, the dam of Merry Legs was known for her high spirit and readiness to

This lovely Tennessee Walking foal exhibits the alert expression and attractive head so characteristic of the breed.

Kellie Rahm and JET enjoying their outlandish costumes at a horse show in Oregon.

Ready to trailer off to a great adventure on the trail. Owners: Larry and Carol Hays of Reno, Nevada.

GREEK REWARD, with successful Horsemanship Badge Girl Scout Troop of Menifee, California.

travel, Merry Legs herself was just the opposite. When one of her riders was asked if she would trot or pace if turned loose, the answer was neither, because she would simply stop. Before a show, her trainer would give her a half-pint of good whiskey to boost her spirits.

Merry Legs' greatness as a show-horse was matched by her potency as a broodmare. She mothered seven fillies and six stud colts.

Another Allan F-1 grandson that made a tremendous mark on the Tennessee Walking Horse of today was Wilson's Allen. This great sire was the product of the intentional breeding of Roan Allen F-38 and his half-sister Birdie Messick.

Johnson Hill, a neighbor of Bud Messick, was anxious to get a colt from Burdie. So when the colt was born, he bought it for $200 and brought it home to his farm. Wilson's Allen's list of names tells the story of his difficult early years: "Johnson Hill Horse;" "Crooked-Tailed Johnson Hill Horse;" "One-Eyed Crooked-Tailed Johnson Hill Horse."

In 1923, after spending his life as a farm workhorse pulling heavy hillside plows around the steep slopes, the long-striding stallion was sold and became known as "The One-Eyed Kirby Horse." During this obscure period, he sired Haynes Peacock, and after being sold

At the ready, a group of Tennessee Walkers and their riders waiting to exhibit the versatility of this special breed.

to Frank Wilson in 1928, he came into his own as sire to Pride Of Memphis. For ten years, until his death in August of 1938, Wilson's Allen was treasured for the excellent horse he had been all along as he sired five World Grand Champions, including Midnight Sun and Strolling Jim (Strolling Jim finished his first year in competition undefeated as well as winning the World Grand Championship at the first National Celebration in Shelbyville).

During the 1939 season, Strolling Jim was entered in 12 competitions and won 12 blue ribbons. Unfortunately by the end of that year, Jim was foundered and had to be sent home to Wartrace (Wartrace became the "cradle" for the breed in the early 1900's) for treatment and rest. By the following year, Jim returned to the arena as World Champion Walking Horse, only to be defeated at his first "Challenge Show" at Baton Rouge by his brother The G Man. In the same competition, the third place horse was Jim's brother Haynes Peacock - three sons of Wilson's Allen in head-to-head competition.

Another of Roan Allen's sons that deserves mention is Merry Boy. This great horse was destined to live in the shadow of his brother Wilson's Allen. All too often his get would come in second, third and fourth to Wilson's Allen's. But in the end, Merry Boy sired two World Grand Champions – Merry Go Boy and Black Angel. Other famous children were Little Merry Legs, Honey Girl, Midnight Sue, and Merry Bird. Looking back at the statistics, it's plain to see that Merry Boy contributed an invaluable investment to the strength of the Tennessee Walker breed

An advertisement for this horse, DUTCH, ran in Denniston, Kentucky, by horse owner Will Ratliff: "This fine yellow saddle stallion, with white mane and tail will make the season at my barn. Terms: $8.00 to insure a living colt; $2.00 in hand paid at time of service; and balance when colt is foaled. Care will be taken to prevent accidents, but I will not be responsible should any occur."

PRIMADONIS, owned by Elizabeth Haynes of Palos Verdes. Photo: Locke Photography

WINDIGO'S INVINCIBLE ADONIS owned by Tom and Donna Doran. Trainer Beth Jennings, up. Photo: Forrest Bliss

MERRY MAN STARR, bought in 1951 for $13. She is the great grandmother of TWH, REBEL ROUSER and SSHBEA World Grand Champion, FAMOUS AMOS.

Herbert Staggs aboard GENERATOR'S SUMMER GIRL.

A good day for stallion SNOW CHIEF DELIGHT and his get. From left: Filly DELIGHTS KITTY DILLON, filly CHIEF'S SUNDAY PRIDE, stallion SNOW CHIEF DELIGHT, colt WHO'S WHO, filly CHIEF'S TOBASCO KITTY, filly THREAT OF SNOW; with handlers Esther Goodchild; Linda Akers; stallion owner and breeder, Sherry Duriga; Stacie Hotchkiss; Bob Hotchkiss; and Dick Polch. They all came home with ribbons from the Buckeye Walking Horse Summer Show, Hillard, Ohio.

Kellie Rahm and friends during a day at the beach.

through the super mares he sired.

One of Merry Boy's lifelong peculiarities was that he did not like to be ridden. Ray and Mac Tenpenny, neighbors of Merry Boy's farm, were determined to enter him in a show. After a day of "eating dust," Mac finally made it into the ring with Merry Boy. The audience was thrilled to watch him win the blue ribbon for performing a perfect running walk. Merry Boy was unimpressed and never returned to ring.

Many years have passed since Merry Boy died in 1958. How does the modern Tennessee Walker measure up to the fine horses of yesteryear? The breed is more than alive and well!

Today's Tennessee Walker is a strong, well-built horse from 14:3 hands to 17 hands. Its most engaging quality is a superb disposition, which makes this horse an excellent choice for children and timid or elderly riders. It is also an animal with great heart and loyalty, making it a fine companion for trail riding, camping, hunting, field trials, harness, handicapped riding programs, and pure pleasure.

The gaiting gene has found a remarkable host in the Tennessee Walker. The classic gaits are the walk, the flat walk, the running walk and the renowned "rocking chair" canter.

The flat walk is a brisk, long-reaching walk that can cover anywhere from 4 to 8 miles an hour. This is a four-cornered gait, with each of the horse's feet hitting the ground sep-arately at regular intervals. The horse will glide over the track left by the front foot with its hind foot. (Right rear over right front, left rear over left front.)

DELIGHT'S SUPERSTAR owned by Tom and Judy Henry. Photo: Rick Osteen

CLASSY'S GLORY owned by Terese Tan, of Pamona, California. Photo by Forrest Bliss

Showing at halter is a popular class to exhibit the beautiful conformation and style of a Tennessee Walking Horse. Photo: Forrest Bliss

TWHBEA

The Tennessee Walking Horse Breeders and Exhibitors Association is the official Registry, established in 1935.

The Tennessee Walker will nod its head in rhythm to the cadence of its feet. This nodding head motion, with the overstride, are two features that are unique to the Tennessee Walker.

The running walk is an extra-smooth gliding gait that is basically the same as the flat walk with a marked increase in speed. The horse can travel 10 to 20 miles per hour at this gait.

In doing the running walk, most Walking Horses overreach. In other words, they overstride by placing the hind foot ahead of the print of the forefoot from 12 to 50 and more inches. This is not necessary to good gait, but it is desirable.

The horse should go straight, placing the feet in line and not winging or weaving in motion. There should be no pace and no wobble or swaying. Most horses have a lot of shoulder motion, and a good horse reaches out with its forefeet and pushes with its powerful hind legs.

Walkers with short necks, hips and rear cannons who have extra length from hip to hock perform the running walk better than their long and flat-shouldered counterparts; wide angles in the stifle, elbow, hip, shoulder and hock joints give a natural edge in the gliding motion of the gait. Extra length from hip to hock enhances its ability to reach under with his hind legs. Shorter necks also contribute to the ease of performance because the forelegs' forward action is regulated in part by neck length. Though ample length is necessary for speed and balance, excessive length places extra weight on the forelegs and may inhibit action.

The "trademark" canter is a forward movement performed in a diagonal manner to the right or to the left. In the canter, the horse gives one the abundance of ease with lots of spring and rhythm, with the proper rise and fall to afford a thrill from sitting in the saddle. The

Headquarters for the Registry are located in Lewisburg, Tennessee. Photo: Courtesy of TWHBEA

GOLDEN GENERATION with Jill Iverson, up.

ORATANA ROCKET'S JET with Kellie Rahm, up.

Supreme Versatility Champion ORATANA ROCKET was trained and ridden by Penny Thomas. He now lives and is loved by his "own person," Kelsey Olsen (pictured).

canter lifts with the front end, giving an easy rise and fall motion that is likened to a rocking chair.

Quality should be apparent. Solid bone, adequate to the proportions of the horse, is desirable. The neck should be well set at the shoulders. The back should be short, but the underline long. The head should not be large and the ears, of medium size, should be reasonably close together. Legs should not be long in proportion to the body, and should sit well under the horse. The horse should be loose in its way of going, and should be able to reach out before and behind with plenty of freedom of motion in its hips and shoulders.

Today we are enjoying a resurgence of interest in the versatility of the original Walking Horse. Some breeders have held on to the old bloodlines, and the original gaits and standards are being brought back. Plantation and versatility shows are springing up across the nation and the Tennessee Walking Horse is finding itself competing in many different equine disciplines. It is no longer unusual to see Walking Horses competing in such events as jumping, driving, English and Western pleasure, trail, endurance riding, gymkhana, field trials and even dressage. The Tennessee Walking Horse Breeders and Exhibitors Association (The Official Breed Registry), sponsors a national Versatility Program.

Kellie Rahm and ORATANA ROCKET'S JET

Kellie Rahm and Oratana Rocket's Jet are a team! Their partnership grew out of the love and dedication of this young woman and her baby-green but sound-minded Tennessee Walker.

Kellie remembers the first time she saw a Tennessee Walker: "It was in the late 80's at a fund-raiser poker ride. I am sure I had seen pictures in magazines of Tennessee Walking Horses before, but nothing had impressed me before I saw them in the flesh, floating across the meadow."

This encounter stuck with Kellie, and she swore to herself that someday she would have a Walker of her own.

Several years later, Kellie was able to acquaint herself with the breed firsthand, when her mother bought a double-registered Spotted Saddle Horse/Tennessee Walker. When they rode together, mother would glide along, while daughter Kellie continued to post the trot, unwilling to give up her stock-type horse that she was so fond of.

It was several years more before she made the plunge and purchased a registered Tennessee Walker, three-year-old Jet.

Jet had been in the hands of well-respected Northwest trainer, Penny Thomas, who agreed to let Kellie take Jet home for a trial period.

Penny had called Oratana Rocket's Jet "green broke," so he and Kellie did some slow easy trail rides. They crossed water, wooden bridges and logs. After the two-week trial period, the sale was made and Jet came home to stay.

Kellie recalls a conversation she had with Penny at that time: "I asked Penny how many times she had actually ridden Jet, and she said about seven rides. Seven rides! I am sure I must have shouted into the phone. Seven rides does not make green-broke in my mind. Penny just laughed and said seven rides is green-broke when you have a horse with a good mind." Penny speaks from great experience. She took Jet's sire, Oratana Rocket through to his Supreme Versatility Championship.

Quoting Kellie: "So began the journey of learning for Jet and me. As our lessons have progressed, so has our feel, timing, balance, collection, gait and most importantly our relationship. He is now truly my partner and friend."

Kellie and JET carrying the Colors, at Horse Expo in Oregon.

Kellie goes on to say: "We spend most of our time trail riding, but also enjoy participating in pleasure shows where we demonstrate versatility in English, Western, and Trail Reining, and we love to run speed events such as Barrels and Pole Bending. We have ridden with the Easy Rider's All-Gaited Horse Drill Team and have also learned to drive."

Kellie and Jet also participate as volunteers to the Adaptive Riding Program. They go on trail ride campouts each year, and act as trail guides and as the runback team in case of emergencies.

In 2001, this special team won the High Point Versatility Award at the Northwest Pleasure Tennessee Walker Show in Boring, Oregon. What an outstanding picture they made as Kellie, riding sidesaddle aboard Jet, carried the flag into the arena!

The crowning glory of the TWHBEA Versatility Program, is the "Supreme Versatility Champion" Award.

Participation in this program enables the horse and rider to enter as many as twenty different events. Some of the divisions are more challenging than others. Some can be as uncomplicated as English Pleasure, Western Pleasure, waterglass or model.

Stallion, MY COLONEL JOE, being loved by his owner Tamilynn Arndt of Wishing Wyoming Ranch in Wheatland, Wyoming. Joe is a liver chestnut, powerfully built with a thundering gait, soft gentle eye and a real romancer.

GOLD VOLTAGE, ready for a mountain outing with his owner Maggie Stillwell from Carson City, Nevada. The kind and willing disposition of the Tennessee Walker make it an ideal companion.

HEADMAN'S MOUNTAIN MYSTERY, a registered and bloodtyped Tennessee Walking filly pictured at two months of age. Exceptionally well-bred, with seven World Grand Champions on her papers. A real black beauty with refined head and awesome gait. She floats! Her temperament is kind, gentle, willing and loving.

A rainbow of equine colors are displayed in this show line-up at a Northern Nevada All-Gaited Horse Show. Photo: Forrest Bliss

Shannon Sheldon aboard BEE GEE'S HEART BEAT. They have become the second team to reach the 1,000 hour pinnacle in the Tennessee Walking Horse Breeders and Exhibitors Distance Program. Photo: Ted and Joyce Brown.

The Versatility Program is a self-achievement program that is custom-designed for both horse and rider. The individual sets the goals they wish to accomplish.

Another TWHBEA-sponsored program is the Distance Award Program. It provides a source of recognition for the horse and rider who enjoy the benefits gained from pleasure trail riding on a regular basis.

Riding hours are recorded in the horse's Log Book, by the owner/rider. These Log Books are supplied by the TWHBEA, and there are no limits to the number of horses each member may enter. However, a person must be a member of the TWHBEA, and the horse must also be registered with TWHBEA, to participate in either the Versatility or Distance Award Programs.

In the Distance Program, hours will be accumulated throughout the horse's life with recognition noted at various levels of accomplishment. A jacket patch is awarded for the completion of 50 hours with additional items awarded for 100, 200, 500 and 1,000 hours in the saddle.

These programs truly promote strong relationships between horse and rider. One such team is Shannon Sheldon and her Ten-

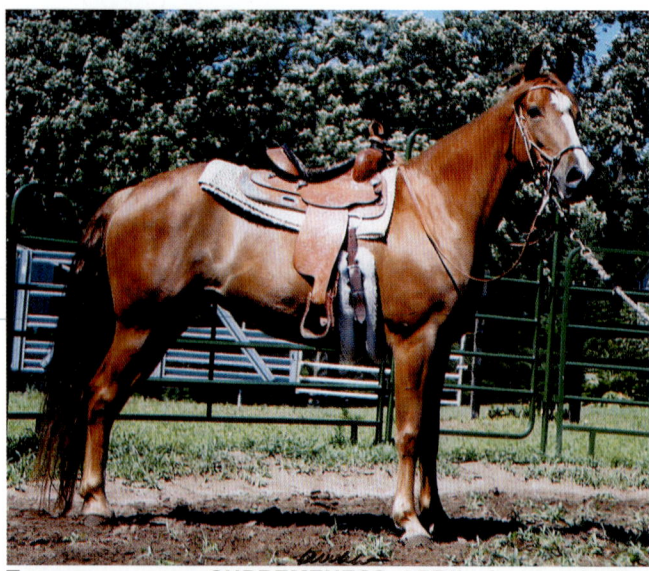

Tennessee mare SUPREMENESS APRIL, is so talented that she can perform multi gaits on command. She will demonstrate a walk, flat walk, running walk, trot, stepping pace, rack, pace, canter and gallop. Photo: Darlene Wohlart Photography

Here we see the tall and the short of the Tennessee Walking Horse. On the left, a six year old, 14 hand tall TWH who takes an Arab sized bridle. On the right, a 23 year old, seventeen hand tall TWH who is truly "draft-sized."

184

Sharon Hanson aboard her endurance Spotted Saddle Horse/Tennessee Walker, **PROVEN WILD SPIRIT**. They are a team that has accomplished numerous endurance competitions and lots of hours on the trail.

nessee mare Bee Gee's Heart Beat. These two were the second team to reach the one thousand-hour pinnacle in the TWHBEA Distance Program.

After they finished in the top ten at the Grizzly Mountain Endurance Ride, and placed 5TH overall, Shannon refered to her sixteen-year-old mare as "easy" and all heart.

This team has the magic ingredient of trust. They trust each other and with trust, they can continue running the mountain as one.

Here is the author on two different Tennessee mares. To the left, **MELISSA**; to the right, **MAGGIE**. "After the tragic loss of Melissa, I shopped for many months for another young Tennessee mare. When I found Maggie, and knew she was the one, to my heartfelt surprise, she turned out to be Melissa's niece."

ALLAN F-1

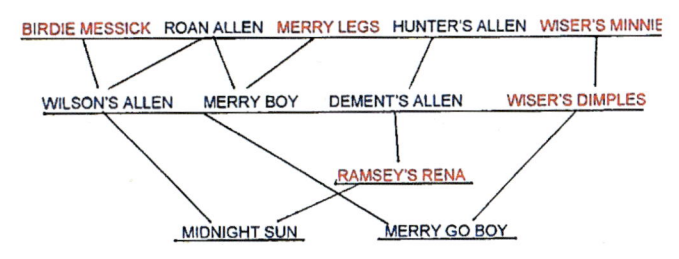

BIRDIE MESSICK ROAN ALLEN MERRY LEGS HUNTER'S ALLEN WISER'S MINNIE
WILSON'S ALLEN MERRY BOY DEMENT'S ALLEN WISER'S DIMPLES
RAMSEY'S RENA
MIDNIGHT SUN MERRY GO BOY

This diagram shows the impact ALLAN F-1 has had on the Tennessee Walking Breed. Line breeding has brought this fine blood into most of the Walking Horses being enjoyed today. Of 11,800 pedigrees listed for the horses registered and recorded in the first five stud books issued by the original registry, more than 10,000 showed ALLAN blood, and 2,785 actually bore his name in some way.

Quoting Shannon: "We are having so much fun in the Distance Program. It's great to get credit for doing something we love. Thanks to TWHBEA for making it possible."

The Tennessee Walking Horse offers so many avenues of enjoyment, from Versatility to Distance, to Carting, to Show Ring, to Family Companion. Its kind and willing nature make it an ideal choice for anyone who wants a great pal who will take you into the mountains, or down the center of the street in parade glamour. This is a breed of tremendous heart, class and presence; a great legacy from the little black horse who wouldn't trot, Allan F-1.

Elizabeth Graves with Tennessee Walker, **DARK MIDNIGHT SHADES**. Photo: Darlene Wohlart

REGAL'S LUNAR EXPRESS
Photo: Darlene Wohlart

HIGH HAT'S BUBBA
Photo: Darlene Wohlart

MAGGIE and filly, SPOTLESS EBEN

JJ
Jack & Terry Hodge
Pocatello, Idaho

MISSOURI FOX TROTTING HORSE

CHAPTER 12

Fox Trotter, FREE SPIRIT
Owner: Betty Mings
Photo: Dawn Lindsay

HEIGHT:	14 - 16H
GAIT:	Flat-foot Walk, Fox Trot, Canter
COLOR:	Any color, including pinto
TRAIT:	Sensible & Kind

Chapter 12   The Missouri Fox Trotter

Westward Ho! The settlers were on the move. The west was calling, and the name of the west was Missouri. The Little House On The Prairie was being lived in for real. Crops were being raised and the cattle industry was to find its second-largest producing state in Missouri.

When Missouri became a state in 1821, more pioneers came flooding from across the Mississippi River, Tennessee, Virginia and Kentucky. They brought the soft-gaited horses that had served them so well in their home states. But the rugged Ozark Mountains held new challenges for these hardy trail-blazers.

Horses that could perform the broken gait called the foxtrot proved to be the most useful for the purposes at hand. It didn't take long for a selective breeding program to begin. As early as 1820, there was a conscious effort to develop a true fox-trotting horse.

So, what is so special about the foxtrot gait? C.H. Hibbard, historian and charter member of the Fox Trotter Association describes the gait as "a broken gait, with the animal walking with the front feet and trotting with the back feet. The back foot disfigures the track made by the front foot." Hibbard goes on to say: "The foxtrotting horse was not a high-stepping horse, but an extremely sure-

Stallion, PATRIOT'S GOLDEN TAHOE S. from Big Cedar Ranch in Ava, Missouri. Photo: Dawn Lindsay

PANHANDLER CLASS ACT with foal getting to know Carrie Bruns at Calico Creek Fox Trotting Horses.
Photo: Jane Bruns

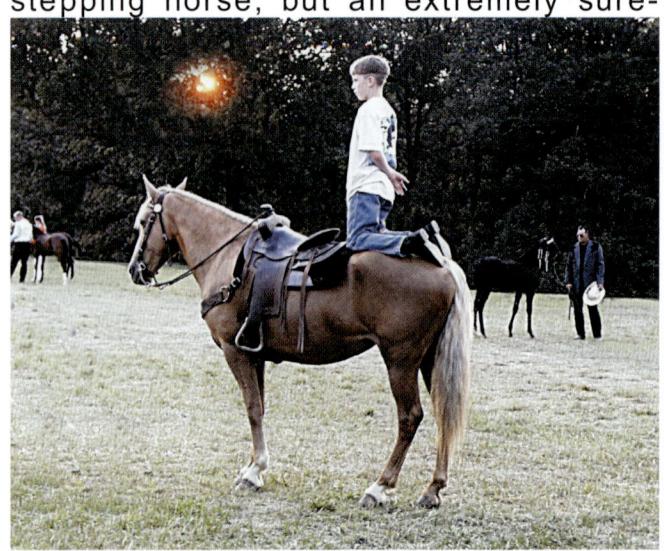

MISTY with Eric aboard at the opening of a local show.
Photo: Dawn Lindsay

YANKEE'S HITCHHIKER, "JOEY", long-time companion to Suzanne Kiechle of Studio City, California.

footed one because of its shuffling gait. Further, because of the sliding action of the rear feet, rather than the hard step of other breeds, the rider experienced little jarring action and was quite comfortable in the saddle for long periods of time."

Attorney General John Ashcroft (former Missouri Senator) at opening ceremonies of a 2001 Show and Celebration. Photo: Dawn Lindsay

The Fox Trotters are indeed cousins to the other soft-gaited horses of the eastern areas, but they retain their own distinctive gait in the foxtrot. Like their namesake the fox, their hind track matches or "caps" the track made by the front foot (on the same side). In the snow, they leave only two tracks per stride.

Looking at the classic foxtrot being performed, the head and tail are slightly elevated, giving the animal a graceful carriage. The rhythmic beat of hooves, along with the nodding action of the head, give the horse a look of relaxation and poise. The head should nod, the ears should indicate the step, and the tail should be a part of the rhythm. The step should be springy and consistently smooth with a little up-and-down motion. The natural rhythm of the Fox Trotter starts at the tip of the nose and goes back to the tip of the tail in one continuous motion.

Most soft-gaited horses can demonstrate the fox trot in addition to their breed-specific gait. While the rack and the running walk can be flashy in appearance and efficient road gaits, the foxtrot can be used as a working gait in rough country as well. From its

Stallion **SUNRISE GOLDEN DUSTY C** with Herman Cantrell up, from Strafford, Missouri. Photo: Dawn Lindsay

earliest development to the present day, the Fox Trotting horse was a useful horse not only on the farm, but in running cattle. From its establishment, well into the 20TH century, the Fox Trotter maintained a solid reputation with cowboys who both pioneered and later ranched cattle from New Mexico to Colorado, as well as in Missouri.

Present-day Fox Trotters are increaseingly found on western ranches. In the Big Horn Basin county of Wyoming, the Stock Growers Association uses them almost exclusively. The U.S. Forestry Service has more than 1,000 Fox Trotters registered to its name. A Fox Trotter horse has claimed top honors with the NATRC[1] on numerous occasions over the years.

What makes a breed of horse this special? Where did it come from? As with many of the other soft-gaited breeds, the Fox Trotter was a part of the culture and life of the community long before it was an official breed.

A family named Alsup settled in the Ozarks before the Civil War. They were known for their racing horses. The prepotent stud they brought with them was Bremmer, and he soon established a line of horses known as Bremmer. Likewise a family called Kissee, also renowned for their good horses, was responsible for establishing the Diamond and Fox strains. To own one of these horses was quite prestigious. Another line of horse that was to influence the Fox Trotters was the Dunn line, named for horseman William Dunn. Old Skip was an important member of that family and contributed much over his prepotent twenty or more producing years.

Old Skip sired horses that had great dispositions and a lot of life-staying qualities. Best of all, his offspring could foxtrot. Many of his colts continued on as studs, and the line continues to the present.

Tom Overstreet brought Chief, an American Saddlebred, and descendant of the

The Missouri Fox Trotter: A horse for all seasons!

---

[1] North American Trail Ride Conference.

Herman Cantrell enjoying his colts at Cantrell Farms, in Strafford, Missouri. Photo: Dawn Lindsay

WILLY, a 3-year-old stud with owner/rider Kim Smith at Mt. Magazine, Arkansas. Photo: Craig Smith

great sire Denmark, to Missouri where he sired many good foxtrotting horses. Horses like Steeldust, Seafoams and Cotham Dare were all active in developing the Fox Trotter we know today. Golden Govenor and Ozark Golden King are but two of the more important foundation sires to this special breed.

Let's take a look at a few of these early Fox Trotting Horses. Old Fox was a Kissee horse. Although no one in the family is sure exactly where he came from, his important time as a stud was in their care.

Old Fox was probably born around 1913. He was raised northeast of Bolivar, Missouri by the Roberts brothers. (Ellis Kissee may have bought him during a Cattle buying trip.) Old Fox was a muscular horse of 15 or 15:1 hands. He had strong shoulders, an angular jaw, and an arched neck with a beautiful flowing mane. He was deep chestnut in color, darker in winter. He had a solid gait with a terrific overreach of about eighteen inches.

Kissee's ten-year-old son, Richard, was given the responsibility of bringing Old Fox around to the farms where there was a mare to

Keith Johnson taking a Championship Pass on GMC'S GOLDEN NUGGET from Johnson Stables, Rogersville, Missouri. Photo: Dawn Lindsay

MFTHBA 2001 Show & Celebration Youth Western Pleasure Class. Photo: Dawn Lindsay

**Dreamaker Farms buckskin stud colt in a field of daisies, owned by Ann Quinn of Niangua, Missouri.
Photo: Dawn Lindsay**

COUNTRY GIRL with filly CRYSTAL being loved by her owner Kelsey Olsen. Photo: Ann Thompson

be bred. Quoting Richard Kissee: "I recall when I took Old Fox to meet a gentleman and his mare to be serviced. He almost had a coronary when I took the saddle and bridle off. However, when he saw how obedient Old Fox was, coming back and putting his head into his bridle, he knew the old boy knew his business."

Kissee's wife, Anna, was surprised that Old Fox built up such an important name. She thought her husband bought him because he was just a good horse. Ellis would talk to the horse and say, "Do you love me, Fox?" The horse would lay his head on Ellis and act as if he could really understand what was being said. The whole family loved the horse.

SONNY with owner/rider Dennis Peleshuck in Washoe Valley, Nevada.

A friend of the family, B. Mills, told about his rides on Old Fox. He said as soon as you got on the horse, he'd go into a running walk that was as fast as the foxtrot of an ordinary horse. For Old Fox to foxtrot, all you had to do was pinch him on the neck, give him a bit of a kick, and he'd move out with such gusto that you could hear his teeth clatter from the nodding of his head.

Old Fox (1913), was the sire of Ozark Golden King (1938), who was the sire of Golden Governor (1943), who was the sire of Golden Rawhide (1957).

Ozark Golden King was foaled April 15, 1938, near Nixa, Missouri. He was owned by Ray and Willie Hedgpeth, and they stood him for twenty years. During his years with the Hedgpeth brothers, Ozark Golden King sired nearly fifteen hundred foals. For the Hedgpeths, there would never be another horse to equal Ozark Golden King.

Golden Governor belonged to Dale Esther, a notable Fox Trotter breeder and promoter. As his name implies, Golden

MFTHBA 2001 Show & Celebration Youth Western Pleasure Class. Photo: Dawn Lindsay

BOBBI JOE, a two-year-old filly, with owner/rider Kim Smith on a cross-country trail ride in Eminence, Missouri. Photo: Lynn Photo, Eminence, Missouri

Governor, out of Betty Fox, was a stylish golden palomino with excellent conformation and good rhythm to his gait. His head, neck and shoulder contributed to his success as a model horse and he was hard to beat in rail classes. It was said the Golden Governor was a horse you could not only show, but use with cattle. Many of his offspring inherited his good "using" qualities.

Golden Rawhide had a short but impressive life (1957 to 1970). Both his sire, Golden Governor, and his dam, Nancy Ann, were grandchildren of Old Fox. Golden Rawhide was the first stallion to win the Fox Trotting Celebration 1966 Grand Championship. His record of winning the Senior Stallion Performance Class for five consecutive years has never been challenged.

Dale Esther, who also owned Golden Rawhide, operated a rodeo company and

Stallion REX'S WHITE LIGHTNING from Calico Creek Fox Trotters. Photo: Jane Bruns

used the stallion as a rodeo pickup horse. Golden Rawhide could be trusted to perform well for anyone. He was frequently ridden by celebrities making personal appearances on the pro rodeo tour. Esther's children used the stallion to gather cattle and horses, and when their father couldn't take them, hauled Golden Rawhide off to shows themselves.

Golden Rawhide had a very important full sister in Lady Anne. When she was bred to Tennessee Walker Sterling Merry Boy, she produced the spectacular stallion, Zane Grey. He was a wonderfully colored dappled grey

RAMBLIN ROSIE and her champagne filly – Dreamaker Farms RHYTHM AND STEP. Photo: Dawn Lindsay

NELLIE with Brenda Foley, up.

EARTH ANGEL, a daughter of MACK K'S YANKEE, with her filly by SOUTHERN JAZZ.

FIZZ'S MOONLIGHT SPIRIT – Marv Davis, Reno, Nevada.

horse foaled on May 10, 1964. He had a natural foxtrot that was both durable and ground covering. In 1968, as a four-year-old, he won the Fox Trotter Grand Championship, but that didn't affect his "using horse" status at the Esther Ranch. What Zane Grey lacked in conformation he made up for in gait and ability. He reportedly had sickle hocks, or at least legs set well under him, but he had exceptional rhythm. He was not a large horse, but he had tremendous heart. His pre-potency put his grey coloring on most of his foals. It is difficult to find an extended pedigree today that does not carry his name.

Zane Grey was bred back to his mother Lady Ann E, producing another important Fox Trotter sire, Missouri Travler. Travler was an impressive deep red horse who lent his name to the term "Travler Red." Like his father, Travler generated strong reaction. People either loved him or hated him. Also like his father, Travler's name is found on a large portion of today's pedigrees and in many instances, multiple times.

Missouri Travler E was known as a "hotter" horse than most, and at the same time his progeny has a reputation for gentle-

ZANE'S BLUE MAX D. – son (from the last foal crop – 1973) of ZANE GREY, giving up his winter coat in his last spring (2001). Owned and loved by the author, Barbara Weatherwax, Washoe Valley, Nevada.

An Arizona trail ride for Valley Springs Fox Trotters from Black, Missouri. Photo: JoAnn Becker

FOX HILL MOONSHINE owned by Julia Tarnawski, Sunland, California. Photo: Judy Frederick

ness accompanying their extra flare of energy and intelligence.

Other important sons of Zane Grey are Frosty Zane F; Frosty Zane; Grey Warrior; Zane's Cap-a-Lot; Zane's Lad; Zane's Cadillac; Zane's Roan Lad; Zane's Ben Blue; and Zane's Dusty Diamond, among others.

In the previous few paragraphs, we have followed the Old Foxline of horses from the early 1900's to the early 70's. Now let's take a step back to the early 40's and take a

YANKEE'S HITCHHIKER, "JOEY," with another Fox Trotter pal, ready for the trail. Owner: Suzanne Kiechle

look at Cotham Dare.

Cotham Dare was a registered American Saddlebred stallion foaled May 9, 1941. He was sired by Cyclone Dare, by Mountain Dare, by Chester Dare, and by the immortal Black Squirrel. His dam was May Cotham by Dink Not. Cotham Dare was brought from Arkansas to Missouri when he was six years old, by Clyde Norman. Norman sold him to Charley and Beulah Rowland in 1948. Rowland insisted that Norman have the stallion registered as a Fox Trotter before the deal was closed. Cotham Dare was described as "taking the eyes" of many people wherever he went. He was well-mannered and strong with a cool head. He was truly a grand, naturally gaited horse that passed his positive qualities on to lots of foals. His progeny, "the Dare Line," was known for its conformation and beauty. And even though Cotham Dare was a Saddlehorse, you didn't have to *make* him foxtrot - you would *"let"* him fox trot.

The Cotham Dare horses, back in those days, were cap tracking - that is to say, their back feet would disfigure their front track whenever they fox trotted. One of Cotham Dare's sons was Dare's Trigger. He was inclined to be a little short in his gait. But he had wonderful conformation and was a pretty, smooth-looking horse.

Lawrence Barnes had another Cotham Dare son, Baldy. He was a big stout horse weighing around 1,400 pounds. It was said

Barbara Weatherwax with Fox Trotters ZANE'S BLUE MAX and RINGO'S PISTOL PETE on a New Year's Day morning ride 1986, Malibu Creek, California.

George Becker from Valley Springs Fox Trotters, riding in Colorado with SMOKEY and IMAGE.

Missouri Fox Trot Registry Headquarters, Ava, Missouri.

Missouri Fox Trotters from Dreamaker Farms at Equine Affair in Ohio, 2002. Michelle Kilburn (center) is riding her gelding CHIBANI.

198

⬅ Photos at left:
Top: Marvin Davis on RED'S RAMBLING VIGILANTE, versatility winner at the 6th Annual All-Gaited Horse Show presented by the Northern Nevada Gaited Horse Club, '02.
Middle: Kathleen Keely on ZACHARY SCOTT, a grey gelding who always presents himself as a winner.
Bottom: JET'S BAY RIBBON, owned by Frank and Jeannie Murphy. Ridden by Frank, RIBBON had a long and successful show career. All 3 Photos: Forrest Bliss.

you could set a glass of water on him and he would never spill a drop. He was as smooth as a clock. Baldy was a fine foxtrotting horse.

The last Cotham Dare son, Ranger, was one of the first Fox Trotter stallions to be registered. His owner was W.D. Singleton. Apparently the people in his town offered to pay the registration fee.

Later generations produced many more special foxtrotting horses like Zane's Quick-Silver. This lovely mare was to bring together the Old Fox and Cotham Dare lines. Her dam was Bonnie G by Dare's Trigger, and her sire was Zane Grey.

Quicksilver had great speed. She was a vigorous competitor that might not always look the best, but she would give the rider her all.

The 1960's produced many of the most influential stallions. In 1963, Danney Joe W., a deep golden palomino, was foaled. His sire was Golden Rebel T. and his dam: June (by Dare's Trigger). His owner Dale Wood used

**Homozygus stallion PURE LUCK with Diane Saddler, up. Owned by Chuck and Sherry Hartley of Missouri.
Photo: Dawn Lindsay**

199

used him for ranch work as well as a show horse. Danney Joe was noted for his quick, fast foxtrot and his sensibility and gentle nature.

Mack K's Yankee was foaled on April 16, 1964. His sire, Midnight Mack K was sired by the well-known Tennessee Walker, Midnight Sun. In truth, Mack K's Yankee was 31/32 Tennessee Walking Horse with only one obscure line going to old-time Saddlehorse. He was one of the most influential breeding stallions of his time and his blood changed both the look and gait style of the breed in large part. His line produced not only successful show horses, but World Champions as well.

Another Tennessee import during the 60's was Giles Hot Toddy. He was a black sabino horse sired by Roger's Perfection, out of Glory's Lady K. One of his important sons was Toddy's Perfection, out of one of the breed's finest mares, Waldren's Golden Nelly, a descendant through her dam, Flicka, to Golden Governor. Toddy's Perfection was not only a most influential breeding stallion, but he was a very successful show horse. He stood stud in the Humansville, Missouri area during the 1980's and 90's, well into his twenties.

By looking at individual horses, grad-

SKIPS BONNIE BLUE with Keri Henson up in the 2001 Versatility Arena at a Show and Celebration in Texas. Photo: Dawn Lindsay

ually the picture of the Fox Trotter begins to take shape. Let's put it all together. The Missouri Fox Trotter may be a chestnut, black, bay, grey, piebald, skewbald, palomino, white, buckskin or any other equine color. Its head should be well-proportioned with a straight profile. Its ears are pointed and its eyes are large and expressive. Its neck is well formed and of medium length. Its chest is broad and deep while the shoulder is sloped and muscular. Its legs are sturdy, well-muscled

SUGAR COOKIE, the first mare honored by the Horseman's Association of Middle Missouri, for her outstanding get.

DOLLY, a SUGAR COOKIE daughter. Notice the similarity in their top lines.

SUNRISE SWEET BETSY C. – Herman and Norma Cantrell, Strafford, Missouri. Photo: Dawn Lindsay

and have good joints with clearly defined tendons. Its hooves must be well formed and proportionate to the size of the horse.

In 1948, fifteen men gathered together at the home of Homer Harley to organize a registry protecting the future of the fox trotting horses. Only a couple of these men were horsemen, but all of them knew the importance of ensuring the future of this most valuable living asset for the State of Missouri. Association Charter members were: G.E. Dye, C.S. Neiman, Ralph Cromer, Ranse Gaston, Clyde Norman, Ernest Uhlmann, D.H. Hibbard, John Dunn, Granville Prock, Ovle House, and Paul David. Bernie Lewis served as attorney for the group.

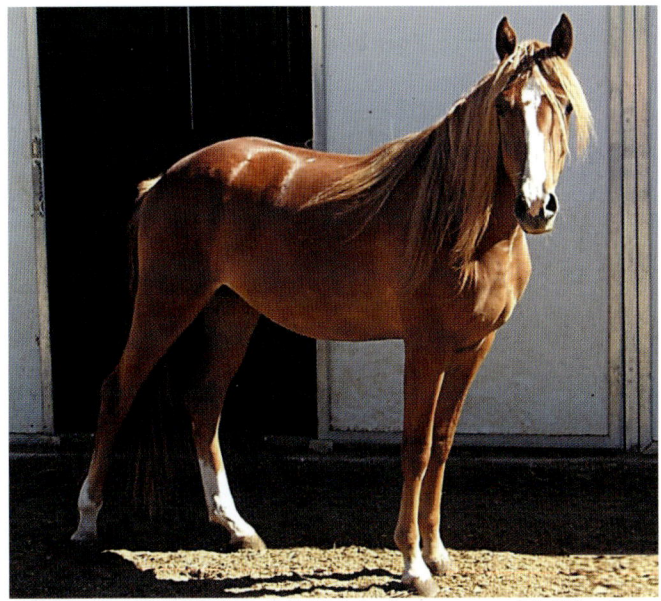

Claude Hibbard was the first president. He is credited with most of the legwork in getting the Association up and running. World War II had just come to an end and as folks were feeling the need for renewal, cars were taking over and the horse was put on the back burner.

The Association limped along for the next ten years, registering less than 500 horses. John Dunn was the first secretary of the Association, and in this position kept all the records in his home. Disaster struck when Dunn's home burned to the ground, turning all the Association records to ash.

Enter Joe Heinz and Dale Esther. In 1958, these two gentlemen, along with Claude Hibbard as secretary, reorganized the Association. With their enthusiasm and determination, they charted a course of rapid expansion.

Through Lawrence Barnes as a member of the Board of Directors, the Missouri Fox Trotter Journal began. The Journal has continued as a monthly publication for the membership, to this day.

JEWEL'S MOUNTAIN CADILAC, two year old filly from Foley's Fox Trotters in Carson City, Nevada.

NO SPEED LIMIT – owned by Pat & John Anderson from Sunhill Farms, Estacada, Oregon. Photo: Dawn Lindsay

ROWDY TWISTER, a homozygous Spotted from Free Rein Farms owned by Ann Quinn, Niangua, Missouri.

PRINCE by SOUTHERN FIZZ out of **A SAINT SHE AINT**. Carson City, Nevada.

The year after its reorganization, the Missouri Fox Trotter Association produced the first Jubilee Celebration, held at the Ava Missouri Fairgrounds. The gathering of the Fox Trotters became an annual event and is traditionally held in September of each year. In 1976, the Association purchased land and established a showgrounds.

In 1981, an office building and a Hall of Fame were constructed on the Celebration Show Grounds in Ava, Missouri. Each year, the growth of the Registry is reflected in the growth and new additions to the show grounds and office headquarters.

Stallion, **SOUTHERN SUNRISE**, owned by Larry Stevens in Marshfield, Missouri, has produced more Champion Fox Trotters at his age than any horse in Fox Trotter history.

Gelding **LION TAMER**, owned and ridden by Jack Keely, is a favorite Fox Trotter to watch in the arena. He has great brio and personality that comes across to the audience.

Stallion FINAL JUSTICE performing at the 2001 Celebration. He has multiple championships at halter, wins consistently at performance, is several times Trail Champion of the South West Region, and is the pride of his owner, Anita Pate of Diana, Texas.

Palomino mare, SAFFRON SILK owned and cherished by Janice Handel, being ridden by Stephen Brook-Blaut of Germany as an introduction to Fox Trotters. Grey gelding BUD is the favorite trail buddy of owner Dennis Handel.

The Fox Trotter breed is frequently the first gaited horse that people discover. Its popularity as a forestry horse and availability in most every section of the country make it a realistic choice.

Steve and Brenda Foley are a couple who have enthusiastically embraced the breeding of these wonderful horses.

When Brenda was only a child, she had an unforgettable experience of riding a spotted, gaited gelding. At that time, she made a secret pact with herself to find a horse just like that for her very own.

Fifteen years later, Brenda and her

Stallion ROYAL HERITAGE at the Celebration. The photo to the right shows the same horse enjoying his retirement.

Quoting owner Lee Yates: "Today, ROYAL HERITAGE is retired to stud and is our babysitter horse for our grandchildren. He is also the horse we drag out when a 'greenie' comes to ride, when we need to work cattle or check fence. We also use him in playdays doing barrels, poles, etc. He is also broke to drive (looks pretty fancy pulling a buggy, grin) and pack. Truly he exhibits the versatility of the Fox Trotter."

Steve Foley on a hunting trip with his stallion, SOUTHERN FIZZ G.

Brenda Foley enjoying her stallion, NUGGET'S REBEL. "CODY" is double-registered in the Spotted Saddle Horse Registry, as well as Missouri Fox Trotter. Brenda and her husband both really enjoy and ride their stallions. They are truly "using horses!"

husband moved to Carson City, Nevada and began their search for "smooth, strong, athletic horses with gentle willing temperaments."

Brenda had the opportunity to ride Zane's Blue Max D. a son of the well-known sire Zane Grey. The dye was cast. Their first purchase was a lovely chestnut gelding and the second, a red chestnut mare. It wasn't long before they owned a stallion Southern Fizz G. and then another, Nugget's Rebel, and soon, with the purchase of more mares, they found themselves seriously in the Fox Trotter breeding business.

Quoting Brenda: "Steve and I never planned on breeding, raising and training Missouri Fox Trotters, we sort of fell into it. I have become obsessed with gait and am enjoying learning to train Fox Trotters. It's very

ZANE'S BLUE MAX D with "the author" aboard.

Stallion, MISSOURI RED WING. As of 2002, he is the only stallion ever to make a consecutive clean sweep of all four World Grand Championships. 1985: World Grand Champion 2-year-old. 1986: World Grand Champion 3-year-old. 1987:World Grand Champion 4-year-old. 1988: World Grand Champion. Owned by Guy and Wilma Hare of Rogersville, Missouri.

Northern Nevada is a trailrider's dream. Pictured are Brenda and Steve Foley on their Missouri Fox Trotting stallions, CODY and FIZZ.

important to me to have a horse reach its potential and gait properly. I always demand an even 4-beat gait without a tendency to pace or trot. I don't allow lazy gaiting. I like a relaxed, stylish way of going with rhythm, reach, and most importantly, smooth.

"Fox Trotters are in our blood now. Sometimes it's difficult balancing our careers and children. Steve is a registered nurse along with owning a commercial sign business and an esophageal studies business. I am a registered nurse, specializing in maternal and child health.

"Steve and I chose the Missouri Fox Trotter Horse because of its gentle even temperament, ease of training, athletic, balanced build, variety in gait, versatility and trail-wiseness. We also like the fact that the Missouri Fox Trotters come in almost all colors."

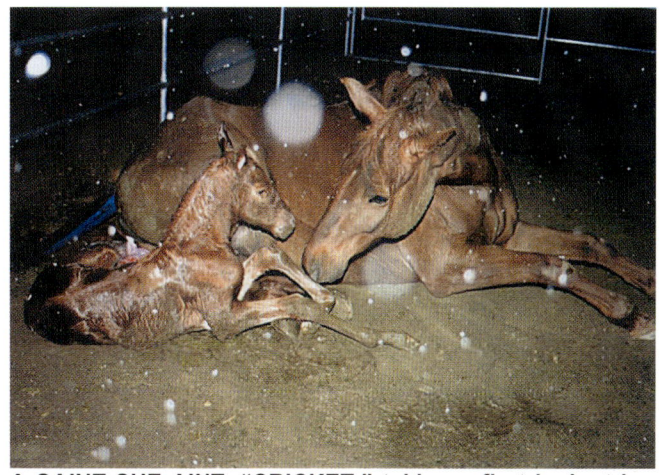

A SAINT SHE AINT, "CRICKET," taking a first look at her new foal, PRINCE, in her home with the Foley's.
Photo: Steve Foley

Stallion WIZARDS TRAVELIN JOE, from Dreamakers Farms where he is sire to buckskins and palominos.
Photo: Dawn Lindsay

Julie Tarnawski riding her stallion FOX HILL MOONSHINE.
Photo: Ann Thompson

Stallion RAMBLIN' LEMON TWIST from Rebel Spring Ranch in Norwood, Missouri

Jenna Murril on RISKY BUSINESS

A wonderful outing with riders at Valley Springs Fox Trotters

Fox Trotters come in a rainbow of colors.

Renee Mack's mare, with her foal by SOUTHERN FIZZ

Jumping competition at the Missouri Fox Trotter Celebration.

Stallion SOUTHERN FIZZ G.
with owner Steve Foley, up

SPOTTED SADDLE HORSE

CHAPTER 13

Spotted Saddle Horse, TODAIN
Owner: Barbara Weatherwax

HEIGHT: No limits

GAIT: 4-beat

COLOR: Any color, with white

TRAIT: Versatility

Chapter 13 – The Spotted Saddle Horse

Pinto horses have been a sought after commodity and source of fascination since before recorded history. Twenty thousand years ago, cavedwellers scratched out pictures of pinto horses on their walls.

Pinto markings appeared throughout the centuries for the purpose of camouflage. Spots, in fact, may have been the original markings on horses. Having a coat that blends into the background is an added advantage, since the horse depends on alertness and speed for survival. A pinto horse can conceal itself in the shadows of foliaged landscape. Zebras and giraffes are other examples of animals who benefit from this type of "natural protection."

Pictures and statuary in the tombs of ancient Egypt record pinto horses as early as 1600 B.C. One painting shows a chariot pulled by a horse with a sorrel body and overo[1] markings. The horse appears to be an oriental type, perhaps a Barb, Arabian or a Turk.

Pinto horses were also depicted in the early artwork of China, Tibet and India. A statuette from the Hun Dynasty portrays a horse with definite pinto markings. Surviving art-work from Medieval China reveals that emperors favored pinto horses because they signified royalty and power.

Ancient Greeks were renowned for their horsemanship. To provide the horses they needed for their races and games, they inaugurated horse-breeding establishments in the nations east of Athens. The Caliph of Motassen operated one of the largest. His horses were described as spotted, speckled, and splotched circus-type Arabians.

The Romans preferred pinto horses for their parades and pageantry. If pinto horses weren't available, they simply painted the spots on for decorations. From ancient times to

---

[1] See page 213 for a description of overo coloring.

Top: PRIME'S SUPERMAN, Triple registered in TWHBEA, SSHBEA and NSSHA from Woodview Stables; Carla & Greg Hester, Morrow, Ohio. Middle: SILVERDEW'S FOXY LADY, Double registered TWHBEA and SSHBEA. This 1990 mare stands 15:3 hands and is a broodmare at Woodview Stables. Bottom: BARNEY FIFE'S GENERAL IKE, standing at Brushy Creek Lodge and Resort, George & JoAnn Becker, Black, Missouri.

the present, European circuses have placed a high value on pinto horses.

Some Iberian vases dating from the third century B.C. verify that the pinto horse was already in residence in Spain before the arrival of the Arabian and Barb horses some 1,000 years later. Spanish pottery depicted pinto horses that appear to be well-bred with smooth, trim body lines and clean, slender legs.

Throughout the history of Europe and the Middle East, breeders of Thoroughbreds, Arabians, Barbs, and Andalusians have, at one time or another, bred specifically for spotted coats. French Arabians, in particular, were noted for their colorful markings.

Spotted horses found their way to the new world when the Icelandic ponies liberated themselves from the Viking ships that crashed on the shorelines of the North American continent. These little horses had a natural soft gait and were often pinto. As war horses, they were exceptionally strong and had great stamina.

Horses arrived again in the Americas with the Spanish conquistadors. Father Bernal Diaz, who accompanied Hernen Cortez on his explorations, specified that at least one pinto be among the horses brought to Mexico in 1519. Many of these found their way into Native American possession. Indian tribesmen people held these pinto horses in high esteem and nurtured their survival.

The pinto horses became an important part of the Native American culture. They were appreciated for being colorful and bright, but there was also a practical reason for owning them. The pinto was the perfect horse for the Indians, who were experts in the art of camouflage. Their colors were easiest to alter to coincide with the changing seasons. The Comanches and Cheyennes coveted a type of pinto they called Medicine Hat. These could be ridden only by warriors who had proven themselves in battle. The Indians believed that they would not be wounded if they were mounted on such a colored horse.

Native Americans started to adapt to a horse culture fairly early in the 17TH century. Intertribal trading, raiding, and trading

Top: CHRISTY'S CANDY MAN, from Teton's Walkers; Rod and Stacie Hill, Tetonia, Idaho. Middle: DILLON'S SHADOW MAKER. This young mare (1998) is a daughter of MARSHAL DILLON and is owned by Woodview Stables; Carla and Greg Hester, Morrow, Ohio. Bottom: STEPPIN OUT TONIGHT, Beech Mile Farm, Bedwell Stables – Janie Rowland from Nashville, Tennessee.

Stallion, REVELRY'S LITTLE BANDIT, from Mane Gait Farms owned by Lisa Brown, Glendale, Arizona.

Filly, HARLEY, Beechmile Farm, Nashville, Tennessee.

with the colonists resulted in the migratory dispersion of pinto horses throughout the country to be bred with the local horses.

The ancestors of the Spotted Saddle Horse that we know today are the Standardbred, the Red Squirrel, the Mustang, the Spanish Jennet, and the Narragansett Pacer. More recently, the Tennessee Walkers and Missouri Fox Trotters have been used in breeding programs to reinforce and lock in the gaiting abilities and overall physical qualities of the Spotted Saddle Horse. The Spotted Saddle Horse is truly the "Sports Model" of the equine world.

With this lovely breed, a person can have the pinto horse they fancy without losing the wonderful four-beat gait.

Terminology for the pinto horse can be confusing. With the great variety of coat colors and patterns, the pinto horse has been called by many names. In Arabia it is called "Kanhwa," which means "blotched with white and chestnut or black." In India, they call it "Lathiawari" and "Pulwahri," which mean a "white horse that flowers with black spots." In Tibet it is called "Tanghan." In Spain it is called "Pintado," which means painted or mottled.

Mares and babies at Beechmile Farm, in Nashville. Owner: Janie Rowland.

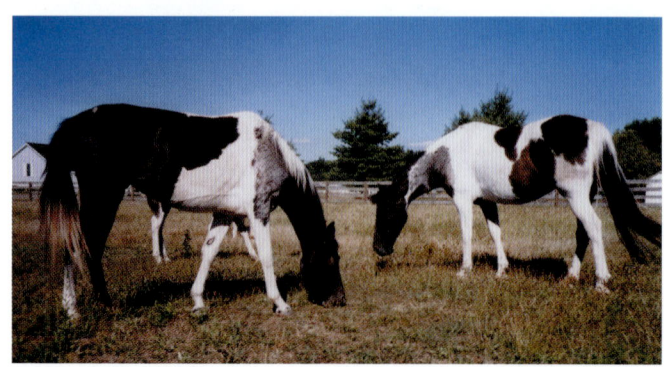

Two great riding mares from Woodview Stables, Morrow, Ohio. Left: BO'S RAMBLING ROSE. Right: FROSTY MORNING WHISKEY.

All these descriptions of the various types of spotted coloring are shared by the primary pinto registries: The Spotted Saddle Horse, The Pinto, and the Paint. In fact the Spotted Saddle Horse can also be registered as a Pinto, because the Pinto Registry is a color registry. The Spotted Saddle Horse *cannot* be registered as a Paint. A horse must be registered as a Thoroughbred or a Quarter Horse to qualify for the Paint Registry.

The following are some common terms used to describe the multi-colored coats of the pinto horses.

Tobiano is a color pattern created by a dominant color gene. The color pattern must be visible for the gene to be present. The white area starts on the back and spreads downward in a regular or clearly marked pattern. The head is usually a solid color, often with a star or snip or small blaze. The legs are usually white below the knees. For a tobiano foal to be produced, at least one parent must possess the tobiano gene.

Overo is a color pattern created by a recessive color gene. To produce an overo foal, both parents must possess the overo gene; however, they need not display the overo coat pattern. The white areas start on the belly and extend upward. The legs are usually dark and the head is usually white. There are three face patterns that are frequently found in an overo colored horse; bonnet face, apron face, and medicine hat.

The **bonnet face** has colored ears and eyes. It gets its name because it looks as if a bonnet were tied onto the horse's head. The

Stallion, TODAIN, from Ophir Hill Station in Washoe Valley, Nevada, owns the kind nature and beautiful face found in the Spotted Saddle Horse. Photo: Ann Thompson

Stallion, NUGGET'S REBEL, from Foley's Fox Trotters, in Carson City, Nevada. "CODY" is a prepotent stud who puts his incredible bone and gentle personality on his get. Photo: Forrest Bliss

The zebra exhibits similar ancient camouflage markings found in the spotted saddle horse.

horse is frequently white-bodied or has little or no color on the body.

The **apron face** has colored ears and color around the jaw. It looks as if a large white apron were tied around the horse's head. Both upper and lower lips are white.

The **medicine hat** has colored ears, and color on top of the horse's head, as if it were fitted with a skull cap. There is usually color around the eyes, chest, flank and base of tail.

Sabino is a term describing a speckled pattern. This horse will have a lot of white on the face. Unless it is a heavily marked horse there is not, usually, white over the back. Any white appearing on the legs, flanks, neck, underbelly, jaw and throat-latch are merely patches, flecks and wisps. The hairs are roaned where the white blends into the colored area. Sabino is sometimes confused with overo, but they are genetically and visually different.

Sabino is a dominant gene. An important stallion in the foundation stock of the Tennessee Walker Registry, Roan Allen F-38 had both the sabino and roan patterns. This was a common combination in the old fashioned Walking Horse. Overo, sabino and roan are independent genetic patterns.

There are several terms associated with the Spotted Saddle Horses which are useful to

FROSTYY MORNIN' WHISKEY, SILVER DOLLAR QUEEN and MR. PENNINGTON, camping out with Pam Stubbs from Doe Run Farm in Roopville, Georgia.

Photos: Courtesy: SSHBEA.

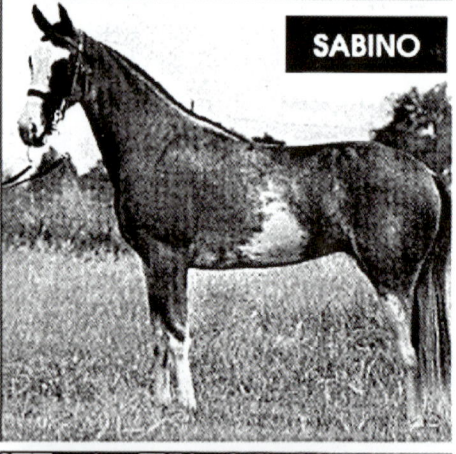

TOBIANO

OVERO

SABINO

TOVERO

214

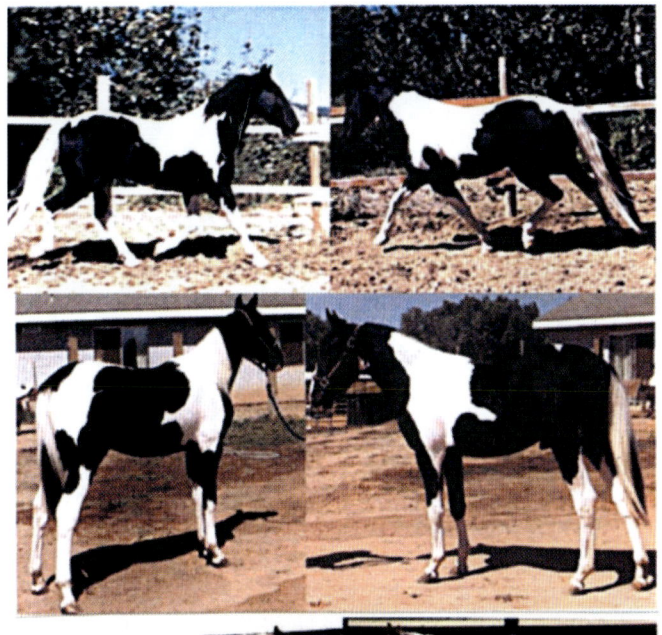

Here are both sides of five different Spotted Horses. They display great variations of color distribution on each side.

common in overo coloring. **Distal** or **ermine spots** are roanish spotted edging around a dark colored spot. Skin under these edgings will be dark. **Ink Spots** are dark skin spots with white hair covering them. They are usually found in large white spots and sometimes found on the legs of high-stockinged horses. These spots are sometimes referred to as **"spots on spots."** **Todainian** is a color pattern found in tobiano horses. It is white over the back and the hind quarters.

Wall eyes, china eyes, and **glass eyes** are all terms describing blue eyes, which are a frequent characteristic in spotted horses. The blue pattern does not impair vision.

Genetic study of the multicolored horse has made tremendous advances in recent years. There are definite "recipes" determining "get."

The tobiano gene is dominant. If the sire has a tobiano gene **T** and a non-tobiano gene **t**, and the dam has the same combination, there are only four possible combinations.

Since **T** is dominant, the get from 1,2, and 3 would be tobiano. The product of 4 would not be tobiano. So the chances of getting tobiano from such parents would be 3 out of 4.

The overo gene is recessive. The horse must have two overo genes before it will display the overo pattern. If the sire has a non-overo gene **O** and an overo gene **o**, and the dam has two overo genes **oo**, the four possibilities would be: 1) **Oo** 2) **Oo** 3) **oo** and 4) **oo**. There would be a 50-50 chance of producing an overo foal: 3) and 4) would be overo and 1) and 2) would not.

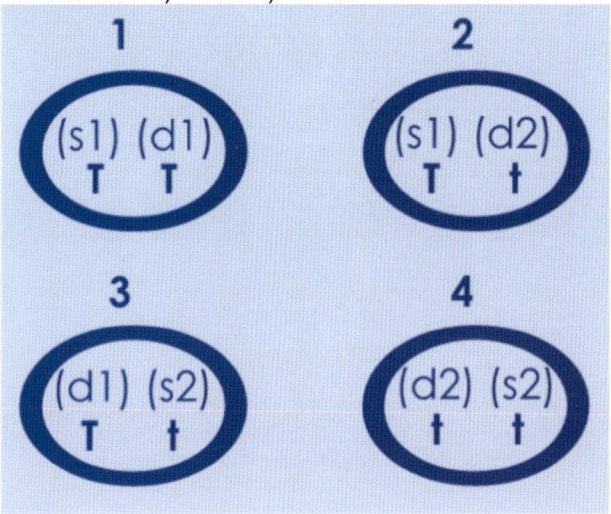

know. **Tovero** is a cross between tobiano and overo. **Piebald** is always black and white - in tobiano, overo and sabino. **Skewbald** is any combination of color other than black and white. Both palomino and white, and bay and white would be considered skewbald. **Calico** is usually found in overo and sabino horses that are roan and spotty white. **Rebecano** (also known as Squaw Tail) describes white at the base of an otherwise colored tail. It is most

1
(s1) (d1)
T   T

2
(s1) (d2)
T   t

3
(d1) (s2)
T   t

4
(d2) (s2)
t   t

OVERO OVERO OVERO OVERO OVERO OVERO OVERO OVERO OVERO

TOBIANO TOBIANO TOBIANO TOBIANO TOBIANO TOBIANO TOBIANO TOBIANO TOBIANO

Unfortunately, there is no blood test to identify the overo gene in advance. Trial and error has validated the formula, as illustrated on page 215.

Two other terms that are part of the Spotted experience are *heterozygous* and *homozygous*. Heterozygous is designated by the symbol (Tt) and it means the tobiano horse will produce tobiano offspring 50% of the time. When the tobiano gene (T) is passed to offspring, the resulting foal will be tobiano. When the solid color gene (t) is passed to offspring, the resulting foal will be solid color. Most tobiano horses are heterozygous.

Homozygous is designated by the symbol (TT) and means the tobiano horse will produce tobiano offspring 100% of the time. The homozygous horse has no other gene to give the offspring. In breeding practice, if a horse produces or sires a solid-colored foal, the horse is heterozygous. The homozygous horse is very valuable in Spotted Horse breeding programs. Homozygous foals are produced by breeding tobiano to tobiano. Of

Makenna Lincoln aboard D'S DOLL competing in the versatility program of an All-Gaited Show. They "ran off" with the high point awards. Photo: Forrest Bliss

Who could resist including this photo of the author taken at a road-side attraction somewhere on Route 66.

216

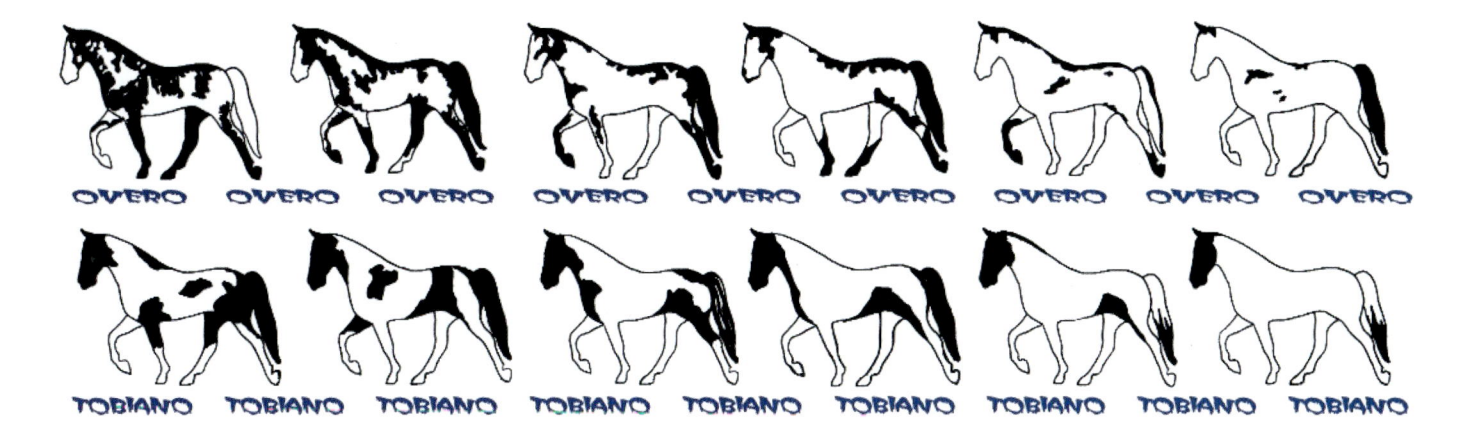

OVERO OVERO OVERO OVERO OVERO OVERO OVERO OVERO OVERO

TOBIANO TOBIANO TOBIANO TOBIANO TOBIANO TOBIANO TOBIANO TOBIANO TOBIANO

this mating, 25% of foals will be solid, 50% will be heterozygous tobiano and 25% will be homozygous tobiano.

With the development and rapidly growing popularity of the spotted horse, the formation of a registry was inevitable.

The National Spotted Saddle Horse Association, Inc. (NSSHA) was formed in 1979 and has headquarters in Murfreesboro, Tennessee. The NSSHA established a Breed Standard which includes: Height and Weight: Most horses registered range in height from 13:3 hands to 15:2 hands, with an average of 15 hands. Weight is proportionate to height. NSSHA tends to aim toward the larger individual as ideal, but does not discriminate because of size.

The Spotted Saddle Horse is surely the "Sports Model" of the equine world. Photo: Forrest Bliss

This double-registered stallion, (SSHBEA & Paso Fino) demonstrates how the Spotteds "Can Do." Owners: Remolino Ranch, Washoe Valley, Nevada. Photo: Forrest Bliss

Muscling: The horse should be well muscled and heavier built than the Tennessee Walking Horse, but not as developed as a Quarter Horse. The muscling should be balanced with muscle that is equally developed in forehand and in the rear. (This is true with most breeds that perform smooth or easy gaits. They must push with the rear and pull with the front.)

Disposition: The disposition should be typically gentle and easy to handle.

Shelbyville headquarters of the SSHBEA

In 1985, the Spotted Saddle Horse Breeders and Exhibitors Association (SSHBEA) was formed and became the official registry for the breed. It was established as a nonprofit, state-chartered organization, operat-ing out of Shelbyville, Tennessee. The SSHBEA maintains a registry, develops the rules and regulations governing all aspects of the breed, licenses judges and affiliates shows.

In maintaining the pedigrees, ownership, transfers and color information, the SSHBEA keeps lists of stallions as well as get, produce and show records. To be registered as a Spotted Saddle Horse, the horse must have at least one parent that is registered with SSHBEA. If a horse meets all the requirements of the association, it is possible to be included in the registry without known parentage, based on the individual's own attributes.

The Spotted Saddle Horse is a wonderful combination of color, temperament, refinement and movement and truly provides the best of all possible worlds for horse lovers. Unlike the showy exterior found on the Spotted, it possess a gentle, sweet temperament. Matching its lovely disposition is its way of going. The Spotted has a walk, an intermediate 4-beat

Donald Hinke,l owner and rider of DM'S DREAM ON TOO. Photo: Forrest Bliss

"Color in the fields" Woodview Stables – Morrow, Ohio.

Joyce Barcus of Overton, Nevada aboard TODAIN.

LIZZIE CAYUSE, registered ASHA mare owned by Jim and Barbara Alexander and ridden by Samantha Deputy.
Photo: Forrest Bliss

TIOGA, a homozygous stud colt at Free Rein Farms.
Photo: Dawn Lindsay

Makenna Lincoln carrying "the Colors" aboard DOLLY.
Photo: Forrest Bliss

gait, a canter and a gallop. The Spotted Saddle Horse must meet gait and color requirements. Its unique color patterns make each one different from every other. The spectrum of colors ranges from almost solid with minimal white markings to almost solid white, and encompasses all of the hues known in the horse world.[2]

On January 1, 1999, the SSHBEA closed one side of the registration books. Any horse born since that time must have at least one parent registered with the SSHBEA and meet all the other requirements in order to be eligible for registration.

The Association has retained the Hardship Clause, which allows horses meeting all SSHBEA requirements except parentage to be registered. These horses are required to be inspected by a SSHBEA inspector, who will make a proper application for registration and collect all appropriate fees.

The horse must possess one spot above a level line, midway between the center of the knee and the floor of the chest and midway between the point of the hock and the center point of the stifle. If a horse has only a high stocking or an extended face marking then it must also exhibit a spot of 2 inches in diameter or more or the tail must exhibit contrasting color and skin 2 inches or more. (Facial markings do not count.) The horse must exhibit a saddle gait and the application must bear the signature of a SSHBEA licensed inspector.

ASHA
American Spotted Horse Association

The year 2000 brought a new and important registry to Spotted Horses. Jay Vincent, from Manchester, Tennessee, developed a registry directly addressing the versatility and natural talents of the Spotted Saddle Horses. Show standards include honor-

---
[2] See page toppers on pages 216 and 217.

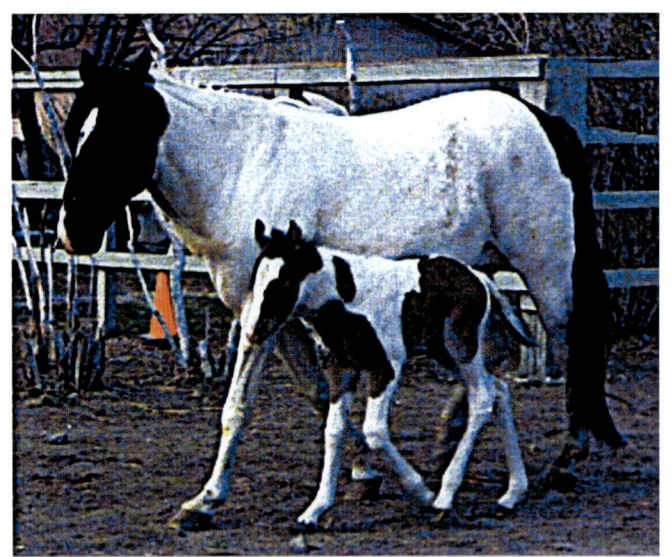

COMET'S MISS JOLESON, "Josie" is owned by Sue Sigler of Reno, Nevada. Colt sired by NUGGET'S REBEL.

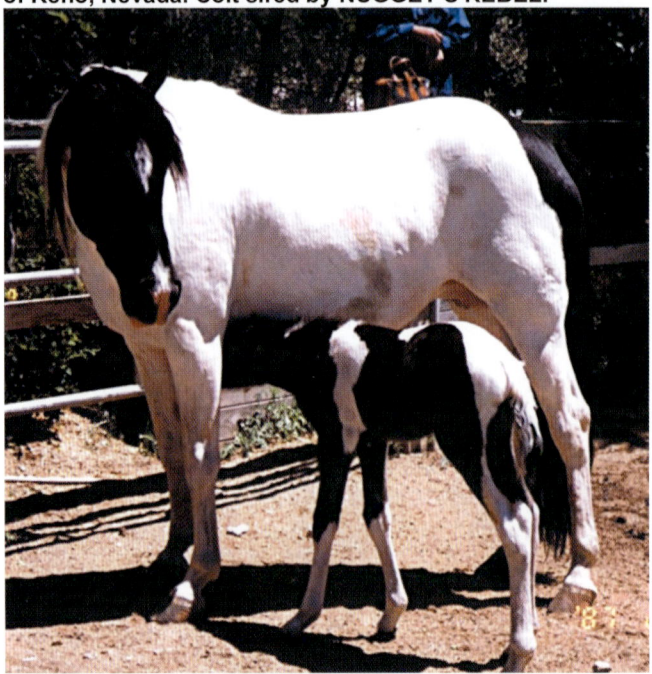

COMET'S MISS JOLESON with filly sired by TODAIN.

D'S DOLL with her filly GRACE. The Lincoln Family, Lake Tahoe, California.

ing all the various gaits performed by soft-gaited horses. Unlike the other Registries the Tennessee gaits are not preferred above the foxtrot, saddle, rack, and the other ways of going.

SSHAW

In 1997, a Spotted Association grew up in the West to encourage the ownership, registration and showing of the Spotted Saddle Horses. It is not a registry, and it requires its member horses to be registered with either NSSHA, SSHBEA or ASHA.

Spotted Saddle Horse Association of the West, (SSHAW), acknowledges the Spotted Horses may include a variety of gaited horse breeds that meet the color requirements. These horses will perform a unique gait depending on their breeding. The horse and rider team is judged on the performance level of their particular gaits that they have chosen to exhibit. One type of gait will not receive preference over another. The important factors are smoothness and consistency.

SSHAW sponsors and promotes a Sport Horse Pentathlon to encourage fun and competitive sportsmanship, and the all-around versatile strengths of the Spotted Saddle Horse. The series requires Spotteds and their

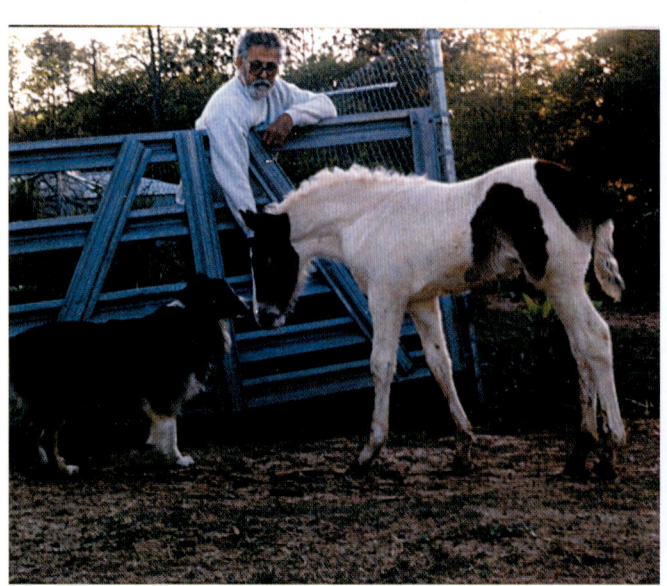

Colin Stubbs with Spotted colt PRIMO, and canine buddy Gus at Avalon Farm in Shelbyville, Tennessee.

riders to demonstrate consistent, well-rounded equestrian skills. The riders will demonstrate the Spotted's smoothness and gaits at the rail; versatility in performance: athletic abilities in running events; and thinking minds over trail obstacles.

Dan Wilson and his wife Monica have been the heart and driving force for SSHAW, and their enthusiasm and organization drew other spotted owners and trainers to the challenge. The Board of Directors has included horse-fanciers from several states, including Lisa Porter from Las Vegas, Nevada; Kristen Lincoln from South Lake Tahoe, California; Loralee Sulik from Brea, California; and Beth Jennings, a well-known gaited horse trainer from Southern California.

Looking at the Spotted Saddle Horse through the eyes and hearts of those who own and enjoy them is probably the most accurate and telling description of this breed.

One such horse is D's Doll, a lovely black and white tobiano mare. She is a handsome 15:3 hands with a natural way of going. Her gaits include a smooth show walk, a speedy and flashy show gait, and the traditional Walking Horse collected "Rocking Chair" canter.

Kristen Lincoln, her owner and "partner," calls her Dolly, and describes her as a bit high-strung but ever so cooperative. Dolly and Kristen are a wonderful example of the joyous magic that happens when the right person finds the right horse. (It doesn't have to be a bad horse to be the wrong horse!)

DANDY D, a.k.a. Mr. Attitude, (by FLASH'S DREAMAKER out of DREAM CRUISE) from Free Rein Farms.

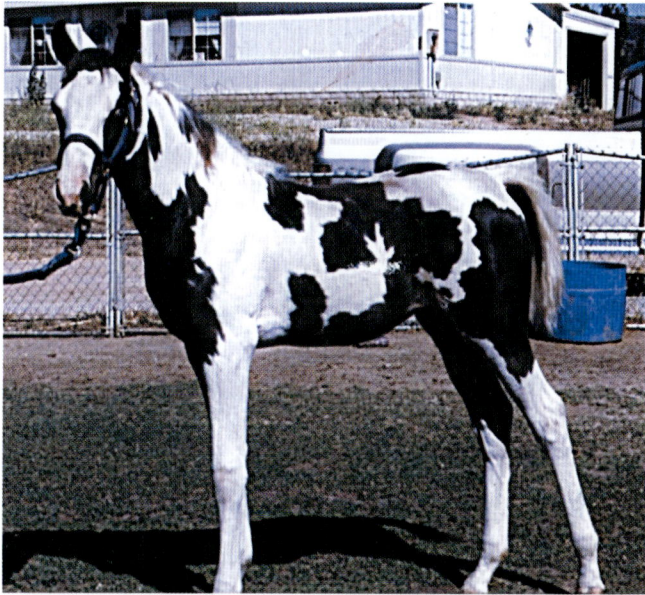

Lots of spots Fox Trotter - Pete & Dawn Gould – California

PUNKIN – Janie Rowland – Beech Mile Farm.

PERFECT HARMONY – Pam Stubbs, Roopville, Georgia.

Kristen Lincoln collecting her first in a long list of Blue Ribbons with D's DOLL. Photo: Forrest Bliss

When Dolly first went home with Kristen, she was definitely a green horse. Someone had been on her back (for registration purposes), but she had had very little training. She was a bit fearful and somewhat unpredictable. Street crossing just wasn't on her agenda. But Kristen had "fallen in love" with Dolly, and was determined to bring her along.

And bring her along she did. Kristen is an amazing wife and mother and executive. She home-schools her three terrific children, volunteers as a midwife, sings at her church, runs a successful home-school organization, trains her horses, and still looks gorgeous in the ski clothes she wore when she was the spokesperson for a National promotional Ski Team!

Dolly has proven herself to be a spectacular trail horse. Kristen and Dolly have spent many hours in the mountains of Lake Tahoe. They climb cliffs, jump logs, cross creeks and even wade in the lake.

Kristen is proud of Dolly's bloodlines, and has raised one filly already. She knows that nature has been enhanced by the meticulous training and loving care she has given to Dolly.

Kristen likes to show off her wonderful horse so others can see and enjoy her too. The

Rebecca Lincoln with filly GRACE

Alaina Clark on ITSY

Kristen Lincoln with DOLLY and KELLY

Pam Stubbs on HARLEY (inset: a young Pam)

LADY'S PRIME SPIRIT known as "GIRAFFE"

Laura Kidder and friend

Trainer of the spectacular TENNESSEE WHISKEY, renowned trainer of Spotted Saddle Horses, Charlie Moore, as a young lad in Shelbyville, Tennessee.

Charlie Moore, of "Whiskey Run" breeding, training and sales center in Shelbyville, Tennessee, riding MISS LIBERTY - 2 year old trail pleasure. Photo: Leverette

Chip Pyle, of Carson City, Nevada with his two Spotted Horses: tovero color to the left, tobiano color to the right.

Stallion, NIGHT CHIEF BANDIT, owned by Ken and Patricia Ward. This attractive boy, with an Indian head on his side, stands at Ward's Horse Farm in Strawberry, Arkansas.

elegant and talented duo often leave their happy trail excursions to enter arenas of competition. Their blue-ribbon display case is chock full after their performances.

In Kristen's hands, Dolly has become all that a Spotted Saddle Horse can be. She has proven to be a versatile and exciting, rough-and-ready.

For the last few years, Kristen is enjoying the role of "show Mom" because her daughters Makenna and Rebecca have followed in her footsteps in the show arena. The Lincoln girls continue to bring home the Blues!

No chapter on the Spotted Saddle Horse would be complete without a look at the renowned trainer, Charlie Moore.

As a child, there were always horses and horse shows in his life. His father was at first a part time horseman, who soon became fulltime when he accepted a position as Farm Manager and Stallion Master at a large farm in Shelbyville, Tennessee. At that point, any semblance of the world beyond horses ceased to exist for Charlie and his sister Pam. In fact, from this point, the Moore kids were learning a lifestyle that would stay with them forever.

As a young man, Charlie decided to strike out on his own and took a position as

This handsome stallion is skewbald tobiano; this describes his bay and white coloring.

Broodmare and great riding horse, LADY'S PRIME SPIRIT.

A young son of NUGGET'S REBEL, at his first show.

NUGGET'S REBEL, known to family and friends as CODY.

Stallion Master at a large breeding operation. It was a good move for him and established him as an individual, knowledgeable and capable and experienced. Later, it led to Peggy, and Tennessee Whiskey, and Spotted Saddle Horse success.

Peggy Edwards bought a young stallion from Mack Motes[3] and brought it to Charlie to be trained. This stallion was the impressive Tennessee Whiskey. The combination worked all the way around, because the stallion became nationally known for his performance and his offspring, Peggy and Charlie soon married and have worked together side by side, ever since.

Today "Whiskey Run Center" trains and breeds show-quality horses with a focus on the Trail Pleasure and Sport Horse divisions. Their commitment to the Spotted Saddle Horse is indisputable; their attention to detail, presentation, and quality makes them stand out in the industry.

Whether world champions or backyard pleasure mounts, Spotted Saddle Horses are extraordinary and special. No two will ever have the exact same markings. This alone makes owning one a unique experience. Add to that their disposition and smooth "way of going." It's easy to see why this breed is generating enthusiastic support from horse lovers all over the country.

---

[3] Mack Motes was the engine behind the organization of the Spotted Saddle Horse Breeders & Exhibitors Assoc.

BERTS BLAZE OF GLORY

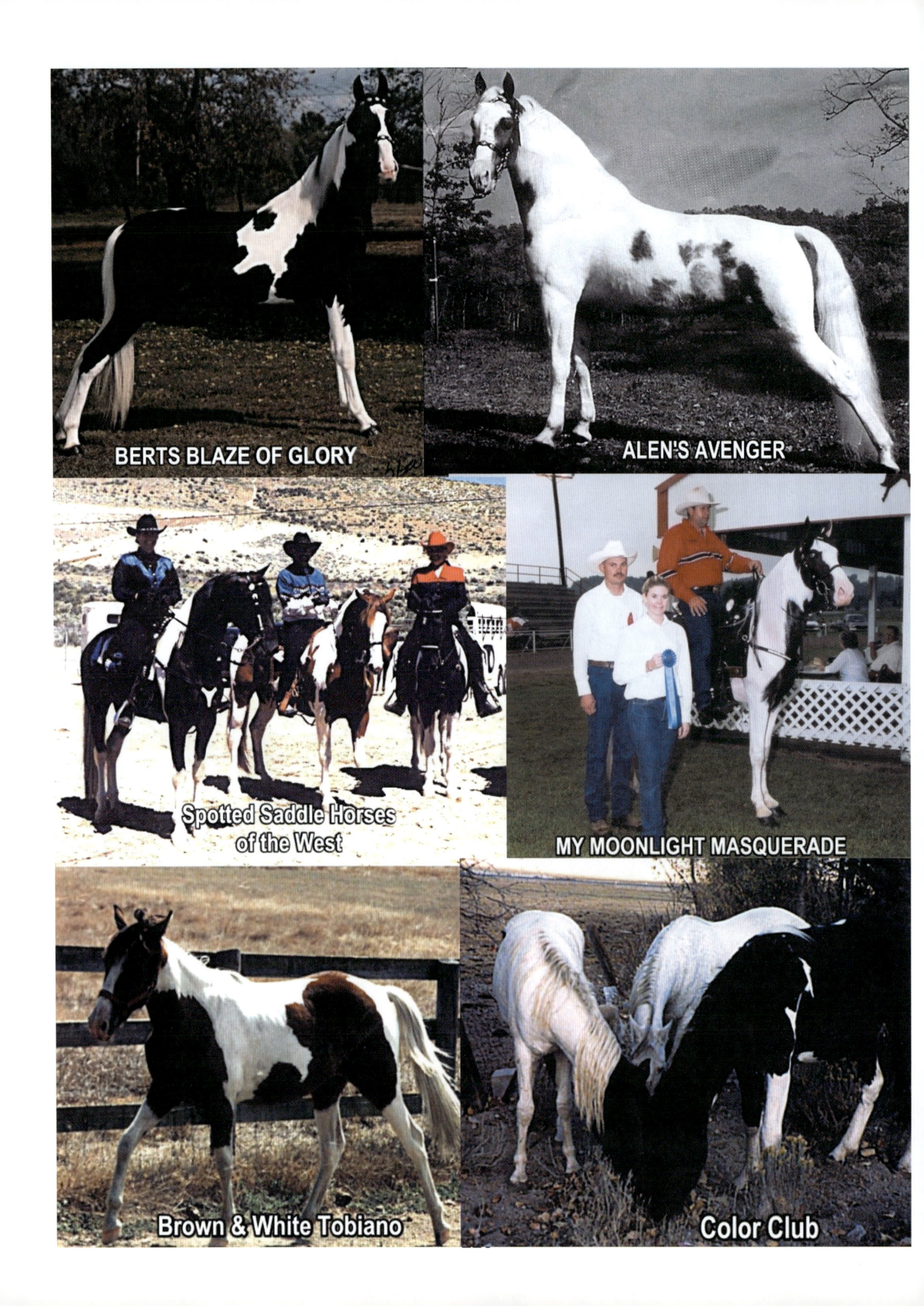

ALEN'S AVENGER

Spotted Saddle Horses of the West

MY MOONLIGHT MASQUERADE

Brown & White Tobiano

Color Club

PAINTS SPARKLES
Owned by: Futrell Farms - Robin Duncan and Earl Futrell
Farmington, Kentucky

PASO FINO HORSE

CHAPTER 14

Paso Fino stallion. TOTAL ECLIPSE CENTELLAS
Owners: B.J. and Gary Schuler

HEIGHT: 14H - 15H

GAIT: Walk, Paso Fino, Paso Corto, Paso Largo, Canter

COLOR: Any color, including pinto

TRAIT: Luxurious comfort

Chapter 14 The Paso Fino

It was in the Antilles Archipelago that a true flower of the soft-gaited family was born and nurtured. The Paso Fino s ancestors first stepped onto American soil in Santo Domingo in 1493. We don t know the exact number of horses, but we know there were at least twenty- five horses and mares. A Royal Decree from Barcelona allowed for the delivery of these horses for the Granada Guild.

We also know that the captain of one of the ships, Alonso de Ojeda, brought his own horse with him. It would seem likely that other caballeros did the same.

Christopher Columbus sent a note to the King and Queen through Antonio de Torres, complaining about the quality of horses sent. He described them as common nags. Most probably they were Asturians, Sorraias or Garranos - the foundation stock for the Iberian horses. They were also the source of the special ambling gait of the Jennet.

Even though Columbus may have preferred the flash and beauty of the Andalusians, these early horses possessed the hardiness and strength to foster the development of a great line of horses. Once crossed with the Andalusian, the offspring of these Spanish horses would display the *brio condido*, or hidden fire, so identified with the Paso Fino we know today.

Within twelve years of this first landing, it was decided to colonize the island of Puerto Rico by letting pigs, cattle and goats go free. It is highly doubtful that they turned any horses loose, since they were still a precious commodity. But in 1509, Don Juan Ponce de

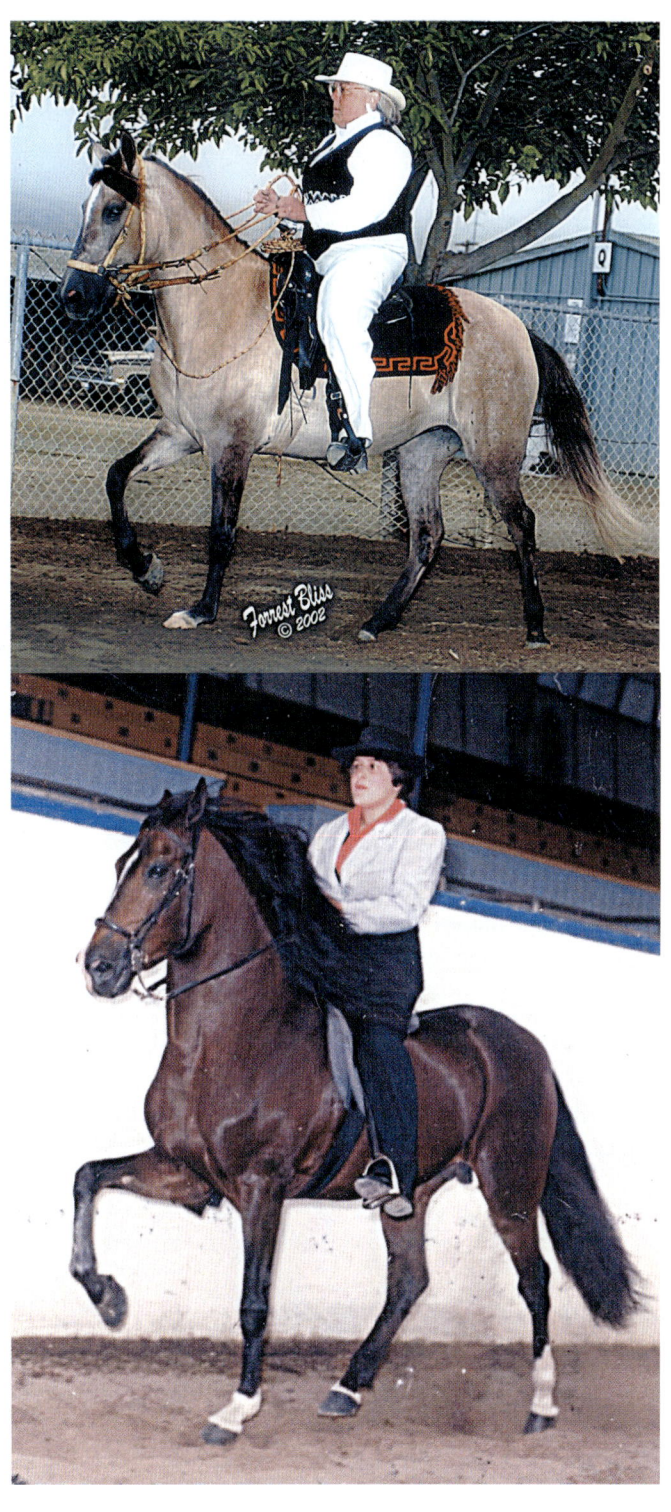

The relationship between horse and rider can be magical. This picture tells a story that certainly brings a smile. Photographed by Terry Wallace.

Leon, the first governor of San Juan Bautista, sent some of his own horses to the island.

A year later, the ban of 1507, which had been set upon the export of horses from the Dominican Republic, was lifted and King Ferdinand allowed the export of horses to Puerto Rico. The colonists were allowed all the cattle they wanted, but were limited to two mares each. Within a year, horses and cattle surpassed the production of gold as a source of riches for the islanders.

In 1521, Ponce de Leon and fifty head of horses landed on the gulf coast of Florida in his search for the fountain of youth. He received a mortal wound while in Florida and was taken to Cuba, where he later died. The true fate of the horses that had accompanied him to Florida remains a mystery. Indian attack, foul weather or other hardships may well have contributed to their demise. On the other hand, they may well have survived and remained on North American soil to become

⇦ **Photos on facing page, Top: EL PASO DOBLE DE REMOLINO** with trainer, Vickie McQuinn up. Owned by Remolino Ranch, in Northern Nevada. Photo: Forest Bliss. **Middle: YANQUI DE ARROYO MARACA**, grandson of **AMADEUS**, and imported from the Dominican Republic. Owner: Peggy Roos. Photo: Tina McKenna. **Bottom:** Paso Finos sharing a secret. Photo: Terry Wallace.
Photos to the left, Top: Janice Russ riding her four-year-old filly, **REGGAE BRAVO**, in Vallejo, California. Photo: Forrest Bliss. **Middle:** Stallion **CORSARIO**, with Carmen Bruce, up. **Bottom:** Paso Finos at play. Photo: Terry Wallace.

Foundation sire LUCERITO, by artist Marilyn Todd/Daniels.

Foundation sire, FAETON LaCE, portrayed by artist Marilyn Todd/Daniels.

the foundation stock for mustangs and other North American breeds such as the Florida Cracker.

1524 marked the true beginning of expansion for the paso horses. The first ones were sent to Colombia; forty more were sent from Puerto Rico and Hispaniola to Florida. At the same time, King Charles V allowed eighty horses to accompany his troops to Venezuela to assist in the conquering and colonization of that country.

Eventually, Asencio de Villanueva imported horses from Andalusia to be bred to the horses being developed locally. Broodmares arriving from Andalusia acclimated themselves and rapidly multiplied. More good stallions were imported from Seville. The horses of Puerto Rico and Hispaniola began to take shape.

Later in the century, an English Count arrived on the shores of Puerto Rico with his expeditionary force. His chaplain described the local horses: Never have I seen a more beautiful or taller horse than those normally seen in England. They are numerous and well-formed, but it seems to me they lack some qualities found in our speedier, lighter English horses. If there were better breeders, there would be more horses; even so, they make a good livery horse, to which use they are destined.

The 17TH century saw the continued expansion of land and horse alike. The raising of cattle increased, and the equine herds were developed in many new stables designed for that purpose. Puerto Rican horses were taken as mounts for the armies of Hern n Cort s into Mexico in 1519, and of Francesco Pizarro into Peru. At that same time, Puerto Rico had become a fully equestrian community. Horses were the only source of efficient transportation in this country without roads.

Toward the end of the 18TH century, Friesian[1] horses were imported from North America and cross-bred with the local horse. The offspring of these breedings were more spirited than either parent, but this would diminish by the second generation. French

This map illustrates the geographical relationships of Florida to Puerto Rico and Colombia.

---

[1] The Friesian is a large carriage/draft horse breed in the Netherlands. It is always black in color and stands between 15 and 16 hands, weighing between 1,250 and 1,400 pounds.

Foundation sire, HILACHAS by artist Marilyn Todd/Daniels

Foundation sire, BOLERO LaCE, by artist Marilyn Todd/Daniels.

scientist Andr Ledrin, described them by saying : I doubt if our Parisian beauties could compete with your amazons with as much grace and daring. Although small, these horses are very agile and are trained[2] while they are very young, in a special type of walk.

A lively export business in horses flourished in the 19TH century. From 1815 to 1827, Puerto Rico exported 2,779 horses. 15 to 40 pesos per head was the price for a draft horse, while racing and paso horses drew a hefty 400 to 500 pesos. Historian Victor Schoelder said: "The Puerto Rican horses are famous in the Antilles and constitute an important branch of the island s commerce."

In 1824, the island was reported to have 38,054 horses and in only ten years, the number had swelled to 43,918.

The Secretary for the Royal Council for Commerce reported on the horse breeding business: Progress in horse breeding is moving along. Existing stables and breeders are consulted and attention is given to the roans that showed their soft and delicate paso. The speed in the native paso and beauty of form during the races is also apparent. There exists among the breeders a healthy spirit of competition that will insure the preservation of the purity of breed of the Puerto Rican horse which is delightful for pleasure, comfortable, enduring, and sure-footed on long trips.

The late 19TH century brought Morgan horses to the Antilles to be bred with the local horses. Most agree that this infusion of Morgan blood was an excellent addition to the Paso gene pool. The great stallion Faron, known by some as the father of the Paso Fino breed, traces his genealogy back to these Morgan horses.

The second decade of the twentieth century saw the birth of Dulce Sueno[3] and other horses that would become known as the family chiefs: Toledo, Regalo and Principe. These fine stallions were all sired by the horse Cayetano, who was himself sired by

Foundation sire, MAR DE PLATA as depicted by artist Marilyn Todd/Daniels.

---

[2] Even though the amble was very popular in Europe at that time, in all probability, Mr. Ledru had never seen a four-beat paso gait. He incorrectly assumed it was taught to these horses.

[3] In the 1930 s, the president of the Dominican Republic sent a blank check to Genaro Cautino of Puerto Rico, asking that DULCE SUENO be delivered to the Dominican Republic. The check was returned, still blank.

TOTAL ECLIPSE CENTELLAS, black Paso Fino stallion, owned by Hillside Farms Paso Finos and B.J. and Gary Schuler of Telford, Pennsylvania. Photo: Darlene Wohlart

Son of **CASTELLANO**. Photo: Darlene Wohlart

SCF THE DRAGON SLAYER, owned by Melinda and Tom Williams of Tennessee.

RAINFOREST BRIBONZUELO. Photo: Darlene Wohlart

DIAMANTE DE CASTA. Owned by Remolino Ranch, and Joe and Jeanne Leisek. Photo: Darlene Wohlart

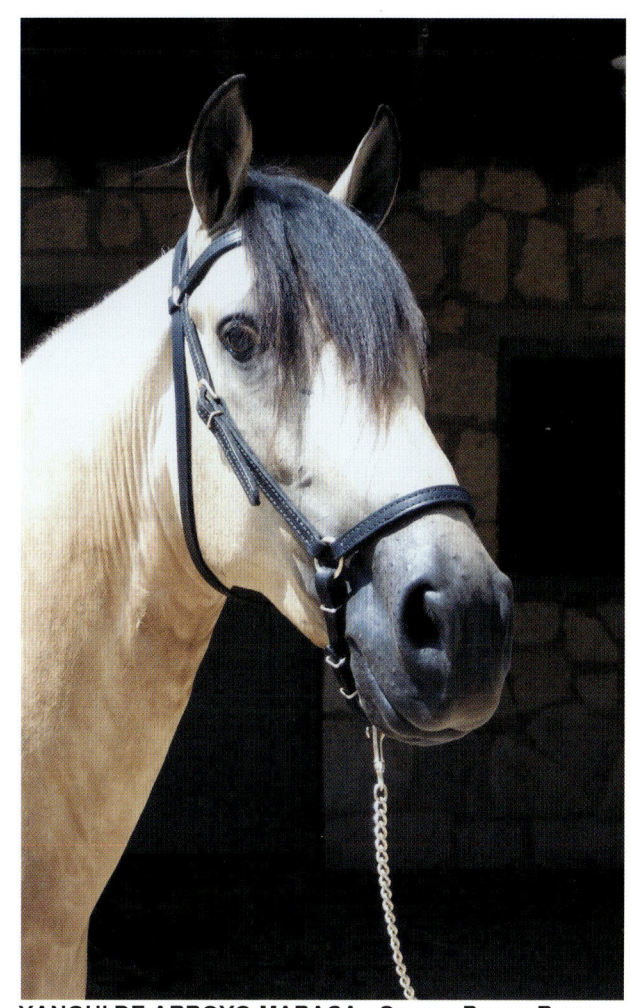

YANQUI DE ARROYO MARACA. Owner: Peggy Roos

DIAMANTE DE CASTA, at a younger age than he is in the photo at top. Photo: Darlene Wohlart

BRIO SADE POWER, photographed by Terry Wallace.

Stallion, CELEDON.

Faraon. Cayetano was a horse of superior color and great talent for the paso gait.

The Puerto Rican Paso Fino Registry was closed in April 1970. This organization registers Paso Fino horses from all countries of origin: Brazil, Colombia, Cuba, Dominican Republic, Peru as well as Puerto Rico. It also administers to the large numbers of horses bred in the U.S.A. (which frequently represent a blend of these different countries of origin).

When the Paso Fino Owners' and Breeders' Association was formed in 1972, they named to their list of Foundation Sires, stallions that had not only performed exceptionally, but produced superior get as well.

There was, however, a young stallion who would *not* be named as a foundation stallion. As a two-year-old, he had not yet proven himself to be the outstanding contributor to the Paso Fino horse we now know him to be. This stallion who has so left his mark on the horses of today, was Resorte IV (Resorte Cuarto), the chestnut son of Resorte III and Cascanueses.

➪ **Photos to the right, Top:** Joe Leisek riding the stallion, **CORSARIO**, in the Holiday Parade, Sparks, Nevada. **Middle:** Joe Leisek riding the mare, **DEB**. Photo: Rick Osteen. **Bottom:** Mare, **TAMBORINA DE PASO LARGO**, at the 2002 Colorado State Fair. She is participating in the Mare Class, as a five-year-old. Photo: Russell Pitts

Susanne Haug riding LA ELEGANCIA DE REMOLINO for Remolino Ranch in Washoe Valley, Nevada.

Quoting Alex Amador: "His conformation was excellent, his temperament gentle, his legs lightning quick, his hocks and forefeet like pistons. The overall impression he gave to all was poetic beauty in motion."

Resorte IV was soon declared "Fuera de Concurso," which means he was out of regular competition. He did compete with Contrappunto and Bochica, other stallions in his category of excellence; for the title of Champion of Champions.

Although he did not win every time, he was truly undefeated in the breeding arena. Showring champions from 1984 - 1997 in Colombia, Venezuela and the United States can all trace their lineage to this prepotent stallion.

His mark of action, his quickness, his style, his conformation and grace, and his beauty can all be seen in both his sons and daughters. But perhaps his ability to produce magnificent sons is why his bloodline is so sought after and prominent in the breed today.

Resorte's sons read like a list of "Who's Who" in the Paso Fino world.

⬅ Photos to the left, Top: CARILLON BRAVO, with owner B.J.Schuler, participating in the parade of breeds at the Bucks County Horse Park, located in Revere, Pennsylvania. Middle: TOTAL ECLIPSE and his rider/trainer German Higuera in 2001 winning 4th National Champion Pleasure Stallion. Photo: Larry Williams. Bottom: Gelding TECADAMA, with owner/rider Lynne Peleshuck of Northern Nevada. Photo: Ann Thompson

Capuchino is a stallion whose show record has never been equaled. Capuchino has not only been on the top 10 list of Sires for more than six years; he has headed the list for two.

Amadeus is a prepotent stallion who has also been named Fuera de Concurso as well as one of his sons, Atrevido Del Ocho.

Resorte's list of sons also includes: Castellano, Piloto, Carmin, Nevado, Contratrista, Cosmos, Resorte De San Juan, El Astro, Romancero and Retorno.

The Paso Fino Horse is medium in size (ranging from 13 to 15:2 hands), and must be thoroughly natural in its way of going. It is a horse of great beauty and vivacity but at the same time has a docile disposition. Its head is fairly small with a slightly convex profile and large eyes[4] spaced widely apart. The ears are comparatively short, set close, and curved in-

DIAMONTE DE CASTA. Photo: Darlene Wohlart

ROMANTICO EL BATEY. Photo: Darlene Wohlart

Stallion, **CORSORIO**, owned by Joe and Jeanne Leisek, and Remolino Ranch in Washoe Valley, Nevada.

RAINIERO, owned by Carmen Bruce of Paso Largo Farm in Willeston, Florida.

---

[4] The eyes should not show white sclera.

DON PEPE DE REMOLINO, described by Dr. Deb Bennett as a true Jennet type.

TORNADO DE GURABO

TORNADA NEGRO is a magnificent solid black Paso Fino stallion with a powerful performance gait and superior hock action. He was born in April 1999 out of two black parents and is 15 hands tall. His sire is the legendary Champion EL BANQUERO CON VIVO (HILACHES) and his dam is CORALITO S CORTEJA (CORAL LaCE). He is managed by Syndicated Equine Enterprises, LLC, Ocala, Florida

ward at the tips. The lips are firm and well shaped with nostrils that are wide and expanded. The neck is of medium length, upright and arched. The shoulders are oblique and deep through the heart with a chest that is moderately wide. The withers are definite but not extremely pronounced and the back varies from long to short.[5] The legs are straight and delicate in appearance with strong tendons, well separated from the bone. The hooves are small without excess heel. The mane and tail are encouraged to grow as long and full as possible.

The Paso Fino gait is a 4-beat gait, in which the time intervals between consecutive footfalls are equal, or almost equal. The footfall sequence is the same as in the equine walk. The sound produced is rhythmic and square in the sequence of independent footfalls, which cannot be perceptively paired. The footfall sequence is 1) Left rear; 2) Left front; 3) Right rear; 4) Right front.

This gait is performed at three speeds, with collection decreasing as speed increases. The first gait is the classic fino. This is the classic show gait (parades, competition etc.). It is performed with the horse fully balanced and

GARLITO, caught in a moment of joy by owner, Terry Wallace.

---

[5] Extremely long or short back is cause for disqualification.

POCO BRAVO, 1998 Grand National champion Pleasure Driving Horse with owner and driver, Gary Schuler. Photo: Larry Williams

collected and demonstrates a rapid, steady, unbroken rhythm of the hoofs. Extension is absolutely minimum. Forward speed is extremely slow, whereas the footfall is exceedingly rapid.

The paso corto is performed with the horse moderately collected and with light contact on the bit. The forward speed is ground-covering but unhurried. Movements should be fluid, willing, relaxed, balanced and free-flowing. The head carriage is natural and relaxed. The corto is an ideal trail and pleasure type gait.

The paso largo is the speed form of the gait and is performed with minimal collection. The same 1-2-3-4 beat is maintained and the rider appears almost motionless in the saddle. Extension and flexion must be harmonious with no tendency to become "light" on the front or "strung out" behind. This gait is smooth, balanced, collected, bold and animated with a rapid forward motion.

Parallel to the development of the Puerto Rican Paso Fino was the development of paso horses in Brazil, Peru, Cuba and Colombia. The foundation stock for these horses was the same. It is interesting to see the diversity and the similarities in these horses

⇦ **Photos to the left, Top: TOTAL ECLIPSE CENTELLAS.** The rider is his trainer, German Higuera at the Virginia Horse Center in Lexington, Virginia. Photo: Darlene Wohlart. Middle: Joe Leisek riding stallion, CORSARIO, at his ranch in Northern Nevada. Bottom: The lovely faces of two young Paso Finos at the Remolino Ranch owned by Jeanne and Joe Leisek.

The first snowfall of 2001 brought out Paso Finos **TOTAL ECLIPSE CENTELLAS, AQUACERO DEL LADERO,** and **FURIOSO DEL LADERO** and their riders, B.J. Schuler, Maryan Schlesman, and Sarah Galante.

five hundred years after the arrival of the first Spanish horses in Santo Domingo in 1493. Different topography, and variations of culture, shaped the Pasos to their individual countries.

If the first horses to arrive were indeed the Sorraias, the Sorraia/Iberian cross-breeds, and Asturian horses from the Andalusian region, we have accounts about their appearance. They would have had convex faces, high withers and short backs. They possessed sloping croups and low-set tails. Their hooves were small, hard and upright. They had remarkable temperaments.

From this early stock, Brazil developed an amazing paso with great brio and a unique marching gait. It's called the Brazilian Marchador. Peru's Paso is known today as the Peruvian Paso. In Cuba, the original horses became feral. They roamed the pleasant Cuban terrain. With natural selection, due to the easy climate and challenges of the native topography, they developed into a new type of paso.

Canadian pacers and trotters were imported to work the sugar fields. These horses were bred into the local herds and the present-day Cuban Paso began to take shape. The Cuban Paso has energy, animation and vigor. It has maintained many of the character-

➪ Photos to the right, Top: Johnny Lanier riding **ZORRITA DE COLOSO**, for the Remolino Ranch. Photo: Forrest Bliss. Middle: Judy Tallman on stallion, **TESORO**. Bottom: Another Terry Wallace classic; "Twig-Tug-O-War," featuring two playful Paso Finos.

241

Filly daughter of ECLIPSE S CASSINO PISADAS: Southern Comfort Farm. Tim and Melinda Williams.

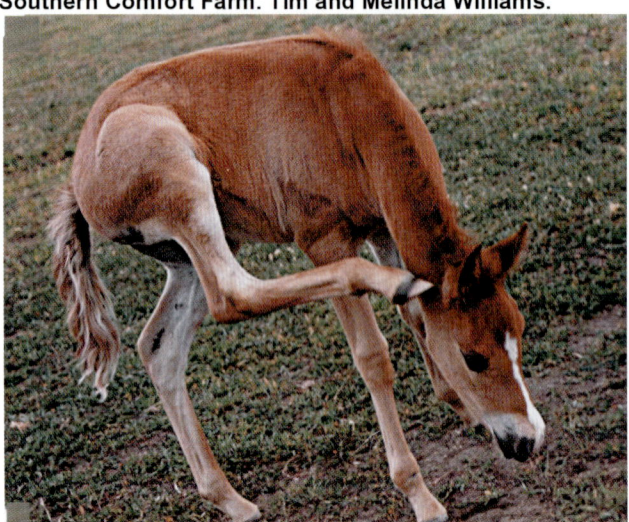

RULETA DE REMOLINO, from Washoe Valley, Nevada.

TORPEDO ESCOLAR, here one week old with his mother, **OKSANA LA MARIA.**

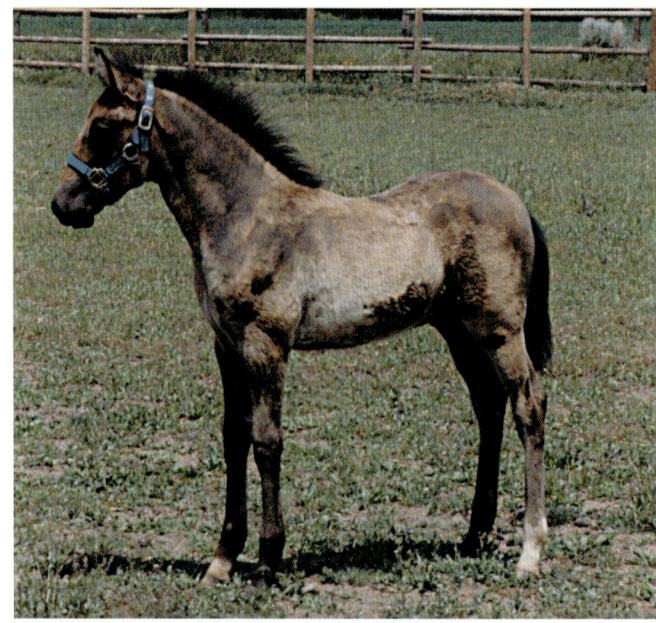

TORNADO son, **VIENTO DE TORNADO;** Robert Haug

CONCHA DEL MAR.

BANJO and **DUMAS,** both Paso Fino stallions, visiting on a winter day at JF Ranch, in Northern Canada.

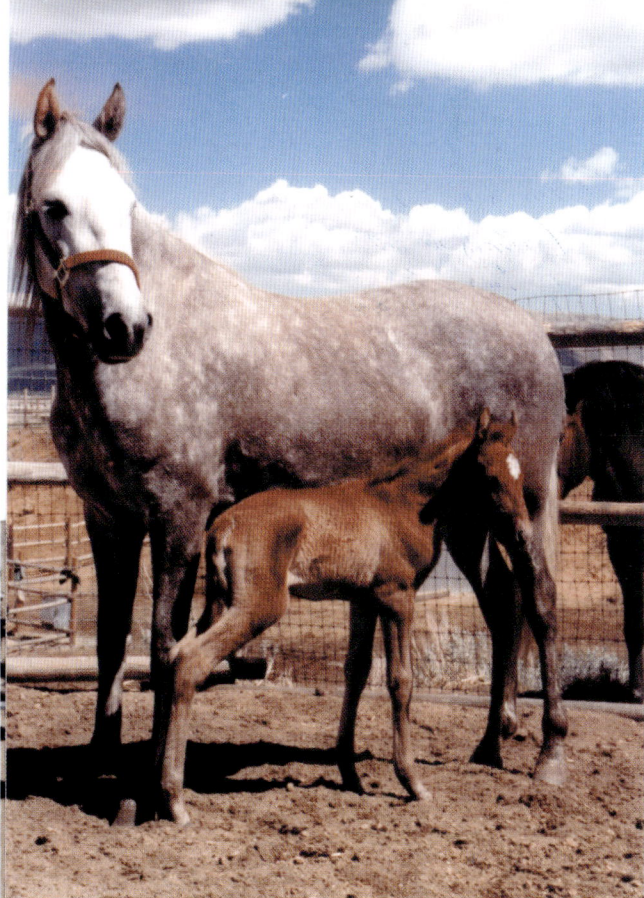

↑ Photos Top: SIERRA VISTAS ULTIMO TANGO "BANJO," from JF Ranch, home of gaited ranch and trail horses, in Northern Canada. Bottom: CADENCIOSA DE CAPUCHINO and her filly.

⇐ Photos to the left, Top: ECLIPSE with her foal, both owned by Southern Comfort Farm. Middle: EZAND filly bred by Legends of the Stall, Toledo, Ohio. Bottom: CHA CHA and dog, Samantha, in the daily ritual to see who is the fastest. Owner and photographer: Mariann Deering

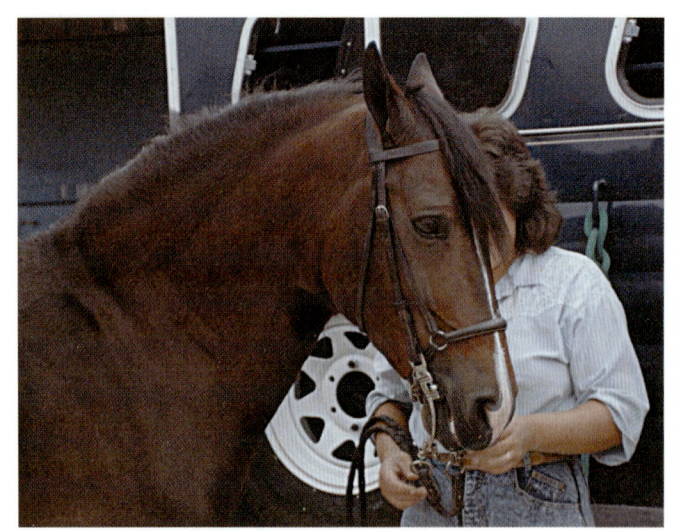

Stallion CORSARIO, chatting with a friend.

istics of the ancient Iberian horse in its regal bearing.

The Cuban Paso has a small, refined head with small ears and large expressive eyes. Its forehead is wide and straight and the neck is medium in length, but arched and muscular. Its chest is wide and well-muscled, and its loin is short and sloping. The croup is also wide and muscular with legs that are short with strong knees. It has well defined tendons and short cannon bones, which surely enhance its gait.

GALENO DE LEYENDA is a son of EL CLASSICO DE PLEBEYO, a top ten Paso Fino sire. He is 14 hands and born in January 1996. Owner Linda Holst reports he is a push-button stallion who can go pleasure or fino, and truly a joy to have around. She would trust him with anyone. Rancho Linda Marchadores, Bonsall, California.

Lacy J. Dalton, at Remolino Ranch, with CORSORIO. Photo: Jeanne Leisek

The Colombian Paso Fino, or Colombian Walking Horse, or Colombian Criollo, was developed over the same five hundred-year period as the Puerto Rican Paso Fino.

When the Spanish displaced the Chibacas Indians and founded Bogot in 1538, the paso horse was introduced to Colombia. With the mild climate and fertile land, the horses flourished and large herds were developed. By 1543, mares from Cordoba, Herez and Seville were imported to develop this paso horse. The Paso Colombiano was to possess the bloodlines of not only the Iberian, but the Berber as well. Within six years, there were breeding and training facilities established throughout Colombia and the Caribbean. The conquering Spaniards kept a constant demand for comfortable saddle horses.

Paso Fino Judge, breeder, trainer and writer, Jorge de Moya, chatting with a prospective student.

DOMINO, getting a kiss from owner Joe Leisek in 1993.

Looking into the more recent past, we see that the breeders in Puerto Rico were developing a showhorse with style and action. In Colombia, the goal was a more versatile horse because horses were needed in the cattle industry. Many Colombian breeders preferred an elevated and elegant trot, and for that reason made use of more Andalusian blood. The Troche y Gallope modality became popular and fathered the Trochadores.[6]

The horse that could perform all the gaits, including the paso, trot and foxtrot, became the most highly prized. One of the important foundation stallions for this multiple modality line of Pasos was Don Danilo. This horse was produced by the mating of a Paso Fino mare, La Diana, to a Spanish imported Andalusian, Lucitano. The product of this mating, the mare La Danesa, was bred back to a Paso Fino stallion, Rey Cometa (Resorte), and Don Danilo was born.

Don Danilo was shown as a Paso Fino, as a Troche y Gallope and also as a Trote y Gallope.

The temperament of the Colombian Criollo is both sprightly and regal and at the same time, gentle. This is a breed distinguished by its extraordinary brio. There are three main manifestations of this. Brio to the rein is the willingness or nimbleness a

Jeanne Leisek, Paso Fino Horse promoter and breeder with gelding, INCA EL BATEY.

LA CODORNIZ EL BATEY with Stephanie Jenson.

Stephanie Jenson getting acquainted with a CORSORIO foal at Remolino Ranch.

---

[6] The troche is a rapid 4-beat diagonal gait known more commonly as the foxtrot.

245

Photographer Terry Wallace has captured a wonderful moment and titled it "Weed Wars." Horses are so very social, and some are more playful than others.

Some horses are more enthused about showing than others. Here OLIVIA hides out. Owner: Mariann Deering

➡ Photos to the right: Top: Stallion, BANDITO DE LA ISLA (owned by 2-W Paso Finos), wearing a jaquima with quick-change snaps, and has a bosal and barada, with a double rein setup and considered to be training gear. Middle: Stallion DOS TAMBIEN DE MOSSY OAKS (owned by Paso Finos de Vega), wearing a traditional rawhide jaquima with a pisador, and a Paso Fino bit. Bottom: Stallion, ROJO TEJAS (owned by Carol Nelson of Lazy IDH Paso Finos) wearing the traditional Bella Forma setup with long reins that have chain ends.

246

Traditional saddles include close replicas of the McClellan and the Dressage saddles. The illustration above shows a Dressage to the left and a McClellan to the right.

CINCO DE MAYO, all decked out in training tack. Note the harness over the hind quarters

⬅ **Photos to the left, Top: A full bridle, or Jaquima, with the traditional woven leather. Bottom: A closeup of the training headgear that is pictured at the top of the facing page. All tack photos, courtesy of Terry Williams.**

horse shows at any movement of the rein. Brio to the ear denotes a response by the horse to any sound produced by its rider. Brio to the heel or leg is response to the slightest pressure. It is not uncommon for a Colombian horse to exhibit all three types of brio.

Paso Fino tack has its own character as well as Spanish names. The *Barada* is the same as a curb strap. The *Bosal* is the same as a noseband. The *Jaquima* is the same as a headstall, and it can be made of rawhide,

247

CORSARIO photographed by Darlene Wohlart

Joe Leisek out checking fences and visiting with his horses at Remolino Ranch, Washoe Valley, Nevada.

NINA DE REMOLINO with her colt, CRECIENTE DE CORSARIO in the pastures of Remolino Ranch, Nevada.

Lynn Bovee riding DUMAS at branding time at the JF Ranch in Northern Canada.

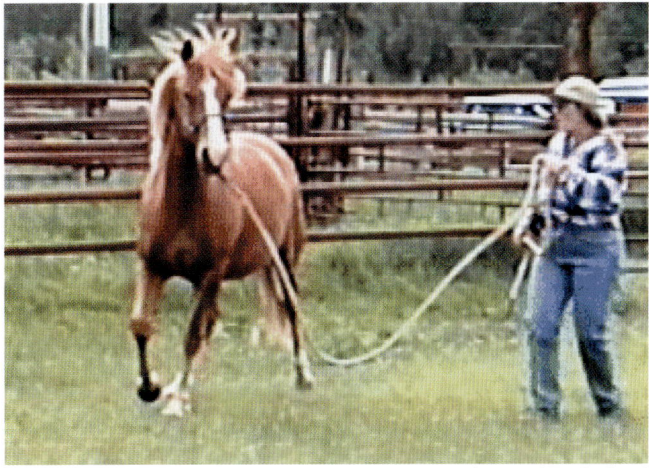

ESPEJA on the longline. Owner Jani, from JF Gaited Horse Ranch, works her, using Paso Finos with much care and attention to their all-around development.

leather or nylon. The *Pisador* is a long lead that is attached to the *Jaquima*, to tie up your horse, instead of using the reins.

The *Romal* is like a quirt attached to the center of the Western Pleasure single rein. It buckles on and can be removed if not being used.

Today, there are many folks who show their support of this lovely breed by establishing breeding facilities across the country. From small to medium to large farms, the Paso Fino horse enjoys great enthusiasm on the part of these breeders.

Jeanne and Joe Leisek established their farm, Remolino Ranch, in a scenic valley between Reno and Carson City, Nevada.

The Leiseks were drawn to the business after the purchase of a Capuchino filly and a Mar De Plata LaCE mare. That was followed by the purchase of Corsario, a bay stallion trained by Carmen Bruce. Corsario won the 1988 National High Point Performance Award and has gone on to be the main sire on the Remolino Ranch.

With their latest acquisition of Remolino Que Norta, a Resorte Cuatro and Hilachas grandson joining their stallion lineup, the Leisek herd represents first- and second-gen-

Stallion, YANQUI DE ARROYO MARACA, a grandson of AMADEUS, and imported from the Dominican Republic.

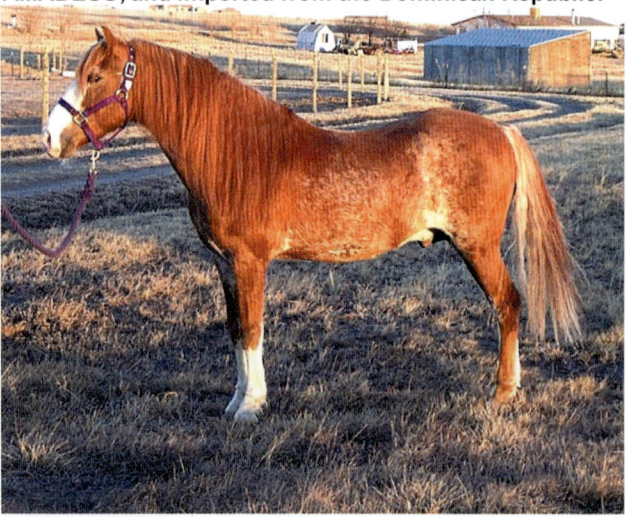

Stallion, BANDIT, owned by Rick and Terry Wallace of Peyton, Colorado.

Stallion, ECLIPSE'S CASSINO PISADAS from Tennessee.

eration horses from the top producing bloodlines in the United States.

The partnership of Joe and Jeanne is a perfect example of what it takes to produce and promote their choice of breed. Joe is a superb rider who looks fine in the saddle as he shows his horses in many venues. He rides in lots of events, from 4H competitions in State Fairs, High Point Official Paso Fino Shows; to the prestigious Rose Bowl Parade in Pasadena, California.

Jeanne has all the instincts for promotion. For several years she kept the exhausting schedule necessary to produce a major exhibition and annual show extolling the virtues of the Spanish Horse. The Reno Livestock Events Center was home to the "All Spanish Breed Horse Show," which generated a whole new audience for the Paso Fino Horse.

The Leisek goal is to raise, train, and sell horses. The ranch is a business, but other objectives are to introduce the Paso Fino Horse to the Nevada population of Arabian and Quarter Horse fanciers.

⬅ Stallion, DIAMANTE DE CASTA at the 1995 Paso Fino Nationals.

Joe Leisek riding stallion, CORSARIO.

PERUVIAN PASO HORSE

CHAPTER 15

HEIGHT: 14:1 H - 15:2H Range

GAIT: Walk, Paso Llano, Sobreandando

COLOR: Varied solid colors. No pinto markings

TRAIT: "pisos" (gait)

Chapter 15 The Peruvian Paso

The Peruvian Paso is the purest link the modern world has with the ancient gaited horses of Spain. Old-time Peruvian breeders claim with a smile that the animal that most resembles a horse is the Peruvian Paso. You can verify this by lining up horses of various breeds. The Peruvian Paso will stand out as unique.

There are many reasons for this singular appearance. Centuries of isolation and careful selection from the available gene pool are but two. The sum total of developing influences have produced a breed of horse that can guarantee 100% that a purebred foal will possess the paso gait.

Francisco Pizarro landed in Ecuador in 1524. Six years later, he was granted authority by King Charles of Spain to conquer and rule Peru. With about 180 men and horses, Pizarro conquered the Inca Empire and established the capital city of Lima.

Denise Boyd and her "dancing" stallion EL PUMA AZABACHE performing in a mid-show exhibition at the Northern Nevada Classic All-Gaited Horse Show.
Photo: Forrest Bliss

Beautiful foals take years of consistent breeding to produce. Pictured are two excellent examples from CHR Eastwind Farms, in Santa Maria, California.

The Spaniards knew that further conquest depended on the strength and excellent quality of their horses. After the acquisition of Peru, development of the Peruvian Paso was underway. Breeding stock was imported into Peru from Spain, Jamaica, Panama and other areas of Central America. Selected prototypes were brought by viceroys from Spain. The foundation stock present in Central America had arrived with the early ships coming from Spain in the late fifteenth century. Ancient breeds such as the Asturian, Sorraia and Garrano were certainly represented along with the Barb, the Spanish Jennet, the Andalusian, the Friesian and Nordic horses. Each of these breeds would contribute their own special qualities to the Peruvian Paso. The Barb was known for its conformation, its striking colors, and its ten-

Lee Bolton aboard her gelding, NIETO DE CHANCHANI.
Photo: Forrest Bliss

dency to amble. The Spanish Jennet had an even temperament and an extremely smooth ride due to its square gait and sloping shoulders.

The Andalusian and Friesian were not soft-gaited; however, their contributions were important. The Andalusian had a beautiful appearance with its straight profile, large expressive eyes, long mane and tail. It also had sloping shoulders and extremely showy high action of its front legs.

The Friesian supplied physical substance with a proud but cooperative temperament. It was a larger horse with high action, elegant head carriage and abundant mane and tail. Its lowset tail is characteristic of modern Peruvian Pasos.

The Nordic Horses were stylish in action with a steady beat, long stride and an arrogant way of going. All these breeds together represented a gene pool with great potential for creating a super line of horses.

Trekking across the sand of the California coastline. Is there any horse more comfortable?

From the beginning, two distinct types were developed. One was an "ordinary" horse, used in their expeditions and for conquest. The other was quite luxurious. This "fancy" horse was used to practice equestrian sports and the riding styles of Spain.

The development continued with no further addition of outside horses until the early 19th century, when Peru declared independence from Spain. At that time, breeders imported European "Old World" horses. Judiciously, they fused Arab, Hackney, Friesian and Thoroughbred blood into the local herds.

Three types of horses emerged from this careful selective breeding: Costeno de paso,[1] Costeno de pasa aclimatado a la altura,[2] and Andean. The Andean has two different types: the Morochuco and Chumbivilcas.

It's easier to understand the brio and specialized talents of the Peruvian Paso when one considers the exotic and dramatic topography of their native terrain.

---

[1] Costal gaited horse
[2] Costal gaited horse acclimated to high altitudes.

The least developed of these types is the Morochuco. It is a strong, small animal of the Andes. It was developed to withstand the rigors of living in altitudes of over 9,000 feet. The Morochuco has a huge lung capacity and a dense coat. It has many characteristics reminiscent of the Tibetan breeds, such as a heavy head with a convex profile set on a short muscular neck. It has an angular overall appearance, unlike its more refined cousins. The Andean has great stamina and is able to climb steep hills at very high altitudes.

The Chumbivilcas is a magnificent horse with enormous endurance. It was the breed of choice as military mount because of its strength, agility and ability to maneuver in high-altitude regions. The Chumbivilcas thrives on sparse natural grasses.

The Costeno de paso aclimatado a la altura, or "high altitude" Costeno horses, are elegant saddle horses. They have been used extensively in the Peruvian cattle industry.

They are sure-footed and possess a renowned "cow sense." They have the smooth,

BKA ISOLA BELLA, Breeding Mares four years and over at Los Amigos Championship Show at Santa Barbara, Calif. Jim Alexander, up. Photo: Debbie Pye

Looking at a map of Peru, one can see the relationship of Northern (Piura), Central (Lima) and Southern (Arequipa) areas. Each one has contributed to the breed development.

MLM CARMEN with Barbara Alexander, up. Barbara and her husband, Jim are breeders and promoters of the Peruvian Horses at their Clear Creek Ranch, located in Carson City, Nevada. Photo: Forrest Bliss

RSV INOLVIDABLE A U.S. National Champion of Champions Breeding Stallion being ridden by Gorge Valenzuela in Santa Barbara, July 1998.
Photo: Debbie Pye

CONQUISTO (AMIGO DE ORO – DULCE DE ORO) with Linda Hallimore-Richardson winning National Championship.

square gait of the old Spanish Jennet, combined with amazing endurance over long distances at elevations of more than 9,000 feet.

The Costenos have small, broad-faced heads with large, expressive eyes and a small muzzle. They have a strong resemblance to - and share most of the characteristics of - the Costeno de Paso, better known in the U.S.A. as the Peruvian Paso.

The Costal Costenos, or Peruvian Pasos, were primarily used on plantations and farms. These costal communities needed horses that could assist in the production of important crops such as cotton, sugar cane and rice. The horse had to be of superior working ability with smoothness and brio. Over the years, three different areas in Peru have developed three slightly different versions of the same horse.

In and around Piura, in Northern Peru, attention was given to smooth gaits and development of termino. Termino the brilliant action typified by high lift as the knee and

Hugh Richardson taking another blue with **ANGEL (FENIX ELIANA)**, a multi-champion mare.

Young stallion, ORO Y PLATA, for his first time at the beach with Hugh Richardson, up.

Many times regional Champion of Champion Breeding Mare, MLM ANTRACITA, ridden by Jorge Valesezuela at the Southern California Pacific Coast Championship Show at Ventura, California. Photo: Debbie Pye

AMAZONA CM, sired by REMIEL CM out of HE LA CHINA. Bred by Crescent Moon Ranch – owners Dale Downey and Mimi Busk-Downey from Alberta, Canada.

Scott and Hugh Richardson riding SONRISA DE ORO and RDS CANELA FINA, with their 1994 foals, in the ocean at Pismo Beach in Central California.

ROSA DE MONTANA, competing at the Northern Nevada All-Breed Classic Horse Show in 2002 with owner and rider Susan Fitz of Yerrington, Nevada.
Photo: Forrest Bliss

The Peruvian Paso Judge will sometimes ride competing horses to assist in making an honest placement. Pictured is Judge Hugh Richardson on CABALLERO DORADO. Photo: Forrest Bliss

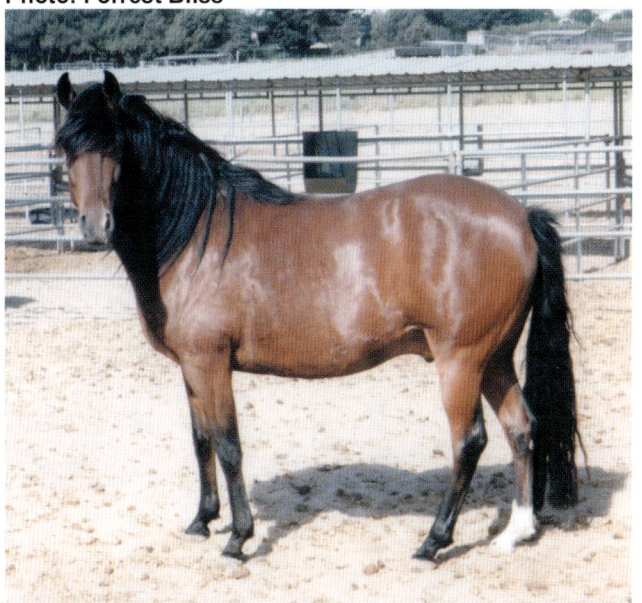

Peruvians come in many colors, although gait and conformation are more important. This filly is both, classic and a black roan.

CESARIO BENDITO, son of NACIO BENDITO-ALELI.

BKA ISOLA BELLA with Barbara Alexander in Mares Zootechnico at Southern California Pacific Coast Championship Show at Ventura, California. Photo: Debbie Pye

CHR Peruvians in Canada. They dominated the show ring in the Northwest for two decades. (far left) RIQUEZAS PERFECTAS, with Hugh Richardson, up.

AMIGO DE ORO (AMIGO FITO – ESTRELLITA DEL SUR) 13- time Champion of Champions Stallion. 1972-1992

Stallion, RDI ALEMAN, sire of the filly pictured below, with owner and trainer, Jerry Restani up.

Filly, RDI PRINCESA ISABELLA, winning a Halter Championship against much older horses. Owned by Robin Posmanter, trained and shown by Jerry Restani.

A beautiful foal from CHR Eastwind Ranch in California.

Palomino mare, MORADA DE RDI, mother to the filly pictured to the left, from Rancho de Isabella, owned by Jerry and Isabella Restani. Photo: Forrest Bliss

fetlock flex, combined with a movement of the front legs similar to the loose outward rolling of a swimmer's arms when performing the Australian crawl. Termino originates from the shoulder, and should not be confused with paddling or winging, which are faults generated by poor conformation. These horses tend to mature at an earlier age.

The Southern area of Peru, in and around Arequipa, has concentrated on stamina and strength. Along with these qualities, comes the foundation attribute of brio. Brio is a quality of spirit that enables the horse to perform with exuberance. This thrilling quality, joined with stamina, give this horse its willingness as well as the ability to perform tirelessly for many hours and many miles.

The central coast of Peru, in and around Lima, wanted a horse with locked-in gait and extreme beauty. Wonderful conformation and beauty of head and neck was important to the plantation owners of this region. As Lima became the Vice Royalty of New Spain, the owners of Peru's large hacienda favored horses with fast, smooth gaits.

The Peruvian Paso that reached the shores of the U.S.A., of course, possesses qualities of all three Peruvian regions. To greater or lesser quantities and qualities, the Peruvian horses move out with brio and energy in their marvelous gaits.

The two basic smooth gaits performed by the Peruvian Paso are the *paso llano* and the *sobreandando*. The *paso llano*, or "smooth walk," is the most commonly seen. The horse's

Linda Hallimore-Richardson riding COMINICA DE ORO, following her half sister AMBROSIA DULCE in her favorite way of riding: bareback.

knee and hock on the same side appear to be joined together, but the feet do not strike the ground at the same time. An even 1,2,3,4 cadence can be heard. The hind foot strikes the ground just before the forefoot. The longer path traveled by the front foot is a key to their incomparable gait. As the rear foot glides straight forward, the forefoot arcs out, then strikes the earth squarely a split second after the rear one.

The horses that can walk in this described sequence, and which overreach and advance because of the extension of both rear and forelegs, are the best gaited horses and are said to have *profundidad de pisos*, - depth of gait, or good thread.[3]

Pisos is the word used to describe the coordinated action of the four legs of the horse - timing, advance, termino, lift, extension, metal (sound), smoothness, and beauty, all combined effortlessly into one fluid motion. The pisos of the paso llano is the 4-beat lateral gait, easily recognizable as three feet on the ground, one in the air, and the staccato "paca, paca" sound, the signature of the Peruvian Paso horse.

A highly praised interpretation of the paso llano is the paso llano *gateado*. Gateado refers to a cat-like way of going. The horse resembles a cat stalking. If you visualize a cat on

Winner of the Canadian National Jr. Championship mare ULTIMA CTR at two years of age, with her elated owner, breeder and trainer, Hugh Richardson.

Stallion, SOBERANO++ from Crescent Moon Ranch, winning another Championship with owner and rider, Mimi Busk-Downey, Alberta, Canada. Photo: Kim Jaserie

---

[3] Thread, is the ability of the horse to begin at a walk, go into a paso llano then a sobreandando and finally a huachano. There should be no sign of hesitation between gaits.

the hunt, you will see the legs moving, but the body will be very quiet. There doesn't appear to be much movement or sound. It is said to be the easiest or quietest way of going, and it should not affect the quality of pisos.

The *sobreandando* is kind of an "overdrive" that is a shade closer to the pace, while still maintaining the 4-beat cadence. The sound of the paso llano is square; the sound of the sobreandando is rectangular.

The *huachano* is a 2-beat gait which is, in effect, a pace. The performance of this gait can be called upon in the show ring to demonstrate the full range of gaits achieved by the individual horse. It is not necessarily a comfortable gait to be used in pleasure riding. Of course, the Peruvian Paso can also perform the plain walk, the canter and the gallop. But it is the paso llano and the sobreandando that set the breed a part. No matter the gait, the naturalness of the Peruvian horse is brought to the forefront with such emphasis that competitions in Peru and the United States require it to be shown without shoes and a short, natural hoof.

The Peruvian Paso horses are surrounded by a wealth of tradition. Peruvian tack is unique to the breed and each piece has a specific use. Most owners and fanciers of Peruvian horses use the Spanish terms to describe each part of the traditional tack.

The headgear is called the *jato*. This consists of three separate items that are placed on the horse in a specific order. First is the *jaquima* and *cabestrillo,* or halter and lead line. With this, the horse can be led to the saddling area and tied in place until the grooming and saddling are completed. Before mounting the horse the *cabestrillo,* or leadline, is wound around the saddle (under the side flaps). It remains in place while the horse is being ridden until it is once again needed to secure the horse after dismounting.

Secondly, there are the *tapaojos,* or eye covers. This item is placed on by a strap placed behind the ears and under the chin. The eye covers remain above the eyes until they are needed to be lowered over the eyes themselves. Traditional training utilizes the tapaojos for several purposes. Its primary use

Jato: Headgear
Cabezada, Riendas y Bocado: Headstall, reins and bit
Tapaojos: Eye covers
Jaquima y Cabestrillo: Halter and Leadline
Gamarrilla: Nose piece

Fine Peruvian straw hats, and both cotton and wool ponchos. The saddle is a Classic. The undercarriage/ tree is shown to the right. Apparel and saddlery are from Hacienda La Encantada and Alberto Lummis from Austin, Texas, and on the net at: http://wwww.peruvianhorse.com

The headgear worn by the Peruvian Paso has evolved over many years. At first look, it seems very complicated, and it's interesting to learn that there is a purpose for each part. Compare this photo with the illustration on the opposite page, top. Match the color of the words with the headgear. Photo: Courtesy of the AAOBPPH

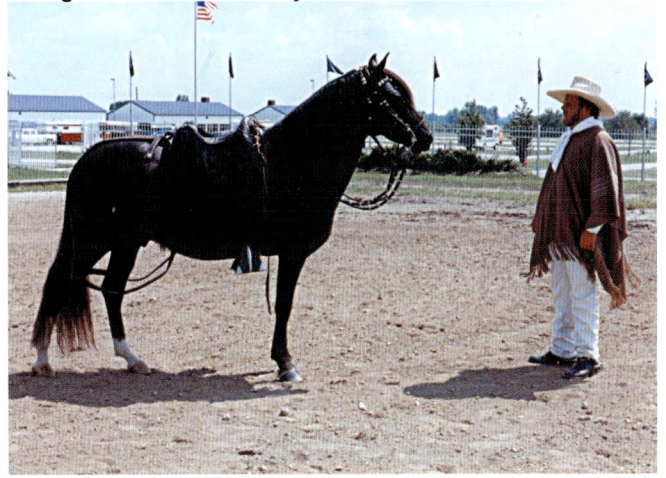

Traditional tack and attire as presented in the show arena. Photo: Courtesy of the AAOBPPH

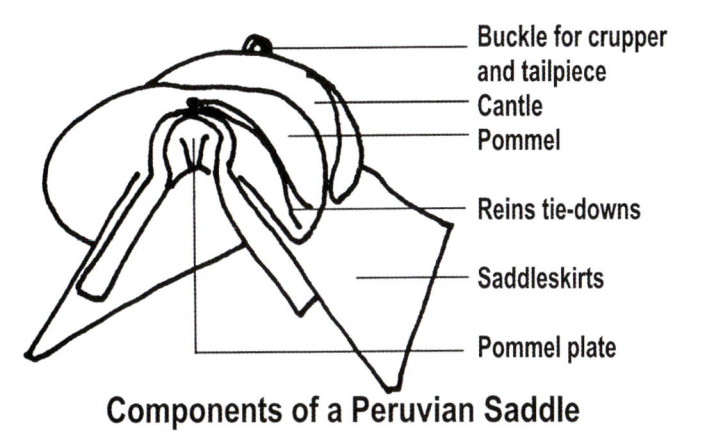

- Buckle for crupper and tailpiece
- Cantle
- Pommel
- Reins tie-downs
- Saddleskirts
- Pommel plate

Components of a Peruvian Saddle

is to cover the eyes of the horse in the first stages of *bozal*[4] training. It also allows an untrained horse to be saddled more easily, or to calm a horse during stressful situations, such as having its hooves trimmed. Trailriders make use of *tapaojos* to keep a horse from wandering when it is not being ridden and there is no convenient place to tie it.

The last parts of the jato are the *cabezada, riendas y bocado,* which means headstall, reins and bit. The headstall is the unit that holds the bit in the horse's mouth. The reins are attached to the bit and act as the brakes and steering wheel.

Before the Peruvian horse is ridden with a bit, it goes through a prescribed series of training stages. Initially, the young horse is started utilizing the *bozal*, and the bozal headgear. This consists of the jaquima and cabestrillo (halter and lead line), and the tapaojos (eye covers). The headstall and reins are attached to a bozal nosepiece instead of the bit. The nosepiece is tied snugly around the horse's nose, and the reins are attached to leather rings above the nostrils.

Other pieces of headgear designed for the Peruvian Paso are the *bozalillo* (caveson) and the *gamarrilla* (nose piece). The bozalillo might be described as a bozal without reins. It fits around the horse's nose, just above the bit to prevent the horse from opening its mouth. The gamarrilla is a horseshoe piece of metal placed over the horse's nose and attached to the bit with adjustable straps.

The Peruvian saddle is unique in appearance. Patterned after the Moorish cavalry saddles of the 1700's, the saddle is used with a crupper, a garnicion, several pads, and detachable stirrups.

First, a saddle blanket or *jerga* is placed on the horse's back, followed by a felt pad, or *fieltro*, and finally a leather pad, or *carona*

---

[4] The *bozal* is a special kind of headgear used for training. It is made of rope or leather and fastened tightly around the muzzle above the nostrils of the horse. It is used in place of a bit.

Texas breeder and trainer Jack Walkins, on his Luxury Gelding, WF PISCO, a multi-champion, and Best Gaited Peruvian Paso.

Elizabeth Graves, trainer and rider of the stallion MAESTRO DEL VIENTO. Photo: Darlene Wohlart

Hugh Richardson on gelding PUCHACHO, in the Pacific.

The Peruvian Paso Horse Registry of North America is an important force in the past and the very bright future of the Peruvian Horse. It is committed to the advancement of the breed and its increasing acceptance by the pleasure-riding public.

Stallion, EL CUERVO CM, by NVG GLORIOSO out of SELECTA PD. Bred and owned by Crescent Moon Ranch in Alberta, Canada. Pictured at 4 years old.

An example of the Barrida. Photo: Judy Frederick Courtesy of the AAOBPPH

Picture-perfect sidesaddle photographed by Jackie Jacobson. Photo: Courtesy of the AAOBPPH.

The logo of the American Association of Owners and Breeders of Peruvian Paso Horses.

Stallion, CONQUISTO (AMIGO DE ORO-DULCE DE ORO) 1979-2001

FANTASMA DE ORO (ORO Y PLATA – ZANTINA CHR), six-year-old cremello mare owned by the author, and living in Washoe Valley, Nevada. Photo: Ann Thompson

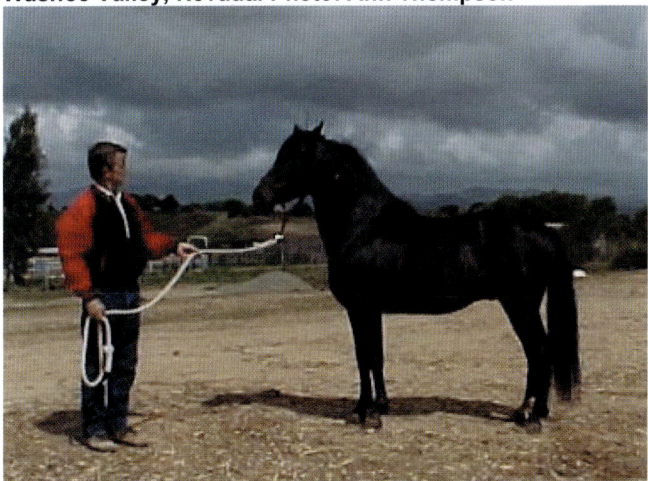

Breeder Hugh Richardson with DANZANTE DEL VIENTO, (DANZANTE DEL SOL CHR – COLUMBIA). This stallion is the cross of CHR Peruvians (Canada) and Eastwind Ranch (California). Photo: Ann Thompson

Stallion NACIO BENDITO (BENDITO DOMINGO – LA TIZONA). Foaled 1986.

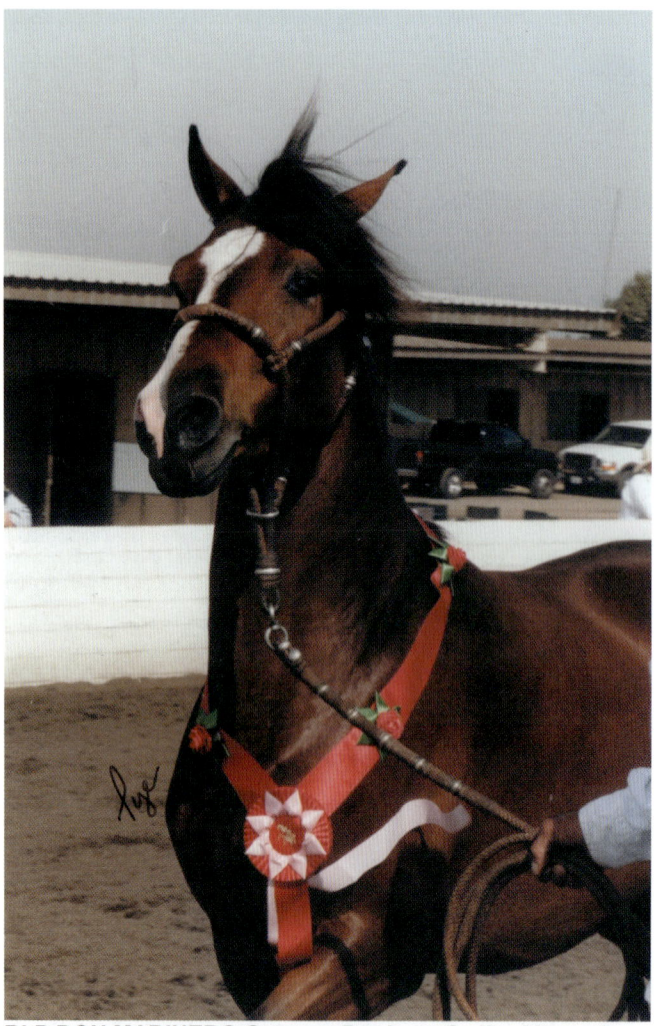

RLP DON MARINERO Owners: Barbara & Jim Alexander. Reserve Champion Halter Stallion, at the Southern California Grand Championship Show in Pamona, California, in October 2002. Photo: Debbie Pye

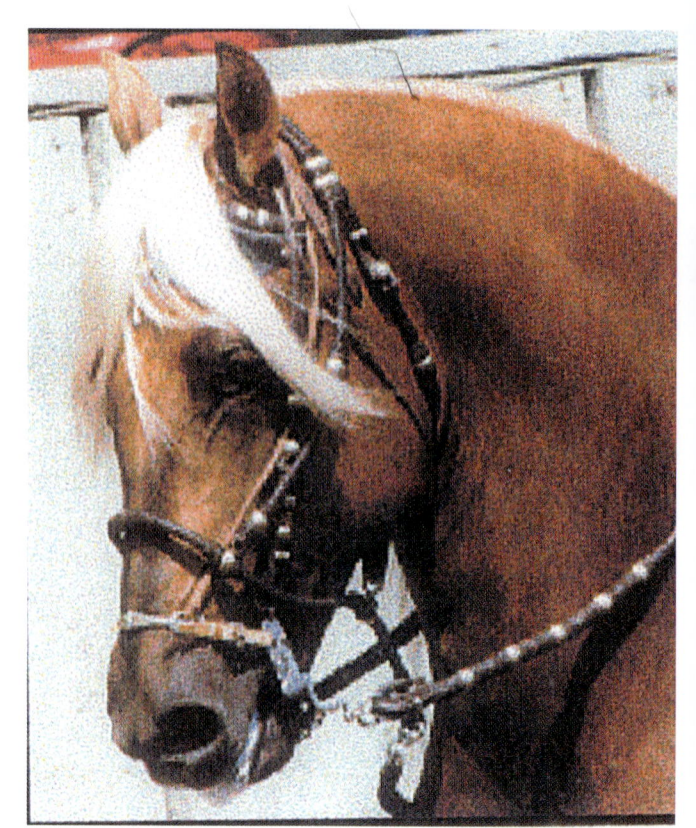

Stallion, CABALLERO DORADO, owned by Nola Giddings of El Sobrante, California. Photo: Debbie Pye

that takes the shape of the saddle on the horse's back.

The saddle itself is made up of a seat and pommel with a square skirt that covers an underskirt where the stirrup buckle, the cinch buckle and the guarnicion buckle are attached. The *muchachera*[5] is mounted to the front of the saddle. The *crupper*[6] buckle is attached to the back of the saddle behind the seat. The *guarnicion* consists of the *floron,* which covers the tail, the *retrancas* (the strap that encircles the hocks) and the *caidas* or *tiros*, which join the retrancas to the top of the floron. This portion of the gear is decorative and traditional

only, and does not make the horse work any differently than he does otherwise.

The detachable stirrups are perhaps the most interesting and useful parts of the saddle. Originally these were made of gold or silver and could weigh as much as 40 pounds apiece. Modern stirrups are hewn from a solid block of dense wood, such as walnut. Many are decorated with carving and metal trim. The stirrups can be most helpful to recreational riders and campers. One can be used as a candle holder or drinking cup. It can actually be buried up to the loop on top and used to tether the horse. With the handle, size and weight, they can be used as formidable weapons as well.

Jack Walkins is a dedicated breeder and promoter of the Peruvian Paso in Texas. He actually went to Peru to see the horses there, to be better able to evaluate the quality of his own horses. Most of his horses came from imported bloodlines and he felt it was important to see what those bloodlines were

---

[5] The muchachera is a small tether used to tie up the reins when the horse is not being ridden.
[6] The crupper is a leather strap that wraps around the base of the tail and attaches to the saddle. Its purpose is to keep the saddle from slipping forward.

Elizabeth Graves, trainer and handler of the lovely stallion MAESTRO DEL VIENTO, from Minnesota. Photo: Darlene Wohlart Photography

The great stallion, SOBERANO++, an ideal combination of gait and strength. Crescent Moon Ranch. 1979 – 2002

doing in Peru.[7] Traditional Peruvian trainers focus their training on the intermediate gaits.[8] Jack looks at the Peruvian horse as a horse, and believes that cantering and galloping are a part of the overall conditioning of a horse. Quoting Jack: "The canter, especially, has improved the gait on my horses because it conditions many muscle groups rather than using only one muscle all the time. In fact, we even let them trot at times, because it conditions them overall."

He goes on to say: "To have an athletic breed, the horses have to be in balance and move off the rear end. The ones that I've seen that don't gait well, aren't working off their rear end. They haven't been trained correctly…and conditioned correctly. One of the worst problems about training is bringing a horse into collection before it has been conditioned. You will wind up with false collection, which is very difficult to correct."

Jack's goal in his breeding program is to breed strong Peruvians that are capable of trailriding where they can maneuver mountains and deserts or whatever. He doesn't wish to compete with the Arabian horses in 100-mile endurance contests. But he feels that the strongest horses for trail will have the quality that can be tops in the show ring. He doesn't believe you breed horses for show or trail. They must be bred for both. And he believes the north/south cross is the ideal way to do it. Jack believes it's important to utilize the Peruvian's many talents when making breeding choices.

The Lima horses come from the vicinity of Lima, Peru.[9] It is the largest city and the *cherados*[10] are more like gentlemen farms around any metropolitan area. They are small, and the horses are used primarily for pleasure, riding and showing.

The Northern horses were developed from the same gene pool but were developed on large agricultural facilities. These ranches might have a thousand horses on hundreds of thousands of acres. The horses were used every day. They were used for transportation from one end of the huge ranch to the other.

---

[7] Peru didn't allow exportation of their horses until the early 70's. That population grew in the United States to around 11,000 by the mid 90's.
[8] The *paso llano* and the *sobreandando*.

[9] Centrally located on the coast.
[10] Breeding farms.

Nola Giddings on CABALLERO DORADO, winning Best of Show at Northern Nevada's All-Gaited Horse Show (pointed for Peruvians), with Judges Hugh Richardson, Elizabeth Graves and Lee Ziegler in 2001. Photo: Forrest Bliss

They were for riding. The best ones were used by the overseers and the owners - the aristocrats. The culls were all neutered and never bred, then ridden by workers.

So it came to be that the very prettiest horses are from the Lima area. They had the long elegant manes and very attractive appearance of the Spanish horse. The Northern horses - though not physically as attractive - had the pisos that most people consider the very best. They possessed the very essence of the gait - the delivery, not extreme, not extreme advance, but just excellent timing.

The Northern Peruvians are known for their termino, smooth gait and early maturity. The Lima Peruvians are appreciated for a locked-in gait, beauty of head and neck and excellent conformation. The southern Peruvians boast of their brio, stamina and strength and a tendency to late maturity.

Jerry and Isabella Restani, from Wilton, California, (pictured on page 260) are enthusiastic about Peruvian Pasos, too. They have been breeding, training and offering top quality Peruvian Pasos for over fifteen years. Their ranch, Rancho de Isabella has won over thirty Champion of Champions awards as of 2002.

Jerry is the rider and trainer. They do lots of trail riding, as well as showing. They believe strongly that it is important to breed

Mare, FIESTA DE CANADA CM, sired by SOBERANO++ out of DULCECILLA. FIESTA is a Champion of Champions mare in Breeding Division and Performance, and a multiple winner of Best Gaited Horse of Show. Owned by Dale Downey & Mimi Busk-Downey and bred at their Crescent Moon Ranch in Alberta, Canada. She is ridden here by Milciades Alvarado.

Respected Judge and trainer Liz Graves aboard Peruvian Paso Horse SATIRA, competing in Cannon Falls, Minnesota.

horses capable of doing both. They breed first and foremost, for strength and pisos (gait), and they find that flash just seems to come.

The Restanis credit their friend Don Faulstich for inviting them to their very first Paso show back in 1987. It was at this show in Monterey, California, that they decided to buy their first Paso. Their plan was to find a gelding they could enjoy and show. Within a year, they had purchased over fifteen breeding animals, under the direction of Eusebio Rodrigus Baca. During that first year, they began winning multiple Champion of Champions ribbons.

The motto at Rancho de Isabella is to breed and train their own champions. For them, this motto has certainly become reality.

After an injury, Isabella thought she might never ride again. But with her Peruvian Paso horse, she is able to ride all day long at her favorite riding place, Point Reyes. It isn't difficult to see why the Peruvian Paso Horse is so important to the Restani family.

Hugh and Linda Richardson have a truly unique story. Hugh, a serious horseman and licensed judge of Peruvian Paso Horses, has been breeding and promoting Peruvians at CHR in Canada for more than thirty years. Linda Hallimore has been dedicated to the Peruvian Paso Horse at her breeding facility Eastwind, in California for close to thirty years. When Hugh and Linda married in the early nineties, they not only became husband and wife but joined their separate farms, creating CHR Eeastwind in Santa Maria, California. What a pair they are! They are both impeccable riders, and they both have all the excellent instincts that make them fine trainers.

A lovely example of stride and termino. Photo: Judy Frederick. Courtesy of the AAOBPPH.

A little equine conversation. Photo: Jackie Jacobson. Courtesy of the AAOBPPH.

Showing in the traditional whites. Photo: Judy Frederick

North meets West on this wedding day for Hugh and Linda Richardson and CHR and Eastwind Peruvian Paso Farms.

Elizabeth Graves with stallion, MAESTRO DEL VIENTO
Photo: Darlene Wohlart Photography

VENTO DE LOS DIOS

ALTEZA DE PRINCESA

A two-day-old colt. Look at the stride!

An orphan foal tags along on a trail ride.

Peruvian mares in Santa Maria, California

A filly sired by NACIO BENDITO

Teeth aleignment is essential in breeding stock.

AMERICAN PASO LARGO HORSE
CHAPTER 16

Largo stallion, AIRIOSO DE JOY

HEIGHT: 14 to 16 hands

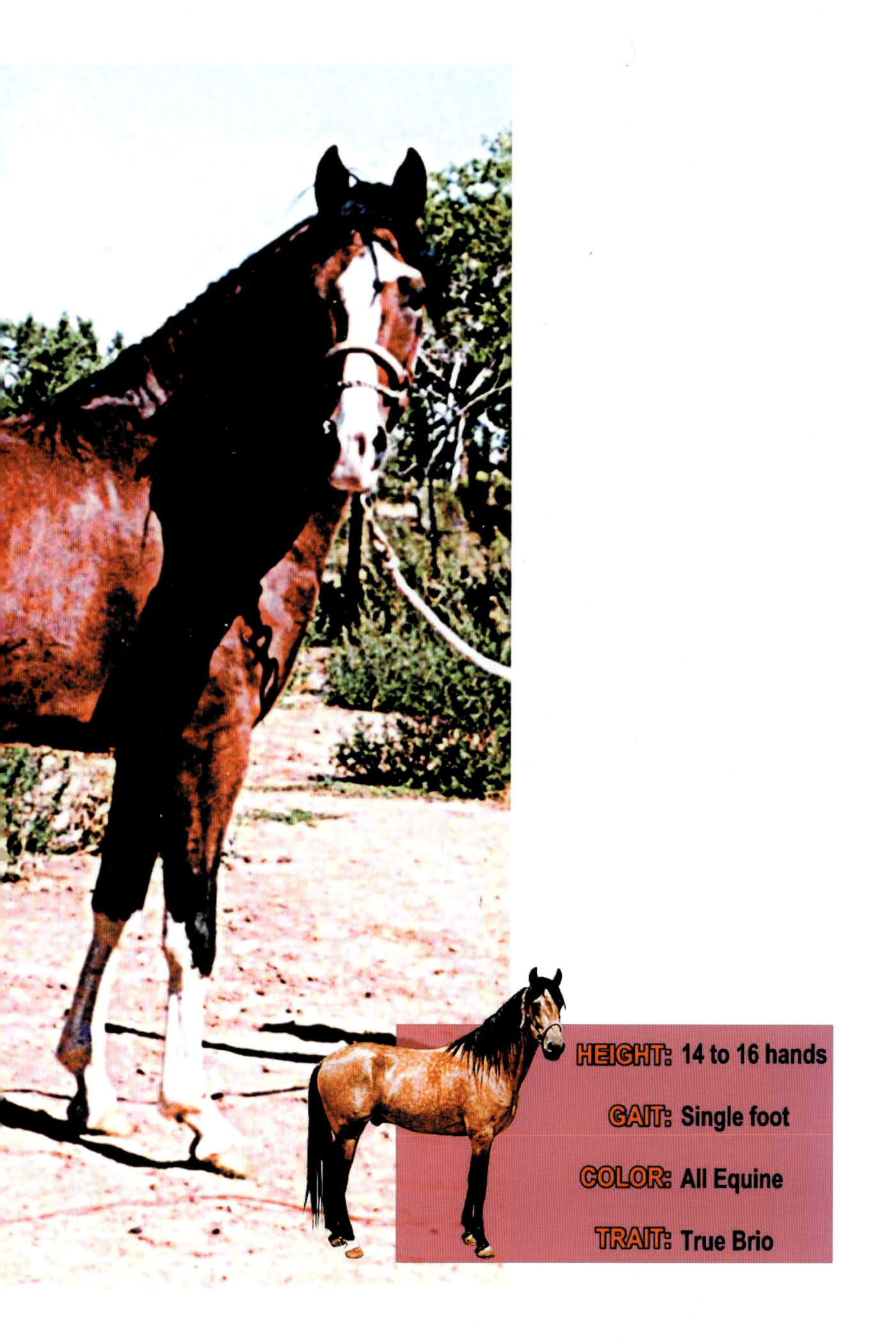

GAIT: Single foot

COLOR: All Equine

TRAIT: True Brio

Chapter 16 The American Paso Largo Horse

The horses in this chapter share their past with the Paso Fino horses in Chapter 14. However, in this chapter we will present a developing new registry born out of the Paso Fino, and one that lay the groundwork for an exciting future.

The concept of the Paso Largo Horse has been budding in the determined hearts of breeders who have been striving for a breed that is smooth, elegant, swift and full of true brio.

The integral parts of what makes a Paso Largo Horse special have been broken down into five main categories: Largo, Corto, Fino, Conformation, and Temperament. It is believed that no one division or gait should be given preferential treatment. Each is given ten points in the scoring system being developed by the Registry; each is extremely important in creating the Paso Largo Horse.

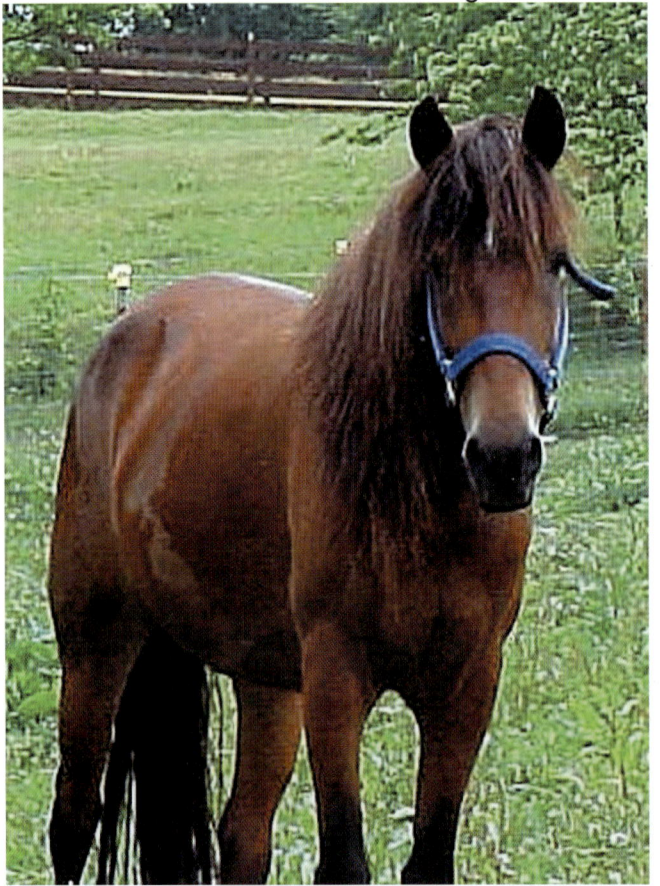

MONARCA'S ECLIPSIA PISADES, from Southern Comfort Farm, owned by Melinda and Tim Williams in Jonesborough, Tennessee.

DON DORADO deVEZ as a six-year-old, from Pisadas de Oro Stables, owned by Isaac Wyler in northern Arizona. The front legs on this horse are desirable in Largo breeding.

ECLISPE'S CASSINO PISADAS, stallion at Southern Comfort Farm in Tennessee. This gorgeous fella is as sweet as he is beautiful, and he passes on his disposition to his get.

CORALS LE VEZ MONARCA as a two-year-old.

Isaac Wyler is at the helm of this significant project. The many years he has spent as a conscientious horseman and breeder have supplied the foundation for the task. At his ranch, Pisadas de Oro Stables in northern Arizona, Isaac has established an amazing herd of horses. His guidelines are strenuous, his direction clear.

When the human becomes involved with the genetic direction of a species, there are bound to be changes. As we have seen with most of the members of the fabulous floating horses, an entire breed undergoes alterations as ego, customs and current trends effect not only showring specimens but pleasure animals as well.

Isaac was concerned that the Paso Fino horse was losing its size and length of stride because the smaller articulate fine-stepping specimen was being favored by Paso Fino judges.

Instead of turning his back on his favorite breed, Isaac began using the same prized bloodlines to produce a longer-strided, larger, easy-natured horse. It wasn't long before he was achieving consistency in his herd. He called it the Paso Largo Horse.

Once Isaac began touting his lovely branch of the Paso family, it didn't take long for other horse enthusiasts to join the project. Today, the Paso Largo Horse is found throughout the country.

From Melinda and Tim Williams at their "Southern Comfort Farm" in Jonesborough, Tennessee, to Judy Tallman at "Dancing Horses, Inc." in Port Orchard, Washington, diligent breeders are jumping on the Paso Largo bandwagon.

The plan was not to shape a new horse, but rather to reestablish the original one. The

Paso Fino is now an acknowledged breed with a powerful organization, the Paso Fino Horse Association, Inc. The registry was founded in 1972 and registers Paso Fino horses from all countries of origin including Brazil, Colombia, Cuba, the Dominican Republic, Peru, and Puerto Rico. There are, however, a great number of registries and associations that have come and gone since the first Paso Fino horse organization was established in 1943.

As we have seen in most of the other soft-gaited horse registries, once the standard is agreed upon by significant numbers of breeders and interested parties, the breed actually becomes the standard.

This being said, the American Paso Largo Horse definitely shares common ancestors with the Puerto Rican and Columbian/P.F.H.A. horses. There is also a great resemblance. The biggest differences are the average, much longer length of stride and larger size attained by the Largo horse. It is also desirable that the Largo Horse be calmer in temperament and more consistent in an even gait transmission. Basically, Paso Largo breeders are looking for the capability to extend the stride, like an exceptional North American Single-Footer or Racking Horse. They want the even footfall of a really good Columbian/P.F.H.A. Paso Fino, the natural gait and brio of the Puerto Rican Pasos, and the size of the Peruvian Paso. The goal is an honest-to-goodness, Spanish-American, true Racking/Single Footing Horse.

Isaac Wyler is quick to point out that there is certainly nothing wrong with the existing registries. They have a devoted membership that is pleased with the development of their breed and the direction of their registry. The Largo Registry, officially founded on November 25, 1996, is simply serious about addressing the needs of breeders concerned with the production of "using" horses that will serve the needs of pleasure and sport-horse enthusiasts.

The primary objective of the Largo Horse Registry is to keep accurate, DNA proven, records of the genealogy of pure-bred Paso Largo Horses. They want to educate people on the unique precise gaits these horses execute that gives such a smooth ride.

CORAL'S CLASSICA DE VEZ, with Charles Lessenger, up. (by CORAL LaCE out of HYA de los VIENTOS)

EL BORILLO SALAGO, with Isaac Wyler, up. This horse is a good example of the desired shoulder and chest conformation.

Isaac Wyler aboard MONARCA at the 1994 Parowan Paso Fino Show. He finished 40 lengths ahead of the second place horse.

ARDEJAR (showing as a Pleasure Stallion) and Isaac Wyler at the 1997 Utah State Fair.

They want to promote the Largo Horse to the American horseriding public as smooth, fast-gaited, mentally and physically sound companion horses. They want to celebrate the beauty of the horse and continue to strive for a good temperament. It is important that the Largo Horse be worthy to be considered a first choice in any situation where a working horse is called for; particularly if a smooth gait would make doing the job easier on the rider.

Quoting Isaac Wyler: "We have adopted a system that gives equal glory and attention to largo, corto, fino, conformation and disposition. The breeders and horse buyers can decide which direction they want to go, and equal recognition will be given to each division. For example, I am a speed-gaiting nut. I have what my wife calls 'a serious addiction to largo.' She says I'm way beyond even professional help.

"Someone else may want a smaller, really calm and lovable horse to slowly gait down a picturesque trail at 6 miles per hour without jarring a back that may have been injured years earlier. Someone else may want a horse with absolutely stunning conformation, elegance, and fire, with no preference as to which of the three gaits it best performs, as long as it stays square.

"There is a best horse, or best type of horse, for all of us. In the end, beauty is only in the eye of the beholder. The main thing is that we all pull together in the same direction. The whole point of the Largo breed is to have a versatile, utilitarian horse, with room and flexibility to grow so that everyone interested can find a niche and be happy with this breed."

In selecting for the Largo gene, it looks like they have started a new breed, but that's not so. They are going backwards in time and have arrived at what looks like a brand-new breed when compared to the Classic Finos of today's Columbian/P.F.H.A. showrings. Actually, they are striving for a horse closer to the one ridden by the Spanish Conquistadors.

They are taking their breed, conformation and gait characteristics from written descriptions of the Conquistador horses and their descendants from 1494 to about 1950.

SC FLA MORANA - Southern Comfort Farm in Tennessee.

ALEXIS DE EMBLEMA as a two-year-old.

Photo: Jim Reynolds

Photo: Jim Reynolds

This intention is to bring the Largo back by breeding horses that matched the descriptions they had to each other. This might work, provided a strict culling program be adhered to. This selecting of specific genes has, and is, doing for the Largo breed what a similar program has done for the Auroch and Tarpan in bringing them back from extinction.

This new Paso Largo Registry began selecting horses within the herds that had exceptional largo, or single-foot, gaits. Much of the foundation stock comes from old-time breeding from such Paso Fino breeders as Ray Free and Henry Richards, who established the "Meadow Herd" of their Salago line of horses. Their bloodline mix was Sorte Bras/Siscocho/Somtre cross-breeds put on the Columbian blood of Hilachos and Muneco.

Betty Klein of Mako's Breezy Oaks Farm always had a soft spot for an elegant, square-moving Paso Fino that could turn on quite a largo. She had slowly been accumulating solid-gaited, speedier-type Pasos for years. It took her awhile, but when she was finally able to talk Frank Noya out of Coral LaCE, she founded what she called the "Coral Largo Dynasty."

More important horses came from Randi Scott and David Lugo. Together they created the Regalo SL Breeding Farm in the United

States. They began adding some Columbian blood into their breeding program from the Que Tal[1] horses. Many of the Largo horses of today can be traced directly to the SL horses of the 1960's and 1970's.

Stan and Mary Wadsworth, of Cabal fame, were the last owners of Hilachos and were major contributors to bringing Largo bloodlines out west. This Cabal blood nicked really well with the Salago and SL herds of the Pasos that already existed out west.

Jim and Loretta Stevens were some of the first to import Puerto Rican horses into the U.S.A. in the early seventies. Their horses were well-gaited, using type horses, with nice conformation and good dispositions. Several speedlines trace back to this original stock. Their stallion, Pegasus Esteban, was a black and white pinto, who brought both color and speed into the gene pool.

There were six stallions chosen to be foundation sires in the Paso Fino Registry: Faeton LaCE and Bolero LaCE from Puerto Rico; Mar de Plata LaCE, Hilachos Que Tal, and El Pastor from Columbia; and Lucerito; from the Dominican Republic. Of those horses, only Hilachos earned a wide reputation of being capable of producing true Largo-type horses. The Columbian stallion's blood still figures heavily in the pedigrees of the fastest Largo horses today. He was a top ten sire three years in a row and was on the top ten sire's list with the PFOBA 11 times.

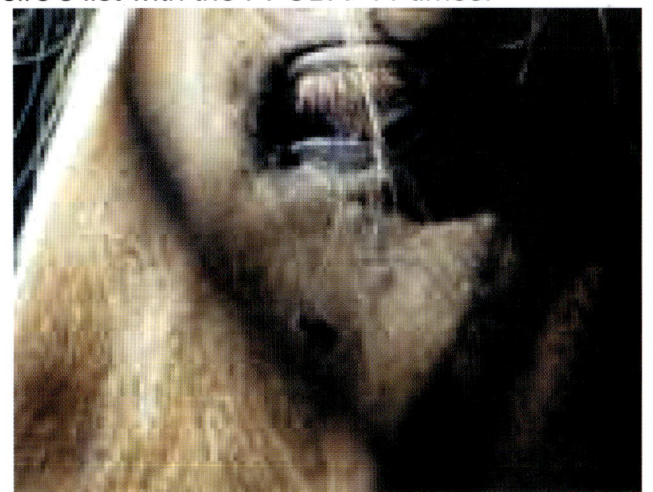

Photo: Jim Reynolds

Photo: Jim Reynolds

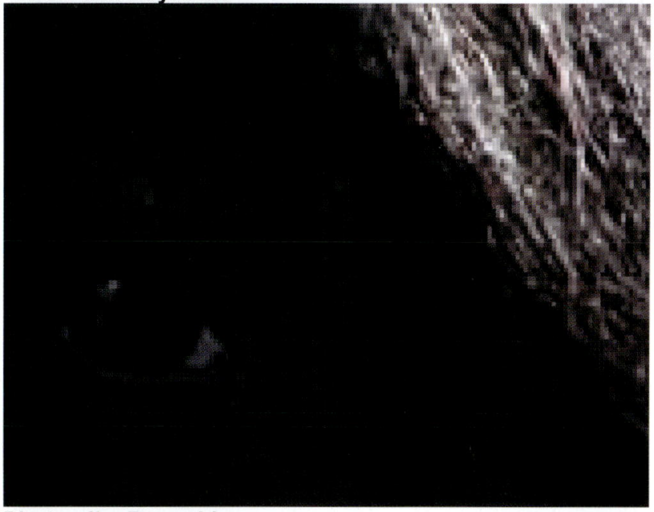

Photo: Jim Reynolds

[1] The Que Tal Columbian Paso breeders, founded by Colin Phipps and Dave Jones, strictly promoted and advertised their Pasos as "working stock horses."

Stallion, ECLISPE'S CASSINO PISADAS owned by Melinda and Tim Williams of Jonesborough, Tennessee.

SC BELTOBIAS, owned by Melinda and Tim Williams.

NEVADA SNOW PRINCES MAKO, with 2-month-old foal by CORALS M ONARCA DE VEZ. Below: A CASSINO filly.

Hilachos was extremely intelligent, had fair conformation, a beautiful head and great extension at the Largo gait. His bloodlines can be a real asset to a Largo breeding program if judiciously used (if breeding lines include classic Fino bloodlines, the largo gait is often canceled out).

The purebred Puerto Rican horses, like the Peruvian horses, always get a lateral, four-beat gait transmission when typical good type is bred to typical good type. The Columbian breeders are not so concerned with consistency of gait, because they honor all modes of gaiting, including the trot and foxtrot. They have a show class for fino, troche (fox-trot), trote (trot) and allow the horse to determine what gait modality it wants to excel in.

In 1943, there was a big annual show in Puerto Rico. It is interesting to see that two divisions recognized back then were the Volteo and the Condiciones Generales (which was the hardest class of all).

The Volteo was the workinghorse class. These were extremely well-gaited horses that were used by the owners and managers of the

VALENTINA DEL CIELO and foal by BOCHICA

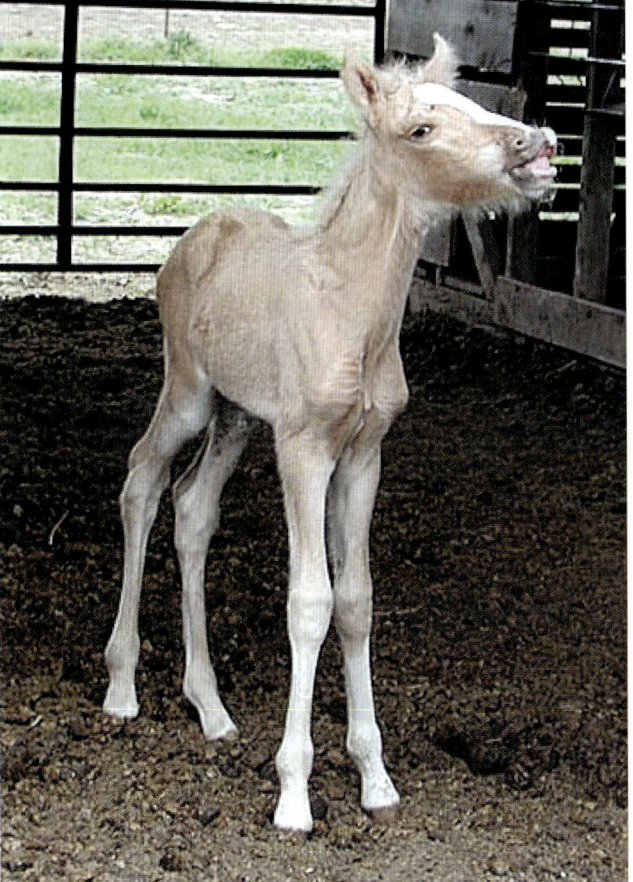

Filly by ECLISPE'S CASSINO PISADAS.

GITORO (exhibiting a desired neck conformation) at seven years of age, with newborn.

large sugar cane plantations to check on the workers and make sure things were running smoothly. This was similar to the way we use a four-wheeler on a big farm today. These horses also had very mellow temperaments and could be ridden by anyone, gaiting wherever they went. They were also the horses chosen to work the cattle on ranches and farms.

In the Condiciones Generales Class, the horse is required to do the paso corto (short step) gait, with the same identical footfall sequence and even timing as the Fino, but much faster forward speed with a stride extension (called "a working trot" in the United States). The same horse must then show a distinct transition in speed from corto to largo. The paso largo (long step), maintains the same identical footfall as the fino and corto, except now the tempo has distinctly increased along with the length of the stride. This is a speed form of the paso (stepping) gait and can't be expected to be maintained for long distances or periods of time. The overreach might approach 200% or more of body length, making this a long-strided gait. All the while, the horse must maintain the even four-beat gait. (A similar gait in the United States would be called to "rack on.")

MONARCAS ECLIPSE PISADAS exhibits stout legs.

RO JO at six years of age, also exhibiting stout legs.

MARIA DE MARIMAC, a twenty-year-old mare in foal.

Now for the hard part of this class. The horse is asked to break its square largo gait without going into a gallop and hit a hard, flying Two-beat pace (similar to the Icelandic flying pace). The horse must maintain brilliance, a good brio and elegance at all times from one gait transition to another and back again.

It took a real athlete to do this class - a performance sport horse, if you will. Only the best applied. Now, six decades later, this amazing sport horse is being resurrected in the American Paso Largo Association and Registry.

As you would expect, the specifications for acceptable gait in the Largo Registry are quite exacting. Here we will share an excerpt from the book *Largo: Resurrecting the Forgotten Gait*, by Isaac Wyler.

Definitions for the Largo, Corto, Flat walk, and Fino gaits as described by the Largo Registry: These isometrically (independent but equal leg spacing) timed, four-beat gaits drift neither diagonally nor laterally. They switch exactly between the two, hold an even stride, and create an isochronous sound. This gait spends exactly the same amount of time on the laterals as the diagonals. The sound "pacapacapacapacapacapacapaca" is repeated. The footfall sequence would fall this way, if started with the left hind foot: Left hind, left front. Right hind, right front. A big mistake has been made by a lot of people calling this a lateral gait, simply because they started the sequence of the footfall from the left hind foot. Instead, let's start the sequence from the left front foot. The footfall sequence would be left front, right hind, right front, left hind. That footfall sequence description does not make this a diagonal gait. If the gait is executed isometrically, both footfall descriptions are describing an even, four-beat gait with no drifting, diagonally or laterally. These two footfall descriptions also describe the perfect equine flat walk that is done correctly. The only difference in footfall between a walk and largo gait would be tempo and stride extension.

"A Largo horse, in proper gait, would go from a flat walk (approximately four miles per hour), to fino (approximately 0-3 miles per hour) or corto (approximately 5 to 13-15 miles per hour, depending on the horse). Upon reaching 13-15 miles per hour, the horse can no longer maintain two and sometimes three feet on the ground at all times as in a walk, fino and corto. To pick up more speed with an increased tempo and extension of stride, and still remain isochronal, the horse now keeps just one foot (single foot) on the ground at a time, but it is still isochronous.

"You have now reached the largo (single-foot) gait. This gait is done in the 'up position.' For example, the whole neck and back is upright and the head has a slight tuck to it. The horse seems to move effortlessly, even though there is incredible walking speed evident. Even with this speed, the ears are still in the perked-forward, or the paying-attention-to-things position. The Largo Horse enjoys this gait, and it shows in the horse's demeanor.

Continuing, with a description of the Carrera Paso Largo:

"Translation of this gait is 'racing long step.' The transition from fast largo to carrera is when the horse goes from it's 'up' position to the 'get down' position. Length of stride and tempo increase considerably. The whole demeanor of the horse changes, even though the synchronous footfall remains isochronous. The neck and back lowers, the neck stretches out, and the nose stretches out to its utmost. The ears sweep back and remain still in utter concentration and effort. The length of stride increases substantially and the tempo increases dramatically. The transition from largo to carrera is much more spectacular than the transition from corto to largo and can rarely be done in an arena. The Paso Largo horse that can execute the carrera paso largo is extremely rare."

When asked what he looks for in a young horse, Wyler is quite specific: "As a breeder, look for foals that gait evenly and naturally as youngsters; then, as they grow awkwardly over the next two to three years, look for a long, bold trot and horse, rather than a pony-looking gallop with athletic ability. In

⇨ **PHOTOS TO THE RIGHT. Top: AIRIOSO DE JOY,** exhibiting an elegant Spanish look. Middle: **LA ARTISTE PISADAS,** a four-yea-old exhibiting a long, round hip. Bottom: **MONARCA'S DEL ORA,** from Southern Comfort Farm in Jonesborough, Tennessee.

GITONO SALAGO, a seven-year-old, performing the corto in western tack, with Isaac Wyler, up.

Isaac Wyler racing MONARCA, at the Bozeman Montana, speed-gait challenge.

MONARCA, exhibiting a natural high action.

Pole bending with Isaac Wyler and MONARCA.

A great display of color at Pisadas De Oro Stables.

Melinda and Tim Williams enjoying a trail ride at their Jonesborough, Tennessee, Southern Comfort Farm.

284

Isaac Wyler and MONARCA, competing in the Speed Gait Challenge at Bozeman, Montana, in 1996.

Judy Tallman aboard her stallion TESORO DE LA DANZA, at her Port Orchard, Washington farm, Dancing Horses, Inc.

Puerto Rican stallion MONARCA, at 20 years of age. He was Puerto Rican Island Champion four times.

American Paso Largo stallion MONARCA, competing in a driving class, with Isaac Wyler driving.

American Paso Largo stallion MONARCA performing a picture-perfect largo gait.

285

CABARITA SALAGO in an all-breed color class.

the pasture, watch for a few steps of a good gait as they are coming down from a galloping speed or perhaps gaiting out of the way to avoid another horse's kick. Being spooked or excited might bring out the gait for a short distance. Those seem to make the best corto/largo horses.

Avoid those horses in pasture that tend to gait everywhere they go and have trouble running like a normal horse. They tend to have a pacey-looking (extremely 4-beat) gallop and usually have a short, choppy stride. In fact, they don't like to gallop at all if they can help it. That short string type of horse tends to drift laterally quite quickly under saddle. It's very difficult to get the elegant, stylish look and ultra-smooth, even gait out of them[2], (the trademark of the Largo Horse).

What are the desired qualities in conformation in a Largo Horse? Well, the first impression of the horse should indicate an elegant, proud, Spanish look. It should be stout, deep-bodied, compact, and long-enduring looking, with attractive conformation as well as an alert, intelligent expression in the eyes. The inherent brio in the horse should be expressed as a courageous animal with presence and lots of heart. Movement should be natural, stylish, with long, fluid action, executed with obvious agility and sure-footedness. The horse should use its head and neck carriage, the whole shoulder, back and entire leg to create a natural, elastic, flexible, free-flowing movement that's breath-taking to watch and addictive to ride.

The Registry wants round, broad front hooves, suitable for a utilitarian horse, and adequate for the size of the animal. The legs,

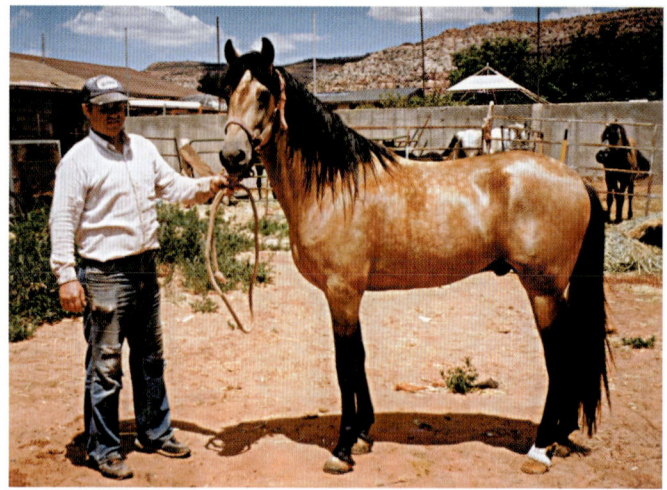

CORALS MONARCA DE VEZ at eight years old, with the desired "uphill to withers" build.

Parading with a stallion and mares with foals at their side.

Judy Tallman enjoying a ride on her lovely Port Orchard, Washington farm. TESORO, a true "using" stallion, and her "best friend."

---

[2] "It's always easier to get a strong gaited horse that drifts slightly diagonally to gait squarely than it is to get a strong gaited horse that drifts slightly laterally to gait squarely under saddle, especially with any animation or speed." Isaac Wyler

Stallion CORALS MONARCA DE VEZ with Isaac Wyler.

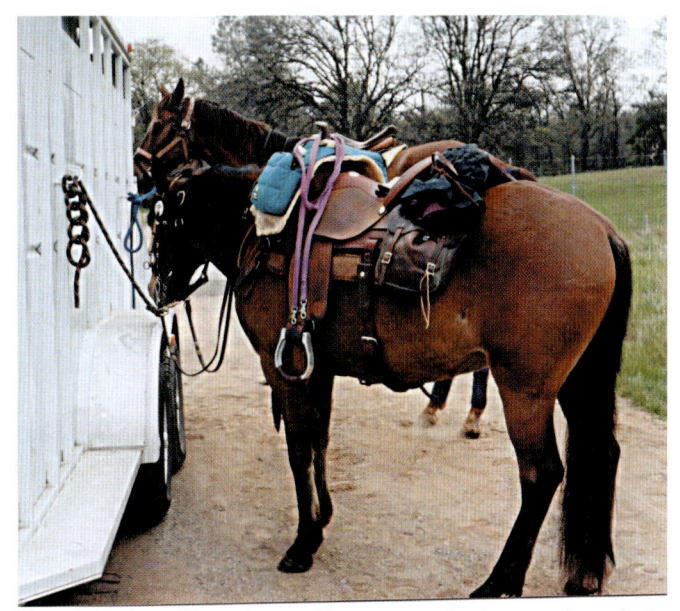

Two American Paso Largo Horses, packed up and ready to go, one in Western tack, the other in English tack.

Tim Williams at his Southern Comfort Farm in Tennessee.

when viewed from any angle, must be clean and straight. They must have substance and still remain refined.

The back is slightly short to medium in length. It is close-coupled and well-muscled, with a well-sprung rib cage. The hindquarters are to be moderately muscled, with a well-rounded appearance, and the chest is of medium width, with long, moderately muscled shoulders that are well-laid back (allowing for a natural, high-neck carriage that ties in well with the mid-section). The neck is strong and well-muscled, medium to slightly long in length. The head is of medium length allowing for a straight or slightly concave profile, with good width between eyes that are large, round and expressively alert. Their broad cheek gives a triangular look to the head, which tapers to a refined muzzle with firm lips and large nostrils. The ears are medium to slightly short with moderate curving in at the tips.

The American Paso Largo Horse will ideally stand at 14:3 hands and weigh between 800 and 1,000 pounds. Being Spanish-bred horses, all colors were imported from Spain and can be represented, as are all equine markings, eye color, and dorsal stripes.

The temperament is extremely important. These horses should possess a willing disposition and sweet temperament. They are gentle at hand, but spirited under saddle. Enjoying the company of people is a highly desirable trait. Good Paso Largos are energetic, exuberant and courageous horses with presence and lots of endurance, vigor, and heart. They are reluctant to quit on you, and will always give 100% at any task required of them. They tend to mature late (six or seven years old) and are generally usable into their twenties, living into their thirties. They are easy keepers and are successful as breeding stock well into their twenties. Sofia la Negra, a direct

Roundup at Rush Lake.

Stallion TESORO DE LA DANZA, a real Dancing Treasure.

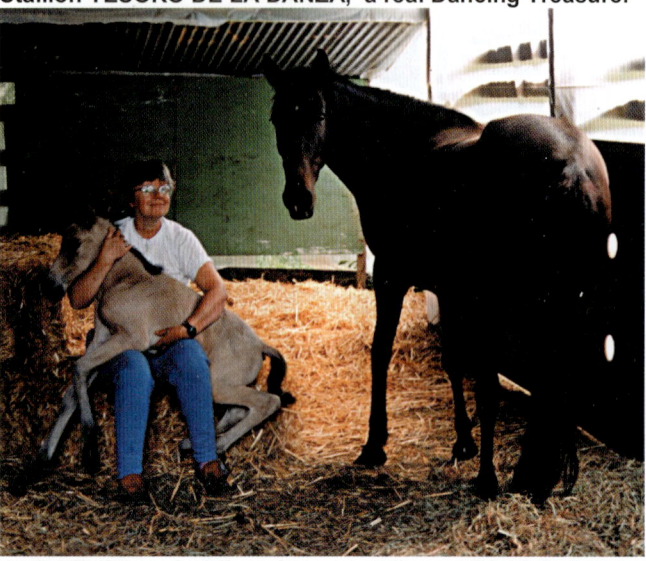

Judy Tallman holding future stallion TESORO DE LA DANZA as a newborn.

SCF ALICIA PISADA, a Paso Largo mare.

Dulce Sueno daughter, was said to have had her son Marichal at the ripe old age of 36!

The Registry itself continues not only to continue registering horses but will maintain a library of video trials for the breeding stock, generated from a non-mandatory breeding stock trial. The Paso Largo registries breeding stock scoring system is based on the performance of each horse's gait, movement, conformation, and temperament and will be rated and evaluated on a scale of one to ten against the breed standard at the trials. A horse can be reevaluated and rated higher, several times if need be, but having achieved a peak rating, they cannot be rated or scored lower than their highest rating. These trials are optional and being conducted so that breeders may have a serious tool to work with while selecting breeding stock.

The registry's shows will be as unique as their horses, with one-mile speed-gait races, gaited endurance races, competitive trail, gymkhana, and fun classes. Impeccable and consistent gait supported by vigorous endurance will be the desired goal. A highlight of their shows takes place the day before ring competition begins, with a structured trailride in which all competitors *and* the judge participate.

The Largo horse is also gaining a reputation in speed gaiting circles around the United States, especially where emphasis is placed on square/even gait. Through these competitions, the American equine-loving public will see the product being fostered in the Largo horse that is considered by many to be

Isaac Wyler and MONARCA (far left) participating in an all-breed show in California.

the ultimate pleasure and trail horse.

Judy Tallman, an enthusiastic breeder and promoter of the Paso Largo horse, is certainly one who supports this idea. Judy had wanted a horse all her life, but her time and energies were spent raising a family. This didn't leave much time or money to realize her dream. Then, when she was forty-eight years old, she thought her hopes were being fulfilled when she rescued a 16-hand Standardbred. He had been trained for the track and thought his only speed was full-tilt. Needless to say, he was not an ideal mount for a beginner rider. Predictably, she fell off him, broke her back and sustained a concussion. Her search for a calm, smooth horse began in earnest.

She was initially attracted to the Paso Fino horse because she felt they were the smoothest. Further investigation found there to be two types of Paso Finos – the hot little horses bred for the show ring, and the larger, calmer horses bred, as the old-time cowboys used to say, as "using" horses with a great largo. These Largo-type horses were extremely versatile and could go all day at about the speed of the trot, only smooth. This was the kind of horse she wanted.

She found Bonita Estrella, a wonderful mare who was an Hilachas granddaughter out of an excellent dam. She was bred to a Majestuoso son when she went to live with Judy. Bonita was sweet, elegant, smooth and extremely fast. She could go all day long on the trails and still be ready to race at the end of the ride.

Her son, Tesoro de la Danza, was born

Stallion, EL BORILLO SALAGO performing the corto.

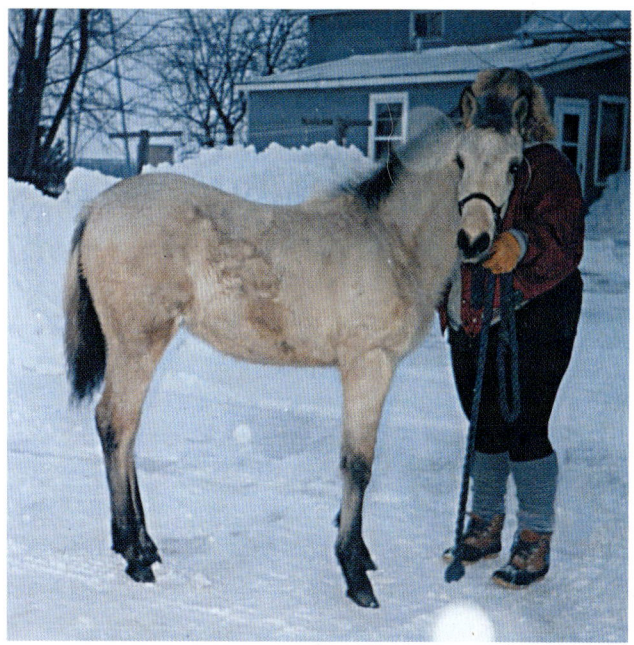

ARIZONA STEPPER at 6 months, in the Wisconsin snow.

FINESS REGALO SL exhibiting the desired smooth point of hip.

QUISADILLA PISADAS, a yearling exhibiting a natural largo.

on August 23, 1995. Quoting Judy: "He was so beautiful and charismatic! My 'Dancing Treasure!' From the time he was born, he was my friend. Baby Tesoro napped with his head in my lap."

As Tesoro grew older, he developed a glorious grulla color with a gorgeous head and outstanding conformation. Judy felt blessed because Tesoro stayed just as sweet and loving as when he was a foal. He had plenty of brio, and she had misgivings about starting her own horse under saddle, but they went slowly with the natural horsemanship methods, using trust and understanding.

Tesoro has definitely learned to trust Judy. He takes her anywhere she wants to go for as long as she wants, and he does it with style and grace.

Another story of horse love and dreams comes from Jo Seabold. Jo had loved horses all her life and dreamed that one day she might have one of her own. When she was 60, she purchased not one, but four Quarter Horses that she enjoyed for two years before the bouncing and jarring got the best of her. Facing serious health problems, Jo followed her doctors advice, and gave up her horses.

No longer able to ride, Jo satisfied her passion for horses by poring over horse-re-

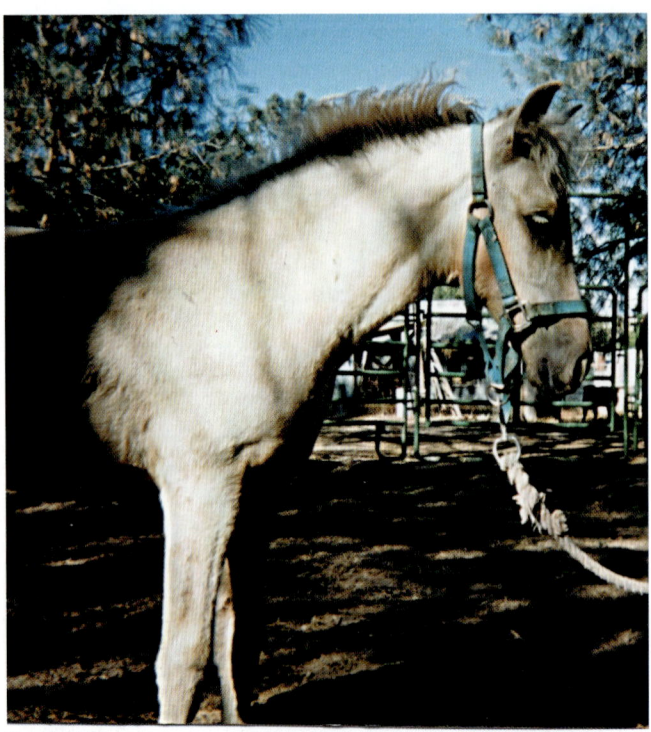

Jo Seabold with her American Paso Largo horses - mare, DAMA, and foal CHICA.

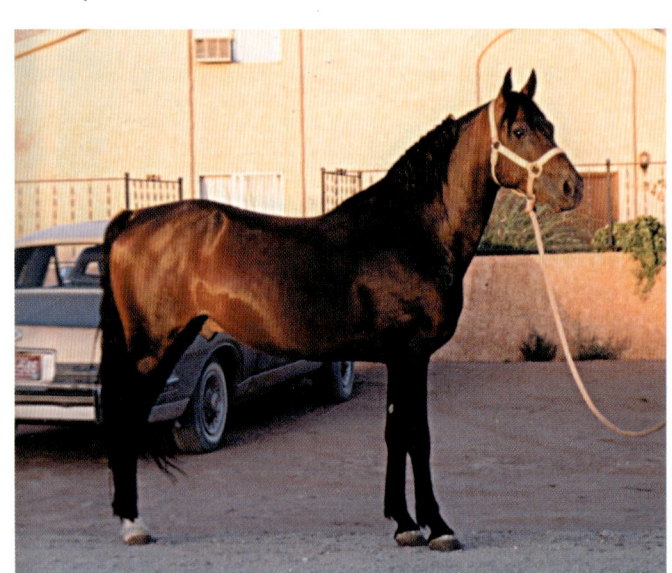

8-year-old KING GLADITTERE, exhibiting correct rear legs.

DANCER, a 3-month-old foal out of QUESADILLA by MONARCA. His gentle nature is evident on his kind face.

MARIA DE MARIMAC at 22, ready to foal again.

lated magazines where she discovered the existence of "gaiteds." After investigating several breeds, she contacted Isaac Wyler at his Pisadas de Oro Ranch in Arizona.

Presently Jo has three Largo horses, with five more on the way! She says these horses are not only a pleasure to ride but are entertaining to simply watch.

Quoting Jo about her grey gelding, Brazo: "Picture this if you will. Brazo, the gelding, takes his rubber feed pan, puts his front feet in it, and prances. Next, he moves up a bit and fiddles his back feet around into the pan and proceeds to prance his back feet while flipping his rear from side to side. He continues at this 'Mexican hat dance' for half an hour, or until I fill his water trough. Then, he must drink from the hose and when the trough is full, splash his nose in it. He makes his 'curtain call' by flipping his lip back and giving me a big smile. The harder I laugh, the more he does it. He is quite the entertainer. Yes, the Paso Largo has made this little ol' lady very happy."

Clearly, the Paso Largo horse is coming into its own. As the "New Millennium Crop" of Largo youngsters comes of age, the bar of excellence is about to be raised again. The future looks bright for this truly versatile and unique type of Spanish-gaited Largo horse.

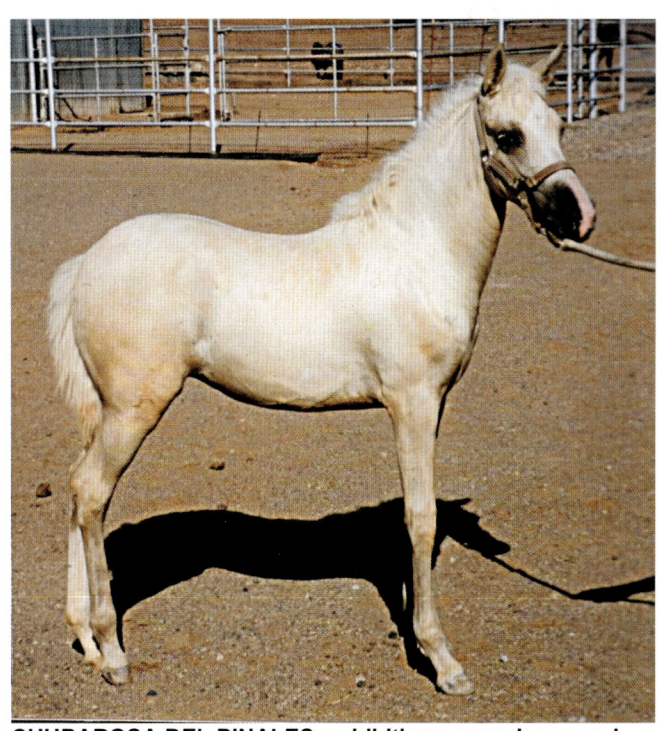

This Largo Paso Fino youngster exhibits an unusual buckskin pinto coloration. (Owned by Melinda & Tim Williams of Jonesborough, Tennessee.

EXQUISITA & '97 filly by ECLIPSE AURAS

JOKER, showing a smooth line from point of hip at one month of age.

CHUPAROSA DEL PINALES, exhibiting a round rear end.

PRECISION

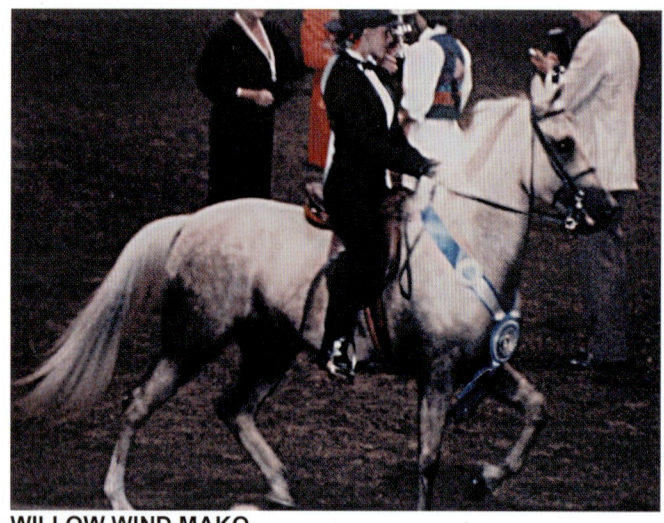

WILLOW WIND MAKO

COQUETTE PISADAS

CORALS OMEGO MAKO

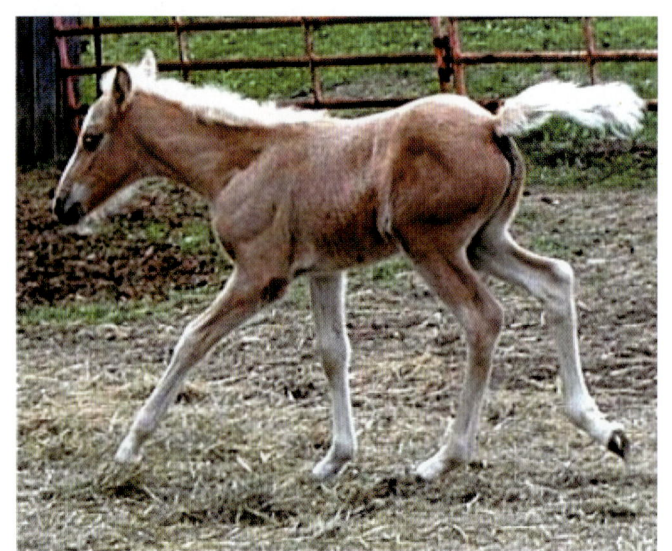

CASSINO DAUGHTER

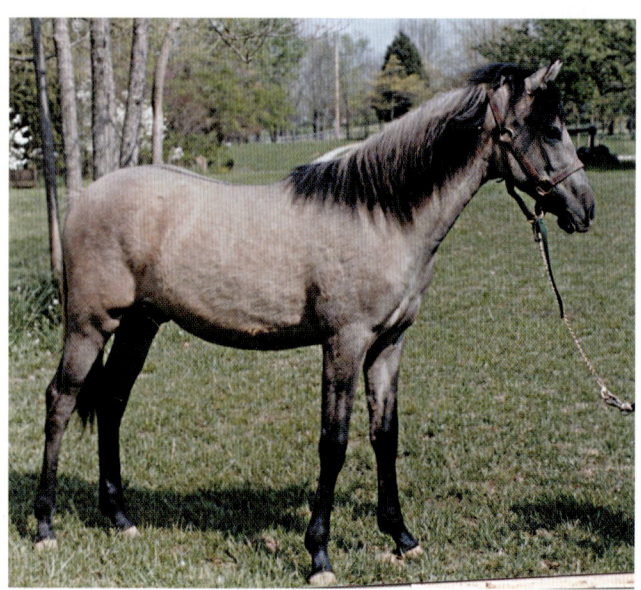

ROYAL OAK PRIMETIME

The American Paso Largo Horse
A Horse For All Seasons

Mc CURDY PLANTATION HORSE
CHAPTER 17

McCurdy yearling filly, MISTY MARIA McCURDY

Height:	14.2H to 15.2H
Gait:	McCurdy Lick, saddle gait, running walk, canter, walk
Color:	Grey factor present at birth, or develops with age
Trait:	Disposition, strength, stamina

Chapter 17 The McCurdy Plantation Horse

In 1865, the McCurdy brothers, Lewis and W.D., operated a breeding facility for Standardbred horses in Lowndesboro, located between Montgomery and Selma, Alabama. They were excellent horsemen with a reputation for standing high-quality stallions. Well-known racers the Tramp, McCurdy's Hambletonian, and Dr. Long all wore the McCurdy colors. Their plantation boasted a regulation race track and premium show barn.

In 1874, Lewis's son Ed was born. Ed and his brother George went on to pursue the family tradition of breeding fine horses. In 1940, an item appeared in the Advertiser in Montgomery:

"The McCurdys of Lowndesboro have for several generations been engaged in raising and handling horses. It is said that Ed McCurdy before he was 24 hours old was taken on horseback by his father over to his grandfather's house for exhibit. Ed McCurdy has spent a large part of the more than 60 years since that time in the saddle."

The famous old barn on the McCurdy plantation from which came some of the most outstanding horses of Alabama were born and raised.

Ed S. McCurdy on McCURDY'S FOX in 1935.

In some areas, draft horses for heavy farmwork would be the choice of breeds. In other areas the light fancy, riding horses would be the best choice. The McCurdy brothers joined with breeders from Middle Tennessee who were developing a light riding horse that could be used for farmwork as well. The McCurdys were to Alabama what the Hunters, Dements, Walkers, and Brantleys were to Tennessee.[1]

In the early 1900's, Ed and George McCurdy purchased McCurdy's Doctor (F-79)[2]. Doctor was sired by W.C. Oats, a popular Alabama stallion named for a one-time Senator from that state. His dam was Nancy McClain, by Slippery Jim, by Pat Malone (F-27).

McCurdy's Doctor became the fountainhead of the McCurdy breeding program. He sired many outstanding horses, which

---
[1] The Brantleys, Hunters, Walkers and Dements were the first important breeders and founders of the Tennessee Walking Horse.
[2] "F" identifies a Tennessee Walking Foundation Horse.

Mrs. Ed S. McCurdy leading a son of McCURDY'S FOX. Mrs. McCurdy was always keenly interested in the development of Walking Horses of Central Alabama and proud of the contributions made by her husband.

enriched the Plantation Walking blood of Alabama by breeding him to some of the finest Alabama Walking mares. For many years, McCurdy's Doctor was sought by the leading breeders of that area. Two important sons were John McCurdy and McCurdy's Fox.

McCurdy's Doctor was foaled in May of 1905. He was a grey horse and passed along that grey gene to many of his offspring. Generally in conformation, the horse resembled a picture of Robert E. Lee's "Old Traveler." His appearance was also handed down to the other horses of the McCurdy line. This prepotent stud was not only beautiful; he had great heart and stamina as well. In fact, when other horses with his reputation might have slowed down, he was still going strong. When he was 25 years old, he was ridden twenty miles to the State Fairgrounds in Montgomery.

In the early days of the breed, the plantation-era folks needed a horse that was versatile. It had to be comfortable, calm and dependable. Many were often ridden thirty-five miles a day to oversee the plantation work. They were also hitched to a wagon, plow or buggy and driven to town for business or supplies. Herding livestock and participating in a fox hunt and transporting children safely to school were other tasks expected of the McCurdys.

During the 1930's, two separate categories of McCurdy horses evolved. The McCurdy family registered their horses with the Tennessee Walking Horse Registry. The McCurdy horses were a positive influence on that registry. Many of the McCurdy horses carry the foundation "F" on their registration number.

At the same time, others began breeding their stock to McCurdy family horses. During the great Depression, many sharecroppers brought their mares to the McCurdy stallion in exchange for work. The horses produced from these breedings were used to plow the fields, pull logs, and transport goods. They would work all week and then carry their owner to town on Saturday. The McCurdy horses were tough and by no means pampered. As their reputation and prominence grew throughout Central Alabama, a true independent breed was born. They were never registered, but they were judiciously bred and maintained as a true breed.

Here we see how consistently this breed has been bred. On the left: 1910 MOORE'S DICK TAYLOR with Wiley Kirby up. On the right: 2001 DIAMOND CATE with Colleen Cates in the saddle. Almost a hundred years separation!

McCurdys are medium in size and are refined overall. They are born black, bay, sorrel and roan, with or without white markings, with a large number of them turning grey as they mature. Not all McCurdys carry the grey modifier gene, but it is the preferred color by many.

The McCurdys outstanding qualities are a calm disposition and easy, comfortable gait. Many of them have natural cow savvy and excel at such various tasks as trail riding, field trailing, driving and working livestock. But it's their easy-going temperament that makes them un-equaled as personal and family horses.

McCurdy Plantation Horses are naturally gaited. They require little training. It is said that you just get on and ride. Their natural saddle

Bo Lassic riding his McCurdy stallion.

Roy A. Rogers, of Greenville, Alabama, founding member of the McCurdy Plantation Horse Association, aboard his young McCurdy stallion.

Herbert Mims on his three-yea-old McCurdy mare.

gait is commonly referred to as the "McCurdy Lick." It is a straightforward square, four-beat, single-footing gait that is extremely smooth. The horses also perform the flat walk and running walk, and many will perform the fox-trot. Newborn foals can demonstrate the gait naturally from birth and can be seen hitting the
lick as they hurry to keep alongside their dams.

In 1993, the McCurdy Plantation Horse Association was formed on an informal basis to bring together owners and fanciers of the old-time McCurdy Plantation Horse. Three horse-

A. Grey Till, Jr. (center) and three of his McCurdy mares.

Colleen Cates and RED'S LETOHATCHEE LEGEND with 2nd place trophy at the Rough String Ranch "Cow Girls On The Run" Endurance clinic and Ride in 2002.

McCURDY'S NEW TRADITION, a young stallion owned by the Cates of Athens, Texas.

Kim McCurdy riding her 2 _ year-old McCurdy Family bred stallion, **McCURDY'S LITTLE IRON MAN -** in Lowndesboro, Alabama.

men were veteran field-trialers: J. Richard McDuffy Sr., of Aiken, South Carolina; Roy A. Rogers, of Greenville, Alabama; and Ron H. Mann of Cullman, Alabama. They got together to make plans for preserving and promoting the old McCurdy Plantation Horse breed. McCurdy family members Lewis H. McCurdy and Edward S. McCurdy Jr., joined the pioneering team with the legal counsel and technical support of A. Grey Till Jr.

In 1995, the McCurdy Plantation Horse Registry was founded for the purpose of registering horses of known McCurdy ancestry that met the breed standards. The McCurdy Plantation Horse Association was incorporated

McCURDY'S CONFEDERATE JASMINE, at her first show.

in 1995, to assure that there would be an ongoing organization to promote the attributes of this historic breed. Both the Registry and the Association are nonprofit corporations incorporated in the State of Alabama.

The common purposes of both the Registry and Association are to preserve this historic bloodline as a distinct breed, promote their use and enjoyment, and enhance the public's knowledge and appreciation of the McCurdy Horse as a treasured legacy of the Old South.

The first McCurdy Trail Ride took place in the Association's inaugural year. It set the identifying focus of the breed - an unequaled

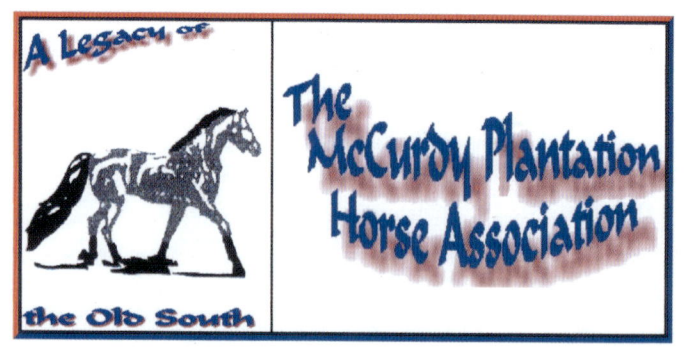

In 1993, the McCurdy Plantation Horse Association was formed by veteran field trialers.

and versatile trail pleasure horse. It was held in Lowndesboro on the McCurdy family plantation property and was so successful that it has become a bi-annual event. 190 riders participated in the Fall 1999 ride, hosted by the Southern Sportsman Hunting Lodge. Members came from Texas, South Carolina, and all points in between.

Teddy Pouncey's black McCurdy stallion, shown at the Alabama Horse Fair in Montgomery, with Keith Pettus up. Photo: Harold Wilson.

The McCurdy horse is enjoying a growing popularity throughout the country and internationally as well because it exhibits a calm, intelligent disposition with tremendous fortitude of mind and body. Its gaits are smooth and natural, and many in the breed have natural cow-herding instincts.

An example of this "cow savvy" was present in a foundation stallion Big Red (1970 - 1977), owned by cattleman Dickson Farrior of Hayneville, Alabama. Farrior reported: "Once he locked on a cow, he would not give up until it was roped or penned. No cow or Quarter Horse ever bested Big Red."

The McCurdy horses also shine through the rigorous demands of the field trial world. Their common sense and work ethic allows them to stand quietly while the dog is on point or the judge is making his evaluation.

But perhaps their most outstanding trait is their versatility, which has become their trademark. The McCurdy is at home on the pleasure trail, working cattle, riding fences, babysitting children, driving, jumping, participating in 4-H projects and in speed events.

A beautiful pair of girls in a McCurdy trailside photo.

They are shown in both English and Western Pleasure Classes at horse shows. Some McCurdy Horses are registered as Tennessee Walking Horses and as commissioned Racking Horses.

June and Barry Snook of Canby, Oregon are enthusiastic supporters of the breed. At their J-Bar Farm and Kennel, they put the talents of the McCurdy Horses to the test in field trialing. They know that in the game of upland bird dog field trialing, it takes a special kind of horse to handle all the requirements necessary for a dog handler or scout or even bird planter to perform their job. Quoting the Snooks: "Field trialing is probably the ultimate test of the temperament and stamina of a horse. Ropes all over, chasing dogs, shotguns, up and down steep mountains at a hefty pace, long hours, long hauls in trailers, 'roading' of dogs in harness, riding in high desert heat, covering up to 30 miles a day and expected to be smooth in gait and calm in attitude."

They go on to say they believe they have found the perfect horse to fit the demanding requirements. "The McCurdy Plantation Horses have a calm and willing disposition, smooth forward gait, athletic ability,

McCURDY'S ROAN LIGHTNING with Eva McCurdy Milligan, daughter of Ed S. McCurdy of Lowndes County, Alabama, at Stewart Ranch.

strong legs, and deep chest providing great bottom for endurance. They are goodlooking animals, built right - short backs, good bone, large hindquarters and very deep chests. Their

Sherry Wood on her McCurdy mare at the trailside.

McCURDY'S HIGH SIERRA, a three-year-old McCurdy mare owned by Jackie and Gale Johnson of Terrell, Texas.

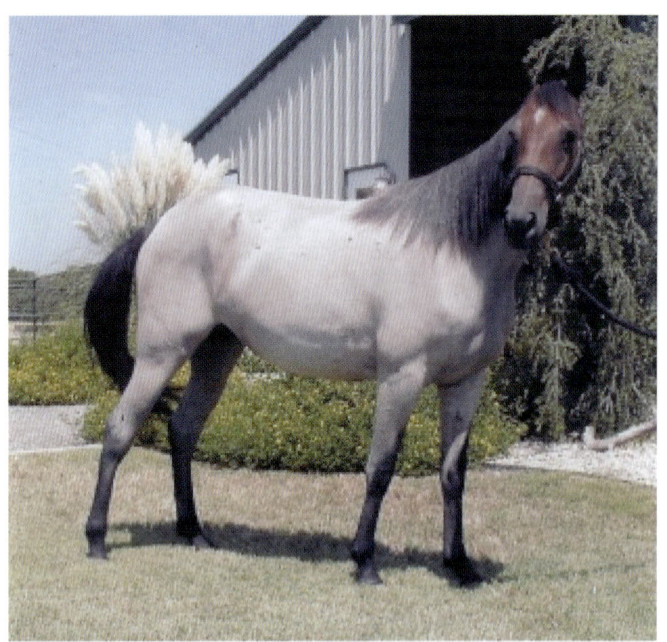

LADY ROAN McCURDY, a classic bay roan McCurdy mare at 3 years of age, bred by Ed & Kim McCurdy of Selma, Alabama.

ACE HIGH McCURDY, a four-month-old colt, going grey.

McCURDY'S CAMEO CATE, a two-year-old mare.

heads are extremely attractive with small ears and the kindest eyes anyone has ever looked into. They seem to have a great intelligence that allows them to pace themselves and be ready to provide everything necessary for a field trialer when they need it."

Once folks discover this special breed they seem to stick with it. Director Richard McDuffie tells of his introduction to the breed: "I was introduced to McCurdy Plantation Horses in the mid-1950's as being 'the world's best backyard horses.' I have used them exclusively since then because they do so many things well. I trail ride, field trial and work them in harness. In the past, I have worked cows, hunted and entered them in gymkhana events. They excelled at all."

Richard continues with a glowing testimonial: "They are very low maintenance. They thrive on pastures or feed that most breeds would suffer on. Most are not accident-prone. They tolerate both heat and cold without shelter. They are calm and laid-back in temperament. They can be left in pastures for months, then caught and ridden or driven as if used the day before."

Two more important supporters of the McCurdy Horse are Ron and Colleen Cates at the Destiny Hills Ranch in Athens, Texas. They were responsible for introducing the McCurdys to Texas after they moved there from Lowndesboro, Alabama, where they were friends with the McCurdy family. Quoting Colleen: "I have bred, raised, trained, and shown three different breeds of gaited horses. If I had to choose only one horse to own and ride, I'd say make mine a McCurdy! They are so easy to train and ride, easy to love, and easy to maintain. They possess an inherent strong constitution of mind and body, with a natural desire to please their rider. If your dream is to ride a horse you can trust in any situation and to be your partner for a lifetime, get a McCurdy."

While living in Alabama, the Cates family were drawn to the McCurdy horses when they observed the disposition, strength, stamina, and gait as the horses were ridden by many veteran field-trialers and dog handlers.

Jackie Johnson tells a heartwarming story about her association with the McCurdys.

She and her father saw their first McCurdys at a gaited horse show in Athens, Texas. They watched a mare being shown by a local breeder who answered their questions, and told them about the breed. They arranged to go to the ranch the following day, to see more McCurdys.

Jackie's father fell in love with the foals and decided he wanted a mare he could have bred and then raise a foal of his own. Plans were made for a later purchase. In the meantime, he had a cardiac arrest.

Jackie's Dad survived the attack, but he had severe damage and a long rehab ahead of him. The one thing that kept him going was the decision to buy a young McCurdy filly, Rose. The stroke had affected his speech, but it was easy to get him to talk about Rose. It was several months before he got up the strength to see Rose, but when he did, they gave him a brush and the filly stood quietly for him to brush her. She was only about 18 months old, yet she stood quietly while he held on to her, to steady himself. Quoting Jackie: "Just before Rose turned two, we started some roundpen work. The hardest thing was to get her to move away from me. Then the day came that I showed her a saddle. She decided it was no big deal and accepted me putting it on her back. The next day, I mounted and rode her. So much for breaking. Rose and I have been on several trail rides encountering water crossings, cows, mules with wagons, and dogs. She takes it all in stride, alert but not excited. I expect her to only get better and better."

Here's a followup letter received from Jackie's husband Gale. "Jackie and I married in March 2001, and since Rose could not be ridden at that time, we were able to purchase High Sierra (in foal), so now we could ride my Arab and one McCurdy. We'd swap out now and then, but the Arab couldn't keep up without trotting some. Well, that bump, bump, bump had to go. We sold Shockerr (yup, two R's) and though he was a fine horse with a good personality, we felt we had one too many (with another on the way). We have been blessed with three fine McCurdy horses and when we can find the larger piece of land that fits our budget, we'll have some more."

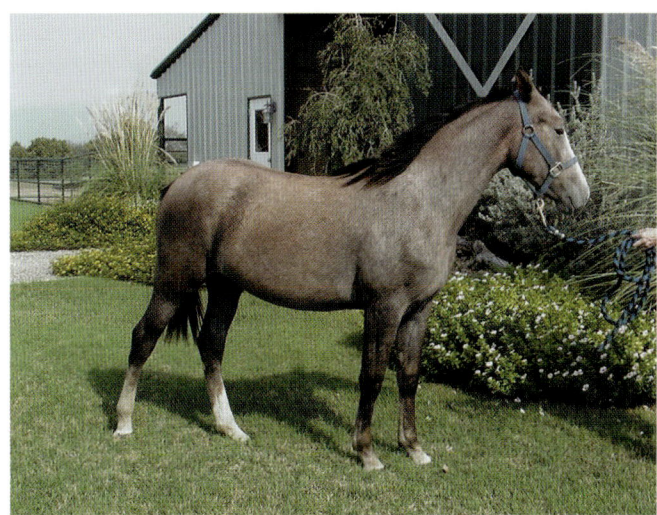

CATES McCURDY ROSE at fourteen months of age. Owned by Jackie and Gale Johnson of Terrell, Texas.

Friends **McCURDY'S TEXAS RANGER** (sorrel) and **FATE** (grey).

McCURDY'S HIGH SIERRA with her foal **McCURDY'S CHOCOLATE SUNDAY** and Gale Johnson. Photo: Ken Lewis

The McCurdy Plantation Horse Registry establishes breed registration requirements and carries out the registration program.

Debbie Seale riding ROOSTER.

Vicki Lipscomb riding GOOD GOLLY MISS MOLLY OF DUNROVIN.

McCURDY'S CONFEDERATE JASMINE at three years of age, winning "Blues" in Pleasure Mares of all breeds at the 1999 Gaitway Open Horse Show in Texas.

First of all, the offspring of two registered McCurdy horses is automatically eligible for Pedigree Registration by simply completing the form within one year of foaling. There are also rules of registration for foundation horses: Only horses of McCurdy ancestry shall be accepted as foundation sires and dams.

1. They must be traced back to McCurdy's Doctor and foundation Mares or to horses that are publicly known to be McCurdys.
2. All horses that meet the above requirements must then meet the breed standard relative to physical conformity, temperament and natural gait.
3. In the event a stud or mare meets all other requirements but is known to carry a percentage of other genes (such as Tennessee Walking Horse), the pedigree should show such, even to the extent of ancestors' names and registration number.
4. Only studs and mares shall be accepted as foundation horses. The letter F shall precede the number assigned foundation horses.
5. Any horse registered or eligible for registration in the Tennessee Walking Horse Breeders and Exhibitors Association Registry, or any other gaited horse registry, must be proven to have genetic lineage to the McCurdy foundation in the registration documents, in addition to meeting the standards of physical conformity, temperament and natural gaiting ability.
6. In order to be registered as a foundation sire, one of the following must exist:
    - A grey stud of known McCurdy ancestry, or
    - A stud with proven lineage (TWHBEA documented) to be within four generations of McCurdy's Fox 410353 or

McCurdy's Doctor F-79 and carry grey characteristics[3] in color, or

- A stud with proven lineage (TWHBEA documented)[4] having a substantial influence of descendants from McCurdy's Doctor F-79 and McCurdy's Fox 410353 on both the sire and dam pedigree and carry grey characteristics in color.

7. To register any stud or mare as a foundation sire or dam, at least one director of the registration office must personally see the horse in question, see them worked under various conditions to the point of being able to ascertain temperament and physical conformity as well as gait. Then a videotape must be made that shows the horse gaiting on unleveled footing, as well as under ideal conditions. A copy of the videotape shall be sent to the registrar. All directors must agree to accept the horse in question. Each director has veto power and any one that objects will deny the acceptance of the horse as a foundation animal.

8. All horses, both studs and mares, must be at least two years of age and broke before being considered for registration as foundation horses. In case of their being bred before they are registered foundation horses, once they have achieved registration status, the offspring must follow the path of all foundation horses to registration.

9. A color photo (s) showing front and one side of the applicant horse must be attached to the application.

---

[3] Grey characteristics are defined as unusual grey markings on the hips and around the head of the tail, combined with definite black points below the knees. Grey characteristics may be present at birth or may develop and become more obvious with age.

[4] TWHBEA is the Tennessee Walking Horse Breeders & Exhibitors Association, which is the official Tennessee Walker Registry (see chapter 11).

CATES McCURDY ROSE, owned by Jackie and Gale Johnson of Terrell, Texas.

Mr. Lewis McCurdy, at a youthful 83 years old, riding his two-yea-old McCurdy stallion, MAC on the October 2000 trail ride.

July 2002, McCurdy Board of Directors. From left: Ron Mann, Ed McCurdy, Lewis McCurdy, Richard McDuffie, Roy A. Rogers and A. Grey Till, Jr.

As horse fanciers discover the natural abilities of the McCurdy Plantation Horse, this Registry is bound to grow in popularity and number. Breeders are now located across the country.

RED'S LETOHATCHEE LEGEND on 1999 Spring Trail Ride

McCURDY'S LADY GRAYSTONE

12-year-old Will Mc Curdy on his 23-year-old gelding, BJ

A rare palomino McCurdy DESTINY'S DIAMOND RIO by LEGEND out of DIAMOND CATE

Director Richard McDuffie leading the trail ride on a McCurdy

CHASE'S FLAME a two-year-old gelding

ROOSTER
Gary and Debbie Seale

MANGALARGA MARCHADOR HORSE

CHAPTER 18

Marchador stallion, CAMAFEU DA BOA FE
Owner: Adhemar Magon

HEIGHT: 14:2 - 16:2 Hands

GAIT: Walk, Marcha, Canter

COLOR: All equine colors plus burgundy

TRAIT: Disiposition, Versatility & Endurance

Chapter 18 The Mangalarga Marchador

Known as a "breed without frontiers," the Mangalarga Marchador is the national horse of Brazil. Since the formation in 1949 of the ABCCMM[1], or Brazilian Association of Breeders of the Mangalarga Marchador, it has become the largest horse breed association in Latin America. The ABCCMM was formed to set standards in conformation, disposition and gait. Today the greatest numbers of this breed are found in Rio de Janeiro, Minas Gerais, São Paulo, Bahia and Espirito Santo.

The Mangalarga Marchadors share a history with other Iberian breeds. 200 years ago, the breed was developed by crossing the Andaluz, the Lusitano and the Barb. This produced a horse known for its rhythmic, smooth gaits, sensible intelligence, docile temperament, and amazing stamina that is hardy and adaptable to all climates, feed and terrains.

In 1808, while the armies of Napoleon threatened their homeland, King K. João VI and the royal family of Portugal fled to Brazil. They brought along selected stallions from *Coudelaria Alter do Chao,* an Alter Royal Farm, established in 1751. These horses were known as the Royal Alter breed, formed from the Spanish Andalusians and selected breeding horses native to the Iberian Peninsula, Madeira, and the Canary Islands. The Alter breed was known for its elegant stature, good stance and docile temperament. King D. João VI designated St. Jao Francisco Junqueira, a famous horse breeder, to cross the Royal stallions with imported Barb mares from Africa.

TIGUARA HYPUS is one of the first two foundation sires to arrive in the United States in the early 1990's. He is a product of HERDADE CADILLAC, the watershed stallion of the early to mid-twentieth century Mangalarga Marchador breeders, and who sired numerous National Champions in Brazil. Between the 40's and the 80's, the Herdade breeding farm won more conformational awards at Mangalarga Marchador expositions than any other farm in Brazil.

Trainer Antonio herding beautiful Mangalarga Marchador mares at Haras Joatinga. Photo: Vida Z. Ward

---
[1] Association Brasileira dos Criadores do Cavalo Mangalarga Marchador

JALLAIO DA BOA FE RL, is a full brother to Grand National Champion, CAMAFEU DA BOA FE, out of ABAIBA, A.J. and BELA CRUZ bloodlines. His graceful diagonal batida gait lends itself to dressage.

A Marchador stallion performing a four-beat gait.
Photo: Vida Z. Ward

Brazil is the fifth largest country in the world, with a total area of 3,286,470 square miles. The basin of the Amazon River comprises more than one-third of the surface of the country.

Even after the French occupation of Portugal ended, King D. João VI remained in Brazil, and in 1815, made it a separate kingdom. He maintained both thrones and ruled the home country of Portugal through a Council of Regency.

In 1812, Prince Pedro I, who was later named emperor of Brazil, gave one of the most important of these Real stallions, "Sublime," to his friend and Baron of Aldenas, Gabriel Francisco Junqueira. The Baron was owner of the established breeding farm, Hacienda Campo Alegre, located in the south of the state of Minas Gerais. This farm was to become the birthplace of the Mangalarga Marchador.

With the exceptional stallion "Sublime," Junqueira began a breeding program that utilized the Real bloodline and native mares of Barb and Spanish Jennet blood. The first animals produced were known as the "Sublime Horses." Many were fast and smooth amblers and became the foundation of the modern-day Mangalarga Marchador horses.

Gabriel Junqueria had a nephew, Jose Frausino Junqueria, a deer hunter and sportsman who became an enthusiastic champion of the breed. He appreciated their resistance and agility on long journeys. His enthusiasm carried over to a friend and owner of the Mangalarga Farm near Pati do Alferes in Rio de Janeiro. It was not long before the farm

Linda Tellington-Jones on stallion, OXUM DO REGAL, owned by Cascade Marchadores. As an internationally renowned trainer and clinician known for her T-touch methods, she enthusiastically states, "One of the great gifts to the horse world is to have the Mangalarga Marchador horse breed introduced at this time for pleasure riders who want an athletic, exotic, magical, yet sensibly personable equine companion. They ride as smooth as a 'Porsche.' With their romantic Iberian heritage, there is no comparison among gaited breeds."

Bill Kambic, one-time Tennessee Walker breeder and enthusiast, now champions the Mangalarga Marchador at his Haras Lucero Farm, in Kingston, Tennessee.

The Marchador comes in a rainbow of colors. Pictured is a tobiano pinto pattern. Photo: Vida Z. Ward

bred so many of these horses that its name became associated with the breed itself.

The horses became known as Mangalargas. The name "Marchador" was added to identify the pure naturally gaited horse and distinguish it from the Mangalarga Paulista. The Paulistas were created in Brazil in the 1930's by a group of breeders in a state of São Paulo by crossing the Mangalarga with Thoroughbred, Arabian or Standardbred. A separate registry of Mangalarga Paulista Horses was formed in 1934.

For more than 180 years, the traditional breeding of Mangalarga Marchador horses concentrated on the original pure foundation lines from Hacienda Campo Alegre. They also included famous lines such as Tabatinga, Abaiba, Angahy, Traituba, and JB, still in existence today with some of the original families breeding on the colonial plantations.

Today, there are more than 350,000 registered Mangalarga Marchador horses in Brazil, still more are found in several countries outside of Brazil. While there are less than thirty-five foundation Marchador horses in the United States, they began catching the attention of the horse world in 2002. They have been seen marching in the 2002 New Year's Rose Parade in Pasadena; on Horse Talk TV; at Fiesta of the Spanish Horse at the Western States Horse Expo in Sacramento, California; Equine Affair; Southern National Exposition in Perry, Georgia; and Equitana, in Lexington, Kentucky.

The judge studies the line-up of participants in the morphology class. Each horse has to qualify individually for the class by showing the judge how they gait and transition.

Quoting Mangalarga Marchador enthusiast Linda Holst: "Have you ever discovered something so exciting and fun [like riding gaited horses], that you wanted to share it with everyone? Imagine speeding along in the latest luxury sports car convertible with the top down, and enjoying a ride so comfortable that you barely realize how fast you are going! Next, think about all the things you like to do on horseback, like pleasure, trail, endurance, dressage, jumping, Western roundups, and cutting. Is there one horse breed that's versatile enough to do all of this? As a matter of fact, there is! The Mangalarga Marchador, built like a Paso in front and Quarter Horse in the rear, solid and sturdy with classic Iberian features."

The United States has approved and granted a trademark to the American Mangalarga Marchador brand, logos and name. This trademark is protected under U.S. Customs law and provides that only authorized registered Mangalarga Marchador horses may be imported. A Mangalarga Marchador is identified with the letter "M" inside a horseshoe on the right shoulder and is registered with the MMHAA, located in Ocala, Florida. A Marchador horse without this identification or registration with the authorization of MMHAA, which is recognized by the American Horse Council and the Brazilian ABCCMM, is "just a horse."

To appreciate the unique attributes that make the Mangalarga Marchador horse breed

Rider and horse owner receive an award from Jose Maur, regional Brazilian ABCCMM association president and Jeronimo Mesquita, Brazilian vice president of MMHAA of the U.S. at the Leopoldina City Fair in Minas Gerais, birthplace of the famous ABAIBA Mangalarga Marchador bloodline.

Sandy Kambic riding her Marchador mare, demonstrating the 4-beat diagonal Batida gait.

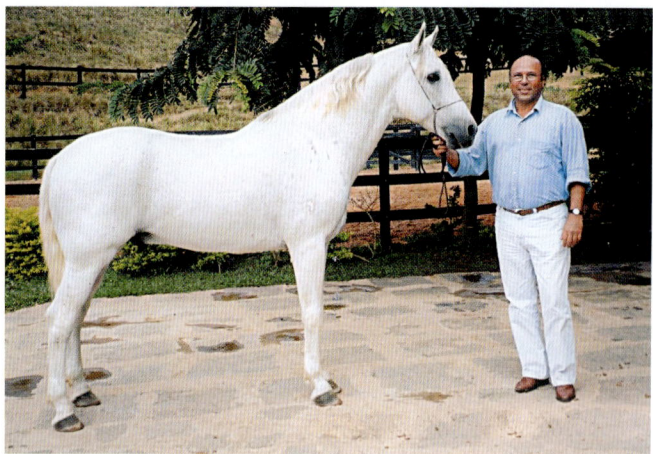

Carlos Ernanny de Mello e Silva with his champion herd sire LACAIO DA CACHOEIRINHA. Photo: Linda Holst

JORDAO DO REGAL out of FESTIN PASSO FINO and whose grandsire is legendary MOLECULE TABATINGA, with ANGAI, TABATINGA and SAMA bloodlines, has been awarded numerous championships in Brazil. Now a United States foundation sire, this striking red bay roan was born in March 1998, is 15:2 hands and stands at Rancho Linda Marchadores, in Bonsall, California. "I feel that it's a privilege to be standing four fabulous foundation stallions out of the few found in the United States," says owner Linda Holst. "As stallions, they are amazingly easy to handle and impressively well behaved
(a quality found in the breed). They keep easily in pipe corrals in a boarding environment."

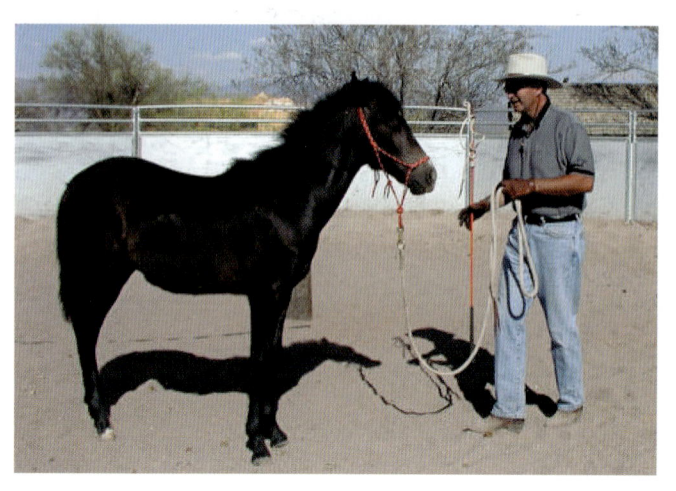

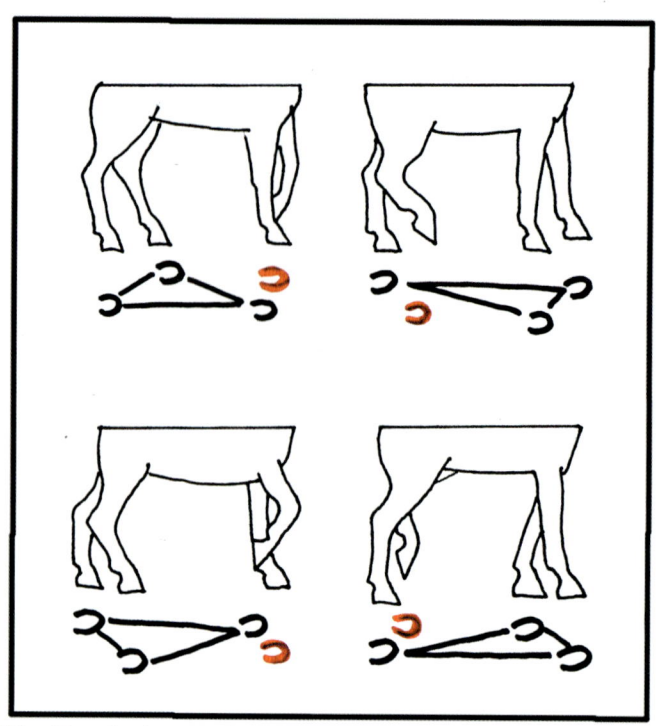

The Marchador produces a very smooth gait by utilizing a stabilizing nano-second triple-hoof support during the extended four-beat reach in front that is propelled from behind.

special, some understanding of the characteristic gaits is needed. In addition to the walk, canter, and gallop, there are two long-reaching, four-beat gaits. They can perform both lateral and diagonal gaits. This ability makes this breed a joy to work with and a pleasure to ride. Their extended four-beat reach in front is propelled from behind and stabilized by a nano-second triple hoof support.

MARCHA PICADA – *Picada* is a Portuguese word meaning "light touch." The picada gait is four-beat, characterized by lateral leg movements, with the sequence of the hoofs being: right rear, right front, left rear, left front, with the hind foot touching the ground a fraction of a second before the front foot. The continuous triple-hoof support and the overreach of the hind hoof makes the gait very smooth. At extended speed, the head and body lift up like a speedboat in front to create a "plane-like" sensation that makes you feel as if you aren't even moving. This gait is similar to

⇦LIBERTAD DO REGAL (CAMAFEU DE BOA FE X RAJA FUGA) was born on September 11, 2001, and is proudly owned by Lynn and John Kelley. Shown with John Kelley, using the Parrelli carrot stick, Marchador yearlings learn quickly and are easy to train. He will be an important future sire with ABAIBA, ANGAY and grandsire FIESTA A.J. bloodlines.

MANGALARGA MARCHADOR HORSE ASSOCIATION OF AMERICA™

the Paso Fino's fino, corto and largo, or the Peruvian Paso's paso llano, without the termino. It can be sustained for long periods of time.

MARCHA BATIDA – *Batida* means "to hit." The batida gait is a diagonal four-beat sequence along with movements of triple-hoof support. Although this gait is similar to the trot, it never has a suspended moment with all its legs in the air but, instead is always in contact with the ground. The longer and more frequent the moments of triple-hoof support, the more comfortable its gait. Three hooves touching the ground simultaneously, are characteristic of these, "marching" horses. The horse makes a semicircle with its front legs and uses its rear legs for leverage, thus propelling it forward. If it marches on level ground at a normal rhythm, the tracks of its two hind feet will cover or pass slightly beyond the tracks of the front feet. In motion, the horse executes alternating diagonal and lateral supports, always softened by an intermediate pause of triple support. It can be compared to the Colombia Paso Fino's troche and the Missouri Fox Trotter's namesake gait.

The Mangalarga Marchador's head is triangular (not concave), with a large, flat forehead tapering to a small, fine muzzle. It has a straight profile and large dark eyes set wide apart and extremely vivacious, typical

➪ VIKING, a beautiful dark bay stallion, performs the Spanish Walk.

Eduardo Saad, owner of Haras Libertas, works closely with Raul Junqueira, incorporating famous TABATINGA bloodlines into his breeding program. Pictured is trainer Marcinho, on DOMINO DA JOATINGA. Photo: Linda Holst

"My adventure began in November 2000, when I met Marsha Sielbeck, president of MMHAA, an importer and breeder of the Marchadores from Brazil at EqWest in San Diego. Intrigued with the breed, I went to Toledo, to see her prized Paso Finos and two Marchadores. After riding all of her Pasos, there came the most exhilarating ride in my entire life. The next thing I knew, I was demonstrating this breed at the Del Mar Nationals." Linda Holst shown on stallion, BATUQUE DO REGAL in Del Mar, California.
Photo: Quince Tree Photography

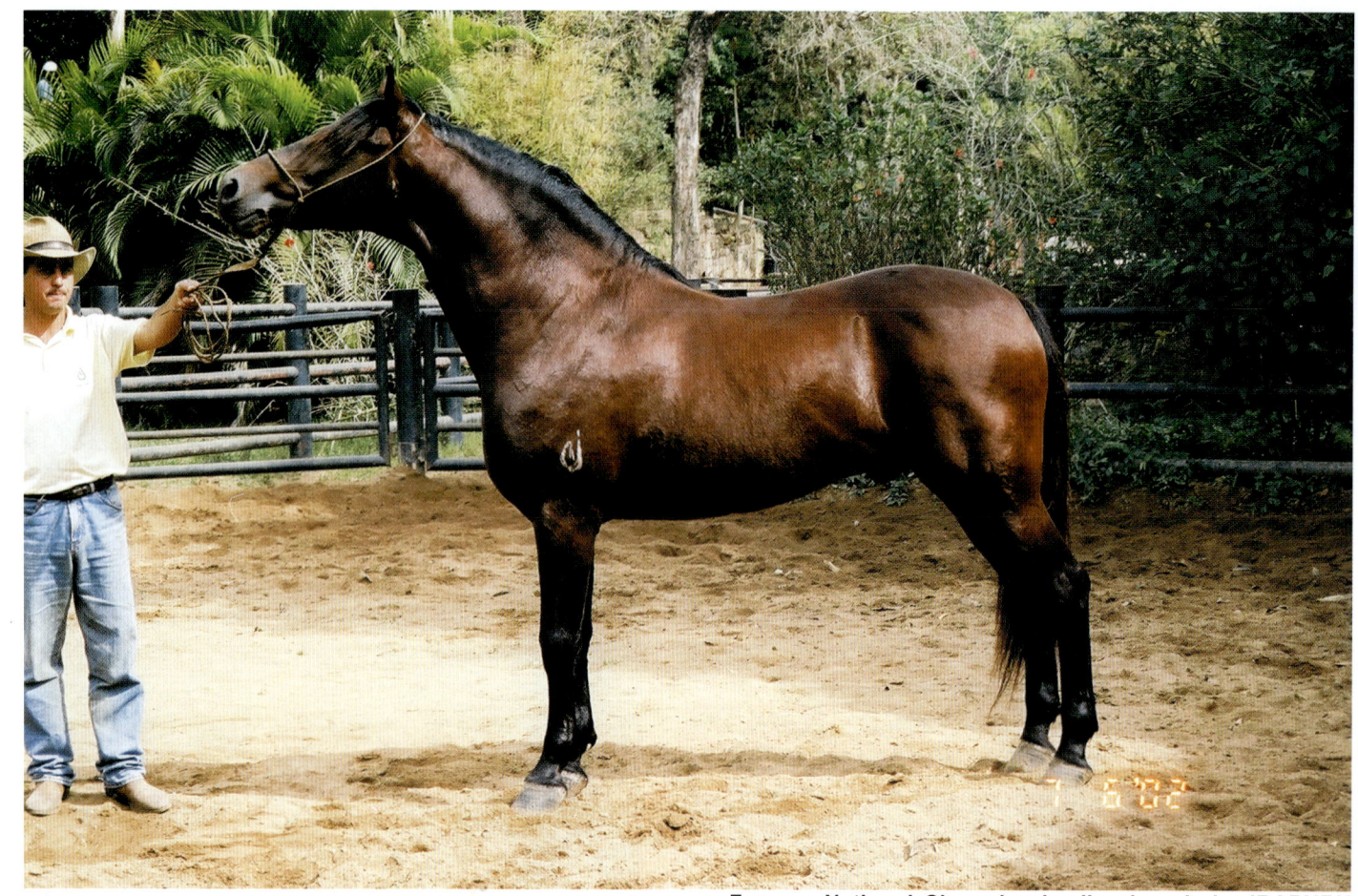

Famous National Champion leading heard sire IRAPURU DA JOATINGA, Haras Joatinga.

of the Barb Horse. The ears are proportional to the head, mobile, parallel and well set-erect, with the tips turned inward. They have an alert, attentive attitude and the upright ears echo the firm look in the eyes that are up to the challenge of any obstacle encountered along the way.

The mouth is of medium width and sensitive to the bit. The nostrils are large, dilated and flexible. The neck is of medium length, sufficient for the horse to be well-balanced for riding and reining. It is well-arched and muscular, inserted into the top third of the chest to allow for a proud, high carriage. The thorax is deep and capable of great lung capacity - one of the reasons for the legendary stamina of the breed. The back is of medium length with short and well-muscled loins. If the distance from the back to the loins is of lesser or equal distance to the length of the croup, it is a sign that the horse possesses excellent conformation. The croup is slightly sloping and long, the tail is set at a medium height, with a short, fine dock pointed down but lightly raised when the animal moves.

The gaskin and forearm tend to be long, well-muscled and articulated, and the cannons are short. The pasterns and hooves are at the slightly lower angle typical of Spanish horses. This allows it to overreach well and without excessive stress to its suspensories. In Brazil, unless the horse is worked hard every day, it is kept barefoot, with only an occasional hoof trim required. It has very thick and tough feet. The Mangalarga Marchador is considered a light horse but stands strong and well-muscled, between 14:2 and 17 hands, and weighs between 850 and 1,100 pounds. Its coat is fine and silky with a full mane and tail. The most common colors are grey, bay and chestnut, but it can also be found in most of the equine colors including pinto and an exotic burgundy peculiar to the breed.

"I believe their versatility and intelligence makes them the horse America has long been waiting for," says Marsha Sielbeck, founding president of the Mangalarga Marchador Horse Association of America (MMHAA). Marsha shares a special relationship with her beautiful stallion, JALLAIO DA BOA FE. "The Mangalarga Marchador stallions are a joy to have around. They are personable and easy to train."

The Mangalarga Marchador is sturdy and well-suited for any terrain. They flourish in any climate. They are easy feeders, resistant to disease, and can travel long distances without fatigue.

These qualities contributed to an amazing feat accomplished between May 1991 and June 1993, when three Brazilian horsemen in their sixties rode their Mangalarga Marchadors over 8,694 miles, through varied terrains and altitudes, from sea level to 15,000 feet, in temperatures ranging from 0 to 115° to prove stamina. Their accomplishment was recorded in the Guinness Book of World Records and memorialized by a bronze and marble statue.

The Marchador is surefooted, graceful, comfortable and excellent in temperament. They are playful, love people and have a docile nature. Stallions are unusually easy to handle. The Marchador is very intelligent and easy to train. The horse is never put under saddle before it is at least thirty months old, and the training is done quietly and patiently. After rudiments of discipline have been achieved, they are prepared for specific skills, which are many. Competitions, endurance contests, cattle herding, and functional performance evaluation are some of the disciplines where the Marchadors shine. They have a natural ability to maneuver around obstacles and are highly valued for their endurance during long-distance travel. Of course, the smoothness of their gait enhances all of these disciplines.

The tack used in Brazil with these horses is simple. The Brazilian saddle is similar to an Australian stock saddle and the headset is cleancut with a snaffle bit. The riding

Linda Tellington-Jones riding stallion, BATUQUE DO REGAL in a clinic session at the Western States Horse Expo, Sacramento, California. "This breed is very intelligent and truly a pleasure and joy for all to partake of."

With long strides in front and tremendous power from behind, BATUQUE, a stallion, powers up like a speedboat lifting up to plane and clocks over 25 mph. The sensation of the picada gait shown (lateral) is one of a "floating" and exhilarating ride! Owner Linda Holst, up.

BATUQUE DO REGAL, a seven-year-old, 15:1 hand son of TIGUARA HYPUS - (one of two original U.S. foundation stallions imported from Brazil in the early 1990's) - is a beautiful dappled golden buckskin stallion. Here he demonstrates his spectacular picada gait at the Western States Horse Expo, Sacramento, California. Owner Linda Holst, up.

apparel seen in the showrings varies from region to region, but is unique. A colorful neck bandana is frequently worn, as is traditional among Brazilian cowboys in and out of the ring.

The ABCCMM holds annual tests and competitions, judging conformation, type, gait and functional performance. The national points ranking system highlights winners and breeders and attracts competitions and exhibitors with cash purses. Gait classes are rigorous and normally last about an hour. The horse is judged for how it executes its gait. Important are carriage, brio and elegance with consistent timing over a wide range of speed. The horses also participate in functional performance testing including reining competitions, cross-country events and endurance tests that can cover distances from 31 to 62 miles.

Their versatility extends to dressage, cutting, jumping, polo and pleasure riding. The population of horses descends directly from Iberian stock. These lovely animals give us a wonderful peek into the past to appreciate the horses of the Conquistadors, the Spanish Jennets.

BRAUNA LIBERTAS with her brand new filly SAMBA DE LAZY T at the Lazy T Ranch in Montana. The filly was sired by SANTANA JUNCO.

CAMAFEU DA BOA FE is a full brother to JALLAIO DA BOA FE, in the United States and a National Champion in Brazil.

Marchadores saddled for a tranquil ride in the Brazilian countryside.

Owner Linda Holst: "I never dreamed that I would meet my equine soulmate in the form of a Mangalarga Marchador stallion. Topping it off is the sweet disposition, ease of handling and intelligence of this beautiful animal with large topaz eyes, who has become my partner and friend. We play almost daily in a large arena. I take off his halter and he will lunge free liberty the direction of my arm. I run with him at my shoulder in a game of stop-and-go, where at any time, I'll put on the brakes and he will immediately stop. He then matches my steps as we run circling in either direction. His favorite game is to take a carrot bowing down with his head between his two front legs. Yes, I confess, he has me 'trained' to give him carrots!"

BATUQUE DO REGAL (TIGUARA HYPUS X VERBENA DA CALCIOLANDIA) as a colt.

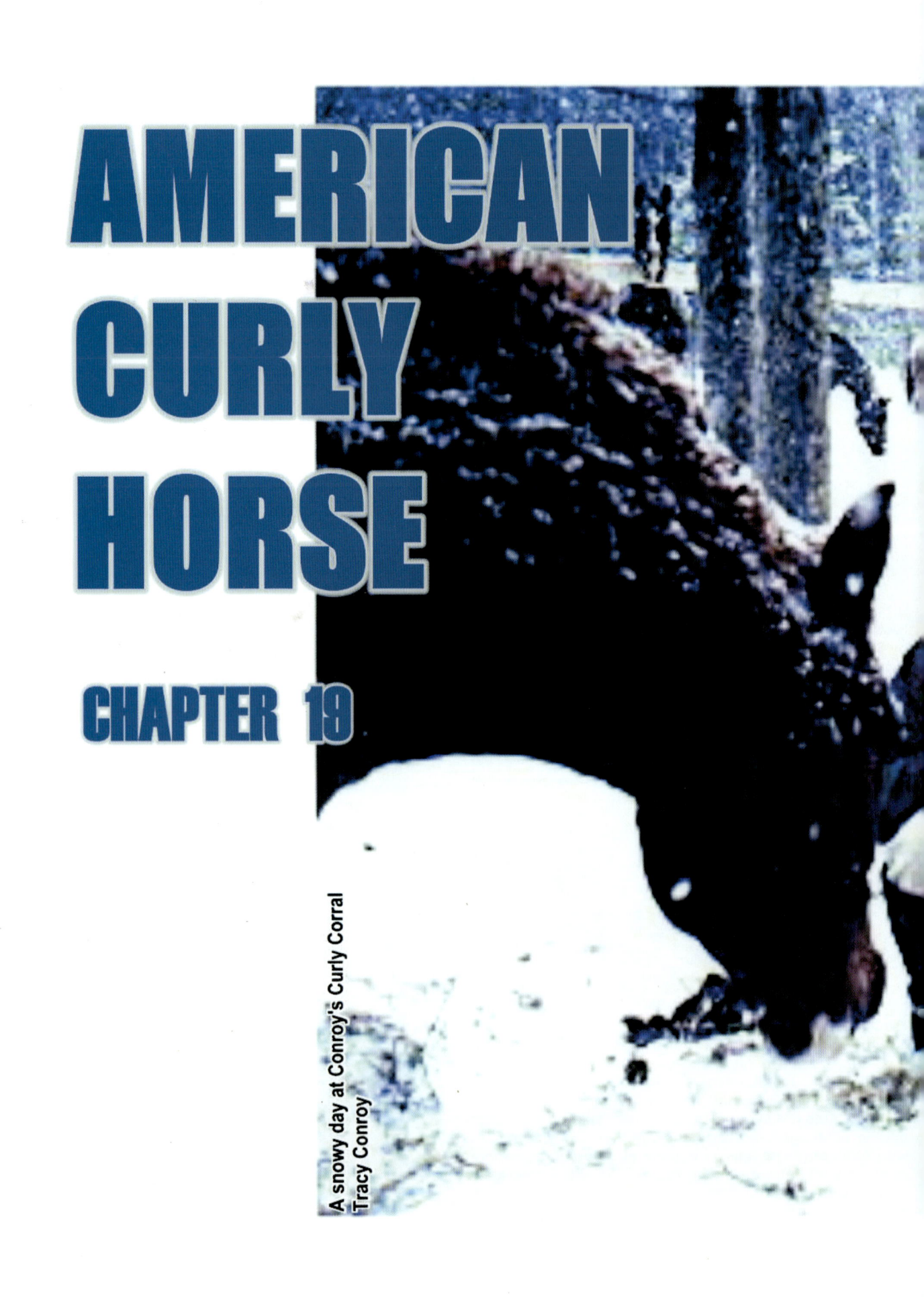

AMERICAN CURLY HORSE

CHAPTER 19

A snowy day at Conroy's Curly Corral
Tracy Conroy

HEIGHT: 14:2 - 15:3 H

GAIT: Running Walk, Fox Trot, Trot, Canter

COLOR: all colors, including pinto and Appaloosa

TRAIT: Stamina & good nature

Chapter 19   The American Curly Horse

The American Curly is a horse with a bright and promising future and a past shrouded in mystery.

The mystery began when a western rancher by the name of Tom Dixon claimed to have brought two curly horses to Nevada from beyond the Kayper Pass in the 1880's. It continues with the discovery of these horses roaming free in the high country range of central Nevada. There is also mystery surrounding their being named after the Bashkir horses of Russia. Someone incorrectly associated the curly coat with Russian Bashkirs. However, Russian Bashkirs don't have curly coats, unless an individual horse is crossed with one of the Soviet breeds that do have curls like the Lokai[1] or the Kuznet.[2]

The American "Bashkirs" do share other characteristics with their Russian namesakes. The traits typical of ancient mountain horses and ponies are: an abiding love of people, uncanny intelligence, stamina, surefootedness, hard feet, compact physique, thick mane and tail, and ease of care. They are versatile and useful animals and in Russia serve not only as riding and draft horses but are used for milk[3] and meat production as well.

---

[1] A breed of horse from Tadzhikistan (former Soviet Union.)
[2] Or Kuznetsk. A breed of horse from Western Siberia.
[3] The mare's milk is made into a product called *koumiss*, a long-time staple and health food used throughout Russia.

Foal, TD'S BLACK EYES BUCK, owned by Tom and Denise Conroy from their Conroy's Curly Corral in Cedarville, Michigan.

Stallion, WALKER'S PRINCE T II is a red roan, registered American Bashkir Curly and Missouri Fox Trotter. He is owned by Johnny Brooks from Circle B Stables in Mountain View, Missouri.

Stallion, LUCKY TOUCH, owned by Jim Howard and Wendy Sauers Smith from their Deserter Creek Curlies in Western Kentucky.

Stallion, WILLOW CREEK CALL ME Mr., registered with American Bashkir Curly Association and truly gaited with a natural running walk. He's owned by Conroy's Curly Corral. As a four-year-old, he was trained by the Conroys' fifteen-year-old daughter.

Diane Mitchell, from Curly Country in Acton, California aboard her stallion BB COPPER SUN, a naturally gaited Curly who performs a square running walk, and is busy starting a Curly line of his own. Photo: Peggi

If the American Bashkir is indeed descended from one of the soviet breeds, the mystery thickens. There are no records of horses being transported in any numbers from Russia to the North American mainland, let alone Nevada.

There is no mention of the importation of horses on any of the ship's logs that brought Russian settlers to the west coast of North America. When they occupied Alaska and parts of the North American coast during the late 1700's and early 1800's, horses were used in a very limited way. A few were used as experiments with farming during that period. Records show there were only sixteen horses in Russian America in 1817.

They did use packhorses to transport goods to the Siberian coast. This was very difficult, and only half the horses could be expected to survive the trip. So there simply were not the numbers that would allow horses to break away from the Alaskan settlements and travel over the extremely hazardous terrain between Alaska and Nevada.

Some have theorized that the Bashkirs came to America across the land bridge during the Ice Age. There is, however, no evidence of fossils or other archeological support of this theory. It appears we have to accept the

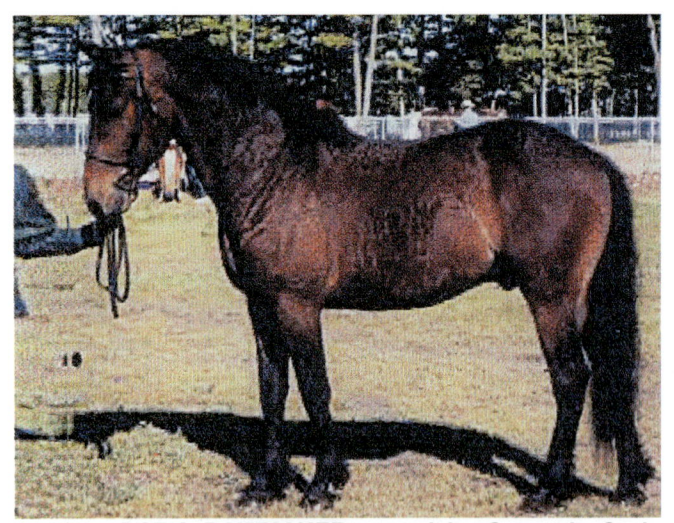

Stallion, D&T'S RAINMAKER owned by Conroy's Curly Corral – Denise and Tom Conroy, in Cedarville, Michigan.

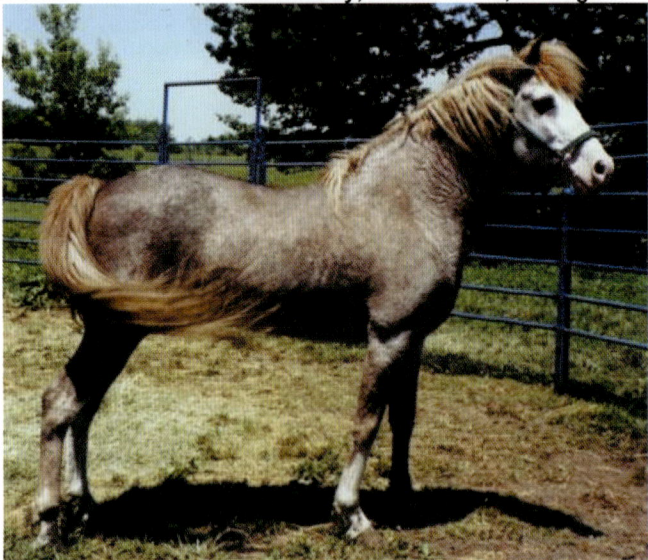

Stallion, SIR PATRICK, a double-registered (ABC and MFTHBA), owned by Richardson's Curlies – Jacqueline Richardson in Woodburn, Iowa.

Stallion, LUCKY TOUCH, from Deserter Creek Curlies – Jim Howard and Wendy Sauers Smith, Owensboro, Kentucky.

presence of these unique and hearty horses without benefit of a clearcut history.

In an attempt to shed a little light on the mystery, 200 horses were studied in the Serology Lab at the University of California at Davis. After blood-typing, it showed that many other breeds have been used in the development of the American Bashkir Curly Horses. Some of them showed bloodmarkers of the Quarter Horse, some of the Morgan breed. The only consistent markers belonged to feral horses or breeds based on feral herds.

Perhaps this breed of horse has managed its own selective breeding program, because it does indeed have qualities peculiar to the breed. The curly coat is particularly interesting. It is transmitted to its offspring approximately half of the time even when mated to horses without the curly coat. Horses with this characteristic have been known to exist throughout history.

Artwork found from 161 A.D. depicted ancient Chinese curly-haired horses. Charles Darwin wrote of Curlies in South America. Napoleon reported seeing "poodle horses" in Vienna at the Schonbrunn Zoo.

"I love taking pictures of J. SILVER HEELS, a.k.a. JAKE - he just fascinates me...he looks like a fairy horse or a unicorn without the horn," says owner Sharon Williams of Frostfire Curlies in Williamsburg, Indiana.

P.T. Barnum exhibited a curly horse in his circus that had been acquired in Cincinnati around 1848. In 1880, Curlies were found and captured from wild Nevada herds by John Camaila. These horses were described as "wholly ones," and "buffalo horses."

In the 1880's, Curlies were not only prized by the Indians, they were believed to be sacred; only a chief could own one. Most prized was the animal possessing a "medicine mark" - a small dark spot in the coat. Their perceived powers of insuring a successful hunt made them the perfect horse to run the buffalo. Drawings from the Indian Chief and artist Red Cloud depict Curlies being ridden at the battle of Little Big Horn. Today, many Curlies can trace their roots back to the Indian Territories of the Dakotas.

The Curly horses have heavy winter coats. They can have kinky, corkscrew curls, or the appearance of crushed velvet, or even a slight wave. Amazingly, unlike other breeds of horses, the Curlies, hair has been found to be hypoallergenic. This makes it ideal for spinning, producing a fine, hypoallergenic cloth. In fact, their hair most closely resembles angora than it does horse hair. Their manes and tail may also be curly, and the mane and sometimes even the tail will shed, along

WALKER'S PRINCE II owned by Johnny Brooks from Circle B Stables in Missouri.

This foal demonstrates a 4-beat gait.

Stallion WELCOME TO HOUSTON, owned by Cheryl Reed, Meanwhile...Back At The Ranch, Bellingham, Washington.

WELCOME TO RIO PONDEROSA, owned by Cheryl Reed.

325

with their winter coats.

Many Curlies are found to have no ergots[4] and small soft chestnuts.[5] Their eyes are characteristically wideset and hooded, like some Asian breeds, which can give them an almost sleepy appearance. It also gives them a wider range of vision to the rear.

Perhaps their most special quality is their trainability. They will stand and face a new or threatening situation without shying or bolting. Their very nature is gentle and "people friendly," making them ideal family horses.

The American Bashkir Curly that possesses all these characteristics today is very much like the Curly horse discovered in 1898. A young boy named Peter Damele was riding with his father across their land in the Peter Hanson mountain range. In the remote high country of central Nevada near Austin, Peter and his father saw three horses with tight, curly ringlets covering their entire bodies.

For almost fifty years, these curly-coated horses roamed freely over the Nevada rangeland owned by the Damele family. But in the winter of 1952, severe weather changed

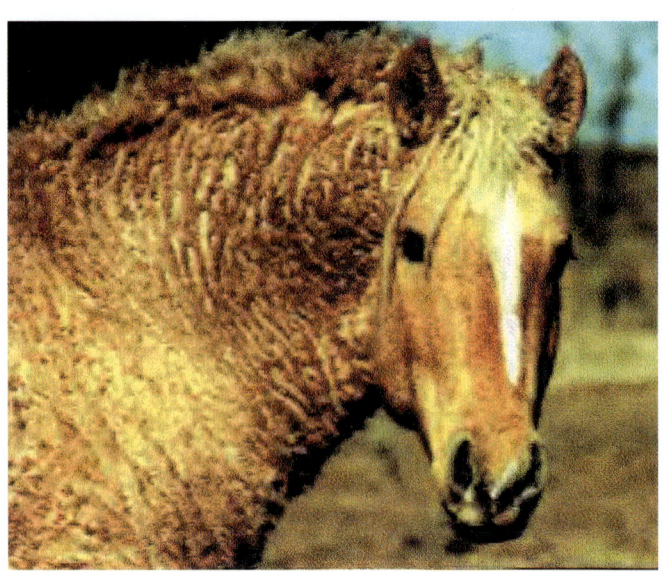

Stallion, FOX FARMS CLASSY, from known as THOR, is from Damele blood lines. He is the son of COLONEL MAJOR CURL and the grandson of COLONEL AUSTIN, great grandson of DIXIE D. P-34. THOR is a wonderful mover. He appears to float across the ground. He keeps his lovely full tail and most of his mane in the summer. Owned by the Hatlestad family from Alva, Oklahoma – and their Red Earth Stables – Classic Curlies.

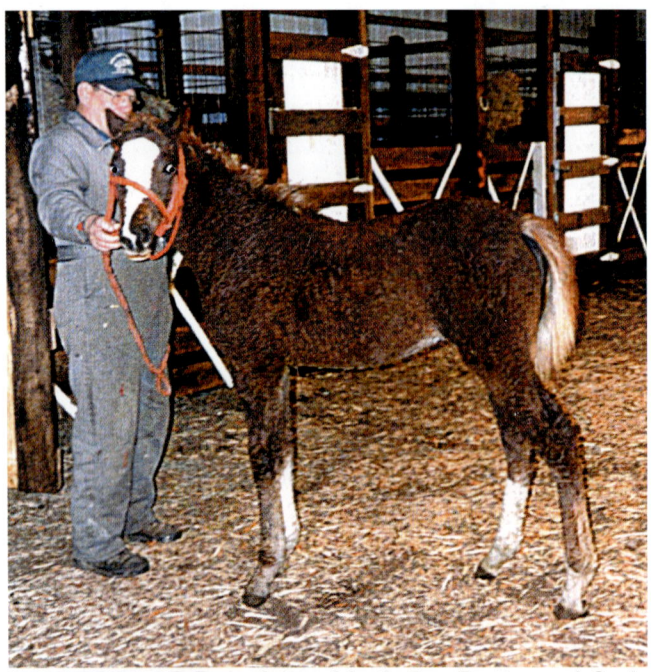

WALKER'S LAD B, registered both Fox Trotter and Curly Horse. Son of WALKER'S PRINCE II.

Colt, MOCHA, out of ND'S BLACK QUEST by COLONIAL'S DUTCH TREAT.

---

[4] A horny growth at the back of the fetlock joint.
[5] A horny growth found on the inside of all four legs, about three inches above the knee, on the inner part of the hock joint.

the future of the hardy herd. The weather was so brutal that most of the horses on the Damele Ranch perished. The family had no choice but to round up the feral herd and bring the Curly horses into the ranch corrals.

To their surprise and pleasure, they found the Curly horses to be extremely tractable and intelligent. Not only were they easy to train; the ranchers were also delighted to discover that many of the curly horses were soft-gaited. Their gait of choice was either a foxtrot or a running walk.

Once the discovery was made that the Curlies were excellent ranch horses, a regular breeding program was initiated on the Damele Ranch that remained in place until 1992. As their herd grew, the Demales began selling horses to other ranches and private parties. Gradually the horses found homes all over the country. At the same time, Curlies can still be found in feral herds. They often come through the government's Adopt-A-Horse program where they are frequently adopted because of their people-friendly attributes.

In 1971, the American Bashkir Curly Registry was founded. People who had become familiar with this unique breed were anxious to create an association that would protect the future of the Curly. In order for a horse to be eligible for registration, it must have curly hair. All colors, including spotted patterns, are acceptable. The horse must exhibit a three-to-six inch long wavy, curly or kinky winter coat. Other attributes must be present as well.

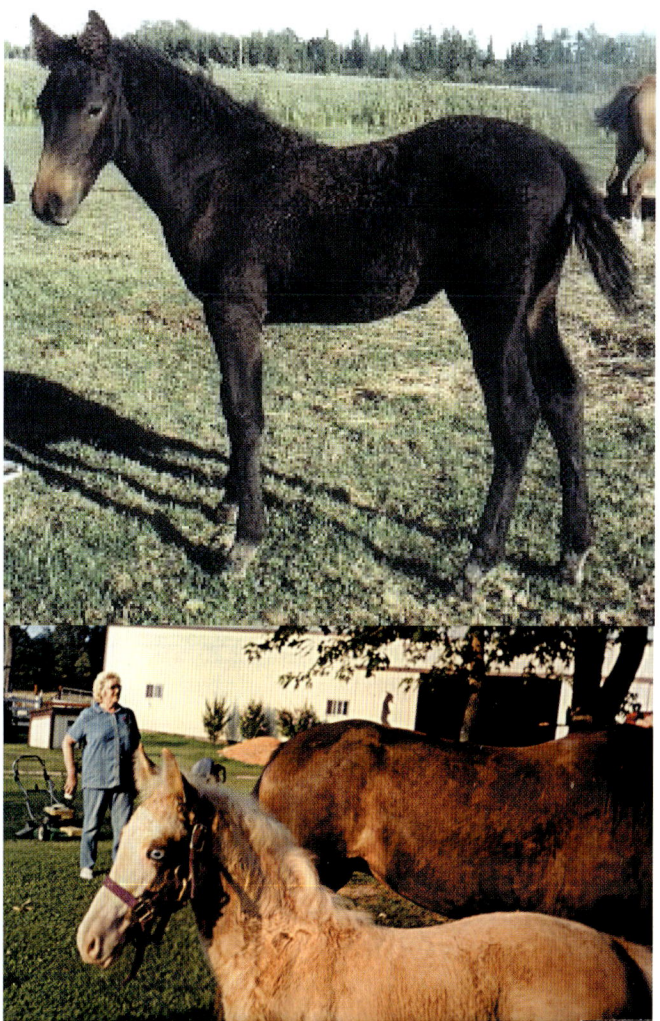

Top: AMY'S BABY. Middle: TD'S PLAIN JANE. Bottom: KALA BABY B, son of AMY'S BABY (Circle B Stables).

PRINCESS ANNIE with Wendy Sauers Smith.

2001 ROSE BOWL PARADE with the Classic Curly Riders (from left to right) Ingrid Fulcher on TOIYA SOLDIER; Marni Malet on EBONY'S MAY DAY; Laurence Washington on BUCK MT'S DAKOTA; Nicole on ROMAN RED; Carrie on JASPER; Tiffany Washington on CHAVEZ; Jim Washing-ton on WOOLLY BULLY; Jim Vail on WINGED VICTORY; Grant Evenson on PEACOCK D; and Jeanette Stone on WRANGLER.

Typically, a Curly horse must be of medium size, 14:2 hands to 15:3 hands. (curly coats appear in both Pony and Draft breeds.) They often resemble early-day Morgans in conformation. They are alert and have a proud carriage. Their hooves are black and hard, and almost perfectly round in shape. At one time, they were thought to have an exceptionally high concentration of red blood cells which would enable their blood to carry more oxygen. They are capable of withstanding extremely cold weather. They have been known to survive temperatures of between 22 and 40 degrees below zero, and they can forage for food under three feet of snow.

Their white cell count, at rest, compares to other breeds at work. A pair is said to be able to draw a sleigh 75 to 85 miles in a 24-hour period without being fed.

At work their breath is quick; in fact, they can actually pant. Their respiration and pulse recovery is unusually efficient. The veins are deep under a layer of fat and an extra-thick hide. Their ability to assimilate feed more readily makes them very "easy keepers."

Their bones are dense, they have stout round cannon bones, and straight legs with flat knees. They have strong hocks and short, strong backs with five lumbar vertebrae, and a round, creaseless rump. Their shoulders are rounded over a strong "V" chest, and their barrel is round. When they are born, they have thick curly coats. Even their eyelashes and the hair inside their ears is curly. Foals tend to hold their tails over their back, like white tailed deer, when they run.

Curly owners are as unique and varied as the horses themselves. Johnny Brooks has raised Curlies for the past 45 years. He was the first trainer of Curlies in Missouri. Many of Johnny's horses are double-registered as Fox Trotters.

Jim Howard and Wendy Sauers Smith live in Western Kentucky on their Deserter Creek Curlies Ranch. Jim began his association with the Curlies in 1986; Wendy started in 1991. Although they now share common goals of conformation, disposition and athletic ability, they have distinct personal preferences that affect the horses being bred at their ranch.

Jim prefers Curlies of size and color. He strives to produce quality Curlies well over 15 hands, many of them with flashy pinto coloring.

Wendy prefers gaited Curlies. She strives to produce quality Curlies with a natural, smooth, fox trot gait.

"Between the two of us, we have Curlies

that are from 14:2 to 16 hands, in all colors, gaited and non-gaited. We both want a horse with good legs, hard hooves, excellent bone, strong top-line, and willing attitude. The thing we like best about Curly horses is their fabulous disposition. We feel this is what really sets a Curly apart from the other breeds. In our breeding program we want to produce the best curly-coated horses we can, whether breeding for size, color, gait – or all three!"

Diane Mitchell at Curly Country in Acton, California, directs her breeding program toward the gaiteds.

"I had been involved in horses all my life, working with Tennessee Walkers for several years. I was looking for something else, but wasn't quite sure what. I hate to jump on a bandwagon, so I responded to an ad in a local paper for 'Curlies for sale.'

"When I went to look, I was quite intrigued by the personality as well as the curls. During the search, the owner commented that they had a stallion whose 'feet went in all directions at the same time.' I asked to see this stallion move.

"When I saw him take his first step, I knew Copper Sun was gaited. They let me ride him and I was ecstatic. I knew I had to have him!

" Since then, I have tried working with all Curlies, and am now working on a line of

Diane Mitchell on her gaited stallion, BB COPPER SUN.

Tracy Conroy aboard CAPT'S CREAMY TAFFY.

In 1971, the American Bashkir Curly Registry was founded. People familiar with this unique breed were anxious to create an association that would protect the future of the Curly.

gaited Curlies. Not all Curlies gait. Actually, only about 30% gait, and most of them have Fox Trotter blood in them. My stallion BB Copper Sun is a horse that gaits and has no Fox Trotter blood. Where his gait came from is hard to say, but it is definitely there when you see him move. Copper is a foundation sire for the ABCR. He is also standing stud at Curly Country, and happily starting a gaited Curly line of his own!"

Tom and Denise Conroy, of Conroy's Curly Corral in Michigan came to the breed by way of Tom's allergies. For many people, the Curly horse proves to be hypoallergenic. This proved true for the Conroys, and led to their becoming enthusiastic breeders and supporters of the breed. Denise goes on to say:

"Regardless of size, color and bloodlines, we have chosen Curlies because of their superior curly traits. They have incredible dispositions, intelligence, very hard feet, excellent conformation and are very easy keepers."

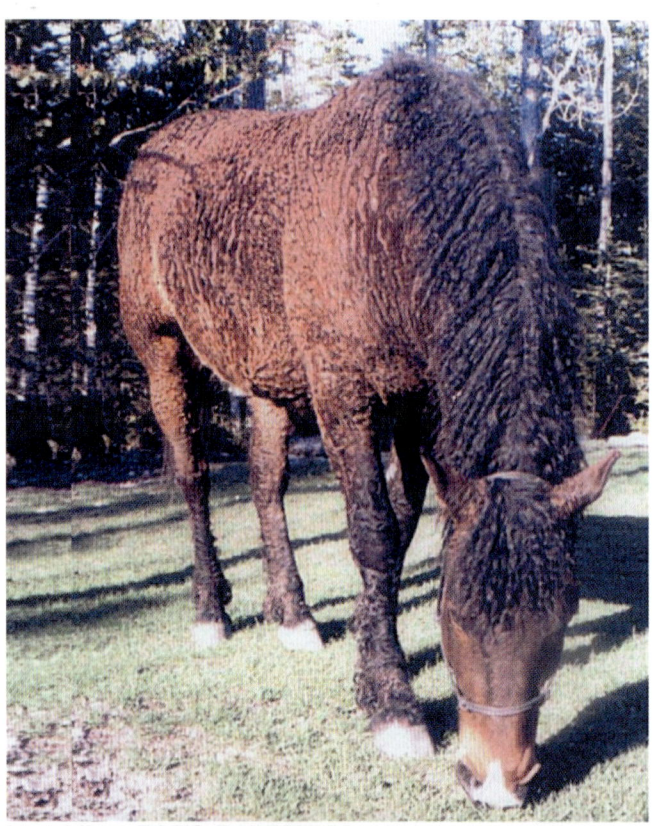

Stallion, WILLOW CREEK CALL ME MISTER. Conroy's Curly Corral in Cedarville, Michigan.

A pasture conversation at Circle B Stables in Mountain View, Missouri.

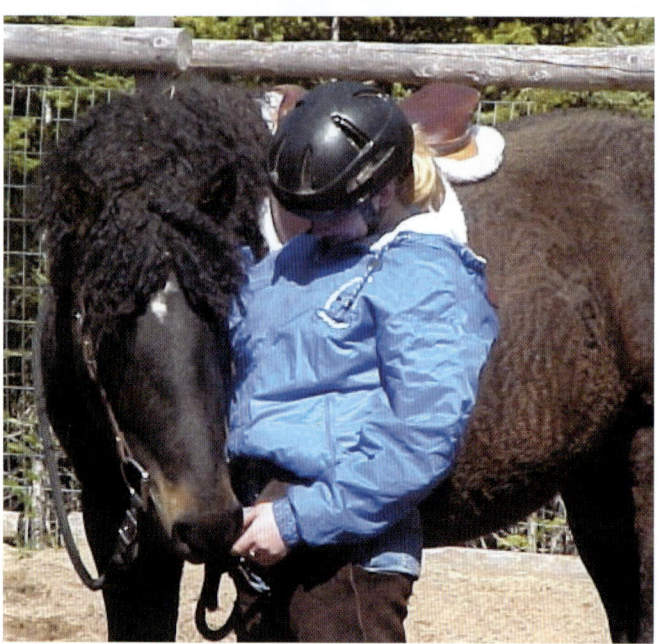

In gelding, D&T'S RAINMAKER, all the visible characteristics of the American Bashkir Curly Horse are evident. He has the roundness of conformation, the curly coat and the curly mane and forelock. RAINMAKER is from Conroy's Curlies.

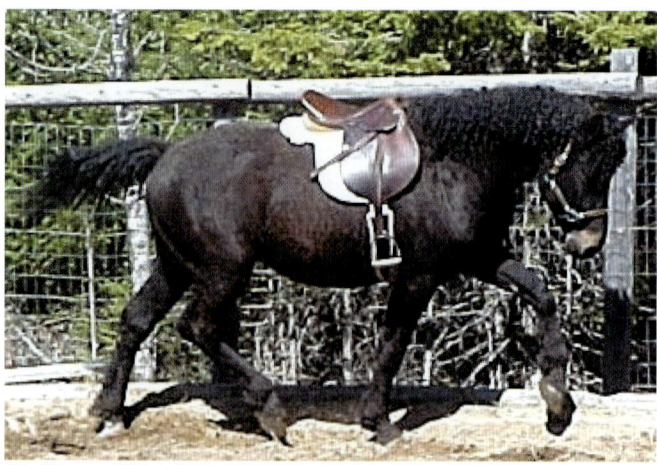

Fifteen-year-old Tracy Conroy, owner and trainer of the stallion, WILLOW CREEK CALL ME MR.

International Curly Horse Organization
North American Curly Horse Registry

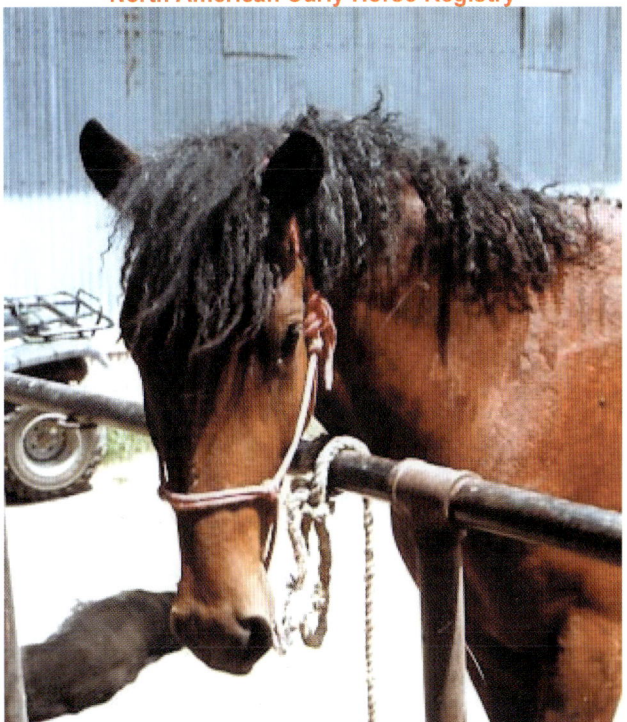

Curly Horses have a disposition to match their beautiful faces.

A pair of exhuberant stallions running free at Hansen's Colorado Curlies owned by Julie Hansen in Macos, Colorado.

In January 2000, a new and important registry was established. Its purpose was to act as a world-scale network for Curly horse preservation, promotion, registration and research. They are, and will remain a democratic, membership-run organization, working hard for the Curly horse.

The ICHO has a comprehensive staff to address the needs of its membership. They have a Member Support Office (for general information, questions about membership or member support issues); a Registrar (for any questions regarding registering a Curly horse with ICHO); an Office of International Affairs (for questions about intergovernmental requirements, breeding, or registering Curly horses outside the U.S.A.); and a Curly Horse Re-search Council (for questions regarding research about the North American Curly Horse). The ICHO also publishes a quarterly newsletter for its membership.

Meanwhile...Back At The Ranch, in Bellingham, Washington, stands palomino stallion, WELCOME TO HOUSTON, sus-pected homozygous for curl. He stands 15:3 and is still growing. He's big-boned and solid, an "old style Curly" with a beautiful head and rocking-horse smooth movement. Super curly in winter, crushed velvet in summer. Full flowing double mane that sheds to 3" in summer and grows back in long silky ringlets. Guaranteed Curls!

Windy McNabb and her son admiring WELCOME TO RIO.

This is PRINCESS ANNIE, a four-year-old, 15:2 hand fox-trotting Curly mare. True to Curly temperament and trainability, after only thirty days training in harness, she went to her first show and placed 2nd in Pleasure Driving. With only harness training and no experience under saddle, she was entered on a last minute whim in the trail class at the Kentucky State Championship Fox Trotter Show. She placed 5th out of 8 riders - Not bad for a horse that isn't "broke to ride." Pictured is Jim Howard of Deserter Creek Curlies Farm in Western Kentucky.

Founding president Donna Vickery maintains a presence, and the Association also has an elected president. Membership is represented by Regional Directors from eight different areas, including the U.S.A., Canada and International.

ICHO is also supported by an Advisory Panel of experts which includes Gus Cothran,

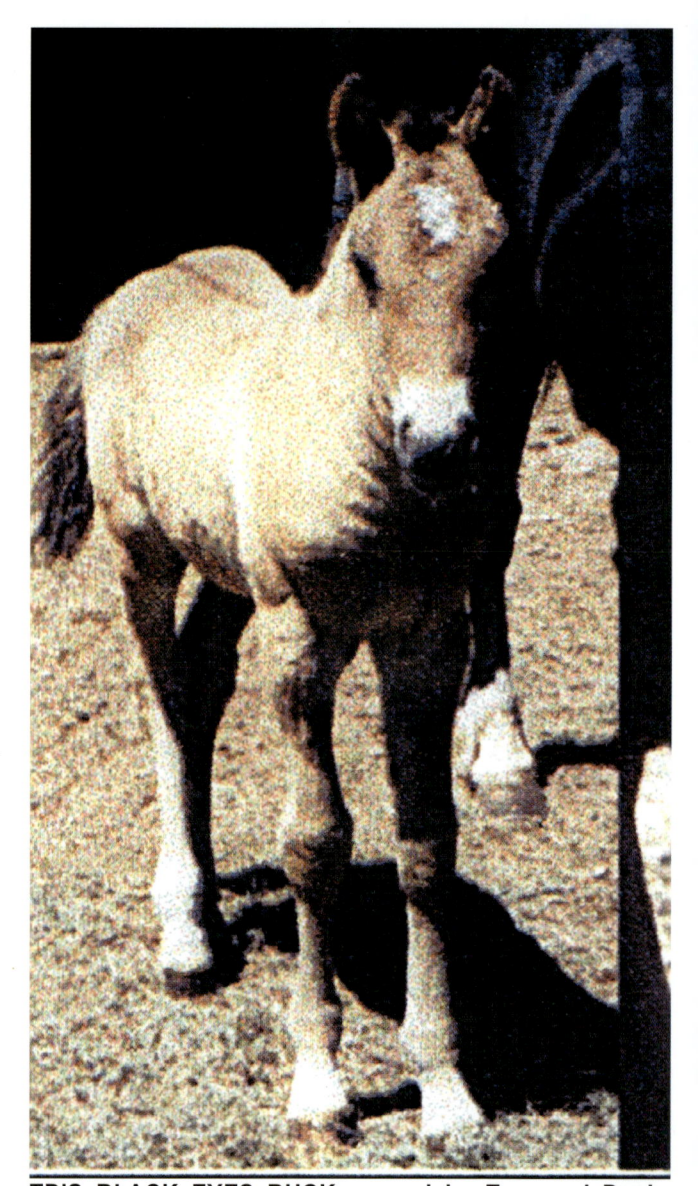

TD'S BLACK EYES BUCK, owned by Tom and Denise Conroy – Conroy's Curly Corral in Cedarville, Michigan.

The magical face of stallion J. SILVER HEELS, owned by Sharon Williams of Williamsburg, Indiana.

Martha Diaz aboard Sparlock, a Curly Horse in the Sport Horse Division. Martha excels in Dressage, Hunter, Jumper and Eventing at Redwind Horse Farm, in El Paso County, Texas.

Meanwhile...Back At The Ranch in the scenic Washington countryside, mothers and babies run free.

The Curly colt WELCOME TO RIO PONDEROSA at four months of age.

The Curly colt, WELCOME TO RIO PONDEROSA with his mother at the farm in Bellingham, Washington.

Another lovely scene at Meanwhile...Back At The Ranch.

Ph.D.,D.Phillip Sponenberg, D.V.M.,Ph.D.,Fred Benker,DVM, and gait clinician, Lee Ziegler.

Important to the Curly Horse fanciers as a group is the Curly Horse Rescue Mission. Herds and individual Curlies alike are rescued, rehabilitated and released for adoption.

The ICHO is developing a framework for research to uncover some of the mysteries surrounding the Curly horse. Current study is focusing on such areas as: Curly horse blood comparisons; gene isolation; epidermal biopsy research; Curly hypoallergenic research and discussion of the genetics of curly hair in horses - or how curly genes may interact.

Within the International Oranization, an ICHO Gaited Curly Association exists to support Gaited Horse owners. Clearly, the Curly horse is a branch of the gaited horse family family tree growing in numbers and importance at a vigorous rate. Shedding their mysterious shroud, they are moving into the twenty first-century with gusto!

Stallion, WELCOME TO HOUSTON

Stallions at play
Hansen's Colorado Curlies

Stallion, BB COPPER SUN, naturally gaited Curly owned and ridden by Diane Mitchell, from Curly Country, in California.

ICELANDIC HORSE

CHAPTER 20

Icelandic stallion, S.C. SOLFARI
Owner: Elisabeth Haug
Photo: Jo Larmour

HEIGHT: 12:3 - 14:3 Hands

GAIT: Walk, Trot, Tolt, Pace, Gallop

COLOR: All colors and markings

TRAIT: Multi-talented

Chapter 20 The Icelandic Horse

The Icelandic's pedigree is unique - unlike any other breed in the world. For almost 1,000 years, these horses have remained totally apart from other equines. The early Viking chieftains of Iceland issued a decree against the importation of live animals. Today, after sporadic attempts to change the law, the ban is still upheld. What began early in the 9TH century as a protection against the plagues affecting much of Europe, remains even today as a prohibition against the importing of any horses into Iceland.

This isolation gives us a perfect look into the ancient horses we only read about. Those horses of long ago such as the Scottish Galloways, Irish Hobbeys, English Palfreys, Spanish Jennets and Asturians were found in great numbers throughout Europe. It was only natural that the early settlers of Iceland would bring these comfortable-riding and good-natured animals with them.

From 874 through 1300, horses in Iceland were bred according to specific rules of color and conformity. But from 1300 through 1900, the lives of the Icelanders and their horses were frequently challenged by the elements. Harsh weather and frequent volcanic eruptions took the lives of many humans as well as horses. From a population of 32,200 many were lost to a bad spell of the illness Moduhardindi. All the Icelandic horses currently in the world are descendants of the surviving 8,600 horses.

The Icelandic horses we know today were developed by both the tough demands of nature and their intimate relationship with the Icelandic people. The cold, wet weather caused the horses to grow shorter legs, shorter necks and longer coats. They adapted to the lack of good feed in the winter by growing very fat in the summer. They can gain weight very quickly, making them very easy keepers.

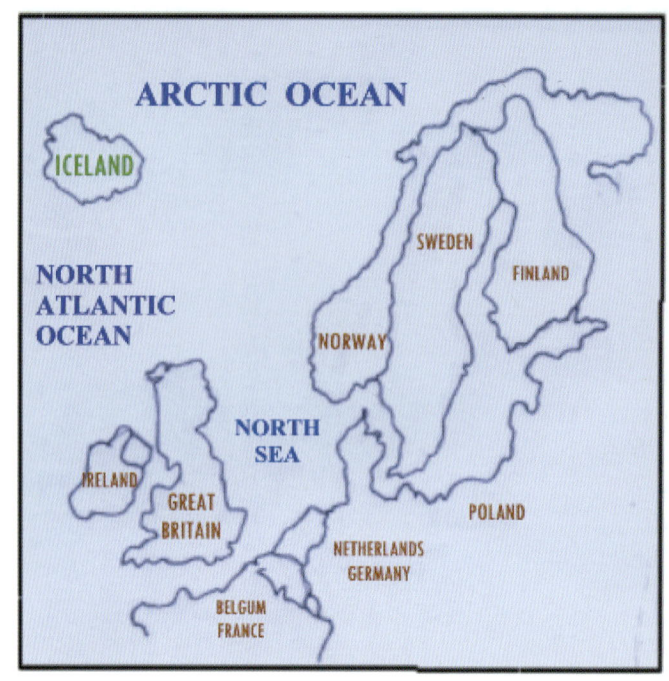

These horses have no natural predators in Iceland, so after nearly 1,000 years, their

A joyful stallion at American Icelandics in Carlsbad, California.

Matheas Kruse on the 32-year-old GLETTA followed by friend, GFOED.

Fight-or-flight instinct has all but disappeared. They are extremely docile by nature but are also highly independent. They exhibit intelligence, common sense, and people-oriented good nature. They do not respond well to intimidation.

The history of the Icelandic horse is intertwined with that of the Icelandic people. In the early days of the Norse settlement, the horse was worshipped as a deity and a symbol of fertility. Icelandic myths and legends incorporate the horse on many levels. It worked side by side with the farmers in the field and supplied much of the entertainment for these hard-working countrymen. The horses were used as transportation and in some cases were consumed as food.[1]

SNOEFAXI from Hredavatnsskali. Photo: Karen Sorensen

German National Championships.

Beginning cart training. Photo: Hasse Hovgaard

A good horse often served as a status symbol. It would be given extra rations and special care at times when even the richest of people went hungry. The horse

---

[1] Even today, if an animal doesn't possess the desirable qualities of an excellent all-around horse, it may be "culled," to make sure it won't leave its mark on future generations.

was more than a helpmate; it was a companion and friend, who in the end might well be buried with its master.

Iceland abounds with glaciers and volcanoes. It is truly a land of fire and ice, where only the strongest survive. The people of Iceland have a more respectful relationship with their horses than any other nation. Only in the last thirty years or so has Iceland begun to build sufficient roads. Throughout the history of the island, horses have been the only means of transportation. In a land of many waterways and few bridges, the Icelandic horse even served as ferries, navigating passengers and supplies across deep glacier rivers. In some instances, the horses were asked to stand in small boats to be transported across a waterway.

Icelanders still go trekking much as they have for hundreds of years. Traditionally, each rider travels with two to four horses. They ride one and pony the rest. The Icelandic horse is especially suited to this type of activity because of its comfort and bonding with other members of the herd. Most breeds are in need of more breathing space, as traveling in a tight bunch would be too difficult. Throughout the day, the rider will alternate the horse he's riding, distributing the workload equally among the horses.

These horses have the wonderful sure-footedness born out of centuries of breeding specifically for this purpose. Today, as in the past, the Icelandics must travel across bad roads, rocks, moors and steep hillsides in all types of weather. These strong individuals have been forged by an unforgiving nature. One concession is made during the icy months of winter, when many of the horses are shod with studded shoes to facilitate travel over slippery roads and slopes.

Norse mythology makes use of the horse in many stories. The supreme god Odin possessed an eight-legged horse named Sleipnir, depicted with his eight legs extended in the ultimate flying pace. Sleipnir was the offspring of the trickster god Loki who had turned himself into a mare to lure the giant's stallion, preventing him from winning the hand of Freyja, goddess of beauty.

Three stallions: SC SOLFARI ridden by Elisabeth Haug, with SC FAGRI JARPUS & KISI.

SC SOLFAXI. Photo: Karen Sorensen

The art of relaxation!

SC INGRIDWELT and filly SC INDIO

Elisabeth Haug riding five stallions. Photo: Karen Sorensen

SC ARI a 4-year-old stallion

1978 Copenhagen International Airport "California here we come!"

Icelandic National Champions - Stallion presentation. Photo: Anette Heaster

Competing in an endurance ride.

SC KISI "Blue ribbons galore!"
Photo: Genise Inman

Solvang Christmas Parade. Photo: Karen Sorensen

SC INDIO with owner Lin Campbell.

SC DIDI and Elisabeth Haug. Photo: Karen Sorensen

SC MORGANBIRTA

Anette and SNAEFAXI.

SC KISI & SIGURBODI

A handsome team of Icelandic horses in harness.

A country scene in the Netherlands.

A country scene in Las Vegas, Nevada.

The first Icelandic horse known by name was the mare Skalm, who is described in the 12th century *Book of Settlements*. The story goes that the Chieftain Seal Thorir settled where Skalm lay down under her load.

Icelandic literature frequently revolves around the special relationship between man and horse. They still cultivate the "horse-rhymes" and stories of great achievements of horses and horsemen. The ratio between horses and humans in Iceland remains a world record. In a country of only 250,000 people, there are an incredible 100,000 horses!

The adult Icelandic horse normally weighs between 750 and 900 pounds. The horse ranges in height from 12:2 to 14:2 hands, with the ideal height being between 13:0 and 13:2 hands tall. There are those who have experimented with increasing the size of the Icelander, but the results have been disappointing. A taller frame diminishes the horse's balance, agility, flexibility, handiness, elasticity, lightfootedness, and surefootedness.

Because their center of gravity is closer to the ground, and their bones are so dense, an Icelandic horse can out-pull other breeds of horses. Their amazing pulling strength ratio alone sets this fine breed apart. Its pulling power is estimated at 1.6 times that of most other breeds.

Coupled with their extreme athletic abilities, this super strength makes the Icelandic an ideal riding horse for almost every type of rider. Unlike other breeds that carry up to one fifth of their own body weight, the Icelandic can carry a remarkable one third! It can carry a rider weighing more than 300 pounds over challenging terrain at a spirited clip. It can also carry a small child with the same brio. It would be a mistake, however, to view this diminutive equine as a child's horse. The Icelandic is a bundle of energy that will match the skills of the best of riders.

Quoting Elisabeth Haug: "The Icelandic horse is very kind, cooperative, strongminded, and sensible. On the one hand, this makes him difficult to brainwash into a push-button machine. On the other, it makes him a great,

Photo: Rick Osteen

Elisabeth Haug on SNOESFARI, from Hredavatnsskalli.

Elisabeth Haug, author of the book "Living Your Dream," on GLELTA from Holl. Photo: Karen Sorensen

SINDRI, the "Mighty Midget."

safe friend on the trail. Like any other horse, he's at his best when not ridden solely by children, and some of them have a personality that makes them better babysitters than others. Icelandic horses are well aware of how much stronger they are, mentally as well as physically, than children. They regard children as two-legged foals and will humor and pamper them as long as they find it reasonable. After that, they'll not put the child in danger but merely remain standing still or go about their

SC SOLFARI. Photo: Karen Sorensen

Icelandic National Championships

Benni & ELJAN, from Langelands Gaarden.

own business in an orderly manner."

The Icelandic doesn't mature until it reaches seven or so and is considered in its prime well into its twenties. A record lifespan is credited to an Icelandic mare named Thulla, who lived to be 57. When her elderly owner died, Thulla simply stopped eating.

Because of this gradual maturing, Icelandics are best trained starting at age four. After basic lessons, the horses are put to pasture again until they turn five. At this time, full weight can be put on them, and their training resumes. Much time and patience is devoted to developing the performance of the gaits unique to the Icelandic. First, attention is given to the walk, the trot and the canter. The "tolt," which translates to "running walk," is the premier gait, and demands careful attention. It is a traveling gait, in which the feet move in the

Here is an example of the incredible connection possible between man and horse. This rider is totally blind.

same pattern as the walk. However, in the tolt, there is a higher action of the legs and an energy that produces quite a speed. Primary consideration is given to ground-covering movements and a look of harmony and balance. The gait is tested for smoothness by having the rider carry a full mug of beer; the amount spilled determines the quality of the gait.

The fifth gait - the flying pace - is known as the gait of the gods. Tremendous care is lavished on developing the muscles necessary for this powerful gait. Not every animal will

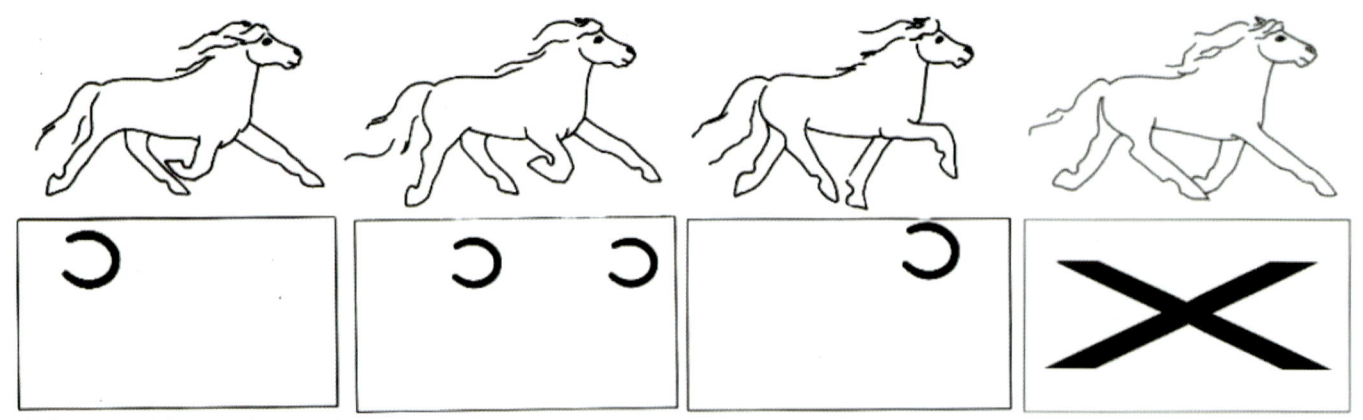

1) Leads with rear foot. 2) Same side; 2-leg support. 3) Pushes off with front foot. 4) All 4 feet off the ground.

The flying pace is known as the "Gait of the Gods."

have the talent to perform this unique gait. Those that do are cherished within the breed.

In the flying pace, or "flugskeid," the feet move in a lateral fashion, with both feet on a side acting together. The result is an extremely rapid gait that has been clocked at 35 mph. The feet move so quickly that with each stride, all four feet are off the ground. At this moment, the horse is truly "flying"!

The breed standards set down by the The Federation of Icelandic Horse Associations (FEIF) are quite specific as to conformation and breeding. First, the Icelandic horse is bred for use, not for show. The primary concern is the rideability of the animal. It must be courageous and resourceful, cooperative and willing, with good forward action. The robust-

The Icelandic horse is judged very carefully. Greatl care is taken to maintain a horse with precise conformation. Here we see the ideal body fitting into a rectangle.

ness typical of the Icelandic must always be preserved along with a flawless disposition.

The Icelandic horse should be well-proportioned and somewhat rectangular. The head must be cleancut and expressive, the neck long, supple and well-set so that the horse carries itself well-balanced when ridden. The shoulder should be comparatively long and well angled, the back flexible and the croup sloping, wide and well-muscled. The limbs must be strong, with well-defined joints.

The horse must give an impression

Lyn and SC KISI

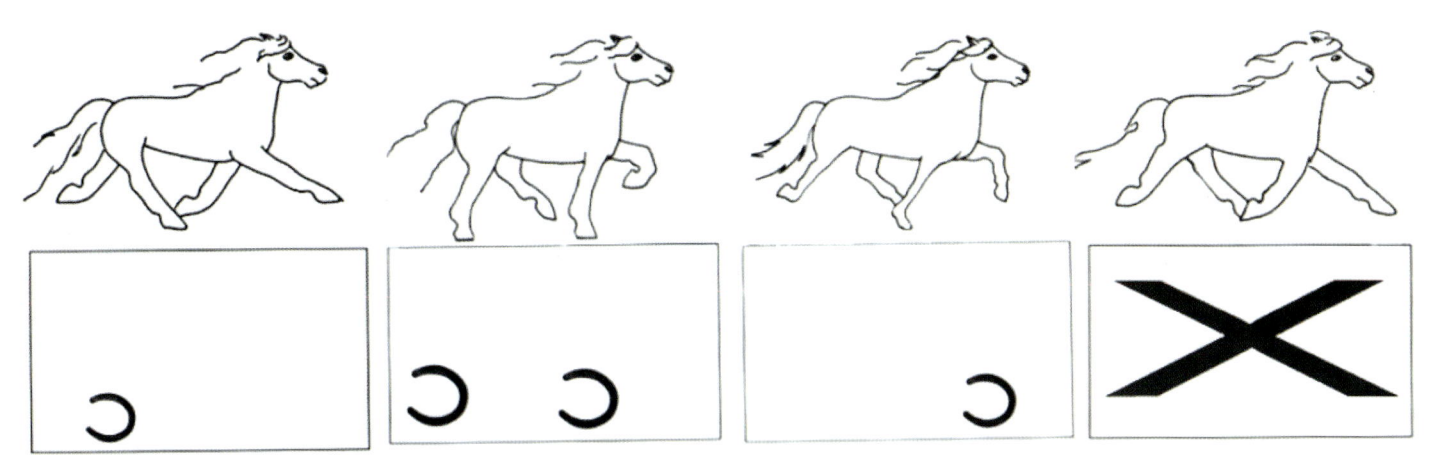

5) Leads with rear foot. 6) Same side; 2-leg support. 7) Pushes off with front foot. 8) All 4 feet off the ground.

This gait is highly praised in an Icelandic Horse.

Reynir Adelsteinsson on a trek across the Icelandic Highlands.

of courage and power, with a proud and attentive expression, especially when ridden.

Almost every possible horse color is available in the Icelandic. Fanciers boast of more than 42 different colors and patterns. From black to white to black and white, a veritable rainbow of choices is available.

The hair and coat of the Icelandic is "teddy bear" fuzzy in the winter, sleek and glowing in the summer. The mane and tail are thick and full, so coarse that tangling is not a problem.

Willingness to work, and performance of the tolt are the most important qualities of the Icelandic horse. In the official scoring process, each of these categories is appointed a factor of 10, which equals 10% of the overall evaluation. If a horse demonstrates irritability or unpleasantness of any kind, it is deemed unworthy to be considered for breeding stock.

Comfort of gait and ease of disposition contribute enormously to the enjoyment and versatility of these very special equines. This is a horse that can swim in summer and skate in winter. In Iceland, seeing folks cling to the horse's back as it swims about in the many waterways, is a common sight. When the same waterways are frozen in winter, these resilient animals can navigate their way across with athletic aplomb.

How do these horses endure outside their homeland? This is an important question, because they can never return to Iceland once they have traveled outside its boundaries.

Stallion, SC ARI with Elisabeth Haug

Fortunately, they do extremely well. There are numbers on the continent equal to those in Iceland itself - a growth that took place over a mere 40 years - and they remain the most popular trekking horse in Europe today. The numbers of horses in America are not yet great, but as people become aware of their fine qualities, they are sure to match the European popularity.

Canada, Texas, the West Coast and the Northeast have all established breeders who are enthusiastic and conscientious about promoting the Icelandics. Riders all over the country are enjoying ownership of these unique animals.

Even the hot, dry desert community of Las Vegas, Nevada[2] is the unlikely home to several of these Nordic exports, one of whom is a 1985 colt named Sokki fra Sleitustodum, owned by Sue Ryzdynski.

Sokki was born on a farm in northern Iceland and imported into the United States as a demonstration horse in 1990. He was a spirited youngster and traveled all over the country to represent his breed after he was gelded.

Although Sokki's grandsire was the famous Hrapn 802 fra Holtsmula, and his sire was Adam 978 fra Modalfelli, he was registered in neither Iceland nor in the United States. Sue purchased him in 1993 and has developed a terrific bond with this "very patient and mellow" fellow.

Sue uses Sokki for pleasure trail riding and says he is great with children and timid adults. He watches out for "personal" space and takes good care of his rider, always aware of how he negotiates the terrain. Sue's initial decision to buy an Icelandic Horse was based on its temperament, smooth way of going, and ideal size (neither too tall nor too short). Sue's expectations were matched and surpassed. She adds a word of praise for the breed's super thick mane and tail. Apparently they act as both fly protection and sunscreen.

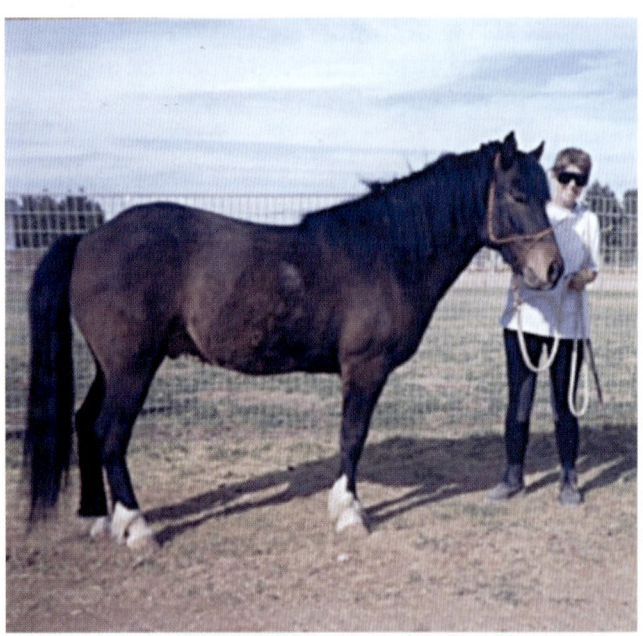

SOKKI FRA SLEITUSTODUM with owner Sue Ryzdynski.

Verner Bruren on RHEIM from Ghato

---

[2] In southern Nevada, the temperature can rise to between 105° and 115° with humidity levels of 10% - 35% during the summer.

Anette on SNAEFAXI. Photo: Karen Sorensen

Dan and SC ELSKA

All ready for a pleasure ride.

SC KISI

Two lovely faces.

SC KRAKI and friends. Photo: Jo Larmour

SC SEGURBODI

Musen on KNALDTORA

SC ELDING and son SC THOR

Young stallions. Photo: JoLarmour

BOERKUR and BRUNKA old friends.

SC BLESI

Getting acquainted.

"California Trek" SC SOLFARI. Photo: Karen Sorensen

"Iceland Trek"

Three Stallions. Photo: Jo Larmour

Nap time. "ZIPPER" (SC KRAKI) and owner, Donna

TIGER HORSE

CHAPTER 21

Tiger mare, Hi Bar's Flashy Color and foal
Tye Dy's Summer Color
Owner: Monica Denney

HEIGHT: 14 -16 hands

GAIT: 4-beat middle

COLOR: Lp characteristic

TRAIT: Calm versatility

Chapter 21 The Tiger Horse

Does it have stripes? Does it roar in-stead of neigh? Well no, but the Tiger Horse is certainly worth roaring about. The history of this colorful, easy-gaited breed is also the history of both Europe and the New World. These horses carried the conquerors as well as the conquered. They carved out new empires all over the world.

Thirty thousand years ago, pictures of horses wearing rope halters were painted in Spanish caves. The models for these paintings were members of the huge "proto warmblood" herds that roamed Europe and became the base for the develop-ment of the Spanish Jennet. Gradually, over the course of centuries, a smooth-gaited, high-spirited horse emerged with added infusions of the blood of horses from northern climates, the Orient, and North Africa.

The Jennet was highly regarded by European horsemen throughout the 15th to 18th centuries. In 1593, Salomen de al Broue, Horsemaster to Henry IV of France, wrote: "Comparing the better horses in order to appreciate their greater perfection, I must place the Spanish at the top, and give it my vote for being the most noble, the best conformed, the bravest and the most worthy of being mounted by a Great King."

In 1759, when Ferdinand came to the Spanish throne, he passed the "Gentleman's Law," which stated that all gentlemen must ride stallions. The law intensified the breeding of horses that had great presence but were gentle and docile in nature.

This ancestor of all North American gaited breeds was quite popular in color patterns found today in the Appaloosa, Knabstrupper and Noriter horses. The Spanish referred to these uniquely marked horses as *Caballo Tigre*, or Tiger Horses.

By the time the English began colonizing the New World, tiger-patterned horses began to loose favor as the English Thoroughbred became more popular. Consequently, many Tiger Horses were exported to the Canadian colonies.

KIMBARS ANGELIC CHEROKEE was born pure white and gradually developed the exotic coloring displayed in this picture as a two-year-old.

The Tiger Horse creates such a dramatic picture in Western tack. Owned by Kellswater Farm.

The Ni Mee Poo (Nez Perce) Tribe of the Pacific Northwest has been singled out and erroneously credited with having developed the spotted horses found so frequently in the Northwest today. The Ni Mee Poo themselves deny that they developed this breed. They did, however, love them, and traded to acquire them whenever possible.

The Ni Mee Poo Indians were perhaps the finest horsemen and horse breeders of the Native American tribes. They acquired the Tiger Horses from Canadian traders. Tribal oral history also tells of special stallions bought from Russian traders. These horses must have been obtained by the Russians from the Spanish in California, because there is no evidence of any Russian importation of livestock.

The Spanish influence on these "Native American" horses produced excellent stock. We have evidence of this from a journal entry written by Merriweather Lewis during the Lewis and Clark expedition of 1804. Lewis wrote: "Some of those horses are pied with large spots of white, irregularly scattered and intermixed with black, brown, bay or some other dark color, but much the larger portion are of a uniform color with stars, snips, and white feet, or in this respect marked much like our best blooded horses in Virginia, which they resemble as well in fleetness and bottom as in form and color."

"Lady Conaway's Spanish Jennet," by Wooton. Painting owned by the Marquess of Hertford.

Lewis was a horse breeder himself, and he recognized the quality in the Ni Me Poo herds. He was familiar with the strong Spanish influence on the British Hobby and the Narragansett Pacer so popular in the colonies at that time.

One of the most notable traits retained by Tiger Horses was the ability to perform an intermediate 4-beat gait, or as it became known later, the "Indian Shuffle." This comfortable riding gait was much easier on both the horse and the rider. Cowboys would pay as much as fifty dollars more for a "shuffler," and this at a time when a good broke cowpony would go for around thirty dollars.

In 1877, war between the Ni Mee Poo and the U.S. Army brought the conquest and relocation of the Tribe. At that time, there was a nearly complete dispersal of the huge herd of Indian horses. Many of these Tiger-type horses

Bay leopard stallion, TS WIND WALKER, "DILLON," owned and ridden by Karen Shead.

This newborn foal appears to be dark, but who knows how it will mature? The coloring and markings of the Tiger horse change with age.

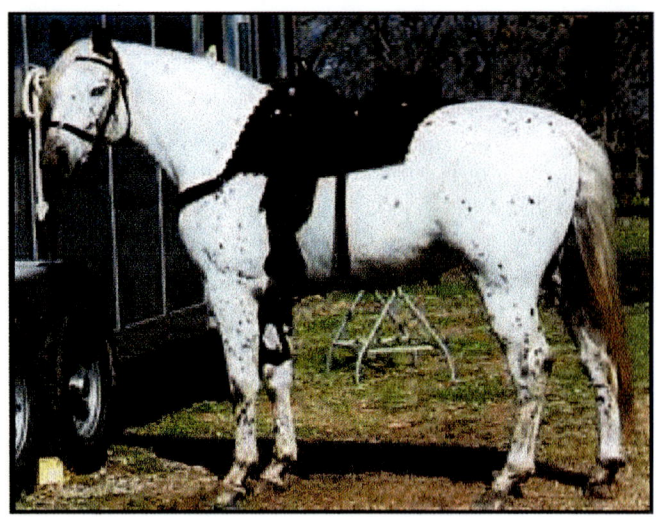

Photo: Courtesy The Tiger Horse Association.

turned up in the Pacific Northwest because they had been distributed among the Native American Tribes by trade. Some ranchers either owned, or held portions of, the Ni Mee Poo herds against the eventual return of their rightful owners.

In 1938, Claude Thompson, an Oregon farmer, established a registry to preserve the spotted horses. The founding of the Appaloosa Horse Club did bring attention to these horses, and prevented their total extinction.

Unfortunately, the ApHc embarked on crossbreeding programs, using Arabian, Thoroughbred, and Quarter Horse bloodlines. This all but eliminated the original Tiger characteristics from the modern Appaloosa Horse. Pockets of the original Tiger-type horse have remained, however, in Canada, remote areas of the Pacific Northwest, and in those herds held in trust by ranch families for the Ni Mee Poo Indians. There are also breeders who have continued to adhere to the "Foundation" breeding stock that regularly produce horses of the ancient Spanish type with their 4-beat gaits.

In 1991, two individuals were brought together by chance with a desire to uncover the origins of the 4-beat gait in their own Appaloosa horses. Their curiosity launched three years of intensive research into the real history behind their Appaloosas.

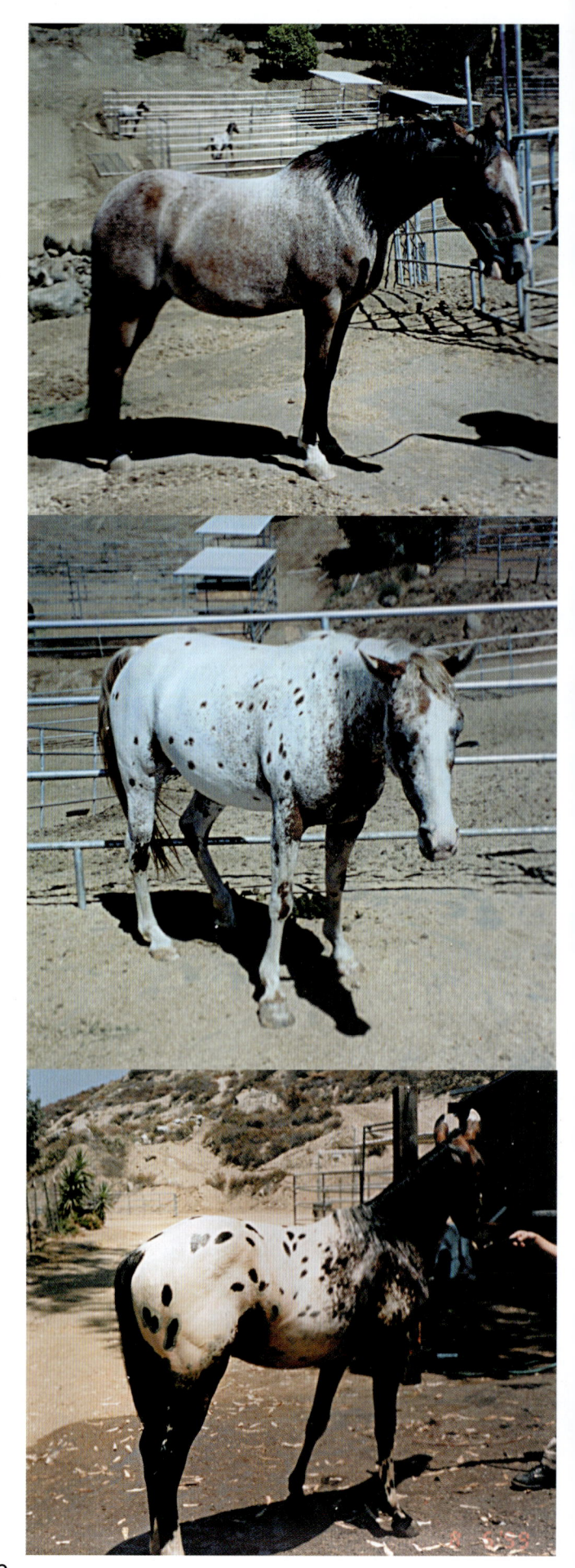

Once a significant amount of information was discovered that directly contradicted accepted Appaloosa history, it was decided a new organization was needed. They were determined to find, preserve and perpetuate what was left of the ancient Tiger-type horses. In 1994, they launched the Tiger Horse Association. It was felt that the best approach was to start with an open club, and to gradually move toward incorporation with the growth of membership. In 1994, the Tiger Horse Association "opened for business" as a membership-driven unincorporated registry. In 1998, the association became incorporated. The founding members, as stock owners, appointed the Board of Directors, who then adopted the Mission Statement and Bylaws of the of the Tiger Horse Association Inc.[1]

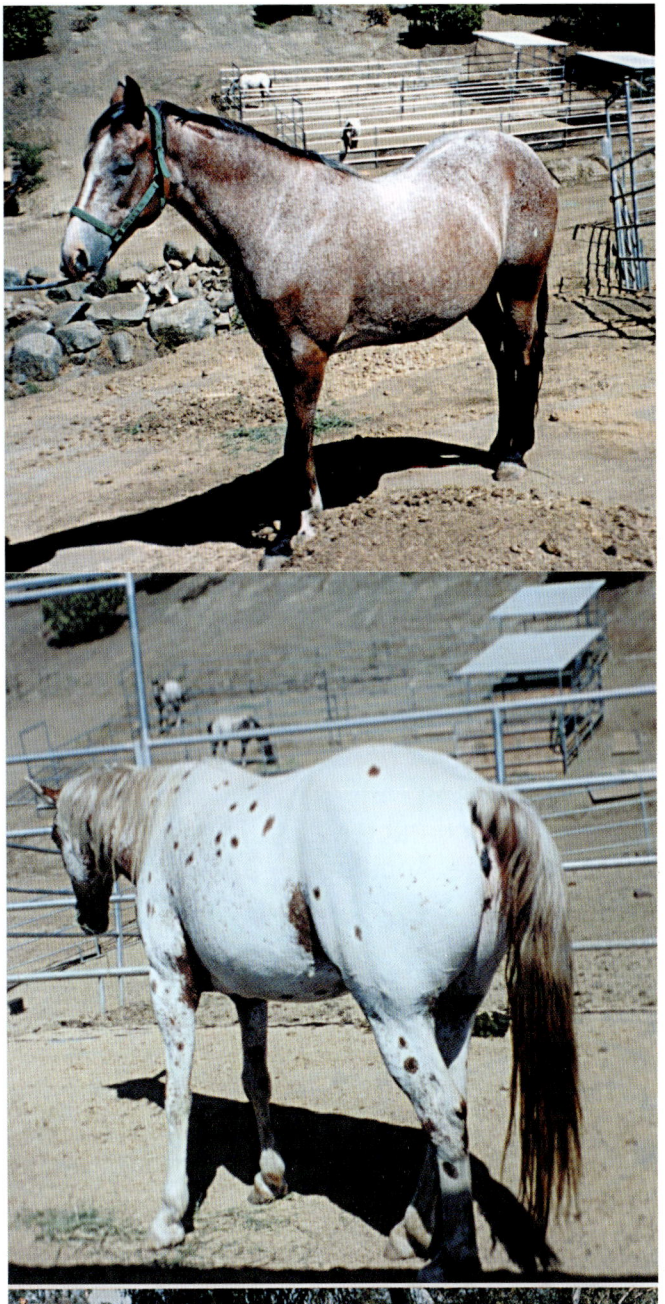

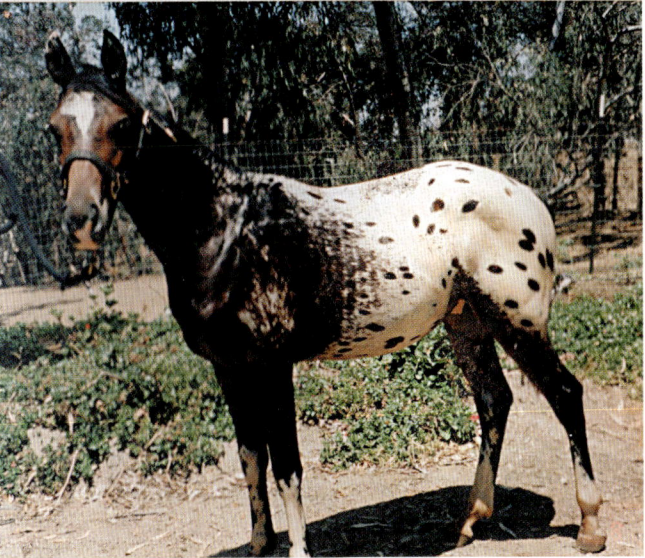

From the time of its incorporation, the THA has been poised to launch an all out campaign to find and register as many horses that still resemble the ancient type as possible. This should ensure survival for these special horses into the 21st century. The job of getting the Tiger Horse breed on the right track - and into the public eye - began in earnest.

The Association went cyber, published a website and established an e-mail address, which has attracted quite a bit of notice, and new members. They have also gathered together an impressive group of experts to develop a comprehensive breed standard.

⇦ **Photos to the left on both facing pages, picture both sides of the same horse. Top: TAL'S ANGEL ROSE, a nine-year-old mare standing 15:3 hands. Middle: HY BAR'S FLASHY COLOR, also registered as an American Indian and Appaloosa. Bottom: TYE DY, a four-year-old, standing 14:1 hands, registered as both Tiger and Appaloosa. All three horses are owned by Monica Denney and The Spotted Rears Tiger Horse Ranch.**

---

[1] These bylaws are found in the official Tiger Horse Association Inc. Handbook.

A 4-year-old chestnut varnish roan mare with blanket. Owned by Wits End Ranch.

An eight-year-old bay varnish roan stallion, ROCKET'S SPOTTED EAGLE, owned by Shufflin'B Ranch

A four-year-old peacock spotted bay leopard stallion, SKYE'S APACHE CLOUD, owned by Shufflin' B Ranch.

Dr. D. Phillip Sponengerg of the Virginia Tech College of Veterinary Medicine is an expert in color genetics and Spanish Horses; Deb Bennet, Ph.D., is a horse historian and conformation expert; members of the Ni Mee Poo Tribe contributed oral history to the research; and Dr. Gus Cothran and the University of Kentucky are doing D.N.A. work for the association to assure proper parentage records and genetic health of the Tiger Horse Breed. Dr. Cothran is also charting the advances made toward the establishment of a true breed.

The name Tiger Horse was chosen not only because it honored the horses of Spanish origin, but alluded to its colorful coat patterns and courageous character.

As foundation stock, the association is actively seeking horses that display the Tiger Horse characteristics of Leopard complex (Appaloosa) color patterns, an even, four-beat intermediate gait, and at least some Spanish conformation characteristics. These horses can come from the Appaloosa, Spanish Mustang, or any of the Paso breeds; Native American herds; wild horse herds; or some of the less well-known based breeds, such as the Florida Cracker.

Because the ability to gait has been actively bred out of the Leopard Complex horses, it is understood by the association, that outside gaited blood must be brought in to strengthen the gaiting ability of the Tiger Horse. However, the association will not allow wholesale out-crossing. Such practices have been the down-fall of other breed organizations by destroying the very characteristics they were designed to protect.

⬅ The bottom two photos to the left are those of father and son. ROCKET'S SPOTTED EAGLE, a.k.a. SKYE, is the result of the blending of Appaloosa and Walker bloodlines, retaining the basic original Spanish traits of both breeds. Skye was selected by the Tiger Horse Associationas a foundation-registered horse in 1994, and he has since produced both sons and daughters to carry on the heritage of his ancestors. SKYE has a true singlefoot gait, being a fine example of a "champagne glass ride." His son, SKYE'S APACHE CLOUD, is the result of further addition of foundation Appaloosa blood to the Shufflin B breeding stock.

All outcrossing will be one generation only. Foals from outcross breedings will have the letter O put at the end of their registration number. These O-number horses must be bred back to a regular registered Tiger Horse or to another O-number horse to produce a registered Tiger Horse. Any further out- crossing of O-number horses will result in the offspring not being accepted for registration. Tiger Horse breeders who wish to use approved outcross horses must submit an out-cross approval form and a video clearly showing the gait, color and conformation of the horse in question to the Tiger Horse Association for approval.

All horses accepted for foundation registration will display the ideal combination of conformation, gait and color. The offspring of registered Tiger Horses may not all, however, show the color traits. These offspring are still fully registered Tiger Horses, but they will not be accepted in the Model Category.

In order to be considered for foundation registration, a video clearly showing the Tiger Horse characteristics and the 4-beat gait of the horse, as well as a completed registration application, must be submitted to the Board of Directors and Advisors of the association and all foundation breeding stock must be both blood-typed and D.N.A. typed.

Once a horse is accepted for registration, it is eligible to participate in the "Tiger In Your Tack" awards program. A Tiger horse may achieve a Certificate of Merit for accruing 100 points in a category. A horse that accumulates 100 points in the Model Category, 100 points in the Road Gait Category and at least 100 points in any other Performance Category will earn a Permanent Championship. Thus, the Permanent Champion horses will be the ideal toward which all breeders can strive. They must prove not only their color heritage but their gaited working ability as well. Any horse not clearly demonstrating an intermediate four beat gait will not be accepted for registration.

This system was put in place to assure that the Tiger Horse will always be what the Spanish and the Native Americans knew and loved: a superior, beautiful, working, travel horse.

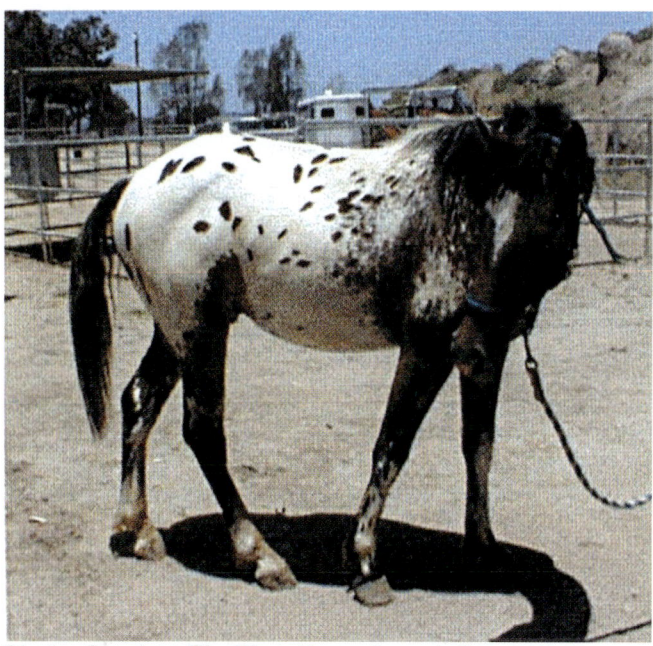

Photo: Courtesy The Tiger Horse Association

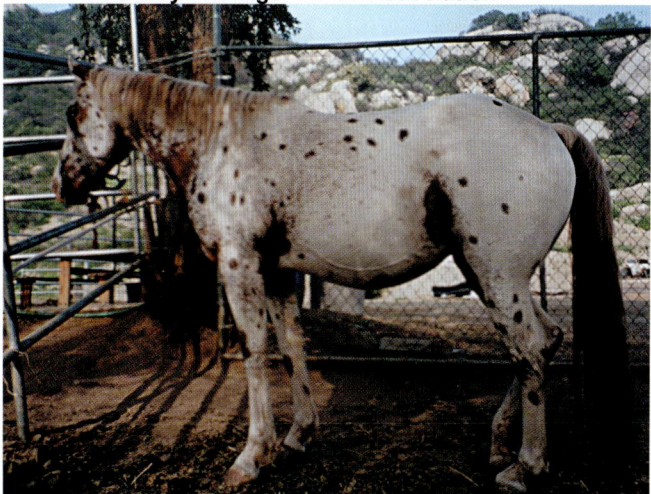

HY BAR'S FLASHY COLOR, owned by Spotted Rears Tiger Horse Ranch in Bonsall, California.

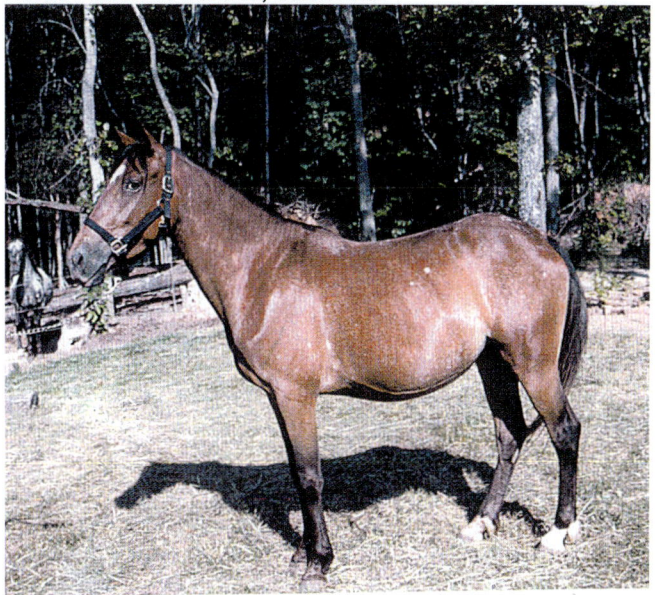

Fou-year-old bay snowflake mare, owned by Wits End Ranch.

The general impression of a Tiger Horse is of a colorful, gaited, light horse breed that is well-balanced and sturdy, with no extreme muscling.

Starting at the head, the ears should be of medium length and generally curved and notched. They should be mobile and alert. The eyes are large and prominent with white sclera surrounding the iris, which can give a surprised expression. Viewed from the front, the head should look lean with no cheekiness. A broad flat forehead between widely spaced eyes should taper to a fine muzzle with large, sensitive nostrils. The profile can be straight to slightly convex.

The neck should be set high, and be moderately long and well-balanced, blending smoothly into the wither. The wither should be well-defined with a sloping shoulder. Viewed from the front, the chest is of medium width, frequently with a well-defined V between the forelegs. The back is short-coupled and strong, with a well-muscled loin and a sloping croup that is level with or lower than the withers, with a low-set tail.

The legs should be sturdy with dense substantial bone with clean, strong, dry tendons and moderate, strong flexible pasterns. The hooves are dense, resilient,

➪ Photos to the right: Top: A five-year-old bay with a blanket and spots and roaning, owned by Wit's End Ranch. Middle: A modern-day Tiger. Photo courtesy The Tiger Horse Association. Bottom: Stallion, CENTAURO LA ESTRELLA. "TORO" is a true Largo horse, with consistent gait. He is a perfect gentleman, with a strong, surefooted way of going, and he is an approved outcross horse for the Tiger Horse Association. (Registered NASHA) Owned by Wits End Ranch.

TYE DY'S SUMMER COLOR with mom, HI BAR'S FLASHY COLOR.

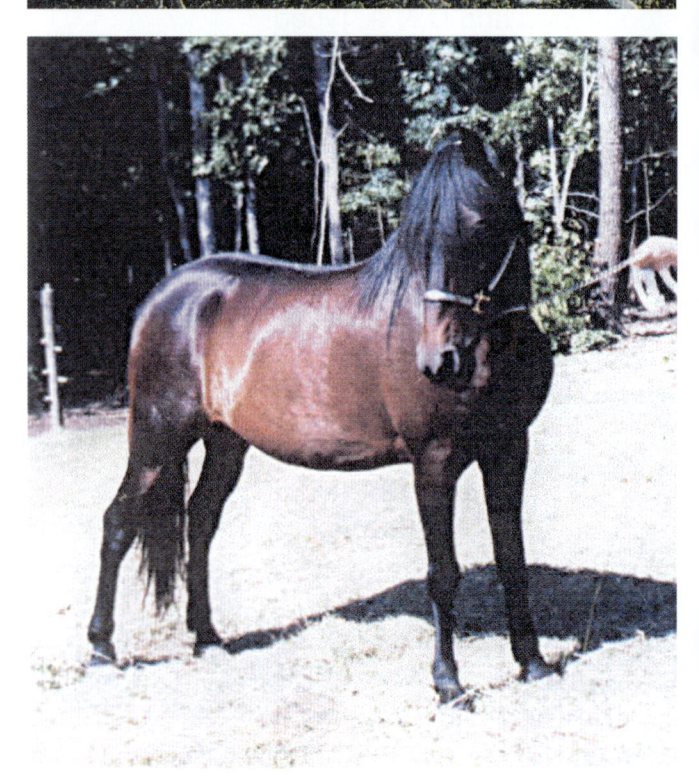

TBA HOLLYWOOD EAGLE, color producing stallion owned by Wits End Ranch.

Photo: Courtesy The Tiger Horse Association.

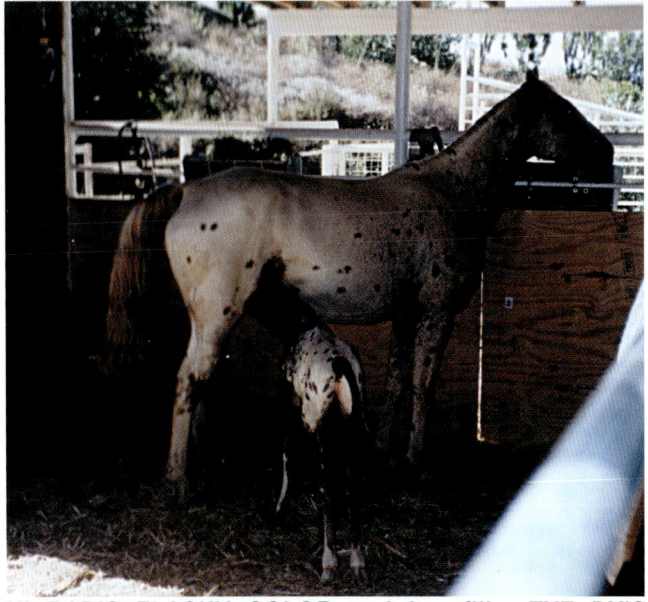

HI BAR'S FLASHY COLOR and her filly, **TYE DY'S SUMMER COLOR**.

substantial and usually striped.

The Tiger Horse ranges in size from 14 to 16 hands, with 14:2 being most typical and desirable. Their weight can range from 700 to 1,300 pounds. Mane and tail hair can range from nearly nonexistent to extremely long and full, but should always be completely natural.

Careful attention is given to temperament, which should be affectionate, gentle, and sensible, with excellent learning capability and a good deal of heart. A controlled spirit and great sense of pride, often referred to by the Spanish as brio, is common.

The Tiger Horse is primarily a gaited, working saddlehorse which, in addition to walk and canter, must perform an even, natural, intermediate four-beat gait. Evenness of gait and an ability to hold gait are very important. The athleticism, soundness and smoothness of the gaits are of great importance. All gaits should have good fluid movement with excellent reach and drive. Termino, while allowed, is not a sought-after characteristic, and if present must be carefully evaluated for soundness. All gaits must be totally natural.

The Tiger Horse is a gaited breed with a color preference. Any base coat color (black, bay, etc.) is acceptable. Common coat patterns include leopard, blanket (with or without spots), roan (with or without spots), and snowflake.

El Caballo Tigre has a long, proud history that stretches back into the mists of antiquity in Spain. In the New World it has changed the course of history for many Native Americans. These smooth-riding, colorful horses have evolved in sheltered pockets al-

This mare has snow flakes on her rear, and her foal exhibits a full blanket. Photo: Courtesy The Tiger Horse Association

most unchanged, and the Tiger Horse Association exists to ensure that they will survive for future generations to enjoy.

With their solid footing now in place, The Tiger Horse Association has established exceptionally high standards for their horses and breeders. It is expected that the horse-buying public will be able to trust that a *true* Tiger Horse will be a *truly gaited* horse, and this will be true for all future generations.

Darlene Salminen, supporter and guardian of the Tiger Horse Association, is developing a breeding program at her Wits End Ranch in Huddleston, Virginia. Her ranch is a small, family-owned and operated horse facility nestled in the foothills of the Blue Ridge Mountains in south central Virginia. The ranch has a strong focus on the rare and beautiful Tiger Horse. It may occasionally breed a registered Appaloosa or North American Single-footing Horse, but its primary mission is to save the Tigers, a rare slice of American history, from extinction.

As a founding member of the Tiger Horse Association, Darlene feels that her breeding program must maintain the highest standards for the breed. To ensure this, only the soundest, best-gaited, most intelligent and best-colored horses are kept as breeding stock. Her goal is eventually to have such consistency in their bloodlines that virtually all foals will be born with good color patterns and a gait that is strong enough to cross-register with the North American Single-Footing Horse Association.

Bonsall, California, is home to the Spotted Rears Ranch and owner Monica Denny. Quoting Monica: "As a little girl, I felt I was destined to be an equestrienne, and some day have my own ranch. But Daddy wouldn't provide the horse, so I had to find another way

This lovely Tiger Horse comes from Kellswater Farm.

This foal exhibits one of the truly exotic colorations found in the Tiger Horse.

⇨	Photos to the right. Top: Stallion SIZ HE'S HOT STUFF, "GUMBY," is an example of a ghost horse. He is homozygous for exotic coloring. He is pictured at 13 years of age. He stands 16 hands tall. The Ghost Horse is the most desired in breeding operations, because of the guarantee to produce color in its get.
Bottom: The lovely expressive face of a Tiger Horse. Photo: courtesy the Tiger Horse Association.

⇦	Demonstration of the smooth soft-gait of the Tiger Horse DILLON with Karen Shead, up. Courtesy of the Tiger Shead.

to my goal. I began nine long years of riding lessons, bareback, English and Western. In summers I went to horse camp. It would have been cheaper for Dad to buy the farm and horse!"

Through the years, Monica owned a panoply of horses: an Arabian, a Quarter Horse, a Tennessee Walker, another Quarter Horse, and another Tennessee Walker. Though she was drawn to the Appaloosa's bold coloring, she couldn't let go of the gait of the Tennessee Walker. So began her search for the Tiger Horse.

Monica feels she was lucky to find good breeding stock right off the bat. Her horses all have blankets with spots, and her foals have been well-gaited, beautiful and kind in disposition. She does advise those folks just starting out to make an effort to start with a registered Tiger Horse. She goes on to say: "If you aren't able to find one, run an ad in your local horse magazine for gaited Appaloosas."

Quoting founding director Darlene Salminen: "The Tiger Horse Association intends to be around for the long haul. This is not a personal hobby by one individual, but a mission by many people, intended to last well beyond the lifetime of a single person. The eventual goal of the association is to switch to a nonprofit membership organization as soon as it is on firm enough footing and has a solid enough membership base to take on the tasks of running the organization. By bringing together a Board of Directors of top-quality horse people, and setting high standards for registration and breeding, the Tiger Horse Association is setting the tone for the future, and ensuring members and the horse-buying public of consistent and fair treatment, as well as an organization that will be in existence far into the future, to preserve the past."

Demonstration of the desired smooth 4-beat gait of the Tiger Horse, DILLON, with Karen Shead, up. Photo: Courtesy The Tiger Shead

WALKALOOSA HORSE

CHAPTER 22

HEIGHT: 13 to 17 hands

GAIT: Natural Singlefoot

COLOR: Appaloosa

TRAIT: Pleasure Trail

Chapter 22 The Walkaloosa Horse

The Eohippus was the first horse to walk the earth. It had three toes and spots. There is evidence that these small creatures inhabited the North American continent. For unknown reasons, they became extinct here and moved on through the Bering Straits to the Don Region of Russia.

What remains important in their development is the coat pattern they displayed. This was most likely a natural protection device. With this spotted shading and coloration, it was easy for the horse to disappear into the surrounding landscape. Like many other wild creatures with distinctive coat designs, these ancient horses owe much of their survival to their exotic coats.

Early cave drawings exhibit the spotted characteristics of prehistoric equines. Spots on horses have been held in high esteem throughout history.

The first horses that "returned" to the New World came with the early Spanish explorers. The Spanish Jennet, a primary-foundation horse of the North and South American herds, was named for the Arab word *genet,* which describes a kind of spotted civet cat. So truly, our equestrian heritage has spots.

In the early 1700's, the Ni Mee Poo or Nez Perce Indians of the Pacific Northwest became infatuated with the spotted horses. They became the first tribe to practice selective breeding, and soon they became closely associated with these dappled beauties. The tiger patterns were quite rare and therefore were the most prized and treasured.

By the mid-1700's, the "Spotted Iberians" began losing their popularity in Spain and France, so large numbers of them were sold to the colonies. Many went to Canada and the American west. These taller, well-gaited specimens contributed to the Native American Nez Perce herds. Chief Joseph, leader of the Nez Perce tribe, rode a roan horse, and there is evidence that only medicine men were allowed to own and ride the speckled appaloosa-type horse.

In addition to the coloring, the horse's "shuffling" gait provided the nomadic Indians a way of moving their households quickly without undo jarring of belongings, or rider.

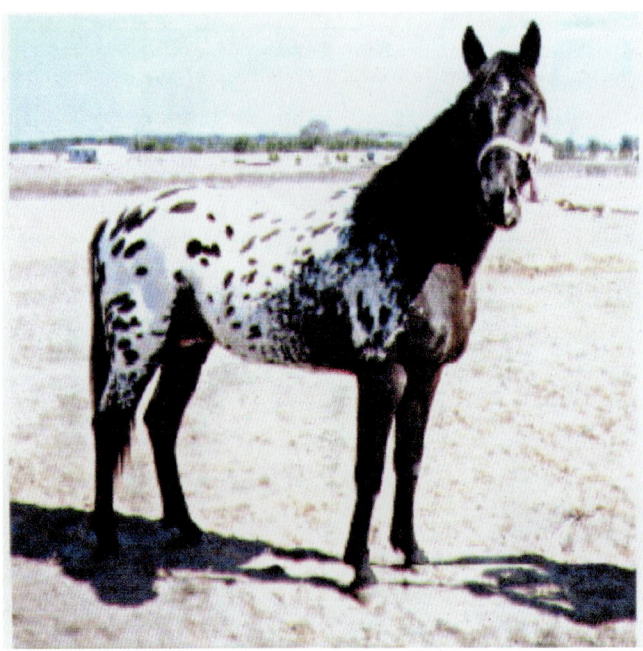

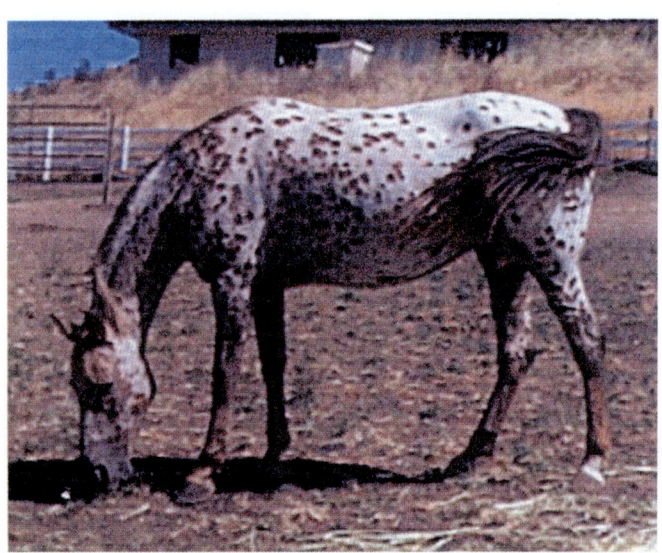

Photo courtesy the Walkaloosa Association.

STRAWBERRY SHORTCAKE, owned by Lee Waddle.

Unfortunately, when the Indian tribes were decimated and disbursed, the horses also entered a delicate period of near-extinction.

In 1938, the Appaloosa Horse Club was founded. Its emphasis was on color, and gaited and non-gaited alike were eligible if spots were present. Once the Appaloosa was given a name, attention was given to the redesign. Breeders introduced Arab blood to refine the horse, and Quarter Horse blood to standardize its characteristics.

A horse with soft gait was not only discouraged, it was retrained or quietly sold. What goes in the showring is all too often what breeders strive for. An intermediate gait other than a trot is cause for disqualification.

So in 1983 the Walkaloosa Horse Association was born. To qualify as a Walkaloosa, a horse had to meet one of three criteria:

1. Be the progeny of a registered Walkaloosa stallion and mare.
2. Show Appaloosa coloring and demonstrate an intermediate gait other than a trot.

THEY CALL ME BEAUTY, a blue roan leopard.

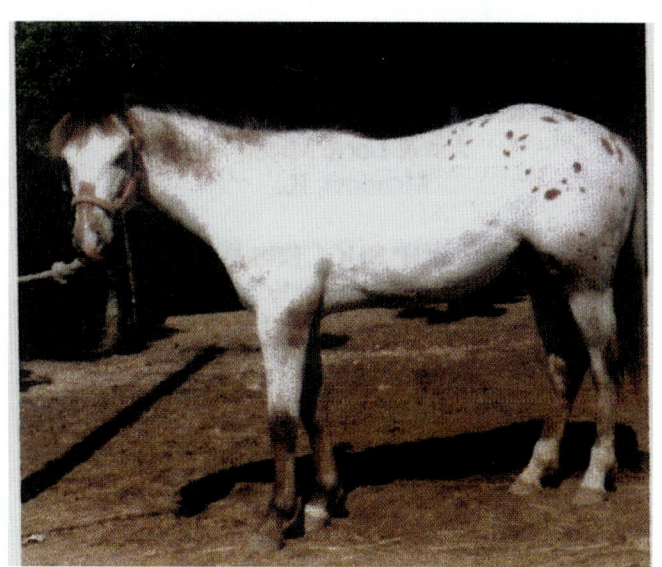

LEGENDARY CISCO. Cindy Winter, Tuscumbia, Missouri.

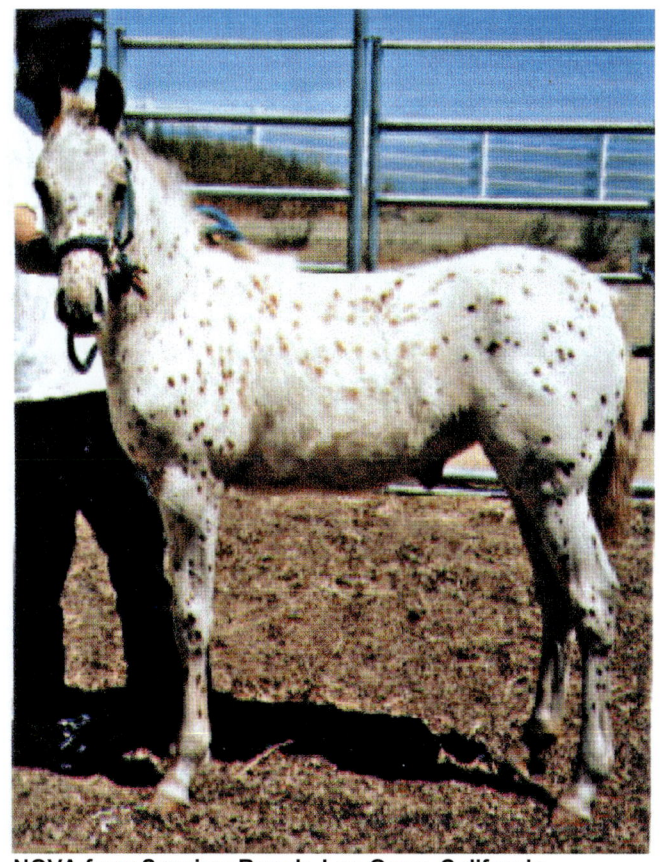

NOVA from Seaview Ranch, Los Osos, California.

GHOST, a Walkaloosa-producing stallion at Seaview Ranch (Pem Meyer)

GUNSMOKE BO JANGLES.

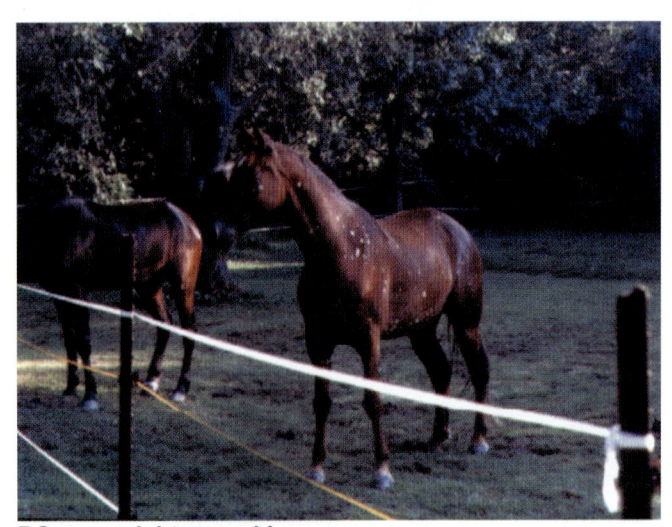

BO as an eight-year-old.

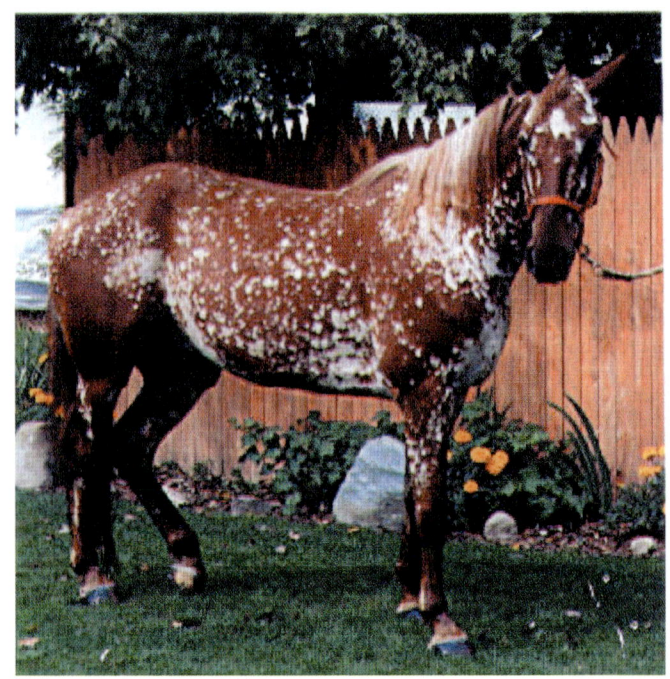

BO as a nine-year-old.

BO JANGLES Walking Horse, turned Walkaloosa.

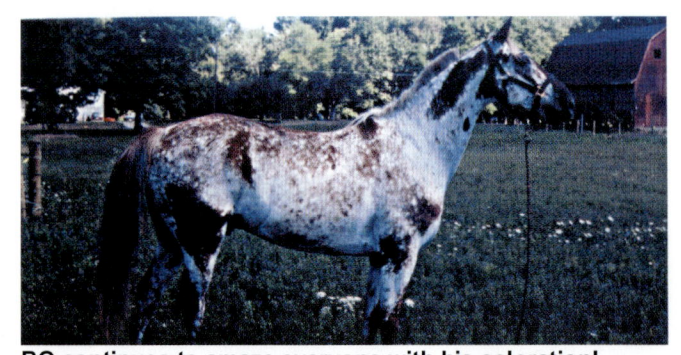

BO continues to amaze everyone with his coloration!

On this page, we see the story of the lovely Gunsmoke BO Jangles, owned by Wade and Sharon Dennis from Farmington, Ohio.

When Sharon first brought BO home, she didn't know she owned a Walkaloosa. When the spots began appearing, she had no idea what was happening. The veterinarian thought maybe the sun was causing the "problem." Then Sharon met someone on a trail ride who told her she had a Walkaloosa!

BO was a three-year-old when he went to live with the Dennis family, and his coat was solid chestnut. Gradually his coloration began to change. When BO made this color transition, Sharon's neighbors thought she had bought another horse.

His story is testament to the fascination of all the variations found in the coats of the soft-gaited Walkaloosas.

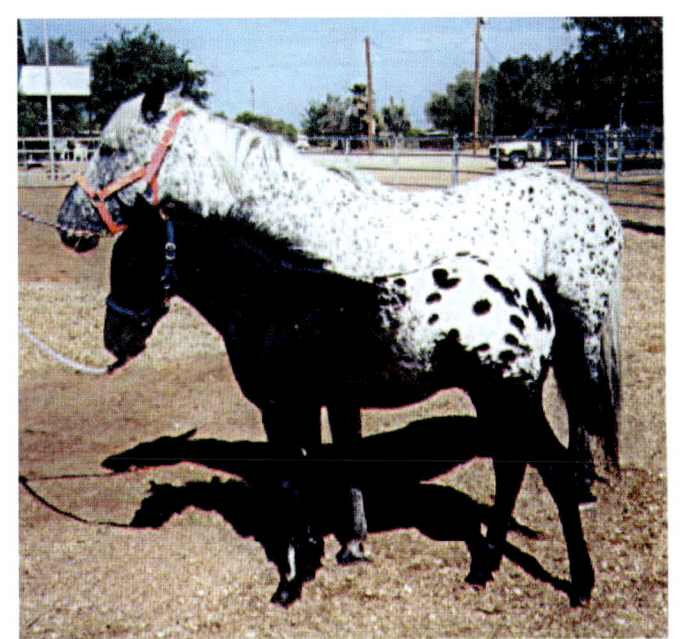

3. Be the product of verifiable Appaloosa (color) and Paso, Fox Trotter, or Tennessee Walker blood.

Walkaloosas come in many shapes and sizes. Their smooth natural gaits and colorful coat patterns make this wonderful horse unique.

The eyes should be ringed with white sclera, be large and kind and widely spaced. The horse's profile may be either straight or slightly dished. Their muzzle should be clean and fine and the skin should have mottling around their eyes and or lips. An attractive head is important. A coarse head or Roman nose is not desirable.

The neck should be well-set on the shoulders and be medium-to-long in length. The throatlatch should be well-defined with a slight arch to the neck.

The forehand, a sloping shoulder with good depth through the heart girth and a moderately wide chest is preferred. The horse should be well-muscled but not muscle-bound. The withers should be well-defined but not pronounced; and the back should be short and strong.

Mare THEY CALL ME SPOT, owned by Pem Meyer, with her colt UNIQUE, owned by Carol Pappas.

Leopard-coated SHOCKER.

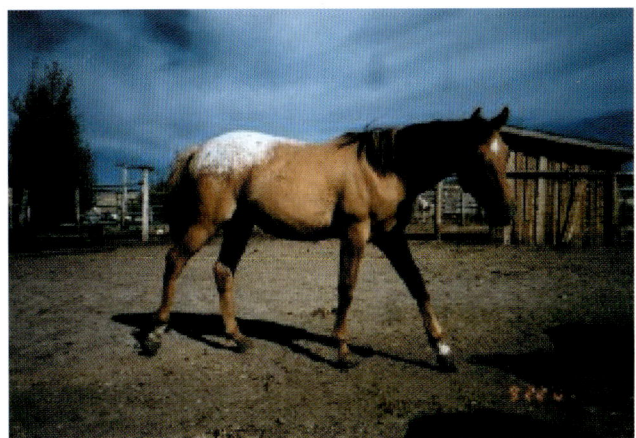

SUNDANCER from Tetonia, Idaho.

Betty Ellis and SHADO'S CRACKER JACK. Betty had wanted a Walkaloosa for years. She visited an Appaloosa breeding facility in Missouri in the hope of finding a gaited version of the spotted beauties. Later she found an ad for a gaited colt from the same Appaloosa breeders. She sent for a video, but someone else had already purchased the colt. She continued to search for a new horse, but changed her focus to Tennessee Walkers. While visiting various sites on the net, she discovered the very same colt advertised for sale again. He is now at his new home with Betty where he was obviously meant to be!

Photo courtesy the Walkaloosa Association.

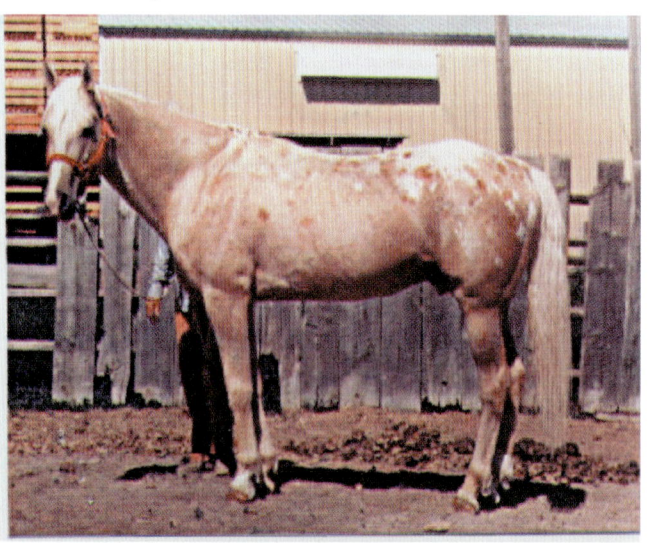

Photo courtesy the Walkaloosa Association.

Registered Walkaloosa stallion SUNDANCER

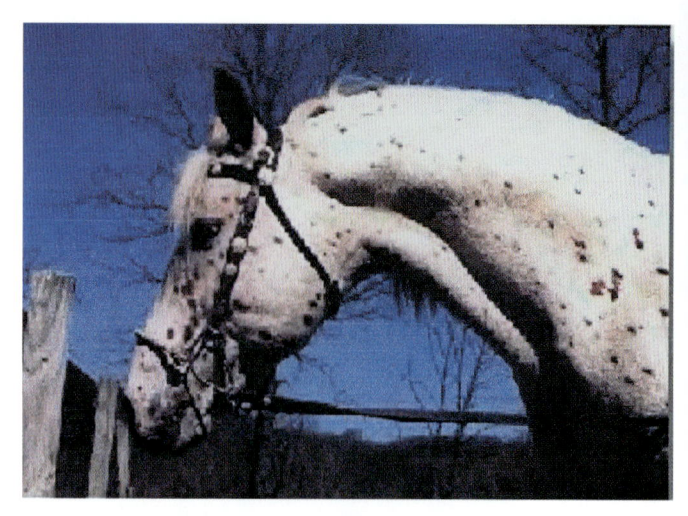

WL'S PRINCE SARKE "SHARK" (1985) owned by Dodie and Marc Sable of New Promise Farms in Kutztown, Pennsylvania. In their words: "There are not enough words to describe how special this stallion is to us and to the many people who have taken lessons with him as their mount, or watched him work. He is truly a prepotent stallion, passing along his disposition, temperament, conformation and agility to every foal, no matter what the breed of mare."

The hip should be long and reaching, topped off with a slightly sloping croup and a well-set tail that is carried gracefully. The legs should be straight, clean and flat-boned, with striped hoofs that are able to easily carry the horse's weight. Extremely fine bones and small feet are not desirable.

The Walkaloosa horse can stand anywhere from 13 to 17 hands tall, but its most typical height ranges from 14:2 to 15:3 hands. There is also a large variation in weight – from 600 to 1,300 pounds with an overall appearance being either stout or refined.

Their coloration is typical of that found in the Appaloosa. They honor patterns including- but not limited to - leopard, blanketed, roan, and snowflake. A gentle, kind and willing disposition is extremely important. They must be suitable for amateurs, where they can be used as pleasure mounts or in field trials, range work (including cattle), and in the show-ring.

SON OF SKIPA TENA, registered Appaloosa, is half AQHA by blood, sired by a palomino Fox Trotter. He has a lot of big gait, loves to "cruise," and is a splendid trailhorse. Owned by John and Pat Anderson.

SUNDANCE'S PRIDE, owned by James A. Kinser.

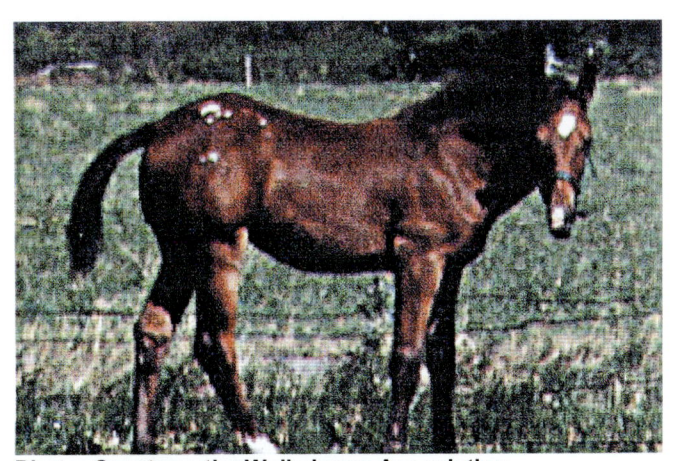

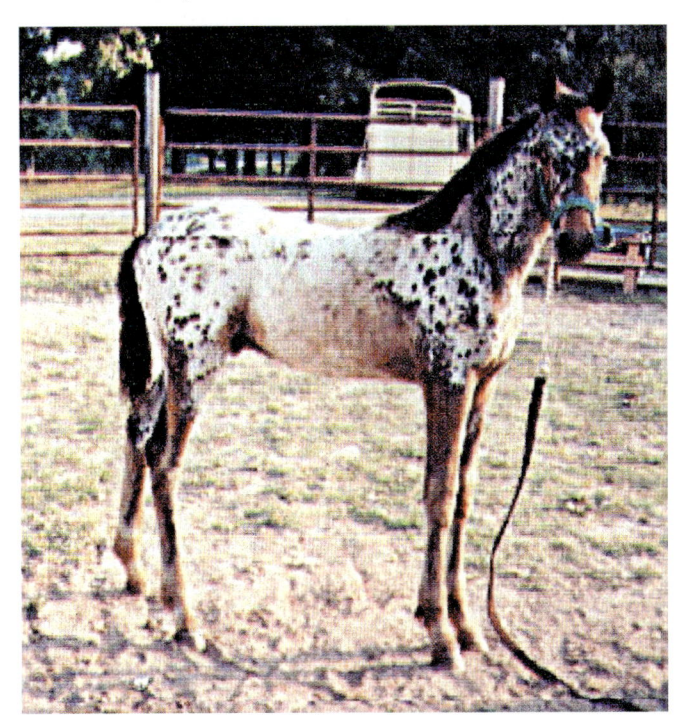

Photo: Courtesy the Walkaloosa Association

THUNDERHEART, owned by Pem Meyer.

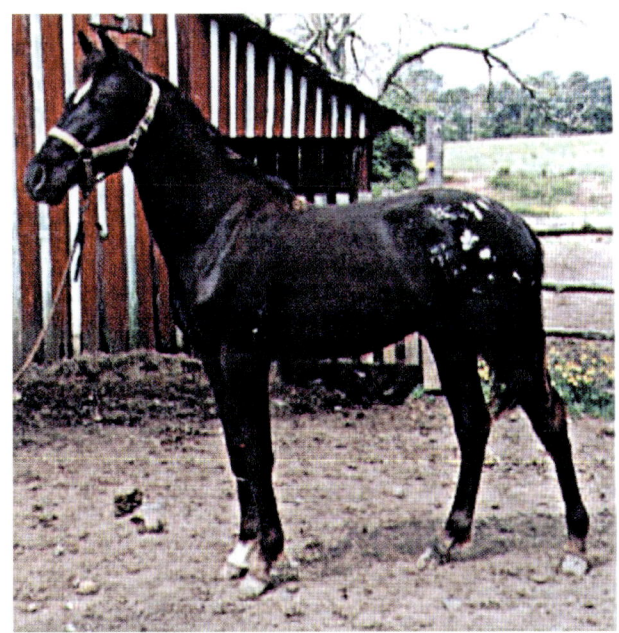

Photo: Courtesy the Walkaloosa Association

Photo: Courtesy the Walkaloosa Association

MIDAS'S JESTER
Sired by a palomino Fox Trotter
out of an ApHC mare.
Owned by Jo O'Brien,
Flight Of Fancy Farms
Colton, Oregon

SUGAR FROSTED
Appaloosa sire, Fox Trotter dam.
Sun Hill Farms
Estacada, Oregon

PLAYFUL ANGEL
Sired by a palomino Fox Trotter
out of an ApHC dam.
John and Pat Anderson, Sun Hill Farms, Oregon

Mare, SIOUX Z, sired by a Fox Trotter out of a Walkaloosa mother. She does whatever you ask and does it with great flair.
Sun Hill Farms, Oregon

SPOTS SPOTS SPOTS SPOTS SPOTS

Stallion, WL'S PRINCE SARKE "SHARK"
Driven by Jen Davidson,
owned and enjoyed by Dodie and Marc Sable.
New Promise Farms, Kutztown, Pennsylvania

TIGER HORSE REGISTRY

CHAPTER 23

HEIGHT: 15 H Average

GAIT: Variations on the 4-beat gait

COLOR: Lp characteristic (no pinto or grey)

TRAIT: Unique in appearance & sound of gait.

Chapter 23   The Tiger Horse Registry

The story of the Tiger Horse is prehistoric and at the same time brand new. The spotted, three-toed Eohippus was the first horse-like creature to inhabit the earth. It began its existence on the North American Continent, but for some reason, became extinct in its homeland.

There is evidence that Eohippus traveled over the Bering Straits to the Don Region of Russia. There the gaited, spotted and white horses became native to the Siberian Steppe of Asia. They were secretly preserved by nature in a hidden valley in the Tian Shan or "Heavenly Mountains" region near the Chinese and Siberian borders.

The Mongolians claimed them as their own and prized them highly as war horses. They became very important to the daily lives and culture of the Mongolian tribes.

In an article about the Turkoman horses found in Iran today, Louise Firouz details the interaction of these ancient horses with their present-day counterparts.

Modern-day "ancient" horses that remain, share a number of the characteristics present in these gaited, spotted horses. The Yamud and the Goklan[1] all display the gift of natural ambling action. The Yamud and Goklan

This antique drawing of a red and a black ghost horse makes an interesting comparison with the photograph to the right of modern-day Tiger Horses with the same coloring.

ANNANDALE'S HEAVENLY and ANNANDALE'S WINTER FOX from Annandale's Tiger Horse Farm in Santa Fe, New Mexico.

ANNANDALE'S LOVE STORY and ANNANDALE'S FAIRY TALE, out for a graze with their canine friend, Digger.

---

[1] The Yamud and Goklan are both strains of the Turkoman horse from Iran.

ANNANDALE'S GHOST STORY and **ANNANDALE'S FAIRY STORY**, two lovely youngsters celebrating the return of the ancient Tiger Horse Gene. See how similar their coloring is to the ancient horses seen in the antique drawing on the top of the previous page.

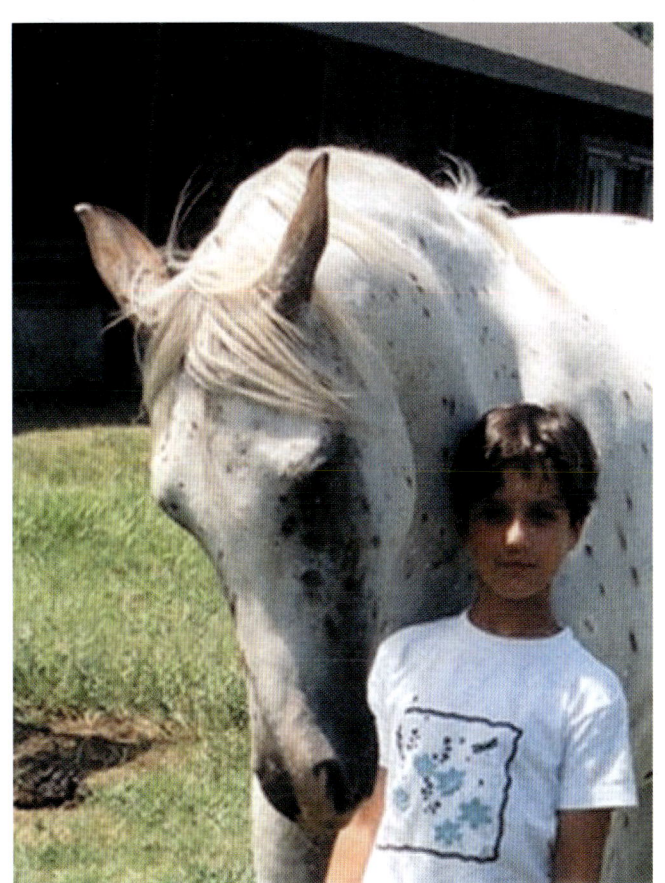

ANNANDALE'S FAIRY TALE, with her friend Maddy.

horses also have rather scant manes and tails, similar to those found in the modern Appaloosa horse.

A Chinese emissary, who first saw the spotted horses of Ferghana from a distance, in battle, mistook their glistening sweaty spots for blood. He reported back to his Emperor with a grand tale about magnificent "blood-sweating horses." These white or "Ghost Horses" were seen continuing to fight even after losing their

ANNANDALE'S FAIRY STORY on her day of birth.

The Indian "Ghost Horse" in action.

377

ANNANDALE'S GLIDER SPIDER and **ANNANDALE'S CINNAMON BLIZZARD** almost create an optical illusion,

their riders. Stories like this, made their way back to the Emperor of China and created a great desire for ownership. Its is easy to understand how these marvelously strong, brave and beautiful creatures were treasured then as now.

In 3,000 B.C., they were coveted by the Chinese Emperors who began crossing them with their small potbellied horses. This breeding program developed horses that were fit for use in hunting Siberian tigers!

These tiger-hunting horses picked up their name somewhere along the way from the Russian steppes to the Iberian shores. They were referred to as El Caballo Tigre (from the French word for tiger) or Spanish Jennet (or Genet, an Arab word for a kind of spotted civet cat).

We have graphic evidence of these

ANNANDALE'S ZEUS, eight months before the picture to the right.

horses from the early colonizing period in Europe. Many paintings depict very colorful Spanish horses displaying numerous coat patterns - overo and tobiano (pintado or pinto);

ANNANDALE'S WINTER FOX.

A herd of mares at Annandale's Tiger Horse Farm.

ANNANDALE'S ZEUS, eight months after the picture to the left.

sabino (roan-like in appearance); and the patterns that can be called "blooded," "blood spotted," "trouite," "leopard" or "tiger" (Lp patterns).[2]

ANNANDALE'S STORYTELLER & ANNANDALE'S LADY-BUG

---

[2] A single dominant gene called the Leopard complex gene (Lp) is responsible for some of the manifestations of Appaloosa characteristic, and this gene can be transplanted to any horse breed.

ANNANDALE'S SNOWBIRD visiting with friends.

In his book *Appaloosa*, Francis Haines claims the spotted horses were more common among the Andalusian stock of Spain in the 16th Century - which brings us back to the American Continent.

Many of the shipments from Spain to Mexico in the years 1512 - 1519 included these spotted Andalusians destined to become part of the herds of Juan de Onate in the settlement of New Mexico. It is also be-lieved that horses from the Lipizzaner herd, near the city of Trieste, were shipped directly back to Vera Cruz in about 1621.

In his book *The Ghost Wind Stallions*, Don Lalonde writes about an Indian known as George Long Grass, who told of four white stallions brought to America by Russian seamen. Because of stormy weather, they pushed the horses overboard to awaiting Native Americns.

ANNANDALE'S GLIDER SPIDER with friend Danny.

ANNANDALE'S FAIRY TALE at four years of age.

ANNANDALE'S FAIRY TALE as a two-year-old.

who were required to pay a much higher price than usual because these white "spirit horses" were as rare then as they are today.

From the early 1500's into the 1600's, horses from Spain secured a foothold on the American Continent. During this period, numerous breeding facilities were established throughout North and South America. Once the American Indians began to adopt these horses, their development was rapid all across the country.

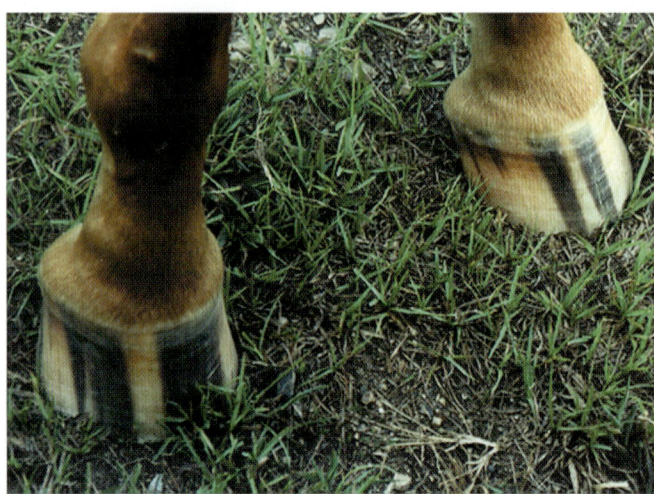

ANNANDALE'S LOVE STORY displaying his gaiting ability.

One of the characteristics often seen in the Tiger Horse is the striated hoof.

ANNANDALE'S FAIRY TALE as a one-year-old.

During the early development of the North American continent, while all the horses were of Spanish blood, the purest Jennet blood was found in the Southern and Western states. They not only represented all colors and patterns, they possessed the very special "four-beat gait" gene and exhibited the ambling gaits.

The loudly patterned horses were highly prized by the American Indians, and in time,

ANNANDALE'S TIGER LILY.

horse and Indian became identified with one another. The tiger patterns were quite rare and therefore most prized and treasured.

Sometime between 1700 and 1730, the

SNOWLINE ROMEO, exhibiting a 4-beat gait.

ANNANDALE'S EAGLE FEATHER with her fan club.

ANNANDALE'S TEQUILLA.

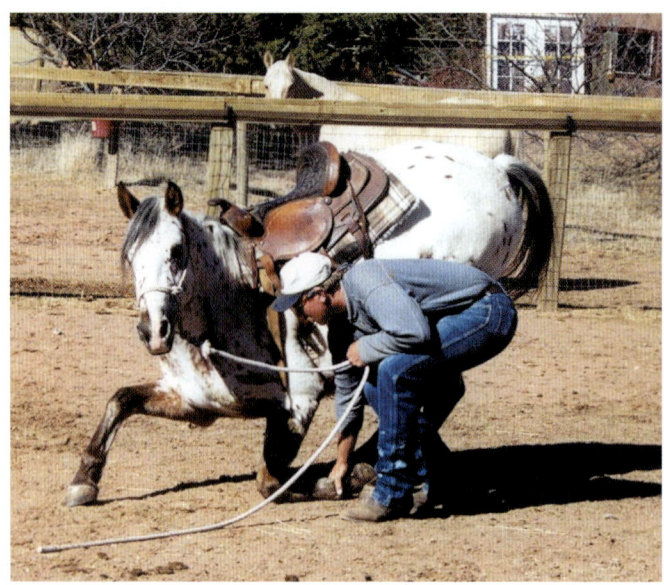

ANNANDALE'S FAIRY TALE taking a bow.

Cayuse tribe introduced the horse to the tribe of their kinsmen, the Ni Mee Poo. The Ni Mee Poo or Nez Perce Indians of the Pacific Northwest were known for their love of novelty. They were often referred to as the most adopting and adapting tribe in the country. Their love for the horse was immediate, and it wasn't long before they were trading with the Shoshone for their first horses.

These horses were undoubtedly of pure Spanish blood. The herds soon were upgraded beyond those of the many other tribes because the Ni Mee Poo developed quickly into premier horse breeders.

In the meantime, back in Spain, Philip of the Netherlands became king. He brought to the throne his love for the Dutch Warmbloods. He began upgrading the native Spanish Jennets by breeding them with the Warmbloods and Thoroughbreds. The result was a horse similar to our modern Lipizzaner and Andalusian. They became instantly popular throughout Europe. The most popular of all was the leopard-spotted version.

By the middle of the 1700's, the "spotted Iberians," as they became known, began losing their popularity in Spain and France. Large numbers were sold to the Colonies. Many were sold directly to Canada and portions of the American west. Populations of these Spanish horses grew throughout the southwestern parts of Canada and the Pacific Northwest.

The Ni Mee Poo or Nez Perce tribes have been linked with Appaloosa coloring. It has been said that their breeding program was directed toward producing the Appaloosa coat patterns. In fact, Chief Joseph himself rode what appears to be a brown or blue roan horse - his favorite mount. There is evidence that

ANNANDALE'S JESSIE and Kate.

ANNANDALE'S LADYBUG with Emiko up.

ANNANDALE'S ZEUS with friend Maddy.

only medicine men were allowed to own and ride the speckled appaloosa-type horse. This alone would point to the fact that they were not available in large numbers but were, instead, rare treasures. More often their horses of color would best be described as pied or pieded, a term commonly refering to pintado patterns, not the speckled appaloosa type.

In 1877, the Ni Mee Poo or Nez Perce Indians saw a near-total dispersal of their tribes and dissolution of their huge herds of horses. Most of the horses were shipped back East. The spotted horses were not that numerous to begin with, so they never reached significant numbers until recently.

In 1938, a group of people started an organization to preserve the spotted Indian horse. They called the horse the Appaloosa. Initially they allowed Arabian blood in hopes of refining the appearance of the horse. Gradually they introduced Quarter Horse into the strain, further allowing the breed's gaiting ability to drift into oblivion. Sometimes an Appaloosa horse will echo the gaiting gene of its ancient forebears and perform a 4-beat gait, but the Appaloosa Horse Club (ApHC) of today discourages this soft gait, and the horses are either retrained or quietly sold.

Enter Victoria Varley, who had the fortitude and determination to recreate an updated version of ancient horse by reuniting the soft-gait and the Lp gene.

In 1993, her first Tiger Horse was born from a gaited Spanish Mustang dam named Star and an Arabian-influenced leopard-spotted Appaloosa stallion named Raf's Sweet Flame. Annandale's Pepper Stepper has remained the poster boy for Tigre, the Tiger

Stallion ANANDALE'S ZEUS with Tigre founder Victoria Varley.

383

ANNANDALE'S LOVE STORY.

BLAIR'S CHEYENNE, sired by ANNANDALE'S STORY-TELLER

Horse Registry and stands at stud near Dallas, Texas. He has produced a number of colorful Tiger qualified foals.

With her husband Mark Varley, Victoria has raised over 40 colorful, gaited Tiger horses during the first ten years of breeding experiments. Many of these have been sold or given to members in order to allow the breed to continue to grow. Their ideas quickly caught fire, and people began jumping on the "Tiger Horse Express" to be part of the exciting new project. The Tigers are great family pets, excellent competitors and command greater prices than many.

Quoting Victoria: "The Lp color gene has been conserved in a variety of breeds, as has the comfortable fourth gait. While I believe one has been separated from the other in man's attempts to 'improve' a breed, I also believe - and am proving - those two components will very quickly gravitate toward each other like magnets or separated chemical components do when brought within range of each other. They lock on or reunite to complete their original chemical makeup."

Victoria reports on her discovery that gait is gender- related 99% of the time. In other

Here is an example of the mottling common to the Tiger Horses.

ANNANDALE'S SNOW BIRD.

Tiger Horse Registry Logo taken from a burial site mound tomb, on display in a museum in Seoul, Korea, entitled, "Spirit or Heavenly Horse." This white birch tree bark carving was found together with the bones and golden crown of an important king, or shaman, from Siberia.

Stallion, ANNANDALE'S STORYTELLER.

ANNANDALE'S LADYBUG

words, sires to daughters and dams to sons. Further discoveries show that the homozygous Ghost Horse patterned horses (white with few spots) tend to be more muscular than their heterozygous siblings and perform a soft-gait she calls the "Indian shuffle" which can be compared to the soft-gait of the Andalusian used in dressage.

The Tiger Horse of the 21st century has no tigers to hunt but is still strongly built, of moderate size and averages 15 hands with excellent legs and feet. All of this makes the Tiger an outstanding using animal that is influenced by contemporary, soft-gaited horses and those carrying the leopard-complex gene. The Tiger Horse comes in all base colors such as black, bay and chestnut, but it is especially noted for the exotic Tiger coat.

Since the Lp characteristic is the pattern of choice, the Tiger Horse Registry will not register a horse with known pintado, grey or genetic white. Any base color is allowed, but in order to establish and maintain maximum contrast, it is suggested that dilute colors be avoided.

The Tiger Horse Registry has established categories of registration and runs two registries side by side. The Tiger Horse Reg-

ANNANDALE'S FAIRY TALE and ANNADALE'S ZEUS

ANNANDALE'S LADYBUG and her one-day-old filly, EAGLE FEATHER

Three "Ghost Horse" fillies, two "Ghost Horse" patterns

istry is a probationary file that accepts all original entries that can prove gait and color and also accepts the sabino gene (but as breeding stock only). Once stallions have produced five fully qualified Tiger foals, and mares have produced three, they qualify for Tigre's Royal Stud Book International and are entered in this permanent file. Foals of two Royalty-registered Tiger Horses automatically qualify as Royalty. All other horses are on probation.

A wide variety of gaited breeds are being used by various breeders to give new life to the Tiger Horse, among them the willing and spirited Fox Trotter, the gentle Tennessee Walker, the sensitive and refined Peruvian Paso, and the Spanish Mustang, among others.

Varley reports that occasionally a Tiger Horse appears from nowhere, usually from Appaloosa parents that are not obviously gaited. Horses like these are quite acceptable to Tigre for probationary registration. They must, however, be proven before being transferred to Tigre's Royal Stud Book International.

Many of today's lovely horses closely resemble the original Spanish or Russian imports[3] to the U.S.A. Although the Tigers are possibly larger than their ancient forebears, their antiquity is never in doubt.

Victoria Varley feels that "this adventure is not for the fickle-minded or faint of heart, but for the enduring owners or breeders determined to enjoy the reestablishment of a very proud and beautiful horse. This rare and illustrious animal has continued to tease its way in and out of existence since time immemorial. Reproducing this lovely animal brings results that are both exciting and unpredictable."

An ancient treasure recaptured

---

[3] There is a four-gaited spotted pony sized horse still being bred in Russia, called the Altai.

386

ANNANDALE'S BUTTERFLY at one month of age. She was the result of line breeding a half sister to her half brother to cement the genes.

ANNANDALE'S EAGLE FEATHER is a "Ghost Horse" filly pictured at ten days of age

ANNANDALE'S HEAVENLY

ANNANDALE'S ZEUS exhibiting a 4-beat gait

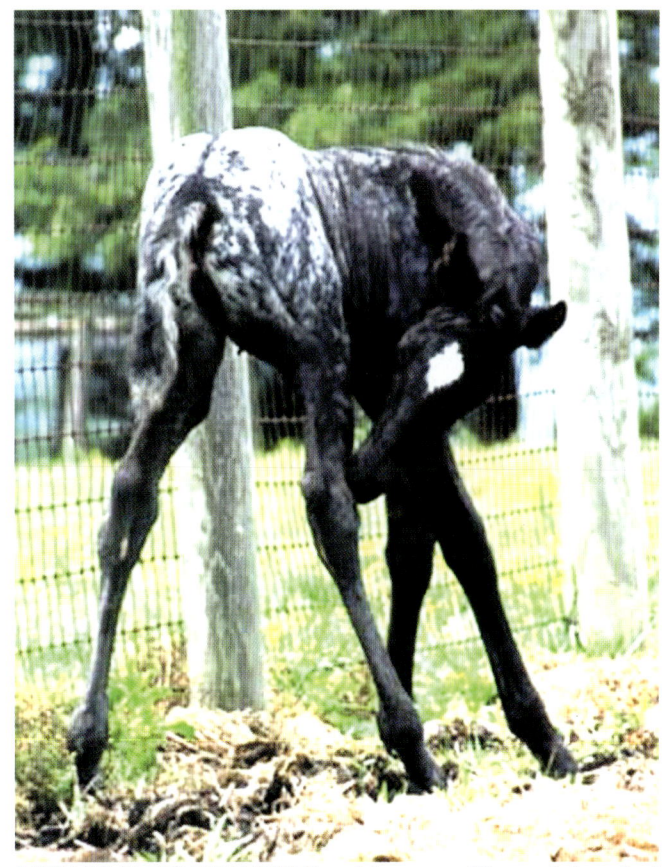

ANNANDALE'S HEAVENLY, a blue roan Tiger pictured at only three days of age.

THE GAITED MORGAN HORSE

CHAPTER 24

Stallion, MARY MELS BAR NONE
Owned by Don Bahr - Do More Morgans - Mineral Point, Wisconsin

HEIGHT:	14:1 - 15:2 Range
GAIT:	All
COLOR:	Bay, black, brown (no greys or spots
TRAIT:	Versatility

Chapter 24   The Gaited Morgan Horse

Imagine a dark horse weighing in at about 1,000 pounds and standing a modest 14 hands tall, outdoing every horse challenging him, whether walking, trotting, running, or pulling!

Today, stories of the horse Figure are told and retold by fanciers of his magnificent progeny. This outstanding horse of the late 1700's is one of the few horses in history to have sired an entire breed by implanting his image on his offspring. After 200 years, his blood runs through the veins of an entire breed now known as the Morgan horse.

Justin Morgan, a blacksmith, music teacher, one-time tavern owner, and jack-of-all-trades, moved from Vermont to Massachusetts. He later returned to Vermont to collect a debt, in the form of two horses. One was a big young gelding, the other, an undersized three-year-old stallion by the name of Figure.

To convert the debt into dollars, Justin sold the gelding, and when he couldn't find a buyer for the stallion, he leased him to a neighboring farmer for a few silver dollars a year.

Figure turned out to be a superb working machine. While under the charge of Robert Evans, he would spend an entire day strenuously dragging logs out of the woods, and yet he would return to his barn as fresh and peppy as if he had spent the day at leisure.

⇨ **OSIRUS**, stands 15:3 hands and is a black chestnut. He consistently puts substance and cow sense in his offspring. The bonus is that he will also single-foot. Owned by Linnea and Michael Sidi at their Meadowlark Morgan Ranch in Loveland, Colorado. Photo: Gary Gray

ADIEL'S CASINO GOLD stands 14"3 hands and produces foals of color as well as beautiful balance. Owned by Meadowlark Morgans in Loveland, Colorado.

The late Dr. Hughes with PATCHETT HILL, sire of CADUCEUS MOSES. Photo: Dennis Nelson DVM

MYSTERY CARAMEL, gaited Morgan, son of MARY MEL'S MYSTERY.

There's a story told about Evans stopping by the local pub, enjoying his share of ale, and bragging about his remarkable little bay horse. Some men at the pub were talking about a large pine log that the teamsters were unable to move. After hearing the Evan's boasts, they challenged him and his horse to accomplish the task.

Evans not only accepted the challenge, he brashly suggested that the men sit on the log. Three of the largest men climbed aboard the log and Figure was hitched up. Figure strained and pulled a little to the side. As the tugs lost their slack and the chains squeaked, the log began to move. Pausing only once, the little bay wonder accomplished the feat in only two pulls as his piston-like feet astonished everyone.

Figure went on to secure his place in history as a true champion and prepotent stud, he foundation sire to an entire breed. Although his exact origins are sketchy, once he became famous, it was natural for people to want to give him a pedigree worthy of his accomplishments. At the time of his birth, the English Thoroughbred, newly arrived on the American shores, was the rage of the day. What better horse to be given credit for the splendid little bay stallion?

As research on the genetics and bloodtyping of various breeds becomes more sophisticated, people who maintain that the Morgan horse developed from the Thoroughbred and Arabs find their position being challenged. Bonnie Hendricks, in her excellent work, *International Encyclopedia of Horse Breeds*, proposes that Justin Morgan, or Figure,[1] was more likely a product of the French-Canadian and Friesian horses. But the politics of the day couldn't imagine giving credit for this awesome American original to anything French or Canadian.

We can look back to the time when Figure was conceived and recognize the available breeding stock in the New England area. There were Norfolk Trotters from England, Friesians from Holland, Norwegian Dun (Fjord) from Norway, Cobs from Whales

---

[1] Figure wasn't known as Justin Morgan until after the death of his owner Justin Morgan.

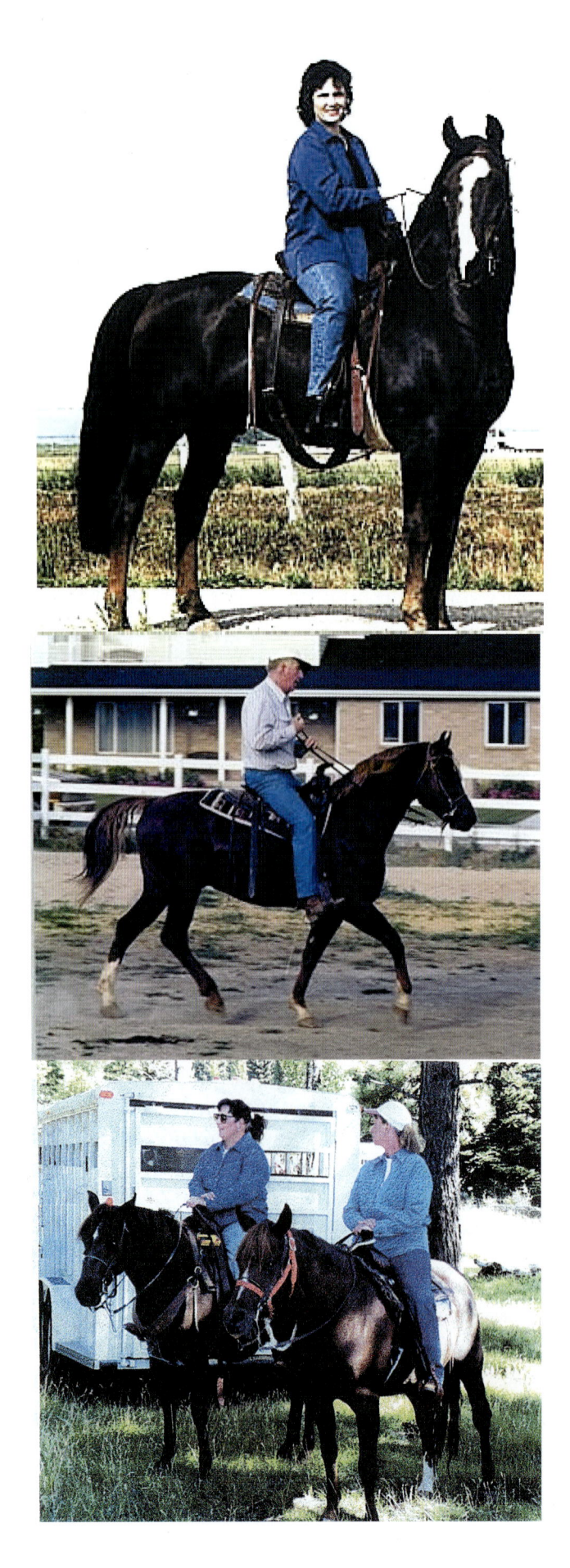

and, of course, thousands of the French Canadian horses.

The French-Canadian horses were small, blocky and powerful. They were excellent trotters able to pull far more than their size and weight would indicate. They were sure of step, curious, bold, had feet of iron, strong legs and powerful quarters and shoulders. Their manes and tails were profuse and wavy and their necks were brawny and crested. These are all characteristic of the Morgan, not the Thoroughbred or Arab.

The origins of the French-Canadian horse also support the theory of their influence on the Morgan breed. These horses came to the new world from French breeding stock that were known to possess blood of the Andalusian from the Spanish Netherlands as well as the blood of the Dutch Friesian.

Perhaps we will never know the exact origin of the marvelous horse Justin Morgan, but we do know a good deal about his famous sons. If Figure himself wasn't a French-Canadian horse, then his offspring certainly were. Some of his most important sons went on to sire families of their own.

Quoting Bonnie Hendricks: "Bulrush, one of the most outstanding sons of Justin Morgan, was out of a Canadian mare; bred back to a black Canadian mare, Bulrush got Randolph Morgan. Randolph Morgan, mated to a Canadian mare, produced Jennison Horse (sire of Old Morrill). Woodburry, another famous son of Justin Morgan, was likely from a Canadian mare, and the dam of Black Hawk was a Canadian."

Research into the early Narragansett Pacers crosses paths with the Morgan's early development. The look of Figure suggests the qualities of the Spanish horses such as the Andalusian; and the fact that the Morgan breed has always harbored a recessive gaiting gene suggests a valid connection.

⬅ **Photos to the left, Top:** The stallion OSIRUS, with Diana Merritt, up. Photo: Steve Merritt. **Middle:** Stallion, MARY MEL'S MYSTERY being ridden by his breeder and trainer, Mel Frandsen. **Bottom:** Shery Jesperson and Linnea Sidi enjoying their Gaited Morgans on a trailride.

Perhaps the most compelling evidence of Figure's French-Canadian background is the fact that prepotency is a quality born of linebreeding and inbreeding. While it is possible for mutant genes to suddenly appear in an individual of any species, sudden genetic prepotency is so remote as to be impossible.

While it is interesting to investigate the origins of the horse himself, what is important to us now is knowing that Justin Morgan established an important breed that amazed and thrilled horse fanciers of his day in much the same way his offspring amaze and thrill horse fanciers today. His strength, brio and athletic abilities were in demand throughout New England, and, soon thereafter, the entire country.

Although the recessive gaiting gene has always been in the Morgan horse, breeders have not honored it until recently. The pace genes that combine with the trot genes to produce the gait or singlefoot are recessive. By definition, a recessive gene cannot be bred out of a gene pool like a dominant gene. This explains why a single-footer can pop up from two apparently non-single-footing parents. Obviously, the odds for getting a single-footer are better if both parents have these genes and both parents exhibit the gait.

Before a soft-gaiting horse became in demand, breeders would quietly dispose of the animals possessing the gaiting gene. In the late 20TH century, some brave souls have begun promoting and breeding for the gait within the Morgan Registry.

Well known gaited horse proponent Annette Gerhardt had made contact with breeders in several different breeds through her informative writing on the soft-gaited experience.

Quoting Annette: "I had a bunch of the 'I have a horse that does that, but it's a Morgan, and it's the only one that gaits; Morgans don't gait' stories come my way, and I was an active member of the North American Single-

➪ Photos to the right, Top: Mel Frandsen riding MARY MEL'S GOLDILOCKS. Bottom: Linnea Sidi aboard a Mel Frandsen horse at the MFHA gathering in Utah in 2000. Photo: Shery Jesperson

SILVERSHOE AUGUSTUS, with Dusty Hackett, up, at the Ranch Horse Rodeo, April 2002. Photo: Linnea Sidi

Footing Horse Association[2] for which I am also a Gait Judge, so I knew about gaited Morgans through NASHA. That winter, I think it was, when I had some time on my hands, I wrote to Jackie Heib, Bruce Olson, and other people I'd gotten the 'I have a horse that does that...' stories from, and said, you don't all know me and you don't all know each other, but you should all start talking to each other because you all have or want gaited Morgans, so why don't you do something about it?"

Annette continues: "It was apparently an idea whose time had come. I was told they were kind of thinking of something along that same line, but needed a catalyst to get things moving. They started the newsletter, a few months later, which ultimately resulted in the Morgan Single-footing Horse Association (MSHA)."

The association is a recognized service branch of the American Morgan Horse Association (AMHA).

The MSHA promotes all Morgan types and disciplines, with particular emphasis on (and promotion of) the inherent four-beat gaits found within the current registry of the Morgan breed. They are committed to research, education and promotion of these horses, due to their outstanding athletic ability. They are fully affiliated with the AMHA, and serve their members as such.

The MSHA promotes those horses that perform four beat-gaits in addition to or in place of the gaits commonly associated with the Morgan breed, i.e. the walk, the trot and the canter.

Here are the definitions the MSHA uses as a standard to describe the gaits of their horses:

Pace – A two beat gait in which the lateral pairs move in total unison.

Trot – A two beat gait in which the diagonal pairs move in total unison.

MARY MEL'S INDIGO, bred by Mel Frandsen. Photo: Gary Gray

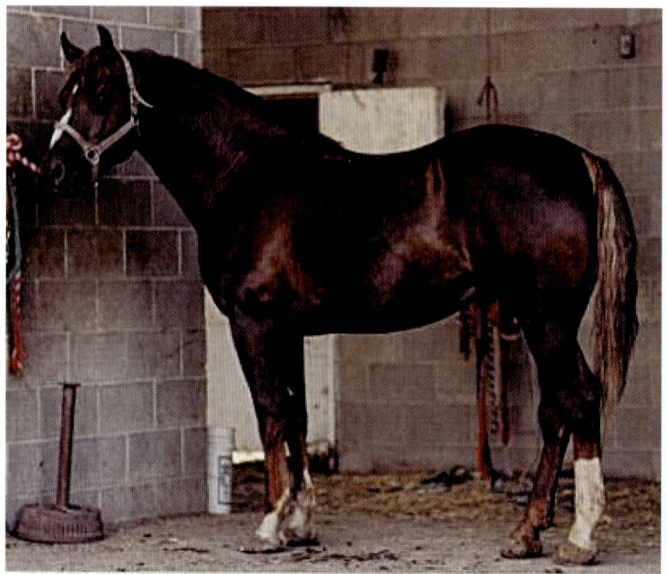

A six-year-old **MARY MEL'S MYSTERY**, photographed by "The Gaited Horse" Magazine after he won first place in the Gaited Morgan Competition.

---

[2] See Chapter 34

394

CADUCEUS MOSES – PATCHETT HILL x MERRY MIRANDA. Born 1992, 15.2 hands. MOSES is homozygous for black points and is a natural single-footer.

Stepping Pace – an uneven, four-beat pace.

Fox Trot – an uneven, four-beat trot.

Running Walk – an uneven, four-beat fast walk in which the horse lengthens stride (thus showing overstride) and continues to nod, as in the flat walk.

Rack – an even, four-beat fast walk in which the horse does not lengthen stride and does not nod its head.

The association is still developing its stand on what specific gaits will be accepted as the intermediate soft gait. They are reaching out to respected authorities on gait from other gaited breeds to help them in their planning. Unquestionably, the emphasis will be on natural and absolutely no action devices. For this reason, they will probably accept any of the intermediate gaits including the diagonal foxtrot. They are also developing a panel of gait experts to evaluate each of the horses within the association. They wish to develop guidelines that will assist them in protecting the integrity of their horses, and help them market these horses to the public. For those gaited-horse enthusiasts who have spent time, money and energy protecting and improving the lives of horses who have been mistreated in the name of vanity, it's joyful to see an organization finally addressing these problems *before* they arise.

Quoting Mel Frandsen: "I should think at this stage of their evolution, we could all agree on the desirability of producing an even four-beat singlefoot. All it takes is a touch of arthritis to know that the more even the beat of cadence, the more even or smooth the ride. I'm not sure we are ready to embrace running walk to the exclusion of the rack for instance. Certainly the most valued mare I have has a great four-beat natural gait, which is a rack; her head doesn't nod and she doesn't overstep. All my grandchildren learn to ride on her and can keep up with any of the other gaited horses, even the overstepping running walk ones."

Mel continues: "She is valued not only because of her very good gait, but for her

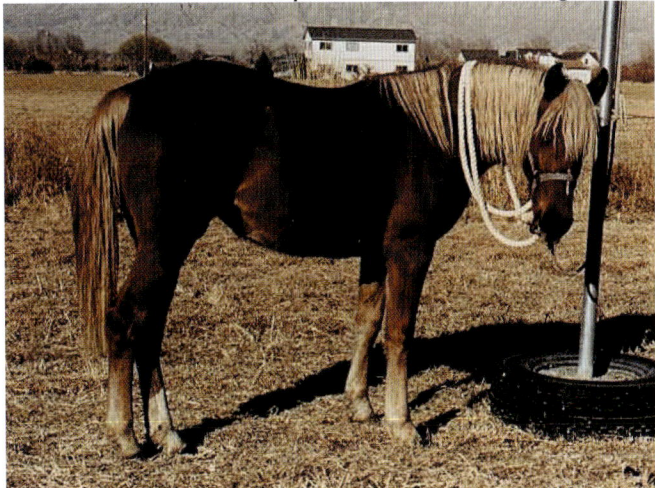

A yearling Morgan filly sired by MARY MELS MYSTERY. Her Morgan mother is also gaited.

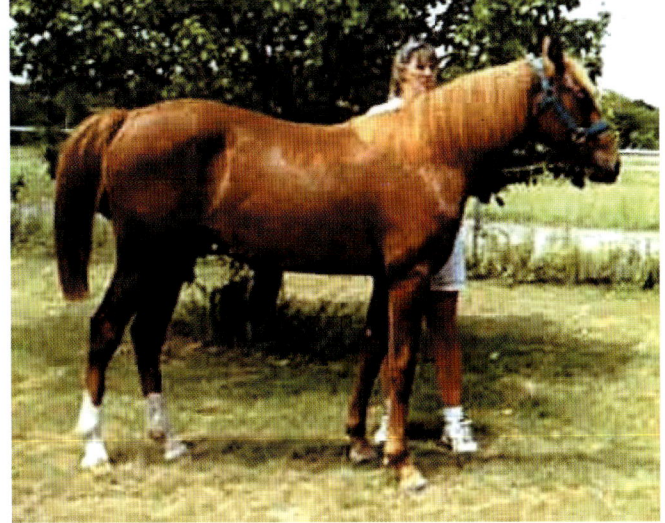

Colt MYSTERY CARAMEL, owned by the Messengers of Liberty Mountain Ranch in Bismarck, Arkansas.

temperament and good old Morgan type. I would hope that each one of us are committed to the Morgan type, with substance, yet refinement - one that can be seen a half-mile away and be recognized as a Morgan, one that has the great temperament that can be enjoyed and is a pleasure to be around. Don't forget good head and legs and bone and all the other Morgan characteristics."

So what makes a Morgan a Morgan, gaited or not? A Morgan is distinctive for its stamina and vigor, personality and eagerness, and strong natural, way of moving. Correct Morgan type and conformation is the same in each section of the Morgan Horse division where conformation is considered. There is only one standard for type and conformation of the Morgan Horse. The Morgan is a spirited and courageous horse but easily handled and intelligent.

The head should be expressive with a broad forehead; large, prominent eyes; straight or slightly dished short face; firm, fine lips; large nostrils; well rounded jowls. The ears should be short and shapely, set rather wide apart, and carried alertly. Mares may have a slightly longer ear.

The body should be compact with a short back, close coupling, broad loins, deep flank, well-sprung ribs, croup long and well muscled, with tail attached high, carried gracefully and straight. The neck should come out on top of an extremely well-angulated shoulder with depth from top of withers to point of shoulder. The legs should be straight and sound with short cannons, flat bone, and an appearance of overall substance with refinement. The forearm should be relatively long in proportion to the cannon. The pasterns

WNS WINDERSTONE with Mel Frandsen. Photo: Linnea Sidi

A painting of the lovely stallion, OSIRUS, created by Karen Barton. OSIRUS stands at Meadowlark Morgan Ranch. Artist Karen Barton – KarenFb@trib.com

A MYSTERY filly that has a non-gaiting Morgan mother, but this filly is a gaiter, and lives in Oklahoma.

The great stallion STELLAR, source of soft-gait in many Morgan Horses. Photo: Courtesy AMHA

GLO BUG and PUMPKIN, two Gaited Morgan mares owned by Leon D. Bess at Pat & Lee's Montana Morgans, in Paradise Valley, Arizona.

Well-known foundation stallion **STELLAR**. Photo: Courtesy AMHA

ADIEL'S CASINO GOLD – SWEET DEXTER x EDEN ROSE, standing at Meadowlark Morgans in Loveland, Colorado.

should have sufficient length and angulation to provide a light, springy step.

Champions of the Gaited Morgan are growing in numbers. Anita Messenger and her family in Arkansas have been involved with both gaited Morgans and gaited Morabs. Quoting Anita: "Over the years we had a few foals turn out gaited who were born out of non-gaited parents. This got us to thinking about it, and then we began to look for a top-quality gaited Morgan stallion to bring in to our breeding program. That's when we discovered that they are not easy to find anymore! In the last few years they have been gaining in popularity again due to the buying public looking for gaited horses. The gaited Morgans are not only smooth to ride, but are attractive horses to boot."

Anita continues: "We finally found that special stallion we were looking for in northern Utah, in the Mary Mel Morgan herd. Mel Fransden has been one of the very few Morgan breeders who unabashedly continued to breed good gaited Morgans during the years when others would never admit they had a gaited foal born. We bought the six-year-old stallion, Mary Mel's Mystery, from Mel. We had two video tapes of Mystery analyzed by Lee Ziegler of Colorado, and she nailed him down doing six gaits, including walk, trot and canter. This was under saddle and at liberty. She also believes that he would rack (which would make him 7-gaited) if the right person got to ride him."

Renowned breeder and Gaited Morgan enthusiast Linnea Sidi tells a wonderful story about modern-day rancher and cowboy Dusty Hackett of the Arapaho Ranch in the Colorado High Country. "He speaks rather highly of his

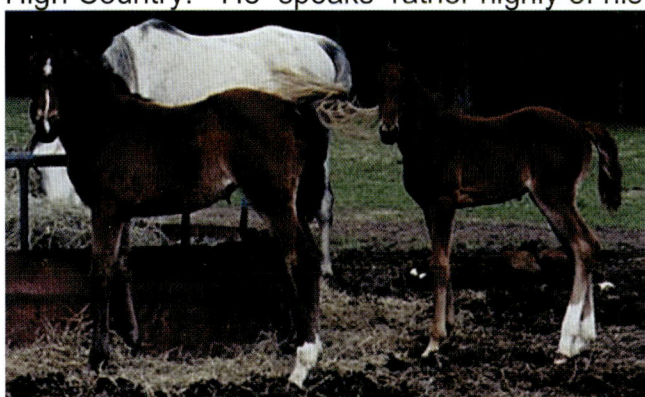

These two foals were sired by **MARY MEL'S MYSTERY**. The chestnut to the right is a full Gaited Morgan colt.

Riders Greg Manley, Bob Laitsch, Scott Durfey, Frank Pulley and Anne Karberg heading out for a great day on the trail.

"Branding 2000" – Dusty Hackett riding GUS.

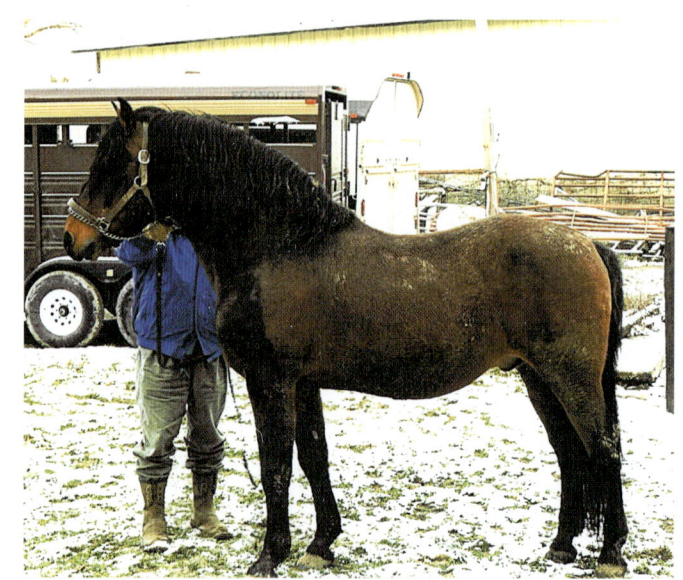

Stallion, PATCHETT HILL with the late Dr. Hughes. Photo: Dennis Nelson DVM

Mel Frandsen riding MARY MEL'S GOLDENROD

Mel Fransden riding MARY MEL'S THE BLACK WIDOW.

Mel Frandsen enjoying his lovely Gaited Morgan Horses.

gaited Morgan gelding, Silvershoe Augustus. Dusty rides more miles in one morning than most of us do in a week. Gus is the number-one pick for saddle duty on days that Dusty needs to cover a lot of ground in a hurry. He knows he can put the trusty gelding into a gentle single-foot and eat up the miles and be back for a good hot meal at noon.

Linnea continues: "When I asked Dusty specifically what he liked a gaited Morgan for, as far as ranch work, he stated: 'Everything. There is nothing I can't do on this horse and I don't feel like I have been riding all day when I get off him.' Gus, as he is known on the ranch, has proven himself time and time again to be a traveler beyond compare. Dusty gets the biggest thrill when he takes the horse to Ranch Horse Competitions – he just eases him into one of those optional gears and goes to work beating Quarter Horses at their own game."

Telling her own story, Linnea exclaims: "There is nothing like a ride on a good Morgan Horse. I started in horses as a small child. A lot of my youth was spent in California and I remember watching the old Vaqueros ride their spade-bit horses. Many of those were part Morgans. I have always liked the old-style stock horses that came from Morgan blood, and I breed for that classic look. These horses are sensible and well-mannered as well as having classic old-style Morgan conformation and looks."

Perhaps the best known name in the Gaited Morgan world is Mel Frandsen. Living in Utah, Mel has consistently produced excellent specimens of Morgans that gait. The following excerpt was taken from one of his articles, and it is a paragraph that definitely puts into perspective a truly productive approach to developing gait.

"Michael Jordan and Karl Malone were not born, nor did they arrive at age 22, as the best basketball players in the world. They were born with the potential to be, but they needed work, and lots of coaching. People have the ability to reason as to how to improve their abilities. Horses don't have that ability, so we must be their coaches. The gait of any genetically gaited horse can really be enhanced with coaching."

With the attention now being given to the Morgan Horse as a gaiting individual, folks who have always admired the Morgan as a breed can celebrate this new dimension.

SPANISH MUSTANG HORSE

CHAPTER 25

Twenty-year-old stallion, SEQUOYAH
Josie Brislawn, Oshoto, Wyoming

HEIGHT:	13:2 - 15 H
GAIT:	Amble, running walk, single foot
COLOR:	Most equine colors
TRAIT:	Stamina, Intelligence

Chapter 25   The Spanish Mustang

The Spanish horse plays an important part in the history of most of the horses described in this book. The first horses brought to American shores were Spanish. The Sorraias, Asturians, Jennets, Garranos, Andalusian and Barbs were the nucleus for both the American breeding facilities, and for those horses that, for a number of reasons, become feral.

The first immigrants were the Spanish, world renowned both for their horsemanship and their fine horses. Horses were an integral part of their civilization. They were used for battle, agriculture, and transportation, each of which demanded different qualities. Undoubtedly, the first shipments sent to America were of Sorraias, because they were smaller and better able to survive the ocean voyage. The Sorraia was also uniquely designed to participate in the development of communities. Its hardiness and comfortable 4-beat gait made it an ideal choice for riding, ranching, and farming.

It was reported that Columbus complained to the Queen that he had been sent "common nags." After his second voyage, every ship headed for the New World carried select Spanish breeding stock by order of the Crown. Many of the early deliveries of stock contained the personal riding horses of the conquistadors.[1] Today, we have living testimony to the hardiness, brio and replication of these early Spanish horses. Today they are known as North American Colonial Spanish

---
[1] Alonso de Ojeda, captain of one of the ships, brought his own horse with him to the New World.

Kiger filly, JUBILEE. Quoting Linda Holst (see chapter 18), "I sought out JUBILE because she is the most perfect representative of the Kiger breed to cross with my beautiful buckskin Mangalarga Marchador stallion BATUQUE DO REGAL. The Kigers, which are considered a pure Spanish Mustang, have strong bones, substance, are savvy and can often gait. This combination, along with the smooth gait of the Mangalarga Marchador, should prove to be a superior combination for endurance competition."

David Frey riding NORTHERN SONG "CAJUN," competing at the American Indian Horse Registry Nationals in September 2002.

Stallion, MAGNETO (MAGS) and owner/rider, Susan Tuscana waiting their turn while the judges ask another rider to back her horse. "We're next in line. MAGNETO isn't nervous, just curious. It's as if he's watching the other horse, trying to get pointers on how to back up properly. This was his first time to ever be in a pleasure class of any kind. He's just standing quietly, like he belongs there."

EL DUC, a Kiger stallion, is owned by Gerald O. Thompson at Springwater Station, Estacada, Oregon. EL DUC is 15 hands and a lineback buttermilk dun and grulla color producer. His foals have good conformation and are long muscled with long legs and bones of steel.

Horses and Spanish Mustangs.[2] They survive and thrive through five general categories: feral, rancher, mission (Mexican), Native American, and Southeastern. Several registries have been formed to represent and protect different segments of the general population.

The development of the Spanish Mustangs was influenced by environmental culling. They didn't start out, as a general population, to be feral, but ultimately they survived and actually thrived by adjusting to the various locales that became their rangeland.

It is interesting to note that these modern horses give us a closer look at the historic horse of the golden age of Spain.[3]

The differences within modern Spanish Mustangs can be attributed to the different selection goals in South and North America. All these horses may be different, but they are still related and share important qualities. Quoting renowned endurance rider Frank Hopkins: "You can't beat Mustang intelligence in the entire equine race. These animals have had to shift for themselves for generations. They had to work out their own destiny or be destroyed. Those that survived were animals of superior intelligence."

As tenacious as these plucky horses were, the evolution of time and fashion took a heavy toll on their survival. At one time they covered the landscape in enormous herds. Many Native Americanan tribes became adept at training and utilizing these horses. Even the U.S. Army Cavalry began using them in their battles with the Indians. They found their American-bred horses were no match for the Spanish-descended war ponies, particularly in the difficult-to-reach nooks and crannies of the West. They chose to "fight fire with fire."

Little by little, however, these horses became scarce. Entire herds were annihilated by the cavalry, "buffalo-" type hunters, and ranchers/farmers. Even horses that were owned and protected were interbred with other

---

[2] Not to be confused with the many feral horses that are managed by the BLM (Bureau of Land Management), known as mustangs.)

[3] Due to divergent selection, the horse currently in Spain is different from the horse known as Iberian at the time of Columbus.

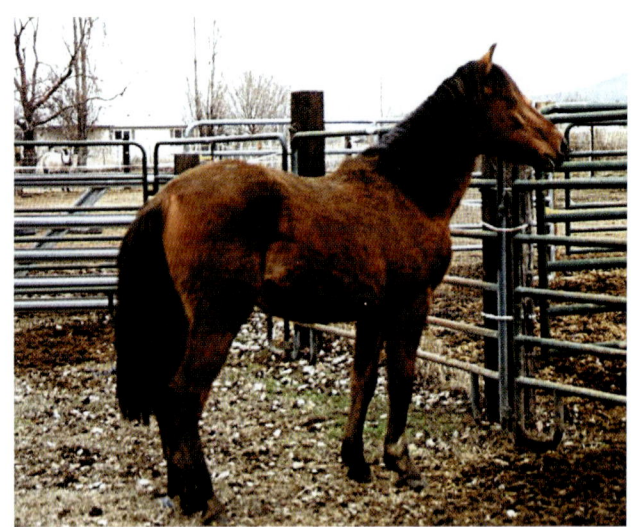

A very athletic dun stud, WARRIOR'S CON-QUISTADOR "FIDO." Owner: Nancy Pearson

Mare, WARRIOR'S KEEPSAKE, (KEEPER) is a 1999 dun overo. (PRAIRIE WARRIOR X SLATEY LADY). KEEPER is owned by Day's End Ranch and Kay and Chuck Day.

types of horses, further eroding the purity of the gene pool.

It wasn't until the early twentieth century, when the horses were on the brink of extinction, that Robert I. Brislawn of Oshoto, Wyoming, began the long journey toward reestablishing the presence of the Spanish Mustang.

Brislawn, born in Palouse County in 1890, worked as a miner, rancher and freight driver. Over the years his preference for the Spanish Mustang continued. He found these horses could not only survive on the poor forage, but they remained strong and never seemed to tire. He respected their agility, speed and loyalty. His personal horses were never hobbled or tied, yet they stayed with him, much as pet dogs might do. Most of all, he respected their will to survive.

In 1925, he began a project to preserve the horses of pure Spanish blood. He launched a search for horses that were essentially pure Spanish types. His first stallions were sons of a horse named Monte, captured from the wild in 1927. Seventeen years later he escaped back to the wild with his herd of mares. (He was never recaptured.)

When Brislawn found himself in Oklahoma, he introduced horses owned by Gilbert Jones into his breeding program. The Jones horses traced back to the Romero family from the 1800's. These horses represented some of the Choctaw and Cherokee horses that sported flashy calico paint patterns.

Taking a historical look at these horse, we find that the original Spanish horses were relatively unselected. Initially they arrived in the Caribbean Islands. Gradually they were exported onto the mainland. Mexico became home to horses that were basically crosses between Caribbean horses and those coming directly from Spain. Many of the horses from Yucatan in Southeast Mexico are responsible for the leopard-type markings.

Padre Eusebio Kino, a Jesuit priest in Sonora, Mexico, was an important figure in the preservation of the Spanish Mustangs. As Kino traveled north establishing missions, he brought the horses with him. Each mission became a new breeding facility for the horses. The Apache Indians also contributed to the expansion of these horses, frequently ravaging and pillaging the missions and taking horses they later went on to trade with other tribes. They became one of the primary causes of spreading the Spanish horses throughout the west.

Today the horses of Mexican strains are generally found one at a time, rather than in herds. The Ita Yates horses are one exception. Usually small and either dun or grulla in color, they are found in the care of Tally Johnson. With only two stallions in 1950, - one of which was sterile - this band of horses has grown and survived to this day as proof that inbreeding need not always result in the decline of a line.

The stallion MAGNETO, co-owned by Rockin B Ranch of Mabank, Texas, and Karma Farms of Marshall, Texas. He only measures about 14 hands in height, but he has a heart of gold!

Stallion EL DUC, the pride of Springwater Station, located in Estacada, Oregon, was captured in the wild in 1993, in the Steen Wilderness on Riddle Mountain.

There is some overlap between the Mexican and Rancher strains. Horses that came from the Mexican herds found their way into the sanctuary of some of the Rancher herds. Remnants from Padre Kino's horses were brought into the United States from Mexico in 1885, by a horse trader named Juan Sepulveda. He sold a group of horses (25 mares and 1 stallion) to a rancher, Dr. Reuben Wilbur. These animals were turned out into the high desert mountains surrounding the Wilbur Ranch. Over the years, the herd was tapped for riding horses needed to run the ranch.

Today, more than 100 years later, these horses, known as the Wilbur-Cruce herd from Saddabe, Arizona, have been sorted and disbursed by the American Livestock Breeds Conservancy (ALBC) under the direction of Dr. Phillip Sponenberg DMV, Ph.D. They divided the herd of 77 into groups and distributed them among conservation breeders.

The Waggoner horses followed the path of many Spanish horses that were diluted over the years. They were, for the most part, mixed with Morgans and Thoroughbreds to produce the American Quarter Horse.

Ilo Belsky, in Nebraska, was one important rancher who kept his horses pure to the Spanish breeding. These horses tend to be heavier than other Spanish Mustangs. They are most often roan, grey, dun and the darker colors.

There are two Romero families that influenced the Mustangs. One, in New Mexico, has all but disappeared, even though it was raised for generations. The other flourished in the 1800's. Together with Gonzales and Marques herds, the flashy calico paint patterns were produced. Both color and Mustang have survived to this day under the protection of Bob Ele and Gilbert Jones.

Native American strains are represented in the Cheyenne, Lakota, Paiute, Navajo, Choctaw, and Cherokee tribes. Family names that remain important are Whitmire, Corntassie, Brame, Crisp, Locke, Self, Helms, Thurman and Carter.

The deaths of several elderly breeders of Spanish Mustangs effected the current numbers considerably. As recently as 1975, hundreds of Choctaw and Cherokee horses were available. Currently, sanctuary and growth of the two herds has been assumed by Bryant and Darlene Rickman. Their dedication to this effort has had a wide impact on the general Colonial Spanish horse population today.

Horses that trace back to the herds of Sitting Bull are now under the protection of Frank and Leo Kuntz from Litton, North Dakota. Horses that escaped the confiscation of the Sitting Bull herd fled to the Dakota Badlands. Many joined feral herds, but others were bred and prospered with the Indians. This branch of the family are mostly black, blue roan, and grey, with some bay and overo. Perhaps the largest source of pure Spanish Mustang blood can be found in feral herds. The Cerbat Herd in the Arizona mountains, the Pryor Mountains herds in Wyoming and Montana, the Kiger herd from Oregon, and the Sulphur Creek herd in Utah represent the most important numbers.

The 21-year battle by Velma Johnston, "Wild Horse Annie," to protect the feral herds, and the scientific advances that allowed Dr. Gus Cothran of the University of Kentucky to identify the frequency of Spanish markers in the blood are major factors in the current healthy condition of the Spanish Mustangs.

In 1966, a national magazine published an article concerning the Neal family who had settled in the Arizona mountains in 1860. Rancher John Neal told of the horses in the area at the time. Even the Indians reported that the horses had "always been there." With an altitude in that area ranging from 5,000 to 7,000 feet, it speaks to the tenacity and hardiness of these Cerbat Mountain Horses.

Unfortunately, during a severe drought in 1971, the horses' ability to dig for water was not considered by the local ranchers when they decided the horses were taking needed water by herds of cattle. A number of horses were "water trapped" and dispersed to Mustang fanciers from Arizona to Washington State.

In 1990, the BLM facility in Hines, Oregon discovered a small herd of horses believed to be remnants of the original Cerbat herd. This was confirmed through blood testing. It was also interesting to find these horses were not negatively affected by the Inbreeding that had allowed for their survival.

➡ Photo to the right: Mare, WARRIOR'S LADY B, "MISS B," is black/dark bay, by PRAIRIE WARRIOR out of SLATEY LADY owned by Tami Atchison. Tami was pre-vet when she bought MISS B and had worked with many horses she called "push-button horses that you can make do anything when training but never remember until it is drilled for some time." Tami is happy to report that the Spanish Mustangs are so smart, they pick up where they leave off and don't miss a beat. After owning MISS B for less than a month, she bought another.

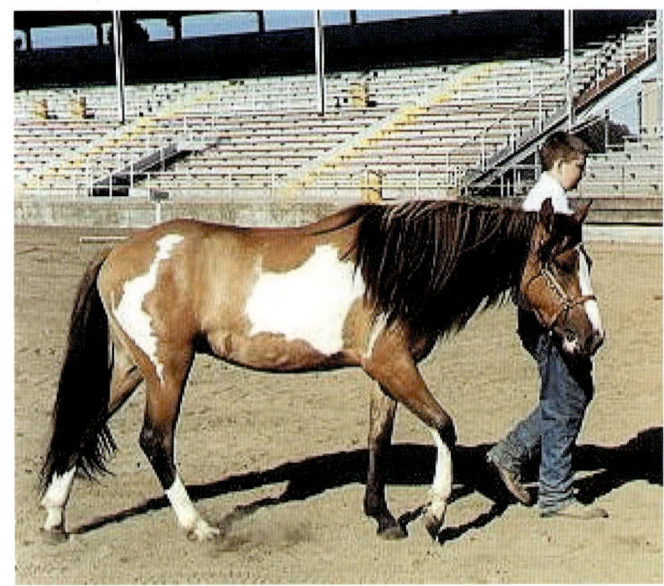

Mare WARRIOR'S KEEPSAKE participating in a 4H Competition with Kay and Chuck Day's grandchildren representing Day's End Ranch.

Stallion NORTHERN SONG (a.k.a. CAJUN) is a perfect example of a Northern-type Colonial Spanish Horse. Owned and shown by Susan Tuscana from Rockin B Ranch.

Judy Shulter riding WHITE WING DOVE, a treasured mare at The Rockin B Ranch in Mabank, Texas. Her owner Susan Tuscana reports that she is one of their best mares and is asked for by name by many of their dude riders – especially the handicapped or special needs children, because she is smooth at any gait and very easy to ride.

Gelding WARRIOR'S PRAIRIE FIRE (a.k.a. ELBE), was sired by PRAIRIE WARRIOR out of dam SLATEY LADY (it was her first foal). He was purchased by Theresa Carney as a long yearling, and started under saddle as a two-year-old. Theresa and ELBE tried out for the Mounted Search and Rescue team, and were licensed in the state of Washington, when he was a three-year-old.

(It is probable that this new group had no more than five ancestors and no less than three, according to the blood tests.) In the wild, nature is a "natural culler" of animals that suffer from abnormal or imperfect genes resulting from inbreeding; only the strong, healthy, superior animals survive.

Many herd members have dark-pigmented areas about three to four inches in diameter on one or both hips, and many have blood markers also found in the Peruvian Paso. The lateral 4-beat gait is also common.

Marye Ann Thompson, of Wilcox, Arizona, has been a major influence on the preservation of the Spanish Mustangs. She has provided sanctuary and growth to the numbers of Spanish Mustangs. She uses the Cerbat horses as a source of pure Spanish blood for her breeding program. Even though she has had excellent results from crossing the Cerbat stallions with other Spanish Mustangs, the ultimate goal is to preserve the Cerbat horse in its pure form.

Recognition of the Pryor Mountain horses was established in 1968, when a Wild Horse Refuge was set aside in the Pryor Mountains by Secretary of State Stewart Udall. The Pryor Mountain Wild Horse Association in Lovell, Wyoming was a guiding force behind the blood testing of 75 horses from the Pryor Mountain herd. Gus Cothran determined a Spanish connection with the Pryor Mountain Horses. Blood markers are Spanish and the general coloration within the herd is consistent with Spanish origin.

In 1977, a herd of horses that looked to be Spanish were brought into BLM. These and several other subsequent additions to the herd were uniform in size and color, shades of dun and displaying dorsal stripes down their back and zebra stripes on their legs. The horses were so distinct that Ron Harding and Chris Vosler of BLM committed to their protection. Twenty of these horses were turned out onto the East Kiger Herd Management Area, seven to the Riddle Mountain Herd Management Area. They were careful to keep other feral horses from the Kiger Horse range. It was deemed important to keep the herd as pure as possible.

SUN DOWNER is a 15-year-old stallion

A yearling stud colt on the Cayuse Ranch in Wyoming

Eight-year-old grulla stallion IKKITSI-PETA GREY EAGLE

Stallion, WARRIOR'S SPIRIT WIND Joe Haynes' herd sire.

Stallion, WAR DANCER 15-year-old at Cayuse Ranch

A buckskin overo yearling filly.

Stallion, WARDANCER and his mares at Brislawn's Cayuse Ranch

GITANO, a 19-year-old mare. Cayuse Ranch, Wyoming

CHOCTAW THREE a 16-year-old stallion.

A buckskin yearling filly Cayuse Ranch, Wyoming

Stallion, SIRBEE A 24-year-old bay roan.

Grulla mare, with a graying gene, JAZZARITA MY LOLITA, was born in 1995. JAZZ is sometimes called FLOPSY because of her damaged ear. She was on the range until she was a year old and was probably kicked in the ear, causing a hemotoma. She had surgery to keep it from flopping down and hitting her in the eye. The ear still doesn't look perfect, but it doesn't effect her babies. She is a great momma and very sweet. This photo was taken when she was two by her owner Nancy Pearson.

JAZZARITA MY LOLITA as a baby, when Nancy Pearson first saw her. The photo to the left shows JAZZ as a mature mare.

The Kiger Mesteno Association was established in 1988 by residents of Oregon, Washington, California, and Michigan. Its mission is to protect and preserve the Kiger Mustang. Attention is given to guidelines for the adoption of individual horses from this herd. They also are promoting an educational program through the BLM Wild Horse Program to ensure the Kiger Herd will remain intact for posterity. They established a registry to track the offspring of the Kigers and plan to maintain pedigrees.

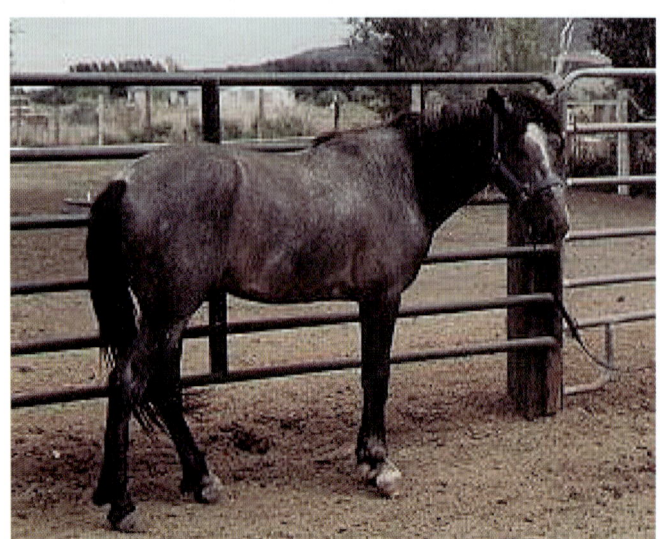

Utah is home to the Sulphur Creek Herd. In 1993, Dr. Sponenberg said: "This is one population that should be kept free of introductions from other herd-management areas, as it is Spanish in type and therefore more unique than horses from most other BLM management areas."

During the 1800's, raids by Indians and mountainmen brought Spanish horses from missions and settlements in Southern California over the Cajon Pass into the Mojave Desert and up to Utah. Many of the horses escaped into the isolated Mountain Home Range and multiplied. Ranchers who later settled in the surrounding areas turned stallions out into the feral herds in the hope of increasing their size. Their attempts backfired; the larger horses settled into the valleys, while the hardy Spanish horses, with their tough little feet and robust natures, moved up into the remote canyons. This served the Mustangs well in the long run, because during the first half of the 20th century, it was acceptable to hunt wild horses and shoot them for meat and byproducts. The horses of the lowlands were easy pickings for the "Mustangers," while the little Spanish horses remained safe in the hard-to-reach areas, to be rediscovered in the early 90's.

WARRIOR'S WIND DANCER, "DANCER" is a grulla roan stud by PRAIRIE WARRIOR out of JAZZARITA MY LOLITA. She possesses a very kind and willing disposition.

The Southeastern strains of the Spanish Mustang are represented in the registries as individuals rather than herd members. There is

Stud colt, PRAIRIE WARRIOR, is the same horse pictured to the right as an adult stallion.

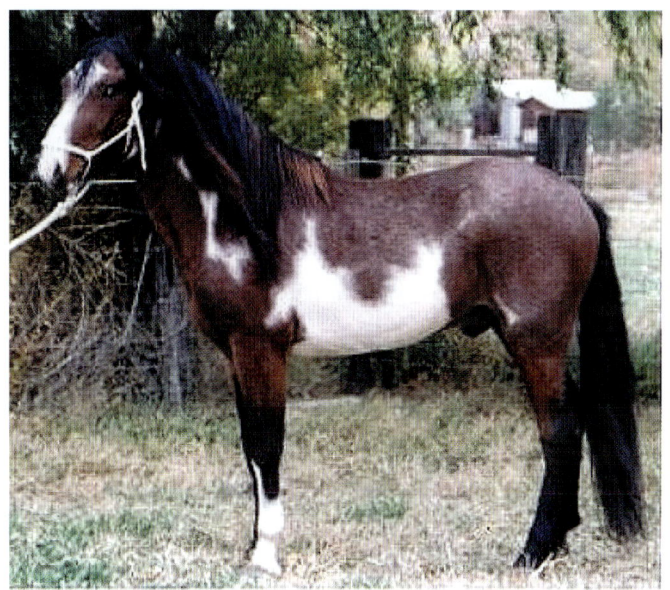

Stallion, PRAIRIE WARRIOR SMR 2217, a bay roan overo, born in 1994. Owner Nancy Pearson says: "This is my first stallion, and I couldn't have been luckier He has an awesome disposition. My mares run with him year round, as do his babies, until they are weaned."

controversy surrounding the purity of blood in these horses. The Florida Crackers are one registry that has a legitimate claim to their Spanish heritage, but (with the inclusion of some Cuban horses) they have evolved into a special category, all their own.

The Banker Ponies, from the outer banks of Virginia and the Carolinas, are clear descendants of the Spanish horses, but because of the introduction of other blood on some of the islands, their purity is in doubt. Some of these horses have proven to be pure enough to be included in a Spanish Mustang Registry, but they have had to be evaluated on a case-by-case basis, not as a herd.

In 1975, Bob Brislawn headed a group that incorporated the Spanish Mustang Registry, the oldest Mustang Registry in the country. It is a nonprofit organization designed to preserve and perpetuate the last known remnants of the true Spanish Mustangs. Initially, they registered twenty animals. Over the years this number grew, and within forty years, more than 2,500 horses had been documented as pure Spanish Mustangs.

The Spanish Mustang Registry describes their horses as "a medium-size horse ranging from 13:2 to 15 hands with an average size of approximately 14:2 hands with proportional weight. They are smooth-muscled with short backs, rounded rumps and low set tails. Coupling is smooth, and the overall appearance is of a well-balanced, smoothly built horse. The girth is deep, with well-laid back shoulders and fairly pronounced withers. They possess the classic Spanish-type head with a straight or concave forehead and a convex nose, in contrast to the straight forehead and nose of most breeds. Ears are

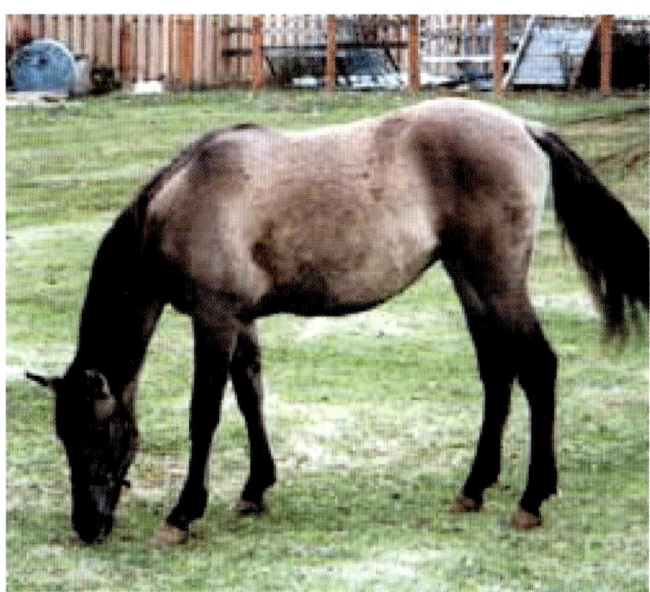

SPRING WATER STATION'S JUBILEE is an ELDUC filly. She is 18 months old in this photo. As a three-year-old, she was 15:2 hands and growing, super-sharp, and placed reserve at Kigerfest 2000. JUBILEE is owned by Linda Holst at Rancho Linda Marchadores, Bonsall, California.

Filly, WARRIOR'S SHADOW LADY with her mother SLATEY LADY. Owner: Tami Atchison

medium to short and usually notched or curved toward each other. Necks are fairly well-crested in mares and geldings, and heavily crested in mature stallions. Chests are narrow but deep, with the front legs joining the chest in an "A" shape rather than straight across. Chestnuts are small or missing altogether, particularly on the rear legs. Feet are extremely sound with thick walls, many having what is typically known as a "mule foot," which resists bruising due to the concave sole. Canons are short, the upper foreleg is long, with the canon bone having a larger circumference than other breeds of comparable size and weight. Long-strided, many are gaited, with a comfortable 4-beat gait such as the amble, running walk, or single-foot. Some individuals are laterally gaited and do a very passable "paso" gait, though without extreme knee action. They are hardy animals and tend to be less prone to injury, particularly of the legs and feet, than other breeds. They have a very different mentality than "domesticated" horses. They are not push-button horses and will not abide abuse; however, they bond well with their owners and once bonded, become very attached to that person. Highly intelligent with an innate sense of self-preservation, they are not prone to place themselves in any situation that might be destructive or dangerous. Compared to "domesticated" breeds, they retain a great many of the instincts that allowed

This beautiful buckskin is a twenty two-year-old mare named YELLOW ROSE. She is owned by Josie Brislawn, at her Brislawn's Cayuse Ranch in Wyoming.

them to survive in the feral state. Colors are extremely varied - the inheritance of the early Spanish Horses who came in many colors and patterns, including dun, grulla, buckskin, paint, appaloosa, as well as the more common bay, chestnut, black and white."

Another registry representing the Spanish Mustang is the Southwest Spanish Mustang Association (SSMA), founded by Gilbert Jones. Jones had been a fancier of the Spanish Mustang since his boyhood, when he was given a Spanish Mustang mare whose descendants are still present on his Medicine Spring Ranch. Jones believes there are actually two branches of the Spanish Mustang Tree - the Spanish Mustang, derived from horses left in Florida by the Spanish explorers; the other, is the strain developed from horses left in Mexico, and known as the Western Mustang. The SSMA has two basic purposes: 1) To keep the purest stock in existence by keeping strict breeding records, and 2) To make the public aware of the stamina and endurance capabilities of the breed.

The Spanish Barb Breeders Association was formed by Susan Paulton of Hot Springs, South Dakota. Their purpose is to perpetuate the breeding of a particular type of Spanish Mustang that favors the Barb-appearing horse.

In this registry, each horse is inspected

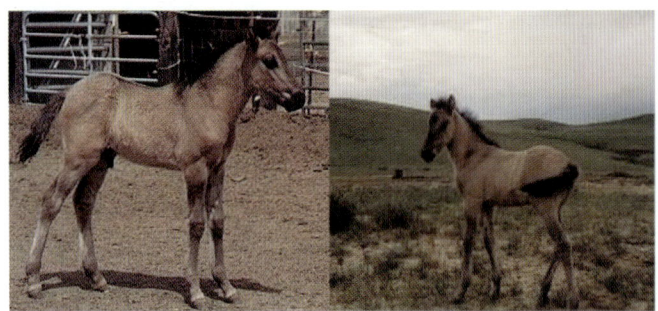

Left: WARRIOR'S PRAIRIE OUTLAW, "LITTLE ELVIS", who grew up to be a herd sire for Canadian breeder, Sheila Archer. **Right:** A baby picture of **SLATEY LADY** (mother to ELVIS), who is pictured on facing page.

individually and has to stand on its own merit, regardless of its parentage. There are two divisions in this Registry: 1) Foals and adult horses that score in the median to low range; and 2) Horses that are inspected again after reaching 3 years of age and score in the upper percentile. Breeders are encouraged to select their breeding stock from the second division.

The Spanish Mustang today is frequently represented in endurance and competitive riding. They are particularly well-suited for the long-distance trials. Hundred-mile, and two-hundred-fifty-mile multi-day rides are venues in which the Spanish Mustangs can utilize the amazing stamina, strength and durability inherited from their ancestors.

Modern-day horses have lost none of the traits found in foundation horses. Bob Brislawn, founder of the original registry, has passed his passion for these horses to his son Emmett. In 1966, Emmett took his sixteen-year-old Mustang Yellow Fox out of retirement and entered him in the Bitterroot ride. This Cheyenne-bred buckskin stallion won championships for Heavyweight, All-Around-Horse, and Best Out-Of-State Horse carrying over 200 pounds. They say that when Yellow Fox approached the finish line, the old horse threw back his head, still looking for the wild horses!

These splendid Spanish Mustangs are true royalty in the family of the Fabulous Floaters. The numbers of enthusiastic breeders are growing, and the future looks bright for these living historical treasures.

One of those breeders is Susan Tuscana at the Rockin B Ranch in Texas.

Quoting Susan: "These horses have really bonded with us and seem to do anything we ask of them." Susan goes on to recount a story that exhibits the can do personalities of these fine horses. Her mule-riding friend wanted her to show him some steep grades in preparation for a ride he was planning in Oklahoma. So, being a good trail-boss, I showed him one of the best (and steepest) creekbeds I have here at the ranch. After trying to go down it a few times and having his mule balk, he was getting pretty upset. I asked him to move over - maybe if Mags (my Mustang stallion), went first, the mule would follow. The other riders assumed Susan and her horse had been on the path before, but she assured them it was a first time for Mags, too.

Susan continues: "I rode him to the edge, let him sniff the area for a few seconds, then gave him the cue of 'get up.' He hesitated, trying to find a way down. When I squeezed my legs a little and said 'hit it' he did the prettiest move you could ever imagine. He calmly went up to the edge of the creekbank and stepped off as if there was nothing there, sitting back and sliding on his haunches as if he'd done it a million times before. It was so elegant, he never even jarred me. When we got down to the bottom, I turned him around and told the group of guys, well...I'm waiting. Needless to say, they think he's one amazing critter."

Nancy Pearson, from the Wild Side Ranch, in Benton City, Washington explains why she became a champion of the Spanish Mustang: "I had adopted BLM mustangs and was totally impressed with their stamina, intelligence, and kindness. While doing research on BLM horses, I read Hope Ryden's book, *America's Last Wild Horses*, and a chapter on the Spanish Mustangs and the Brislawn's Cayuse Ranch. I was planning a trip to the Pryor Mountain Wild Horse herd and decided to add the Cayuse to my trip. When I got there, studied them and their herd behavior (it was June, so there were many babies), and I listened to the Brislawns tell the history, I just fell in love. I picked my first two while I was there! It was the best decision I ever made, and I can assure you, these horses have taught me more than I will ever teach them!"

SLATEY LADY (a.k.a. BRISSY) is a grulla mare born in 1994. She is the pride and joy of owner Nancy Pearson, who describes her as craving attention. She even shakes hands!

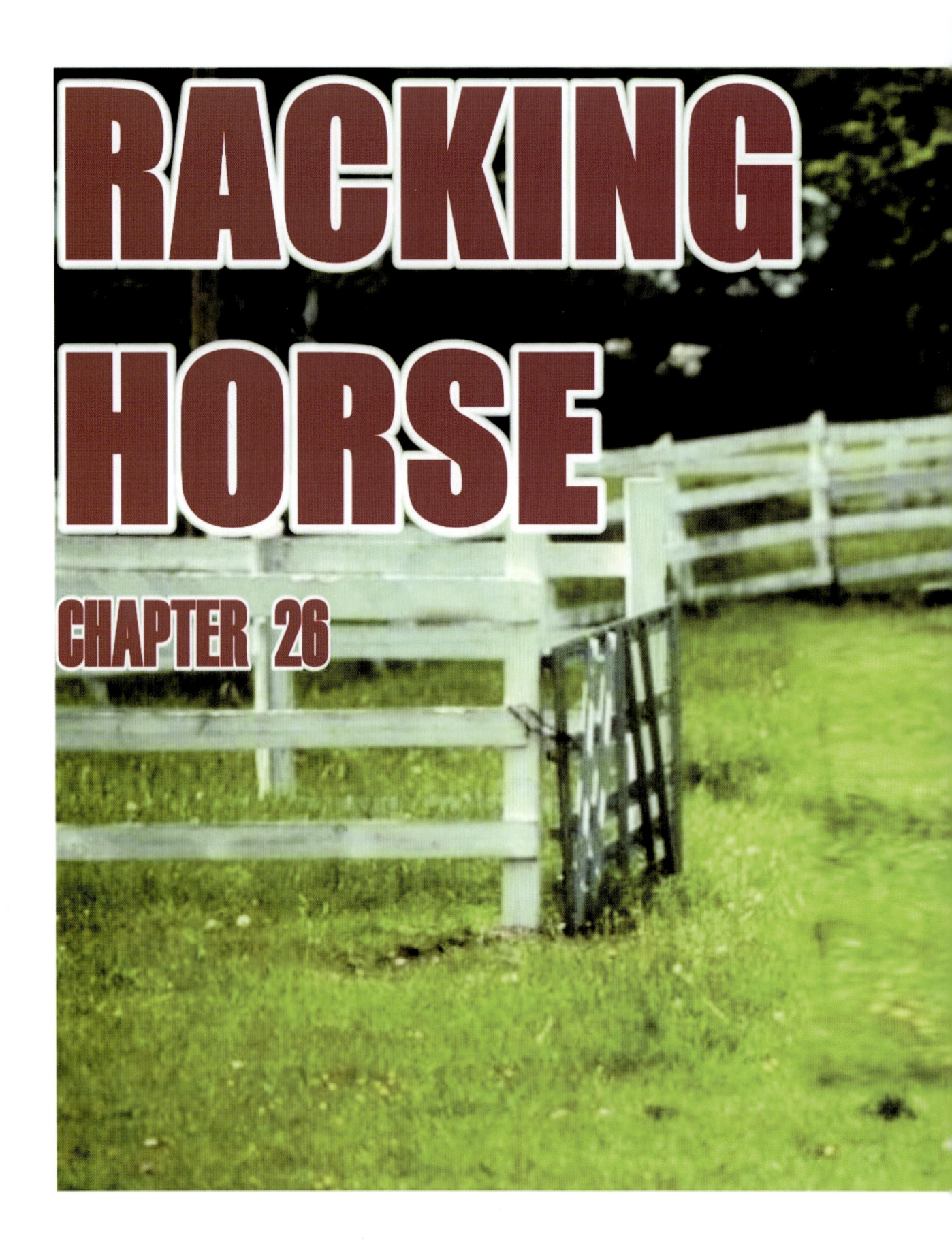

RACKING HORSE

CHAPTER 26

A natural rack being performed by a 3-day-old son of WINDJAMMER

Chapter 26 The Racking Horse

There are horses in every soft-gaited registry that are capable of racking. The Tennessee Walker fanciers have included a speed-racking class in their shows for years. Some other breeds give their own breed-specific names to the rack gait.

There are two basic racking speeds - the stepping rack, which is the slower and smoothest gait, with an alternating foot support of two feet on the ground, then three feet on the ground, and the speed rack, moving so fast that the alternating foot support appears to be two feet on the ground flying into just one foot on the ground. This is one gait that is easily seen in photographs.

The racking horse has been with us for as long as there have been soft-gaited horses. A registry, The Racking Horse Breeders' Association of America (RHBAA) is the first to isolate the gait as being breed-specific. In 1971, a group of Alabama horsemen formed the RHBAA. That year, the United States Department of Agriculture granted a Registry and Stud Book to the organization. A new breed had became official. In 1975, the House and Senate of the Alabama state

⇨ Photos to the right: Top: Susie Wright aboard mare BLACK FANCEY GIRL, "GRANNY," a natural Racking Standardbred with a natural front-end and registered RHBAA. Photo: Sandra Hall. Middle: Shawneen Magrum riding stallion HERICHO from Turning Point Training Center. Photo: Aaron Archachi. Bottom: B. Weatherwax riding mare GOLDEN GIRL, "TESSA," a double-registered KMSHA and Racking Horse. Photo: Forrest Bliss

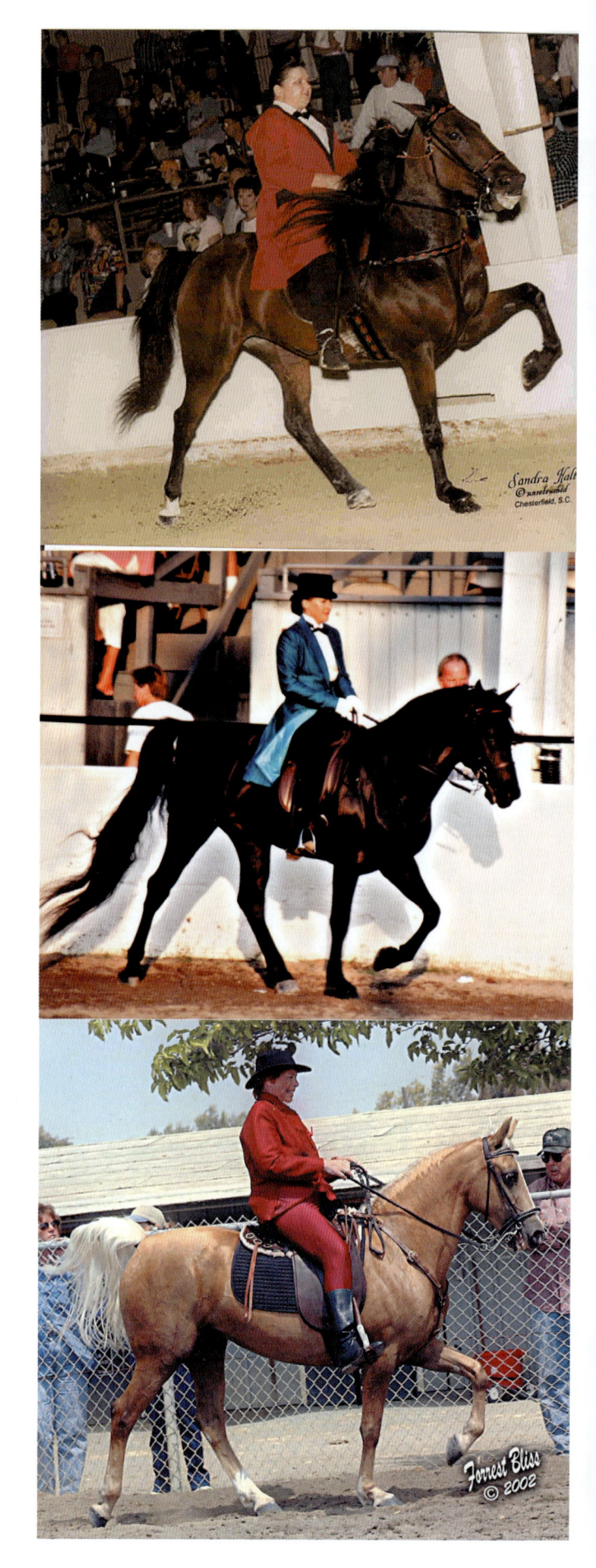

Alabama headquarters for the RHBAA, Racking Horse Breeders' Association of America.

legislature named the Racking Horse the official state horse of Alabama.

The Racking Horse has a distinct Southern heritage, but its ancestors are found in the same roots as many of the other soft-gaited breeds. They descend from Thoroughbred, Saddlebred, Standardbred and Morgan bloodlines. They were being bred on Southern plantations before the Civil War. Their smooth, rolling gait and amazing endurance made them ideal for transportation at that time. They were put to work in the field, asked to carry riders for days on end with little rest, and might be needed to pull the family's wagon to church on Sunday.

Today's Racking Horse is a popular show horse. In the open show division, it performs the show walk, the step rack and the fast rack, which is a true speed gait.

A rapidly growing show division among Racking Horse enthusiasts is the Trail, Field and Pleasure Division. Over the last ten years, this division has expanded tremendously with classes such as trail pleasure, country pleasure, western pleasure, park pleasure, show pleasure, style pleasure and others. The important feature of these pleasure horses is an ability to be comfortable, efficient and "pleasurable" on an all-day ride with a smooth gait.

A more recent addition to the Racking Horse world is the Pleasure Racking Horse Versatility Program. This program was developed to promote the utilization of the flat-

↑ Top: Sandy Preston riding the remarkable stallion WINDJAMMER. Photo: Debbie Bush. Middle: Sandy Preston riding CRIMSON TIDE. Photo: Sandra Hall. Bottom: John Demetris aboard the equine legend EZD'S FALCON ROWDY. (Very nearly performing a pace) Photo: Courtesy NASHA

shod pleasure Racking Horse in all aspects of the pleasure horse industry. It consists of a merit program by which Racking Horses can earn points by participating and succeeding in a wide variety of classes, including English trail pleasure, pleasure driving, western pleasure, halter, trail obstacle and even endurance riding.

"Rack Across America" is an new competition set up by the RHBAA to reward Racking Horse trail riders. To participate, the horse must be registered with RHBAA. The recorded hours go with the horse. The rider must also be a current member of the RHBAA and the Pleasure Association. Prizes are given for time spent (in forward motion, not lunching) in trail riding. Accomplishments will also be published in The Racking Review.

A chapter on racking horses wouldn't be complete without looking at the Horses of Osborne Gap. EZD'S Falcon Rowdy and his progeny from Osborn Gap, Virginia, are not a registry, not a breed - they are a phenomenon.

A hundred and fifty years ago, an amazing branch of the Mountain Horse family, known as the Kentucky Walker, flourished. This horse was known for its speed and impeccable single-foot gait with a normal speed of 12 to 15 miles per hour.

By the mid 1930's, the breed had all but disappeared except for a few horses tucked away in the Osborn Gap area of Virginia. Typically, these horses have short backs, deep chests, small alert ears, straight front legs, and long, well-angulated hind legs. The dominant color is dun, with bay, chestnut and black being common. Tight breeding and hard use has helped to develop a fast-traveling hardy horse that likes to go.

In Beef Hide Creek, Kentucky, an outstanding horse named The Colonel came to live with Robbie Johnson. His origins are a mystery, but he was believed to be of Morgan or old-time Saddlebred bloodlines. The Colonel was known throughout Virginia and Kentucky for his smooth gait and disposition. He stood about 14:2 hands tall and weighed around 950 pounds. He had fine, keen legs supporting a stocky body with short back and broad chest. His short, thick neck ended in a small, flat head with small fox-like ears. He was a dark mahog-

Racking Mountain Horse, GOLDEN GIRL "TESSA" exhibits one of the many colors found in the Racking Horse. Photo: Brenda Foley

NASHA registered, ROWDY'S LIL RASCAL, son of EZD'S FALCON ROWDY, demonstrating a speed rack. You can clearly see the one-foot-on-the-ground-support. J.B. Stanley, owner and rider.

any bay. This description of the horse is but a fraction of what makes him memorable. The Colonel had stamina, reach, bottom and quickness, and, he could blister the ground, becoming a single footing, four-beat racking machine. The Colonel was never beaten in a four-beat gait race.

John Demetris was a champion of The Colonel and his remarkable offspring. John's breeding program produced a stallion named EZD'S Falcon Rowdy, who continued to astound everyone who saw him perform throughout his life. "Falcon" had the ability to demonstrate a true traveling single-foot, a gait that was in danger of disappearing. It is being rediscovered with open mouthed, jaw-dropping awe as people see for the first time what a true traveling single-foot is.

Rowdy was twice World Champion Speed Racking Horse. He did it once in 1976 and returned to do it by lapping everything in the class at age fourteen. He often went to the races in the bed of a pickup truck or after a 45-mile mountain ride to get to the races. He raced on a Standardbred track in Sherbrook, Quebec, Canada. He worked at the huge Callahan Ranch near San Antonio, Texas. He lived in temperatures from 67° below to 123° above. And just for fun, he participated in any number of gymkhana events. He was valued by his owner for more than his reportedly incredible turn of foot. After a freak injury broke his thighbone, he was nursed back to full health.

Falcon was just 14:1 hands tall. He had a glistening dappled dun coat, and like his father, The Colonel, he was the fastest gaiting horse in the world.

Quoting John Demetris: "When you ride him at his great speeds, the tears in your eyes blind you and the wind against your body feels like it's going to pull you off the back of the horse, but the adrenaline runs through your body and the rush is so strong, gravity sort of pulls you deep into the saddle and the horse does the rest."

The pair of Demetris and Rowdy have been described as looking as if they were one,

EASY FALCON, grandson of **EZD'S FALCON ROWDY**, out enjoying the trail with owner Dale Downey, up. The attractive buckskin coloring is common in the Falcon bloodlines.

Stallion, **ROWDY RAWHIDE'S ROCKET**, a grandson of **EZD'S FALCON ROWDY**, owned by Doug and Jan Stanley of Clintwood, Virginia.

Stallion, WINDJAMMER, second from left, with three of his get.

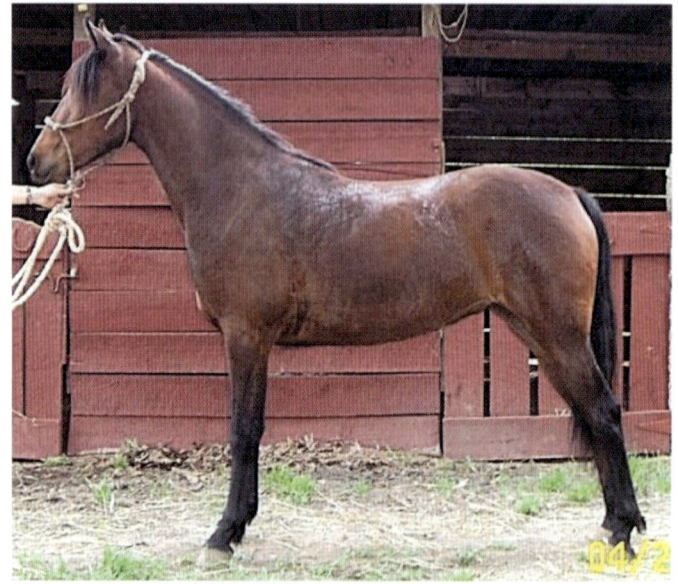

Filly, WINDS OF CHANGE RS, (ECHO), as a yearling. She is a daughter of WINDJAMMER, and is owned by Patricia Clark.

MY PRECIOUS STAR, with owner Patricia Clark, up, in Western tack and attire. Photo: Debby Bush

WINDS OF CHANGE (ECHO), under saddle as a two-year old, with trainer Sandy Preston.

Eight year old registered Single-footing mare, MY PRECIOUS STAR, in English tack, with Patricia Clark. Photo: Debby Bush

sailing over the road with the grace and speed of the wind.

John Demetris hoped to preserve the breed he had grown up with in the Kentucky Mountains. They were all similar in appearance - short, stocky, sure-footed, smooth, and most of all, tremendously fast, with unbelievable endurance.

Demetris collected seventeen individual horses. Sadly, in the early 60's, he was involved in a horrible mining accident and lost his right arm at the shoulder. One by one, he had to sell his precious horses to pay the many medical bills. But he never parted with Rowdy. This colt would give back not only John's life but his dreams as well. John claimed the only time he was not in excruciating pain was when he was on the back of a horse. He thought nothing of leaving the house at 10 a.m., riding 100 miles through the Jefferson National Forest, and returning at night fall, echoing the exploits of his younger years. When their spirits were daring, Demetris and his good friend Jackie Potter would ride their horses to the "honkey tonkes," and when they closed at midnight, the two men would ride the 30 miles home.

Rowdy died at the age of 29, and Demetris passed away in 1997. But their legacy remains. Both the men and the horses on top of the mountain in northwestern Virginia are unusual and unique.

The Rowdy offspring all seem to possess the unique traits that John Demitris began trying to preserve some thirty years before in his childhood dreams. He knew the true single-footing horse and how it was made. He understood horse conformation very well. He was no fad breeder or breeding randomly crossing or breeding whatever came along. He remained true to the real single-footing horse no matter what.

There are a number of EZD'S Falcon Rowdy progeny still reproducing. In fact, at least 75 to 80% of the breeders involved with

➡ Photo to the right: The Headless Horseman. Ken Ward, principal of the Airport School in Berkeley, played the headless horseman in the reenactment of *the Legend of Sleepy Hollow*. His target, Ichabod Crane, is portrayed by Vernon Mitchell, assistant principal at Berkeley Senior High School. Ken has performed this reenactment on his racking horses for 30 years!

CRIMSON TIDE, with trainer Sandy Preston, up.
Photo: Debby Bush

Susie Wright riding mare BLACK FANCEY GIRL.
Photo: Sandra Hall

the North American Single-Footing Horse Association are using The Colonel lines as the foundation stock in their breeding programs. What a gift from the Virginia Mountains! The horses of the Osborn Gap continue to enrich the options available in the world of the soft-gaited horse.

Doug and Jan Stanley of Clintwood, Virginia, are proud owners of a Falcon grandson, Rowdy Rawhide's rocket. This fine stallion is not only passing along the precious Falcon genes, he is Doug's rough-and-ready partner on the trail. Quoting Doug: "Rocket is the son of Rowdy Rawhide, grandson of EZD's Falcon Rowdy, and the great-grandson of The Colonel. He is fast, smooth, and has an excellent disposition and fine conformation."

Another Falcon grandson is Easy Falcon, who is standing at Crescent Moon Ranch in Alberta, Canada. Owners Dale Downey and Mimi Busk-Downey, have been raising Peruvian Paso horses for twenty-five years. They have a smaller breeding program de-voted to the Single-Footing Horses. Most of them are registered with NASHA (North American Single-Footing Horse Association). The Downeys believe the racking horses to be fast and smooth. "They have good minds and efficient gaits that will make them an ideal choice for endurance and competitive trail- riding or ranch work."

Earl and Susie Wright have a small stable in southeast Kentucky, where they own and train speed Racking Horses. Susie rides and her husband Earl watches (and growls) if Susie doesn't do it just right. Earl is also the farrier and shoes all of their horses.

The Wrights like to show horses, but they also enjoy their horses on the trails. Susie's mare Skip's Fancy Pants, a Standardbred by breeding and a speed racker by performance, is in the Rack Across America Program. Fancy has reached 1,000 trail hours.

The stallion, Windjammer SP, owned, shown and loved by Sandy Preston of Lexington, Virginia, is a multi-Champion Racking Horse. His origins are unknown, but he has the characteristics that - at the time of his birth in 1971 - would have been commonly referred to as a Kentucky Walker or an Old type Morgan horse.

Top: Pam Stubbs on ROLEX. Middle: Doug Stanley on ROWDY RAWHIDE'S ROCKET. Bottom: WINDJAMMER.

Windjammer SP has been a part of Sandy's family since he was a two-year old, but they didn't become a real team until he was 14. His first major speed competitions were in 1988, when he gained the name "The Bay Bullet." His fierce rivalry with Speck, nicknamed "The Strawberry Jet," and Speck's rider, Robert Skimhorne, were known as the "speed wars," and the crowds loved every minute of it.

Windjammer is in his thirties, and he and Sandy are still together. Quoting Sandy's good friend Patricia Clark: "He is a grand old stallion and still carries himself with the look of eagles. He has that special appeal that only truly great animals have, and he will never be forgotten in the minds of those who have seen him."

Although the Speed Racking Horse can come from different breeding (Standardbred, Walking Horse, Single-footing Horse, etc.), there is a body type that is pretty consistent with the ability to rack. According to the RHBAA (Racking Horse Breeders' Association of America), the Racking Horse is attractive and gracefully built with a long sloping neck, full flanks, well-boned, smooth legs, and finely textured hair. The Racking Horse is considered a "light" horse in comparison with other breeds, averaging 15:2 hands and weighing 1,000 pounds. Colors may be black, bay, sorrel, chestnut, brown, grey, yellow, cremello, buckskin, dun, palomino, roan, champagne, and even spotted.

The Racking Horse comes by this gait as naturally as walking or striking a bold trot comes to other breeds. It may be shown under saddle, in hand, or in harness.

Beginning riders have found the Racking Horse to be the answer to their prayers not only for his extremely comfortable ride but also because of its unusual friendliness to humans. Beginners and veterans alike can appreciate the opportunities generated by this intelligent, family-oriented steed.

Registered Racking Horses are presently found throughout the United States and in several foreign countries. Over 80,000 of them are registered with the RHBAA at its headquarters in Decatur, Alabama.

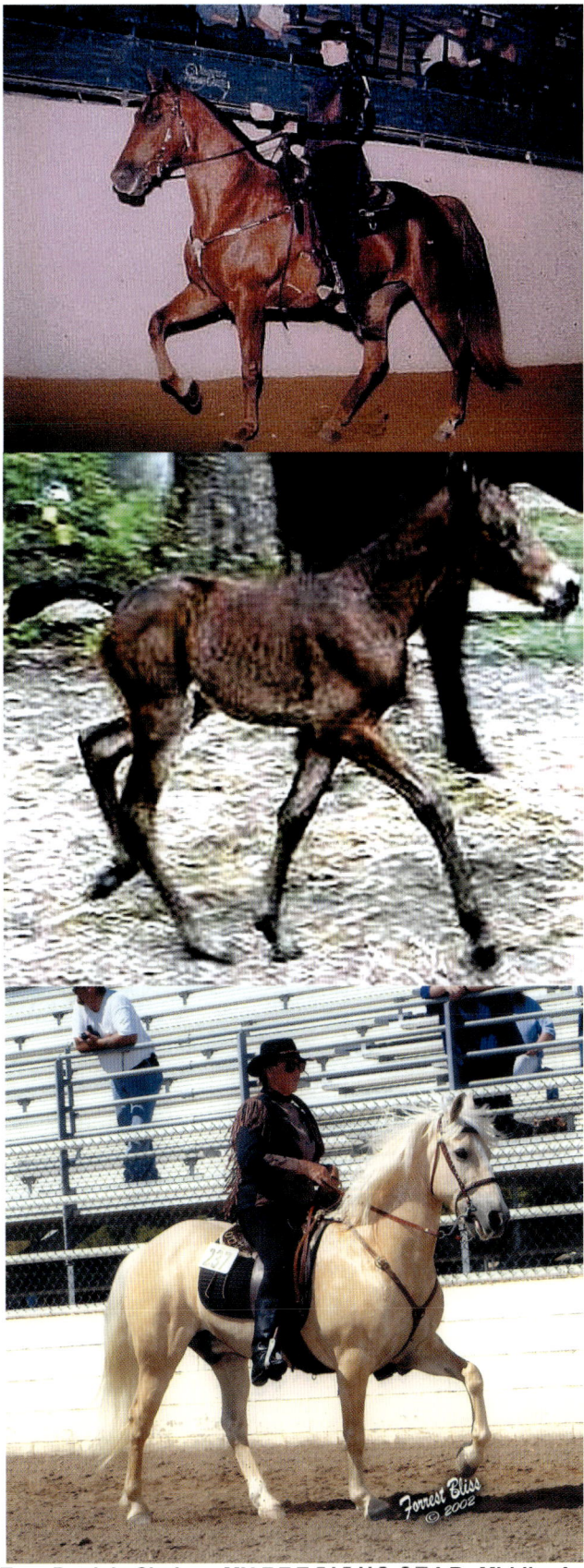

Top: Patricia Clark on MY PRECIOUS STAR. Middle: A three-day-old filly, WINDS OF CHANGE (ECHO), demonstrating a natural rack. Bottom: Double-registered Kentucky Mountain Saddle Horse and Racking Horse KENTUCKY GOLDRUSH, with Barbara Weatherwax, up.
Photo: Forrest Bliss

PART WALKING HORSE

CHAPTER 27

Tennessee Walker stallion, GOLDUST ROYAL TRIGGER
Owner: Grace Larson

GOLDUST ROYAL TRIGGER is a Registered Tennessee Walker and is sire to many Part Walkers.

Chapter 27 The Part Walking Horse

The Tennessee Walker has been a popular and available horse since the 1930's. For many horse lovers, the Tennessee Walker is the only soft-gaited horse they have ever heard about. The official Breed Registry has registered well over 300,000 animals. It's not hard to imagine how many horses, both of pure and mixed blood, were never registered.

Purebred Walkers Merry Boy Sensation, Jet's Gay Strutter, Ebony's Town Clown, Banner's Shepherd, Go Boy's Jet K, and part Tennessee Walkers like Zane's Cadillac, Zane Grey, Mr. President, Mack K's Yankee, and Tody's Perfection, were all important sires in the development of the Missouri Fox Trotter Breed.

Using the Tennessee Walker as a major ingredient, other breeds were developed. The Tennuvian is principally a cross between the Tennessee Walker and the Peruvian Paso. While many Walkaloosas are developed from within the Appaloosa breed, more often they are a cross between the Appaloosa and the Tennessee Walker. Many pure-blooded Tennessee Walkers are registered with one of the Racking or Mountain Horse Registries.

The 1990's produced a plethora of new registries and associations. Breeds that were once represented by a singular Registry/Owner Association were now developing new groups that chose to honor different aspects of the same horse.

The Tennessee Walker was no exception. While the Tennessee Walking Horse Breeders and Exhibitors Association (TWHBEA) remains the principal record-keeping registry, the International Pleasure Walking Horse Registry (IPWHR) is gaining the confidence of pure-bred Tennessee Walking Horse owners for registration

For a period of time, horse owners were ignoring the registration process, claiming it was too expensive, complicated, or just plain unnecessary. Once there is a breech between horse and registry, there is no way to undo the decision. Only a few of the important registries allow for registration on the strength of the horse's own talents. The unbroken line of family as defined on a pedigree is the only ticket into most registries. So it is with the Walking Horse.

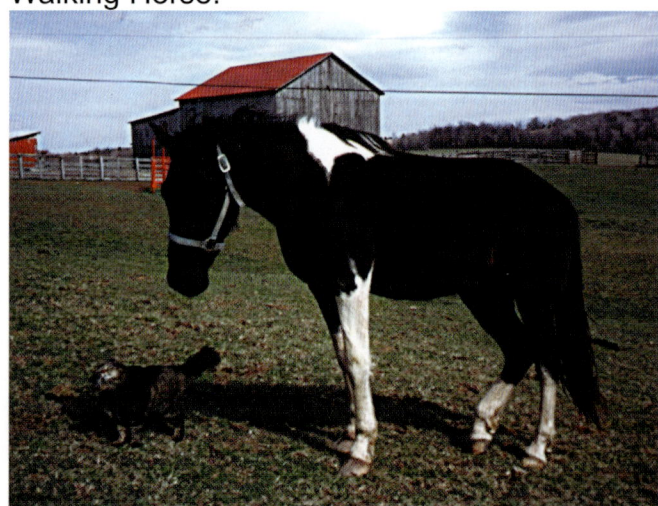

TIGO'S HARLEQUIN, 3-year-old gelding. Part Tennessee Walker and part Saddle Horse.

TIGO ACE'S SHADOW, 4-year-old gelding. Part Tennessee Walker and part Morgan.

428

Eventually, the benefits of registering a horse became better understood. Keeping records about parentage and family lines is of the utmost importance to the breeder. The Registry is also an important validation of ownership. While a simple bill of sale is sufficient for ownership transfer, having the sale recorded in an impartial organization, accompanied by photographs, specific descriptions of the particular animal, and (in some cases) videotape, blood-typing, and DNA information, is certainly a more complete verification.

While these services are readily available to pure-blooded animals, they weren't for the part-bloods.

Fortunately for those part-blood horse owners, Grace Larson and her husband Lyle took on the enormous task and responsibility of setting up a Registry for Part Walking Horses. In April 1998, the forms and requirements were designed and the appropriate paperwork submitted to the state of Montana. They announced their existence in various periodicals and they were open for business.

Within a couple years, their numbers grew to well over 350. Justifying the confidence given to them by horse owners, they have received a good number of ownership transfer registrations. In 2000, the Part Walking Horse Registry (PWHR) was appendixed to the International Pleasure Walking Horse Registry (IPWHR). This affords the horse that gaits properly an opportunity to participate in shows. They can be entered in classes that are approved and acceptable to IPWHR registered horses.

BLACK, 16-year-old mare. Part Tennessee Walker and part American Saddle Horse. Owned by Susan Young, Mathis, West Virginia.

The PWHR is open to half, three-quarter, seven-eighths and purebred Tennessee Walkers whose dam or sire was not blood-typed.

The PWHR helps both the stallion and mare owners by giving them the option to register their offspring. It can recognize that the foals' sire or dam may be Arabian, Appaloosa, Quarter Horse, Paint, Pony Breed, Warmblood or any such breed. It can provide

ARROW'S A.J. cremello stud colt with blue eyes and a star. Owned by Janie Haines, Monte Vista, Colorado.

ARROW'S BEAU DANDY, a cremello stud colt with a blaze and blue eyes. Owned by Janis Haines.

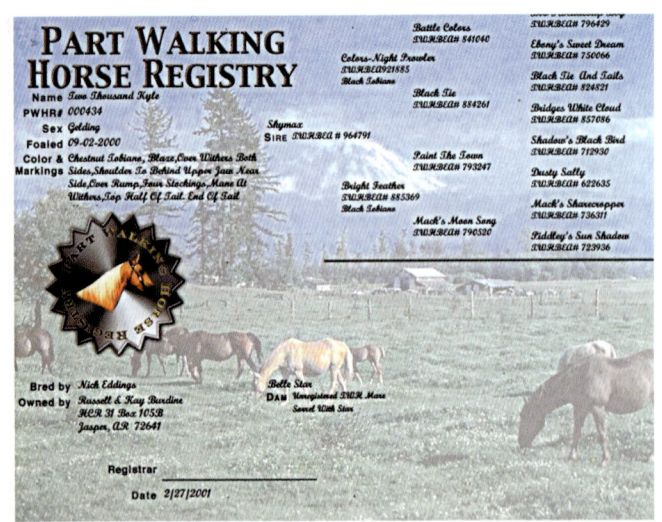

The Part Walking Horse Registry provides a lovely pedigree, suitable for framing.

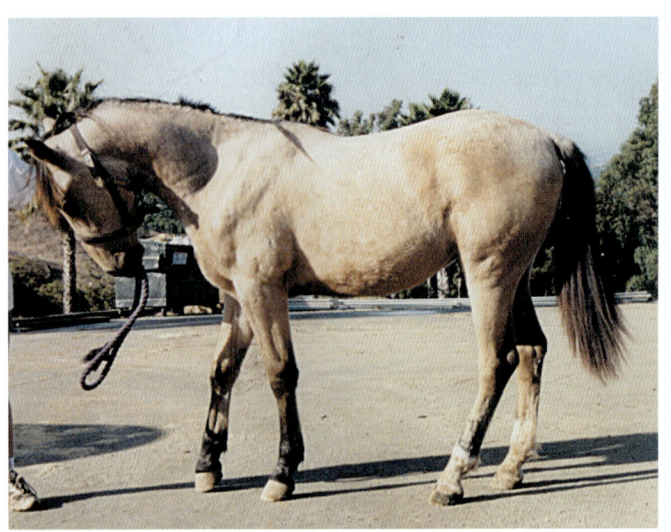

ATRAYO, a gelding, is registered as both Part Tennessee and Buckskin. Pictured at 3 years of age.

a link between sellers and buyers looking for the Tennessee-type horse. The PWHR does not require gait but does require proof of the sire or dam's TWHBEA or IPWHR or Canadian registration.

So what is the background of these folks now providing such a critical service? Quoting Grace Larson: "I was raised with Tennessee Walkers during the late 1940's and 1950's. My husband's family used horses for farming while our use was always ranching with a land base that required miles of riding. After being away from horses for many years, we purchased our first registered mare in 1989. As the saying goes, 'Ride one today & own one tomorrow.' Our 'one' ended up being 15 head by 1998. By then we were standing three registered Walking stallions at stud to outside mares."

Grace works to keep the registry on track via the Internet. From her website, she reaches interested horse owners over the world. All pedigrees are entered into a Pedigree Research site, and photos of PWHR registered horses are scanned into the data base.

Most of the horses are products of the breeding of non-registered mares to registered stallions. Grace has plans to compile statistics of the various breeds that have been crossed with Walking Horse stallions or mares.

The vitality of this registry is apparent in the horse owners who are participating in it.

Owners of Part Walkers are quick to tout the wonderful qualities of their precious horses.

One such owner is Susan Young from Mathias, West Virginia. Quoting Susan: "Little Bits is my favorite because I had her at birth. My father had the stallion and the mare. Little Bits was born in June 1975. Dad gave her to me and helped me train her. She is such a part of my life, words are not strong enough to express. I've been around horses all my life. Little Bits is truly the smartest horse I know. We communicate 100% and are a great team. My brother said, 'She's above horse smarts.' God blessed my life with her. She will always be my #1 horse."

Susan has twelve others. Most are

DIXIE TWO (right) a 10-year-old mare and mother of DIXIE'S PRIDE (left), a yearling Part Tennessee, part Saddle Horse gelding.

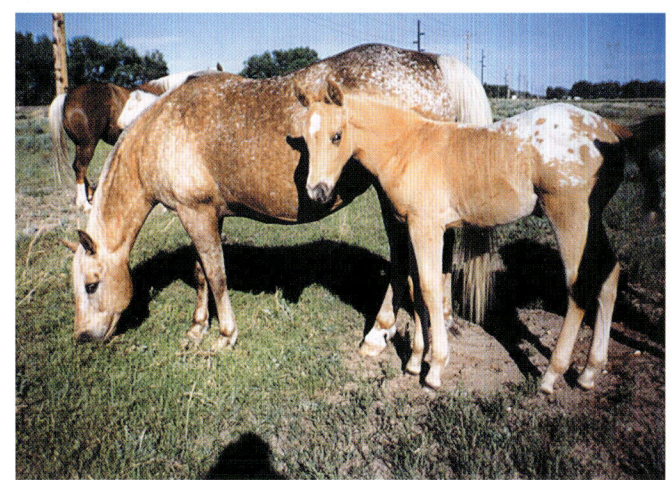

WYOMING GOLD RUSH, a registered Part Tennessee Walker with his dam, GOLDIE, a registered American Quarter Horse, bred and owned by Patricia Haines of Torrington, Wyoming.

Part Walkers. Another "special" member of her herd is a three-year-old colt named Coal. She reports he is "Soooooooo sweet!" She believes his confident "boss" behavior and trusting disposition will contribute to an easy training period.

Janis Haines, of Monte Vista, Colorado, has loved horses ever since she was a child. At sixteen, when her classmates were hoping to get a car, Janis was working and saving to buy a horse. Her family lived in town, so she had to board Halleujah at a ranch in the country. Thirty years later, Janis and her

CUSTER, a 3-month-old Part Walking Horse.

ZARA, Part Walker mare, five years old, and mother to CUSTER.(pictured below).

husband have added several Part Walkers to their lives. Janis says: "We just love them. They have friendly, gentle dispositions and have been easy to train. Our horse family consists of one full-blooded Tennessee Walker mare, one quarter horse/mustang-mix mare, and two half-Tennessee Walking Horse colts. They are brothers, and though they are 11 months apart in age, they could pass for twins. We enjoy watching them play games together, teasing and chasing each other at times. And others they just stand side by side with their heads together, appearing to be talking. Recently we bought a horse trailer. As I was working on it in the pasture, the brothers were so curious toward the trailer, I decided to open up its rear door to see what they thought of that. Neither one had seen a trailer before. Would you believe that they just walked right on into it? They stood in it all proud, as if to say, 'well, what are you waiting for, let's go for a ride and try it out !"

Elizabeth Lyons, originally from Georgia, has her own story about a beloved horse. She has always had gaited horses beginning with a blood bay named Pat. Pat was a part Morgan, part Thoroughbred. Both Elizabeth and Pat were eight years old when their association began; it continued until they were twenty four. In 1978 Elizabeth was given a Tennessee Walking mare as a first wedding anniversary

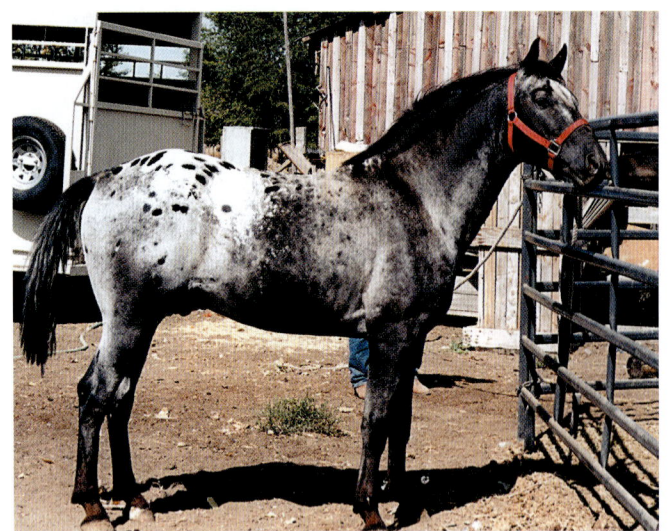

Stallion, MIDNITE EBONY STAR, registered both PWHR and Walkaloosa, owned by Dale Rohnert, Wilder, Idaho.

gift. This horse was a beautiful, dappled palomino with a perfect star. Her name was Duchess, and she was destined to become a trusting and true friend who was so gentle she could be caught anywhere and ridden with only a piece of baling twine around her neck. Duchess was Elizabeth's perfect horse, and her constant companion until the mare passed away at 28, in 1991.

When Elizabeth remarried in 1996, she and her husband Wally Lyons brought many new horses onto their busy ranch in northeast Wyoming. The offspring of these original horses, three Arabian mares, eight Tennessee mares and a Tennessee tobiano stallion, are now the heart-beat of the ranch.

Wally has become a convert to gaited horses. With his Tennessee mare Dolly, he rides in many parades and through parked cars at Shriner Circuses.

Elizabeth's new favorite is a Tennessee bay mare named Jay, who reminds her so much of her earlier friend Duchess.

Quoting Elizabeth: "I know it must be silly, but when I think of Duchess, tears come to my eyes. It seems like only yesterday that beautiful creature was still here nuzzling my cheek and standing by my side. No other mare can ever take her place in my heart."

Bob Adams and Patricia Haines are owners and operators of Horse Play Farms. They have several Part Walker horses that they use in a therapeutic riding program especially designed for troubled youth.

Sheri Branson's association with gaited horses began when she was just a youngster with the Tennessee Walker mare, Zara. She says her knowledge of horses came from this association. Sheri says of Zara: "She always had a lot of energy, never seeming to tire. She was gentle, loving and a joy to be around."

Sheri is now the mother of three, has earned a master's degree in special education, and with her husband Mark raises both Missouri Fox Trotters and Part Walkers. As residents of Missouri, Sheri and Mark stand a Fox Trotter stallion. But since they both prefer a Walker type, they continue to breed their Walker mares to the Fox Trotter for their own personal use. For the Bransons, the Part Walker is their breed of choice.

Dale Rohnert of Wilder, Idaho, is a man with an amazing family history of horsemen and horse adventure stories. His great great grandfather was a horse rustler in Russia. They stole horses, kept them for awhile, then sold them to the Russian Army. When he was "found out," he emigrated to the United States in the late 1800's. Since then, the family has been involved with horses of some kind. From Budweiser Clydesdales to race horses to pleasure horses, the family's association with horses continued to the early 1980's when Rohnert discovered the gaited horse. When he sustained injuries in an auto accident, the doctors suggested he find a good gaited horse if he wanted to continue riding. Rohnert owned a gaited Appaloosa mare that he bred to a Walking Horse, thus beginning his Walkaloosa/Part Walker breeding program.

Rohnert's mom suffered a stroke which caused physical disabilities. She participates in *Hippo Therapy*, which is simply horseback riding. She has to be helped on and off, as well as during the ride, but the results have been very encouraging. She plans to continue riding for the rest of her life.

Grace Larson with
GOLDUST ROYAL TRIGGER

Inset: Grace's granddaughter,
Amber Czerwinski with GOLDUST's filly, PWHR Reg.
MONTANA LOVEN'S SUGAR BABY

FLORIDA CRACKER HORSE

CHAPTER 28

Cracker stallion, TICO
Owner: Bobby Hall

HEIGHT: 13:0 to 15:2 hands

GAIT: Walk, trot, single-foot, canter

COLOR: Common colors - solids and greys predominate

TRAIT: Strength, endurance, "loaded with cow"

Chapter 28 The Florida Cracker

"Don't get on your high horse." Ever wonder what that means? Well, in the same time frame as Christopher Columbus (1492), Spanish military horsemen customarily had two mounts. One of these would be a small marching horse, a soft-gaited horse that was comfortable to ride across the country terrain. The other would be a large trotting warhorse trained for maneuvers on the battlefield. There was a ritual performed before these military encounters when the soldier stepped from his small gaited horse onto the large "high" horse to embark into battle (thus getting on your "high horse").

During the "Conquest" years, the Spaniards bred these two distinct types of horses. The larger was a non-gaited work horse suitable for both war and herding. The smaller horse was ideal for travel and "gentle folks."

On his second voyage to the Americas, Columbus brought these Spanish horses with him. Developing a remount station in Hispaniola [1] was considered a priority. This first shipment consisted of twenty-four stallions and ten mares. Most likely, they were the smaller soft-gaited horse rather than the larger war horse. They were used not only for military and government exploration, but by the pioneers and settlers as well. Comfort was a consideration, plus the smaller horse was better designed to survive the ocean crossing.

Spanish tradition held that the true "macho hombre"[2] would only ride a stallion, which explains the large number of stallions in the first shipment. All but a few of these horses would be used as riding mounts.

St. Augustine was the first European settlement in North America. The Spanish colonists brought their livestock, and their long black snake whips to control them. Unlike their counterparts in California and Mexico,[3] the St. Augustinians rarely used ropes. Their skill with the loud-cracking whip set them apart, and they became known as Crackers. It wasn't long before the plucky little horses they rode were also called Crackers.

The whip became an all-purpose device for these early Colonists. With it, they could control the cows, individually and as a herd; they could hunt small game; they could use it as a weapon; and they used it to communicate with each other from as far away as three miles.

Out west, the cattle men were known as cowboys. But in Florida, they called themselves "cow hunters," or "Cracker Cowmen." They maintained an active trade with Cuba, which meant a regular and continual introduction of Spanish horse genetics into their herds.

Stallion, SILVER, owned by Ralph Weeks, of Lakeland, Florida. Photo: Sam P. Getzen

---

[1] Today, we know Hispaniola as Haiti.
[2] "Real Man"

[3] The Cracker was being developed in Florida at the same time as the Spanish Mustang. The Spanish Barb were developing in the West.

436

Post-Civil War trading with Cuba brought more gaited stock into Florida aboard cattlebarges. The gaited Cuban Steppers, which had been trained by the Cubans, were folded into the existing "Cracker" gene pool. A three-hundred-year Spanish influence throughout the Florida peninsula[4] carried over into the local development of horses and horsemanship. The Piney Woods cattle and the hearty Cracker Marshland horses assisted the survival of the early Florida settlers throughout these three centuries. Both horse and cow were partners with their human counterparts against the hardships of the swamps and marshes. Military massacres and diseases had totally eliminated the original tribes, but there were still Indians in the area who cultivated their own little smooth-riding Spanish horses known as "marsh tackies."

These Indians, collectively known as "Seminole,"[5] became efficient, solid horse trainers who often 'liberated' local horses. They also began breeding the horses when the land

AYERS BLUE, a Cracker stallion in the Ayers Line. He is owned by Doyle Hazellief of Okeechobee. BLUE is a working cow horse who has been ridden in Bridless Reining Exhibitions, and also performs various Riderless Exhibitions in response to voice commands. He is pictured being ridden by Dewaine Hazellief.
Photo: Sam P. Getzen

around them was changing hands frequently. First it was the Spanish, then the French, then the English, then the Americans - both Confederate and Union. As Ranches collapsed, the equine stock was left to roam free and forage for their existence in the coastline marshes.

In 1838, Comte de Castelnau wrote: "The Floridian horse, such as it is today, and which is called generally 'Indian Pony,' is small, long haired and bright-eyed, lively, stubborn, and as wild as the Indians themselves. It has a wonderful endurance of fatigue and hardship. It has a singular instinct in finding its way in dense woods. Its food consists only of the high grass that covers the prairies and it does not require any care."

In describing the importance of the Cracker Pony, Ed Smith noted in *Them Good Ole Days*, that some hands could ride for over sixty hours on the same horse, riding all day and most of the night, and both would be ready to go the next morning. He doubted if any horse had ever had more endurance.

During the many Indian Wars throughout Florida, much of the cattle and horses were destroyed by the U.S. Military. Many officers would "salvage" the riding horses. After one

SPANISH DOLL, at age fourteen, owned by Sam P. Getzen, and part of the broodmare band at the Bobby Hall Ranch, tSan Antonio, Florida. Photo: Sam P. Getzen

---

[4] From the 1500's until the 1800's, when Spain turned Florida over to the United States, a definite Spanish influence was felt in that area.
[5] Seminole became the white man's term for all Florida Indians. It is the English-language version of the Muskogee tribe's word "Simanoli," which the Muskogee derived from the Spanish word, Cimarron, meaning wild, or runaway.

battle, General Andrew Jackson sent a herd of "smooth gaited" Seminole ponies back to his farm in Tennessee. Through adversity, the magic soft-gaited gene was being spread throughout the country.

In the 1930's, the screwworm changed the fortune for the Florida Cracker Horse. It was during the Great Depression that the fateful decision was made to move cattle from the Dust Bowl into Florida. Before that time, cattle in Florida were driven from horseback by use of the whip. The crack of the whip would control the movement of the herds, and little contact with the individual steer was necessary.[6] The cattle were small, tough, wiry and possessed long, sharp horns that made working them dangerous and requiring a rather rare horse to drive them.

Necessary attributes were endurance and quickness. Even though many of the range riders were large, and their tough and tireless Crackers weighed between 750 to 800 pounds, they were able to cover ground at very high speeds. These little horses could travel over scrub ground riddled with gopher holes and pitfalls without developing serious leg ailments.

Unfortunately, the larger cattle coming in from the Dust Bowl were infested with the screwworm, and it became necessary to use a rope and hold each animal for veterinary treatment. No longer was the small, smooth fleet-footed Cracker appropriate for the job. The heavy, stronger Quarter Horse was imported into Florida.

During this period, John Ayers feared that all the wild Spanish horses on his range would be killed by the Government in their drive to eradicate an outbreak of fever ticks. Desperate to save the Cracker Horses, he paid some government riders to pen several horses (about six in all). Ayers loved the horses and refused to believe that horses could take grass away from the cattle.

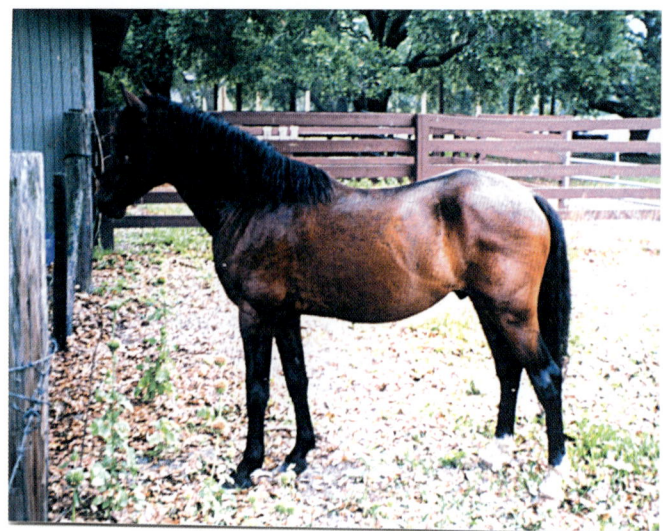

JOHNNY REB BOY, an Ayers-line Cracker stallion, owned by the Florida Park Service. He lives at the Lake Kissimmee State Park. Photo: Sam P. Getzen

ESPERANZA, mare, owned by Faith Sasser of Pahokee, Florida. Bred and photographed by Sam P. Getzen

HERNANDO DE SOTO, an Ayers Line Cracker stallion owned by Barry Farm. Photo: Sam P. Getzen

---

[6] The use of a whip is also used in Australia. The numbers of cattle are so great and their nature so wild, that the cattle are driven into shoots for medical attention, rather than being singled out with a rope for individual handling.

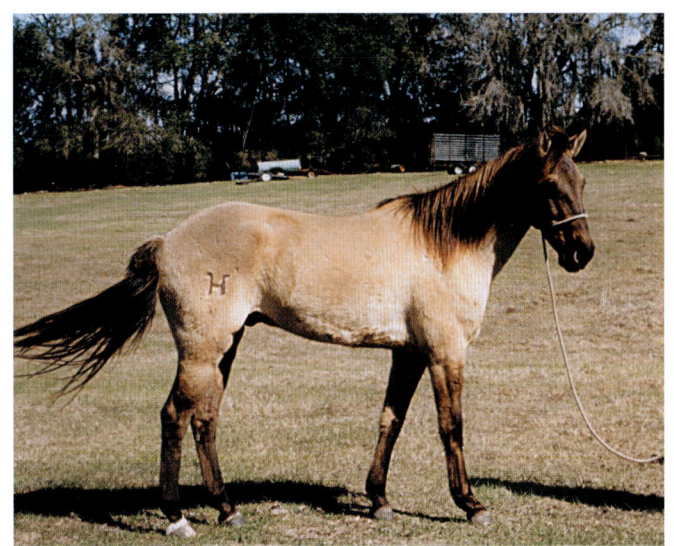

DUN RAT, a Harvey line Cracker gelding (May 2000) owned by Kenny Holder of Newberry, Florida. Photo: Sam Getzen

Sam P. Getzen, from Newberry, Florida with his Cracker mare, SPANISH DOLL.

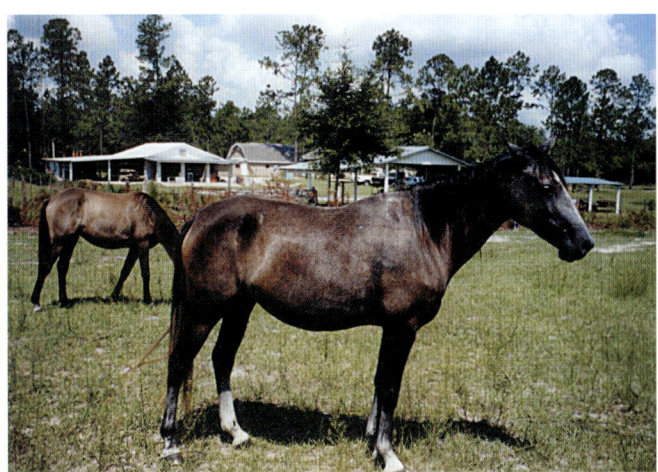

An Ayers line Cracker broodmare owned by Ellison and Will Hardee of Chiefland, Florida Photo: Sam P. Getzen

In 1935, the Heart Bar Ranch in Kissimmee, Florida, began importing Quarter Horses from Texas.

Quoting Sam Getzen: "The first recorded arrival of a Quarter Horse in Florida was when Geech Partin of Kissimmee bought a Quarter Horse stallion in Texas and shipped him to Kissimmee in a railroad car with a bunch of bulls. When the stallion was unloaded, he was an awful sight, as the bulls had chewed off all his mane and tail hair."

Once the Quarter Horse gained a strong foothold, it didn't take long for the numbers of wild Cracker[7] herds to decline. They might have remained nothing more than a curious footnote if it weren't for John Ayers and some Florida ranchers, who refused to cross the Crackers with newly imported larger horses. Sumpter County in Central Florida remained prime Cracker Horse territory up to the 1950's. Some of the older Florida cattlemen kept small herds of Crackers up to the 1970's. These herds would provide cow pony replacements for cattlemen from all over the state.

Unfortunately, as ranchers who had protected and preserved the Cracker Horse began retiring, and passing away, the various herds were dispersing and being outbred to other breeds. Many of them became feral, as they were range bred and raised. They were never given shots, never wormed and the horses themselves selected the breeding stallions. They shared pasture with the cattle, and inevitably, as the human population grew, their range land began shrinking.

In 1984, John Law Ayers, owner of the Ayers Cattle Co. donated horses from his Cracker Horse herd to the Florida Department of Agriculture and Consumer Services. Doyle Conner, the FDACS Commissioner, grew up riding Cracker Horses on the open ranges of Bradford, Florida. Along with several Florida cattlemen who had also spent much of their lives on the backs of Cracker Horses, Mr. Conner went to the Ayers Ranch and selected the horses to be received by the

---

[7] Over the years, these little horses came to be known by a variety of names - Chicksaw Pony, Seminole Pony, March Tackie, Prairie Pony, Florida Horse, Florida Cow Pony, and Grass Gut, among others.

FDACS. Publicity for the event opened up a public awareness of what a Cracker Horse was, and just how few of these animals were left.

In 1985, the Friends of Paynes Prairie, Inc. purchased five mares and a stallion and released them on Paynes Prairie to start a Cracker Herd there.

Robert J. Barry of Newberry, Florida, had been a champion of the Florida Cracker for more than forty years, and when he realized how near to extinction they were, he said, "something should be done to save these horses for future generations." He decided to track down Cracker Horse owners and breeders throughout the state and encourage them to form an association and registry for the purpose of preserving and promoting the Cracker Horse as a distinct breed.

By 1987, Bob Hall of San Antonio, Florida and a business associate of Mr. Barry, became involved by purchasing several Cracker Horses. When Buck Mitchell joined Bob Hall and Robert Barry in starting Cracker Herds of their own, they decided it was time to start contacting other Cracker Horse owners to set up a meeting.

In 1988, an ad was placed in the Florida Cattleman Magazine inviting anyone who owned or was interested in Cracker Horses to become involved.

In January 1989, sixteen people attended a meeting in Osceola County Center to consider starting a Cracker Horse Preservation Association. Fourteen questionnaires filled out at that meeting represented ownership of ninety Cracker Horses. Subsequent to the meeting, Commissioner Doyle Conner assured the assistance of his department.

The first Officers and Directors were Bob Barry, President; Bobby Hall, Vice President; and Sam P. Getzen, Secretary and Treasurer. Directors were Harvey Ayers, Doug Partin, Kevin Whaley, Charles W. Harvey, Elwyn Bass and J.C. Bass. The Charter of Incorporation was granted on April 21, 1989.

The Bylaws provided for the Board of Directors to act as an Evaluation Committee, and the first horses deemed eligible for registration as foundation horses were those in the State's three Cracker Horse herds, the Ayers Cracker Horse herd; horses in the Bobby Hall Cracker Horse herd, the Charles W. Harvey Cracker herd, a Harvey-bred mare owned by Elwyn Bas, and three Cracker Horses owned by Doug Partin. The oldest horse approved for the Foundation Registry was 30-year-old Dan B, owned by Everett Boals from Gainesville, Florida.

Gus Cothran of the University of Kentucky has been testing and grouping blood-

SAN ANN DOLLY, an Ayers line Cracker filly. Owned by Dudley Farm State Park. (A family type farm from the 1850's) Photo: Sam P. Getzen

The Florida Cracker Horse Association, Inc.
Illustration of the Florida Cracker by Caroline Smith

work from many different horses and has identified a number of modern breeds that carried bloodmarkers of the Spanish horse. He has compared the Cracker blood with that of the Andalusian, Sorraia, Lusitano, and Alter Real breeds, and made a clear distinction between horses of Spanish descent and those with no Spanish ancestors.

Over the last fifty years, the Cracker breed has continued to survive because several families have bred with the sole purpose of keeping the bloodlines alive in their herds. The Ayers, Harvey, Bronson, and Whaley names are still very important within the breed. Only about 35% of all Cracker Horses are soft-gaited. All branches of the Cracker family produce some horses with soft-gait, but the Ayers line has the highest percentage.

Florida Cracker horses are small saddle-horses, standing 13:0 to 15:2 hands at the withers and weighing between 750 and 1,000 pounds. The head is refined and intelligent in appearance. The profile is straight or slightly concave. The throat-latch is prominent and the jaw is short and well-defined. The eyes are very keen with an alert expression and have reasonable width between them. The eye colors are dark, with a white sclera, grey or blue. The neck is well-defined, fairly narrow, without excessive crest, and is about the same length as the distance from the withers to the croup. The back is short, narrow, and strong with well-sprung ribs. The croup is sloping and short. Tail is set medium low. The breed is found in any color common to the horse; however, solid colors and greys predominate. Enticing leads of paint and roan strains still persist, and these other colors (historically present in the breed), may yet be located in some remote corner of Florida.

While this external type is distinctive, breed proponents insist that the best way to tell a Florida Cracker horse is to ride one. Horses that are soft-gaited will demonstrate gaits including the flatfoot walk, running walk, trot and ambling or paso-type gait. Cracker horses are willing workers whose action shows spirit, not laziness. They are always characterized by a very smooth walk, enormous endurance and a strong herding instinct. Local lingo would describe their strong herding instinct as "loaded with cow."

Perhaps the most unique aspect of this horse is its staying power and stunning quickness. Pound for pound, probably no other horse in America can compare to this tough little cow-pony for quickness and endurance.

The FCHA is one of the newest registries in the United States addressing one of the oldest breeds in this country - the Spanish Horse brought to the Americas by the conquistadors.

The use of the "Cracker" whip is not for the faint of heart. Much practice is necessary. Historically the whip was used to control the cattle; as a weapon; to hunt small game; and to communicate over a distance of three miles.

SPANISH DOLL at four years old, owned by Sam P. Getzen, pictured with Kenny Holder of Newberry, Florida. Photo: Sam P. Getzen

THE SPANISH GAITED PONY

CHAPTER 29

HEIGHT: 11 - 13 hands

GAIT: Any 4-beat

COLOR: Mostly bay, some chestnut

TRAIT: Gentle with endurance

Chapter 29   The Spanish Gaited Pony

The very special family of gaited horses continues to grow. Breeders are reaching out and developing new breeds and registries as the demand for soft-gaited horses increases. Diverse tastes and special interests dictate the growth of assorted types in all directions.

One category that hasn't had too much attention is that of gaited horses specifically for children and small adults. Larry and Shirley Davidson at Davidson Ranch have been preparing to fill that vacancy for a number of years.

In 1983, near Tacoma, Washington, Larry and Shirley Davidson started developing the Spanish Gaited Pony. Twelve small, bay-colored and very refined pony mares were bought, mostly in the midwest, because of the greater selection available there.

The mares were bred to a Champion Peruvian Paso bay stallion standing 14:2 hands tall. Later, a Paso Fino stallion was added to the program. The goal was to produce a gaited pony with a super-smooth ride, lots of refinement, and a good disposition with plenty of life and energy in a package 11 to 13 hands tall.

➡   Photos to the right: Top : A yearling Spanish Gaited Pony colt. Middle: The desired coloration is solid, as this youngster exhibits. Bottom: Stallion TOMÉ at five years of age. He stands 12:2 hands tall.

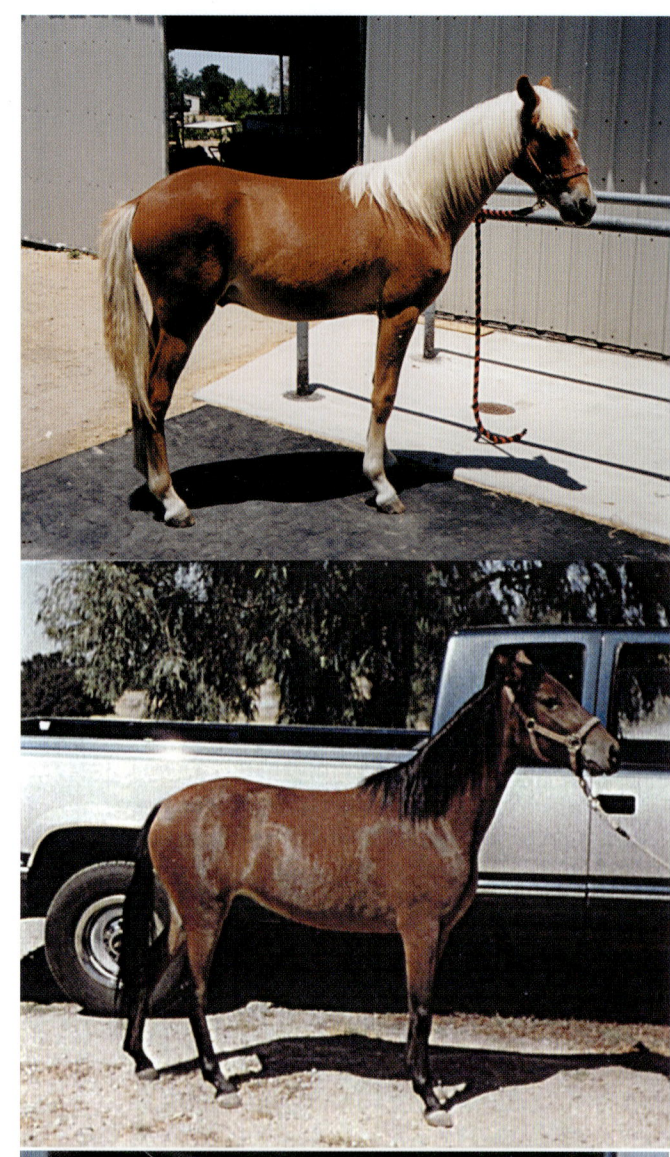

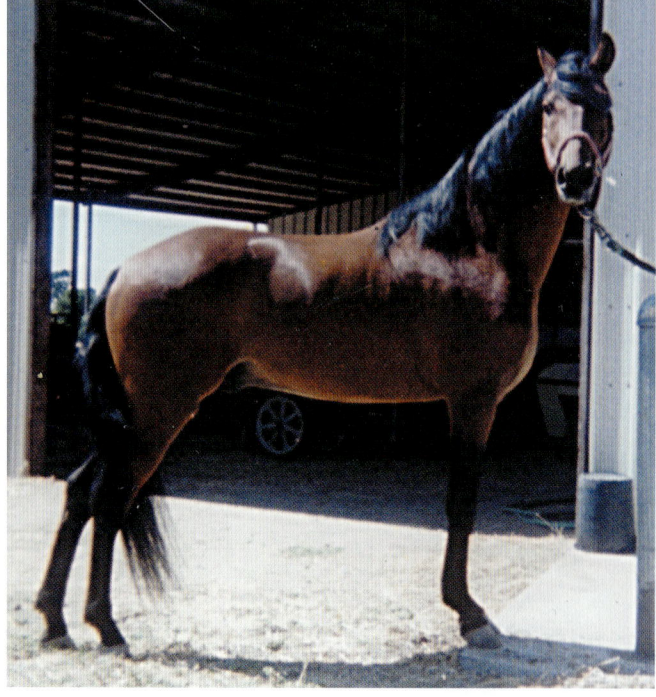

In 1990, the Davidsons and their ponies moved to California and continued the line breeding program that was producing even better-than-expected results.

The original stallion and mares are now gone and their great grandsons and daughters are carrying on the breed. The fourth- and fifth-generation foals have arrived and the newborn babies are gaiting naturally in the pasture beside their mothers, bringing smiles to the faces of all who see them. The number of ponies is rapidly growing.

Those sold through the years were geldings or ponies that did not meet breed standards. They were not registered or sold as breeding stock.

This breed has been line bred and closely selected for gait, conformation, disposition, size, color and endurance. Maintaining beauty and refinement are also important features.

Strict standards for disposition, conformation, and color have been set. These smooth gaited saddle ponies range in height from 11 to 13 hands with an upper limit of 13 hands being strictly adhered to. Their weight ranges between 400 and 600 pounds.

Their shoulders should slope to enhance smoothness of gait and their withers are

Below: Three two-year-old fillies.

CORDERO, son of TOMÉ

Above and below: A field of mares and their foals, 1997.

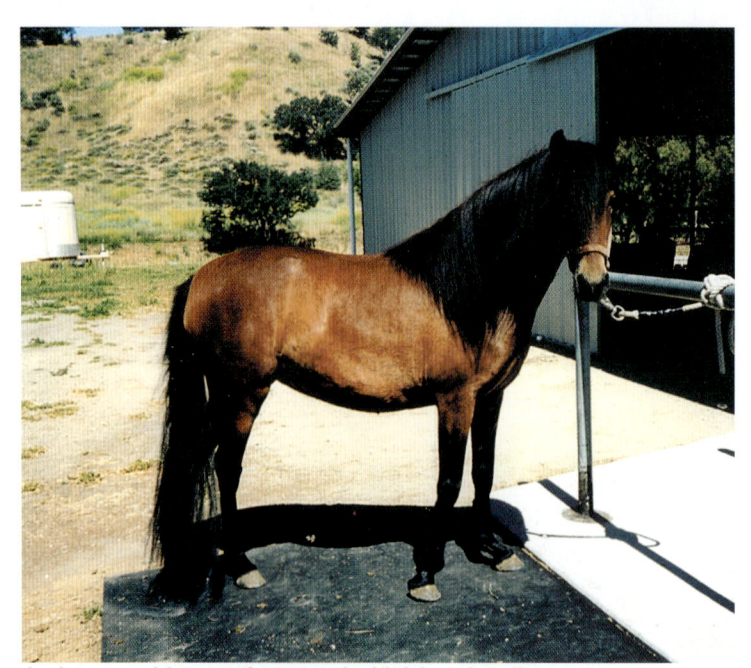

A six-year-old mare that stands 11:3 hands tall.

White markings are not desired.

Above: A five-year-old stallion that is 12:2 hands tall.

➪ Top: 11-year-old mare – 12: 1 H. Bottom: 1-year-old colt.

defined and slope smoothly to the back. The neck is arched gracefully and is of medium length.

The midsection is moderate in length, with a chest that should be moderate in width and depth under a strong and muscled back. The croup is mildly sloping, and the hips are rounded with broad loins.

The legs are refined, straight and strong, with well-defined tendons. The forearms are long and the cannons tend to be short. The thigh and gaskins are strong but not heavily muscled, and the hocks are strong but not to the point of being coarse or heavy. The pasterns are sloping and medium in length, not stubby or excessively long and weak. The hoofs are well-rounded and proportionate in size for the pony. The mane and tail and forelock should be full and natural. The tail is set and carried low. The head should be refined and in proportion to the body. The ears are medium length, not too long, and definitely not short and stubby. The eyes are large and well-spaced, very expressive and bright. The muzzle area should be fine.

The gait of the Spanish Gaited Ponies is an evenly spaced 4-beat lateral gait. The footfall is the same as a natural equine walk with speeds varying up to approximately 15 m.p.h. The speed depends on the size of the pony. They also perform a walk, lope and full gallop.

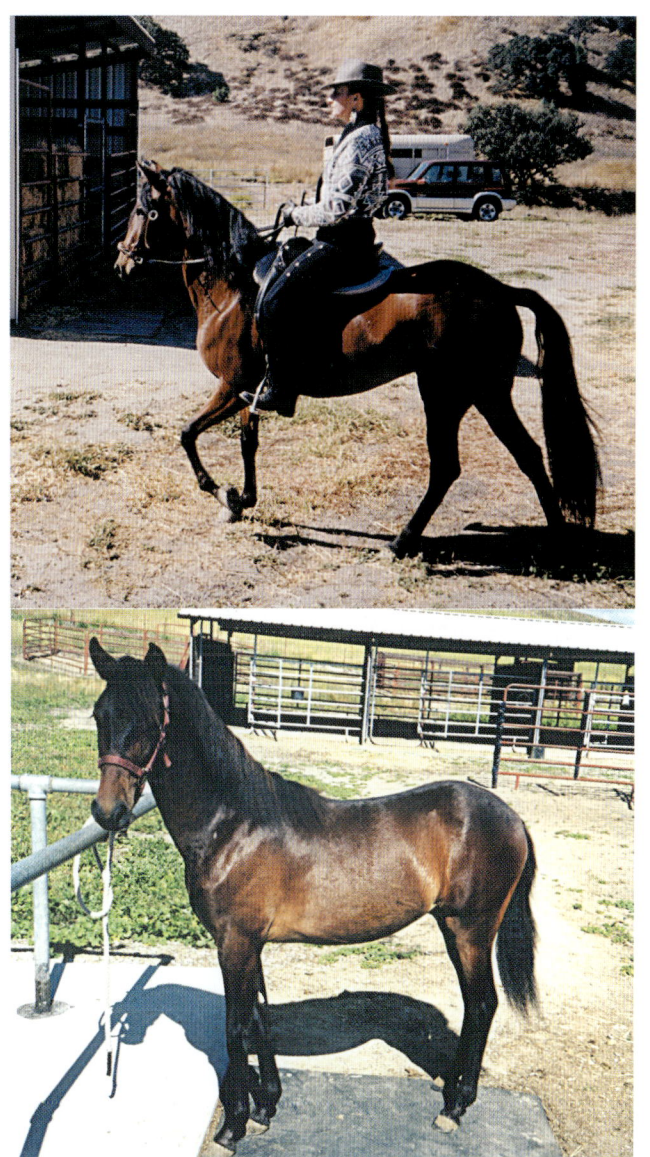

A very important ingredient is the disposition. The Spanish Gaited Ponies should be spirited, willing and responsive under saddle and at hand.

The colors include bay, chestnut and related colors. It is preferable to have no white markings, but in no case shall there be any white above the knees or hocks, except small stars, strips and snips on the face.

The ponies are bred to be strong, spirited, willing and manageable for pleasure, trail and show. The registry is reserved for offspring of sires and dams who are also registered in the Spanish Gaited Pony Registry.

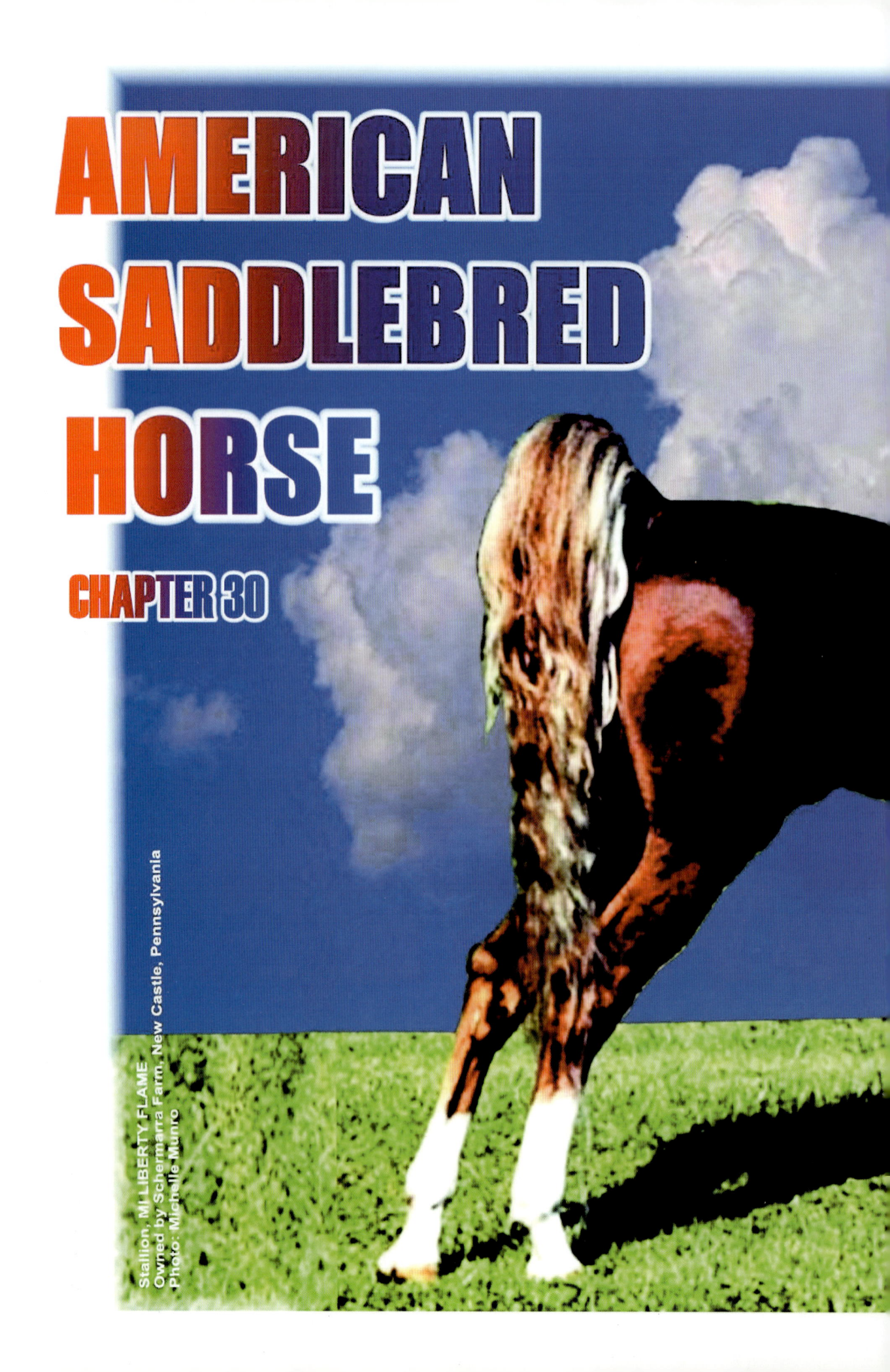

AMERICAN SADDLEBRED HORSE

CHAPTER 30

Stallion, MI LIBERTY FLAME
Owned by Schermarra Farm, New Castle, Pennsylvania
Photo: Michelle Munro

HEIGHT: 15H - 16H

GAIT: 5-gaited

COLOR: Most equine colors; fine and silky

TRAIT: Elegance

Chapter 30 American Saddlebred
"The Peacock"

As we have seen in other breeds featured in this book, foundation horses are frequently the same in several breeds. The horse that would become the American Saddlebred was a major contributor to most of the soft-gaited horses described in this book. In chapters 7, 8, 9, and 10, the Mountain Horses of Kentucky, as descendants of the Narragansett Pacers, are shown to be a breed having great influence on most of the soft-gaited American breeds.

Principal contributors were the Thoroughbreds, Narragansett Pacers, Morgans, Canadians and the Spanish horses. There were numerous important stallions from this list that were considered foundation sires. When the fledgling Saddlebred Association met in April 1908, they decided to list Denmark (by Imported Hedgeford), as the sole Foundation Sire. Other sires were given numbers and acknowledged, but Denmark had so many descendants that the other sires could not compete with him for prominence.

⇨ Photos to the right: Top: Stallion ANACACHO'S GOLDEN CADILLAC, 16:2 hands tall, pasture breeder. CADILLAC keeps his gorgeous dark golden color, even in the winter. He is a 3-time Futurity Winner and by age seven, produced 2 Futurity Champions. CADILLAC has the bloodlines of CH WING COMMANDER and STONE-WALL KING, up close. He's a big, powerful stallion of the strong-boned build. Owned by Buresh Farms, and Joe and Joyce Buresh. Middle: Stallion ANACACHO'S CRÈME SODA, by ANACACHO'S GOLDEN CADILLAC, out of SOVEREIGN'S THREE TIMES CHARMED (by SOVEREIGN SEA). This rare cremello is owned by renowned athlete George Foreman. Bottom: The equestrian statue of Civil War hero General John Hunt Morgan was unveiled in 1911 in Lexington, Kentucky. The horse: a Saddlebred.

450

Denmark was foaled in 1839. He was a brown horse of great beauty, and able to compete successfully in four-mile races. It is probably his son, Gaines' Denmark, out of a fine pacing Cockspur mare that is the true "Foundation" Denmark. This handsome black stallion, foaled in 1851, was the chosen mount of Civil War General Hunt Morgan. More importantly, he was sire to Washington Denmark #64, Diamond Denmark #68, and Sumpter Denmark #65.

Unlike the rest of the horses that are considered soft-gaited, the Saddlebred holds the trot as an important gait. To this end, they made use of both the Arab and the Thoroughbred. The blood of the Thoroughbred Messenger, a grey horse standing close to 16 hands, was important in the development of the Standardbred breed, and he also played a major role in producing the Saddlebred.

Kentucky became a primary producer of good saddle horses after the War of 1812. The settlement of the Ohio Valley, Tennessee and Missouri was dependant on good 'usin' horses. The Thoroughbred Denmark blood, coming from Gaines' Denmark (whose mother was naturally gaited), down through his descendants, coupled with Harrison Chief, and his Thoroughbred Messenger genes, was the foundation for future Saddlebreds.

These Saddle Horses were definitely using horses. Their development was linked to the need for a horse that was easy gaited and wouldn't tire the rider as he rode over extensive groumd. The horse had to be gentle enough not to injure women and children. It had to be fast enough not to disgrace the owner in a horserace and able to jump well enough to ride the hounds; sensible enough go to town on Saturday night and stylish enough to hook to the carriage on Sunday morning, taking the

⇐ Photos to the left. Top: Stallion, MI LIBERTY FLAME, owned by Schermarra Farm in New Castle, Pennsylvania, at the West Virginia Tri-State show in 1997. Photo: Debbie Scherder. Middle: Mare, DIAMOND BOUQUET, sired by ATTACHE'S BORN BELIEVER and out of a PENNY'S SUPERIOR STONEWALL dam, as a four-year-old. She is one of the outstanding broodmares at Far Field Farm in Petaluma, California. Bottom: Stallion, MI LIBERTY FLAME at home at Schermarra Farm, owned by Deborah and Joseph Scherder, in New Castle, Pensylvania. Photo: Michelle Munro

Four-yea-old filly, UMAIDMELUVLU, was Reserve World Champion as a weanling. Sired by PERIAPTOR, she is now part of the lovely team of Saddlebred and 12-year-old owner, Stephanie.

family to church.

Shows developed from the local horse —men showing off in town, and especially courthouse days and other special events. By 1846, the American Saddle Horse was established as a breed and by 1856, the nation's first major horse show was a feature of the first great fair in Saint Louis, Missouri.

During the Civil War, most of the officers' mounts were privately owned. The overwhelming choice was the American Saddle Horse. General Lee had Traveller, General Grant used Cincinnati. General Sherman rode Sherman's Lexington and Stonewall Jackson rode Little Sorrell of pacing stock.

From the Civil War battlefields to the modern 21st-century horse shows, the American Saddlebred has been a willing and capable partner for all equestrians.

This magnificent cousin to the soft-gaited horse still occasionally conceals the magic "soft-gait gene." These horses are able to be developed into the ultra show horse - the five-gaited Saddlebred.

The two gaits that are added to the conventional walk, trot canter are the "slow gait" and the rack. The slow gait is a slow stepping pace. The rack is the same 4-beat square gait that most of the soft-gaited horses are able to perform.

The ideal American Saddlebred mare, REEDANN'S COUNTRY TALK. This five-gaited mare, a World Champion in her fourth year, is both a thrill and a joy to ride. "ANNIE" is now a broodmare at Far Field Farm in Petaluma, California. Photo: Howie Schatzberg

The silhouette of the Saddlebred is truly unique. The line is vertical from the front toe tips to the throatlatch. Their swanlike neck is long, arched and well-flexed at the poll. The ideal American Saddlebred is well-proportioned and presents a beautiful overall picture. Their eyes are wide-set and expressive and their ears are gracefully hooked and set close together on top of their head. Their facial profile is straight with a relatively fine muzzle and large nostrils.

The withers should extend well into a back that is strong and level with well-sprung ribs, a level croup and a tail that comes out high. Trainers of the five-gaited horse often prefer a croup that slopes very slightly from the hip to the dock, because this type of conformation facilitates performance of the slow gait and the rack.

For both the trotting and gaiting type of Saddlebred, the legs should be straight with broad flat bones and sharply defined tendons and sloping pasterns. The cannon bone should be flat and strong. The pastern should be fairly

Three-year-old naturally gaited gelding ESTERO, sired by CATALYST, with his owner Alexandra, who is also his trainer. Both young woman and young horse are doing very well, exhibiting the exceptional disposition of these Saddlebred horses.

The great-grandson of famous WING COMMANDER, the American Saddlebred colt, HUSTLE TIME. As a four-year-old, HUSTLE TIME stands 17:1 hands and is a talented athlete. Bred at Far Field Farm, owned by Barbara Molland.

long and sloping, but strong. It should have enough angle to be able to reduce concussion. Their feet should be hard, smooth, and flat without any ridges, dryness, or flaking and be in proportion to the size of the horse.

The show ring "peacocks" perform all their gaits with tremendous style and flash. Natural Saddlebreds, used for trail, pleasure and versatility are similar to their soft-gaited relatives in temperament and tractability. American Saddlebreds have found their place in ultimate tests of fitness, durability, and refinement. They are excellent jumpers, are naturally light on the forehand, and have tremendous stamina. While many people associate the Saddlebred with Saddle Seat performance in the show ring, they excel in many other disciplines - Dressage, Cross Country, Western Pleasure, Reining, Roping, Jumping, Hunter, Driving, Therapeutic Riding, and of course pleasurable trail riding.

Dorothy Cable, respected Saddlebred breeder, historian and horsewoman, shared a few stories that are of interest to the story of the breed. According to Dorothy:

A horse named Rex Rysdyk was owned by a Pittsburgh attorney who did his own training. He very successfully trained and showed this horse five gaited, then entered him in a 300-mile Eastern Cavalry Endurance ride, where he placed fourth. The next year he first showed the horse three gaited and again entered the same ride competition (although the weight requirements were substantially increased) and came out with a 100% perfect score and a third-place win.

Another wonderful story is that of Flower

ASB stallion, MI LIBERTY FLAME, photographed by Michelle Munro, during a visit to Schermarra Farm. At that time, FLAME had been retired from the show ring for several years.

King. He was a Saddlebred stallion who went to a Montana cattle ranch. When his master died way off in the mountains, the stallion stayed and guarded the body until help arrived several days later.

Demonstrating the versatility of the Saddlebred, Dorothy tells the story of a beautiful chestnut Saddlebred who performed along with the Lipizzaners in a demonstration in Greenville, South Carolina.

Another tale is that of Col. T.W. Minton. From 1920-1930, in the last 10 years of his life he rode Gladys Gilbert everywhere on business, through traffic, mountains, rivers, on fox hunting trips, and when it was too rough for riding, he turned her loose and she'd ➡

Photos to the right. Top: Nineteen-year-old gelding, SOVEREIGN SEA, now living in California and enjoying his new life on the trail. (Sire: GLENKNOLL'S GOLD STANDARD by ROBERT E. SEA. Dam: FANCY HILLS by HICKORY HILLS.) Bottom: PARTY TRAIN, former World Champion five-gaited mare as both a three year old and a four-year-old. His trainer and rider in this photo is Don Harris. PARTY TRAIN is now a broodmare at Far Field Farm, Petaluma, California. Photo: Elizabeth Glenn

Two lovely faces, so richly demonstrating the kind eye at the heart of the Saddlebred horse.

follow him. At big fairs, she won in model classes, high school, led parades, cleared 5 _ feet in jumping class and was ridden by a stable boy in a running race. She won against two horses direct from the race track. Gladys Gilbert was also five-gaited.

In Dorothy's own words about her personal experiences: "There is so much to say about Saddlebreds. They are a very special breed having wonderful dispositions as well as beauty. I'm too old to do it now, but I used to mount my unbroken Saddlebreds bareback having skipped most of the usual

⇦ **Photos to the left: Top: Stallion, SOVEREIGN SEA** had a marvelous show career that included Championship at halter, fine harness, and three-gaited. He was retired to breeding at six and ridden in street parades and trail. His tail was never set, and in this photo you can see the fake tail he's wearing (the photo on the facing page shows him as a gelding with his natural tail). Owned by Buresh Farms and Joe and Joyce Buresh, in Oxford Junction, Iowa,. Photo: Pro Photo, Pam Olsen. Bottom: A playful stallion, **MI LIBERTY FLAME**, showing in New York, as photographed by Michelle Munro.

A young Mark Bisby getting acquainted with Saddlebred gelding ROBERT.

Stallion, MI LIBERTY FLAME with owner, Debbie Scherder's granddaughter, demonstrating the gentle nature of this elegant horse.

Yearling fillies at Far Field Farm in Petaluma, California.

ground training. I just talked to them. They listened and I never had any of them try to throw me. Now I can't step foot outdoors without the horses I have here at home noticing. (The mobile home sits in one of the pastures.) Unless shut out, they come to me demanding immediate attention. Some of them call or sometimes paw at the porch. One mare, now gone, used to take her nose and knock on the door.

"It is also not unusual to find one or two sleeping just outside the wall nearest to my bed. They know their names, come on call, and follow me. At feeding that figures, but at other times it is just a matter of companionship.

"One thing I've always been careful about: I never lie to a horse. If I call and promise feed, they get it. If I call without making that promise, they're happy with a few words and a pat. I also talk to them and explain things I need to do to them. If hurt, they come to me. Many people do not realize or develop the intelligence of their horses. They can and do learn language."

Barbara Molland at Far Field Farm in Petaluma, California is another Saddlebred breeder and enthusiast who is passionate about her devotion to the breed.

Quoting Barbara: "I would like to give you the reasons why I am so devoted to this breed. While I, like so many Saddlebred enthusiasts, still thrill to the five-gaited stake, my reasons for owning and breeding them all these years stem from the characteristics that make them fundamentally such superlative

OLEMA and SAIL AWAY, two young Saddlebreds enjoying a "beautifying mudpack." Certainly nothing can hide the quality and style of these youngsters from Far Field Farm in Petaluma, California.

riding horses - the horseman's horse, as I like to say. For whatever reasons, in my own experience I have found a correlation between the Saddlebreds that will rack and a willingness to go forward and move on without hesitation or fear of what is ahead of the horse. This courage coupled with forward energy, is a horseman's dream because this characteristic of the horse enables the rider and horse to move forward with speed and comfort without fear of mishap. In the days of widespread use of the riding horse, this was a requirement. The farther we have come from general use of, and familiarity with the horse, the more we forget about this fundamental characteristic.

"I have watched the facial expressions of people who come to the farm and try out a five-gaited horse for the first time. Even the best riders will be a bit awkward at first, if they are unaccustomed to gaited horses. Once they are going with the horse (which usually takes a couple of times around the arena), their facial expressions begin to completely change, and they begin to smile, realizing they are having the ride of their lives. They suddenly understand what all the hoopla is about, and then we can't get them off the horse!"

➪ Photos to the right: Middle: Two day old colt with five-year-old Evan. The newborn CACHE CREEK is sired by RADIANT SULTAN, and his dam is SUGAR MOVES by STONEWALL'S MAIN EVENT. As a grown-up, he has proven to be naturally gaited with the even temperament of his line. Bottom: Weanling colt, CORMAC, out of the HARLEM GLOBETROTTER daughter, HARLEM'S FAIRE MAIDEN and sired by RADIANT SULTAN, whose bottom line has produced some wonderful athletes. Owner: Barbara Molland

CADILLAC'S GOLDEN GYPSY, daughter of ANACACHO'S GOLDEN CADILLAC, out of BEAU'S LIL LUV, by BOLD AND THE BEAUTIFUL. Owned by Joe and Carrie Byrd.

American Saddlebred stallion, MI LIBERTY FLAME, owned by Schermarra Farm in New Castle, Pennsylvania, at the West Virginia Tri-State Show in 1997. Photo: Debbie Scherder

FAR FIELD TABASCA is a pinto American Saddlebred, sired by PHI SLAMA JAMA, and out of the good pinto Saddlebred mare, the Champion, DOZEN ROSES. As a three-year-old, this young mare took to the saddle as if she had always been ridden…a breeze to train! Here she is pictured at her first show with her trainer and assistant trainer.

The author's Mom, Mary Thompson (Miss Chicago of 1926) riding her elegant Saddlebred mare PRINSETTA MACDONALD, in front of her home in 1938.

SUGAR MOVES, by STONEWALL'S MAIN EVENT, with her brand new, day-old "gaited" filly, HARVEST MOON, a true candidate for performing the five gaits. Her sire is HARVEST COMMANDER, a great-grandson of the famous WING COMMANDER. Photo: Barbara Molland

➡ Photo to the right: SWING TIME, daughter of FLIGHT TIME (a son of WING COMMANDER), with her new foal in the pasture at Far Field Farm, in Petaluma, California. This is a very strong ASB line. Photo: Barbara Molland

"The Girls" ready to steal hearts, at Far Field Farm in California. Owner Barbara Molland reports all of these yearling fillies are sired by World Champions and out of well-bred dams.

Barbara goes on to explain: "There are those breeders who would differ, but most would say that the rack and slow gait have traditionally been the focus of the Saddlebred breeder — certainly as important as the trot, which holds a sacred place in the show horse. This is evidenced by the fact that the Open Five-Gaited Championship is always the last class of the World Championships and of virtually all our top horse shows. It is the culmination of everything we love about these horses, the thrill of it all.

"While there have always been individual horses within the breed that were strictly three-gaited or walk-trot horses, as we call them, it wasn't until breeders began to breed for ultra refinement in the 20th century that we found a significant percentage of our horses losing their racking ability. There are trainers within the industry who will tell you that they 'rack everything,' but it is undoubtedly more difficult for a horse to do the extra gaits if its conformation and genetics don't facilitate that. That is why I consider it so important to continue breeding those lines that exhibit the ability to gait. Finally, I would not want the readers to believe that the three-gaited horse is all the American Saddlebred is about because that is far from being true. One only needs to see the large numbers of five-gaited pleasure horses being shown by amateur riders to appreciate how wildly popular these horses are."

I have had important connections with both basic categories of the breed. As an infant and youth, I accompanied my parents with two lovely Saddlebreds hitched to a buggy for memorable outings through the Forrest Preserves of Chicago in the early 40's.

My mother's special mount Prinsetta Macdonald, a jet black Saddlebred mare, was a viable contender in the show rings during that period. Prinsetta went on to be an elegant parade horse.

As an adult, I've had the joy of owning my first major "heart bonding" horse, a bay Saddlebred gelding named Robert.

"Robbie" came into my life as a rescue and went on to be a great love and a great companion. Although he has been gone for almost two decades, his picture remains on my desk at this very writing.

Robbie was the epitome of what a person needs for trail riding. His heart was deep, his conformation and mind so very solid. He had enormous brio but was calm in the face of challenge. He loved to go, but was content to stay at home and graze. There were times when circumstances made riding infrequent, but when asked to go under saddle, it was as if no time had intervened. Adventures on this noble Saddlebred surely provided the bedrock for this book.

The Saddlebred is a magic ingredient of many soft-gaited breeds enjoyed today. Their gentle spirit and magnificent physical appearance are treasures to anyone who has been lucky enough to know one.

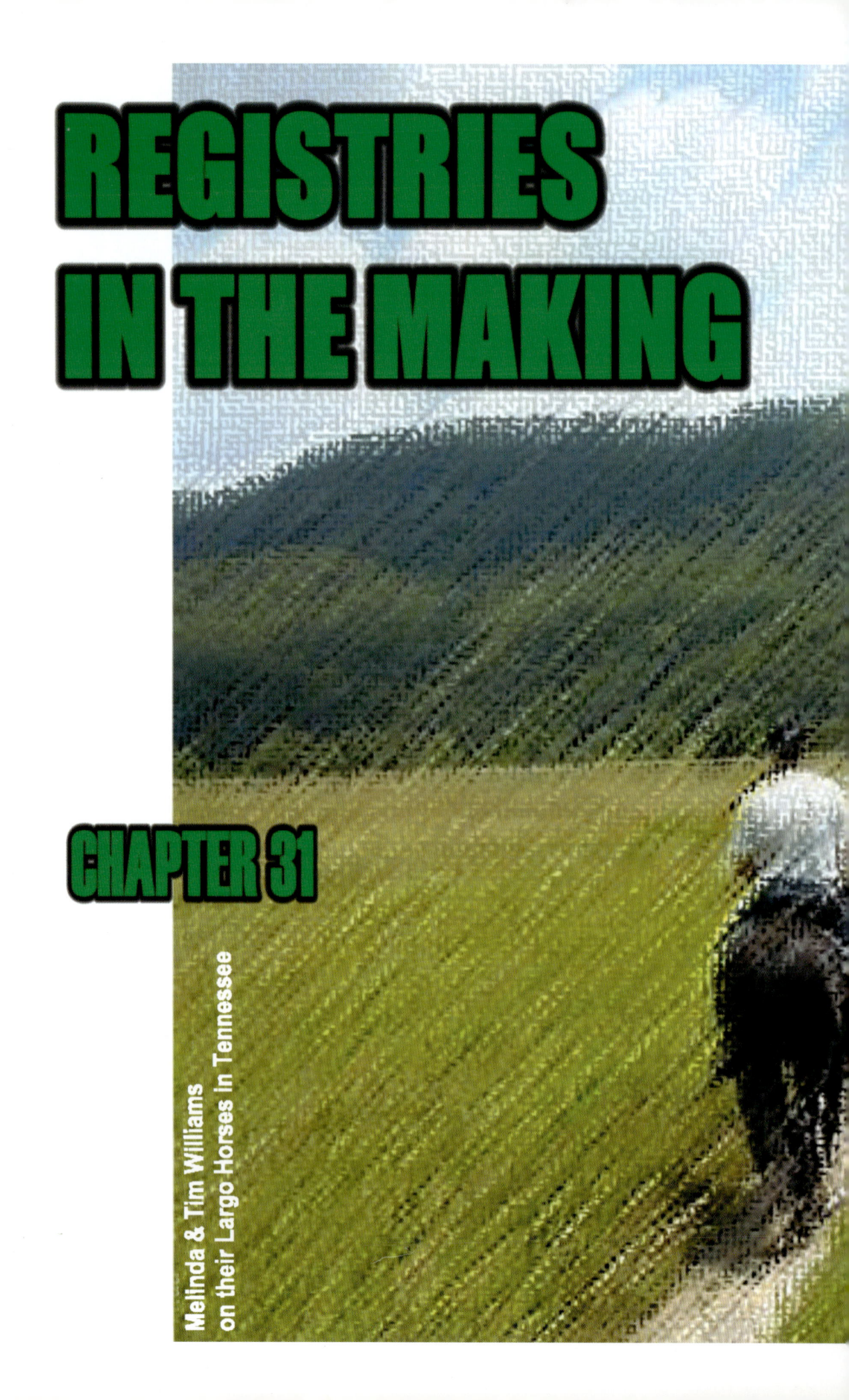

REGISTRIES IN THE MAKING

CHAPTER 31

Melinda & Tim Williams
on their Largo Horses in Tennessee

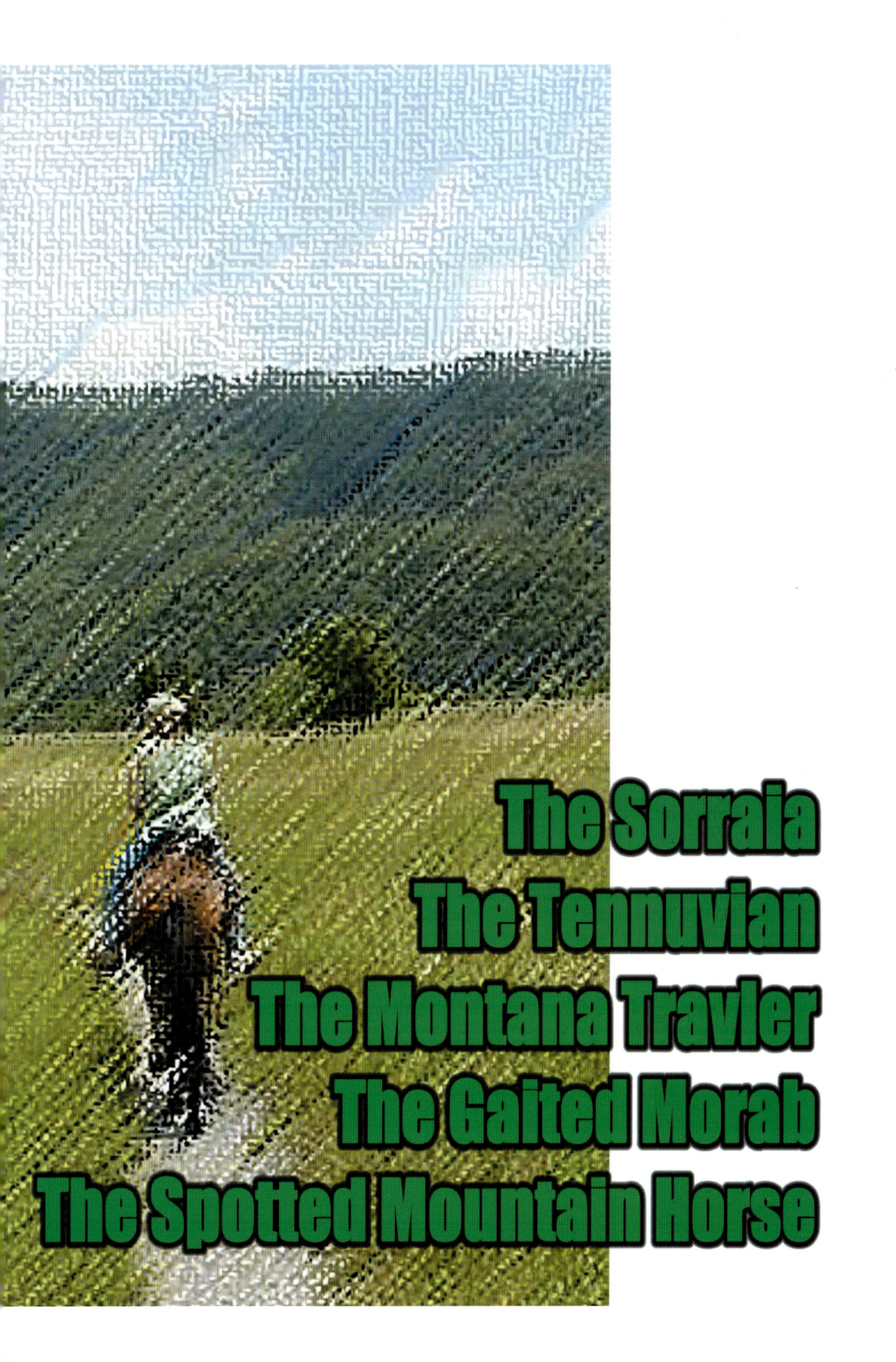

The Sorraia
The Tennuvian
The Montana Travler
The Gaited Morab
The Spotted Mountain Horse

Chapter 31   Registries In The Making

In this chapter, we will take a look at several breeds and registries that are developing their own following. From the ancient Sorraia to the fledgling Spotted Mountain Horse, these equines are finding their place in the world of the soft-gaited horse.

The Sorraia

The Sorraia appears to be the predecessor of many light horse breeds. Prehistoric cave paintings in Escoural in Portugal and la Pileta in Spain, give us evidence of the early existence of these important equines. As it is not unusual for a Sorraia to be gaited, there is a possibility that it is a source of the soft gait in horses.

Although there could be a strong tie to the now extinct Tarpan, Dr. Ruy d'Andrade, the Iberian scientist and horse expert who discovered and saved the Sorraia, considered him to represent "Equus stenonis," and a prototype of the Form III wild horse. Many researchers believe there have been four forms of wild horse that became the predecessors of the horses we know today: I - Pony; II – Draft; III – Sorraia (warmblood); IV - Oriental.

The Sorraia sought refuge in the western region of the Iberian Peninsula, a swampy and isolated area located north of Lisbon. Although the Sorraia was known by some as the "swamp horse," it was named after the Sorraia River by Ruy d'Andrade.

Dr. d'Andrade discovered these horses in 1930, and since that time he and his family have been responsible for their preservation.

Today the Sorraia is nearly extinct. Most are privately owned in Portugal and Germany. But of the 150 - 200 head still existing, most are in the herds of the d'Andrade family and the Portuguese National Stud. All of these horses are direct descendants of the original group of 7 mares and 4 stallions secured by Dr. d'Andrade.

The Sorraia is a walking history book. Their appearance, showing no outside blood, may give us a window back through thousands of years to see what these early and ancient horses looked like. Their unique appearance has brought to our attention the encouraging information that we may have, here on the American shores, similar, if not the same, living relics. Quoting Hardy Oelke, a world renowned expert on ancient equines: "The ancestor of the Iberian breeds still exists. Some of America's mustangs are zoological treasures and of the same type – they represent a chance to rescue this endangered subspecies."

When testing the DNA of American Mustangs, some proved to have not only similar, but identical DNA patterns to that of the Sorraia. These results are scientifically accomplished with the use of DNA analyses, indicating that similarity in phenotype may not be freak occurrences. Sorraia-type Mustangs have been found in several BLM Herd Management Areas and Mustang registries.

With these discoveries, the Sorraia Mustang offers a chance for a second leg in the preservation of the subspecies world wide. To this aim, preservationist breeders are supporting the Sorraia Mustang Studbook, which was established to keep the records and promote the breeding and preservation of the Sorraia Mustang.

The Sorraia typically stands around 14 to 14:2 hands tall. It is a refined, slender, leggy horse with a narrow wedge-shaped head, and chest, prominent withers leading to a rather

The Sorraia exhibits a primitive coloration of some shades of dun or grulla with a dorsal stripe, black-tipped ears, and bi-colored mane and tail. Photo: Courtesy Hardy Oelke

The Sorraia has the ability to withstand extreme climate and survive on very little food, while maintaining good health. Photo: Courtesy Hardy Oelke

straight back of medium length, on to a rafter-shaped hip and a medium tail set. The legs are fairly long and clean with round, long cannon bones that produce a rather high knee action. Their feet are medium-sized and don't have excessive hair around the fetlocks.

The Sorraia exhibits a primitive coloration of some shades of dun or grulla with a dorsal stripe, black-tipped ears, and bi-colored mane and tail (usually fringed with the light, often almost white color.) Its legs are striped with bars or zebra stripes. It often has a stripe across its shoulder, and it usually does not have white markings.

This is an extremely limber and flexible horse, both laterally and vertically. Many of today's gaited breeds inherited this ability to flex at the poll, to collect and to work off the hindquarters and to carry itself proudly.

Modern soft-gaited horses can thank the Sorraia for the tendency to gait laterally and the talent for cow work. This gratitude should also extend to the ability to withstand extreme climate and survive on very little food while maintaining good health.

The Tennuvian

Paula Bonser, founder of the Tennuvian Registry, initiated the development of this breed by cross-breeding the Peruvian Paso and the Tennessee Walker. A horse is eligible for registration if its parents are either a Tennessee stallion and a Peruvian mare, or a Peruvian stallion and a Tennessee mare. Tennuvian to Tennuvian is also becoming more common.

To be registered, a horse may be of any color, but must not exceed 14:3 in height. Paula reports these horses are beautifully gaited, gentle and intelligent. They are excellent for trail riding, endurance riding, ranch work or for driving carriages. They can be shown in open breed, gaited horse competitions.

The Montana Travler

In the early 1930's, horse lover Tom Eaton began his quest for the ideal horse. At that time, he didn't imagine he would be responsible for developing an entire new breed.

He began with a Thoroughbred-Hamiltonian mare and a Hamiltonian stallion named Mugs. To this combination, Eaton added Morgan, American Saddler and Tennessee Walker. He wanted a horse with a flat-footed running walk, good toplines and an excellent disposition.

In the early 1940's, Tom turned his top mares loose into a secluded Montana canyon with a half Morgan - half American Saddlebred stallion. There they remained until Tom returned from World War II. He was pleased with the 45 head of young horses waiting to be trained; and was even more pleased at the ease in which these young horses accepted training.

That same year Tom Eaton began a pack train business in the Montana mountains and used these young horses from the canyon in his string. All of these horses performed a flat-foot running walk, had good dispositions and had backs well-suited for a saddle.

Years later, in 1974, Eaton realized the ultimate reward of his breeding program with the birth of the lovely Montana Travler (who was sired by a Tennessee Walker stallion).

Tom Eaton with foundation stallion MONTANA TRAVLER A1.

Quoting Eaton: "From the very first, this colt caught the eye of every horseman who saw him. Many agreed with me that this colt would become a good prospect as a stallion. As a two-year-old, he sired four foals in 1977, and nine in 1978. All showed excellent quality."

From that time on, Eaton continued his development of the "Montana Travler Breed," with Montana Travler, the stallion, as its foundation.

Montana Travler is a flashy, ground-covering 16:1-hand chestnut stallion, who could, in fact, walk flat-footed at a rate of 8 miles an hour. His offspring have an over-reach of 8 inches or more as foals, and are consistently possessing the special qualities of the foundation sire in size, disposition, way of going and general appearance.

In 1984, the American Horse Council approved and registered the Montana Travler as a new breed of horse and it was selected as the official Montana Centennial breed in 1989.

Quoting Senator John Melcher: "The many patient years of breeding have certainly paid off. Producing the first unique breed of horse developed in the State of Montana is certainly a worthwhile accomplishment."

⇐ **Mark A. Engle, Vice President of the Montana Travler Horse Association.**

DAKOTA FLASH, Grandson of MONTANA TRAVLER, owned by Mel Atkinson of North Dakota.

To be eligible for registration, a horse must be at least three years of age and trained to saddle. It must carry genes from Montana Travler A1, and must exhibit the conformation, disposition and gait consistent with the foundation sire.

The Montana Travlers are being used on ranches in Montana, in the National Park Service, as hunters, jumpers, endurance horses and as rodeo pickup horses.

With the development of the Montana Travler Horse Association, numerous breeders are embracing the goals of Tom Eaton. It is a Registry destined to grow.

The Gaited Morab

There are several registries for the Morab (Morgan crossed Arabian) Horse, but the one championed by the country's largest breeder of *gaited* Morabs is, the International Morab Breeders' Association Inc. (IMBA) – the cornerstone of the Morab Community Network.

Anita Messenger and her husband have been breeding Morabs since the 1980's. In 1995, they began addressing the element of gait to their breeding program.

Quoting Anita: "Since the Morgan and Arabian breed both have 'gait' lurking around and popping out every once in a while, it was only natural for the Morab to show up with it, too. Over the years, we had a few foals turn out gaited who were born out of non-gaited

Two Gaited Morab yearling fillies: LM MYSTERY DEBUTANTE, and LM MYSTERY SHILOH. Both are out of 50/50 Morab mares, so they are _ Morgan and _ Arabian.

A Gaited Morab colt sired by MARY MELS MYSTERY, out of an Arabian mare.

parents. This got us to thinking about it, and then we began to look for a top-quality gaited Morgan stallion to bring into our breeding program. We found that special stallion in Northern Utah in the Mary Mel Morgan herd."

Mel Fransden has been one of the very few Morgan breeders who unabashedly continued to breed good-gaited Morgans at a time when others would never admit they had a gaited foal born.

We bought a six-year-old stallion, Mary Mel's Mystery, from Mr. Fransden. Then we had videotapes of Mystery analyzed by Lee Ziegler of Colorado.[1] She nailed him down doing six gaits, including walk, trot and canter. This was under saddle and at liberty. Lee also believes that he would rack (which would make him 7-gaited) if the right person rode him."

At Liberty Mountain Farms, the Messengers are the first breeders to actively breed for registered gaited Morabs. In 2002, they had their second foal crop by Mystery. By the end of 2003, Mystery will have sired over 30 foals on the ground in at least 8 different states, and most of them will be Morabs.

The Morab breed is one of the fastest - growing breeds in the country, and it looks like the Gaited Morabs are going to become highly sought after.

Quoting Anita: "After all, what more could you want? All the wonderful attributes that the Arabian and Morgan breeds can give you, plus 'smooth' gaited on top of that. It's only a matter of time."

LM Sterling Sundance, a Morab gelding belonging to Elaine Parker in Florida, is an endurance horse. He also works cattle, and his trainer thinks he needs to be started in jumping. Elaine says he has an awesome running walk in addition to a normal walk, a ground-eating trot, and a rocking-chair canter.

Elaine used to own and show Quarter Horses and now feels that owning Sun-

LM STERLING SUNDANCE, with owner, Elaine Parker.

---

[1] Lee Ziegler is known as a gait analyst and clinician. Lee is nationally recognized for her expertise.

dance is more than she could have ever imagined. The vets at the vet checks in the endurance rides are telling her Sundance needs to be in longer races. The more mileage she adds, the better he gets.

LM-Ark-Three Smokey and his owner Paul Gleitz of Missouri have earned the Gold Medal Award level in the Morab Breeder's Association, and did it mostly on trails.

The combination of Morgan and Arabian is a powerful package, and when you add the ability to gait, it's safe to say that this is a breed with a dynamic future.

The Spotted Mountain Horse

A recent addition to the gaited horse family, the Spotted Mountain Horse has taken off at a gallop. Within the first months of opening the Registry in 2002 more than a hundred horses were accepted, and the future of this organization was enthusiastically guaranteed.

The Spotted Mountain Horse is also included in the United Mountain Horse (UMH) shows. They can compete for high points in the three divisions, Trail Pleasure, Classic Pleasure and Park Pleasure. They show under the KMSHA/UMH rules book, which among other things, requires that horses be shown in standard keg shoes.

The "Sports Model" of the Mountain Horse Family.

CHAMP, the first horse registered in the Spotted Mountain Registry. His owners Billy and Debbie Caudill of Mount Sterling, Kentucky report he is a great gaited horse and a perfect trailhorse in the woods. He also does tricks!

The characteristics of the Spotted Mountain Horse are identical to those of a Kentucky Mountain Saddle Horse, except for color. To register a horse, the owner must be a current member of the Kentucky Mountain Saddle Horse Association. To qualify for registration/certification in the SMHA, they must meet the following criteria: 1) Show a willing and gentle disposition; 2) Demonstrate to an examiner - either in person or by video - a smooth, natural, even, four-beat gait; 3) Be of good conformation, i.e. well-proportioned with regard to body, head, hind and legs, of medium structure, not too fine or too coarse; 4) Have white body markings other than the face and legs.

The growing numbers of soft-gaited horses, registries and associations are an exciting product of the 21st century. As horse fanciers discover these gems the proliferation is bound to continue.

Spotted Mountain colt SIZZLIN STARBUCK pictured with his mother MOUNTAIN LADY is a great-grandson of Rocky Mountain foundation sire, TOBE.

PART THREE

ASSOCIATIONS and ACTIVITIES

32. The Pleasure Trail - A Place To Shine
33. Let's Show Our Horses !
34. North American Single-Footing Horse Association (NASHA)
35. Competitive Trail Riding (NATRC)
36. American Gaited Horse Association (AGHA)
37. Gaited Horses on the Net
38. United Mountain Horse Association (UMH)
39. Hollywood Horses
40. Moms and Babies

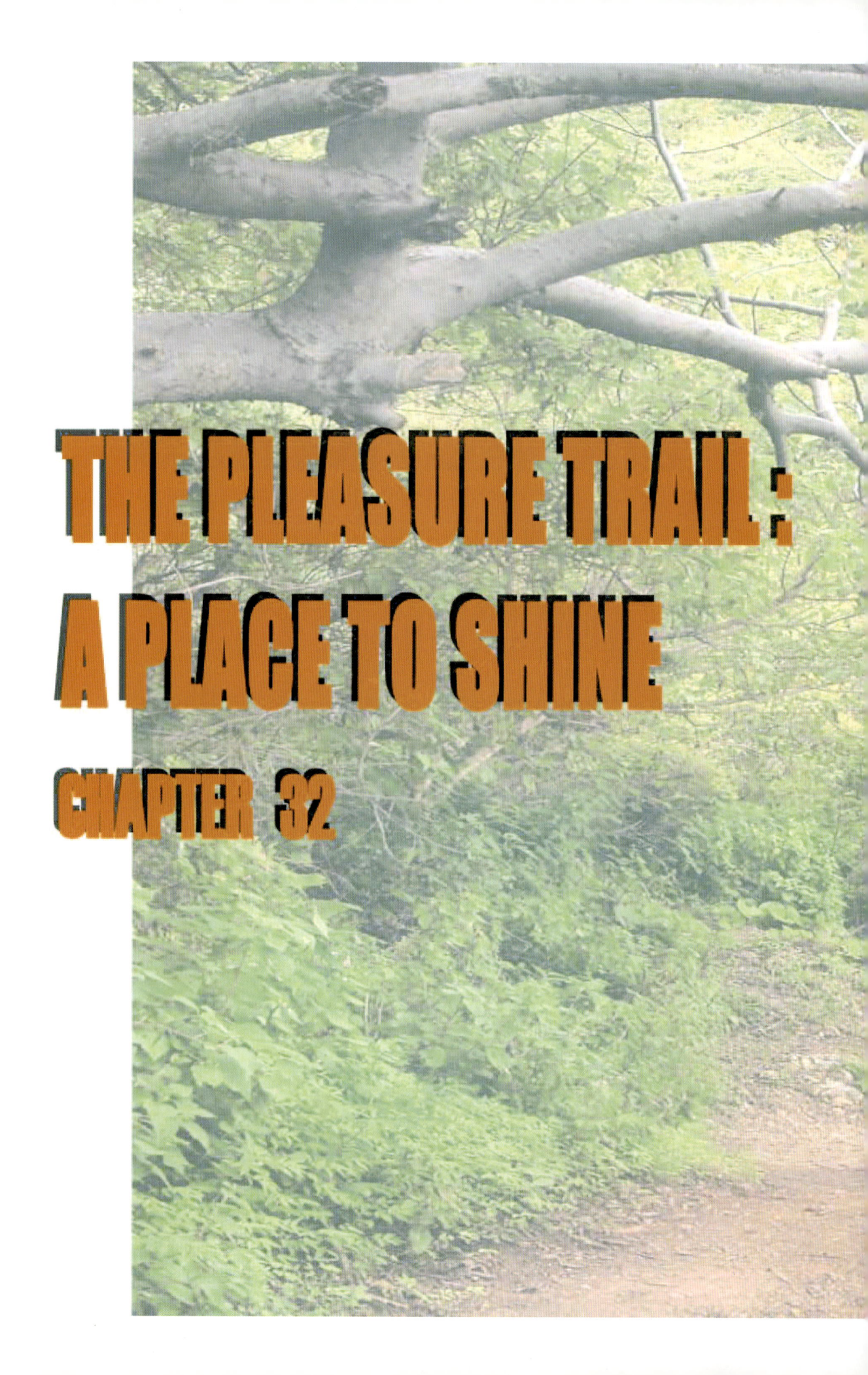

THE PLEASURE TRAIL : A PLACE TO SHINE
CHAPTER 32

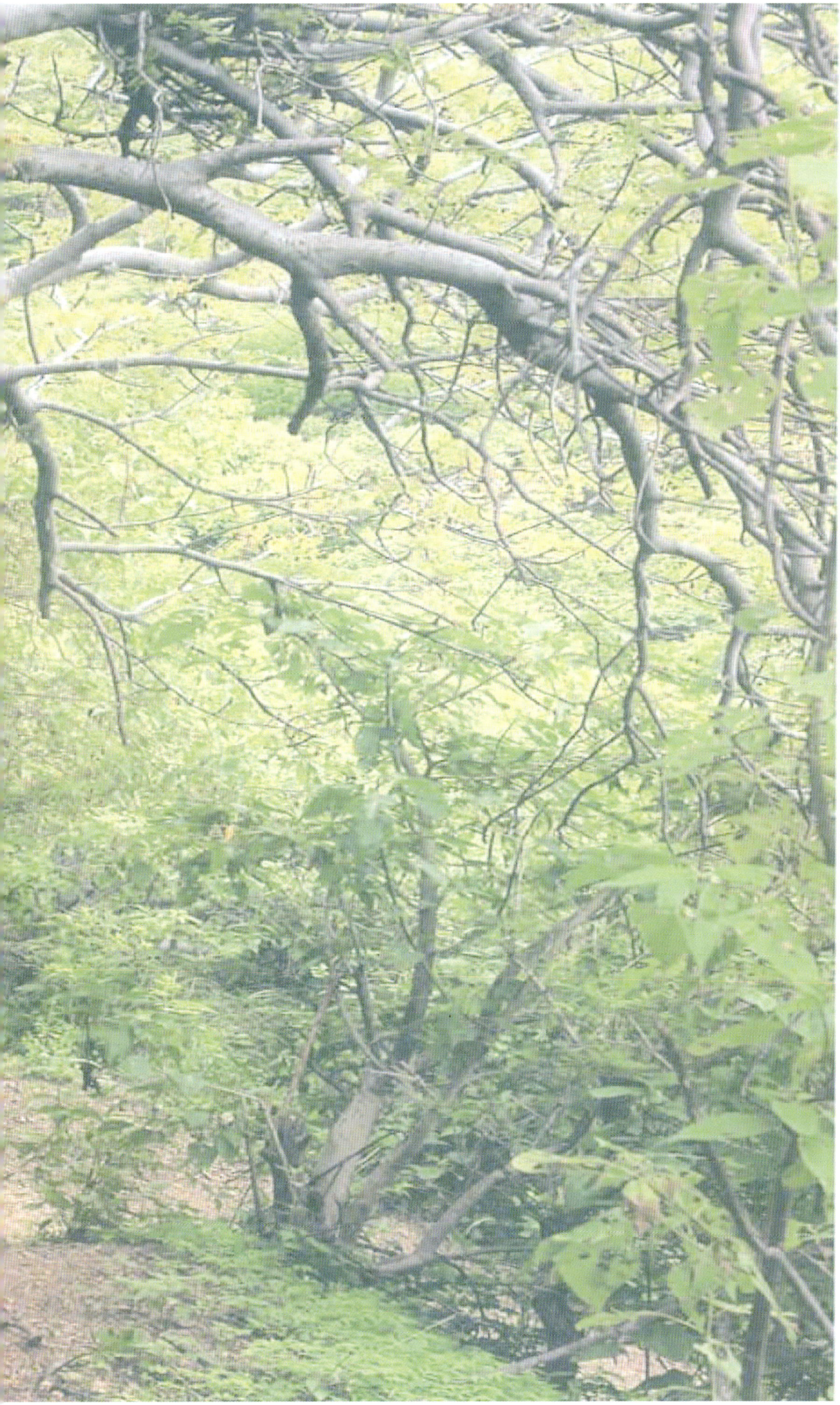

The pause that refreshes. Darlene Rubin, and Fox Trotter, Pistol Pete enjoys a picnic with Joyce Barcus and Tennessee Walker, Maggie on a Sierra ride.

Chapter 32 THE PLEASURE TRAIL: A PLACE TO SHINE

There are many ways to enjoy the trail experience. The relationship between horse and rider will determine the type of riding you most enjoy.

The terrain that is available to you will naturally affect the riding you do. Some riders time their rides, and enjoy making it to the top of every available peak. Others are happy meandering around their neighborhood or over gentle paths. Others would rather be with a large group of riders. Yet others prefer riding alone. Many riders participate in a variety of trail activities and styles.

Add the variable of weather to the mix of multiple terrains and different riding styles and you can see there is a massive array of trail choices.

Whatever ride you choose, there are guidelines that will help to ensure a pleasant outing. The health and condition of your horse should be of primary concern. Matching the condition of you and your horse to the demands of the particular ride is most important.

Although the resting pulse rate for every horse is different, it should range from 32 to 44 beats per minute. When exercising, the pulse rate will rise, but within 10 minutes or so, it should drop to less than 70 beats per minute. Practice checking this pulse rate both at rest

Washoe Valley, Nevada, is the meetingground for this group of riders, all members of the Northern Nevada Gaited Horse Club.

Irma Lloyd with Paso Finos, DUMAS AND TALENTO, taking a break while checking stock at JF Gaited Horse Ranch, in Northern Canada.

470

A gathering of riders ready to head out onto the trail in Sutton's Bluff. Photo: Valley Springs Fox Trotters

CHEETAH and DELLA (Paso Fino and NASHA) both proved their abilities on the ranch before they were used for breeding. Both took to dominating cattle right away, stopping hard and jumping out fast, and turning on a dime. They have great stamina and are both fearless and surefooted.

and during exercise. You will feel more confident about conditioning your horse if you have this information at hand.

There are five important items to keep in mind when you head out onto the trail: 1) Let someone know where you are going and approximately when you plan to return; 2) Dress appropriately for the time you're leaving and plan for any changes in the weather; if you're taking off on a warm summer afternoon, carry a jacket for warmth, in case you may be out longer than you plan; then, even though you may be starting out on a cool morning, take some kind of headgear to protect you from bright sun); 3) Carry a trail emergency kit (see illustration, P.9); 4) Don't endanger yourself; and 5) Make sure you and your horse are properly conditioned for the chosen trail ride. Preventative maintenance and planning ahead can definitely improve the overall success of your trail riding experience.

You will continue to learn about your horse and your own riding every time you venture out onto the trail. This learning process is what establishes the bonding between you and your soft-gaited horse.

Try not to start something new on an important ride. For example, if you intend to use hobbles, familiarize your horse with them on its own home ground. If you want to add electrolytes to its drinking water (which may be a good idea on long hot rides), make sure it has tasted the mixture and will drink it without hesitation. If you are making a change in the tack your horse is used to, do so in a situation where the familiar tack is still available.

Trail riders in training, Katie and Jennifer Grant on INCA.

A pair of Tennessee Walkers with their "Moms" Shannon and Kellie.

Different weather brings with it specific concerns. First let's look at the general items that will apply on each and every ride.

Make sure your horse is up-to-date on all vaccinations. Cuts and bruises are not uncommon, and a current tetanus shot is a safeguard against a needless yet serious infirmity.

Develop teamwork between you and your horse. Take whatever measures necessary to ensure a positive relationship. Spend time with your horse both on the trail and at home in your yard or at the stable. Some of the most productive times can be spent in casual and informal ways. Walk around with your horse looking at various things. Leading it up and down a street will often provide new insights and help develop a mutual trust. Don't discount any hours that can be spent together. Simply grooming your horse, can bring you to a closer connection.

It can be most helpful to see your horse interacting with other horses. Watching your horse in a field with other horses can be very

⇨ Photos to the right, Top: Missouri Fox Trotter stallion, PATRIOT'S GOLDEN TAHOE S., owned by Don and Marlene Smith, standing at Big Cedar Ranch in Ava, Missouri. Photo: Dawn Lindsay. Middle: Paso Fino crossing a bridge, photographed by Terry Wallace. Bottom: Mountain stallion GENERAL JACKSON, with Barbara Weatherwax, up.

Jani London, from Charlie Lake, British Columbia, riding Paso Fino, DUMAS TM, on his first 25-mile endurance race as a six-year-old.

revealing. Where does it fit into the pecking order? Does it take charge or is it submissive? To see the horse react to other horses may help you understand the reaction it has to various activities and situations you experience together.

Talk to your horse and develop a strong vocal communication. In an emergency, voice control can make a tremendous difference in the outcome. Tell your horse what you want of it. Talk to it in soothing tones when it is upset. Maintain a vocal connection.

As the familiarity between you and your horse evolves, so does the potential for wonderful trail riding.

Don't rush your horse's development. If you want a calm and relaxed horse, then you must be calm and relaxed. Especially if you are new to the soft-gaited horses, the best thing you can do is walk. Whatever breed you have selected, the quickest way to develop a strong gait is to have a strong walk. All of the soft "second gears" come out of the walk. If you

⇦ **Photos to the left, top:** Racking stallion ROWDY RAWHIDE'S ROCKET with owner/rider Doug Stanley up. **Middle:** Three-year-old Fox Trotter stallion, WILLY, with Kim Smith up, at the Lonesome D Horse Camp, Midway, Arkansas. Photo: Janie Britton. **Bottom:** Mangalarga Marchadors out for a spin. This foal was carefully bred with champion bloodlines at Haras Trimonte.

Riding with only a lightweight rope, Chris Martin is on Missouri Fox Trotter, CAROUSEL, owned by Sandy Brown. Photo: Dawn Lindsay

A view through the ears - The view that trail riders absolutely relish! These belong to a Tennessee Walker.

push your horse to speed, it will probably resort to its own "tricks" to accommodate you. Pushing a horse to gait before the musculature has developed, or before you are confident in what you are asking for, can lead to pacing or trotting. The quickest way to a solid gait is to take your time developing a brisk and energized walk.

The canter is also a marvelous aid to conditioning your horse. You can spend plenty of time in a canter developing athletic stamina without the confusion tentative gaiting can cause. But treat the canter as a separate gait. Don't let the horse break into a canter from its second gear. Always start the canter from a walk or a standstill.

Remember, that magic soft-gaited gene is in there. It doesn't need to be taught and it will develop naturally as the horse is properly conditioned.

Perhaps one of the best training tools is another experienced trail horse. If at all possible, it should be a soft-gaited trail horse. You horse will listen to the foot-fall. Matching the rhythm of a well-gaited horse will reinforce your training. Spending a lot of trail time with a trotting horse could complicate the learning process for both you and your horse.

An experienced trail horse can also serve as a steadying presence and companion as well as a teacher. At bridges, water cross-

⬅ Photos to the left, Top: Sharon Henson and Kellie Rahm on their Tennessee Walkers. Middle: Paso Fino, CHEETAH, babysitting the kids. She is registered as ELECITAS ELAN, with both PFHA and NASHA. Bottom: Sharon Henson on her Spotted Saddle Horse.

Vasquez Rocks in Southern California, where Juan Filipe Orrego is riding a Missouri Fox Trotter. The ears belong to a Tennessee Walker and a Fox Trotter.

ings and other "scary" places, the seasoned horse can reassure a green horse.

Try not to take your horse on a trail that is beyond its ability. If you respect its fears, you will be able to work to overcome them. There's one "cowboy term" that definitely comes into play - "the horse needs plenty of wet blankets." This means that there is no substitute for experience. Many trail experiences will develop a solid horse.

Of course there is work you can both do that doesn't need to be done on the trail. Teach your horse to respond to leg pressure. Side passing is a basic maneuver for a trail horse. Another important factor in body control is back in a straight line. Mount and dismount your horse from both sides.[1] On the trail you may run into situations where the right side of the horse is the only one that can be safely

⇨ Photos to the right, Top: Two Fox Trotters - a twelve-year-old sorrel gelding, LEVI, with rider Janie Britton; and a three-year-old palomino filly, SUGAR DUST, with Kim Smith, up. Photo: Sharon Fenske. Middle: Hugh Richardson in his favorite winter outfit, "sweats," enjoying a ride at his Canadian Peruvian Paso Farm. Bottom: Fox Trotter stallion, SOUTHERN FIZZ, with Brenda Foley, up; and Kentucky Mountain Saddle Horse stallion GV MAN'S MASTERPIECE, with Skeeter Savage riding in the Sierras of northern Nevada.

---

[1] Mounting from the left is a tradition dating back to the time of warriors on horseback. Since most people are right handed, most soldiers would hang their saber on their left side, making it easier to pull it from its scabbard with the right hand. With a scabbard and saber hanging from your left side, it would be very difficult to mount a horse from the right side.

mounted or dismounted. Don't wait for that occasion to teach your horse.

Quarter turns are also a valuable aid to successful trail riding. Quarter turns are simply the ability of your horse to move its hind quarters around in a circle while the front legs remain in one place (turning on the fore quarter), or moving your horse's front end around in a circle while the rear legs remain in one place (turning on the hind quarter). It doesn't take much imagination to see how these maneuvers can be an invaluable aid during an emergency on the trail.

Rules of safety apply to riding alone, riding with others and simply being around your horse. It's a good idea to learn and practice these rules until they become everyday habit and custom.

Never approach a horse from behind without speaking up to warn it of your presence. If you are grooming your horse or simply approaching a friend's horse, the closer you stand to it, the less likely you will be kicked. Many accidents happen when the horse is startled.

Never try to out-muscle a horse. A quick snap on the lead will be more successful than trying to out-pull it. While it is important to keep a secure hold on the lead strap, never wrap it around your hand or wrist or body.[2]

Camping out with your horses and your friends is a unique way to "recreate."

---

[2] The tremendous strength of a horse should always be kept in mind. It is dangerous to attach yourself to a horse without a quick-release option. A finger wrapped with a lead rope can snap off in an instant. A wrist or arm could be broken or severely damaged if it's attached to a horse that suddenly bolts. A body could be dragged and severely injured if it can't get free from a galloping horse. It is always safer to set a horse free than to try and hold it using your body parts!

Riding at all times of the year, will show changes on the very same trails. This is the same trail as the one to the right – covered in snow. It's a whole different experience.

Missouri Fox Trotter A SAINT SHE AINT, "CRICKET," with a friend at Washoe Lake State Park, Nevada.

Here is the same trail pictured on the facing page in autumn. A familiar trail can present many surprises when it is covered in a blanket of snow. For safety sake, save the investigating for clear weather rides.

Mountain mare GRANDVIEW'S CANDY ALAMODE with Makenna Lincoln up, in South Lake Tahoe, California.

When you lead a horse into an enclosure - either stall or corral - turn it to face the door or gate before you release it. Make sure you are not in the path of its hind legs, as it may kick out in a burst of enthusiasm.

Carefully examine your tack as you put it on your horse with special attention to places of wear. Make sure buckles and other hardware are solid and in working order. Leather straps should be supple and cleaned on a regular basis.

Saddle up well before starting out on your ride. This gives your horse's back time to warm up. Check your cinch throughout your ride. It certainly doesn't have to be choking your horse, but it should be tight enough to keep your saddle securely in place. If you tie up for lunch, loosen the cinch, but remember to tighten it again before you start out.

Once you are on the trail, constantly scan your surroundings. Be alert to any surprises that may be lurking in the foliage, be it another horse, deer or even a plastic bag fluttering from a branch.

Watch other riders to see if they are successful at maneuvering any obstacles without trouble. Do not pass riders without first getting their attention and asking on what side you should pass. Then pass only at a walk or slow gait. Never run past another rider.

Tie a red ribbon on your horse's tail if it is known to be a kicker. If your horse tends to be cranky, warn other riders, then use caution not to ride too close. Be careful at up-hills and downhills. Talk to your horse and warn it to

Trail riding allows the horse and rider to find places that might otherwise prove inaccessible. Pictured is a lake in Nevada.

A three year-old-Paso Fino stallion, BANJO, on his 3rd ride, with Lynn Bovee, up. "The most agreeable horse ever"

The Ruby Mountains in North Eastern Nevada provides a spectacular scenery for the adventurous trail rider.

pay attention to its footing. Develop forgiving hands and a centered, balanced, deep seat. Lean back slightly going down steep inclines and lean forward going up.

Losing sight of other horses as they disappear over the crest can also be upsetting to your horse. When you reach the summit or bottom of a hill, don't rush off. Be considerate of other riders and make sure they are coming along safely. Show the same concern at water crossings. Some horses won't want to cross water unless it sees others crossing safely.

If your horse should become frightened and attempts to run, turn it in a circle and then tighten the circle until it stops. If it is frightened by something it sees on the trail, work to calm it and then walk it to the source of fear and let it sniff and examine it. Try not to punish the horse if it is afraid. Do not, however, let the horse buffalo you over something it should be familiar with.

If you come to a pavement or some other slick surface it's best to get off and walk with your horse. On long rides it is a good idea to dismount and lead the horse for at least five minutes out of every hour. It's good for you, and good for your horse.

Your horse's sense of smell and hearing are far better than its eyesight, though its eyesight is quite unique. It has monocular vision, or the ability to see separate objects

Isaac Wyler demonstrating the Largo Horse's ability to do it all.

Weather seldom keeps the avid horseback rider from their favorite pastime. Riding on a bareback pad through the snowy landscape is Anne Savage on Mountain, SAM.

478

Paso Fino, INCA, giving an enthusiastic young lady her first horseback ride.

Doug Stanley riding stallion, ROWDY RAWHIDE'S ROCKET, registered both Racking Horse and NASHA.

each eye at the same time. Plus, the horse can see anything behind it that is not narrower than its body. Its eyes are set wide apart on the sides of its head and can't see objects closer than four feet. In fact it can't see the ground directly in front of itself.

Don't tailgate. In a large group or with only another horse or two, it's important not to crowd. Accidents can be avoided if a horse has enough room to maneuver. A good rule of thumb is to leave at least one horse length at a walk, two while gaiting, and three at the canter.

If you plan to ride with other riders, try to be on time. Horses can work up into a lather if made to stand at the ready, waiting for that expected trailer that never seems to come. You and other riders will appreciate being able to get right out onto the trail at the planned time.

Whether you ride alone or with others, remember that the outside is a natural environment for horses. Don't put off riding just because of the weather. With an attention to safety measures and proper attire, inclement weather will simply expand your options for new trail experiences.

Snow can be a lovely landscape for a horseback ride. Save the exploring for fair-

Donna Middel and HONKEY TONK ANGEL, a three-year-old Fox Trotter filly riding in Colorado. Photo: Valley Springs Fox Trotters of Black, Missouri.

Paso Fino stallion, DUMAS TM, with Lynn Bovee up and ready for the calves at branding time.

A group riding Peruvian Pasos, decked out in traditional attire and tack, enjoying the pleasures of the trail.

weather days. In the snow, even familiar trails take on a whole new appearance. Commonplace items like mailboxes, parked cars, boulders and tree stumps can be mysterious and even scary to a horse when covered with mounds of white. If your horse is new to winter weather, be patient until it learns to accept these changes.

Take your time and stick to trails you're acquainted with. Remember, fresh snow can camouflage holes, drop-offs and poor footing. Don't risk asking your horse to walk on pavement or other slick surfaces that might be frozen.

A hoof pick is a necessity on snowy rides. Snow can pack into the hoof and actually create balls of icy snow that make it difficult and even dangerous for a horse to travel. Check its feet regularly and use the hoof pick to clean the hooves whenever necessary.[3] Since horseshoes exacerbate the problem of captured snow, you might consider leaving your horse barefoot throughout the winter. This should only be considered, however, if your horse's feet will not be damaged without shoes.

⇨ Photos to the right, top: Kellie Rahm on a young Tennessee Walking horse. Second: Terry Wallace and a group of friends on Paso Finos, out for a summer ride. Third: Mariann Deering on Paso Fino, OLIVIA, at Joe Graham Horse Camp at Timothy Lake in the Mt. Hood Wilderness area. Bottom: From left, two Peruvian Pasos, a Fox Trotter, and a Kentucky Mountain Saddle Horse with riders Jim and Barbara Alexander, Steve Foley, and Barbara Weatherwax.

---

[3] To prepare for a snowy ride, applying Vaseline or vegetable oil to the frogs of your horse's feet can help guard against snow buildup. If you ride a great deal in the snow, you might want to have rubber pads mounted under the shoe. This also prevents snow buildup.

From left: a white Racking Horse; a palomino Mountain Horse; (in the back), a bay Tennessee Walker; (center) a chestnut Fox Trotter.

Once a horse's feet get chipped and disfigured, it can take a number of shoeings before they are back to normal. Be advised that going barefoot can be risky. Leaving the rear hooves barefoot and having shoes on the front can be a successful compromise.

Make sure you are dressed warmly. Be careful that your winter boots are not too big to be pulled safely from your stirrups. Don't wear a long and loose scarf that could get tangled in the brush or tree branches. Wear gloves with a good grip, preferably ones that won't become soaked with moisture.

As for your horse's clothes, wear a slicker to cover the saddle in wet weather. You may want to add tapaderos or stirrup hoods to stirrups. Don't put an icy cold bit into your horse's mouth. Hold it under your arm for a while, or run warm water over it.

With its heavy winter coat, your horse will tend to sweat more on a snowy ride. If you ride frequently in cold weather, you may want to consider clipping its belly and legs, so the sweat can be wicked off the horse easier. Make sure you have a warm blanket and an adequate shelter waiting for your horse at the end of the ride.

Hot and humid weather comes with its own list of precautions. Plan a leisurely and

⬅ **Photos to the left, top: Paso Finos on a lunch break. Photo: Terry Wallace. Second: Washoe Valley, Nevada, is the meeting ground for this group of riders, all members of the Northern Nevada Gaited Horse Club. Third: Tamilynn Arndt on a trail drive in Wyoming. Bottom: Valley Springs Fox Trotters enjoying an outing with their "people" in 2001.**

481

slower-paced ride. Prepare for the inevitable insects. Spray you and your horse against these pests.

Your horse's temperature is sure to rise with hot weather exercise. Although normal is from 99° to 101°, it could rise to 103° or 104°. Check to see that it drops quickly once the horse is at rest.

Respiratory rate should normally be from 8 to 20 breaths per minute. In an over-exerted and panting horse it may rise to more than 60. Give your horse an opportunity to rest frequently. Find shade for it if possible.

Check your horse's upper lip to make sure it is pink and moist. If you press your finger against the gum to turn it white, then it should take no longer than one or two seconds to return to pink after you remove your finger.

Lastly, check your horse's hydration. Pinch a section of skin and release it. The skin should immediately fall back into place. With a dehydrated horse, the skin will remain pinched.

If you determine your horse is showing signs of dehydration or excessive fatigue, the area between the hind legs, where large vessels run, is a good place to cool the horse with running water or sponge bath. Don't stress the animal further until it has had the opportunity to recuperate.

⇨ **Photos to the right, Top:** Magical scenery found on a trail ride is even more special when viewed from the back of a much loved horse- here a frozen winter pond. **Middle:** The author out for a trail cart ride in the 1940's. **Bottom:** A break in the winter weather, and riders hit the trail!

Geri Chutuk on Fox Trotter, PISTOL PETE and Barbara Weatherwax on Fox Trotter, ZANE'S BLUE MAX D.

Trailering to ride can be the ultimate in fun. Just make sure you prepare by having your trailer regularly checked for safety. Frequent maintenance checks should be an absolute part of your regular chores.

When you purchase a trailer, take someone with you who is an experienced horse trailer user. Pay attention to other people's trailers to see what you do and don't like. Listen to what they say and assess how the information relates to your needs and your horses. Remember, it takes at least seven feet of interior height to accommodate an average-sized horse.

Pay special attention to your trailer's hitch, floorboard, brakes, latches, bearings, tires and all welds. Keep the hitch covered and greased when it is not connected to your trailer. Regularly remove your mats and hose out the trailer. A coat of water repellant will help the floor retain its integrity. Let the floor dry out before you reinstall the mats. Have your bearings packed as least annually. At the same time have your brakes and tires checked by an expert.

⬅ **Photos to the left, Top: All work and no play - KNGHA stallion TREVER with owner Greg Jenkins. Middle: American Paso Largo breeder, Isaac Wyler on one of his "using" Largo horses, crossing a lake. Bottom: Palomino Valley in Nevada provides a wonderful opportunity to gait with friends.**

Cliff Clemmons with Rocky Mountain Horse, NICK, riding through the back hills of Kentucky.

Keep all metal hinges and latches lightly lubricated to prevent rust. If you have dividers and chest bars, periodically remove them to make sure they don't become jammed from bends or corrosion.

Keep your truck in good mechanical order. A cellular phone is wonderful insurance against the dangers that can befall you if you should have truck problems with a trailer full of horses. You don't want to leave the horses unattended while you go for help. An emergency telephone call will help to insure a safe and happy outcome.

Always use trailer boots or leg wraps on your horse.[4] Use trailer ties with quick-release snaps to secure the horses in the trailer. If you don't have the quick-release hardware, always

Keeping truck and trailer serviced and in safe working order is critical to enjoyable trail riding.

use a quick-release knot when tying your horse in or out of the trailer. Use the quick-release knot whenever you tie your horse in any situation.

Here's a list of trailer supplies that you'll find helpful if you always have them available.

TRAILER KIT

- ❖ Water supply (In summer, if you're not sure about water availability on the trail, fill an ice chest with water. It usually

---

[4] This may not be as necessary in an open stock trailer. While you are becoming acquainted with a horse or new trailer, it's a good practice. It's always advisable to be "over cautious," than underprepared.

484

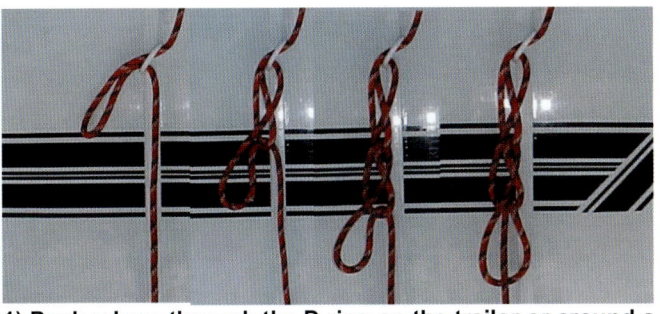

1) Push a loop through the D ring on the trailer or around a post. 2) Reach through the loop and pull another loop through the first loop. 3) Repeat step 2 until there is not much rope left. 4) Slip the end of the rope through the last loop to "lock" the tie (then if the horse pulls on the end of the rope, it will only tighten the knot). To release the knot, pull the end of the rope out of the last loop and pull. The knot will release completely.

travels well in the floor of the trailer's storage area or in the back of your truck).

- ❖ Horse blanket or cotton sheet for each horse in the trailer.
- ❖ Bucket
- ❖ Barley or grass hay in hay nets keeps the horses busy in transit on *long* drives.
- ❖ First Aid Kit
- ❖ Grooming equipment (a hanging shoe holder works well because it keeps the brushes, etc. separate and is easy to hang in the storage area or tack area or simply on the wall of a stock trailer).
- ❖ Trail riding emergency kit (carried in a saddle bag attached to one of the saddles).
    - ❖ Leather thong
    - ❖ Pliers or trail tool
    - ❖ Knife
    - ❖ Halter and lead
    - ❖ First Aid Kit
    - ❖ Cell Phone
    - ❖ Gloves
    - ❖ Duck tape
    - ❖ Conway buckle
    - ❖ Leather punch
    - ❖ Wire
    - ❖ Rope
    - ❖ Vet wrap
    - ❖ Chicago screws
    - ❖ Hoof pick
    - ❖ 6" piece of hose
    - ❖ EZ Boot

Kelsey Olsen riding stallion, SOUTHERN FIZZ, a double-registered Missouri Fox Trotter, and Kentucky Mountain Saddle Horse.

The fun you and your horse have together will establish a special bond. The camaraderie with friends and enjoyment of your soft-gaited horse can be a pleasure that knows no equal. Just remember to be safe and to plan ahead the best you can. The more time you spend on the trail and trailering to the trail, the more you will learn, and the easier it will be to make decisions. The pleasure trail is definitely a place in which you and your soft-gaited horse can shine!

GENERAL INFORMATION FROM THE NATIONAL PARK SERVICE

1. The use of horses and other pack animals on the main roadway is permitted only where necessary for entering or leaving trails
2. Horses are prohibited in picnic areas, near eating or shopping establishments, in most campgrounds and in

Skeeter Savage riding Mountain Pleasure, stallion, CLEMMONS THUNDER, "BEAUTY." Skeeter's daughter, Kelsey Olsen (to the left) is as avid a rider as her mother.

Stallion, CORSARIO, with Jennifer Grant.

Paso Finos CHA CHA and OLIVIA in their "camping trip stalls." Owner Mariann Deering

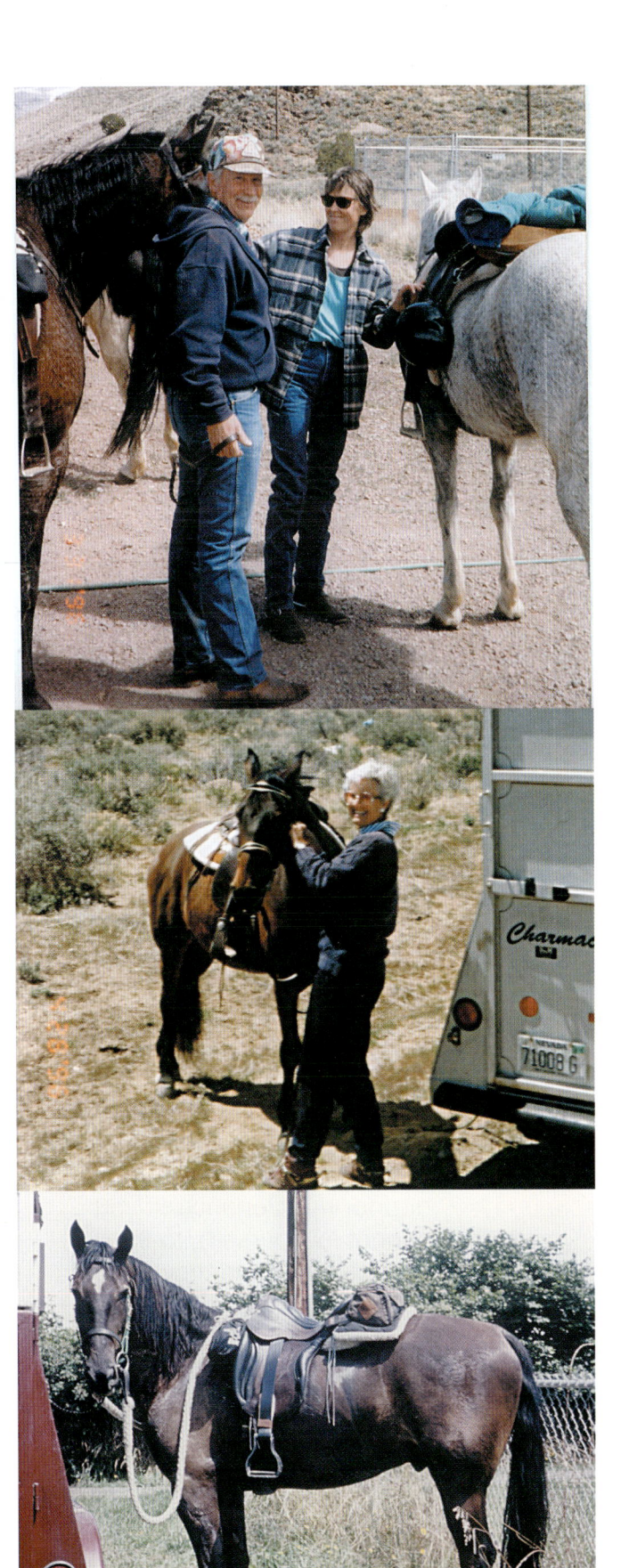

CADENCIOSA DE CAPUCHINO, a Paso Fino, eager to get going onto the trail. Get the message?

other places where the public normally gathers.
3. Horses must be slowed to a walk when passing pedestrians or bicyclists.
4. Horses cannot be picketed or pastured in meadow unless otherwise specified.
5. Wilderness permits must be obtained from the Park Superintendent if you are bringing your own animal into park back country.
6. Check with each National Park for its special rules and regulations.

⬅ **Photos to the left, Top:** Larry and Carol Hays with their soft-gaited horses, planning to ride with friends in the Northern Nevada Gaited Horse Club. **Middle:** Fox Trotter breeder and trainer Kathleen Keely making last-minute tack checks before heading out onto the trail. **Bottom:** Tennessee Walker JET, ready to go.

On the following page, you will find the published do's and don'ts from the Equestrian Patrol. It's best to have information before you venture into the State and Federal Parks.

Paso Finos on parade, with Joe Leisek riding his Buckskin Paso Fino, INCA.

DO's AND DON'Ts FROM THE EQUESTRIAN TRAILS PATROL

DO NOT:
- Carry firearms or shoot across the trail.
- Destroy, deface, remove, disturb any property on or adjacent to trail.
- Cut, carve, destroy or otherwise deface trees and shrubs on the trail. (You may remove or cut down trees or branches that have fallen on the trail.)
- Use threatening, abusive or indecent language on the trail.
- Operate a motor vehicle on the trail.
- Molest livestock on or adjacent to trail.
- Ride a saddle animal in a manner that might endanger any person or animal.
- Trespass from the trail onto private property.
- Smoke, except at designated areas.
- Build a campfire on or adjacent to the trail.
- Litter: What you pack in, pack out.
- Have a dog on the trail unless on a leash. (Some agencies do not permit dogs under any circumstances. Please determine before using a trail.)

DO:
- Close all gates that you pass through that were closed when you approached.
- Report all fires encountered or sighted on or from the trail.
- Pick up litter and transport if possible to litter receptacle.
- Exercise courtesy when approaching another trail user whether mounted or dismounted.
- Approach other trail users at a walk.
- Report all evidences of disrepair or poor maintenance (if you cannot fix yourself), to the administrating agency.

Robert Haug on his Paso Fino, VIENTO DE TORNADO.

Future Trail Delight
Left: PASH'S BWB INAUGURAL BREEZE
Right: PASH'S KISS THIS
Missouri Fox Trotters from Pash Farm in Marshfield, Missouri
Paul and Sharon Carey
Photo: Dawn Lindsay

LET'S SHOW OUR HORSES !

CHAPTER 33

Fox Trotter, SOUTHERN FIZZ G
Photo: Forrest Bliss

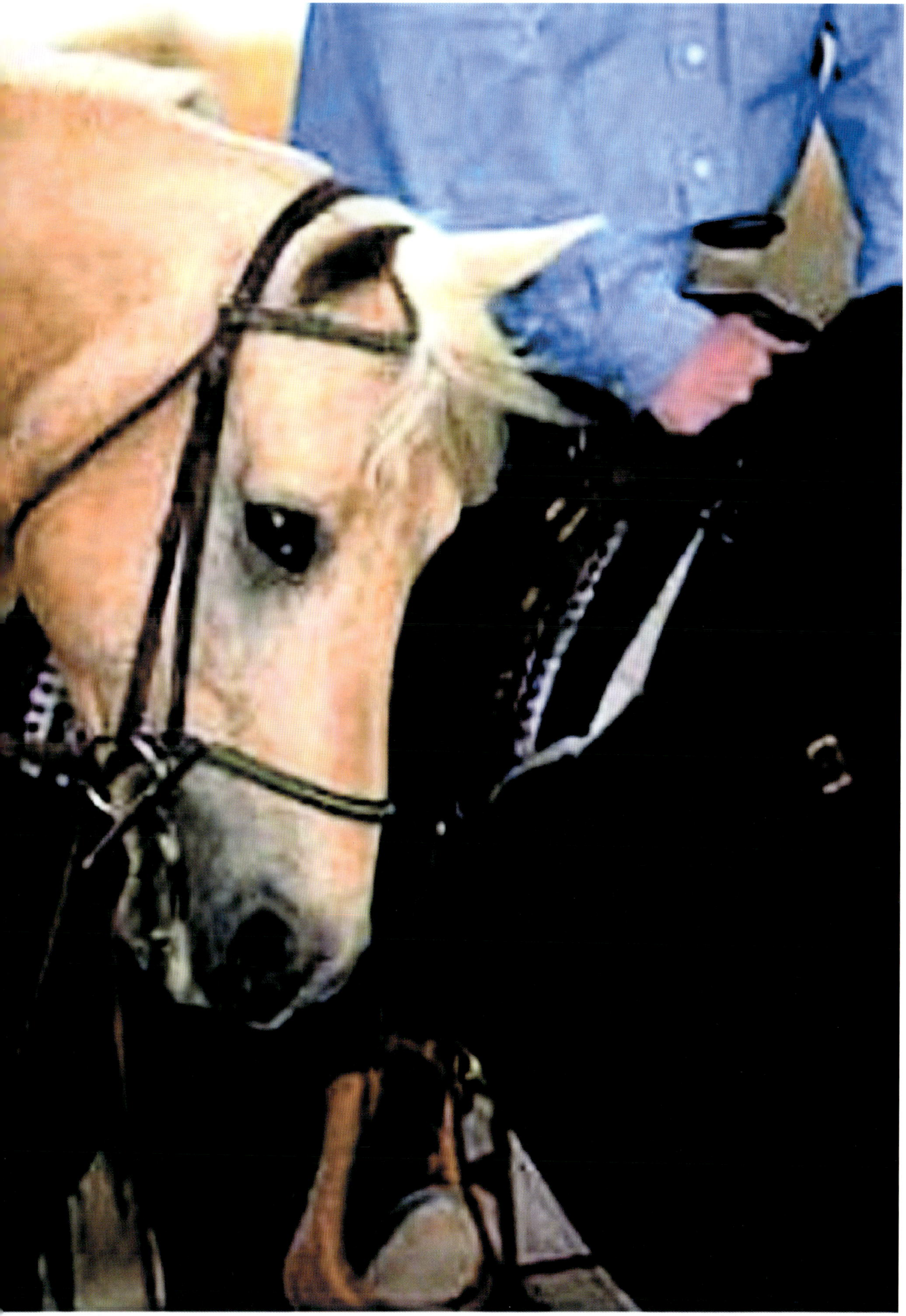

CHAPTER 33   LET'S SHOW OUR HORSES!

Every registry has its own rules and regulations controlling the show venue. Special requirements have been developed for horses of each breed that are designed to best exhibit the horse. Breeders and administrators from within the individual breeds make their determinations based on the way they want their horses presented to the community.

Because these guidelines are not written in stone, it would be unproductive to list them in this volume. What we will present, is a general overview of the soft-gaited horse in the show ring.

Showing is a valuable tool on several levels. For the owner, it's an opportunity to put their horse in a challenging situation. What better way to bond with your horse than by surviving the stress and fun of a show? Training to participate in a show gives the horse and rider a specific purpose to train toward. Preparing for a show also includes the careful cleaning of both horse and tack. Even if you do one show a year, you're sure to start out with a clean horse, and your tack will be guaranteed at least one thorough cleaning.

For those owners who compete throughout the show season, there are numerous awards they can strive for. Most of the major registries have a point system that encourages participation. Many local clubs have point programs designed to reward its members. Even trail riders can win points and prizes for hours spent in the saddle.

For the trainer, it's better than the yellow pages. He or she gets the opportunity to exhibit the "results" of his or her training program. They enjoy the income derived from the actual showing of horses, plus are able to generate new clients.

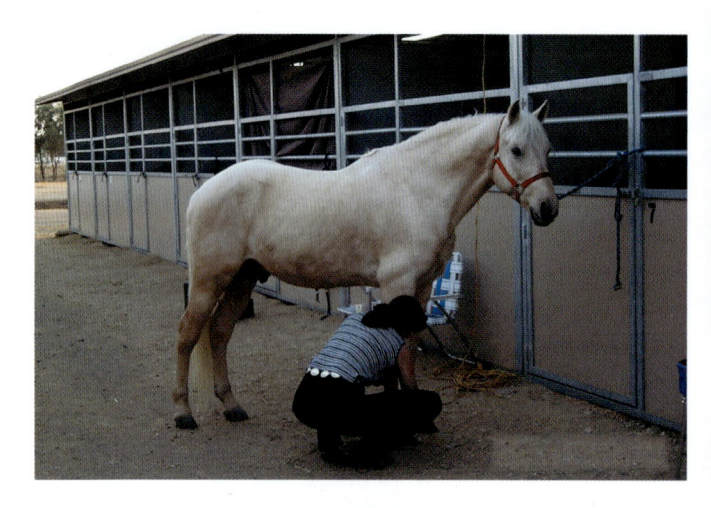

492

Billy Odom, third from left, judging an all-gaited "practice show" for the Northern Nevada Gaited Horse Club in the mid-1990's. Popularity of All-Gaited shows is growing tremendously.

For the breeder, participation in the show circuit is an opportunity to show the products of their breeding program. The halter classes allow young horses to be shown, even though they are often too young to be ridden. Often horses are sold, and interest in horses, coming from a particular farm, can be generated.

Major shows have a true impact on the breed itself. Winning stallions become the desired mate for mares. The prominence of one stud or the other can remain high for a season, or for many years. Even though a stallion will only have a 50% influence over the foal, he can produce literally hundreds of offspring over the span of his lifetime. The mare, on the other hand, will have the same 50% influence, but only over one foal a year.

It's easy to see how a stallion that becomes popular in the show ring can influence a breed for many, many years.

For the audience, a gaited horse show gives attendees a place to go to see the horses in action and meet the breeders, owners and trainers. In the case of multi-breed

⬅ **Photos to the left – facing page, top:** Preparation to show necessitates lots of hard work on the part of the horse owner. Every part of the horse is addressed, including its feet. **Middle:** Brenda Foley winning High Point with her Spotted Saddle Fox Trotter stallion NUGGET'S REBEL. (Photo: Forrest Bliss) **Bottom:** Fox Trotter stallion, SOUTHERN FIZZ, flat walking his way out of the arena with a blue ribbon. (Photo: Forrest Bliss).
This page, top: Like father (SOUTHERN FIZZ), like son, (FIZZ'S MOONLIGHT SPIRIT). (Photo: Brenda Foley) **Middle:** Fox Trotter, RINGO'S PISTOL PETE with Mara Baygulova. **Bottom:** Peruvian tack and attire making a lovely presentation. Photo: Judy Frederick, courtesy AAOBPPH

TRIPPLE S IRON MAN, owned by Tripple S Ranch in Montague, California. (KMSHA & RMH).

CONLEY, owned by CW Registered Naturally Gaited Mountain Horse Farm.

Performance Classes provide a challenge to both horse and rider. Here we see Beth Jennings riding Julie Tarnawski's Fox Trotter stallion, **FOX HILL MOONSHINE**. Photo: Rick Osteen

Missouri Fox Trotter mare, **PERFECTION'S TRAVELING NELLIE**, with Sandy Patterson, of Marshall, Illinois, up

shows, spectators can see the various breeds in the ring together. The soft-gaited horses are wonderful, but each breed has its own charactoristics that are more or less appealing to the individual fancier.

In recent years, there has been a movement to show several soft-gaited breeds at the same show. Financially it allows the smaller registries an opportunity to be seen side-by-side with other gaited horses. It will be important to develop a pool of judges knowledgeable in more than one breed.

In areas where there is this interaction of soft-gaited breeds, there has been a healthy exchange of ideas and an expansion in types of classes available.

At these "all-breed" shows, the *rail classes* [1] are perhaps the most familiar. Basically, these classes allow the horses to enter the ring and demonstrate a specific order of gaits, at the call made by the judge. For example, in a Fox Trotter 2-gait class, the horses enter the ring counter clockwise performing the flat walk, then on command accelerate to the fox trot, and then return to the flat walk. At the call of the judge, the horses will change directions and repeat the gaits in the same order. They will then be called into the center of the arena where the judge will evaluate the overall appearance of the horses in that class, send his lineup of winners to

---
[1] Rail classes are conducted by judging the quality of gait exhibited by the horses as they travel around the arena in both directions.

494

Stallion, MAGNETO, with owner Susan Tuscana representing Rockin B Ranch, home to Spanish Mustangs and Indian Horses of America, in Mabank, Texas.

the announcer, and then the prizes are awarded. A three-gait class is basically the same, except the canter is added to the series of gaits performed.

The *performance classes*, where the horse and rider are challenged with various tasks and patterns is becoming more popular in the soft-gaited horse show lineup. A designed pattern with specific gaits at specific times is drawn out and posted before the class. Each horse performs individually.

Both *English and Western tack* are popular with Mountain Horses, Tennessee Walkers, Icelandics and American Saddlebreds. The Spotted Saddle Horse is always shown in Western tack and attire. This breed has been a strong forerunner in promoting the versatility of their horses. *Spotted Saddle Horses of the West* developed a versatility program called the "Pentathlon." At specific shows, they offer challenging versatility classes as well as rail classes that enable the horses and riders to accumulate points toward the Pentathlon Championship.

Although *Mountain Horses* are shown in both English or Western tack and attire, some classes are specific - for example, "Western Pleasure." In these classes, Western protocol

➡ Pictures to the right: Top: Tennessee Walking Horse at the rail. (Photo: Forrest Bliss) Middle: Peruvian Paso in traditional tack and attire. (Photo: Judy Frederick, courtesy AAOBPPH) Bottom: Champagne Class with a foxtrotting contestant. Photo: Forrest Bliss

495

is held. Reins are held in one hand, and the free hand is not allowed to touch the reins or saddle or exchange with the rein-holding hand. In classes that are not specific, both English and Western tack and attire are permitted.

Mountain Horses are represented by five Registries and one major association, United Mountain Horse (UMH). Participation in a show requires documentation of registration. Each organization holds its own shows, and they also participate in shows together by blending their rules and regulations.

The *champagne* or *water-glass classes* are a prestigious win. The winning horse is the smoothest horse. Drinking or champagne glasses are filled to the brim and given to each of the competitors. Then the judge asks for various gaits or tasks. At the completion of the class, each competitor's glass is examined to find which one has the most liquid. This is a very important win because it honors the "smooth" in a horse.

In the showring, the *Peruvian Paso Horse* is allowed Peruvian, English, Western, Plantation or Australian gear in any class except as noted elsewhere or specified as an exception in the prize list. A fairly consistent rule, throughout most of the registries, is a

➡ Pictures to the right, Top: Spotted Saddle Horse TODAIN in Western tack and attire. Bottom: Tennessee Walker in Western tack and attire. Rider: Maggie Stillwell.

⬇ Below: BEAM'S FLAMING ROCKET, owned by Don and Kattie Freeman and Freeman Stables, with their 4-year-old grandson Aaron Freeman in the saddle.

prohibition against combining or mixing different types of gear. The Peruvian rules do allow the Peruvian bit with Peruvian, or other curb chain, can be used with any headstall. The Peruvian boza (without halter and eye covers) can be used in any class that permits the bozal with any approved non-Peruvian saddle.

Traditional costume is an important part of Peruvian Paso show tradition. Qualifying gaits include the Paso Llano, an equally spaced, four-beat gait and the Sobreandando, a faster, slightly more lateral gait.

There is much to be seen and enjoyed by the audience at a Peruvian Paso show. Their classes are unique. Horses are asked to work alongside another horse and given specific tasks by the judge. It is even acceptable for the judge to ride the competing horses. They have "Pisos" (Gait) classes, performance classes, showmanship under saddle, and the lovely "conjuntos" or pairs class. Many classes or even shows are concluded with a demonstration of the barrida. In this activity, a number of horses perform as a group by traveling side-by-side, pulling into single file in a "follow the leader" style of gaiting around the arena, followed by a return to gaiting side-by-side. It's like watching the Rockettes of the equine world!

Stallion JERICHO, owned by Shawneen Magrum, competing in a halter class at the International Rocky Mountain Horse Celebration in Kentucky Horse park, 2000. Photo: Aaron Archacki

In a Paso Fino halter class called "Bella Forma," the horse can be shown by either one or two people. Photo: Terry Wallace

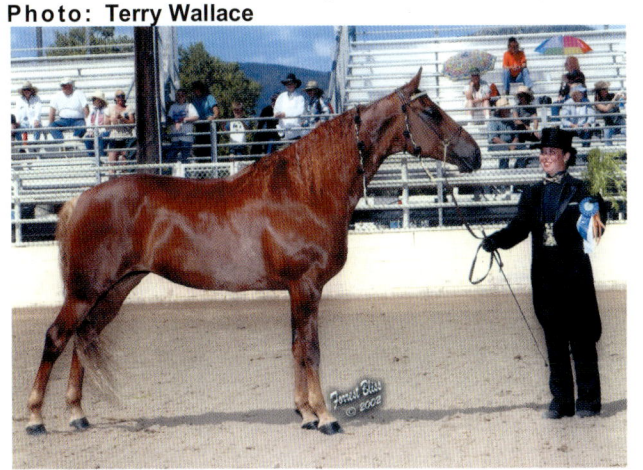

A Fox Trotter competing in a halter class. Photo: Forrest Bliss

Peruvian Paso mare, ZANTINA CHR, with owner/handler Hugh Richardson of CHR Eastwind Ranch in California.

Attending an all-gaited breed show helps to dispel the erroneous beliefs that the soft-gaited horse is not up for the challenges. They have enormous GO!
Photo: Forrest Bliiss

Here the rider is picking up an object that has been placed on the top of the drum. The judge will look to see that the horse is quiet and relaxed while the rider leans from the saddle.

This "L" made from railroad ties is another good obstacle in trail class. It can be backed through, or side-passed over. It is an aid in making specific requests of your horse that can be transferred to your trail riding – i.e. control in an emergency.

This is traditional barrel racing. The barrels are placed in a pattern in the arena, and the horse and rider must negotiate the pattern while being timed. In some gaited horse shows, the horses will be asked to gait around the barrels with time being subtracted if gait is broken. In others, they will gallop, and the winner will be the swiftest.
Photo: Dawn Lindsay

Many competitors in the trail classes have a practice course in their own back yard. A horse trained to compete is a superior trail mount. The classes simply isolate several skills that are helpful in a true trail experience.

498

Jenna Murril on RISKY BUSINESS, demonstrating the sliding stop. When performing more demanding athletic events, shin boots are recommended.
Photo: Dawn Lindsay

Steve Foley aboard stallion SOUTHERN FIZZ provides a wonderful example of a handsome presentation of horse and rider in a vigorous Versatility Competition at the Northern Nevada Classic All-Gaited Horse Show of 2001.
Photo: Forrest Bliss

Tennessee Walking Horse GREEK REWARD, owned by Margot Grissom of McCloud, California and being ridden by Beth Jennings, renowned gaited horse trainer from Hemet, California.

Although the gaited horse is not primarily used for cross country and jumping, it can perform beautifully by adding jumping to its Versatility Classes.
Photo: Rick Osteen

Susie Wright aboard the amazing Speed Racking Horse, FANCY PANTS, from E & S Stables in Southeast Kentucky.
Photo: Terry Young

23-year-old KMH/RMH mare DAPPLE POLLY, with owner and rider Shelly Spradlin, winning first place in the gait class at the Utah State Fair – Judge, Mary Donald.

A great deal of training and conditioning are needed to produce a winning *halter horse*. Different registries have different priorities, but all judges are looking for a well-behaved, well-constructed and well-conditioned animal as defined in their breed standard.

The *Paso Fino* may be exhibited in halter by two handlers, although one is also permitted. This competition is called "Bella Forma." The horse is allowed to move freely in gait (either Classic Fino or Paso Corto) at the end of two (or one) lead lines. Conformation and gait are both judged. The horse should demonstrate pride, style, elegance, and enthusiasm, along with good manners and ready response.

Lead-line competition is a joyful class to observe and an important one for the "lifeblood" of each registry. It is the youth who will preserve the customs and protocol of the horse show. In the lead-line class, the horse is led by an adult (who is in charge of the horse), and the youngster sits in the saddle and holds the reins. Customarily, all participants receive a blue ribbon (with those points not counting toward the high point award). Careful attention is paid to the child's attire. Lead-line contestants are not permitted on stallions.

↑ Photos, Top: Albert Vega, from Paso Finos de Vega Ranch, Midway, Colorado, on his stallion DOS TAMBIEN DE MOSSY OAKS. Albert is wearing the traditional show outfit, including the long, hair-on, traditional chaps, called Zamarros. Photo: Russell Pitts. Bottom: Stallion ROJO TEJAS practicing for Bella Forma competition ('99 West Coast Champion Bella Forma colt). Owner Carol Nelson says "Red"'s calm and gentle temperament matches his beautiful and statuesque appearance. He is a grandson of CAPUCHINO, and great-grandson of CASTELLANO.

⇨ Photos to the right, Top: Trail classes are designed to duplicate situations that might be found on the trail. Here we see a "simulated" bridge. Middle: Kristen Lincoln and DOLLY, in authentic Indian costume. Bottom: "Ladies in waiting," to two Tennessee Walking Horses.

Speed competitions are also becoming popular. Racking Horses and the Tennessee Walkers have included speed classes in their shows for years. With the introduction of EZD Falcon Rowdy bloodlines to Mountain Horses and the North American Single-Foot Horse Association, speed is becoming a desirable trait for many soft-gaited horses.

Watching a speed racker "fly" around the arena is perhaps the most heart-stopping event at any show. It is one class that keeps the audience out of their seats. For those seeing a speed class for the first time, the most frequent comment is one of open-mouthed disbelief. NASHA and the Largo Registry are two organizations that give careful attention to the development of speed in their breeding programs. As these registries grow, we are sure to see more speed in our all-breed shows.

Trail competition is also a part of many soft-gaited shows. A course is developed and posted. Usually there are two levels of judging - novice and advanced. In many cases, the course is the same; only the standards for completing it are different. In other shows, the two courses can be completely different.

Costume classes allow for imagination in traditional and comical outfits on both horse and rider. Either way, it's always entertaining for the audience.

Parades are certainly venues available for showing our horses. Holiday celebrations and community projects are fine reasons to spruce up our steeds and hit the streets.

Participation in shows and parades can definitely be an asset to you and your horse. Membership in local associations as well as a connection with your primary registry can enrich your soft-gaited horse ownership experience.

Owners usually register their horse at the time of purchase. At that time, they frequently join the Breed Association. These memberships have to be renewed each year. This is recommended. Your membership usually comes with a newsletter that will update you for show dates and locations. It will also keep you informed about any changes in the rules and regulations, allowing you a true involvement with your chosen breed.

"Parade Of Lights" a holiday celebration, featuring these wonderful Paso Fino horses, from left to right: Hank Kuiper on TIO VIVO DEL CARDO, Carol Kuiper on CARA CHISTOSA, Erin Holloway riding BRAVADO SKC, Linda Evans riding SANGRIA DE HOLANDES, (then there's a repeat of Carol, Hank, Linda, Erin) and the last riders to the right are Raymond Vega, riding DOS TAMBIEN DE MOSSY OAKS, and Vicki Vega riding DOMINO. Photos: Terry Wallace

Joe Leisek participating in the Rose Parade; held every New Year's Day in Pasadena, California. What a great presentation the Paso Finos made!

Vickie McQuinn, rider and trainer on Paso Fino mare, LA ELEGANCIA DE REMOLINO, where she won Best Of Show at the Northern Nevada Gaited Horse Club Show. Photo: Forrest Bliss

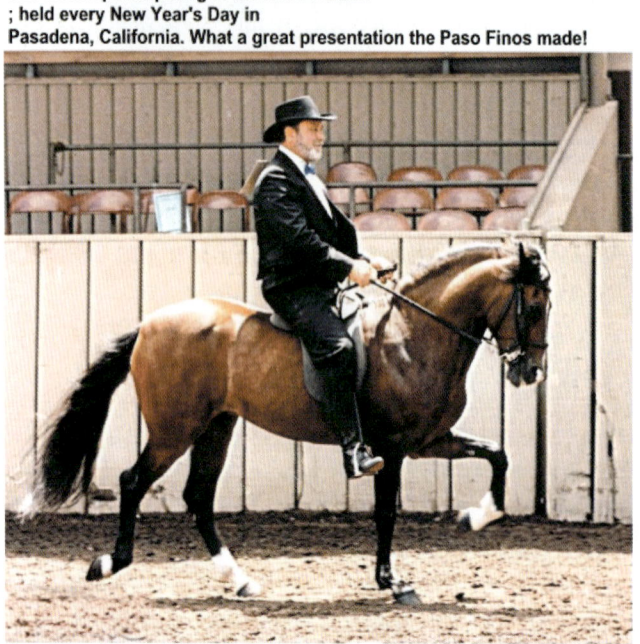

Paso Fino stallion CORSARIO with owner Joe Leisek, from Remolino Ranch, in Washoe Valley, Nevada in the saddle.

Rider and trainer, Johnny Lanier, aboard Paso Fino mare, ZORRITA DE COLOSO. Photo: Forrest Bliss

Keri Henson up on SKIPS BONNIE BLUE, competing in 2001, at the Versatility Arena Show and Celebration in Texas. "Ride 'em Cowboy!" Photo: Dawn Lindsay

NASHA

North American Single-Footing Horse Association

CHAPTER 34

P-DINK, NASHA mare
Owners: Ted and Elsie Neely

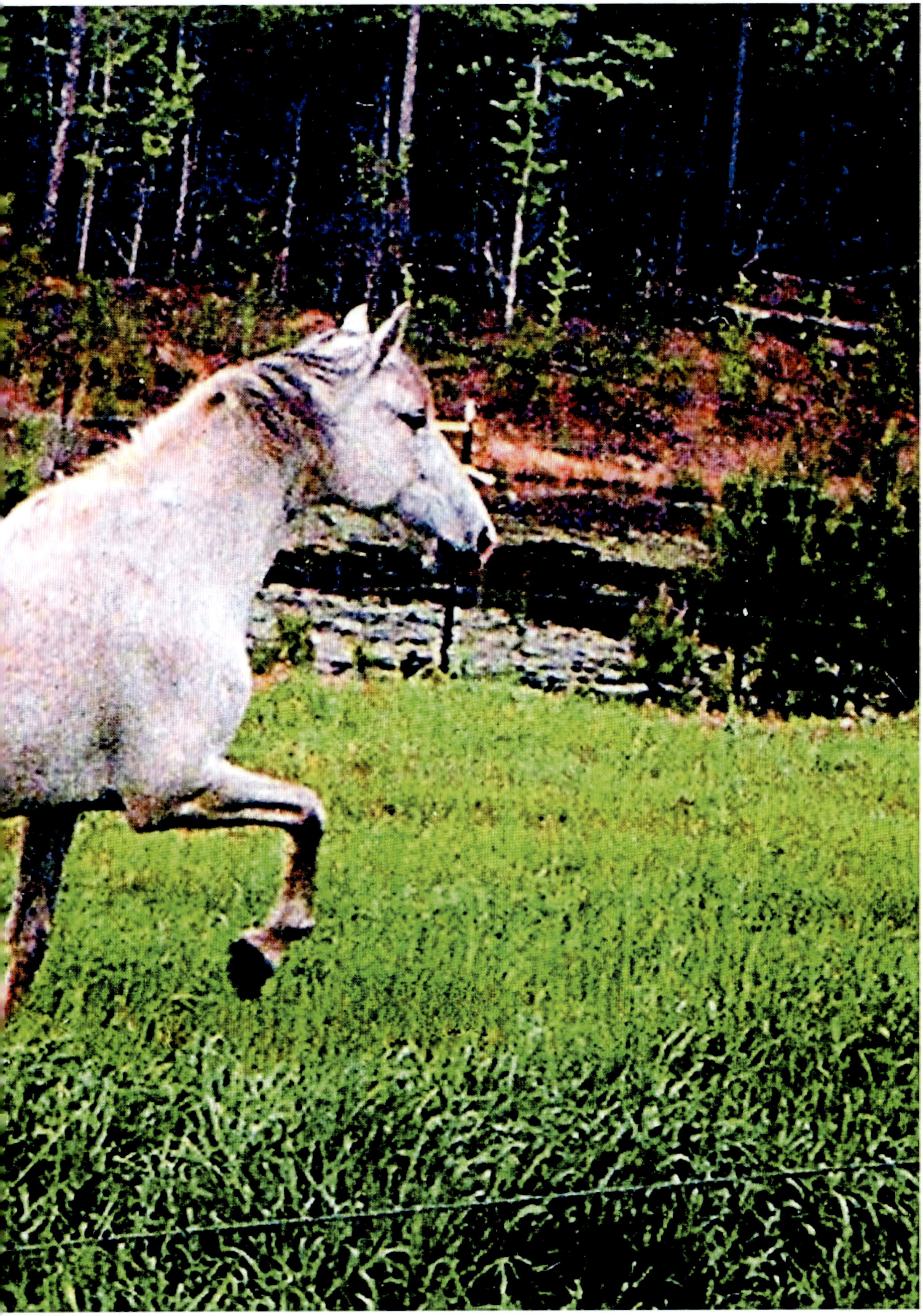

Photo: Courtesy Lavinia Kingery of Breez Krest Farm
Fincastle, Virginia

Chapter 34 North American Single-Footing Horse Association (NASHA)

What a unique concept! Develop a horse that will be comfortable, tractable and dependable as a pleasure-trail and working animal. Actually, it was discovering the North American Single-Footing Horse Association that inspired the writing of *The Fabulous Floating Horses*. Finding this registry heightened the awareness of the many different options we have in the world of soft-gaited horses.

Barbara Bouray was the force behind this important association. It is through her dedication and resolve that we have the North American Single-Footing Horse Association.

NASHA began as a performance-based registry. It honors the old-style traveling single-footing gait, with a goal of producing ranch horses, pleasure horses and competition trail and versatility horses, or what they call "good, usable saddle horses."

The goals for this association were set by avid trail riders and ranch owners who log thousands of miles a year on horses under various conditions. They held a big range of useful speeds and maximum smoothness at all speeds of gait as a major consideration. A tractable willingness to work and a tempera-

Steve Wright, from Clintwood, Virginia, riding his beautiful buckskin stallion, ROWDY RAWHIDE, son of EZD'S FALCON ROWDY.

CM NAVAJO as a three-year-old, sired by EASY FALCON and out of a Peruvian mare, SOBERANA DE LUNA CM.

EZD'S MACON REBEL as a two-year-old. Registered both RHBAA and NASHA, he can gait 21 to 22 m.p.h. for several miles without breaking gait. He can travel faster, but his owners and trainers, Ted and Elsie Neely don't want to push him for long distances at a greater speed.

Stallion, RASCAL'S LIL CHAMP.

ment that is neither hot and explosive nor lethargic and stubborn would be important.

The NASHA horse should display a general working conformation with a strong saddle back, good feet, and good legs. They honor athletic ability and endurance.

Ideally, their gait at the intermediate speed is 4-beat with a near-even timing. The range of actual speed begins at a relaxed trail speed of 7 - 9 m.p.h. to road gait of 12 - 15 m.p.h. and a racing speed of over 20 m.p.h. The horse will have one foot on the ground at all times – thus "single-footing." Speed is a characteristic of the gait, but speed at the loss of proper form is not a goal.

The rear legs should at least cap and often overstride the front feet as speed increases - in other words, the length of stride increases as speed increases. This requires a powerful rear end, and excessive rear hock action or a low skating action in the rear should be avoided.

An efficient working horse should have enough lift in the front end to clear uneven ground without stumbling. The front end needs to get out of the way for the driving hind end at speed.

The head nod that is characteristic of some gaited horses is not a part of the NASHA

ROWDY'S LIL RASCAL, with 82-year- Wiley Stanley, up.

Stallion, ROWDY'S LIL RASCAL

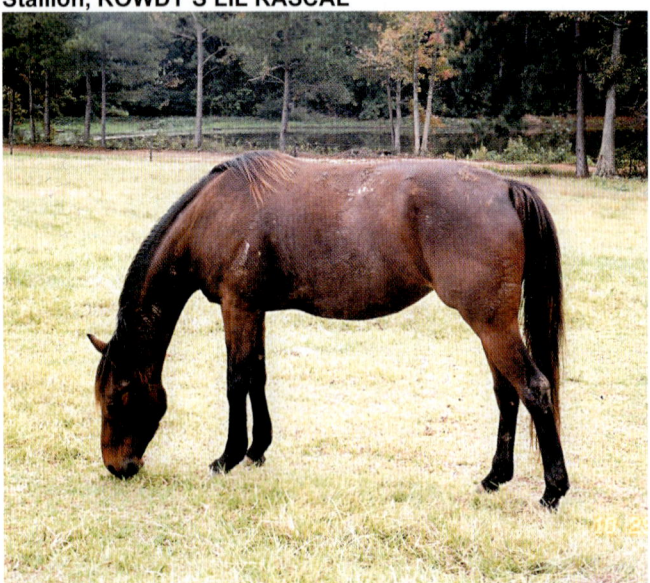

CANDY'S CADILLAC, a six-year-old NASHA horse owned by Ted and Elsie Neely at their 4-Beat Farm in Alabama.

GREY SPIRIT, both McCurdy Plantation and NASHA.

EZD'S CUPID ARROW, son of EZD'S FALCON ROWDY, and sire to EZD'S MACON REBEL.

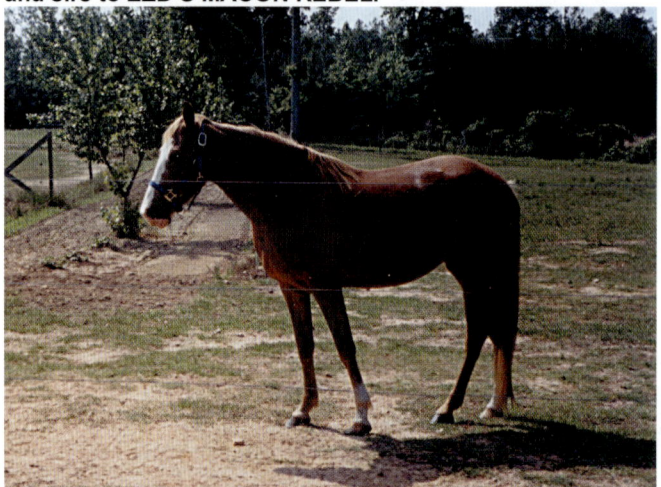

MANN'S MISS MERCEDES, a McCurdy Plantation mare, is also registered NASHA.

EZD'S LITTLE CAN DO, a half-sister to EZD'S MACON REBEL.

Two-year-old RASCAL'S FLASHY LADY with David Stanley, owner and rider.

What a color! This lovely is owned by High Places Ranch and Barbara Bouray, from Goodyear, Arizona.

Stallion, CM LEGACY, is a chocolate dun FALCON grandson, pictured at four years of age. Owners: Dale Downey and Mimi Busk-Downey from Crescent Moon Ranch, in Alberta, Canada.

MONEY FOR NOTHING, NASHA-registered and owned by High Places Ranch.

↓Below: ROWDY'S LIL RASCAL with owner David Stanley, up.

horse. In general, they travel with their head up. In fact they may stretch out, and at racing speed, they will actually lower their head.

Where most of the other registries give credit to horses that are well-trained and expertly shown, the root of the NASHA horse is to be a reliable mount that provides a consistent smooth ride and calm workman-like disposition.

Once the registry was established, finding such horses became the challenge. Locating the few remaining pockets of horses with a true single-footing gait was not easy. The horses were generally very tightly line-bred or inbred. (Outside blood was not necessary.)

Most often, horses were found in the rare pockets of true single-footers, with other gaited breeds where certain lines produced occasional single-footers rather than the appropriate gait for their breed. Frequently wild horse herds and even non-gaited breeds produce "crop-outs."

Initially, any horse with an intermediate 4-beat gait was eligible, but the owners had to

RASCAL'S LIL CHAMP, with Amanda Stanley and Bear, up.

➡ Photos to the right, Top: Stallion, **ROWDY'S LIL RASCAL**. Middle: Stallion, **ROWDY RAWHIDE'S MAJESTIC MYSTERY**. Bottom: **RASCAL'S FLASHY LADY**, a three-year-old mare with riders Brenda Stanley and daughter, Shelby, up.

be dedicated to producing single-footing horses from that point. By 1998, running walk, foxtrot, slick-pace or extremely long striding or short-tight striding were no longer eligible for registration in NASHA.

Although the registry has no intention of closing, it will be placing appropriate restrictions on new applications to insure overall quality and correctness of gait. Most importantly, there is no plan to see the horses become show-horses. A working horse is the premium. NASHA has a design in their awards program that includes a series of checks and balances to insure that these horses are rewarded for their working qualities.

First of all, they allow shoes that are no heavier than a trail shoe. This is to ensure seeing the genetics in a horse, not its training or manipulation. They provide more than 45 categories in their high-point program. Of these categories, only two are showring gait classes.[1]

NASHA is determined to produce and reward the ultimate gaited trail and ranch horse. Their ultimate and difficult-to-attain award of "Premier Champion" requires at least 100 points in at least one trail category. These

ROWDY RAWHIDE'S GO GO GIRL, a spotted buckskin, with owner and rider Jan Stanley, up.

⬅ Photos to the left, Top: The lovely head of EZD'S FALCON ROWDY, owned by John Demetris from Osborn Gap, Virginia. Middle: Stallion, ROWDY'S LIL RASCAL. Bottom: RASCAL'S FLASHY LADY, with riders Jeannie Cassidy O'Quinn and her daughter, up.

---

[1] The two gait classes are Road Gait and Park Gait.

RASCAL'S HIGH SKYWALKER, a three-year-old gelding owned by Wiley Stanley and ridden in this photo by Michael Stanley.

Milli Dold from Goddard, Kansas, riding single-footing horse GOLDRUSH.

⇨ Photos to the right, top: Stallion, ROWDY RAWHIDE'S ROCKET, with owner/rider Doug Stanley, up. Middle: (left) ROWDY RAWHIDE'S ROCKET (NASHA & RHBAA). Bottom: A three-month-old buckskin colt, ROCKET'S MOUNTAIN JEWEL, by ROWDY RAWHIDE'S ROCKET.

512

DUMAS and BANJO, three-year-old stallions, playing in the snow. Both are double registered with NASHA and as Paso Finos. JF Ranch, Northern Canada.

David Stanley riding stallion ROWDY'S LIL RASCAL with David's grandson Austin riding WHITE MAGIC.

⬅ Photos to the left, top: Participants in the "Ted Neely's Single-footer Trail Ride" in October 2002. They rode the trail for two days, enjoyed a BBQ one night, and a fishfry the other. Folks traveled to the festivities from Texas, Louisiana, Virginia, Kentucky, Tennessee, and Alabama. Middle: Dog and horse "hanging out" on Birch Knob, Alabama. The dog is Bear, the horse ROWDY RAWHIDE'S MAJESTIC MYSTERY. Bottom: CM AURORA at one month of age. She is registered NASHA, and sired by EASY FALCON, out of a purebred Peruvian mare MECHE DE ORO CM, from Crescent Moon Ranch in Alberta, Canada.

SOCIETY'S DIXIE, a registered Walking and Racking Horse is a ten-year-old, with her day-old foal by MACON REBEL.

David Stanley riding stallion ROWDY'S LIL RASCAL with David's brother Don Riding SUGAR.

categories include organized trail rides; competitive trail; endurance or organized harness rides.

A conformation is emerging that lends itself to the type of horse NASHA requires. It is on its way to becoming a performance-based "breed." They will officially be considered a breed once the horses selected for their specific purpose consistently reproduce to "type." After three generations of selective breeding producing consistent results, a breed begins to emerge that is distinct from other breeds already in existence.

The NASHA horse is beginning to resemble the "old time Morgan," with the exception of its neck, which is slightly more refined.

The use of the Narragansett-type gaiting horses (known for their speed), combined with heavy use of the Spanish-style gaited stock for improved lateral flexibility is producing a horse type not consistently found in other gaited breeds. As of January 1, 1997, all horses registered with NASHA must fall into one of three categories: 1) Horses with both their sire and dam registered with NASHA can be registered at any age. A video of the horse gaiting must be provided along with a registration application; 2) Horses with one parent

RASCAL'S FLASHY LADY as a six-month-old filly with Austin Stanley.

⇐ **RASCAL'S LIL DYNAMITE** as a 16-month-old colt with members of the Stanley family.

registered with NASHA can be registered. The horse must be at least six months of age. A video of the horse gaiting must be provided along with a registration application; 3) Horses six months or older of exceptional quality and a true single-footing gait may apply for registration with neither parent registered. However, this category will be reserved for exceptional-quality horses only. A video of the horse gaiting must be provided along with a registration application.

NASHA also has a registration category, "FB," for exceptional-quality stallions or mares no longer living who have had a positive and substantial impact on the bloodlines of horses registered with NASHA. The owner or family of the horse must apply for registration.

The NASHA Award program is divided into categories. Each category is of equal value. These categories are divided into five divisions. Each addresses specific uses - Organized Trail or Harness Rides; Parades; Demos; Drill Teams; Endurance or Competitive Trail Rides.

The purpose of the Performance Horse Division is to recognize horses that compete in disciplines requiring specialized or advanced training. This division demonstrates the versatility and suitability of NASHA horses for various types of work.

NASHA registered mare with her first foal, a colt.

Joseph Jr. on RASCAL'S LIL CHAMP, and Joseph Sr. on MAJESTIC MYSTERY at High Knob, Alabama.

ROWDY'S LIL RASCAL, at the Equine Affair in Columbus, Ohio, for NASHA, with David Stanley.

➡ **ROWDY RAWHIDE'S ROCKET with owner Doug Stanley.**

NATRC
North American Trail Ride Conference
CHAPTER 35

Chapter 35 The NATRC Experience: Competitive Trail Riding

The North American Trail Ride Conference (NATRC) is perhaps the most important competitive trail ride organization in the United States.

NATRC shouldn't be confused with endurance riding. A competitive trail ride is not a race, but rather a competition for riders covering a marked course in a given period of time. According to NATRC's literature, the pace for Open Division is about 4 - 6 mph, on a 25 - 35 mile trail for a one-day ride; for a two-day ride the mileage would be 50 - 60 miles; and for a three day ride, 80 - 90 miles.

The pace is accordingly less intensive for the Novice and Competitive Pleasure (CP) divisions. It's about 3.5 – 5 mph on a 20 - 25 mile trail for a one-day and 30 - 40 miles a day on a two day competition. Three-day rides are not permitted for the Novice and CP Divisions.

The horse is judged on condition, soundness and trail ability on natural trail obstacles. The rider is judged on presentation (not showmanship), grooming (no artificial enhancements, polished hooves, etc.), trail equitation (not prettiness of form), trail safety/courtesy, stabling, etc.

Through the promotion of the NATRC, it hopes to stimulate greater interest in the breeding and use of good horses possessed of stamina and hardiness, and qualified to make good mounts for trail use. They also hope to demonstrate the value of a type and soundness in the proper selection of horses for competitive riding and encourage proper methods of training and conditioning horses for competitive trail riding.

There is also an education ingredient in NATRC encouraging good horsemanship as related to trail riding, and the demonstration of the best methods of caring for horses during and after long rides without the aid of artificial methods or stimulants.

For the actual ride competition, there are two components for judging. First, the veterinary judging and second, the horsemanship judging.

For the veterinary judging, there are three divisions: 45% for soundness; 40% for condition; and 15% for trail ability and manners. A horse may be disqualified by the veterinarian judge if it requires medical treatment; if it is unruly and too difficult to examine; or if the horse fails to meet recovery criteria as set forth by the vet judge.

There are also three sections to the horsemanship judging. 50% goes to trail equitation; 30% to trail care (attention to horse's needs); and 20% for grooming, in-hand presentation, and attention to tack and equipment.

So, what's the procedure? Well, you have to get up early enough the morning of the ride to feed you and your horse and be tacked up and ready to go by start time. You will be judged from the very beginning on your horsemanship and manners of you and your horse.

Riders are usually timed out at 30 second to one-minute intervals. After you leave the start, riders travel at their own pace during the day. You must follow trails marked with colored ribbons as well as use the map which shows turns, elevations, and mileage reference points along the route.

The horses are observed several times during the day, often at surprise points in the trail. Some judges will hide along the trail to observe the rider and horse along difficult stretches like a hill or water crossings. Natural obstacles are utilized, like bridge crossing, trees, bushes and even tethered animals such as lamas.

The riders must be careful to time themselves throughout the ride. Pacing is extremely important. Again, this is not a race.

The rewards are numerous. There are, of course, the prizes awarded to the competitors; but beyond that, are the rewards experienced by the horse and rider by bonding throughout the whole experience. Once you have lived through a competitive trail ride together, the joys of knowing and understanding your horse will amaze you.

Our gaited horses are beautifully suited to the challenges of competitive trail riding. The Missouri Fox Trotter has been particularly successful on a national level. But this is an activity, open to all who wish to participate in it.

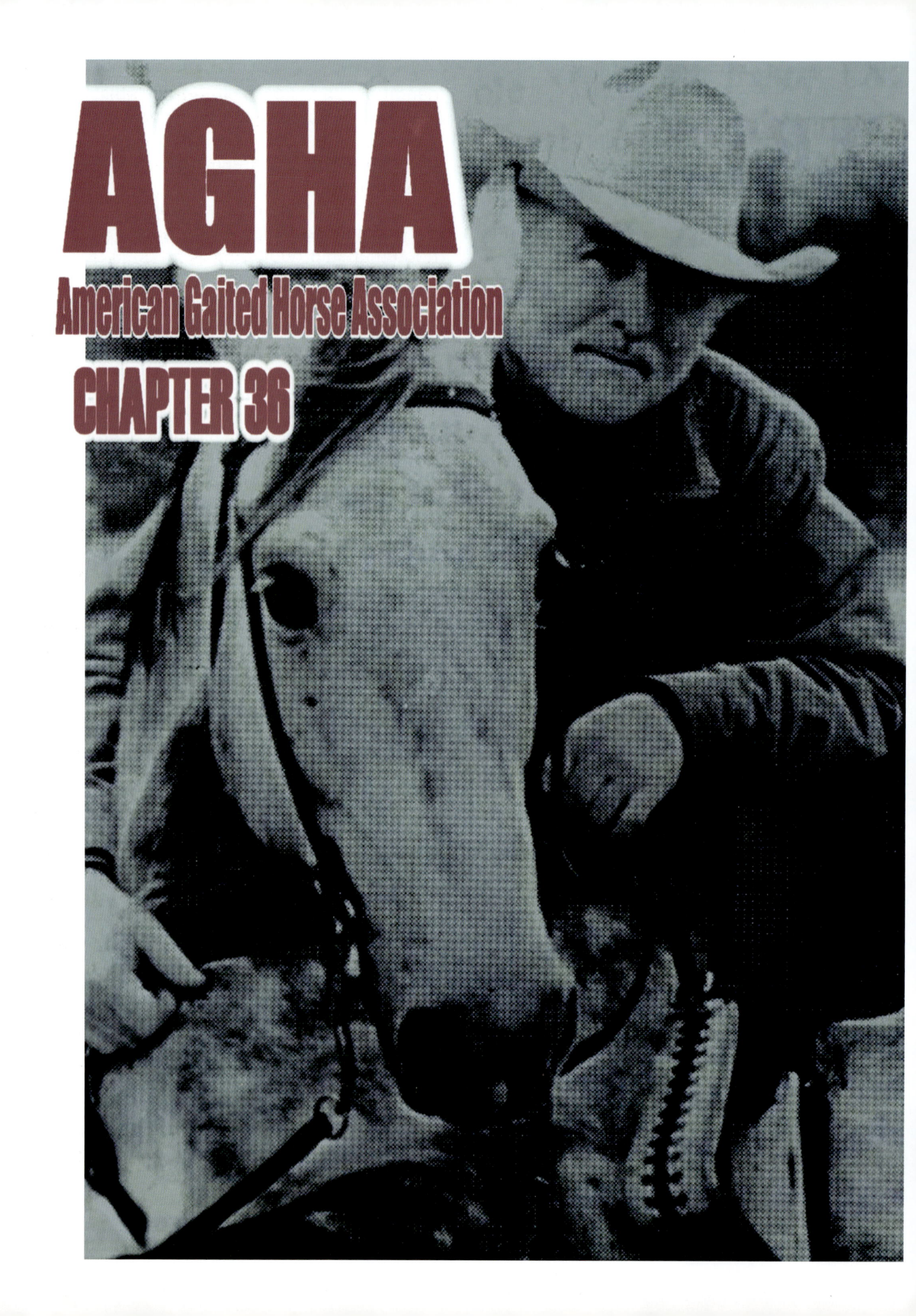

AGHA
American Gaited Horse Association
CHAPTER 36

"America's Other Horse"

Chapter 36 The American Gaited Horse Association (AGHA)

The American Gaited Horse Association is the brainchild of horseman Bob Bounds. Bob is a man of purpose and (as he describes it) "a mission." That mission is the promotion of natural, lite-shod gaited horses.

The AGHA is a national organization standardizing show regulations and judging procedures for natural, lite-shod Walking, Racking, Saddle and Fox Trotting horses. It's an organization with whom all existing pleasure horse organizations can be proud to affiliate, yet retain their local identities.

AGHA has a judging system where every entry is scored in every maneuver, and a scorecard posted for everyone to view following each class, making the judge instantly accountable. It's an important goal of the association to create a nationwide pool of judges, all of whom would be judging by the same regulations and using the same judging procedures.

The show process creates a National Point System where points become a permanent record, remaining with the horse and enhancing its value. It is a point system that automatically moves horses up in class level, making room for new entries.

AGHA shows are radically different from other horse show competitions. Horses show at different levels, so a novice horse has as good a chance to win a class as a long-time veteran, because each competes against animals on their own level of expertise.

When a horse is first shown in an AGHA-sanctioned show, the owner has the option of entering the horse as a Novice, Intermediate, or Class A horse. Once a horse has been entered at a certain level, it can never be shown below that level, but can be shown one level above. The move up the ladder is based on the points the horse accumulates during its showing career.

The point system is: Novice=less than 20 points, Intermediate=less than 100 points, Class A=less than 300 points, and Class AAA= 600 points or more.

As this show network matures, they are adding new classes other than walk, rack and canter, such as reining, obstacles, team penning, working cow horse, hunter-jumper, and more.

The AGHA is a revolutionary organization devoted to recognizing and registering qualified individuals on the basis of gait alone, regardless of color or whatever registration papers a horse carries, or whether he carries any papers at all. All that's important is that if its gait so qualifies it, it can register that and compete for lifetime cumulative points in AGHA shows.

In designing classes for AGHA shows, Bounds has drawn from his background of needing good-minded, smooth riding, well-broke horses that are reliable mounts, whether in the showring, working cattle on a ranch, or trail riding cross-country. Smooth gaits, manners, and training are the backbone of the AGHA judging criteria, and horses that fit this mold will always have widespread appeal to people of all vocations and interests.

The AGHA welcomes all natural, lite-shod gaited horse breeds to compete in recognized shows. The AGHA has also designed a show system that could act as a blueprint to other show organizations, gaited or not, for a fair and competitive show venue.

As support for his show system, Bob Bounds conducts gait seminars that can act as crash courses in identifying gait and analyzing the strengths and correctness of the soft-gaited horse.

Bob has an excellent way of sharing his approach to the psychology of horsemanship and the mechanics of the special gaits of the gaited horse.

GAITED HORSES ON THE NET

CHAPTER 37

Chapter 37   Gaited Horses On The Net

When *The Fabulous Floating Horses* was conceived, there was no such thing as an active Internet. It was most certainly no resource for beginning research. As of the 21st century, the Internet is home to an abundance of gaited-horse information and interchange of ideas. Some sites are designed to be strictly web addresses, while others represent associations and individual ranches and farms. Two such web addresses are the Gaited Horse International, and the Gaited Horse Registry of America.

GAITED HORSE INTERNATIONAL ASSOCIATION
A Non-Profit Organization Dedicated to Promoting Gaited Horses On An International Level

The Gaited Horse International Association is a nonprofit association dedicated to promoting the training, and well-being of all breeds of gaited horses, worldwide. They are asking for the involvement of the public to help them promote the gaited horse breeds.

They offer a membership that includes a quarterly newsletter and a listing in their Website Breeders Directory.

On their web page, you will find a navigation bar that will take you to various places on their site such as the classified page, calendar of events page and a bookstore and a gift shop.

A major feature of this Association is the inclusion of specific gaited-horse information headings for gaited breeds. On these breed pages, they are providing links to the Breed Associations themselves.
http://www.gaitedhorse.com

GAITED HORSE REGISGRY OF AMERICA

With the Gaited Horse Registry of America, you can actually register your gaited horse. It is a nonprofit organization committed to maintaining permanent records and encouragment for activities which aid, promote, and foster the preservation and betterment of purebred Gaited Horses nationwide.

With their goals of education as a guide, their website offers a discussion forum, a bulletin board and a bookshop. They are also soliciting pictures, stories, and information about gaited horses from their members and industry experts.
http://www.gaitedhorseregistry.com

Another contributor to the net is the web magazine, Gaited Horses.Net. It is an interactive forum for the exchange of ideas and discussion of training methods for gaited horses. They have covered such topics as Mounting Aids, Bending at the Poll, Collection and the Bit, and Finding a Suitable Saddle. Information and training guidelines are provided by such guest experts as Liz Graves, Lee Ziegler and Beverly Whittington.

Attention is being given to gaited horse folks on a local level as well as nationwide. They provide an opportunity to connect with people who are close enough to join on a trail-ride.

Another helpful feature is the Quiz Central, where they have several new questions added in the General Horse Information – a more difficult version of the Regular General Horse Quiz. A person can submit a multiple-choice question, along with an illustration (if needed), and it will be added to the quizzes.
http://www.GaitedHorses.net

THE GAITED HORSE
The One Magazine For All Gaited Horses

The popular *The Gaited Horse* is a glossy hi-tech quarterly magazine that has a presence on the net. It offers information about the publication, such as highlights, breed profile, and information "about the cover." You can learn how to subscribe, and how to advertise. Back issues of the magazine are also available and they solicit reader suggestions. A "Web Feature" is provided to all who find their page. www.thegaitedhorse.com

With tremendous "presence" being felt "out there" on the World Wide Web, the future of the gaited breeds is not only enhanced, but assured. With all the soft-gaiteds under one heading, they are certainly a constituency to be reckoned with!

UNITED MOUNTAIN HORSE

CHAPTER 38

Rocky Mountain Horse
ROCKIN' DOBBIN

Kentucky Mountain Horse
JOE BANJO

Mountain Pleasure Horse
SHORT'S GOLD MINE

Kentucky Natural Gaited Horse
F & R'S RED FLAME

Chapter 38 The United Mountain Horse Association (UMH)

The UMH recognizes that most Mountain Horse owners are not interested in showing. After all, the ultimate purpose of these soft-gaited gems is to be on the pleasure trail. But with-out strong, reputable and professional show circuits in existence, no breed maintains its popularity and growth. In the show venue, the public is made aware of different breeds. In the show venue, there is an apparent goal for the breeders and trainers of any breed.

In the fall of 2000, a group of Mountain Horse breeders and exhibitors formed a non-profit Kentucky corporation dedicated to promotion and exhibition of Rocky Mountain, Kentucky Mountain, and Mountain Pleasure horses.

Several important issues were addressed in the development of this Association, that are directed at the longevity and health of the Association itself. First of all, it was decided to hire a horse-industry professional who does not own or show Mountain Horses to handle daily operations as an executive director. They also made provisions for a specialized independent Hearing Board - separate from the Board of Directors, members, or the Executive Director - to handle disciplinary matters and complaints.

Because each of the participating Registries has different goals and even different breed standards, it was decided to provide each "style" of horse with an opportunity to compete with like horses. They chose to provide classes for the full range of action styles naturally found in Mountain Horses, so that these styles would not be lost to the breeds due to political fashion or judging biases. To this end, there are three primary categories of classes: Classic, Trail, and Park.

Prior to the formation of UMH, the preference of most judges in many breed-sanctioned shows, was to reward only the higher-action, Park-style horses when horses with different styles of action appeared in the same class. Moderate-action and trail-style horses were losing the opportunity to successfully compete. There was a concern that this would lead to horses with lower action - always desired by the pleasure horse buying public - no longer being bred or promoted by the major breeders.

In other circuits, only the trail-type horses were seen as acceptable. This did not allow for horses in the higher-action ranges to compete and was also perceived as having a depressant effect on show participation.

So with the inauguration of the UMH, there was a place for all horses to exhibit a full range of naturally occurring styles of going. With the UMH, each style of going, and from any of the registries, has a place to show on their own merits, with equal prestige.

From the UMH's inception, the establishment of separate classes for Park Pleasure, Classic Pleasure and Trail Pleasure was an unquestioned success. Suddenly, new names and faces were appearing as winners.

A fundamental factor in the design of the UMH has been the attention given to the training of judges. Two licensing bodies - the Independent Judges Association and the National Walking Horse Association - have included a complete UMH training program in their clinics for judges. Mountain Horse judging will be offered not only to Mountain Horse specifically, but to judges of different breeds as well. It is important that show managers can have a wide choice of qualified, licensed and independent judges from which to choose.

It is important to note UMH has no desire to expand into a registry, or to compete with existing registries in any manner. It is an association that promotes Mountain Horse ownership and participation in the established Mountain Horse registries. The ultimate objective is to foster promotion and popularity of the Mountain Horse.

In its inaugural year, the UMH drafted and completed its bylaws, published a complete rule book and a training and judging video tape, established a website with updated show schedules and results, and launched a monthly news magazine, the *Mountain Times*.

The crowning aspect of this association is the annual UMH-KMSHA World Championship Show, held each year in late summer, when horses from all the Mountain Horse Registries can compete on a level playing field, according to the talents of the individual horse.

HOLLYWOOD HORSES

CHAPTER 39

Chapter 39   HOLLYWOOD HORSES

Not only have horses driven civilization as we know it today, they have figured prominently in our entertainment. Several talented gaiteds have joined their human partners on film. Not only have many ranglers chosen soft-gaited horses as their anonymous mounts, but stars themselves have shared the limelight with a soft-gaited equine performer.

Here we will look at only a few of the teams we have all enjoyed. It would take an entire volume to do justice to the stories attached to these horses and their famous riders.

Glenn Randall was an important trainer in Hollywood. Not only did he train Champion, Trigger and the Black Stallion, he trained the chicken used in the series "Roots." His experience with celebrity soft-gaited horses led to his involvement with soft-gaited horses throughout the latter part of his career. Glenn worked with numerous pleasure and show soft-gaited horses, well into his eighties.

Gene Autry and soft-gaited CHAMPION, co-starred in more than a hundred films. Photo: Autry Museum of Western Heritage

THUNDER is a big, handsome 16:3 black Tennessee Walking stallion. He co-starred with Mel Gibson in the 1993 feature film, "The Man Without A Face." His full name is GO BOY'S THUNDER, and he carries on the tradition of gentle disposition, incredible eyes and outstanding conformation. He performs a natural running walk and has the ability to excel at any event. Owner: Elizabeth Boyd

⇦ Roy Rogers and Trigger. Photo: The Roy Rogers and Dale Evans Museum

Tom Berringer shared the screen in "Rustlers' Rhapsody" with Racking Horse WILDFIRE. The horse is a real scene-stealer, and the film is a hoot. Photo: Courtesy Paramount Picture Studios.

MOMS AND BABIES

CHAPTER 40

Spotted Saddle Horse
Photo: Sue Sigler

Missouri Fox Trotter
Photo: Dawn Lindsay

Kentucky Mountain Saddle Horse
Photo: Kristen Lincoln

Missouri Fox Trotter
Photo: Dawn Lindsay

Kentucky Mountain Saddle Horse
Photo: Ann Thompson

Tennessee Walking Horse
Photo: Ann Thompson

Missouri Fox Trotter
Photo: Dawn Lindsay

Fox Trotter

Mountain Horse

Mountain Horse

Single-Footing Horse

Mountain Horse

Mountain Horse

Spotted Fox Trotter

Mountain Horse

Mountain Horse

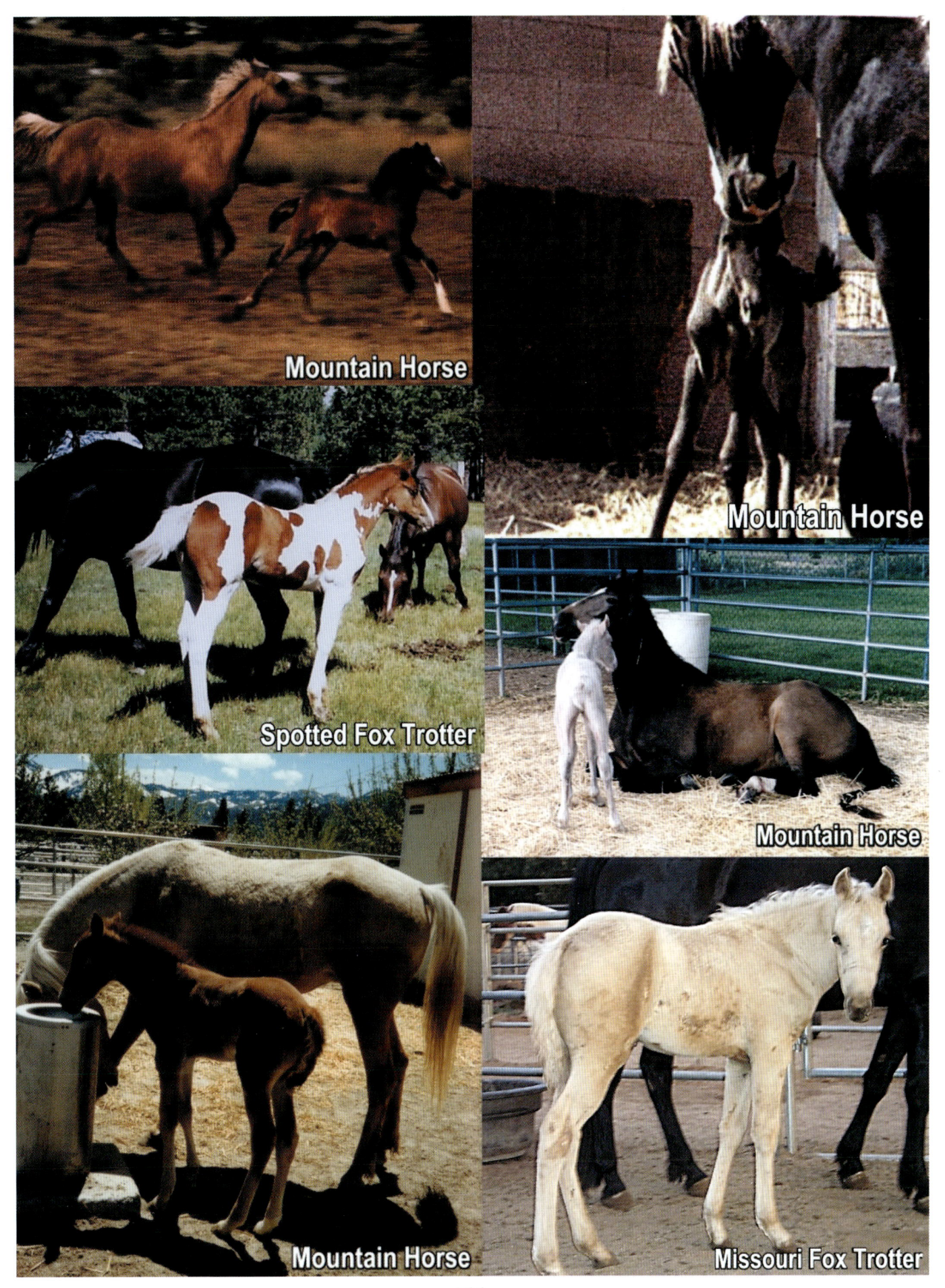

Missouri Fox Trotter

529

Tennessee Walking Horse

Paso Largo Horse

Mountain Horse

Mountain Horse

Single-Footing Horse

Missouri Fox Trotter

Mountain Horse

Fox Trotter
Photo: Dawn Lindsay

Spotted Fox Trotter
Photo: Brenda Foley

Peruvian Paso
Photo: Linda Richardson

Mountain Horse
Photo: Desirai Schild

Kentucky Mountain Horses

Mountain Horse

Spotted Fox Trotter
Photo: Dawn Lindsay

Tennessee Walking Horses

Fox Trotter Horses

Spotted Saddle Horses

Kentucky Mountain Saddle Horse

Kentucky Mountain Saddle Horse

Peruvian Pasos

Missouri Fox Trotter

Mountain Horse and Peruvian Paso

Missouri Fox Trotter

Rocky Mountain Horse

Missouri Fox Trotter colt
Photo: Dawn Lindsay

BREED CHARACTERISTICS

BREED	SIZE	GAIT	COLOR	TRAIT
MOUNTAIN PLEASURE HORSE	14:2 & up	mountain walk, mountain gait and favorite gait	any color, limited white	"Boy Scout" breed
KENTUCKY MOUNTAIN SADDLE HORSE	11:00 & up	trail walk, show walk, slow gait	any color, limited white	people-oriented
ROCKY MOUNTAIN HORSE	14:2 – 16	trail walk, show walk, pleasure gait	any color, limited white	gentle disposition
KENTUCKY NATURAL GAITED	14:2 & up	saddle gaits	all colors including pinto	comfortable
TENNESSEE WALKING HORSE	14:3 – 16	flat walk, running walk, canter, hand gallop	any color, including pinto	elegance/kindness
MISSOURI FOX TROTTER	14 – 16	flat walk, fox trot, canter	any color, including pinto	sensible and kind
SPOTTED SADDLE HORSE	no limits	4-beat, walk, canter	pinto	versatility
PASO FINO	14 -15	walk, fino, corto, largo, canter	any color, including pinto	luxurious comfort
PERUVIAN PASO	14:1 – 15:2	walk, paso llano, sobreandando	solid colors no pinto	"pisos" (gait)
LARGO	14 – 16	single-foot	all equine colors	true brio
McCURDY PLANTATION	14:2 - 15:2	McCurdy lick, saddle gait, running walk, canter, walk	grey factor	disposition, strength, stamina
MANGALARGA MARCHADOR	14:2 – 16:2	walk, marcha, canter	all colors plus burgundy	disposition, versatility & endurance
AMERICAN BASHKIR CURLY	14:2 – 15:3	running walk, fox trot, canter	all colors – pinto & appaloosa	stamina & good nature
ICELANDIC	12:3 – 14:3	walk, trot, tolt, pace, gallop	all colors and markings	multi-talented
TIGER HORSE	15 average	walk, 4-beat, canter	Lp characteristic (no pinto or grey)	unique in appearance sound of gait
WALKALOOSA	13 – 17	natural single-foot	appaloosa	pleasure trail mount
GAITED MORGAN	14:1 – 15:2	all	bay, black or brown no spots or greys	versatility
SPANISH MUSTANG	13:2 – 15	amble, running walk, single-foot	most colors	stamina & intelligence
FLORIDA CRACKER	13 - 15:2	walk, trot, single-foot, canter	any color – mostly solids & greys	strength, herding instinct endurance/quickness
SADDLEBRED	15 - 16	5-gaited	most colors – all fine & silky	versatility
SPANISH GAITED PONY	11 – 13	any 4-beat	mostly bay, some chestnuts	gentle endurance
OSBORN GAP	14:1	single-foot, rack	dun	speed

ASSOCIATIONS AND REGISTRIES

AMERICAN ASSOCIATION OF OWNERS AND BREEDERS OF PERUVIAN PASO HORSES
P.O. Box 476
Wilton, California 95693
(916) 687-6232
FAX: (916) 687-6691
registrar@aaobpph.org
www.aaobpph.org

AMERICAN BASHKIR CURLY HORSE REGISTRY
P.O. Box 246
Ely, Nevada 89301-0246
(775) 289-4999
FAX: (775) 289-8579
Secretary@abcregistry.org
http://www.abcregistry.org

AMERICAN BUCKSKIN REGISTRY
P.O. Box 3850
Redding, California 96049

AMERICAN GAITED HORSE ASSOCIATION
1614 Canadian Avenue
Plano, Texas 75023
(972) 527-6911
FAX: (972) 527-9029

AMERICAN HORSE PROTECTION ASSOCIATION
P.O. Box 170305
Milwaukee, Wisconsin 53217-9962
Or:
1000 29th Street, NW Suite Y-100
Washington, DC 20007
(202-965-0500

AMERICAN MUSTANG ASSOCIATION
P.O. Box 338
Yucaipa, California 92399

AMERICAN SADDLEBRED ASSOCIATION
4093 Iron Works Parkway
Lexington, Kentucky 40511
(859) 259-2742
FAX: (859) 259-1628
Saddlebred@asha.net
www.saddlebred.com

AMERICAN SPOTTED HORSE ASSOCIATION
P.O. Box 36
Manchester, Tennessee 37349-0036
J@cafes.net

FLORIDA CRACKER HORSE ASSOCIATION, INC.
P.O. Box 186
Newberry, Florida 32669
(352) 472-2228
http://www.imh.org/imh/bw/flcrack.html#toc

GAITED HORSE INTERNATIONAL ASSOCIATION
507 North Sullivan Road Suite A-7
Veradale, Washington 99037-8531
(509) 928-8389
FAX: (509) 927-2012
info@gaitedhorse.com
www.gaitedhorse.com

GAITED HORSE REGISTRY OF AMERICA
(509) 232-2698
FAX: (509) 928-2392
info@GaitedHorseRegistry.com
www,gaitedhorseregistry.com

INTERNATIONAL CURLY HORSE ORGANIZATION
Member Support Office
2690 Carpenter Road
Jamestown, Ohio 45335
(937) 453-9829
office@curlyhorses.org
www.curlyhorses.org

INTERNATIONAL MORAB BREEDERS' ASSOCIATION, INC.
RR 3 Box 235
Ava, Missouri 65608-9553
IMR@morab.com
http://www.morab.com

INTERNATIONAL PLEASURE WALKING HORSE REGISTRY, Inc.
P.O. Box 141
Bartlett, Ohio 45713
(866) 479-4746
FAX: (815) 461 6429
IPWHA@ipwhr.org
www.ipwhr.org

KENTUCKY HORSE PARK
4089 Iron Works Parkway
Lexington, Kentucky 40511
(800) 678-8813
(859) 233-4303
info@kyhorsepark.com
www.kyhorsepark.com

KENTUCKY MOUNTAIN SADDLE HORSE ASSOCIATION
P.O. Box 505
Irvine, Kentucky 40336
(606) 723-6551
kmsha@kih.net
www.KMSHA.COM

KENTUCKY NATURAL GAITED HORSE ASSOC.
5154 Hwy 364
West Liberty, Kentucky 41472
(606) 743-7173
Francis@meginc.com

THE LARGO HORSE ASSOCIATION
Pisadas de Oro Stables
Colorado City, Arizona 86021
(928) 875-8117

MANGALARGA MARCHADOR HORSE ASSOCIATION OF AMERICA
P.O. Box 770955
Ocala, Florida 34477
1-866-MARCHADOR
http://www.marchadorhorses.com

MCCURDY PLANTATION HORSE REGISTRY AND ASSOCIATION
c/o Edward S. McCurdy Jr.
1020 Houston Road
Selma, Alabama 37601
(334) 872-5412
Publicity Director:
Colleen J. Cates
(903) 677-4858
mccurdylady@yahoo.com
http://www.mccurdyhorses.com

MISSOURI FOX TROTTING HORSE BREED ASSOCIATION
P.O. Box 1027
Ava Missouri 65608
(417) 683-6144
foxtrot@goinmissouri.org
www.mfthba.com

MONTANA TRAVLER HORSE ASSOCIATION
PMB 442 1106 West Park
Livingston, Montana 59047
(406) 222-8015
(406) 222-5591 FAX
http://www.montanatravler.com

MORGAN SINGLE-FOOTING HORSE ASSOCIATION
2640 S. Co Road 3E
Loveland, Colorado 80537
(970) 669-3822
msfha@msfha.com
www.msfha.com

MOUNTAIN HORSE MUSEUM
Exit 33 – Mountain Parkway (45 minutes from Lexington)
691 Natural Bridge Road
Slade, Kentucky 40301
(606) 663-0928

MOUNTAIN PLEASURE HORSE ASSOCIATION
P.O. Box 79
Wellington, Kentucky 40387
(606) 663-0036
mpha@mtn-pleasure-horse.org
www.mtn-pleasure-horse.org

NATIONAL WALKING HORSE ASSOCIATION
P.O. Box 28
Petersburg, Tennessee 37144
(931) 659-9729
FAX: (931-659-6286

NATIONAL SPOTTED SADDLE HORSE ASSOCIATION, INC.
P.O. Box 898
Murfreesboro, Tennessee 37133-0898
(615) 890-2864

NORTH AMERICA SINGLE-FOOTING HORSE ASSOCIATION
2995 Clark Valley Road
Los Osos, California 93402
(805) 528-7308

NORTH AMERICAN TRAIL RIDE CONFERENCE
P.O. Box 224
Sedalia, Colorado 80135
(303) 688-1677
FAX: (303) 688-3022
natrc@natrc.org
www.Natrc.org

NORTH AMERICAN WALKER
P.O. Box 365
Frederick, Pennsylvania 19435

PART WALKING HORSE REGISTRY
HC 84 Box 3087
Forsyth, Montana 59327
(406) 356-2854
www.hiplainswalkers.com

PASO FINO HORSE ASSOCIATION, INC.
101 North Collins Street
Plant City, Florida 33566-3311
(813) 719-7777
FAX: (813) 719-7822
www.pfha.org

PERUVIAN PASO HORSE REGISTRY OF NORTH AMERICA
3077 Wiljan Court Ste, #A
Santa Rosa, California 95407-5764
(707) 579-4394
FAX: (707) 579-1038
info@pphrna.org
www.pphrna.org

RACKING HORSE BREEDERS' ASSOCIATION OF AMERICA
67 Horse Center Road
Decatur, Alabama 35605
(256) 353-7225
FAX: (256) 353-7266
RHBAA67horse@aol.com
http://www.rackinghorse.com

ROCKY MOUNTAIN HORSE ASSOCIATION
P.O. Box 129
Mt. Olivet, Kentucky 41064
(606) 724-2354
information@rmhorse.com
www.rmhorse.com

SORRAIA HORSE CONTACT & INFORMATION
Hardy Oelke
Othmaringhausen
58553 Halver
Germany
oehorse@aol.com
www.sorraia.org

SORRAIA MUSTANG STUDBOOK
Othmaringhausen
58553 Halver
Germany
oehorse@aol.com

SOUTHWEST SPANISH MUSTANG ASSOCIATION
P.O. Box 148
Finley, Oklahoma 74543
Http://www.Spanishmustangs.com

SPANISH BARB FOUNDATION
Route 1 Box 149
Hot Springs, South Dakota 57747

SPANISH GAITED PONIES
P.O. Box 270
Creston, California 93432
(805) 237-0760

SPANISH MUSTANG REGISTRY INC.
c/o Jane Greenwood
11790 Halstad Avenue
Lonsdale, Minnesota 55046-4246
http://www.spanishmustang.org
zncwboys@means.net

SPOTTED MOUNTAIN HORSE REGISTRY
P.O. Box 505
Irvine, Kentucky 40336
(606) 723-6551

SPOTTED SADDLE HORSE BREEDERS' AND EXHIBITORS' ASSOCIATION
PO Box 1046
Shelbyville, Tennessee 37162
(931) 684-7496
FAX: (931) 684-7215
www.sshbea.org
sshbea@cafes.net

SULPHUR HORSE REGISTRY
WWW.SULPHURS.COM

TENNESSEE WALKING HORSE BREEDERS' & EXHIBITORS' ASSOCIATION
P.O. Box 286
250 North Ellington Parkway
Lewisburg, Tennessee 37091-0286
(931) 359-1574
twhbea@twhbea.com
www.twhbea.com

THE TENNUVIAN HORSE REGISTRY
Paula Bonser, Founder
18443 Moorhaven Drive
Springhill, Florida 34610
http://www.rogueperuvianhorses.com

THE TIGER HORSE ASSOCIATION, INC.
1604 Fescue Circle
Huddleston, Virginia 24104
(540) 297-2276
tigerhorseassoc@worldnet.att.net
http://www.tigerhorses.org

TIGER HORSE REGISTRY
39 Crazy Rabbit Road
Santa Fe, New Mexico 87508
(505) 438-2827
FAX: (505) 438-2828
tigrehorse@aol.com
www.tigrehorse.com

UNITED MOUNTAIN HORSE
P.O. Box 11
Unionville, Tennessee 37180
(913)294-2253
umhorse@aol.com
www.unitedmountainhorse.org

UNITED STATES ICELANDIC HORSE CONGRESS
38 Park Street
Montclair, New Jersey 07042
icecong@aol.com
www.icelandics.org

WALKALOOSA HORSE ASSOCIATION
2995 Clark Valley Road
Los Osos, California 93402
(805) 528-7308
FAX: (805) 528-3128
Pmeyer@walkaloosaregistry.com

BREEDER & TRAINER DIRECTORY

Every effort will be made to update changes in directory listings on the website:
www.thefabulousfloatinghorses.com

AMERICAN CURLY

CIRCLE B STABLES
American Curly
Johnny Brooks
702 CR 3450
Mountain View, Missouri 65548
(417) 934 - 6122
WALKER'S PRINCE T

COLORADO CURLIES
American Curly
Julie Hansen
39364 Road G
Mancos, Colorado 81328
(970) 533-9021
jlhnsn@fone.net

CONROY'S CURLY HORSES
American Curly
Tom and Denise L. Conroy
5643 E. M-134
Cedarville, Michigan 49719
(906) 484-3621
WILLOW CREEK CALL ME MR.
Denise@Conroyscurlies.com
http://ConroysCurlies.com

CURLY COUNTRY
American Curly
Rex and Diane Mitchell
34542 Juniper Valley Road
Acton, California 93510-1007
(661) 269-2282
BB COPPER SUN
curlyco@worldnet.att.net

DESERTER CREEK CURLIES
American Curly
Jim Howard and
Wendy Sauers Smith
6046 Deserter Creek Road
Whitesville, Kentucky 42378
(502) 275-9347 (evenings please)
WALKER'S CURLY T
CurlyHorse@aol.com
bashcurl@aol.com
http://www.dccurlies.com

FROSTFIRE CURLIES
North American Curly Horse/ICHO
Sharon Williams
7020 Edgerton Road
Williamsburg, Indiana 47393
(765) 847-2684
J.SILVER HEELS
shawill@infocom.com

MEANWHILE...BACK AT THE RANCH
American Curly
Cheryl Reed
789 Old Samish Road
Bellingham, Washington 98226
(360) 733-0299
WELCOME TO HOUSTON (palomino)
curlygirls@hotmail.com

RED EARTH CURLY HORSES
Bashkir Curly
Roger & Jo Ann Hatlestad
P.O, Box 612
Alva, Oklahoma 73717
STRIKES HIS ENEMY
FOX FARMS CLASSY
NTS VISION QUEST
hatlestadcurly@yahoo.com

RICHARDSON'S CURLIES
North American Curly Horse
Jacqueline Richardson
1259 310th Ave
Woodburn, Iowa 50275
(515) 342-6180
SIR PATRICK
KRESKIN
Curlhors@pionet.net

REDWIND HORSE FARM
Sport Horse Curlies
Martha Diaz
6345 Charolais Drive
El Paso, Texas 79938
(915) 857-2374
redwindfarm@hotmail.com
http://www.redwindfarm.com

AMERICAN SADDLEBRED

BURESH FARMS
Golden American Saddlebred Horses
Joe and Joyce Buresh
4237 30th Avenue
Oxford Junction, Iowa 52323
(563) 826-2981
(563) 826-3043 FAX
ANACACHO'S GOLDEN CADILLAC
buresh@netins.net
http://www.bureshfarm.com

FAR FIELD FARM
American Saddlebred Horses
Barbara Molland
5000 Carroll Road
Petaluma, California 94952
(707) 876-1885
(707) 876-3412 FAX
bmolland@farfieldfarm.com
www.farfieldfarm.com

SCHERMARRA FARM
American Saddlebred
Deborah and Joseph Scherder
2312 West State Street
New Castle, Pennsylvania 16101
(724) 654-9546
MI LIBERTY FLAME
Schermarrafarm@aol.com
http://www.milibertyflame.com

FLORIDA CRACKER

FLORIDA CRACKER HORSES
Florida Cracker
Sam P. Getzen
P.O. Box 186
Newberry, Florida 32669
(352) 472-2228

FOX TROTTER

BOWMAN STABLES
Missouri Fox Trotters
Stacy Bowman
5128 Stagecoach Road
Pleasant Plains, Illinois 62677
(217) 487-7664
bowmanfxtr@aol.com

BRUSHY CREEK LODGE AND RESORT
Missouri Fox Trotters
George and JoAnn Becker
Rt. 1 Box 173
Black, Missouri 63625
(573) 269-4600
BARNY FIFE'S GENERAL IKE

CANTRELL FARMS
Missouri Fox Trotters
Herman and Norma Cantrell
1090 White Clover Road
Strafford, Missouri 65757
(417859-2308
caddohc@aol.com
www.foxtrottercolor.com/Cantrellfarms

CALICO CREEK FOXTROTTING HORSE FARM
Missouri Fox Trotters
David and Jane Bruns
Gibbon, Minnesota 55335
(507) 834-6962
jbruns@prairie.lakes.com
www.calicocreek.com

DREAMAKER FARMS
Missouri Fox Trotters
Ann Quinn
8114 State Highway M
Niangua, Missouri 65713
ann@foxtrottercolor.com
www.foxtrottercolor.com

FOLEY'S FOXTROTTERS
Missouri Fox Trotter
Brenda & Steve Foley
74 Ruby Lane
Carson City, Nevada 89706
(775) 883-0279
SOUTHERN FIZZ G
sunset@charter.net
http://www.geocities.com/Heartland/Valley/6524/

FREEMAN STABLES
Missouri Fox Trotters
Don and Kattie Freeman
P.O. Box 356
Mansfield, Missouri 65704
(417) 924-8834 (home)
(417) 924-3515 (office)
DARK BEAM
MASTER CHARGE

FREE REIN FARMS
Missouri Fox Trotters & Spotted Saddle Horses
Charles and Dawn Lindsay
192 Sumac Lane
Marshfield, Missouri 65706
(417) 859-6861
dlindsay@usipp.net
http://www.free-rein-designs.com

GUY & WILMA HARE
Missouri Fox Trotters
Guy and Wilma Hare
3444 East County Line Road
Rogersville, Missouri 65742
(417) 753-2946
MISSOUIR RED WING
RED WING'S STRIKE THE GOLD

JOHNSON STABLES
Missouri Fox Trotters
Keith Johnson
6298 E FR 168
Rogersville, Missouri 65742
(417) 889-6768

MANE GAIT FARMS
Missouri Fox Trotters
Lisa Brown
"Horse sense is what keeps horses from betting on people."
4814 W. Banff Lane
Glendale, Arizona 85306
(602) 908-8393
(602) 978-4489
REVELRY'S LITTLE BANDIT
manegaitfarms@msn.com

PASH FARM
Missouri Fox Trotters
Paul and Sharon Carey
Marshfield, Missouri 65706
(417) 859-7661

REBEL SPRING RANCH PALOMINOS
Missouri Fox Trotters
Marshall and Lee Yates
3977 Malone Road
Norwood, Missouri 65717
(417) 741-6293
(417) 741-1428 FAX
palomino@windo.missouri.org

SANDEROSA FARMS
Missouri Fox Trotters
James and Suzanne Sanders
1437 CR 210
Weimar, Texas 78962
(979) 732-5258
TOUCH OF CLASS
sandfoxtrot@aol.com
www.foxtrottersusa.com

SOUTHERN SUNRISE BREEDING FACILITY
Missouri Fox Trotters
Larry Stevens
(417) 859-7977
SOUTHERN SUNRISE

SPRING CREEK FARMS
Missouri Fox Trotters
Kim Smith
3641 SE 82nd Street
Runnells, Iowa 50237
(515) 266-2231
BUCKSKIN WILLY

SUN HILL FARMS
Missouri Fox Trotters
Gaited Appaloosas
John and Pat Anderson
26425 South Hillockburn
Estacada, Oregon 97023
(503) 630-6910
WAKON'S SUGAR SNOW
ApHC 566951

VALLEY SPRINGS FOXTROTTERS
Missouri Fox Trotters
George and Joann Becker
Rt. I Box 173
Black, Missouri 63625
(573) 269-4743
(573) 269-4234 FAX
vsfoxtrt@misn.com
www.missourifoxtrotter.com

GAITED MORGAN

LIBERTY MTN GAITED MORABS
Gaited Morgans and Gaited Morabs
The Messengers
107 Racetrack Road
Bismarck, Arkansas 71929
(501) 617-9855
MARY MELS MYSTERY
libertymtn@yahoo.com
http://libertymtnranch.faithweb.com

MARY-MEL MORGANS
Gaited Morgans
Mary and Mel Frandsen
506 S. 100 W.
American Fork, Utah 84003
(801) 756-4655
MaryMelM@aol.com

MEADOW LARK MORGANS
Gaited Morgans
Linnea Sidi
2640 SCR 3E
Loveland, Colorado 80537
(970) 669-3822
(970) 635-9014 FAX
mlmorgans@aol.com
http://www.meadowlarkmorgans.com

PAT & LEE'S MONTANA MORGANS
Gaited Morgans
Leon D. Bess
6028 N. Quail Run Road
Paradise Valley, Arizona 85253
(480) 948-5356
MtnManLee@aol.com

ICELANDIC

AMERICAN ICELANDICS
Icelandic Horses
Elisabeth Haug
6829 Camino De Amigos
Carlsbad, California 92009
(805) 455-5126
"Living your dream"
Elisabeth@AmericanIcelandics.com
www.AmericanIcelandics.com

FARANDI FARMS
Icelandic Horses
Jo Larmour
Sebastopol, California
(Sonoma County)
(707) 829-2633 (not after 9:00 p.m.)
farandi@sonic.net
http://www.sonic.net/farandi/

LARGO

DANCING HORSES, INC.
Largo and Paso Fino Horses
Judy A Tallman
3805 SW Lake Flora Road
Port Orchard, Washington 98367
(360) 874-0386
TESORO DE LA DANZA (grulla)
Registered both Largo & Paso Fino
judy1@tscnet.net
http://www.dancinghorses.com

PISADAS DE ORO STABLES
American Paso Largo Horses
Isaac Wyler
P.O. Box 690
Colorado City, Arizona 86021
(928) 875-8117
CORAL'S MONARCA DE VEZ
ROYAL OAK PRIME TIME
MONARCA'S ECLIPSE PISADAS
http://www.dancinghorses.com
link to Pisadas de Oro Stables

SOUTHERN COMFORT FARM
Paso Fino – Largo Horses
Melinda & Tim Williams
Jonesborough, Tennessee
(423) 348-8378
ECLISPE'S CASSINO PISADAS
SCF THE DRAGON SLAYER
melwynd@usit.net
www.Scfpasofino-largohorses.com

MANGALARGA MARCHADOR

CASCADE MARCHADORES
Mangalarga Marchadors
16825 Delicious Street
Bend, Oregon 97701
holmsusan@aol.com

HARAS LUCERO
Mangalarga Marchadors
Bill and Sandy Kambic
673 Buck Creek Road
Kingston, Tennessee 37763
(865) 376-1835

IMPERIAL FARMS
Mangalarga Marchador
Tony and Elaine Orta
323 Alpine Drive #20565
Jasper, Georgia 30143
(404) 218-7358
(770) 893-4304
RITMO (a palomino)
Mroorta@yahoo.com
elaineorta@yahoo.com

LAZY T RANCH
Mangalarga Marchadors
P.O. Box 27
Boulder, Montana 59632
www.montanamangalargamarchador.com

MARCHWIND FARM
Mangalarga Marchadors
www.marchwindfarm.homestead.com
lmarch@sowega.net

RANCHO LINDA MARCHADORES
Mangalarga Marchadors
P.O. Box 1008
Bonsall, California 92003
(760) 643-9262
(858) 212-6650
BATUQUE DO REGAL
info@marchadorhorses.com
www.marchadorhorses.com

ROYAL ALTER MARCHADORES
Mangalarga Marchadors
8250 N.W. 136th Avenue Road
Ocala, Florida 34481
(352) 368-5786
info@royalaltermarchadores.com
www.royalaternarchadores.com

MC CURDY PLANTATION

DESTINY HILLS RANCH
McCurdy Plantation Horses
Ron and Colleen Cates
7600 CR 2800
Athens, Texas 75751
(903) 677-4858
FAX: (903) 677-4868

J-BAR FARM and KENNEL
McCurdy Plantation Horses
June and Barry Snook
23338 South Blount Road
Canby, Oregon 97013
MC CURDY'S NEW TRADITION
(503) 266-3411
snook@pdx.net
www.mccurdynorthwest.com

PRAIRIE CREEK RANCH
McCurdy Plantation Horses
Paula Sue Swope
Webmaster of the McCurdy Plantation Horse Association's Website
11691 CR 1200
Malakoff, Texas 75148
Paulasue@swopes.org

MONTANA TRAVLER

MINER CREEK RANCH
Montana Travlers
Mark Engle
222 Cokedale Road
Livingston, Montana 59047
(406) 222-8015
(406) 222-5591 FAX
minercreekranch@msn.com

DONOVAN RANCH
Montana Travlers
Chuck Donovan
602 Robin Ln
Livingston, Montana 59047
(406) 222-3352
ChuckDonovan@aol.com

MONTANA TRAVLERS
Montana Travlers
Mel and Shirley Atkinson
Box 17
Hazen, North Dakota 58545
(701) 748-2816]
DAKOTA FLASH
Montanatravler@westriv.com

MORAB

LIBERTY MTN GAITED MORABS
Gaited Morabs and Gaited Morgans
Anita and Clarence Messenger
107 Racetrack Road
Bismarck, Arkansas 71929
(501) 617-9855
libertymtn@yahoo.com

MOUNTAIN

ALMOSTA PONDEROSA
Mountain Horses
Ron and Desirai Schild
P.O. Box 5429
Chubbuck, Idaho 83202
(208) 237-6413
ANNA'S EL CHICO
GENERAL JACKSON
dschild013@msn.com

A MOUNTAIN HORSE RANCH
Mountain Horses
Gaila Noel
18120 3rd Avenue
Bend, Oregon 97701
(541) 385-0857
SGT. PEPPER and JOKER
noelgaila@webtv.net
www.amountainhorseranch.com

BREEZ KREST FARM
Rocky Mountain Horses
Terry and Lavinia Kingery
149 BreezKrest Lane
Fincastle, Virginia 24090
(540) 473-3016
ljkingery@msn.com

CLASSIC FARM
Mountain Horses
Dave & Sue Stefanic
1215 McCormick Rd
Mechanicsburg, Pennsylvania 17055
(717) 766-5996
FAX: (717) 796-5996
DOCK – SONNY - J.LEE'S ROCK-IT –
SANTA ANNA - CLASSIC SQUIRREL -
NUNCIO'S SKYHAWK - JOE BANJO -
LET'S TANGO
 (all double-registered)
clsfarm@aol.com
www.classicfarm.com

C & W MOUNTAIN HORSE FARM
KMSHA
19497 Ayers Road
Brooksville, Florida 34609
Bill & Linn Compton
(813) 920-7100
FAX: (813) 249-4904
bcompton@tsionline.com

C & W MOUNTAIN HORSE FARM
Mountain Horses
Greg & Danette Williams
(813) 254-6353
FAX: (813) 371-4708
CONLEY, DIAMOND REO,
DEL RIO
gwilliams@tsionline.com
www.cwmountainhorses.com

CW STABLES
KMSHA and Spotted Mountain Horses
Billy and Debbie Caudill
2473 Tipton Road
Mount Sterling, Kentucky 40353
(859) 498-4203
(859) 585-3052 CELL
cwstables@bellsouth.net
www.cwstables.net

CYPRESS LAKE STABLES
Mountain Horses
Al and Tom Prewitt
207 Fairway Drive
Fayetteville, North Carolina 28305
TOM'S PRIDE
(910) 484-1615 p.m.
(910) 484-2104 a.m.
info@cypresstock.com
www.cypresstock.com

DOUBLE W STABLES
Mountain Horses
Mike & Brenda Wattenberger
3651 Kiddville Road
Mt.Sterling, Kentucky 40353
(859) 498-8678
sandwstables@aol.com
www.doublewstables.com

EMERALD ACRES
Mountain Horses
Sandy McCart
1444 Talmage-Mayo Road
Harrodsburg, Kentucky 40330
(859) 865-9277
CRF BOUNTY HUNTER
emeraldacres@hotmail.com

FRANCIS MOUNTAIN FARM
Kentucky Natural Gaited Horses
Nelson and Judy Francis
8257 Rockhouse Creek Road
Salyersville, Kentucky 41465
(606) 743-7173
Francis@meginc.com

GAITWAY FARM
Rocky Mtn. Mtn. Pleasure,
Kentucky Mtn.
Gary, Louise and Julie Neidert
6107 Highway U
Wausau, Wisconsin 54401
(715) 675-3933
www.gaitwayfarm.com

GLEN PECK FARM
Mountain Pleasure Horses
Glen Peck
954 West Maytown Road
Ezel, Kentucky 41425
STARDUST
(606) 725-4781

GOLDEN ARROW FARM
Mountain Horses
Nora Deaton
691 Natural Bridge Road
Slade, Kentucky 40376
(606) 663-0928
GOLDFINGER STAR (triple registered)
A.I. and shipped semen available.
goldfingersstar@se-tel.com

HAWK HILL FARM
Kentucky Mountain Saddle Horses
Bonnie and Robert Robinson Jr.
2875 Crooked Creek Road
Irvine, Kentucky 40336
(606) 723-1297
AMIGO BLUE
drpepperbonnie@hotmail.com

H & S STABLES
Kentucky Mountain Saddle Horse
Hiram & Shirley Combs
939 A Combs Road
Campton, Kentucky 41301
(606) 668-3089
NERO
Vacation cabin and horseback trails
Combshs@hotmail.com

INDIAN HILL FARM
Rocky Mountain Horses
Mike and Diana Medler
10592 S. Co. Rd. 300 W
Williamsburg, Indiana 47393
(765) 874-1091
justa@globalsite.net

JAKE ROSE STABLES
Mountain Horses
Jake Rose
6569 E. Hwy 36
Olympia, Kentucky 40358
(606) 674-2859

JENKINS PLEASURE GAIT FARM
KNGHA – KMSHA - MPHA
Sara and Greg Jenkins
2634 Pricey Creek Road
Salyersville, Kentucky 41465
(606) 349-1567
TREVOR
F & R'S HOT GOLD, and
RED FLAME'S HOT GOLD

KB MOUNTAIN HORSES
Mountain Horses
Kellie, Brad, Brett & Karlee Bretthauer
8261 Scotia Road
Newport, Washington 99156
(509) 292-8033
BLUE RAIN
kellie@kbmtnhorses.com
www.kbmtnhorses.com

K/B STABLES
Mountain Horses
Kim & Bruce Harrison
W361 N9317 Brown Street
Oconomowoc, Wisconsin 53066
(920) 474-7533
MARTIN LUTHER
kbes@gte.net

LAZY-S-FARM
Mountain Pleasure Horses
Raymond and Vivian Setters
333 Corey Road
Salt Lick, Kentucky 40371
(606) 683-3040 (home)
(859) 497-2344 (mobile)
FAIR YANKEE CLIPPER
rsetters@mis.net
www.mountsterling-ky.com/horses/setters

MASTERS STABLES
Rocky Mountain Horses
Carson & Judy Masters
230 Tates Creek Ave
Richmond, Kentucky 40475
(859) 623-5937
(859(625-1921
DOC HOLIDAY
BLUE SMOKIN' SAMBO

MAY FARMS
Mountain Pleasure Horses
Lowell & David May
4616 Falcon Road
Salyersville, Kentucky 41465
(606) 349-3323 (Lowell)
(606) 349-2534 (David)
EMERALD FIRE
vdjjmay@foothills.net

MOUNTAIN HORSES
KMSHA & MPHA
Vernon Brewer
236 Clover Fork
Jackson, Kentucky 41339
(606) 666-8741

MOUNTAIN VIEW FARM
Mountain Pleasure Horses
Paul E. Stamper
P.O. Box 127
Ezel, Kentucky 41425
(606) 725-5635
(606) 725-5636 FAX
paul@mrtc.com

ODOM'S MOUNTAIN HORSE RANCH
Mountain Horses
Billy and Fran Odom
16300 Morrison Road
Oakdale, California 95361
(209) 881-3284
GOLDFINGER'S PRIDE and
BEN JORDAN
Billy@mountainhorses.com
fran@mountainhorses.com
www.mountainhorses.com

OPHIR HILL STATION
Mountain Horses
Barbara Weatherwax
Washoe Valley, Nevada
(775) 849-0676
FAX: (775) 849-3162
OPHIR HILLS HIGHLANDER
GENERAL JACKSON
softgaits@aol.com
www.thefabulousfloatinghorses.com

OVERLOOK STABLES
Mountain Horses
Joyce and Vernon Stamper
692 McVey Road
Sharpsburg, Kentucky 40374
(606) 247-5633
Horses for Sale - Training
overlook@mickrotec.com

PADGETT STABLES
Mountain Horses
Dan and Debi Padgett
3815 Tipp Cowlesville Rd.
Tipp City, Ohio 45371
Distributor: Guardian, Magnum and
Pestel pelleted horse bedding
Mfg: *Fine-Tines* | Stall Fork
Stallions: SAMANTHA'S BIG BOY,
BUDDY'S LAST STAND
(937) 335-3589
debi@aplusequine.com
http://www.padgettstables.com

RAINBOW'S END GAITED HORSES
Mountain Horses
Elen & Charlie Kentnor
3088 AZ Highway 83
P.O. Box 717
Sonoita, Arizona 85637
(520) 455-0202
(520) 455-0303 FAX
Stallion/Sales/Bed & Breakfast
MOUNTAIN MUSIC
ElenKentnor@compuserve.com
www.gaitedmountainhorses.com

ROCKIN' R FARM
Mountain Pleasure Horses
Drexel and Robin Ratliff
P.O. Box 384
Jeffersonville, Kentucky 40337
(859) 499-0545
rockinfarm@hotmail.com

SANDEROSA FARMS
Mountain Horses
James & Suzanne Sanders
1437 CR 210
Weimar, Texas 78962
(979) 732-5258
TOUCH OF CLASS
sandfoxtrot@aol.com

TRIPLE S MOUNTAIN HORSES, LLC
Mountain Horses
Bert & Paula Morgan
6222 Hwy 140
Eagle Point, Oregon 97524
(530) 459-3530
TRIPLE S IRON MAN
CHOCO DOCK
triplesranch@snowcrest.net
www.triple-s-ranch.com

TURNING POINT TRAINING
Gaited Mountain Horses
Shawn Magrum
8315 Avon Lake Road
Lodi, Ohio 44254
(330) 948-3013
JERICHO

VAN BERT FARMS
Mountain Horses
H.T. & Wilda Derickson
Larry & Vera Patterson
800 Derickson Lane
Stanton, Kentucky 40380
(606) 663-9070
Over 200 horses with
15 stallions to choose from
vanbert@mis.net
www.vanbertfarms.com

WESTON CREEK GAITED HORSES
Mountain Horses and Peruvian Pasos
Shelly Spradlin
F & R'S RED FLAME
Westoncreek@aol.com

WILDFIRE FARM
Rocky Mountain Horses
Bonnie Hodge
P.O. Box 402
Viola, Arkansas 72583
(870) 458-3433
rhodge.88@Juno.com

WILLOW CREEK FARM
Mountain Pleasure
Lonnie & Milyne Potter
528 Whitson Road
Cynthiana, Kentucky 41031-5496
(859) 234-6645
CROWN ROYAL
GEVEDON'S TRIGGER

WOODWIND FARMS
Mountain Horses
Joyce Doonan & Will Ferguson
410 Sandrel Lane
Wytheville, Virginia 24382-9585
(276) 228-7009 (evening)
doonan@netva.com
www.woodwindfarms.com

THE WRIGHT PLACE
Kentucky Mtn. and Mountain Pleasure
Renee Wright
P.O. Box 43
Wellington, Kentucky 40387
(606) 768-6139
BLUE, SPIDER

NORTH AMERICAN SINGLEFOOT

4-BEAT FARM
NASHA / McCurdy Plantation
Ted and Elsie Neely
2280 County Road 39
Notasulga, Alabama 36866-2341
EZD'S MACON REBEL
(334) 257-1275
4beatfarm@msn.com

DAVID LEVI STANLEY
NASHA & RHBAA
David and Brenda Stanley
Rt 3 Box 462
Clintwood, Virginia 24228
(276) 926-6688
rascal@naxs.net

HIGH PLACES RANCH
NASHA
Barbara Bouray
2201 S.166th Avenue
Goodyear, Arizona 85338
(406) 581-0073
Borzois@attgobal.net

JOSEPH STANLEY
NASHA Registered Horses
J.B. Stanley
Rt 3 Box 583
Clintwood, Virginia 24228
ROWDY RAWHIDE'S MAJESTIC MYSTERY
jbstanley@naxs.net

RACKING ROCK STABLES
NASHA / RACKING HORSE
Doug and Jan Stanley
Rt.2 Box 303F
Clintwood, Virginia 24228
ROWDY RAWHIDE'S ROCKET
(276) 926-8650

PASO FINO

DANCING HORSES, INC.
Paso Fino and Largo Horses
Judy A. Tallman
3805 SW Lake Flora Road
Port Orchard, Washington 98367
(360) 874-0386
judy1@tscnet.net
http://www.dancinghorses.com

DEERING RANCH
Paso Fino & Trote y Galope Horses
Mariann Deering
12345 S.W. Tooze Road
Sherwood, Oregon 97140
(503) 685-9637 Home
((503) 225-1545 Work
Deering@aol.com

ESTRELLA DE PASO
Paso Fino Horses
Peggy Roos
4190 County Road 154
Elizabeth, Colorado 80107
(303) 646-2656
peggydroos@aol.com

HILLSIDE FARMS
Paso Fino Horses
B.J. and Gary Schuler
Telford, Pennsylvania 18969
bj@netcarrier.com
www.hillsidefarms.biz

JF GAITED RANCH AND TRAIL HORSES
Paso Finos and Single-Footing Horses
Jani London
Box 437
Charlie Lake, B.C. VOC 1HO
(250) 262-3273
DUMAS TM, 1996 bay Paso Fino, also registered with NASHA
gaited@ocol.com
http://www.gaitedranchhorses.com

LAZY IDH PASO FINO RANCH
Paso Fino Horses
Carol Nelson
811 Molasses Road
Dale, Texas 78616
ROJO TEJAS
(512) 398-6084 (phone & fax)
lazyidh@direcway.com
www.geocities.com/lazyidh/index.html

RANCHO LINDA MARCHADORES
Paso Fino Horses
P.O. Box 1008
Bonsall, California 92003
(760) 643-9262

REMOLINO RANCH
Paso Fino Horses
Jeanne & Joe Leisek
75 Lewers Creek Road
Washoe Valley, Nevada 89704
(775) 883-1975
CORSARIO
jjleisek@aol.com

SYNDICATED EQUINE ENTERPRISES, LLC
Paso Fino Horses
8250 NW 136th Ave. Road
Ocala, Florida 34482

TIERRA ALTA
Paso Fino Horses
Carol and Russell Pitts
6325 Echo Ridge Heights
Colorado Springs, Colorado 80908
(719) 495-1792
seajay2002@msn.com

2-W PASO FINOS
Paso Finos Horses
Rick and Terry Wallace
4340 Wileys Road
Peyton, Colorado 80831
BANDITO DE LA ISLA
Twobarwpaso@earthlink.net

PART TENNESSEE WALKER

HIGH PLAINS WALKERS
Part Tennessee Walking Registry
Tennessee Walking Horses
Grace Larson
HC84 Box 3087
Forsyth, Montana 59327
(406) 365-2854
GOLDUST ROYAL TRIGGER
GLL'S SUN CHIEF
www.hiplainswalkers.com

HORSE PLAY FARMS
Part Tennessee Walking Horse
Bob Adams and Patricia Haines
Rte. 1 Box 492
Torrington, Wyoming 82240

DALE ROHNERT
Part Walker and Walkaloosa
Dale Rohnert
19618 Fish Road
Wilder, Idaho 83676
(208) 482-6717
MIDNIGHT EBONY STAR

PERUVIAN PASO

CHR EASTWIND RANCH
Peruvian Paso
Hugh & Linda Richardson
2200 Richview Road
Santa Maria, California 93455
(805) 937-1477
FAX: (805) 937-1899
Chreastwind@aol.com
http://www.chreastwind.com

CLEAR CREEK RANCH
Peruvian Paso
Jim & Barbara Alexander
Carson City, Nevada 89705
(775) 882-6265
jimalex@nvbell.net

CRESCENT MOON RANCH
Peruvian Paso Horses / North American Single-Footing Horses
Dale Downey & Mimi Busk-Downey
Box 449, Acme
Alberta CanadaTOM OAO
cresmoon@netway.ab.ca
http://www.supergait.com

MOOSE VINE RANCH
Peruvian Paso Horses
Denise and Craig Boyd
P.O. Box 182
Mt Aukum, California 95656
(530) 620-6420
EL PUMA AZABACHE
moosevine@innercite.com
www.moosevine.com

NOLA GIDDING'S PERPUVIAN PASOS
Peruvian Paso Horses
Nola and Steven Giddings
887 Solano Court
El Sobrante, California 94803
CABALLERO DORADO
(510) 758-7786
dorado887@aol.com

RANCHO DE ISABELLA
Peruvian Paso
Jerry and Isabella Restani
8903 Voula Lane
Wilton, California 95693
Standing: RDI Aleman & RDI Amante
(916) 687-8598
FAX: (916) 687-4529
Restani@frontiernet.net
www.Peruvianpasos.com

WESTON CREEK GAITED HORSES
Peruvian Pasos and Mountain Horses
Shelly Spradlin
F & R'S RED FLAME
Westoncreek@aol.com

RACKING HORSE

E & S STABLE
Racking Horse / Standardbred
Earl and Susie Wright
(606) 633-9574
ESstable@webtv.net

RACKING ROCK STABLES
NASHA / RACKING HORSE
Doug and Jan Stanley
Rt. 2 Box 303F
Clintwood, Virginia 24228
ROWDY RAWHIDE'S ROCKET
(276) 926-8650

TYLER MOUNTAIN STABLES
Racking Horses
Sandy Preston
4866 Big Tyler Road
Charleston, West Virginia 25313
(304) 776-7578 Stable
(304) 776-4740 Home
Training, Boarding, Lessons, Sales.
WINDJAMMER SP (5 times reserve world champion speed racking horse)
Rackon71@aol.com

SPANISH GAITED PONY

DAVIDSON RANCH
Spanish Gaited Pony
Larry & Shirley Davidson
3785 La Panza Road
P.O. Box 270
Creston, California 93432
(805) 237-0760

SPANISH MUSTANG

APACHE TRAIL RANCH
Spanish Mustangs
Marye Ann and Tom Thompson
4970 South Kansas Settlement Road
Wilcox, Arizona 85643-9748
(520) 384-2886
MAT@vtc.net
http://www.angelfire.com/az/xochitl/

BRISLAWN'S CAYUSE RANCH
Spanish Mustangs
Josie Brislawn
2740 D Road
Oshoto, Wyoming 82721-9705
(307) 467-5394
Josie@CayuseRanch.com
www.CayuseRanch.com

ROCKIN B RANCH
SMR – AIHR - HOA
Robert and Susan Tuscana
17427 Tarlton Road
P.O. Box 708
Mabank, Texas 75147
(903) 887-7034
(903) 880-3953
"Birthplace of Champions"
rockinbranch@earthlink.net
http://www.rockinbranch.cjb.net/

SPRING WATER STATION KIGER MUSTANGS
Kiger Mustangs & American Paint Mustangs
Gerald O. Thompson
35585 S.E. Tracy Road
Estacada, Oregon 97023
(503) 630-3609
EL DUC
Kiger3@prodigy.net
http://www.Springwaterstation.com

WILD SIDE RANCH
Spanish Mustangs
Nancy Pearson
Benton City, Washington 99320
(509) 588-8146
PRAIRIE WARRIOR
Nancy@wildsideranch.com
http://www.wildsideranch.com

SPOTTED SADDLE HORSE

AVALON FARM
Spotted Saddle Horses, Racking Horses & Tennessee Walking Horses
Colin and Pamela Stubbs
325 Blue Stocking Hollow Road
Shelbyville, Tennessee 37160
(931) 680-1018
(770) 596-9398
pstubbs@mindspring.com
http://pstubbs.home.mindspring.com

BEECH MILE FARM, BEDWELL STABLES
Spotted Saddle Horses
Janie Rowland
Spring Hill & Nashville, Tennessee
(615) 665-0642
STEPPIN OUT TONIGHT
beechmilefarm@home.com
www.beechmilefarm.com

DOE RUN FARM
Spotted Saddle Horses, Racking Horses, Tennessee Walking Horses
Pamela Stubbs
141 Jackson Road
Roopville, Georgia 30170
(770) 596-9398 (mobile)
(770) 854-8017
Certified Equine Sports Massage Therapist
pstubbs@mindspring.com
http://pstubbs.home.mindspring.com

FUTRELL FARMS
Spotted Saddle Horses
Robin Duncan and Earl Futrell
3568 Swan Road
Farmington, Kentucky 42040
(270) 435-4148 (farm)
(270) 382-3104 (handler)

WARD'S HORSE FARM
Spotted Saddle Horse, Tennessee Walking Horses, Missouri Fox Trotters, Racking Horses
Ken and Patricia Ward
99 East River Drive
Strawberry, Arkansas 72469
(870) 528-4070
NIGHT CHIEF BANDIT, PAINT'S RED ROOSTER, DOC'S MR EBONY
KPWard@Wardshorsefarm.com
www.wardshorsefarm.com

WHISKEY RUN
Spotted Saddle Horses
Charlie and Peggy Moore
295 Bluestocking Hollow Road
Shelbyville, Tennessee 37160
(931) 685-1876

WOODVIEW STABLES
Spotted Saddle Horses and Tennessee Walkers
Carla and Greg Hester
8572 Morrow Rossburg Road
Morrow, Ohio
(513) 877-3194
woodviewstables@att.net
www.Woodviewstables.com

TENNESSEE WALKER

PALMER'S STABLES
Tennessee Walker/Racking Horse
Kentucky Mountain Saddle Horse
David Palmer
9793 Hwy 52E
Beattyville, Kentucky 41311
Quality Show & Trail Horses
(606) 464-0979
SOUL'S GOLD (also registered KMSHA)

RANCHO ALEGRIE
Tennessee Walking Horses
Tom and Judy Henry
Alpine, California
(619) 445-4163

TETONS MOUNTAIN GAITED HORSES
Tennessee Walkers & Fox Trotters
Walkaloosa Horses
Rod and Stacie Hill
383 W. Wells
Tetonia, Idaho 83452
(208) 456-2379
(208) 456-2479 FAX
PAPA'S EASY PUSH
CHRISTY'S CANDY MAN
TETON'S TRIPLE TREAT
tetonswalkers@cs.com
www.tetongaitedhorses.com

WISHING WYOMING RANCH
Tennessee Walking Horses
Tami Lynn and Brad Arndt
309 N. Hightower Road
Wheatland, Wyoming 82201
(307) 322-4893

WALNUT HILL WALKERS
Tennessee Walking Horses and Spotted Saddle Horses
Sherry L. Duriga
2334 North Ellsworth
Salem, Ohio 44460
(330) 332-4738
SNOW CHIEF DELIGHT
SDuriga@aol.com
http://hometown.aol.com/SDuriga/walnuthillwh.html

WOODVIEW STABLES
Tennessee Walking & Spotted Saddle Horses
Carla and Greg Hester
8572 Morrow Rossburg Road
Morrow, Ohio 45152
(513) 877-3194

TENNUVIAN HORSES

ROGUE PERUVIAN HORSES
Tennuvian Horses
Jon and Cindy Ziegler
3197 Beagle Road
White City, Oregon 97503
(541) 826-4945
(541) 826-4965 Fax
farmrjon@cdsnet.net
http://www.rogueperuvianhorses.com

TIGER HORSE

ANNANDALE'S TIGER HORSE FARM
Tiger Horse Registry
Victoria and Mark Varley
39 Crazy Rabbit Road
Santa Fe, New Mexico 87508
(505) 438-2827
FAX: (505) 438-2828
tigrehorse@aol.com
www.tigrehorse.com

SPOTTED REARS TIGER HORSE RANCH
Tiger Horse
Monica Denney
30977 Via Maria Elena
Bonsall, California 92003
(760) 732-0023
FAX: (760) 732-0029
CELL: (760) 583-9700

THE TIGER SHEAD
Tiger Horses
Karen E. Shead
12540 N 177 E Ave
Collinsville, Oklahoma 74021
(918) 371-0374
TS WIND WALKER "DILLON"
DillonDen@aol.com

WITS END RANCH
Tiger Horses
Darlene Salminen
1604 Fescue Circle
Huddleston, Virginia 24104
(540)297-2276
witsendranch@worldnet.att.net
http://witsendranch.home.att.net

WALKALOOSA HORSE

NEW PROMISE FARMS
Walkaloosa Horses
Dodie B. Sable
593 Old Rt. 22
Lenhartsville, Pennsylvania 19534
www.newpromisefarms.com

SEAVIEW RANCH
Walkaloosa Horses
Pem Meyer
2995 Clark Valley Road
Los Osos, California 93402
(805) 528-4770

SUN HILL FARMS
Walkaloosa Horses
John and Pat Anderson
Estacada, Oregon
WAKON'S SUGAR SNOW
pasunhill@cascadeaccess.com

TRAINERS

INVICTA FARMS
Gaited Horse Trainer
Beth Jennings
Hemet, California
(909) 766-8838
Ridetomuch@aol.com
http://www.invictafarms.com

SHADES OF OAK
Gaited Horse Trainer
Elizabeth Graves
4537 37th Street
Clear Lake, Minnesota 55319
(763) 662-2303
All breed gaited horse clinics, specializing in gait analysis and natural development for beginning to advanced levels. Positive re-enforcement for the horse and rider.
marshal@sherbtel.net
www.lizgraves.com

LEE ZIEGLER
Gaited Horse Trainer
"Gaits Without Gimmicks"
15125 W. Coachman Drive
Colorado Springs, Colorado 80908
Doing a selected number of small clinics on gait identification, conformation and riding gaited horses each year.
Smthrider7@msn.com

PROFESSIONAL PHOTOGRAPHERS

The author wishes to thank these talented photographers for their participation in this project. Excellent photography is the life-blood promoting our Fabulous Floaters.

FOREST BLISS
P.O. Box 1103
Magalia, California 95954
(530) 873-9424
Specializing in Horse Show and Ranch Photography. On location with mobile lab, complete with proof viewing, and enlargements made on the spot.
ftbliss@californianow.com
www.now2000.com/ftbliss

BLUE COUNTRY GRAPHICS
Kim Jaserie
16729 Highfalls Street
Canyon Country, CA 91387
(661) 298-2505
kjaserie@socal.rr.com

DEBBY BUSH
Horse Show Photographer
Chesner, South Carolina
(864) 461-8133
debbush@bellsouth.net

TED & JOYCE BROWN
24770 Springer Road
Sweet Home, Oregon 97386
(541) 367-4842

COMMUNITY PHOTOS & VIDEO
Gary & Sharon Leverette
309 Oak Circle
Unionville, Tennessee 37180
(931) 294-5132
glevgrp@aol.com

FREE-REIN DESIGNS
Dawn Young
192 Sumac Lane
Marshfield, Missouri 65706
(417) 859-6861
dlindsay@usipp.net

SANDRA W. HALL
1230 Shiloh Acres Road
Chesterfield, South Carolina 29709
(843) 623-6652
(843) 623-9103 FAX

JIM HARGROVE
1145 N. Chipman Street #27
Owosso, Michigan 48867
(877) 735-2431
mail@jimhargrove.com
www.jimhargrove.com

ROB HESS PHOTOGRAPHY INC.
P.O. Box 1396
Olympia, Washington 98507

JACKIE JACOBSON
All-Breed Photographer
Specializing in Farm & Ranch
1071 Statler Run Road
Fairview, West Virginia 26570-8554
(304) 449-1696
Bukm55@aol.com

BOB LANGRISH
The Court House
High Street, Bisley
Gloucestershire GL6 7AA
England
(44) 207 452 770140
(44) 207 452 770146
Bob@boblangrish.co.uk
info@boblangrish.co.uk
www.boblangrish.com

LOCKE PHOTOGRAPHY
Lee Locke
P.O. Box 375
Norco, California 92860
(909) 351-8733 PH/FAX
Ranch-Farm-Kennel-Portrait-Action-Conformation
LeeLockePhoto@netzero.net

LYNN PHOTO SERVICES
Box 114
Eminence, Missouri 65466
(573) 226-3418
(573) 226-5466
lynnfoto@socket.net

MILLER PHOTO
Gary & Mardean Miller
12653 W. Reservation
Pocatello, Idaho 83202
(208) 237-7208

MICHELLE MUNRO
9186 Versailles Road
Angola, New York
14006
(724) 654-9546

RICK OSTEEN
20450 Fortuna Del Sur
Escondido, California 92029
(760) 752-4498

V.W. PERRY
5135 Old Boonesboro Road
Winchester, Kentucky 40391
(859) 744-1274
(859) 737-0517 FAX
vwp@meginc.com

RUSSELL PITTS
6325 Echo Ridge Heights
Colorado Springs, Colorado
80908
(719) 495-1792

DEBBIE PYE
P.O. Box 1967
Ramona, California 92065
(760) 789-5410
weppye@earthlink.net
http://www.wepye.com

QUINCE TREE PHOTOGRAPHY
Ed Moore
16261 Sunset Terrace
Valley Center, California 92082
(760) 749-4333
equestrianimage@aol.com

JAMES REYNOLDS
Digital 2 Photo & Video
(360) 440-5300
jimr@digital2.us
www.Digital2.us

HOWIE SCHATZBERG
P.O. Box 1570
Cave Creek, Arizona
85327
(480) 595-2865
Howie@howardschatzberg.com
www.Howardschatzberg.com

MARILYN TODD-DANIELS
Woodsong Institute of Art
Equine Artist, Educator, Author
(903) 364-2649
woodsong@texoma.net
www.woodsonginstitute.com

TERRY WALLACE
4340 Wileys Road
Peyton, Colorado 80831
twobarwpaso@earthlink.net

VIDA Z. WARD
Official MMHAA Photographer
3535 SW 44th Avenue
Portland, Oregon 97221
(503) 292-9449
Vidazward@aol.com

LARRY WILLIAMS PHOTOGRAPHY & DESIGN
Larry & Karen Williams
P.O. Box 771868
Ocala, Florida 34477-1868
(352) 291-2304
(800) 297-6135
www.larrywilliamsphotog.com

DARLENE WOHLART PHOTOGRAPHY
P.O. Box 880236
Port St. Lucie, Florida
34988-0236
(772) 878-6128
An artist that takes photographs. You can always have a photo taken of your horse, wouldn't you rather have his essence captured?
equinephoto@earthlink.net
www.equinephotography.com

TERRY YOUNG PHOTOGRAPHY
P.O. Box 54911
Lexington, Kentucky
40555-4911
(859) 264-8579
terryyoung@yahoo.com

A Special Thank You To:
The Roy Rogers-Dale Evans Museum And Happy Trails Theatre
**Roy Rogers Jr.
President**
3950 Green Mountain Road
Branson, Missouri 65616
(417) 339-1900 – Missouri
(760) 243-7300 – California
www.RoyRogers.com

AUTRY MUSEUM OF WESTERN HERITAGE
4700 Western Heritage Way
Los Angeles, California
90027-1462
(323) 667-2000
(323) 660-5721 FAX
www.autry-museum.org

BIBLIOGRAPHY

The writing of this book was in answer to requests for information about the various soft-gaited horses to be found all in one place. For this reason, the bibliography is a bit unusual. The facts and tradition of each registry and association were found in a few books, but mostly from word-of-mouth and breed-specific magazines and newsletters. When my research began, in 1993, there was no such thing as a viable internet. Over the last few years, that has certainly changed; now there is an enormous amount of information on the net. Our soft-gaited world is destined to keep growing!

BOOKS AND MAGAZINES:
Biography of the Tennessee Walking Horse
   Ben A. Green-Parthenon Press 1960
The Echo Of Hoofbeats
   Bob Womack-Pub: Dabora, Inc. 1994
Fox Trotter Trackings
   Nadine I. Moeller- Light Graphics 1986
Paso Fino II
   Wendy Spring- The Paso Fino Bloodstock Agency, Inc. 1988
International Encyclopedia of Horse Breeds
   Bonnie L. Hendericks- University of Oklahoma Press 1995
4-Beat Magazine
   Produced quarterly by NASHA (North American Single-Footing Horse Association)
   Barbara Bouray, Publisher
GaitWay Magazine
   Tissa Porter, Publisher
Mountain Horse Connection
   Lloyd & Teri Wineland – Owners/Editors/Publishers

NEWSLETTERS AND HANDBOOKS:
   MPHA – Mountain Pleasure Horse Association
   KMSHA NEWS – Kentucky Mountain Saddle Horse Association
   RMHA – Rocky Mountain Horse Association
   KNGHA – Kentucky Natural Gaited Horse Association
   TWHBEA – Tennessee Walking Horse Versatility Handbook
   JOURNAL – Missouri Fox Trotter Horse Association
   SPOTTED SADDLE HORSE NEWS SSHBEA
   PASO FINO HORSE WORLD – PFHA
   The Peruvian Paso Horse Registry of North America Handbook
   ABCR- Curly Cues
   The International Federation of Icelandic Horse Judging Handbook
   Eye of the Tiger – THA
   WHA – Walkaloosa Horse Association Newsletter
   Tale of the Tiger - Tiger Horse Registry
   MSHA – Morgan Single-Footing News
   NASHA – Single-Footing Express

ASSOCIATION SUPPORT:
So many people gave me full support for this project. Here, I'm listing the person who acted as spokesperson for each Association or Registry:

   Mountain Pleasure Horse Association – Brenda Wattenburger
   Kentucky Mountain Saddle Horse Association – JR Robinson
   KNGHA - Nelson Francis
   TWHBEA – Jan Keyser
   American Largo Horse Association – Isaac Wyler
   The McCurdy Plantation Horse Association – Colleen Cates
   The Mangalarga Marchador Horse Association of America – Linda Holst
   Icelandic Horse – Elisabeth Haug
   Tiger Horse Association –Darlene Salminen
   Walkaloosa Horse - Pem Meyer
   Tiger Horse Registry – Victoria Varley
   The Gaited Morgan – Mel Frandsen
   Spanish Mustang – Nancy Pearson & Susan Tuscana
   Sorraia – Hardy Oelke
   Racking Horse – Pam Stubbs
   Part Walking Horse – Grace Larson
   Florida Cracker – Sam P. Getzen
   Spanish Gaited Pony – Shirley Davidson
   American Saddlebred – Dedi Gatlin & Barbara Molland
   Montana Travler – Mark A. Engle
   Gaited Morab – Anita Messenger
   NASHA – Barbara Bouray
   AGHA – Bob Bounds
   UMH – Paula Morgan

INDEX

Ailments 75
Akhal-Teke 14
Amble 33,439
American Bahkir-Curly 137,320
American Saddle Horse 168
Andalusian 15,230,241,245,254,310,379,402
Appaloosa 356,367
Arabian 312,449,463
Asturian 230, 254,338, 402
Australian 89
Barada 247
Barb 254,310, 402,411
Batida 315
Bits 91
Blanketing 76
BLM 406,460
Body parts 30
Bosal 247,263
Breton 15
Brio 260
Cabestrillo 262
Canadian Horse 15,98,16,241
Canon 410
Canter 38
Carona 263
Carts 94
Cerbat 406
Chestnut 326,410
Colors 16,26,108,125,370
Concave 23
Conformation 22
Convex 23
Corral construction 67
Corto 37,282
Courser 14
Destrier 14
Diagonal 35,460
Dorsal flex 23
Ectomorph 22
Endomorph 22
English 88
English Pacer 14
Ergot 326
Facial markings 24,25
Feed 69
Field Trailing 300
FIGURE 390
Fino 37,282
Flat walk 36
Florida Cracker 16,27,232,358
Florida Cracker 432
Flying pace 38,346
Fox trot 36,190,395
Fox Trotter 188,426
Fox walk 36
French Canadian 13, 390
Friesian 15,254
Gaited Morab 462
Gaited Morgan 388

Gaits 33,239
Gallop 38
Gamarrilla 263
Garrano 230, 254
Goklan 376
Grooming 77
Hoof care 28,73
Huachano 38,262
Hypoallergenic 330
Iberian 460
Icelandic 14,336
Irish Hobbie 15,98,116,338,355
Jaquima 247,262
Jato 262
Jennets 402
Jerga 263
Kentucky Mountain Saddle Horse 16,22,26,114,464
Kentucky Natural Gaited Horse 152
Kentucky Walker 418
Kiger 403
Kuznet 322
Largo 37,282
Lateral 34
Leg markings 24,25
Leopard complex 358,379
Lokai 322
Lope 38
Lusitano 310
Maintenance 66
Mangalarga Marchador 27,241,308
McCurdy Plantation Horse 294
Mesomorph 22
Missouri Fox Trotter 16,22,26,188,212
Montana Travler 461
Morgan 15, 169,233,417,46,463
Mountain Pleasure 96
Mustang 212,383
Narragansett Pacer 15,98,116,168,355, 392,448
Ni Mee Poo 355,366,382
Norman 15
Osborn Gap 418
Overo 210,213,378
Pace 38
Palfrey 14,338
Parades 210
Part Walking Horse 424
Paso Fino 16,85,228
Paso Largo 272
Paso llano 22, 37,260
Paulista 312
Peruvian Paso 16,22,27,85,86,241,252,407, 442,461
Picada 314
Piebald 215
Pinto 210

Pisador 249
Plantation Breeds 17
Podarge 14
Prepotency 393
Pre-purchase exam 62
Preventative maintenance 71
Pryor Mountain 137,406
Quarter Horse 437,463
Rack 37,395,450
Racking Horse 27
Racking Horse 414
Rocky Mountain Horse 134
Romal 249
Running walk 37,180,395,439,461
Sabino 214,378
Saddle gait 37
Saddlebred 15,137,157,192,417,446
Saddles 82
Scottish Galloway 15,98,116,338
Single-footing Horse 362
Skewbald 215
Sobreandando 37,260
Sorraia 230, 254, 402,460
Spanish Gaited Pony 440
Spanish Jennet 15,98,116,212,254,338,354,378
Spanish Mustang 400
Spotted Mountain Horse 464
Spotted Paso 27
Spotted Saddle Horse 26,208
Square 34
Standardbred 15, 168, 212,312,417,449
Stepping pace 38
Stepping rack 416
Support professionals 73
Tack 82,317
Tapaojos 262
Teeth 31
Temperament 20,245
Tennessee Walker 16,26,166,212,297,426,461
Tennuvian 28,461
Termino 37,257
Thoroughbred 312,417,449,461
Tiger Horse 27,352
Tiger Registry 374
Tobiano 213,378
Tolt 38,345
Troche y gallope 37
Trot 36, 394,439
Trote y gallope 38
Turkoman 376
UMH 464
Ventral flex 23
Walk 36
Walkaloosa 28,364,426
Warm Blooded 20,123
Western 87
Yamud 376

DATE_____
(Every effort will be made to keep readers updated through the web page: www.thefabulousfloatinghorses.com)

Please enroll me in the "Living Book Project" to be informed about future additions to this volume.

NAME:_____
(PLEASE PRINT CLEARLY)

ADDRESS:_____
_____
_____

TELEPHONE:_____

FAX:_____

E-MAIL:_____

Comments:_____
_____
_____
_____
_____

FOLD LINE

FOLD LINE

Markwin Press
"The Fabulous Floating Horses"
P.O. Box 19898
Reno, Nevada 89511